American Antique Furniture

A BOOK FOR AMATEURS

by Edgar G. Miller, Jr.

IN TWO VOLUMES
VOLUME TWO

DOVER PUBLICATIONS, INC., NEW YORK

Published in Canada by General Publishing Company, Ltd., 30 Lesmill Road, Don Mills, Toronto, Ontario.

Published in the United Kingdom by Constable and Company, Ltd., 10 Orange Street, London W. C. 2.

This Dover edition, first published in 1966, is an unabridged and unaltered republication of the work originally published by The Lord Baltimore Press in 1937.

Standard Book Number: 486-21600-4

Library of Congress Catalog Card Number: 66-20419

Manufactured in the United States of America
Dover Publications, Inc.
180 Varick Street
New York, N. Y. 10014

CONTENTS

APPENDIX

VOLUME TWO CONTAINS A DETAILED INDEX TO BOTH VOLUMES.

CHAPTER XVII

MIRRORS; SCONCES; DRESSING GLASSES

Section 139. General remarks. The story of antique "mirrors", or "looking–glasses",[1] in our country begins about the year 1700. It is thought that at that date the glass was imported and continued to be imported until after the Colonies became States; but that many frames[2] for the glasses were made here, especially those of a plain character, from about 1710.

1. A "Looking–glass" is a descriptive word, meaning a piece of glass coated on the back with a preparation and showing images by reflection; especially a glass into which one may look and see his image. This word was used in the inventories of the estates of deceased persons in the eighteenth century in our country.

The word "Mirror" is broader in meaning than "Looking–glass". A mirror is any polished surface, whether of metal or glass, used to reflect objects. Metal mirrors have been used from remote antiquity, and are now used in some of the Asiatic countries, and also in our country for some purposes.

As all of the mirrors shown in this chapter are of glass, and as those of the eighteenth century were called "looking–glasses", the latter term is perhaps more suitable in a book on antique furniture; but the word "mirror" is shorter and its exact meaning cannot be misunderstood. Mr. Lockwood uses the word "looking–glass"; Mr. Cescinsky uses "mirror".

Convex and girandole mirrors and sconces are defined in section 150.

2. The terms "looking–glass" and "mirror" are commonly used to mean both the glass and the frame which holds it; but in considering the various styles, the frame is the important feature.

Many advertisements of looking–glasses are found in the American newspapers after about 1750.

John Elliott of Philadelphia evidently found that "advertising pays", as he continued his advertisements from about 1756 to 1776. In one published in 1763 he stated that he "will undertake to cure any English looking–glass that shows the face either too long or too broad or any other way distorted."

The Elliotts and their mirrors are also referred to in this volume in notes on pages 611, 622, 629, 632 and 686. *(Note 2 continued on page 608.)*

The amount of the English "luxury tax" was according to the size of the mirror and thus influenced the size of the glass used and the designs of the frames. It is said that the high cost of large glasses was the reason for so many of the mirrors in the Queen Anne style being in two sections, thus using small pieces, as will be seen in section 141. For the same reason, in the time of Chippendale and Robert Adam, the large mirrors were made in several sections, the joints between the parts being concealed by decorative moldings.

The beveling of the glasses in the old mirrors was a difficult operation, usually done while the glass was in a molten condition. The angle of these bevels was very slight, often barely felt by the fingers, and seldom sufficient to create the prismatic colors seen in the modern beveled edges when rays of the sun strike them. This beveling is also referred to in section 44, paragraph No. 2.

An interesting matter in connection with mirrors is the long continuance in style, or the revival, of certain types. It is hard to realize that fretwork mirrors, shown in section 143, began to be made about 1720 and continued in style until after 1800; and that gilded mantel mirrors, shown in section 149, were made from about 1740 to 1830. Moreover, all of these types are now constantly reproduced, which shows their continued popularity.

Many of the fine English mirrors with carved and gilt frames were copied in our country so exactly that it is said to be often difficult to distinguish between the English and the American pieces, especially when on the English pieces a carved American eagle was used, a decorative detail said to have been popular in England[4] about 1780 to 1790. One detail, however, is said to be noticed, namely, that in the English mirrors the board at the back is of a size to fit inside the frame, very close to the glass, but in the American pieces the backboard was generally

(NOTE 2, *continued from page 607.*)

     In 1784 James Reynolds of Philadelphia advertised that he had "just imported and to be sold at his looking–glass store, The Golden Boy, near the Bunch of Grapes Tavern, in Third Street, a great variety of English, French and Dutch Looking Glasses".

     The above quotations are taken from "The Arts and Crafts in Philadelphia, Maryland and South Carolina, 1721–1785", published by the Walpole Society, 1929, pages 196 and 197.

     A comprehensive label of Thomas Natt, of Philadelphia, is quoted in section 152, note 6.

    3.   The cost of manufacture until near the end of the eighteenth century was high. Mr. Cescinsky mentions that in a bill of Chippendale for certain large mirrors made by him the carved and gilded frames were priced at thirty–eight pounds and the glasses at three hundred pounds. Plain transparent glass was proportionately costly. In the case of prints the glass must have been more costly than the print itself. Nearly all of those which were framed and covered with glass had the broad margins cut down; and it is only the prints which were published in a book or kept in a portfolio which have survived to our day with their margins intact; Cescinsky and Hunter, "English and American Furniture", page 255; Cescinsky, "English Furniture of the eighteenth century", volume 1, pages 227–232.

     Notwithstanding the high cost of glass it seems that the famous "Mistress Nell Gwynn", 1650–1687, had one of her rooms completely paneled with mirrors which served as decorations for the room and also enabled her to see herself from all points of view.

    4.   As stated by Mr. F. S. Robinson in his "English Furniture", page 306. See also section 142, note 11, and the clock No. 2055.

larger than the opening of the frame and was nailed to the back, giving a space between the backboard and the glass, a method which tended to protect the back of the glass.[5]

It is said by Mr. Cescinsky that of the entire range of English furniture of the eighteenth century the carved mirror frames of the Chippendale period are the most easily faked, usually in so skilful a manner that it requires expert examination by one having actual workshop experience with the methods used in the period.[6]

Old handmade glass may often be recognized by its thinness as compared with modern glass; and also by its irregularities and its slightly wavy appearance, differing in this respect from the modern glass. A piece of modern glass is generally thicker and heavier than an old piece of equal size. This weight sometimes causes the old frames of mirrors fitted with new heavy glass to break at the lower points where the parts are glued together.

Mirrors intended to be hung on a wall are of two types, one being merely called "mirrors" and the other being known as "pier mirrors". This classification does not include round convex mirrors or "girandole mirrors", as these are not mirrors in which one's image may be well seen, but are merely decorative, as shown in section 150. "Pier" mirrors are so called because they were intended to be hung on a "pier", an architectural word which means the portion of a wall which is between two windows or two doors; and they were also used over tables standing at a wall. These pier mirrors were generally very large, often as much as six or eight feet high, but in other respects they were not noticeably different from other wall mirrors. Other types of mirrors, not to be hung on a wall, include mantel mirrors, which are seen in section 149, and dressing glasses, which are shown in section 152.

In mirrors in which any of the wood of the frame is exposed, that is, not gilded or otherwise covered, the wood is generally the same as that of other furniture of the period in which the mirror was made. Thus in the mirrors in the walnut age of the Queen Anne style the wood is walnut, and in the mahogany

---

5.   This is remarked by Mr. Cescinsky in "English and American Furniture", page 256.

The antique mirrors found in American homes include some which were made in France, so often the leader in styles, and others made in Italy, where the finest early glass was made and whose workmen were brought to England to work in the Vauxhall works. It is difficult for the amateur, and for the writer, to determine whether a particular mirror is of English or other make. See the note to the mantel mirror No. 1231 which was finally found to be of French make. The distinctive features of style which are seen in various other articles of furniture made in different European countries are not always apparent in mirrors, probably because the makers in one country copied the styles of those in other countries.

6.   This is stated by Mr. Cescinsky in "English Furniture", volume 2, page 341.

A similar remark may be made in regard to American mirrors of almost all periods and styles. Small pieces of old wood, taken from old articles of no value, may be used in the frame; new gilding may be "aged" sufficiently to give an appearance of having been "regilded" many years ago, instead of recently. Original glass is not always expected by purchasers; and indeed new glass may be desired by those who prefer to have a "restored" glass rather than an original one which does not reflect perfectly. See also note 1 in section 143.

age of the period of Chippendale and later it is usually mahogany.[7] The kind of wood is mentioned in the sections treating of the mirrors of the various periods and styles. When the wood was gilded or painted or lacquered, pine was commonly used.

Section 140. Early types of mirrors.—The earliest mirrors found in our country, some dating back even prior to the year 1700, were imported, and are now few in number and are seldom seen outside of museums. Examples are shown in illustrations Nos. 1087 and 1088. In these mirrors the main feature is the square or rectangular frame with a curved top.

1087 (LEFT) MR. L. V. LOCKWOOD.   1088 (RIGHT) ANONYMOUS.

In the first type, shown in No. 1087, the frame is made of olive wood and is almost square. The top is in the form of sections of circles. The frame is decorated with inlaid designs of curves and flowers and on the top are inlaid birds which are not clearly seen in the engraving. About 1690–1700.

In the next type, shown in No. 1088, the frame is made of walnut. In this mirror the shape of the frame is similar to that in the previous piece, but the top is in the form of a semi–circle and is elaborately cut in curves with a flower in the centre. About 1700–1710.

These two illustrations are taken by permission of Mr. L. V. Lockwood from his "Colonial Furniture", volume 1, figures 310 and 312.

7. See "Oak and Walnut" and "Mahogany", sections 28 and 29.

Section 141. Queen Anne style mirrors.—The style of Queen Anne, as seen in mirrors, was a favorite one in our country for a long period after the end of her reign, (1702–1714), probably even as late as about 1765,[1] in the middle of the period of the Chippendale style; and this without material changes in its principal features.

These mirrors are most easily recognized by the design of the upper portion of the frame, not including a "cresting" often seen over the top. This design consists of curves at the top of the glass which extend downward on the sides until they reach the straight portion of the sides. Moreover the glass[2] is usually in two parts, both of which are generally beveled. The upper part of the glass is cut in a manner to follow the curved lines of the frame; this upper glass overlaps the lower one, without any molding to conceal the overlapping. An ornamental design of some kind, such as leaves, was often cut on the upper glass. The lower glass was rectangular. A "cresting" over the top of the frame was often used, cut in curved designs, as are the fretwork[3] mirrors shown in section 143. In some cases there was fretwork at the bottom also. All of these features will be seen in the illustrations.

The wood is almost always walnut, solid or veneered on the frame, the cresting being of the same wood but not veneered.

Examining the illustrations, we see four mirrors, Nos. 1089–1092, which are said to be of the period of about 1710–1725. These have the glass in two sections, the upper one decorated with cut-in designs.

In No. 1089 the high cresting, cut in various curves, seems to derive its design from a mirror such as No. 1088 in the previous section. Such crestings are made of thin wood which is liable to warp and break. The frame is veneered in walnut. The top of the upper portion of the frame itself is in the curve of a half circle, below which are two "cyma" curves, which are described and illustrated in section 23. The glass is in two sections, the upper one being beveled and

1. This date is thought to be definitely established by labels found on mirrors of this style made by John Elliott of Philadelphia, the labels being of a kind which were used by him at the date mentioned. See on this subject note 3 in section 143.

2. The glass in these mirrors is not often all original. The first English glass of good quality was made in the time of Charles the Second, about 1662, at a glass factory established by the Duke of Buckingham near Vauxhall, which is now a part of London. In some cases the claim is made that the glasses are original Vauxhall pieces, a claim which should be received with caution.

3. The use of fretwork on the upper and lower parts of mirror frames is so much a characteristic of a large group of pieces that they are made the subject of a separate section, No. 143, entitled "Fretwork mirrors", and it may be thought that some of the mirrors shown in this section with fretwork designs should appear in that section; but such mirrors here shown are so definitely in the Queen Anne style, (except perhaps No. 1098), that it seems proper that they should appear in this section.

    In some early mirrors of the Queen Anne style the cresting was made separate from the frame and was detachable from it; but in later pieces, from about 1725, the cresting was made as a part of the frame.

    In some mirrors of the period the back of the frame extends upwards in a solid piece for an inch or two above the curved portion at the top, as though the piece had not been completely finished. This may have been to hold a cresting.

decorated with cut–in designs; the lower section is new. This mirror is about forty–two inches high. About 1710–1725.

No. 1090 is very similar to the previous one except that there is no cresting, which may have been broken off, or perhaps the piece was made without one. The bevel of the edge of the upper glass is clearly seen. The formal flower design is cut in. The lower glass is also beveled. In this mirror, as in the previous one, the wood is veneered walnut. About 1710–1725.

In No. 1091 the cresting is somewhat smaller than in No. 1089 and the fret-work is less elaborate. Here the molding on the inside of the frame is in a form which is used on several other mirrors shown in this section. The upper glass is shaped in the same curves as the frame around it and is decorated with a design. This and the two preceding mirrors are somewhat more than three feet high. About 1720–1735.

In No. 1092 the character of the cresting again changes, being ornamented with gilded edges and a gilded and concave medallion with a design of a shell. The curves of the upper portion of the frame differ somewhat from those in the previous pieces. The upper glass is ornamented with a cut–in design of fanciful foliage. The entire inside edge of the frame is gilded. This mirror is almost five feet high. About 1725–1735.

In the next group, Nos. 1093–1098, are six other mirrors, four of them with the glass in two parts.

No. 1093 is a tall and narrow mirror, its height being almost five feet. In the centre of the cresting is a pierced and gilded design and on the top are some of the many curves seen on the fretwork mirrors in section 143. Around the upper glass the frame is in a series of short curves. About 1725–1750.

No. 1094 is very similar to the previous one, but without the gilded design in the cresting and with slightly different curves in the upper portion. This also is a tall and narrow mirror. On the back is a label of John Elliott[4] of Phila-delphia, in English and German, the label being of the kind which was used by him between the years 1762 and 1767. The date is thus about 1765 if the label indicates that Elliott was the maker, not merely the repairer of a previously made mirror. The style is that of about 1730–1740.

In No. 1095 the frame is lacquered, or japanned, a kind of decoration which is explained in section 31, and is ornamented with gilding. There is no cresting on the top, which is arched but not in the same manner as in Nos. 1089 and 1090. The height is four feet. About 1710–1725.

No. 1096 is a smaller mirror, twenty–eight inches high and twelve inches wide. The curved cresting is plain in design. Both the upper and lower sections are beveled. Although without elegance, this mirror is a pleasing piece. About 1750–1760.

4.   See note 3 in section 143 in regard to Elliott mirrors.

1089 (Upper) Anonymous.   1090 (Upper) Mr. John S. McDaniel.
1091 (Lower) Anonymous.   1092 (Lower) Anonymous.

1093 (Upper) Mrs. Howard Sill.   1094 (Upper) Mrs. Arthur Hale.   1095 (Upper) Mr. John S.
1096 (Lower) Anonymous.   1097 (Lower) Anonymous.   McDaniel.
                                                                         1098 (Lower) Anonymous.

1099 (UPPER) DR. JAMES BORDLEY, JR.   1100 (UPPER) DR. JAMES BORDLEY, JR.
1101 (LOWER) MRS. MILES WHITE, JR.   1102 (LOWER) ANONYMOUS.

No. 1097 is still smaller, being only twenty inches high, so small that one piece of glass was used instead of two. Here the walnut veneer of the frame is made and applied in numerous small pieces, a method called "cross–banding", because the grain of the veneer is cross–wise. From the appearance of the mirror it would seem that the veneer was badly cracked; there may be some cracks, but the openings are mainly caused by the shrinking of the pieces of veneer. The form of the frame approaches a rectangular shape, only the upper inner corners being curved. The edges of the glass are beveled. About 1750–1760.

No. 1098 is also small, the height being twenty–five inches. The frame is rectangular, having no curves at any point; even the moldings around the glass are not curved at the upper inner corners, differing from those in the preceding pieces. The mirror is probably not strictly in the Queen Anne style but may be a later and simplified form of that type.[5] About 1740–1760.

Nos. 1099 and 1100 are of a different type, being wider in proportion to their height than the preceding mirrors, and having very ornamental crestings.

In No. 1099 the cresting is cut in a group of ornamental designs. In the upper part of the walnut frame six curved and three small and straight portions may be counted, the curves being of the cyma type, which is shown in section 23. The lower portion is plain, as also in the next mirror. About 1725–1750.

In No. 1100 the cresting is low and the forms include flowers and leaves. At the bottom of the cresting will be seen four "C" curves, the outer ones being elongated; these curves were much favored by Chippendale, and many will be seen in the mirrors in the Chippendale style in the next section, as in No. 1103 and others. The top of the frame is almost straight, but on each side are the usual curves extending down to the top of the lower glass. About 1725–1750.

In the next two mirrors, Nos. 1101 and 1102, the frame around the upper part of the glass is not curved in the manner of most of the preceding pieces, being rectangular except at the two upper inner corners, which are curved.[6] This general form of frame was followed in a simplified way in many fretwork pieces shown in section 143. Mirrors of this type are said by Mr. Lockwood to represent the best work of the Queen Anne period. They were generally gilded and were of fine proportions.

In No. 1101 the top has two scrolls in the manner seen in several mirrors in the Chippendale period shown in the next section. Between the scrolls is an ornamental figure called a "cartouche",[7] and the inner ends of the scrolls terminate

5.   A mirror of this kind is illustrated, and is discussed by the editor, in "Antiques", January, 1924, page 11, and the date is regarded as stated above; also in the issue of September, 1924, pages 131–132, where it is said that the label on the mirror was probably that of a repairer, not of the maker.

6.   Mirror frames entirely rectangular in form were also made in the Queen Anne period. Examples are shown in Mr. Cescinsky's "English Furniture", volume 1, figures 238, 249 and others.

7.   This word "cartouche" is defined in connection with highboys in section 87, note 5, as "a carved ornament of fanciful form. It has no similarity in meaning to a cartouche of the Egyptian kings."

in rosettes and vertical leaves. At the upper corners are other scrolls which are duplicated at the bottom of the frame. On the base are two vacant spaces where candle brackets were perhaps attached by nails. In the centre of the base is a carved shell. Almost the entire surface of the frame and cresting is covered with ornamental designs of leaves. About 1725–1750.

No. 1102 is of the same type as No. 1101. The scrolls at the top, the cartouche in the centre, the scrolls at the four outer corners, the two curved upper inner corners and the shell at the bottom are all somewhat similar to those in the preceding piece. In addition, there is a string of flowers on each side. This mirror is copied from Mr. Lockwood's "Colonial Furniture", volume 1, figure 325. About 1725–1750.

A similarity of form will be noticed between some of the mirrors in the dressing glasses of the Queen Anne period, such as Nos. 1255–1258 in this chapter, and some of the wall mirrors of about the same period illustrated in this section.

Section 142. Mirrors in the Chippendale period.—Very few mirrors strictly in the *style* of Chippendale, that is, in a style which Chippendale originated or developed, were made in our country; but many mirrors made in the *period* of Chippendale, which in our country was from about 1755–1785, are commonly called by the name of Chippendale, meaning the "Chippendale period", although in some cases certain features in these mirrors may be in the style of Queen Anne.

For convenience of discussion we consider first the mirrors Nos. 1103–1106 made in the general style which Chippendale exhibited in his book the "Director",[1] published in 1754; next we see a group, Nos. 1107–1112, made in the Chippendale period, but with certain features of the Queen Anne style; these are followed by several others, Nos. 1113–1120, of different types; and in a separate section, No. 143, are the fretwork mirrors which originated in the reign of Queen Anne, 1702–1714, and continued to be popular in our country throughout the Chippendale period and later, and are sometimes called by his name. It is difficult, if not impossible, to fix with certainty the dates of all of these mirrors and some of the dates here given are merely approximate and perhaps conflicting.

In the first group of mirrors, Nos. 1103–1106, in which the Chippendale[2] style is shown, the principal features are that the entire wooden front framework is carved and gilded; the lines of the frame are in a variety of curves, in which a favorite curve somewhat in the form of the letter "C" is almost always seen;[3] and

1. This book is mentioned in "The Chippendale style", section 15.
2. Mirrors in the "Chippendale style" were made by several prominent cabinet makers whose names are mentioned in the books. A number of designs by these men and others are shown in the book "English Furniture, Woodwork and Decoration", by Mr. T. A. Strange.

    Many of these elaborate pieces were "pier" mirrors, which are referred to in section 139, near the end; see also "pier" tables which are mentioned in section 174 entitled "Miscellaneous tables".
3. The presence of these "C" curves on an article of antique English furniture is generally an indication of the Chippendale period, but they were occasionally used both before and after the Chippendale period. Moreover, they were revived in the Victorian period, as shown in the bureau No. 768. This curve follows the French designs.

around a large glass are often a number of small and separate glasses whose junctions are concealed by wooden partitions. Some of these mirrors are highly ornamented by carved designs of birds, leaves, flowers, animals, Chinese subjects or fanciful forms, such as "dripping water", and to them the term "rococo"[4] is generally applied. Elaborate mirrors of this type were probably not made in our country, but a few of a plainer kind were made here and some fine ones were imported from England, where they remained in vogue for a number of years after other articles of Chippendale style furniture had gone out of fashion. The dates of those shown here are about 1755–1790.

Pine wood was generally used for these mirrors as well as for other articles which were entirely covered with gilding, a treatment which is mentioned in section 34.

No. 1103 is a somewhat plain example. The entire frame and ornamental additions are made of wood, which is gilded. Around the large glass in the centre are small glasses, the junctions between them being concealed by the framework. The "C" curves above referred to are clearly seen; the large one on the left of the frame is in the natural position, facing the right; the other large one, on the right, faces the left. Below each of these large C curves is a smaller curve of the same type, and at the bottom are two other small ones; and above the large curves are ten others, some not very distinct. The popularity of these decorative curves is indicated in this mirror. The ornament at the top seems to be an American eagle on a rectangular platform, holding in its claws a shield and several arrows, which may be compared with the inlaid eagles on the much later desks Nos. 803 and 805. This patriotic ornament, not harmonious either in design or date with the mirror itself, must have been substituted for an earlier design. An urn with festoons of drapery is on each side. An oval mirror, No. 1241, with brackets for candles attached, has probably been in the same house with this mirror for much longer than a century. About 1770–1780.

No. 1104 is another mirror in which there is an inner frame enclosing a large glass, around which are smaller panels of glass surrounded by an outer frame carved in leaf designs. This form has a very light and graceful appearance. At the top is a scroll on each side, between which is a small glass, and below are glass panels enclosed by carved partitions. On the sides are other glass panels and at the base are three others, the central one having C curves; other curves of the same kind may be seen in several places. About 1765–1775.

4. This word "rococo" is defined in connection with "Philadelphia style" lowboys in section 92, note 2, as follows: "Generally a meaningless, though often a very rich, assemblage of fantastic scrolls and crimped conventional shell work, wrought into irregular and indescribable forms."

Large mantel mirrors and small wall mirrors of very elaborate "rococo" character, in the Chippendale style, are shown in the English books. None of these were made in our country, but a few were imported. They are not illustrated here.

A mantel mirror in the Chippendale style is shown in No. 1228 in section 149, and elaborate ones are shown in Mr. Lockwood's "Colonial Furniture", volume 1, figures 336–337.

A fine wall mirror in the Chippendale style is one of the series of "Little–Known Masterpieces" in "Antiques", February, 1923.

1103 (Upper) Chase House—Annapolis.   1104 (Upper) Anonymous.
1105 (Lower) Mrs. Miles White, Jr.   1106 (Lower) Mrs. Miles White, Jr.

No. 1105 is another handsome and elaborate mirror in the rococo style of Chippendale. At the top is a Chinese seated figure, apparently Buddha. The painting on the semi–circular glass represents a country scene, with two Chinese figures, a bridge, some flowers and a large bird; the curved portion of the frame around this glass is in six C curves. The mirror glass is rectangular, except that the corners are in C curves. Strings of leaves and flowers are on the sides on which are also large elongated C curves. At least twenty–nine C curves may be counted on this mirror. About 1755–1770.

No. 1106 is another good example of rococo work. There is only one glass and this is in a rectangular frame on the sides of which are finely carved designs of fruits and flowers. At the top and bottom are fanciful carvings. Nineteen C curves may be seen. About 1755–1770.

The next group of mirrors in the Chippendale period, Nos. 1107–1112, are distinguished by a "scroll pediment"[5] at the top. Mirrors of this type are not shown in the "Director", the book of designs by Chippendale, but they were made in the Chippendale period and are commonly called by his name in our country, but in England are often known merely by the name "Georgian".[6] In addition to the pediment these mirrors are distinguished by having some parts gilded and other parts not gilded.[7] A gilded molding extends around the sides and the bottom, with right–angle corners near the top and a lower line connecting them. The base is cut in several curves, among which the cyma[8] curve is always present. On each side there is generally a string of leaves or fruits or flowers. The wood

5. The word "pediment" is an architectural term which, in connection with mirrors and other articles of furniture, means an ornamental feature above a horizontal band or cornice. In the mirrors in this group it consists chiefly of two curved pieces, or scrolls, whose inner ends generally terminate in rosettes; and between the scrolls is an ornament, generally a bird. This ornamental form is seen with variations on other pieces, such as the highboy No. 666, the secretary–bookcase No. 858; see also the mirrors Nos. 1159–1161, and the Index under the word "Pediment".

6. In England, mirrors of this type were made from about 1740, and are called "Georgian", an indefinite term, as explained in section 14, note 2. The four "Georges" reigned from 1714 to 1830.

Mirrors Nos. 1107–1112 are often called "Martha Washington" or "Constitution" mirrors in our country. There seems to be no sufficient reason to justify either of the names.

It is said that the name "Martha Washington" was given to the mirror from the fact that one of this type belonging to Martha Washington was in Mount Vernon, a reason which would make the name apply as well to other mirrors in that residence. The word "Constitution" is often supposed to refer to the United States ship "Constitution", (Old Ironsides), whose victory over the British ship "Guerriere" in the war of 1812 caused its name to be a familiar and patriotic word; but the name is a manifest misnomer when applied to a style of mirror made in the previous century. The word cannot properly apply to the "Constitution of the United States", because there is no connection between the Constitution and a mirror, and also because the Constitution went into effect in 1789, some years after the mirror became the fashion.

7. The word "parcel–gilt" is often applied to mirrors which are partly gilded. Shakespeare used the word in "King Henry the Fourth", part 2, act 2, scene 1, line 78, where the hostess said to Sir John Falstaff, "Thou didst swear to me upon a parcel–gilt goblet . . to marry me." The use of the word at the present time seems somewhat pedantic.

8. The "cyma curve" is explained and illustrated in section 23.

1107 (Upper) Mr. Albert G. Towers.   1108 (Upper) Mr. Albert G. Towers.
1109 (Lower) Mr. C. Edward Snyder.   1110 (Lower) Dr. M. A. Abrams.

is either walnut or mahogany. Mirrors of this type were apparently made in America from about 1760 to near the end of the century.[9]

In No. 1107 we see the characteristic features mentioned above and also other details. At the top are two gilded scrolls, somewhat taller than usual, at the inner ends of which are rosettes from which leaves are hanging. Between the scrolls is a gilded "cartouche".[10] Below the gilded band under the scrolls is a gilded molding with right–angle corners, the inner ends of which are connected by a lower line. The base projects beyond the side lines and is cut in a series of curves. On the sides are carved strings of fruits and leaves. The glass is surrounded by the gilded sides of the frame which is cut in a series of double cyma curves with curved corners similar to those seen in the mirrors Nos. 1139–1141 and in the secretary–bookcases Nos. 849, 898 and 900. About 1750–1775.

No. 1108, also, has a cartouche between the scrolls which terminate in rosettes and leaves. On the sides are carved draperies ending in tassels. The glass is rectangular and the base has projecting ends and is cut in a series of curves. About 1750–1775.

In No. 1109 we see, instead of a cartouche, a pheasant in a defiant attitude, one of the birds which were favorite ornaments of many mirrors of this and later periods, either between the scrolls or in openings cut in the fretwork of the mirrors shown in the next section; birds also appear on some of the girandole mirrors illustrated in section 150. It is said that the pheasants, usually having a long tail, were copied from Chinese designs, not from the European type. Some of the birds are very fanciful and are unknown to ornithologists. They were used as far back as about 1715 on the English mirrors.[11] On the sides of this mirror are carved leaves. About 1760–1775.

No. 1110 also has a pheasant at the top between the scrolls. The frame differs from the previous ones in that there is no carving on the sides, and the moldings at the ends of the base form pointed projections with the moldings on the sides. The moldings on the base turn inward and upward over the surface, as also in No. 1115. The frame is curved at the upper inner corners as in the mirrors Nos. 1101–1102 in the Queen Anne style and in some of the fretwork type. About 1750–1775.

Nos. 1111 and 1112 are tall and handsome mirrors which were no doubt made to hang on the "piers" between windows or doors, and are therefore known as "pier mirrors", as mentioned in the next to the last paragraph of section 139.

9. Several of this type have the label of John Elliott, of Philadelphia, the label being in the style used by him about 1760. See note 3 in section 143.

10. The word "cartouche" is referred to in note 7 in the previous section.

11. As mentioned in section 139 at note 4, it is said that many English mirrors of about the period of 1780 to 1790 used the American eagle. In Mr. Lockwood's "Colonial Furniture", volume 1, figure 333, a mirror is illustrated with a bird which he states has an eagle's head and a pheasant's tail. The French form of eagle may be seen on some pieces of French furniture, especially those in the Empire style. Even the "phœnix", the mythological sacred bird of antiquity which rose from its own ashes every five hundred years, is supposed to be represented on some mirrors; the Japanese "phœnix" is a long–tailed domestic fowl, not likely to be meant when the word is used. Birds are also referred to in section 37.

1111 (Left) Mr. & Mrs. Bayard Turnbull. 1112 (Right) Mrs. Miles White, Jr.

Illustrations of similar mirrors are in Mr. Lockwood's "Colonial Furniture", volume 1, page 392.

In No. 1111 the general design is about the same as in the preceding four mirrors, having gilded scrolls at the top, gilded moldings at the top and base and around the sides and the glass. The framework at the top of the glass, however, is in the curved style characteristic of the Queen Anne style mirrors shown in the previous section. Between the scrolls at the top is a basket with flowers, a decorative feature which is said to have come from Chinese designs and is seen in the English Queen Anne style pieces as well as in later ones. On the sides are long strings of flowers and leaves. About 1750.

No. 1112 is similar in some respects to No. 1110 but is different in general appearance, and is of greater height. The upper part of the glass is not curved in the manner of the preceding mirror. The curves of the sides at the base make projections, and the bird resting upon leaves is of the usual type. This piece has strings of leaves and fruits on the sides. About 1750.

Nos. 1113–1116 are four mirrors which have not architectural pediments but are somewhat similar to the preceding mirrors having those pediments.

In No. 1113, at the top, are gilded scrolls whose inner ends are ornamented with rosettes and leaves. Between the scrolls is a "cartouche", resembling that in No. 1107, which is referred to in the comment on that piece. The frame around the glass is curved at the top in the manner seen in some of the Queen Anne style mirrors. Gilded moldings are around the glass, the sides and the curved base, the latter being in the style of the six previous pieces. The projections at the sides near the base are somewhat similar to those in Nos. 1110 and 1111. We miss, however, the strings of flowers on the sides. About 1750.

In No. 1114 the gilded scrolls at the top terminate without rosettes, and between them is a cartouche, as in the previous mirror. The frame around the glass is curved at the upper corners as in some of the Queen Anne style pieces. The fretwork at the bottom is not gilded. On the sides are designs of drapery, carved as in No. 1108. A gilded ornament is applied on the base. About 1760.

In No. 1115 we again see a bird, probably a pheasant, on a pedestal between the gilded scrolls, and on each side of the pedestal are other gilded forms. Four C curves are on each side of the upper portion of the frame and below them are strings of leaves and flowers. The inner edge of the frame is cut in a series of cyma curves as in No. 1107, projections are on the sides near the base as in Nos. 1110 and 1112, and four gilded moldings extend upward from the bottom, similar to two in No. 1110, between which are three moldings in C curves. About 1770.

No. 1116 is regarded as a modified form of the mirrors having a pediment, such as Nos. 1107–1112, the central part of the gilded band below the scrolls being omitted, and there being no molding with right angle corners. Between the gilded scrolls is a pedestal upon which there is a gilded vase. On the edges of the fretwork portions on the sides of the top, and at the base, indistinct lines are cut into the wood, making incisions called "incised" lines, which are often gilded. Similar incised lines, gilded, will also be seen in some of the fretwork mirrors in the next section, as in Nos. 1139–1141 and others. On the sides are strings of gilded flowers and leaves. Mirrors of this kind are said to be of a transition character, linking the Chippendale with the later styles of Adam, Hepplewhite and Sheraton. The cresting, however, may be a substitute.[12] About 1770.

No. 1117 is another of the mirrors with a broken pediment. In the centre is a gilded "cartouche" in a fanciful design. At the inner ends of the scrolls are rosettes with leaves hanging from their centres. The wide molding around the inner frame is gilded and has curved corners. We miss, however, the gilded moldings on the sides and the base. The wood is walnut. About 1750–1775.

12.   Incorrect restorations are frequently found on mirrors. An eagle may be substituted for a broken pheasant; a new finial may be on the pedestal; a glass may be obviously modern. Accidents are inevitable in the course of a century or more, especially in mirrors. In this chapter, and in other chapters of this book, minor imperfections are not always mentioned.

1113 (Upper) Dr. James Bordley, Jr.
1114 (Upper) Dr. J. Hall Pleasants.
1115 (Lower) Mr. Edgar G. Miller, Jr.
1116 (Lower) Dr. James Bordley, Jr.

The next three mirrors, Nos. 1118–1120, are probably not of American make, but are shown here as interesting pieces.

No. 1118 is fully gilded and is well supplied with rococo designs. It may be compared with No. 1106. The C curves are spread over the entire frame, at least thirty being visible upon close inspection, those at the inner and outer corners of the frame being especially conspicuous. Several other decorative designs may also be seen. About 1760.

No. 1119 is also gilded at all points. At the top is a bird of somewhat uncertain pedigree standing on a platform. At the upper corners are curved designs somewhat resembling the letter "S", and C curves are seen at the inner upper corners of the frame. At the sides are forms of various kinds and at the lower corners are large C curves. These rococo decorations are of a fanciful and meaningless character, as mentioned in note 4 in this section. About 1750.

No. 1120 should perhaps appear in section 141 with other mirrors in the Queen Anne style, the upper part of the frame being curved in the manner of that style. The cresting and the base are ornamented with scrolls and other rococo designs among which numerous C curves may be seen. About 1740–1750.

This section on "Mirrors in the Chippendale period" is now at an end. The dates are not as accurate as those in the later styles of Hepplewhite and Sheraton. As mentioned at note 6 in this section, many English mirrors are attributed merely to the long period known in England as the "Georgian period", 1714–1830, or to the "Early Georgian" or other indefinite part of the period; see also section 14, note 2.

Section 143. Fretwork mirrors.—In this section are mirrors in which both the top and the base are cut in fretwork, because of which they are called "fretwork mirrors". Certain other mirrors have fretwork designs only at the top, such as the early one No. 1088, and others of this type were made in the Queen Anne style, such as Nos. 1089 and 1093; other mirrors have fretwork designs only at the bottom, such as Nos. 1159–1161 in the Hepplewhite style. These mirrors which have fretwork at either the top or the bottom, but not at both, may be regarded as being in the style, for example, of Queen Anne or of Hepplewhite, the fretwork not always being the principal features; but in those which have fretwork at both the top and the bottom the fretwork is generally the main feature.

The fretwork mirrors here shown are commonly said to be in the Chippendale style, although they were not mentioned in Chippendale's book, the "Director", nor were any ever made by him so far as is known; and it is not likely that Chippendale would have associated his name with any article so plain as a "fretwork mirror", which in his time had been in common use for many years. They were, however, made throughout the Chippendale period and this fact seems to be the reason for the use of his name in connection with them.

1117 (Upper) Metropolitan Museum of Art.
1119 (Lower) Miss Helen H. Carey.

1118 (Upper) Mr. C. Edward Snyder.
1120 (Lower) Mr. John C. Toland.

627

An interesting point in connection with these fretwork mirrors is that they were made with but little change for almost a century. The second one here shown, No. 1122, is English and is dated by Mr. Cescinsky at about 1715 to 1725, many years before the time of Chippendale, as mentioned in the comments on that piece; and it is known that such mirrors were made in our country as late as about 1800. During this period there were at times some minor changes in the designs, but none of any very distinctive nature. The result of this long continued sameness of style is that it is difficult or impossible to fix a date of manufacture for many of the pieces unless we have the aid of labels of recognizable date, or other documentary evidence, or moldings or other features used only at certain periods.[1]

In these mirrors, next to the glass, there is almost always a small gilded molding; and sometimes there is in the top or base a round and carved decorative design, often representing a shell. A very popular ornament was a carved and gilded bird, either a pheasant or an eagle, in an opening in the top, often apparently in the act of flying through the hole; and occasionally there is a gilded bird, perhaps made of composition, applied on the surface of the top. The frames are generally of walnut or mahogany, often veneered upon pine or other suitable wood.

Most of these mirrors were made between about 1750 to 1800, a period which included all of the Chippendale, Adam and Hepplewhite periods, and a part of the Sheraton period. As mentioned above, it is not possible to determine the exact dates of manufacture of the various mirrors, for the reason that their styles continued in vogue for such a long period. One distinctive detail, however, is the curve of the upper inner corners of the frame, this being characteristic of the Queen Anne style, as seen in section 141; but in our country these curved corners were used for perhaps fifty years after the Queen Anne style passed out of fashion.

From the large number of available photographs of fretwork mirrors, often differing merely in their size and curves, only twelve, Nos. 1121–1132, are shown in the first group, in which the upper inner corners of the frames are curved; in the six mirrors in the second group, Nos. 1133–1138, all the corners are rectangular. These groupings have no special significance and do not establish a date with certainty.

Beginning with No. 1121 we see a mirror which is definitely in the Queen Anne style, as shown by the two glasses, upper and lower, and by the curves of the frame around the upper glass, both of which features appear in the mirrors in the Queen Anne style in section 141. In the opening in the centre of the cresting

1.   Another result is that it is difficult for the writer to avoid repetition in the comments, as the features are so similar. In the selection of illustrations the aim is to show some of the most pleasing forms of fretwork. These mirrors, especially those made in the latter half of the eighteenth century, are perhaps more often found than any other single article of antique furniture except chairs.

It may be mentioned that many of these mirrors are very easily and frequently faked. A model to copy, a few pieces of old wood, some tools and a modern glass, (the old (?) one said to have been broken), are all that is needed. See also note 6 in section 139.

is a form said to represent a shell. The scrolls in the cresting and at the sides of the top are duplicated on the base, but in a reversed position. The wood is walnut and the date is about 1725.

No. 1122 is an English fretwork mirror which is said by Mr. Cescinsky[2] to be a good type of the ordinary frames which were made in great numbers in England from about 1715–1725. In this mirror are the principal features seen in the fretwork mirrors from these dates to about 1800, when the style passed out of fashion in our country. The cresting at the top with the fretwork extensions at the sides, and the base with its extensions, are cut in scrolls and other forms which may be seen, with some variations, in many later pieces. No special names have been given to all of these various fretwork forms, and in fact it would be almost impossible to find such names for all of the great variety of curves. The gilded design in the centre of the top, and the oval one at the base, are ornaments which are not essential parts of the mirror and are not found in the great majority of pieces. The upper inner corners of the frame are curved. The wood is mahogany. About 1725.

In No. 1123 there is a round carved shell at the top. The curves of the inner upper corners will again be noticed. As is usual, the design of the fretwork at the bottom differs from that at the top and the cresting is somewhat larger than the base. About 1740–1750.

In No. 1124 there is a round opening at the top in which there is a gilded form of a shell resembling that in No. 1121. The carved scrolls at the four outer corners of the frame are very delicate and liable to breakage. About 1740–1760.

In No. 1125 the fretwork is simpler in design, but of the same general character. There are no decorative features. The outlines of the fretwork at the top and base resemble those in No. 1131. On this mirror is a label of John Elliott, of Philadelphia, who is the subject of the note.[3] About 1760–1770.

2. In his "English Furniture", volume 1, at figure 250, which is here copied with his permission.
3. Somewhat lengthy mention may be made of the numerous mirrors of John Elliott of Philadelphia because of his advertisements in the newspapers and his labels on many fretwork mirrors. It is said that he came from England to Philadelphia in 1753 and was in business in that city until about 1776, when he retired. The business was carried on by his son John Elliott, Jr., who in 1804 was joined in business by his two sons who continued it until 1809 under the name of "John Elliott and Sons".

These Elliotts placed their labels on very many of the mirrors which they handled. At least three different types of labels were used by the first John Elliott, in both English and Pennsylvania German, the latter apparently because of the large number of German people who had settled in the neighborhood of Philadelphia; these "Pennsylvania Dutch" are referred to in the chapter on "Chests", section 78, note 1. The first type of label mentioned his store "in" Chestnut Street, where, as appears from his advertisements, he was located from 1753 to 1761; the second type of label mentioned his store "in" Walnut Street, where he was from 1762 to 1767; the third type was apparently used from 1768 to 1776.

In 1756 the first advertisement of John Elliott, "cabinet maker", appeared. It called attention to "a neat assortment of looking glasses, viz., piers, sconces and dressing glasses" which he imported from London. His advertisements generally displayed a dressing–glass of the type of

(*Note continued on page 632.*)

1121 (UPPER) MR. L. V. LOCKWOOD.
1124 (LOWER) DR. JAMES BORDLEY,
  JR.

1122 (UPPER) ANONYMOUS.
1125 (LOWER) MR. ALBERT G. TOW-
  ERS.

1123 (UPPER) FAMILY OF THOMAS
  CRADOCK.
1126 (LOWER) DR. JAMES BORDLEY,
  JR.

630

1127 (UPPER) MR. EDGAR G. MILLER, JR.
1128 (UPPER) MRS. WM. M. ROBERTS.
1129 (UPPER) MRS. WM. DEFORD.
1130 (LOWER) MR. & MRS. CARROLL VAN NESS.
1131 (LOWER) DR. M. A. ABRAMS.
1132 (LOWER) MR. J. F. H. MAGINN.

In No. 1126 the moldings around the glass are well seen in the engraving. The top and base are somewhat larger than usual and are without any decoration. About 1760–1770.

No. 1127 is a large mirror, forty–four inches high and twenty–eight inches wide at the widest point. The sides are ornamented with vertical carved and gilded applied pieces. The carving of the fretwork is more delicate and the design is more intricate than in most of the mirrors of this type. The beveled edge of the new glass may be seen. About 1760–1770.

No. 1128 has a favorite form of cresting, often seen in mirrors of the period, with variations, and there are delicate bits of carving at several points on both the top and the base, with small scrolls at four points on the sides. About 1760–1770.

Nos. 1129–1132, the four other mirrors in the group of twelve having curved inner upper corners, are decorated with birds, three of which have long tails probably indicating their membership in the pheasant family. These birds were carved from wood and then gilded. There is no particular significance in this form of decoration, except that the mirrors of this kind in which birds were used were generally of the period of about 1780–1800. The similarity of these mirrors makes unnecessary a detailed comment on each piece.

In No. 1129 the fretwork is delicately made. The tail and wings of the pheasant here, as in the two following mirrors, extend well over the surface of the cresting upon which it is applied. About 1780–1800.

No. 1130 is a similar piece, with delicate fretwork. On the upper part of the sides are two attachments, not visible in the illustration, by which the mirror was hung upon the wall. About 1780–1800.

(NOTE 3, *continued from page 629*.)

No. 1259; see the note to this dressing glass. He also advertised that he repaired frames and resilvered glasses.

The mirror No. 1094 in section 141, in the Queen Anne style, bears the second type of label, 1762 to 1767, indicating a later use of the Queen Anne style than would be expected. In the period of about 1755 to 1785 the fashionable style of mirror was that of Chippendale, shown in section 142; but the Elliott fretwork mirrors were plain and inexpensive and naturally continued to be made for those who did not wish to buy the more elegant pieces. The fretwork mirrors were made in practically the same design by the members of the Elliott family from about 1753 to 1809, a long period which exceeds the periods of the styles of Chippendale, Adam, Hepplewhite and some years of the style of Sheraton.

The label of John Elliott, Jr., was apparently used by him between about 1784–1803. It mentions "Looking–glasses in neat mahogany frames of American manufacture". The firm of "John Elliott & Sons", 1804 to 1809, also used a label.

It should be borne in mind that the label may indicate either that Elliott, or his successors, made the mirror, or that they repaired it or that they sold it as an importer or dealer. The label cannot always be relied on as fixing the date of manufacture. See on this point the remarks in section 6 at note 10.

The historical matters stated in this note are taken mainly from the "Pennsylvania Museum Bulletin" of April, 1924. See also an article in "Antiques", September, 1924, pages 131–132, and previous articles there cited.

In No. 1131 the fretwork is less delicate, but the mirror was formerly more decorative, having a pheasant at the top and in the base a circular opening with a gilded ornament as in the dressing glass No. 1275. The fretwork at the top is similar to that in No. 1125. About 1780–1800.

No. 1132 is of a different type, having a scroll top with an eagle in the centre, by reason of which the fretwork at the top is confined to the corners. This piece combines features of the usual fretwork mirror with the scrolled and ornamental top of the mirrors in the Hepplewhite style shown in section 145 as Nos. 1159–1161. About 1785–1800.

In the next group, Nos. 1133–1138, the upper inner corners of the frame are rectangular, not harmonizing with the curves of the cresting so well as do the curved corners; and other features will also be noticed.

In No. 1133 the fretwork cresting is higher and the base is deeper than in previous pieces. At the top of the cresting a gilded eagle is applied on the surface. The form of the molding around the glass is well seen. About 1780–1800.

No. 1134 also has a high cresting and a deep base, neither of which are decorated. The design of the cresting may be a variation of the popular design in No. 1128. About 1780–1800.

No. 1135 is also a popular form. It has an oval opening in the cresting in which are five gilded leaves, and also several cut–in, or "incised", carvings on the top and base. About 1780–1800.

No. 1136 differs from other fretwork mirrors already seen, having a gilded string of flowers and leaves on each side and an applied pheasant on the cresting in the popular form of Nos. 1128 and 1134. About 1780–1800.

No. 1137 also has gilded flowers and leaves on the sides. The cresting is in the form of two scrolls between which is a pedestal supporting a pheasant. About 1770–1790.

No. 1138 may be compared with No. 1132, having scrolls at the top with a pedestal between them. The ornament which was on the pedestal is missing, but a gilded eagle is applied under the pedestal. Near the top are small pieces of fretwork, and at the bottom the fretwork is cut in an unusual manner. About 1790–1800.

In the last group of fretwork mirrors, Nos. 1139–1144, several features will be noticed. One is that the gilded inner edges of the frames are generally in a series of "cyma" curves, (as to which see section 23), resembling those on the mirror No. 1107 and on the doors of several secretary–bookcases mentioned in the comment on that mirror; another feature is that several of these mirrors are ornamented with gilded designs "cut in" the wood, or "incised"; the third is that all but one have strings of carved flowers and leaves on the sides; and the fourth feature is the pheasant which was the favorite bird for ornament.

1133 (UPPER) DR. JAMES BORDLEY, JR.

1136 (LOWER) MRS. MAURICE F. RODGERS.

1134 (UPPER) MRS. MAURICE F. RODGERS.

1137 (LOWER) ANONYMOUS.

1135 (UPPER) MR. E. G. MILLER, JR.

1138 (LOWER) MR. & MRS. EDW. H. MCKEON.

1139 (Upper) Anonymous.
1142 (Lower) Mr. C. Edward Sny-
    der.

1140 (Upper) Anonymous.
1143 (Lower) Mrs. Miles White,
    Jr.

1141 (Upper) Miss Mary Dorsey
    Davis.
1144 (Lower) Mrs. W. W. Hubbard.

In No. 1139 the top has two gilded scrolls and a pedestal upon which is a gilded pheasant, and under these is an "incised" gilded decoration of dainty sprays of flowers which are repeated on the base. The four inner corners are in the form closely resembling a "C" curve, and two small distinct curves of this kind are on the sides of the gilded central portion of the base. This mirror is about two feet in height. The wood is walnut and the date is about 1780–1790.

No. 1140 is similar to the previous one, but is less elegant in the incised decorations. Two "C" curves are on each of the scrolls at the top, and two are in the decoration of the centre of the base. This mirror is about four feet high. The wood is mahogany veneered on pine. About 1780–1790.

No. 1141 is more clearly in the form of a fretwork mirror, especially at the top, where there is a round opening within which is an eagle with open wings. Incised decorations of leaves are at the top and on the base. The design of the fretwork at the bottom is plain. About 1780–1790.

In No. 1142 there is a gilded design in the round opening in the cresting, and gilded sprays of incised flowers are on the cresting and the base. The inner edges of the frame of this mirror are not in cyma curves; but the upper inner corners are in a curved form resembling those seen in Nos. 1122–1132. About 1780–1800.

In No. 1143 the top is finely cut and is ornamented with a gilded pheasant in a round opening. On the base are small sprays of leaves. Here there are no strings of leaves and flowers. About 1780–1790.

In No. 1144 there are no incised decorations, but gilded leaves are applied on the top and a gilded shell on the base. The inner edge of the frame is in the form of modified cyma curves. The form of the upper fretwork resembles the popular one seen on No. 1128. About 1780–1790.

This concludes the group of mirrors which have fretwork at both the top and bottom. Others with fretwork at the bottom only will be seen in section 145, which treats of mirrors in the Hepplewhite style.

Section 144. Adam style mirrors.—As mentioned in section 16, entitled "The Adam style", it is not usual for books on American antique furniture to consider the Adam style at any length, because furniture in that style was apparently not made in our country. But although mirrors in the Adam style may not have been made here to any extent, we see in the next section certain features of that style in our American mirrors made in the style of Hepplewhite who followed the designs of Adam in many respects. Moreover the English mirrors in the Adam style are so handsome that the reader will be interested in seeing a few illustrations of them.[1]

1. It has been said that the Brothers Adam will "always be gratefully remembered for the mirror frames they designed, even though all their other work were forgotten"; quoted from "The Practical Book of Period Furniture", by Eberlein and McClure, page 196.

In section 16, above cited, two mirrors, one rectangular and one oval, designed by Robert Adam, are seen in the full page illustration No. 4, containing six articles in the Adam style. The designs of these two mirrors are typical of the style and differ from all others previously made in England or America. In the illustrations in this section several other examples of rectangular and oval mirrors are presented.

The distinctive features of the mirrors in the Adam style are that various parts of the frames are generally of a more delicate design than those of the preceding styles of Chippendale or Queen Anne; over the entire surface they usually are carved, especially with fluting, and gilded; they are generally decorated with strings of flowers, either straight or in festoons; and are also frequently ornamented with a classic urn or other classic designs.

Many of the graceful festoons and wreaths on the mirrors were too delicate to be made of wood, and were made of a plaster composition which was applied on wire and became very hard and could be gilded or painted.[2] The charm of the Adam mirrors is largely based upon these decorations and the harmony of design between them and the frame.[3]

Turning to the six examples of the Adam style in illustration No. 4 in section 16, we see two mirrors in that style, not numbered. The *upper* one is a large rectangular mirror of simple design. At the top is an urn in classic style, containing fruits, and on the sides of the urn are branches with leaves, in graceful curves. Mr. Cescinsky mentions that these ornaments at the top could not be used without the aid of wired composition. The sides of the frame are fluted. The *lower* mirror is oval, and is regarded as being of fine design and workmanship. The leaves and the strings of flowers are of composition, "carved wood being impossible with such delicacy of treatment". At the top, over the urn, is a classic form known as an "anthemion", or honeysuckle, which was a favorite decoration for many years. It is well seen on the chairs Nos. 178 and 179 in the Chippendale style, and on the settees Nos. 522 and 523; see also note 48 in section 51, and the Index. Under the urn are festoons of drapery suspended from

2. This composition, sometimes referred to as "compo", a substitute for carved wood, was developed in Italy. It was introduced into England by Robert Adam, and was a necessity in much of the work designed by him. The strings and festoons of flowers and leaves on mirrors, often not attached to the frame except at their extremities, could not be successfully made of wood. In some mirrors and other articles both carving and composition were used; for example, carved and gilded wooden urns or other ornaments were at the top or bottom and composition strings of flowers were on the sides. Composition work of this kind is known as "filigree". The composition is sometimes called "gesso", which is an Italian word meaning "plaster" or "chalk". The word "filigree" is also defined in note 2 in section 145.

      Pine wood was generally used for such portions of the frame as were to be gilded or carved.

3. As mentioned in section 16, when the Brothers Adam designed a house they also designed the furniture in order that it might be in harmony with the style of decoration of the house; and as many of the houses had lofty ceilings, many mirrors were made very high, one "pier mirror", (see section 139), shown by Mr. Cescinsky in his "English Furniture", volume 3, figure 73, being ten feet high. These pier mirrors matched the decorative scheme of the table or mantel over which they were hung. The mantel mirrors also were often very large.

a horizontal bar, a detail which will also be seen in the Adam style sconces Nos. 1250 and 1251. About 1770.

In the next four illustrations, Nos. 1145–1148, the mirrors are rectangular, and in Nos. 1149–1151 they are oval; all except Nos. 1148 and 1151 are copied from Mr. Cescinsky's "English Furniture", volume 3, chapter 4, with his permission.

In No. 1145, at the top, is an urn from which three festoons of flowers hang, and on the sides are strings of the same flowers. At the base is a ram's head with curled horns, and here also are festoons of flowers. The rectangular frame is ornamented by horizontal flutings in groups which are divided by round applied rosettes. About 1770.

No. 1146 is an unusual type,[4] having an inner glass surrounded by ten smaller ones, all rectangular, the joints between them being concealed by moldings, as in the Chippendale style mirror No. 1103 and others. Here also we see an urn at the top, under which, in a half–circle, is another form of anthemion, or honeysuckle. Festoons and strings of flowers, made of composition and not attached to the sides, ornament the top and sides. About 1770.

No. 1147 is a tall mirror, similar to No. 1145 in having the frame decorated with horizontal flutings and rosettes. In the oval panel at the top is a plaque of Wedgwood ware and above is an anthemion, or honeysuckle, ornament. The two mythological griffins,[5] part lion and part bird, are a characteristic detail of the Adam style. About 1775.

No. 1148 is a large and handsome mirror. At the top is an urn under which is a finely carved oval design. The leaves and flowers and scrolls combine to make a graceful decoration. At the sides are strings of flowers, not attached to the sides, and at the bottom are festoons of drapery. This form of mirror seems to have been the model for several of the drawings of Hepplewhite shown in illustration No. 1152. This mirror and two sconces, one of which, No. 1250, is shown in section 150, form a charming "mirror set by the Adam Brothers" which is the property of the Pennsylvania Museum of Art, through whose courtesy these objects are illustrated here. About 1775.

---

4.   A mirror of this type, but without any ornamentation outside of the frame, is illustrated in "Antiques", February, 1929, page 126, and is said to have been brought by Thomas Jefferson to Monticello from France.

5.   These griffins are also seen on the top of the Hepplewhite mirror No. 7 in illustration No. 1152, and in the wall mirror No. 1221 and the mantel mirror No. 1229. See also the Index.

    The following quotation in regard to griffins is copied from page 425 of the "Accompaniment" to Sheraton's "Drawing Book" which is mentioned in section 18: "The griffin is another fabulous being, existing only in the vain imaginations of the ancient heathen poets. . . They represented it partly an eagle, and partly a lion, that is, the lower part of it. They supposed it to watch over golden mines and hid treasures. It was consecrated to the sun, whose chariot was drawn by a number of them. And these, if you please, may be introduced into subjects intended to represent covetousness; or they may be placed over cabinets where treasure is kept."

1145 (Upper) Anonymous.   1146 (Upper) Anonymous.
1147 (Lower) Anonymous.   1148 (Lower) Penna. Museum of Art, Phila.

Four oval mirrors are interesting. The first is the lower one shown in illustration No. 4 in section 16, referred to in the early part of this section; that mirror and the three on this page illustrate Mr. Cescinsky's remark that "Robert Adam's oval hanging mirrors are among his happiest" works. In these mirrors the frames, as usual, are of wood and the ornaments are of composition.

In No. 1149 the top is ornamented with an "anthemion", or "honeysuckle", design under which is a small rectangular painted panel, and at the bottom is another similar anthemion design under which is still another one in a reversed position. On the top, bottom and sides are gilded leaves and flowers. About 1775.

1149 (LEFT) ANONYMOUS.   1150 (CENTRE) ANONYMOUS.   1151 (RIGHT) MRS. JOHN S. GIBBS, JR.

At the top of No. 1150 is an urn with small openings and in a form which was copied in part by Hepplewhite in some of his drawings shown in No. 1152. Here the curved strings of flowers, made of composition, extend down from the urn almost to the bottom, supported on the sides at several places. At the bottom are leaves and ribbons. About 1770.

No. 1151 is a charming oval mirror in which strings of flowers, rising from the urn, fall in graceful curves to the sides of the frame where they are almost met by other flowers which extend to the bottom and are supported by an oval plaque. The urn is in an uncommon design and at the very top are three flowers. About 1775.

In the next section are drawings and mirrors in the Hepplewhite style in which the style of Adam is frequently followed, with variations.

Section 145. Hepplewhite style mirrors.—In illustration No. 1152 are designs of eight mirrors, copied from Hepplewhite's "Guide" which is mentioned in section 17; in these designs the influence of the Adam style in the work of Hepplewhite is clearly shown.[1] The rectangular form is similar; and the scrolls at the top, the festoons and the strings of drapery, leaves and flowers are all gilded on "composition", as in the mirrors in the Adam style which we have seen in the previous section. In certain of these Hepplewhite designs we see other features characteristic of the Adam pieces; thus in the design 2 the inner glass and

1152—Designs of mirrors in Hepplewhite's "Guide".

1. This illustration is an arrangement of Hepplewhite's designs, by Mr. T. A. Strange, in his "English Furniture", etc., page 277. Designs 6 and 10 are of sconces, as to which see section 150.

These eight designs of mirrors are dated "September 1, 1787", in Hepplewhite's "Guide". In the third edition, published in 1794, they are on plates 116, 117 and 118. The designs of the two sconces 6 and 10 are on plates 113 and 115. The designs of the mirrors appear also on pages 250 and 252 of the book "Chippendale, Sheraton and Hepplewhite" by J. M. Bell.

In reference to these designs it is said by Mr. Strange, pages 275–277, that "the influence of the classic taste is here distinctly discernible. Some of these designs might be taken to be by the Brothers Adam, so light and tasty are they."

It is suggested that the preceding section No. 144 on the "Adam style mirrors" be examined in connection with this section.

the smaller glasses surrounding it are similar to those in the Adam mirror No. 1146; in design 5 at the top is an oval panel and in design 7 are two griffins, all of which are seen on the Adam mirror No. 1147; and other resemblances, such as the frequent use of urns at the top, will be noticed.

Illustrations Nos. 1153–1158 show examples of this Hepplewhite style, or, as it may be called, the Adam–Hepplewhite school or period. It is said that mirrors of this type were made in our country from about 1785–1800. Because of the character of their ornamentation they are sometimes called "filigree"[2] mirrors, a term which is equally applicable to some of the mirrors in the Adam style.

No. 1153 is a pleasing mirror in the Hepplewhite style. At the top are ears of wheat in an urn from which festoons of leaves and flowers extend downward. On the top of the frame are spiral scrolls supporting the festoons and at the base are other floral forms. The rectangular frame is gilded and is decorated with lines of beading. It is said that a number of mirrors of this kind have been found in the neighborhood of New York city. The similarity of the cresting of this mirror to that on the one marked 1 in No. 1152 will be noticed. About 1790–1800.

No. 1154 is a very similar mirror although the urn is of a different type, and the spiral scrolls are smaller, and perhaps even more pleasing, than those in the preceding piece. Here also the frame is decorated with lines of beading and at the base are festoons of leaves and flowers with a central ornament. About 1790–1800.

In No. 1155 the elaborate cresting consists of an urn or vase with fluted sides, containing flowers, from which festoons and strings of leaves and flowers extend over the sides. At the base are other festoons. The edges of the frame are in a wavy design. About 1790–1800.

No. 1156 is a less elegant mirror than the three mentioned above. The frame is plainer and the strings of leaves falling on the sides are not as delicate. The cresting is formed of spiral scrolls and a vase in which are flowers. The frame is hollowed out and has rosettes at the corners. About 1790–1805.

No. 1157 is an example of a type of gilt mirrors which were popular about 1790, showing agricultural products, such as fruits, in cornucopias which were emblems of plenty. Here there are three spiral cornucopias, two with fruits, ribbons and strings of flowers. The frame has lines of beading and spiral columns, with rosettes at the corners. About 1790–1815.

No. 1158 is a small mirror of less elegant design. At the top is a platform upon which is an urn, and from the urn festoons of leaves extend over the sides which are ornamented with applied forms, as are also the corners. At the base

2.   This word is defined as ornamental work consisting of gold, silver, or sometimes copper, wire formed into delicate traceries of scrolls, network or the like; or any kind of ornamental openwork similar to filigree. In a figurative sense the word means anything very delicate, light and fanciful, especially anything too delicately formed to be serviceable; Century Dictionary. See note 2 in section 144.

1153 (UPPER) ANONYMOUS.
1156 (LOWER) MR. E. G. MILLER, JR.

1154 (UPPER) ANONYMOUS.
1157 (LOWER) MRS. MAURICE F. RODGERS.

1155 (UPPER) ANONYMOUS.
1158 (LOWER) MR. E. G. MILLER, JR.

are other festoons of leaves caught up at the ends and centre. This mirror may perhaps be considered as following the style of Adam more closely than that of Hepplewhite. About 1785–1800.

Another type of mirror is shown in Nos. 1159–1161. In each of these are two gilded scrolls on a pediment[3] top and between the scrolls is an urn; and gilded leaves and flowers are on the sides. The large surfaces are not gilded and the base is generally cut in fretwork designs. Such pieces are commonly said to be in the Hepplewhite style, although there are no mirrors with fretwork in his

1159 (LEFT) MR. & MRS. GEO. SHIP-LEY.   1160 (CENTRE) METROPOLITAN MU-SEUM.   1161 (RIGHT) ANONYMOUS.

"Guide"; but they were apparently made in the years in which the Hepplewhite style was in vogue in our country. These mirrors are generally made of mahogany veneered on pine. As in other pieces of the kind, the flowers and other such decorations are very fragile, especially those in the urn, and few of the mirrors are in their original condition. The American cabinet makers evidently did not feel themselves bound to confine their designs to any one style either in form or decoration; in some of these mirrors they introduced patriotic features, such as an inlaid oval with the American eagle.

3. Pediment tops with scrolls are also seen in the mirrors Nos. 1107–1112 and are described in note 5 in section 142. See also the Index under the word "Pediment".

No. 1159 is a large and handsome mirror in which the features above mentioned, and others, are seen. In the urn are ears of wheat, and below the urn is an inlaid oval in which there is an inlaid American eagle. Directly below the eagle is a group of six inlaid vertical bars,[4] and two other groups are at the ends but are not well seen in the engraving. The eagle and the bars are also seen in the Hepplewhite style sideboard No. 955, which belongs to the same owners. Inlaid eagles are referred to in section 33. About 1790–1800.

In No. 1160 the height of the mirror in proportion to its width is somewhat greater than usual, and perhaps on this account a panel is placed above the glass. On this panel a scene on the seashore is painted and there are a number of small lines which represent waves. In an inlaid oval there is an eagle with a shield, over which is an inlaid group of eighteen stars.[5] About 1790–1805.

No. 1161 is similar to the two previous mirrors in most respects, but the urn is of a different type. Three groups of six inlaid vertical bars, not well seen, are similar to those in No. 1159. There is a gilded molding around the frame and within the molding is a line of inlay, giving a pleasing appearance. About 1790–1805.

Section 146. Mirrors in the Sheraton period.—Although Sheraton did not exhibit any mirrors in his "Drawing-Book", (mentioned in section 18), his name has been attached to a large number of mirrors having certain characteristics, and the term "Sheraton style" is commonly, but loosely, used in referring to them. Moreover, it is often not entirely clear whether certain mirrors of this kind should be classified under the name of "Sheraton style" or under the name of the succeeding "Empire style". In these circumstances, it seems best to consider the mirrors shown in this section as being in the "Sheraton *period*", about 1795 to 1820 in the case of mirrors, rather than in the "Sheraton *style*", thus regarding them as having been made in a certain period instead of in an uncertain style.[1]

4. These decorative bars are shown on the left of the centre of the Shearer sideboard "A" in illustration No. 949; also in the mirror No. 1161.

5. These eighteen stars may not have been intended to represent the number of States in the Union at the time the mirror was made, but if they were so intended they indicate the date to be after the admission of the eighteenth State, Louisiana, in 1812, and before the admission of the nineteenth State, Indiana, in 1816, a date which seems to be later than would be supposed from the style of the mirror. In the Appendix, section 208, is a list of the States in the order of their admission.

Similar indications of dates are on the desks Nos. 803 and 805, and on the mirrors Nos. 1168, 1173 and 1196. See the Index under the word "Stars".

This mirror is in the Metropolitan Museum of Art and is shown as No. 147 in "The Homes of our Ancestors", by Halsey and Tower, on page 183 of which book it is said that "the superb gilt and mahogany mirror, figure 147, has the eagle with its clustering stars inlaid beneath the pediment. The painting of the glass panel is characteristic of some Baltimore maker."

1. Of course all of the mirrors made in the Sheraton "period" were not made in the Sheraton "style". Some mirrors in the true Chippendale style continued to be made until about 1800, and some in the Hepplewhite style were made as late as 1810, or even later if the stars in No. 1160 are relied on. But in the period of about 1795–1820, the fashionable style was that of Sheraton. Moreover in

A great number of the mirrors of the Sheraton period have a cornice[2] under which acorns or balls are attached, with columns on the sides, and with two panels, the upper one of glass or wood and decorated, the lower one of clear glass as in No. 1165. Other types of mirrors were made in which certain features of the Sheraton style appear, as in mantel mirrors and dressing glasses; these types are shown in later sections of this chapter.

To us, who are proud of our country's history, the most interesting mirrors of the Sheraton period are those which are decorated with paintings of a patriotic character, especially those portraying the naval battles of the war of 1812–1815, and the ships which contributed to the victorious result. In those days of our young republic, when the national spirit was highly aroused, these mirrors, with scenes of the victory of the "Constitution" over the "Guerriere", or with views of our ships, or with the American eagle as an emblem of sovereignty, or with our flag and its stars and stripes, were exceedingly popular; and with mirrors of this type we begin the Sheraton period, although they are among the latest in date.

In the first group, Nos. 1162–1167, the scenes are of our naval victories in the war of 1812 and of some of the ships which won them. On some of the mirrors

(Note 1, *continued*)

this period many pieces were made in the American Empire style. There was overlapping both forward and backward.

A well illustrated article entitled "Tabernacle Mirrors" by Alice Van Leer Carrick is in "Antiques", July, 1922, pages 11–15. See also section 147, note 2.

2. A. The cornice, meaning the projection at the top, and the columns are architectural features, and mirrors of this kind are sometimes called "architectural mirrors". The word "tabernacle" has also been applied to them because of a supposed resemblance to a tabernacle in the architectural sense, meaning a canopy or projection. Fortunately these terms need not be used unless one wishes to speak in a technical manner.

B. Several frequently used words of an architectural character may be defined in order that they may be clearly understood. They are necessarily used here to some extent in order that the mirrors may be properly described. In several books and many articles it is assumed that the reader knows their proper meaning. The definitions are based upon the Century Dictionary.

C. A "column" or "pillar" in mirrors, as in architecture and in common usage, is an upright piece, cylindrical or slightly tapering, which generally serves as a support to something resting on its top. In mirrors the columns appear to support the part which is above them, but actually they are merely ornamental. They are "applied" on the frame of the mirror.

D. A "capital" is the uppermost part of a column, or pillar or pilaster, the latter being a flat column. In classical architecture the different columns, such as the Doric, Ionic and Corinthian, had their respective appropriate capitals. A capital is indispensable at the top of a column. In mirrors it may be carved or rounded or plain.

E. A "cornice" is a projection which extends beyond the line of the part to which it is affixed; for example, the cornice of a house. In mirrors it is the top which projects forward beyond the line of the lower parts of the mirror. Cornices are seen in almost all of the mirrors of the Sheraton period, and under them acorns or balls are generally attached.

F. "Pendent", sometimes spelled "pendant", means "hanging". In architecture it means a hanging ornament. In mirrors it is used to indicate the hanging strings of flowers or leaves, such as those on the mirrors of the Adam style and Hepplewhite styles; or to the gilded balls hanging from the cornice in the mirrors in the Sheraton and Empire styles. Pendent balls are first seen here on No. 1163 and pendent acorns in No. 1167.

the names of the ships are given. The artists who painted the scenes naturally drew on their imaginations in many details. Each of the gilded frames is different in some features which are mentioned in the comments. The illustrations are too small to present clear pictures of the paintings of the ships.

In No. 1162 the painting shows two war–ships in action, supposed to be the "Constitution" and "Guerriere", on August 19, 1812; the ships are very close together, as are all of the ships in the battle scenes. Here the painter adorned with mountains the scene of battle which was in the Atlantic ocean, far from land; or perhaps the ships are not those they are supposed to be. The gilded frame has an elaborate molding on the cornice, and, with the double columns on each side, presents more of an architectural appearance than is shown in some other mirrors. The border around the painting is in three colors. This mirror is about four feet high. About 1815–1820.

In No. 1163 the words "Constitution and Java" are in the border below the painting, which represents another victory of the American ship, on December 29, 1812. Here the border is decorated with foliage and a shield. Under the cornice are the familiar gilded balls. The ends are hollowed out in a semi–circular form in which are moldings in a spiral form. This mirror is about three feet high. About 1815–1820.

In No. 1164 the words "Enterprise and Boxer" in the border are not well seen in the engraving. The victory of the "Enterprise" was won on September 5, 1813. The frame is similar to that in the preceding mirror, except that instead of the balls under the cornice there is a molding in the same spiral form as on the sides. The border is ornamented with blue and gold foliage. The height is about three feet. About 1815–1820.

In No. 1165 the words "Perry's Victory" on the border refer to the battle of Lake Erie on September 10, 1813, in which our Commander Oliver Hazard Perry announced his victory in the memorable words "We have met the enemy and they are ours." The ends and bottom are hollowed out and are decorated with a beading. The border is in blue and gold and the height is about three feet. About 1815–1820.

No. 1166 is a handsome mirror with double columns on each side, with gilded balls between them and also at the bottom and under the cornice. The painting shows the "Constitution" and several other craft in the lower bay of New York, on a white panel decorated with leaves. This is a tall "pier" glass of fine workmanship. About 1815–1820.

No. 1167 has two types of double columns which meet at the top of the glass, as also appears in No. 1192 and others. Large gilded acorns are under the cornice and gilded balls are below them. Under these balls are several applied decorative moldings. The name of the warship is not given, but it may be assumed that it is the "Constitution". About 1815–1820.

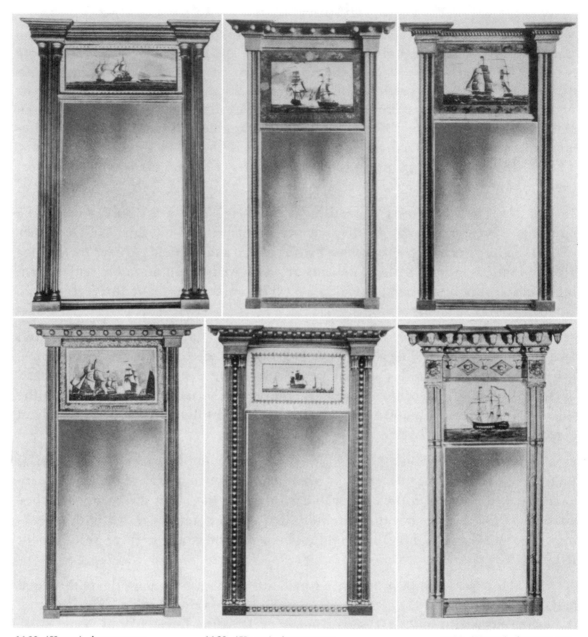

1162 (Upper) Anonymous.
1165 (Lower) Anonymous.

1163 (Upper) Anonymous.
1166 (Lower) Metropolitan Museum of Art.

1164 (Upper) Anonymous.
1167 (Lower) Anonymous.

1168 (Upper) Metropolitan Mu-
    seum.
1171 (Lower) Anonymous.

1169 (Upper) Anonymous.
1172 (Lower) Anonymous.

1170 (Upper) Metropolitan Mu-
    seum.
1173 (Lower) Metropolitan Mu-
    seum.

In the next group of six illustrations, Nos. 1168–1173, we see other patriotic mirrors of the Sheraton period. Each of these mirrors exhibits the national spirit of the new republic without special reference to the war of 1812; and, as in the previous group, the frames are all different, each one showing some particular feature of interest.

In No. 1168 the top is of the architectural "broken pediment" type, and upon the pedestal is an American eagle and below are festoons of leaves. Broken pediments of this kind are also seen in other articles such as the secretary–bookcase No. 851; but here the seventeen stars[3] in the oval indicate a date between the years 1803 and 1812. The decorations in the oval represent the growing commerce of the country; and above is the word "Liberty". On the frame the fluted columns, the horizontal lines of beaded molding and the other decorative work unite in producing a handsome and interesting mirror. About 1804–1812.

In Nos. 1169–1173 the patriotic spirit is shown by the memorials to Washington and by the paintings of the American eagles or flags.

No. 1169 is in honor of Washington, whose portrait appears in the glass panel, with two memorial urns under weeping willow trees. The columns at the sides are hollowed out and in each is a spiral molding. Under the cornice are thirteen gilded balls, perhaps referring to the thirteen original States. About 1800–1820.

No. 1170 is also in memory of Washington, whose name is on the base of the memorial urn which is kept green by the flowers springing from it. On each side of the urn are flags. The frame is plain, but under the cornice is an unusual type of ornamental molding which may be well seen with a magnifying glass. About 1800–1810.

In No. 1171 are the familiar gilded balls, under which are applied decorations of baskets of flowers. In the white painted panel is an oval within which is the American eagle. Around the oval are flags and warlike emblems. On each side of the panel is a large acanthus leaf on a curved form which supports the cornice, and is known as a "corbel", which is illustrated and explained in connection with the mantel mirror No. 1231. Below are two columns on each side. The height is about four and one–half feet. About 1815–1820.

In No. 1172, also, there are two columns on each side, and between them are gilded balls, which are also seen under the cornice and on the base as in No. 1166. On the white painted glass is an oval containing an eagle with a shield, and surrounded on three sides by festoons of flowers. This mirror is four feet high. About 1815–1820.

No. 1173 is a plain but interesting mirror. The frame is unusual in having a small panel at the base, decorated with gilded designs. In the upper panel is an American eagle holding in its beak a streamer containing the patriotic words

3. See the list of States and the order of their admission into the Union in the "Appendix", section 208; also the comments on Nos. 1160 and 1196.

1174 (Upper) Mrs. John S. Gibbs, Jr.
1176 (Lower) Mr. J. Gilman D'Arcy Paul.

1175 (Upper) Anonymous.
1177 (Lower) Anonymous.

"E Pluribus Unum". Around the eagle are sixteen stars, none of which are conspicuous and some of which have become almost invisible. These sixteen stars probably indicate that the mirror was made at a time when there were sixteen States in the Union; if so, this mirror was made between the year 1796, when the sixteenth State, Tennessee, was admitted to the Union, and 1803, when the seventeenth State, Ohio, was admitted. See section 208 in the Appendix for the list of States in the order of their admission. Other mirrors with stars are Nos. 1160 and 1196. About 1800.

Passing from the mirrors with patriotic features, we now examine other mirrors which are shown in groups for ease of comparison. Although there may be some uncertainty as to dates, all of these mirrors are regarded as having been made within the period of about 1795 to 1820.

Nos. 1174–1177 are wide in proportion to their height, and on each side are two separated columns within which is a narrow glass panel generally of the same height as the central glass. These mirrors may be English.

No. 1174 was perhaps intended for a mantel, its width being about thirty-three inches and its height about forty-three inches. At the top are three paintings on glass, the middle one showing a country landscape. Under the cornice are small gilded balls. On each side are long glass mirrors between the fluted columns. About 1790–1800.

No. 1175 is of a similar design, but not so wide as the preceding mirror. The three panels at the top and the two long panels at the side are fully decorated with gilt floral designs.[4] Above the four columns, the divisions separating the three panels are ornamented with applied flowers; and below the columns are applied rosettes. About 1800–1810.

In No. 1176 the two long glass panels at the sides extend from the cornice to the base and are decorated with gilt grapevines on a dark background. There is also a panel at the top, adorned with floral festoons, and one at the base with grapevines, both on a white background. Around the central glass is a reeded border which is stained black in imitation of ebony, as are the circular borders around many of the convex glasses and girandole mirrors shown in section 150. About 1800–1810.

No. 1177 is interesting although similar in general form to the three preceding mirrors of this type. Between the slender columns on each side is a glass panel painted in gilt with leaves twining around a third column. At the top is a panel decorated with a ship, a bridge and rocks upon which there are trees. About 1800–1810.

---

4. The French word "églomisé" is sometimes used in describing glass panels painted in gilt. An eighteenth century French designer, named "Glomi", used a certain method of decorating a glass object, such as a looking glass, with a gold leaf painting. His work was much admired and the word "églomisé", in which his name appears, was invented in 1825 to indicate his method. See "Nouveau Larousse Illustré", volume 4, page 80. Several mirrors with gold leaf paintings are shown in this section.

In Nos. 1178–1181 the panels are decorated with delicately painted and graceful designs of flowers.

No. 1178 has the familiar gilded balls under the cornice, below which is a line of applied oval decorations. In the panel are flowers under which is a festoon of drapery and tassels. On each end of the panel is a front view of a "corbel" supporting the cornice, as explained in note 2 in the comment on No. 1231. About 1800–1820.

No. 1179 is a tall mirror, forty–eight inches high, with a panel in which there is an urn from which several large gilded flowers arise, and a multitude of other leaves and flowers are in unsupported positions. The columns here extend to the top of the panel. On the back of the frame are the remains of a label bearing the name "Barnard Cermenati", of Newburyport, whose work was mentioned in "Antiques", October, 1922, page 153, and September, 1925, page 139. About 1800–1806.

In No. 1180 the panel is white and the decorations are a group of flowers gracefully springing from flower–pots in the lower corners. In the centre is another floral design. Here also the columns extend to the top. About 1800–1820.

In No. 1181 there is a white panel in which are bunches of grapes and leaves in festoons suspended from rosettes. Around the edges of the panel are delicate traceries, not well seen in the illustration, and under the cornice are seven applied rosettes. At the bottom are two brass knobs supporting the mirror, such as are referred to in section 151. About 1800–1820.

In Nos. 1182 and 1183 the upper panels are ornamented with another type of decoration. In No. 1182 the upper panel is fully covered with decorative designs which are not very well seen in the engraving. In the centre is a small landscape and on each side is a round star–like painting of brilliant color. The other portions of the panel are filled with gilded designs of graceful form. About 1800–1820.

In No. 1183 the painting of a castle in the centre of the panel suggests that the mirror is of English make. On each side of the castle scene is a painting with a dark background. The frame is large and is covered with ornamental work, such as the beaded moldings in several places and the acanthus leaves on the "corbel" supporting the cornice as in No. 1178. About 1800–1820.

In the next group, Nos. 1184–1187, are four mirrors in which a lattice–work design is used in the panel. This design, with variations, appears also in the backs of several chairs in the Sheraton style shown in Nos. 234, 269 and 270. It is also seen in a vertical position on the doors of secretary-bookcases, as in Nos. 852 and 854. Two fine mantel mirrors with lattice–work are shown as Nos. 1231 and 1232.

In No. 1184 the panel is of wood and the lattice–work design is applied, and resembles a series of diamond–shaped forms. The reeded columns extend upward to the same height as the glass. Under the cornice is a row of small gilded balls. About 1800–1820.

1178 (UPPER) MR. & MRS. WM. D. POULTNEY.
1181 (LOWER) MRS. JOHN S. GIBBS, JR.

1179 (UPPER) MR. E. G. MILLER, JR.
1182 (LOWER) ANONYMOUS.

1180 (UPPER) MRS. JOHN S. GIBBS, JR.
1183 (LOWER) ANONYMOUS.

1184 (Upper) Mr. J. Gilman D'Arcy Paul.
1186 (Lower) Anonymous.

1185 (Upper) Mr. Edgar G. Miller, Jr.
1187 (Lower) Mrs. Arthur Hale.

In No. 1185 the lattice–work is painted on a glass panel and encloses an oval in which a landscape appears. The frame is decorated with rosettes at the four corners and with three horizontal lines of beaded molding. The columns extend upward beyond the glass and around them are four gilded bands. The cornice projects forward very slightly. About 1800–1820.

No. 1186 is a handsome mirror with a large eagle at the top holding in its beak two festoons of chains and balls which are supported at the ends by urns or ewers. The eagle stands upon a small wooden panel under which is the glass panel decorated with lattice–work. The urns, the festoons and the small wooden panel suggest the Adam style. In the centre of the panel is an oval with a landscape. As in the previous mirror, the cornice projects forward very slightly. About 1800–1820.

No. 1187 has not only a panel with applied lattice–work at the top, but also a glass panel below it with a gilded urn from which gilded flowers extend horizontally in somewhat the same manner as those in No. 1179. On each side are two columns, as in No. 1162, around which there are three horizontal bands. About 1800–1820.

The next four mirrors, Nos. 1188–1191, have in the panel at the top a type of decoration, known as "low relief", or "bas–relief", which projects slightly above the surface of the panel and is made of composition and applied on the panel.[5] Designs of fruits, flowers, shells, stars, leaves and cornucopias[6] are seen on mirrors of this type. These mirrors may be dated at about 1800–1820; but "relief" work is also seen in mirrors of a later date in the American Empire style.

In No. 1188 the panel is decorated with three festoons of drapery, and other forms are suspended and are also on the ends of the panel, all doubtless being survivals of the Adam and Hepplewhite styles of festoons seen in the two previous sections. About 1800–1820.

In No. 1189 the panel is decorated with flowers, and under the cornice are the familiar gilded balls. Horizontal bands are around the clustered columns. About 1800–1820.

In No. 1190, on the panel, is a figure of an angel, as stated in Mr. Lockwood's "Colonial Furniture", figure 384, and also a festoon of flowers and leaves. The columns extend from the base almost to the cornice. About 1800–1820.

In No. 1191 are bunches of grapes on vines in a graceful design. The columns taper gradually to the top and at the base are reeded vase–like forms. Under the cornice is a row of ornamental figures. About 1800–1820.

---

5.   The word "relief", as used in this connection, is defined as "the projection of a figure or feature from the ground or plane on which it is formed. 'Relief' is, in general, of three kinds: high relief, low relief, (or bas–relief), and middle relief. The distinction lies in the degree of projection." Otherwise stated, "low relief", or "bas–relief", is "a form of relief in which the figures or other objects represented project very slightly from the ground". Century Dictionary.

     A design in "relief" which is constantly seen, but seldom noticed, is that of words or figures on a coin.

6.   A cornucopia design is in No. 1196 in this section. See also No. 1220 in section 148 and for other cornucopias see the Index.

1188 (UPPER) MR. E. G. MILLER, JR.   1189 (UPPER) MR. E. G. MILLER, JR.   1190 (UPPER)   METROPOLITAN MU-
1191 (LOWER) ANONYMOUS.   1192 (LOWER) MRS. F. G. BOYCE, JR.   SEUM.
                                                                     1193 (LOWER)   METROPOLITAN MU-
                                                                                          SEUM.

Other illustrations of mirrors in the Sheraton period, Nos. 1192–1199, are of several different types, each type showing some characteristic of the period.

No. 1192 is a fully decorated mirror. Acorns are under the cornice, and below the acorns are four applied rosettes and a festoon of drapery, below which is a painted glass panel with a festoon of flowers. At each side of the panel are two short columns, below which are spiral columns extending to the base, as also in No. 1167. About 1800–1810.

No. 1193 is a handsome mirror which shows features of the Adam and Hepplewhite styles in the three urns, the small panel under the centre urn and the festoons of leaves, such as are seen in No. 1152; in other respects it resembles in general design some of the mirrors of the Sheraton period shown above. In the upper panel is a painting representing "Liberty" and a ship in the background typifying commerce; in this respect it may be compared with No. 1168. About 1800–1810.

In No. 1194 there is a suggestion of the lattice–work seen in the panels of Nos. 1184–1187, but the design is not fully carried out, as there is a painting of a house in the centre, and between the arms of the cross–pieces are painted leaves. At the top are two lines of molding and at the upper corners are rosettes. About 1800–1810.

No. 1195 is a mahogany mirror and has no gilding. The reeded columns are slender and delicate. In the glass panel is a painting of Mt. Vernon with its eight columns and the Potomac river in the background. About 1810–1820.

No. 1196 is of a different type. The large upper and recessed panel, instead of being made of glass, is of wood. On the panel is an applied spray of leaves and a graceful cornucopia with fruits. The sides are wide and flat and the top is carved. On the sides and the base are fifteen stars which perhaps represent the number of States in the Union at the time the mirror was made, and indicate the date to be between 1792, when the fifteenth State, Kentucky, was admitted into the Union, and 1796, when the sixteenth State, Tennessee, was admitted; see the mirror No. 1173 and the list in the Appendix, section 208. This mirror has been gilded. If the so–called stars are correctly understood, the date was about 1795; but they may be rosettes and of a later date.

No. 1197 is a plain mirror of a somewhat similar type, and doubtless is a later form of the previous piece. It has a curved cresting, and is of mahogany and without decoration. The sides are wide, and are flat except at the edges where there are slender reeded columns. About 1810–1820.

In No. 1198 there are no columns on the sides or elsewhere. Over the large panel is a band of light wood and the panel is decorated with inlay, and other lines of inlay are at the base. Four rosettes are at the corners of the glass. Mirrors of the type of this and the preceding one seem to be plain and later variations of those shown in Mr. Lockwood's "Colonial Furniture", figures 370 and 371. About 1815–1825.

1194 (UPPER) MR. E. G. MILLER, JR. 1195 (UPPER) MR. & MRS. JAMES 1196 (UPPER) MR. C. W. L. JOHN-
1197 (LOWER) MR. E. G. MILLER, JR.   CAREY, JR.   SON.
                                     1198 (LOWER) MR. E. G. MILLER, JR. 1199 (LOWER) LOCK. COL. FUR., FIG.
                                                                             385.

In No. 1199 the spiral columns taper towards the upper ends and are of a somewhat heavy type. Under the cornice are acorns, below which are two classical figures, and between them is a large applied shell. At the bottom the columns terminate in reeded forms. This mirror may perhaps be regarded as in the American Empire style because of the heavy columns. About 1820–1825.

Illustrations of many similar mirrors of the Sheraton period would be shown if space permitted; but those here presented are examples of the principal types. In later sections, treating of mantel mirrors and others, are additional illustrations of the fashion of the period.

Section 147. Empire style mirrors.—In mirrors of the Empire style,[1] some of the same features are found as in other articles of furniture in that style, the principal one being the use of larger and heavier parts than in the previous styles and periods. In mirrors this is particularly seen in the columns, which are often larger in size and less elegant in design than those in the Sheraton period. The delicate reeding on the columns of the earlier pieces disappeared and the columns were frequently covered with somewhat coarse carvings of leaves, spirals or rings. In some cases there was a combination of gilded and black portions on the same column.

The cornice and columns which were used so generally in the Sheraton period, giving an architectural[2] appearance to the frame, were sometimes omitted and the frame thus lost the dignity and completeness of the earlier pieces. The mirrors, however, in many cases continued to be made in two sections, the upper one usually containing a painting or an applied decoration; but in the mirrors in which the cornice and columns were omitted there was generally only one section. All of these features will be seen in the illustrations, which are comparatively few in number because there is much sameness in the designs of the mirrors in the Empire style.

Mirrors of this type are not generally considered to any extent in the books, as they are not fine antiques, either in age or appearance. The dates of those shown here are from about 1815 to 1830, overlapping the Sheraton period, which, in mirrors, was in vogue from about 1795 to 1820, as mentioned in the previous section.

1. As to the Empire style, see section 21. The term "Empire" style is commonly used to mean the "American Empire" style, as distinguished from the English and French Empire styles.

2. As to this, see note 2, A in the previous section. An Empire style mirror without a cornice and columns is sometimes called "non–architectural" because their absence deprived the mirror of its architectural features and appearance.

   Several mantel mirrors which well illustrate the Empire style are shown in section 149. An American wall clock with a gilded mirror front in the same style, is No. 2047.

Each of the Empire mirrors Nos. 1200–1203 has a projecting cornice and columns, as most of those in the Sheraton period have, and the mirror is therefore regarded as being architectural in design. In Nos. 1204–1206 there are no projecting cornices and the mirrors are known as non–architectural.[3]

In No. 1200 the cornice is rounded at the ends, giving a somewhat heavy appearance to the top. Under the cornice are acorns, below which are some fanciful designs of applied work. The upper glass panel represents a country scene with a man on a prancing horse. The columns are the principal indication of the Empire style, being carved in rings and lacking the elegance of the reeded or fluted ones of the Sheraton period. The partition covering the junction of the upper and lower glasses is also ringed. About 1820–1830.

In No. 1201 the gilded columns are carved in a spiral or twist in the centre, with a vase–shaped top and bottom, and at the base is a carved horizontal piece. In the panel is a painting of a New York church and other buildings, over which are two urns and a shell. Four rosettes are at the corners. About 1825–1830.

In No. 1202 the cornice is reeded on the edges and the centre is in a curved form. Each column is decorated with coarsely carved acanthus leaf designs between which are ringed portions. Brass rosettes are at the four corners, as in the previous piece. About 1810–1815.

No. 1203 is in a popular form, the columns having a series of three gilded and ringed sections between which are two sections which are "ebonized", meaning that they are stained black to imitate ebony. The glass panel has a painting of what is supposed to be a Chinese building. A similar painting may also be seen on the doors of the clocks Nos. 1928 and 1931. The painting is within a stenciled border. In this mirror and the two following ones the columns are similar. About 1810–1820.

In Nos. 1204–1206 there are no projecting cornices, but the columns are present. Nos. 1203–1205 have the same type of columns, but their appearance is much changed by other features.

In No. 1204, except for the absence of a cornice, the general design of the frame resembles that of the previous piece. The columns are partly ringed and gilded and partly black, the black portions being reeded. Around the glass is a reeded black border which is enclosed within a gilded one. On the glass panel is a painting of a naval battle, presumably of the war of 1812–1815. About 1815–1820.

No. 1205 is another in which the columns are partly ringed and gilded and partly black. Four rosettes are at the corners. This is a smaller and plainer piece than the two preceding ones, having no painting at the top nor other ornamental features. About 1820–1830.

3. In "Antiques", July, 1926, pages 31–35, several similar mirrors in the Empire style are illustrated, with comments.

1200 (UPPER) MR. & MRS. GEO.
    SHIPLEY.
1203 (LOWER) ANONYMOUS.

1201 (UPPER) ANONYMOUS.
1204 (LOWER) ANONYMOUS.

1202 (UPPER) ANONYMOUS.
1205 (LOWER) ANONYMOUS.

1206 (LEFT) ANONYMOUS.   **1207** (CENTRE) MR. & MRS. WM. A.   **1208** (RIGHT) ANONYMOUS.
DIXON.

No. 1206 has a frame of a different type. The columns and the top and bottom are wholly gilded and are ornamented with applied designs. In the panel is a painting of a landscape. Around the panel and the glass are gilded borders. About 1820–1830.

Great numbers of Empire mirrors of the types shown in this section, and other similar types, are to be seen in shops and private houses.

No. 1207 is a mirror of light wood, with a concave frame on the edges of which is a plain molding. Around the glass is a border stained to represent ebony. Although without decoration by gilding or otherwise this mirror is an attractive one and is especially so over a bureau in a room furnished in maple. About 1820–1830.

No. 1208 is a very familiar type in black and gilt. Around the frame and also around the glass is a border of gilt, and between these borders the mahogany is in a concave form. The bright lines at the upper right corner appear to be gilt, but in fact are merely reflections of light. A large mirror of this type may be used either vertically, as over a bureau, or horizontally, as on a mantel or in a hallway. About 1820–1830.

Section 148. Other wall mirrors.—In this section are presented several mirrors of different styles or periods. Some of these pieces might have been placed in previous sections, but they are of special characters which make it difficult to classify them as being in a particular style.

In Nos. 1209–1212 we see a type of mirror which in certain respects resembles some of the fretwork mirrors shown in section 143, but in other respects is very different. The fretwork is on the top and the base, but not on the sides which are straight and not ornamented. The special feature is that the cresting is very high and was decorated with a carved, gilded and applied design which in many cases has disappeared; and the base was decorated in the same manner. Almost all of these mirrors are less than three feet in height. It is said that mirrors of this type are not uncommon and that they were made prior to 1750, and with some changes were again made as late as about 1770 to 1800, perhaps by way of reviving an old style.

No. 1209 seems to be an early example of this type. The cresting is very high and is cut in a series of "C" curves, which were a favorite form of decoration in the time of Chippendale and even earlier, as mentioned in section 142, in note 3. A gilt ornament was no doubt on the cresting, but is now missing, which is natural in view of the warping of the thin wood of which the cresting is made; on the base is a new gilded decoration in the style of the period. About 1750–1760.

No. 1210 is a curiosity. It is on a larger scale than the others on the page and at first sight it appears to have no similarity to the preceding mirror or the next one; but in fact it seems to be a similar piece which has lost its high cresting, and is hung upside down, with the base at the top. The writer purchased this piece some years ago thinking it was a mirror of the same type as No. 1098, in the Queen Anne style, and he now keeps it (and several other articles) as a warning. It is "cross–banded", which is explained in the comment on No. 1097. The date is supposed to be about 1750–1760.

No. 1211 is probably in a somewhat later style than No. 1209. The cresting is in another design and there are no "C" curves. The applied gilded decorations are probably new; that on the base is much the same as in No. 1209. About 1770.

No. 1212 is a later development of the style of Nos. 1209 and 1211, with a tall cresting; but instead of the fretwork on the cresting of those two mirrors, in this one the edges of the cresting are ornamented with graceful molded and gilded designs of scrolls and leaves, and in the centre of the top is a pheasant. At the four corners of the frame rosettes are applied upon the square blocks. About 1785–1795.

No. 1213 is another type which was popular at about the same time as the preceding one. Here the top is in a different form from any previously seen, consisting of a wide central platform upon which are gilded leaves and flowers, and two smaller platforms, with gilded leaves, at the ends. Below the top are lines of molding around the edges and the glass, and four rosettes upon blocks. There are no curved lines in the frame of the mirror except the two concave curves at the top. All of the moldings, blocks, rosettes and feet, and all of the gilded ornaments at the top, are applied, and almost all are of composition. About 1785–1800.

In No. 1214 the top is in an unusual form, having a "broken" effect as in No. 1168, but with concave curves at each side. The ornament which doubtless was in the centre is missing. Below are festoons such as those seen on the mirrors in the Adam and Hepplewhite styles; and on the curved base is a gilded design. The glass is beveled and around it is a gilded molding. About 1785–1800.

1209 (Upper) Mr. E. G. Miller, Jr. 1210 (Upper) Mr. E. G. Miller, Jr. 1211 (Upper) Anonymous.
1212 (Lower) Lockwood's Col. 1213 (Lower) Anonymous. 1214 (Lower) Mrs. E. N. Dunham.
  Furn., Fig. 365.

The next two mirrors, Nos. 1215 and 1216, are known as "Bilbao" mirrors. This name is said to be given to mirrors of this type because they were brought to the seaport towns of New England in ships coming from the town of Bilbao in Spain, not far from the French border. The frames of these mirrors are made of pieces of marble of various colors, cemented or glued on wood; or perhaps of a synthetic marble made in Italy. Around the glass are gilt moldings. Because of the heavy marble of the frame and the delicacy of the scroll work at the top these mirrors are seldom found entirely in their original condition. From the decorations at the top it seems probable that the designs were suggested by those of Adam or Hepplewhite, shown in sections 144 and 145.

No. 1215 is a handsome mirror of the Bilbao type. At the top are two large scrolls with leaves and flowers and between the scrolls in an oval frame is a painting of a woman standing alone in an open landscape. At the ends of the top of the frame are urns. The tapering columns are in two parts, and are seen to be formed of a number of small pieces of marble. At the bottom are feet as in No. 1212. Around the frame, and also around the glass, are gilded moldings. About 1780–1800.

In No. 1216 the top is ornamented with gilded designs of flowers and leaves in scrolls, between which there is a vase with flowers, resting on a platform. Under these is a semi–circular marble arch enclosing a glass. This glass and the rectangular one below are bordered with gilded moldings. The rounded columns at the sides are slender and tapering and rest upon rectangular bases. About 1780–1800.

No. 1217 is a handsome gilded mirror with a cornice which does not project in the usual manner. At the top is a row of leaves under which are flowers arranged in the form of a double cyma curve, as to which see section 23. Around the top and sides of the frame and the mirror are lines of beaded moldings. On each of the reeded columns are six bands and at the four corners are blocks upon which are rosettes. This mirror should perhaps have been shown in section 146 which is on the Sheraton period. About 1800–1810.

No. 1218 is a "courting" mirror, of which a considerable number have been found in New England near the seaport towns, such as Salem. Mr. Lockwood, in his "Colonial Furniture", volume 1, page 328, states that his examination of a large number has convinced him that the original ones were brought to our country from China, for the reasons that the frame is not in any European style, the wood is the same as that used in certain Chinese picture frames, and strips of Chinese paper have been found in the backs. It seems that these mirrors were copied in England and America, as indicated by the use of walnut wood, often with a wide convex molding on the frame. In the illustration of this courting mirror we see the shallow box in which it is supposed to have come from China; the cover of the box is missing. All around the cresting and the frame are wooden moldings between which are pieces of glass crudely painted with unfamiliar flowers and leaves. In the cresting are flowers painted on glass. The height is about sixteen inches. The date is thought to be about 1800–1810.

1215 (Upper) Metropolitan Museum.
1218 (Lower) Anonymous.

1216 (Upper) Mr. Albert G. Towers.
1219 (Lower) Anonymous.

1217 (Upper) Mr. & Mrs. Bayard Turnbull.
1220 (Lower) Mr. Geo. Bradford Simmons.

No. 1219 is an interesting mirror with unusual designs. In the pointed crest-ing are three sunken panels, one oval and two arched, with inlaid shells; and a white carving in bone representing the rising sun, or perhaps a shell, is in the centre. The sides and other parts of the frame are flat and wide as in Nos. 1197 and 1198. At the top of the glass is a row of interlaced semi–circular and Gothic arches, and other openwork is at the base. A line of inlaid molding is around the glass. This mirror was perhaps made about 1800. Its origin is not known.

No. 1220 is an oval mirror in which the frame is formed of two cornucopias which are joined at the top and bottom. The mouths of the cornucopias are seen to be filled with fruits and vegetables, and are connected with each other by strings of flowers upon which an American eagle stands with outspread wings.[1] About 1790–1800.

In No. 1221 the two applied griffins in the panel at the top are a character-istic detail of the Adam style, as mentioned in the comment on the Adam style mirror No. 1147, note 5. They are also seen in No. 7 in the Hepplewhite designs in No. 1152; and with a wreath between them they appear on the mantel mirror No. 1229. In the panel at the base is a leaf design and on the top, sides and base are other leaf figures, with four rosettes at the corners. About 1800–1810.

In No. 1222, a somewhat large rectangular mirror, the top is decorated with leaves and flowers and in the centre is a small rectangular glass panel with painted flowers. As in No. 1217, the cornice does not project. The columns are reeded and the base is ornamented with moldings. This mirror may be compared with the upper mirror in the Adam style, in illustration No. 4 in section 16. About 1800.

No. 1223 is an oval mirror in which the frame, except for its shape, resembles the round convex mirrors and girandole mirrors shown in section 150. Upon a pedestal at the top is an eagle and on each side and at the bottom are leaves. Around the glass is a reeded band of wood stained black to resemble ebony, beyond which are more than fifty gilded balls such as are in the convex and girandole mirrors. About 1800.

No. 1224 is an English mirror in an oval frame which is very similar to the preceding one, but is more highly decorated. At the top is a gilded basket with flowers and with garlands of flowers hanging down on the sides. At the base are gilded oak leaves extending up the sides. The ebonized wood around the glass is not reeded. This is a well proportioned and pleasing piece. About 1800–1810.

No. 1225 is an oval Victorian mirror with a frame carved in designs which faintly recall the "rococo" ornamentation seen in the Chippendale style mirrors Nos. 1118–1120 and there mentioned in the comments. At the top are fruits and on the sides are bunches of grapes, except for which, and the oval glass, the mirror might be mistaken for one in the Chippendale period. Several "C" scrolls with

---

1. A fine mirror of this type is shown in the frontispiece of "Antiques", October, 1929. Others are in Mr. Lockwood's "Colonial Furniture", volume 1, pages 324 and 396.

1221 (UPPER) MR. & MRS. GEO.
    SHIPLEY.
1224 (LOWER) ANONYMOUS.

1222 (UPPER) MRS. M. F. RODGERS.
1225 (LOWER) ANONYMOUS.

1223 (UPPER) MR. ALBERT G. TOW-
    ERS.
1226 (LOWER) ANONYMOUS.

one end terminating in leaves will be noticed. A form of "C" scrolls also appears in the next mirror and in the Victorian bureau No. 768, indicating a revival of the design. About 1840–1850.

No. 1226 is also an oval Victorian mirror in which there are "C" scrolls at the top and the bottom. The outer portion of the frame is pierced with many round openings, and on the inner and outer edges of each space between these openings are four "C" scrolls, almost too numerous to count and too small to be well seen without a magnifying glass; but even with its superabundance of "C" scrolls this mirror could not be mistaken for one of the Chippendale period. A spiral molding is within the outer portion of the frame. About 1830–1840.

Section 149. Mantel mirrors.—Although there are a few mantel mirrors in our country in the styles of Queen Anne and Chippendale they are seldom seen, and therefore we present only one example of each style.

No. 1227 is regarded as being in the Queen Anne style. The base extends in curves at the ends as in Nos. 1107–1113, and on the blank spaces at the ends two candle holders were probably placed. The ends and the glass are surrounded with carved and gilded moldings. The glass is beveled and is in one piece instead of in three parts as in most of the other mantel mirrors shown here. This mirror is also shown in Mr. Lockwood's "Colonial Furniture", volume 1, page 390. About 1730–1750.

No. 1228, in the Chippendale style,[1] is an ornate and fully gilded mirror in three parts, on which we see several of the popular "C" curves of the Chippendale period which are referred to in connection with Nos. 1103–1106. The moldings at the base extend in curves beyond the ends. At the top are two squirrels and under the arch in the centre is a swan. In the left section of the glass is a painting of a man in Chinese costume with white sleeves and a fan; in the right section is a Chinese woman; and in both sections are painted trees. The four upright columns are finely designed and executed. About 1760–1770.

The other mantel mirrors shown in this section are all of a later date than the foregoing ones.

Although No. 1229, with its columns and cornice, is in the style of Sheraton, it has also an indication of the styles of Adam and Hepplewhite in the applied griffins on a raised panel under the cornice. These imaginary creatures are seen in the Adam style mirror No. 1147, in the Hepplewhite figure 7 in No. 1152, in the card table No. 1516 and the wall mirror No. 1221. The griffins hold between them a wreath of laurel, an emblem of victory or distinction. They are described in note 5 in section 144. On each side is a glass panel painted with festoons of

1. Two handsome gilded mantel mirrors in the Chippendale rococo style are shown in Mr. Lockwood's "Colonial Furniture", volume 1, figures 336 and 337. Mirrors of this kind were apparently not made in our country, but a few were imported from England. In recent years reproductions have been made and are very effective in the proper setting, but are generally regarded as having too fanciful decorations for rooms furnished in the styles of our antique furniture.

1227 (Upper) Hammond–Harwood House. 1228 (Next to Upper) Mrs. John S.
1229 (Next to Lower) Mrs. Reginald W. Petre.   Gibbs, Jr.
                                                  1230 (Lower) Mrs. Maurice F. Rodgers.

leaves suspended from a horizontal bar, in the centre of which is a portrait; this design also may be a derivation from the Adam style. This mirror is finely decorated at all points. About 1800–1820.

In No. 1230 the laurel wreaths under the cornice are of about the same type as the wreath held by the griffins in the preceding piece. In the centre is a raised panel with an oval design of flowers. Around the three sections of the glass and on the partitions between them are moldings of the same design as in the preceding mirror; and the lyre–shaped ornaments above the two columns on the ends are also the same in each piece. These similarities suggest that the two mirrors were probably designed or made by the same person. About 1800–1820.

No. 1231 is a well known mantel mirror in the Peirce–Nichols house in Salem, Massachusetts, and belongs to the Essex Institute, through whose courtesy the photograph appears. The purpose of showing on the right a side view of the "corbel" on a larger scale is stated in the note.[2] Under the reeded edge of the cornice and the numerous gilded balls is an applied composition lattice–work in two parts between which is a panel with two festoons of drapery. Under these is a panel with applied composition designs of trumpets at the ends and two branches of leaves in the centre. Three bands are on each of the four columns. The date has been the subject of an interesting difference of opinion, as mentioned in the note.[3]

2. The shape of the curved pieces with a carved leaf, over the two columns at the ends, appearing to support the parts above, is not well seen in the photograph, which was taken from the front, and in order to get a better view a photograph taken from the side is shown. This piece is seen on mirrors, mantels and some other articles. It is known by the architectural name "corbel" and is defined as a projection from the vertical face of a wall, supporting a part above. In furniture it is also known as a "bracket" or "console". As viewed from the side it is almost in the shape of a cyma curve, as to which see section 23. Other examples are in the mirrors Nos. 1171, 1178 and 1183. The presence of a "corbel" does not seem to indicate any definite date for the object on which it appears.

A pleasing illustration of the mirror is in "Antiques", February, 1931, page 119, in an article by Mr. Fiske Kimball, entitled "Furniture carvings by Samuel McIntire".

3. Four opinions as to the date have appeared in well known publications. There is a local tradition that the mirror was bought in 1783 at the time the house was built.

One writer stated that the mirror was probably bought "some few years after the house had been built, for the mirror is in the style which was popular about 1790."

Another writer regarded the mirror as a "war's–end mirror"; the "branches of leaves are the palms of heroic martyrdom"; the trumpets are those of fame. The Revolutionary War having ended, the mirror was probably made shortly thereafter, "between the closing of the war in 1781 and the signing of the treaty of peace in 1783."

A third writer terms the mirror a "McIntire glass", (as to McIntire see the chapter on "Sofas", section 72, notes 5 and 6), and considers that it was "probably made for its present position about 1790."

The fourth writer mentions a tradition that the mirror was "made to fit the panel over the mantel" in a room built in 1783, and accepts that date as the date of the mirror.

Happily for all concerned, all being wrong, it has since been made clear by definite information that the mirror was made in Paris in 1801 as a wedding present for a daughter of the Peirce family. After this disclosure one of the writers remarked that the moral is that in fixing dates of antiques "it is well to distrust all evidence save that of style and of provable contemporary document"; as to which see also section 6 entitled "Dating antique furniture".

1231 (Upper) Essex Institute, Salem.
1232 (Lower) Mrs. Homer Eaton Keyes.

No. 1232 is a handsome mantel mirror with two reeded columns at each end, resting upon blocks which are ornamented with two rosettes. Under the cornice are gilded balls and below these is an applied lattice–work which extends across the entire front and is decorated at each intersecting point with a rosette. As in the preceding piece, the edge of the cornice is reeded. This mirror is forty–eight inches high and fifty–five inches long. About 1790–1800.

No. 1233 has four columns, each consisting of a cluster of three upright wooden rods connected by bands and resting on small gilded balls standing on blocks with rosettes; similar rosettes are above the tops of the columns. Under the cornice is a concave surface, below which in the centre are interlaced strings of leaves. There are no gilded balls or acorns. On the base are two lines of molding and another is under the concave surface above mentioned. About 1800–1810.

In No. 1234 the distinctive feature is that the two columns at the ends are not in a rounded form, but have flat surfaces which are ornamented with bands and raised designs; and similar flat horizontal forms are under the cornice and at the base. The three glasses are not as high in proportion to their width as are those in the other mantel mirrors shown here. About 1810–1820.

No. 1235, in the Empire style, has no gilded balls or panel under the cornice, but the space is occupied by a horizontal half–round piece which is partly gilded and partly stained black to represent ebony; and the same method of decoration is used on the two vertical columns at the ends. Two gilded columns divide the glass into sections. This black and gold decoration is similar to that seen in the wall mirrors Nos. 1203–1205. About 1810–1820.

No. 1236, also in the Empire style, has gilded rings under the cornice and on the columns at the ends, parts of which are carved in designs which may represent pineapples. At the two lower corners are bunches of grapes and leaves and at the upper corners are rosettes over which are acorns. The columns dividing the glass are in an unusual design. The top, bottom and ends are hollowed out, as in Nos. 1163 and 1164. About 1810–1820.

In No. 1237, in the Empire style, groups of rings are on the top and ends and between the rings are fanciful designs, and at the bottom and on the four corners are other decorations.[4] The columns dividing the glass into three sections are also ornamented and around the glass is a decorative border. There are no gilded balls on this mirror. About 1810–1820.

In No. 1238 we see indications of the influence of the Adam style in the festoons and oval rosettes in the upper portion, and also in the panel in the centre with figures in the manner of Wedgwood. The border around the glass and the columns dividing the glass into three sections are reeded and stained black in imitation of ebony, as in the wall mirror No. 1176 and in the convex mirrors and girandole mirrors shown in the next section. This is probably a Victorian revival of previous styles, but might easily be mistaken for an earlier mirror. The date is said to be about 1850–1860.

---

4. A similar mantel mirror is shown in "Antiques", July, 1926, page 31, where fourteen mirrors of the period of about 1780–1840 are illustrated, with brief comments.

1233 (UPPER) MISS HARRIETT R. CHEW.   1234 (NEXT TO UPPER) MISS HELEN H. CAREY.
1235 (NEXT TO LOWER) MRS. WM. M. ROBERTS.   1236 (LOWER) MR. & MRS. BAYARD TURNBULL.

1237 (UPPER) MR. EDGAR G. MILLER, JR.
1238 (LOWER) ANONYMOUS.

676

Section 150.   Convex mirrors; girandole mirrors; sconces.—The term "convex mirror" is sufficiently descriptive to require no explanation other than that it is generally a round mirror in which the glass is convex, not flat; but the meanings of the words "girandole" and "sconce" are somewhat indefinite.

In the dictionaries it is said in substance that a "girandole" is a bracket to hold candles or other lights. It may be a branched candlestick to be used on a table or mantel; or it may be a wall bracket with receptacles for candles, somewhat resembling in form a gas bracket or an electric light bracket. A "girandole", in its proper sense, is complete without a mirror,[1] but it and a mirror are often combined in one piece. In our country a round convex mirror in a gilt frame with brackets for candles is often called a "girandole"; but a more expressive term is "girandole mirror", that is, a round mirror, with girandoles in the sense of candle brackets; and this term is therefore used in this book.

A "sconce", in its proper meaning, is said to be a wall bracket, or group of brackets, holding candles or lights, without a mirror; but although a mirror is not necessarily a part of a sconce, a sconce is often fitted with a flat mirror. Sconces with and without flat mirrors are shown in Nos. 1248–1253.

By way of summary of these definitions it may be said that a girandole mirror is generally round and convex, with candle brackets attached; and a sconce is a wall bracket for candles and may or may not have a mirror attached.

The frames of the convex mirrors and of the girandole mirrors are gilded and are very similar in construction. The round convex glass is usually surrounded by a border which is stained black to imitate ebony, and is fully reeded. Around this border is a molding which is either hollowed out in concave form, in which case the concave portion is generally ornamented with gilded balls, or in convex form. In a few mirrors, not illustrated here, the glass is concave, not convex. Because of their convex or concave form, the glasses always give a distorted reflection; if the glass is convex, the image of the reflected scene becomes a miniature; but if the glass is concave, the image is enlarged. These pieces were made in pairs and were used for decorative purposes, as they could not be used as "looking" glasses. Perhaps some of these mirrors were made in our country, but most of them seem to be of English or French make.

---

1.   To call a mirror which has no lighting arrangements a "girandole" is a misuse of the word because its primary meaning is connected with lighting, not with mirrors.

Flat mirrors in the Chippendale style were sometimes fitted with candle brackets; No. 1241 is an example.

In the Macquoid and Edwards "Dictionary of English Furniture", volume 3, page 57, under the heading "sconces and wall–lights" it is said that "a variety of lighting arrangements are included in this heading, the terms used to define them having a somewhat vague" meaning.

The word "girandole" is not used in the same sense by all of the English or American writers. In "Antique Furniture", by Mr. F. W. Burgess, page 369, it is said that the term is often misapplied. It is here also said that "when coal gas superseded candles, (about 1820), girandoles were discarded, and many were broken up and the metal work melted; but a goodly number survived and are now welcome additions to twentieth century furnishings, especially as they are so well adapted to the new (electric) methods of lighting." This book is an English one.

The ornamental features are of various kinds and quality. At the top the favorite feature was the American eagle as understood by foreign designers, often standing on a pedestal of rocks, from which there is in some cases a "dripping water effect", imitating a design used in the time of Chippendale, as mentioned in the third paragraph of section 142. A dolphin, or sea–horse, was also a popular figure, and baskets of fruit or flowers were sometimes used. On the sides and base there were other decorations, generally of leaves or shells or both, made of composition or of composition on wood.

These convex mirrors and girandole mirrors are all dated from about 1800 to 1820.

Nos. 1239 and 1240 are convex mirrors, not girandole mirrors, as they have no candle brackets. In No. 1239 the round frame is hollowed out and is ornamented with numerous gilded balls. On the top is an eagle with outstretched wings standing on a pedestal of rocks, as also in No. 1245, and on each side are leaves carved in scrolls. At the base are other carved leaves, between which is a gilded shell. The glass is surrounded with a border stained black. About 1800–1820.

In No. 1240 there is a vase at the top filled with fruits and grain, and on each side of the vase are leaves. On the sides are other leaves and at the base are others. In this mirror the surface of the round frame is hollowed out in concave form, but there are no gilded balls within it. The reeded black border around the glass is well seen. About 1800–1820.

No. 1241 is a mirror with attached brackets for candles. The large central glass is oval and flat, not convex, and is surrounded by small glasses, the joints between them being concealed by moldings, resembling in this respect the Chippendale style mirror No. 1103. At the top is an urn from which hang branches with leaves and fruit. At the base are carved and gilded leaves and flowers and in the centre are two brackets for candles; here also, but not well seen, are several "C" curves which were a favorite form of decoration before, during and even after the time of Chippendale, as mentioned in note 3 in section 142. This mirror and the mirror No. 1103 are believed to have been for much over a century in the Chase House, in Annapolis, which was built in 1771. About 1770–1775.

The next six illustrations, Nos. 1242–1247, are girandole mirrors, that is, round convex mirrors with girandoles, meaning brackets for candles.

No. 1242 is ornamented at the top by two dolphins facing each other and provided with very flexible tails; these dolphins may be compared with those on the card table No. 1556. The surface of the frame is hollowed out and numerous gilded balls are attached to it. The usual black and reeded border surrounds the glass. The base is ornamented with leaves and ribbons. Three candle brackets are attached to each side, not to the bottom as in the previous piece. About 1800–1820.

1239 (Upper) Mr. J. F. H. Maginn.   1240 (Upper) Anonymous.
1241 (Lower) Chase House, Annapolis.   1242 (Lower) Mr. Arthur E. Cole.

No. 1243 is a fully ornamented girandole mirror. At the top is a vase in which there are leaves and a shell–shaped design. On the upper part of the sides are bunches of fruits and flowers. The gilded molding around the glass is a half-round one and is divided into four parts by rings and other designs. About 1800–1820.

In No. 1244 there are no leaves or other designs around the frame, nor any gilded balls. At the top an eagle is upon a pedestal and from its beak two chains hang in festoons and extend down to the brackets on the sides. Lines of ornamental molding are on the inner and outer edges of the gilded frame. As the receptacles for candles are well shown here it may be mentioned that the round brass piece made to hold a candle is known as a "bobèche", a French word meaning the "socket of a candlestick". The glass saucers catch the candle drippings. It is often imagined that the saucers and the glass "drops" are of the highly esteemed old Waterford glass. About 1800–1820.

No. 1245 is a fully ornamented girandole mirror. At the top is an eagle on a pedestal of rocks, as in the convex mirror No. 1239. The sides and lower parts have leaves, and a shell is on the base. The frame is hollowed out and gilded balls are attached to it; and surrounding the balls is an ornamental molding. About 1800–1820.

In No. 1246 an unusual feature is that on each side there is an attachment to which the brackets holding the candles are fixed. Over the spiral design of the attachment is a small figure apparently representing a pineapple. An eagle on a platform is at the top and within the frame there is a very large number of gilded balls. About 1800–1820.

No. 1247 also has an eagle at the top and on each side and on the base are gilded leaves. Here the brackets extend further in front of the glass than in the other girandole mirrors, giving a more brilliant diffusion of light. About 1800–1820.

Six sconces are shown in Nos. 1248–1253. The first two of these, Nos. 1248–1249, are examples of sconces in the proper meaning of the word as stated at the beginning of this section, namely, wall brackets for candles, without a mirror attached. The other four sconces, Nos. 1250–1253, are fitted with flat mirrors, not convex or concave. Two of these mirrors, however, Nos. 1250 and 1253, are evidently not intended to be used as "looking glasses", the reflecting glasses being so fully decorated that they are useless for that purpose. All these sconces are effective for lighting purposes and several of them are very graceful and delicate articles, so delicate, in fact, that restorations have no doubt been necessary from time to time. These sconces are regarded as of English origin. They are not often seen in our country, but are so interesting that space must be given to them.

1243 (Upper) Col. Washington Bowie, Jr.
1245 (Lower) Hammond–Harwood House.

1244 (Upper) Miss Eleanor S. Cohen.
1246 (Lower) Mr. & Mrs. B. Turnbull.
1247 (Lower) Mr. J. G. D'A. Paul.

No. 1248 is one of a pair of sconces with spears which suggest the ancient Roman "fasces", a word perpetuated in the "fascism" of modern Italy. An eagle is on a rock and below is a horizontal bar under which two candle brackets are attached and also two festoons of flowers. About 1775–1800.

In No. 1249 the main features are similar in character to those in the preceding piece. Here are three spears, an eagle on the top of a column, and sus-

1248 (Left) Metropolitan Museum of Art.   1249 (Centre) Mrs. John S. Gibbs, Jr.   1250 (Right) Pennsylvania Museum of Art.

pended tassels. The candle brackets, however, are in a different position from the previous ones and are larger and more graceful. On these brackets are glass saucers from which glass drops are suspended. About 1775–1800.

No. 1250 will be recognized at once by those who have examined section 144 as being in the Adam style. The urn with flowers at the top, the flowers falling in graceful lines, the oval in which there are small glasses surrounding a small oval with a classical dancing girl, the horizontal platform from which the candle brackets are suspended, the fluted vase–shaped base with flowers below—all these are in the style of Robert Adam. A pair of these sconces are side pieces of the fine Adam mirror No. 1148. About 1775.

No. 1251 is somewhat similar in form to the preceding sconce. Above the urn in the upper portion are vertical leaves from which long strings of flowers extend down to the base of the oval glass which is supported upon a horizontal bar. At the ends of this bar are small urns and in the centre are two curved candle brackets. Below are festoons of flowers. About 1775–1790.

No. 1252 is also in the style of Adam as is shown by the urn at the top, under which is a vase–shaped form from the sides of which strings of leaves fall grace-fully over the sides of the round mirror below. At the base are two brackets for

1251 (LEFT) MR. A. G. TOWERS.   1252 (CENTRE) METROPOLITAN MU-   1253 (RIGHT) MRS. JOHN S. GIBBS,
                                          SEUM OF ART.   JR.

candles, and furnished with glass saucers from which glass drops are suspended as in No. 1249. About 1775–1790.

No. 1253 answers to the definition of a sconce, having candle brackets, and in this case also a mirror.[2] This is of a different type from the preceding sconces and recalls certain other mirrors in having a Chinese scene, as in the same owner's mantel mirror No. 1228, and a base projecting beyond the side lines as in Nos. 1112 and others. Drapery is suspended, as on a bedstead, from the domed top and on the sides. This piece is small and is one of a pair. About 1760–1770.

2. Two designs by Hepplewhite of very delicate sconces without mirrors are Nos. 6 and 10 in illustration No. 1152.

An illustrated article entitled "Eighteenth Century Lighting Devices", by Mr. R. W. Symonds, is in "Antiques", October, 1932, pages 139–142, in which several sconces are shown.

Section 151. Knobs for mirrors.—In the latter part of the eighteenth century and in the early part of the nineteenth it was the fashion to support mirrors on two small round or oval knobs, with a screw at the back, which were put in the wall at such a height as would cause the mirrors to tilt forward somewhat and thus give a downward reflection. The faces of these knobs were generally made either of enamel in a brass frame, or wholly of pressed brass, and were decorated with a variety of patriotic or other subjects; among these were portraits of American statesmen, naval or military commanders, ladies in the costumes of the times, views of land and sea, ships of war, thirteen or more stars and weeping willow trees in graveyards. The most desirable knobs were known as "Battersea" [1] enamel knobs, from the place of their original manufacture in a section of London; but many knobs made elsewhere in resemblance of them appropriated their name.[2]

In illustration No. 1254 three examples of enamel knobs are given. The first is a portrait marked "Com. Perry", the second "Gen. Washington" and the

1254—ANONYMOUS.

third is a sea scene with a lighthouse and also a dwelling which is alarmingly near the waves.[3]

1. A descriptive and illustrated article entitled "Battersea Enamel Knobs", by Miss Christine Adams, is in "Antiques", August, 1922, pages 73–75. See also the same magazine of November, 1931, page 289, figures 9 and 10; also July, 1929, page 29.

When used on fretwork mirrors, the knobs were placed in the curves of the base; on mirrors with columns they were probably under the columns, but they appear to better advantage if placed nearer the centre of the base.

2. The Battersea factory was in operation from 1750 to 1756, when it became bankrupt.

The word "Battersea" now indicates merely the type of knob; no reliance should be put on the word with respect to age or origin. Moreover many small enamel articles, such as tea caddies, cups or plates which were apparently not made in the factory, are now offered as Battersea enamel pieces.

These knobs are about two inches in diameter. Larger sized brass knobs, made after about 1800, were used to hold window curtains in place.

3. His victorious battle of Lake Erie on September 10, 1813, made Commander Oliver Hazard Perry a national hero. He died in 1819. A mirror with the words "Perry's Victory" is shown in No. 1165.

A large number of mirror knobs are shown in Mr. Wallace Nutting's "Furniture Treasury", Nos. 3564–3602.

Section 152. Dressing glasses.—From the reign of Queen Anne, (1702–1714), until about a century later, dressing glasses [1] were a favorite form of mirror for the dressing room. They were intended to stand on the top of dressing tables or chests of drawers and were made in many shapes; but all of them have the same general character, being small mirrors swinging between two upright posts which were attached to a box–like group of small drawers in which toilet requisites could be placed. In some of the early pieces there were also writing compartments, as in Nos. 1255 and 1256.

In these dressing glasses the lower part with drawers, sometimes called the "box", is as important a feature as the glass, and both parts follow the styles of the periods in which they were made. Thus we see the styles of the Queen Anne, (seldom Chippendale), Hepplewhite, Sheraton and Empire periods; and the reader who has examined the preceding mirrors shown in this chapter will see in these small mirrors some of the styles which were seen in the larger ones; and in the "box" portion some of the same curved fronts, inlay, veneering and, in some cases, handles and feet,[2] will be seen as in the bureaus of the respective periods. These similarities are referred to in the comments. The wood also was the same as that of other furniture of the same period, walnut being generally used in the earlier pieces and mahogany in those after about 1750; but a particular kind of wood was not restricted to any definite period.

No. 1255 and 1256 are dressing glasses which not only have two or three drawers, but also a desk compartment.

In No. 1255 the Queen Anne style will be recognized in the shape of the mirror frame, which resembles those in Nos. 1095 and 1099. The upright supports are "turned" in a round form and rest on feet which resemble the trestle feet seen on the tables Nos. 1300–1302; these feet hold the mirror more firmly in place than those used in some of the later pieces. The open lid of the desk portion is supported by small "pulls" such as those on the desk No. 777; and below the desk is a drawer. The ball feet seem to be small forms of those on the desk referred to. About 1725–1750.

No. 1256 was probably made in Holland or in England with some of the Dutch features and styles. The Queen Anne style appears in the cresting on the top of the mirror, somewhat similar to that in the mirror No. 1100; the glass, however, is rectangular at the inner upper corners. The upright supports of the mirror resemble in form the side supports of the backs of many of the Queen Anne style chairs, such as Nos. 58–63 and others. The curved front of the lower portion resembles in some respects the front of the Chippendale style "bombé" bureau

1. In the English books these glasses are called "toilet glasses". In our country they are sometimes called "shaving stands", a term which is unsuitable, as it limits their usefulness to masculine purposes. The words "dressing glasses" seem to be appropriate.

2. The handles and feet of these pieces were necessarily very small, in fact were miniatures, and were very frequently broken, and when this occurred new handles or feet in a later style were often substituted. Handles, knobs and feet of the various styles are shown in sections 39, 40 and 25, respectively.

No. 724. The corners of the framework are cut in a wide form of chamfering, as to which see the bureaus Nos. 713 and 714. This piece is made of walnut and is about thirty–three inches high and twenty–two inches wide. About 1730–1750.

No. 1257 also shows features of the Queen Anne style, the upper portion of the frame of the mirror being in a series of curves as in the Queen Anne style mirrors Nos. 1093 and 1094. Here the uprights supporting the mirror are straight and rectangular and are held in position by being inserted in holes in the top of the "box". A distinctive feature of the box in this and the next two dressing glasses is the shape of the three small drawers which form the front of the piece and curve inwardly from the bottom. About 1735–1760.

No. 1258 seems to follow the Queen Anne style, which is indicated by the inward curve of the fronts of the drawers, and by the curves of the mirror frame at the upper inner corners, as in the Queen Anne mirrors Nos. 1101–1102 and in the fretwork mirrors in the same style, Nos. 1121–1126; but, as mentioned in section 143, mirrors with these curved inner corners were made for many years, apparently from about 1730 to the end of the century.[3] The finials, the ornaments which were at the top of the uprights, are missing. The tiny brass handles and the miniature bracket feet will be noticed. Perhaps about 1750–1785.

In No. 1259 the frame of the mirror is entirely rectangular and at the top is a fretwork cresting of somewhat the same plain character as in the Queen Anne style mirror No. 1098 which continued to be made until after 1800. Here the drawers are in the same inward curve as in the previous two pieces. The original brass handles are missing. About 1750–1785.

At this point another mirror of about the same period should appear, but it was mislaid for some time and is now shown as No. 1275, the last in this chapter.

The next ten dressing glasses, Nos. 1260–1269, are in the styles of Hepplewhite and Sheraton. It might be possible to determine which of these pieces are in the Hepplewhite style and which are in the style of Sheraton, as in the consideration of sideboards in section 127; but as similar dressing glasses were made by many cabinet makers working in the two styles at about the same time, it seems better to consider them all as being in the "Hepplewhite–Sheraton period" and thus avoid possible errors in making distinctions of little real importance.[4]

In these dressing glasses the mirrors are either shield–shaped, oval or rectangular in form, and the front of the "box", or lower section, is either serpentine,

3.   John Elliott, of Philadelphia, who is referred to at length in note 3 in section 143, advertised in the local newspapers from 1756 to 1776, showing rough sketches of dressing glasses of the type above; but none of the mirrors are in exactly the shape with which we are familiar. Advertisements do not, however, always establish the date of manufacture; even now we may see in the country newspapers advertisements of auction sales showing illustrations of furniture made in the Victorian style of the Centennial year 1876.

4.   In Mr. Strange's "English Furniture", etc., page 273, twenty drawings are shown of the "Hepplewhite and Sheraton period toilet glasses", and in Mr. Cescinsky's "English Furniture", volume 3, figure 301, eight types of "toilet mirrors of the Sheraton period" are illustrated.

1255 (UPPER) DR. JAMES BORDLEY, JR.   1256 (UPPER) MRS. MILES WHITE, JR.
1257 (LOWER) MR. JOHN C. TOLAND. 1258 (LOWER) MR. E. G. MILLER, JR. 1259 (LOWER) DR. JAMES BORDLEY, JR.

bow–shaped or straight. The lower section usually has three small drawers, often inlaid with rectangular or curved designs. Several of the comments on these pieces mention resemblances to features found in bureaus and other pieces of the period. The wood is mahogany and the dates are from about 1785–1810.

In No. 1260 the mirror is in the shape of a shield, with a serpentine top which was seen in so many chairs in the Hepplewhite style, such as Nos. 200–208. The front of the lower section is also in a serpentine curve. There are three drawers, the central one of which is larger than the end ones, as usual in these

1260 (Upper) Mr. John C. Toland.   1261 (Upper) Lock. Col. Fur., Fig.   1262 (Upper) Mr. & Mrs. H. L.
1263 (Lower) Mr. E. G. Miller, Jr.   400.   Duer.
                          1264 (Lower) Mr. Arthur E. Cole.   1265 (Lower) Mr. Arthur E. Cole.

pieces. The feet are small, flat and round. The wooden knobs are probably substitutes for the original brass ones. A dressing glass of this type is commonly regarded as in the Hepplewhite style on account of its shield shape, but is not placed by the English writers mentioned in note 4 exclusively in that style but merely in the "Hepplewhite–Sheraton period". About 1790–1810.

In No. 1261 the mirror is also in the form of a shield, with a top which is not serpentine but is in two concave curves which meet in the centre. The fronts of the two drawers in the lower section are also in concave curves. The feet are of the bracket type and the knobs are small brass ones. This type is shown by Mr. Cescinsky as one of the Sheraton period. About 1790–1810.

In No. 1262 the mirror is oval. Ivory rosettes are at the top and near the bottom of the uprights holding the mirror. In the lower section the three drawers, with lines of inlay on the edges, are in a serpentine form. This dressing glass would look well on the serpentine front bureau No. 729. The feet are in a bracket form and the handles are of brass. About 1790–1810.

In No. 1263 the oval mirror is in a position requiring the lower section to be somewhat wider than that in the preceding piece. The lower section is plain and is in a shape which would match fairly well with the bow–shaped bureau No. 738. The round knobs are of brass and the feet are of the bracket type.[5] About 1790–1810.

In No. 1264 the mirror is rectangular, the top and bottom shorter than the sides, and is supported by rectangular uprights. The frame of the mirror and also the uprights have lines of inlay. Conforming with the shape of the mirror, the top and bottom of the end drawers are shorter than the sides. The front is serpentine in form and is ornamented with lines of inlay. Tiny brass knobs are on the drawers. About 1790–1810.

In No. 1265, also, the mirror is rectangular, and the top and bottom are wider than the sides, with rectangular uprights. The lower section is flat at the ends, between which it is bowed. The ends are ornamented with inlay and the three drawers have lines of inlay on the edges, with glass knobs. The feet are of the ball type. About 1790–1810.

In No. 1266 the uprights are "turned" in a plain design, but the mirror and the lower section are decorated with inlay. The inlay on the finely veneered fronts of the three drawers is in the form of parallel lines with rounded ends as in the bureaus Nos. 737 and 738, a design apparently first shown by Shearer, on a sideboard, as mentioned and illustrated in section 127 and note 6. Small brass knobs are on the drawers. About 1790–1810.

No. 1267 has uprights which are more elaborately "turned" than in the preceding piece. The front is slightly bowed. Here there are two drawers, finely veneered, on which are large brass knobs. A label on this dressing glass bears the name of Thomas Natt, of Philadelphia.[6] About 1790–1810.

5. The spaces between the sides of the frame of the dressing glass and the upright posts were caused by warping of the posts. An attempt to bring the posts closer together by tightening the screws resulted in one of the posts breaking under the strain. After the broken parts of the post were glued together, the spaces between the mirror frame and the posts were filled with washers, and sufficiently tight contact was thus obtained to hold the mirror in any position without putting too much strain on the posts. This cabinet–work detail may be useful to some owners.

6. His label is as follows, mentioning a variety of mirrors, domestic and imported: "Thomas Natt, Looking glass manufacturer, printseller, and importer of British Plate Glass, Mirrors, etc. No. 164, Market Street, three doors above Fourth, on the south side, Philadelphia. Constantly on hand an extensive and elegant assortment of fancy framed looking glasses, gilt mantel and pier glasses, mahogany and curled maple do., toilettes, sconces, swings, etc., etc.—Tablet, stained pillar, and fluted framed looking glasses in great variety... Plain, fancy and ornamental gilding and resilvering... On hand, looking glass plates, prints and mirrors of superior quality and late importations."

See also note 3 in this section in regard to the advertisements of John Elliott.

No. 1268 is an English dressing glass and is of a different type, having no drawers. The oval frame is supported by uprights which are similar in form to those in No. 1262, but rest upon feet of the trestle type. The lower framework is held together by a curved bar. This kind of dressing glass is not often seen in our country, but is illustrated in the English books referred to in note 4 in this section. The form is about the same as that of the usual type of "horse" or "cheval" glasses [7] of the period. About 1790–1810.

1266 (Upper) Sheppard & E. P. Hospital.
1269 (Lower) Metropolitan Museum.

1267 (Upper) Mr. & Mrs. Wm. A. Dixon.
1270 (Lower) Dr. James Bordley, Jr.

1268 (Upper) Anonymous.
1271 (Lower) Mr. E. G. Miller, Jr.

7. This is copied from figure 301 in volume 3 of "English Furniture of the Eighteenth Century", by permission of Mr. Cescinsky.

In Sheraton's "Drawing Book", (as to which see section 18), third edition, 1802, page 383, the large dressing glasses which stood on the floor and in which one's whole figure could be reflected, were called "horse–dressing glasses". The word "horse", as the first part of a compound word, indicated a large or coarse thing of its kind, as in the words "horse–chestnut", "horse–play", etc. The word "horse–dressing glass" was used to distinguish the large dressing glass from the small ones, such as those in our illustrations. The French word for a horse, "cheval", was later substituted for the English word and the large piece became known as a "cheval glass", meaning a "large dressing glass". "Dressing glasses" were thus in two types, one of which, now commonly called merely a "dressing glass", was small and was meant to stand on a bureau or lowboy or table; the other, the "cheval glass", was large and was meant to stand on the floor, as above stated. This large "cheval glass", first made in the time of Queen Anne, again became the fashion in the Sheraton period when the cost of glass had fallen greatly from its high prices in previous years.

No. 1269 is in the style of Sheraton, as will be seen by comparing the lower section of the dressing glass with some of the upper part of the Sheraton style sideboard No. 1002. There are two drawers at the ends above the level of the central portion, with two deep drawers below, and a long drawer in the centre, under which is an arch. Four brass handles with a ring in a lion's mouth are on the three lower drawers, and the feet are of the brass claw type; both of these brasses are seen on pieces in the latter part of the Sheraton period and on several tables and chairs made by Duncan Phyfe. The uprights are reeded, with brass balls at the top and brass knobs at the sides for holding the mirror in any position. About 1800–1820.

No. 1270 is an unusual piece in both the upper and lower sections. The plain rectangular mirror frame, with slightly curved inner corners at the top, is supported by two large and deeply grooved uprights of a kind apparently not seen in other American dressing glasses, but which resemble designs in English books. Feet with somewhat similar grooving are in the tripod table No. 1589. The lower section has four projecting round columns, not reeded or fluted, but apparently for ornament. The feet are of the flat type as in No. 1260. The central drawer is recessed and below it the "apron" is cut in cyma curves. Perhaps about 1820–1830.

No. 1271 is also an unusual and peculiar piece. The oval mirror is supported by uprights which have scrolls both at the top and bottom. In the lower section there is a round projecting column at each end, in this respect resembling the previous piece to some extent. Under the columns are ball feet. There are three drawers, the fronts of which are "blocked" in part. The two outer drawers are concave and the central one is serpentine. The wood is walnut. Perhaps about 1800–1810.

The next three dressing glasses, Nos. 1272–1274, are in the Empire style.[8]

In No. 1272 the upper section, with its rectangular mirror and its "turned" supporting uprights, is not materially different from several others in this section. The lower section, however, departs from the curved form of front and

(NOTE 7, *continued*)

Cheval glasses were occasionally made in our country in the Sheraton period, and until about 1830, but original ones are now seldom seen. One made by Duncan Phyfe is shown in "Furniture Masterpieces of Duncan Phyfe", by Mr. C. O. Cornelius, plate 51. One in the Empire style is in Miss Morse's "Furniture of the Olden Time", No. 389. One of the earliest English pieces is shown in Mr. Cescinsky's "English Furniture", volume 1, figure 185, dated about 1720; another is in Mr. Nutting's "Furniture Treasury", No. 3201. All of these cheval glasses have the same type of feet as in No. 1268 above.

Designs of large fire screens, not mirrors, made in the style of the cheval glasses, are called "horse screens" by Chippendale in his "Director", as to which book see section 15. The same term was used by Hepplewhite and Sheraton in their books.

8. During the period of the Empire style the mirrors began to be attached to the tops of bureaus and thereafter dressing glasses ceased to be made. See the bureaus Nos. 764–768.

Another form of dressing glass made especially for shaving purposes was popular about 1840 and for some years thereafter. It consisted of a round or rectangular swinging mirror attached to the top of a small box of drawers made to hold shaving requisites, the box being supported by a

(*Note 8 continued on page 692.*)

presents a straight one with three drawers which have small glass knobs. The four small round columns at the front indicate the Empire style, as in the bureaus Nos. 763–766. About 1830.

In No. 1273 the Empire style appears in the rounded front of the single drawer, as in the bureau No. 765 in that style. The frame more nearly approaches a square form than in previous dressing glasses. The feet are of the ball type. The handles are of an earlier design. About 1830–1840.

No. 1274 recalls the bureaus Nos. 765–766 in having the supports of the mirror in carved scrolls which if closer together and furnished with strings would

1272 (Upper) Mr. E. G. Miller, Jr. 1273 (Upper) Miss Elisabeth H. Bartlett.
1274 (Lower) Mr. John C. Toland. 1275 (Lower) Mr. Arthur E. Cole.

resemble a lyre. In the straight front are three drawers with circular wooden knobs. The feet here are of the ball type as in the preceding piece. About 1830–1840.

No. 1275 should have appeared in connection with No. 1259, but was mislaid. The cresting is cut in fretwork and was adorned with a leaf or other carving in a circular opening. The lower section has three curved drawers, the central part being in a serpentine form. The upper inner corners are rectangular, as in Nos. 1133–1134 and others. The wood is mahogany. About 1750–1780.

(Note 8, *continued from page 691*.)

single column about four or five feet high under which were feet. These shaving stands were unstable and unsightly, in spite of spiral turnings and fanciful feet. The height of the mirror was made adjustable to the requirements of the user.

CHAPTER XVIII

TABLES AND STANDS

Section 153. In general.—The table[1] is one of the indispensable articles of domestic furniture and has been in use from remote times in all civilized countries. It was a familiar object in every household at the period when our country was settled, but only a few of the early American examples have survived to the present time.[2] The earliest one now known, dating from about 1650, shown as

---

1. The word "table" is defined as "an article of furniture consisting of a flat top, (the table proper), of wood, stone or other solid material resting on legs or on a pillar with or without connecting frame–work"; Century Dictionary. In England the word "table" has a somewhat broader usage than with us; for example, what we call a flat–top desk is there called a "writing table". See also note 1 in section 173.

2. Mr. Lockwood in his "Colonial Furniture", volume 2, page 167, states that "more early tables have survived than early chairs. The reason is perfectly obvious, as the former were intended to hold dead weight and the chairs were put to the strain of live weight."

No. 1276 in the next section, was called a "table board and frame", the "board"[3] being the flat top and the "frame" being the lower part which supports the top.

Few articles of furniture have been made in as many forms as tables, for the reason that tables have been made for so many different purposes, each purpose requiring a special type. Thus we have dining tables, tea tables, serving tables, dressing tables, card tables, sewing tables and others. One term, more frequently used in England than in our country, is "occasional" table, meaning a small movable table suitable for various purposes[4]—an indefinite word which is not often used when a more descriptive one can be found.

In tables a distinctive feature, and one which generally determines the style, is the leg. The principal forms are the cabriole leg with Dutch, or club, feet of the Queen Anne style; the cabriole leg with ball and claw feet, and the straight and square leg, both of the Chippendale style; the straight leg of the Adam style; the straight, square and tapering leg of the Hepplewhite style; the curved leg or the straight, round and tapering leg of the Sheraton style; and several other less important kinds of legs. These types, with certain variations, are easily recognized in our American tables.

The other distinctive feature of tables is, of course, the top. This varies in design and size from the large tops of the long dining tables, such as No. 1317, to the tiny round tops of certain tripod candle stands, such as No. 1398, all of which will appear in the illustrations.[5]

As seen in the list of sections, this chapter is divided into twenty–three sections, two of which, Nos. 161 and 175, are on the subject of stands.

Section 154. Several early types.—In this section we examine certain tables of different types which were in vogue at various times from the date of the earliest American pieces, about 1650. The illustrations do not include two well–known kinds of early tables which, because of their importance, are treated separately in the next two sections, namely, gate–leg tables and butterfly tables; but those which are shown here comprise about all of the types which the amateur collector is likely to find very interesting.

3.   This word "board" in connection with a table continues in use with us in several expressions. Thus there is a "board of directors", figuratively called a "board" because the directors sit around one; and in the expression "board and lodging" we use the word "board" as meaning food, which is served on a board. The word "table" is also used in a figurative sense, meaning that which is placed upon a table for refreshment; Century Dictionary.

4.   In "A Glossary of English Furniture", by Penderel–Brodhurst and Layton, page 115, an "occasional table" is defined as "a small light portable table, used for ladies' work, flowers, ornaments and a variety of other purposes. The shape and adornment of tables of this character are infinitely various." In "American Furniture" by Mr. E. S. Holloway, page 85, occasional tables are referred to as being "for any purpose to which at the moment they might be convenient."

When used in reference to a chair the word "occasional" means an odd chair, not forming part of a set; Century Dictionary.

5.   In this chapter four hundred and two illustrations of tables and stands are presented, a number in one chapter exceeded only by the four hundred and eighty–two illustrations of chairs.

For many persons these early tables, as well as other articles of the period, have a certain charm and interest on account of their age, their simplicity and their association with the founders of our country; but to many other persons they are not very attractive. This diversity of opinion applies especially to the small and plain tables which are often called "tavern" tables.[1] Moreover, wholly genuine tables of the early period are not often seen outside of museums, and are seldom obtainable by the amateur collector. Plain and small tables recently and skillfully made from old parts of other articles are not easily distinguishable from genuine antique ones.

In the note brief mention is made of several early types which are not illustrated here.[2]

No. 1276 is a well–known table, referred to in the previous section, owned by the Metropolitan Museum of Art through whose courtesy the illustration appears. It is said by Mr. Lockwood, in his "Colonial Furniture in America", to be the oldest American table known. A table of this type, used as a dining table, was known as a "table board and frame" and is described in those words in inventories of the estates of deceased persons. The table is in fact an oak frame upon which a removable pine board was placed. Here the board is about twelve feet long

1. These "tavern" tables are now less popular among collectors than they were a few years ago. See note 4 in this section.

  A valuable work on early American furniture is Mr. Wallace Nutting's "Furniture of the Pilgrim Century", Revised Edition, 1924, with more than fifteen hundred illustrations.

2. A. A "chair table" is an ungainly combination of the two articles composing its name. A large table top, either round or rectangular, was attached to a large low back chair in such a manner that the top could lie horizontally over the chair and be used as a table, or could be raised vertically so that the chair could be used. A drawer was under the seat of the chair. When not used in the centre of a room as a table it could be placed against the wall, saving space. A chair table with a long rectangular table top is in the "seventeenth century room" of the Metropolitan Museum of Art. Several are shown and explained in Mr. Nutting's "Furniture of the Pilgrim Century", Revised Edition, pages 450–453. See also paragraph 3 in note 6 in section 46, and figures 439–441 in Mr. Lockwood's "Colonial Furniture". About 1640–1700.

  B. A "hutch table" is similar in construction to a chair table, but, instead of a chair, there is a "hutch", meaning a box on two legs, to which the top is attached. Several are shown in the books mentioned in the preceding paragraph. About 1700.

  C. Small tables or lowboys with a slate top set into the frame are known as "slate–top" tables or lowboys. Around the slate is a wooden border a few inches wide which is finely made and decorated. It is thought that the slate was intended to hold hot dishes which would injure a wooden top. Marble tops were used for the same purpose on the sideboard tables Nos. 1305 and 1306. Mr. Lockwood, in his "Colonial Furniture", volume 1, page 73, states that in his opinion these slate–tops were made in Holland, where Delft tiles were similarly used; see also his volume 2, figures 705, 706. About 1700.

  D. "Drawing tables" were rectangular tables which could be enlarged. One method was by "drawing" out leaves which were placed in the ends and "were supported by wooden braces which drew out from the frame and held the ends firmly on a level with the table." This type of table is illustrated in Mr. Lockwood's "Colonial Furniture", volume 2, figure 675. Another type of "drawing tables" is known as "architects' tables", illustrated in Nos. 1635–1637.

  E. Several tables called by Mr. Wallace Nutting "communion tables" and others known as "refectory tables" are shown in his "Furniture of the Pilgrim Century", Revised Edition; see the Index to his book.

and only two feet wide, the diners sitting on one side only. The frame consists of three "trestles", the word "trestle" in connection with a table meaning an upright supporting piece, or leg, at each end, and sometimes also in the middle, as here. These three trestles are held in position by a horizontal bar which passes through them. The feet are known as trestle feet, a type necessary to keep the uprights firmly in position. Because of the trestles, tables of this kind are called "trestle" tables.[3] About 1650.

No. 1277 is a much more substantial table, having massive legs connected by heavy stretchers. Perhaps originally the piece had feet of a small rounded type. There are two paneled drawers with wooden knobs. The top is of maple and extends considerably beyond the frame at both ends; the frame seems to be of oak. A number of tables of this general form, but often with ornamental features, have been found, and are regarded as being either communion tables, parlor tables, dining or kitchen tables, the latter because of the drawers which were often of different sizes in one table. This piece is about five feet long. About 1700–1720.

No. 1278 is an early English dining table which is shown here as an example of an important type in the development of tables. This piece is in the Metropolitan Museum of Art, through whose courtesy it is illustrated here. The conspicuous feature is the form of the six legs with their massive carved "bulbs", similar to those seen on the bedsteads of the period, which are not illustrated in this book. Tables and bedsteads of this kind have not been found in our country and it is probable that none were imported because of their cost and the difficulty of transporting objects of such large size. About 1650.

Passing on to the small tables we see in No. 1279 a table with spiral or twisted legs and stretchers. The spiral feature was one of the earliest types of ornamentation and was very often used. It is seen, for example, in the gate–leg table No. 1291 to which a note on the subject is appended; the purpose of the references is stated in section 1, pages 9–10. The number and arrangement of

3.   A.   Another "table board and frame" is shown in Mr. Nutting's "Furniture of the Pilgrim Century", Revised Edition, No. 673. On page 465 he states that recently a number of trestle–board tables have been found which were made about 1800 by the Shakers. Recently tables of the same general character have been imported from Sweden. An illustrated article on these Swedish tables and other articles is in "Antiques", July, 1932, page 16. Two other New England tables are shown in the same magazine, July, 1927, page 30.

B.   An interesting matter is mentioned by Mr. Nutting in his book on pages 454, 459–460. He states that it was the custom after meals to remove the trestle dining table from the centre to the side of the room so as to have more open space; and that later when gate–leg tables were used as dining tables the custom continued, letting down the leaves and placing the table by the wall. "We remember one ancient and huge kitchen where only two members of the family were left. Invariably the dining table was closed and pushed to the wall after every meal, leaving a great empty space of no possible benefit. Our grandmothers would as soon have thought of leaving the dishes unwashed as of leaving the table" in the centre of the room.

C.   As is seen in the illustration, the trestle feet are merely blocks of wood attached to the trestle legs and extending out at right angles to the top. Similar forms of trestle feet are in Nos. 1300–1302. Other forms, apparently adapted from trestle feet, were used in the late Sheraton, Empire and Victorian periods, as in the tables or stands Nos. 1632 and 1675.

1276 (Upper) Metropolitan Museum of Art.   1277 (Centre) Mr. John S. McDaniel.
1278 (Lower) Metropolitan Museum of Art.

697

the stretchers will be noticed. Stretchers turned in the form of balls or knobs are also seen on tables of this period, as in No. 1282. About 1650–1700.

No. 1280 has four plain and heavy stretchers, suitable for rough usage. The legs are turned in vase–shaped forms with rings between them. The feet are not rounded as they are in most of the tables of this type. This piece and several others following are of the kind often called "tavern"[4] or "tap–room" tables, indefinite terms which should be avoided. The term "small turned–leg tables", is perhaps sufficiently descriptive if understood not to include butterfly tables and small gate–leg tables. About 1700–1725.

No. 1281 has a round top and the legs slant outward, or, as the term is, they are "raked" or "splayed", as in the Windsor chairs shown in illustration No. 440. The turnings of the legs are in the vase–and–ring style and the stretchers are heavy and plain. About 1700–1725.

In No. 1282 the top is rectangular and the legs are turned in a slender form with rings above and below. The stretchers, as mentioned in section 26, note 4, form an "H" and are known as "H stretchers", and are "turned" in the ball, or knob, pattern. The round brass handle of the drawer is of a much later type. About 1700–1725.

No. 1283 has slender and graceful stretchers instead of plain and heavy ones; and the legs also are slender, as in the preceding piece. The upper portion contains a drawer, and the "skirt" is in a form which suggests that of the highboy No. 651 and the lowboy No. 679. About 1700–1720.

In No. 1284 the legs are turned in the "inverted cup" pattern, as in the highboys Nos. 632–634, and the lowboys Nos. 669–671. The cross–stretchers are turned in a vase–and–ring design. The brass escutcheons and drop handles of the period will also be noticed. About 1700–1720.

4. A. The term "tavern table" has been applied to various kinds of small tables of the period from about 1675 onwards. Because of their small size, compared with gate–leg and other tables, they were easily movable and on this account were much used in the public rooms of taverns; and their small size was equally suitable for use in kitchens and other rooms. They were either square, rectangular, octagonal, oval or round, and generally had an overhanging top. One or more of the feet is often replaced with a new one of incorrect design.

B. It is not possible to divide the tables of this general character into exact classes according to their probable usage; but it is likely that the large tables were for dining purposes, the next in size for taverns and general household use and a still smaller size for use as a "stand"; but the difference between a small table and a "stand" is in many cases uncertain at this early period as well as in the time of Hepplewhite and Sheraton; see the first paragraphs in sections 173 and 175.

C. A "half–moon" table is illustrated in "Antiques", March, 1922, page 113, as a "Little Known Masterpiece". This almost round table is in two parts of nearly equal size and when the table is not in use one part is turned upside down and placed within the other part. About 1725.

D. In a "sawbuck" table the board may be supported by a horizontal bar as in the table No. 1276. The ends of the bar rest upon an X–shaped support or rack of the kind seen in a "sawbuck" or "sawhorse" which is used for holding wood when being cut by a wood–saw; Century Dictionary. In "Antiques", February, 1935, page 63, is an illustrated article on a sawbuck table now in Dartmouth College. Illustrations of similar tables are Nos. 804 and 810 in Mr. Wallace Nutting's "Furniture Treasury". See also illustrations of three "X–trestle" tables in "Antiques", November, 1926, page 358.

1279 (Upper) Metropolitan Museum of Art.   1280 (Upper) Dr. James Bordley, Jr.
1281 (Centre) Mrs. John S. Gibbs, Jr.   1282 (Centre) Anonymous.
1283 (Lower) Hammond–Harwood House.   1284 (Lower) Hammond–Harwood House.

The next five tables, Nos. 1285–1289, are in the Queen Anne style, as to which see section 14, and have Dutch, or club, feet, and are not strictly in the "early types", as they are all of the eighteenth century. On each of the preceding small tables we have seen stretchers, which, as stated in section 26, were frequently used in our country in the Queen Anne period, but not in England until they were revived in the time of Chippendale. The wood of these tables in the Queen Anne style is generally walnut or maple.

No. 1285 has "raked" legs as in No. 1281. These legs are pleasing in form and terminate in Dutch, or club, feet such as are seen on chairs, highboys and other articles in the Queen Anne style. About 1730–1750.

In No. 1286 the "skirt" is cut in arches and curves as in highboys of the period, such as No. 637. The legs are straight, not raked or cabriole in form; similar legs are on No. 1288 and on the large table No. 1308, and are referred to in note 2, A in section 25. The feet are of the Dutch type with a ball under each foot. About 1730–1750.

No. 1287 is a three–legged, or tripod, table. As in the preceding piece, the skirt is cut in curves, here in the shape of two cyma curves, as to which see section 23. The legs are raked, and end in the same type of feet as in the two preceding tables. About 1730–1750.

No. 1288 is a walnut rectangular table with a full overhang at each end and with a drawer in the centre. The legs, two of which in the engraving have an erroneous appearance of being raked, are straight and terminate in Dutch feet, under which are high "shoes" which may be compared with those in No. 1286. About 1730–1750.

No. 1289 is a smaller table than the preceding one, with legs which become round as they extend downward and terminate in the usual Dutch feet. Three arches are cut in the skirt under the drawers in the manner of those on some of the lowboys in the Queen Anne style, as in No. 686. About 1730–1750.

In No. 1290 the legs are slightly curved and are attached to the skirt above its base. The brass ring handle in the drawer is of a later period than the other parts of the table. The balls in the ball and claw feet are more nearly spherical than in many other tables. About 1725–1750.

In connection with some of the plain and originally inexpensive tables shown in this section it should be particularly noted that the dates here given are merely the approximate dates at which the styles were in fashion; and that tables in these styles continued to be made, especially in the smaller towns, for many years after the styles passed out in the large cities. The study of the subject makes it possible to know the approximate dates when most of the furniture styles *began* to be fashionable, but it is not possible to fix the date at which articles in a particular style were no longer made. This subject is also mentioned in connection with "dates", in paragraph 2 of the text in section 6.

1285 (UPPER) MR. ALBERT G. TOWERS.
1287 (CENTRE) MR. ALBERT G. TOWERS.
1289 (LOWER) MR. J. F. H. MAGINN.

1286 (UPPER) MR. J. F. H. MAGINN.
1288 (CENTRE) COLL. OF MRS. J. STABLER.
1290 (LOWER) DR. JAMES BORDLEY, JR.

Section 155. Gate–leg and folding tables.—Both of these tables are varieties of drop–leaf tables. In a gate–leg table the legs which support the leaves resemble gates somewhat in appearance and swing out in the manner of gates. A folding table is similar in having a swinging gate, but the gate operates in a different manner, which is better understood by examining the illustrations Nos. 1300–1302 than by reading a printed explanation.

Gate–leg tables were the favorite tables in our country from about 1650 until the change in style in the Queen Anne period,[1] about 1720, when they were

1.   A.   It is said that in America gate-leg tables continued to be made until about 1750, or later in the country districts. They originated in the Jacobean period, as to which see section 12.

B.   After more than two centuries it is difficult to be certain of the dates of tables of such similar character. Mr. Lockwood, in his "Colonial Furniture", refers to most of the gate–leg tables shown by him as being in the style of the last quarter of the seventeenth century, which was 1675–1700. Concerning dates see also section 6.

C.   It is said that tables on the gate–leg principle again became popular in England about 1750 to 1775 and later, with legs and stretchers of a very light character. In "Old English Furniture", by Mr. G. Owen Wheeler, London, 1924, pages 570–574, these "spindle" or "spider–leg" tables are illustrated and are dated 1775–1795. An example is in Mr. Wallace Nutting's "Furniture Treasury", No. 967, and in "Furniture of the Olden Time" by Miss Morse, No. 239. See also "Antiques", December, 1934, page 220.

D.   The wood used in gate–leg tables was generally maple in New England, but sometimes walnut; further South, walnut was almost always used; but other woods are occasionally found.

E.   The top of the table is the part most likely to be damaged by usage. In pointing out the danger of asserting that a table has its original top, Mr. Wallace Nutting, in his "Furniture of the Pilgrim Century", Revised Edition, page 460, states that "there is no possible method of proving such an assertion"; but that "ancient table tops, however, are often found and are adaptable to ancient table frames, especially in the case of the tavern table with its one piece top." Many gate–leg tables have tops which are not the original ones.

F.   The leaves are attached by hinges to the stationary top in several methods which are difficult to make clear without using technical words which are avoided in this book so far as possible. These methods to some extent indicate the period in which the table was made, although of course any cabinet maker could at any time use any method known to him. By the more usual method the hinges are not visible. See the comment on No. 1297.

G.   The feet on almost all of the gate–leg tables are rounded, and, if original, are usually worn or injured. A few tables have "Spanish" feet, a type which may be seen on other pieces of the period of about 1690–1710, as on the lowboy No. 674, and the chairs Nos. 39–41. See also illustration No. 11.

H.   The stretchers are usually "turned", the vase–and–ring design being most frequently seen; but in some tables the stretchers are plain and straight, indicating, it is said, that the piece is of Southern origin.

I.   In large tables there may be a drawer at each end, but in smaller ones there is but one drawer which is about two–thirds of the length of the table.

J.   Gate–leg tables vary greatly in size, ranging in width with the leaves open from about seventy–eight inches to about thirty–six inches. The medium sized ones are most often found. The very large ones and the very small ones are more desirable because of their comparative rarity.

K.   Several gate–leg tables have been found with four gates, two on each side, with two feet on each gate, that is, eight feet on the four gates and four on the frame, making twelve feet in all. The usual number of gates is two, with one foot on each gate. In No. 1292 there are eight feet in all.

L.   Reproductions of these gate–leg tables have recently had a large sale. A prominent department store advertised reproductions of forty–nine different examples of genuine gate–leg tables. Whether an original or an exact reproduction, a gate–leg table is a desirable article of furniture.

to a great extent superseded by drop–leaf tables in which the leaves were supported by movable legs without the gate features, as in the tables shown in section
162. Anticipating somewhat, it may be said here that later, in some drop–leaf
tables, legs were not used as supports and the leaves were supported by movable
brackets as in the Pembroke, library and sofa tables shown in sections 163–165.
On card tables and some others, however, movable legs continued to be used.

The usual form of a gate–leg table has a top attached to a somewhat narrow
frame and the frame rests upon two legs at each end. On each side of the frame
are the gate–legs which support the leaves, as above mentioned. The leaves were
generally semi–oval in form, but in some cases they were rectangular; and if in
the latter form, two or more tables could be connected, and thus make one large
table. A large gate–leg table was generally used as a dining table, and was no doubt
satisfactory for that purpose, except that it "condemned at least some of those
seated around it to acute discomfort owing to the multiplicity" of the legs.

In these tables the principal features are the size, the character of the turnings, the number of feet and the plainness or elegance of the tables in general
appearance; in other respects they are very similar and call for little comment.

No. 1291 is a small gate–leg table of an early type as is indicated by the
form of the spiral[2] turnings of the legs. The stretchers are all plain, not turned,
and are heavy and strong. As mentioned in note 1, H, it is said that stretchers of
this plain character often denote a Southern origin. Here the inner legs of the
gates do not extend to the floor and have no feet, so that there are only six legs
with feet. About 1650–1680.

No 1292 is a larger table in which the inner legs of the gates extend to the
floor so that there are eight legs with feet. The stretchers of the gates and of the
front and back of the central portion are turned in a vase–and–ring form; but at
the ends of the side stretchers of the central portion are other turnings. About
1675–1700.

In No. 1293 the turnings of the legs are very similar to those in the preceding
table, being of the vase–and–ring type; but the turnings of the stretchers are of a
somewhat heavier form. Here also there are only six feet. A drawer is in the
front and the skirt under the drawer is cut in two cyma curves. About 1675–1700.

---

2. The spiral type of turning, or carving, on legs, stretchers and other parts was used in different
forms and in widely separated periods. In the gate–leg table here shown, about 1650–1680, and in
the table No. 1279, the legs are in an early form which is easily distinguished from the later type. The
spiral turning is seen on the pedestal of the tripod stand or table No. 1394, in the Chippendale style,
about 1760–1780, on which the turning is more delicate. On the legs of the so-called serving table
No. 1446, in the Sheraton style, about 1810–1820, the turning is somewhat heavier. In the table No.
1450, about 1815–1830, the turnings have become less elegant and are characteristic of the Empire
period, in which they were very popular. The slight and somewhat arbitrary difference between the
spiral turnings of the late Sheraton style and those of the Empire style is that the latter are generally
heavier and coarser than the former. Other examples are in the dressing table No. 1472, the card table
No. 1538 and the sewing tables Nos. 1575 and 1588. Spiral turnings are also seen on the bedposts
Nos. 1069 and 1070 and the sideboards Nos. 1015 and 1016. The term "twist" is sometimes used in
the sense of "spiral turning". See also the Index under the word "Spiral".

1291 (UPPER) DR. JAMES BORDLEY, JR.
1293 (CENTRE) MR. J. F. H. MAGINN.
1295 (LOWER) DR. JAMES BORDLEY, JR.

1292 (UPPER) MR. & MRS. J. MARSH MATTHEWS.
1294 (CENTRE) MRS. MILES WHITE, JR.
1296 (LOWER) MR. & MRS. CHARLES E. ELLICOTT.

1297 (Upper) Mrs Miles White, Jr.
1299 (Centre) Mrs. John S. Gibbs, Jr.
1301 (Lower) Mr. J. F. H. Maginn.

1298 (Upper) Mr. Edgar G. Miller, Jr.
1300 (Centre) Lockwood Col. Furn., Fig. 689.
1302 (Lower) Mrs. Miles White, Jr.

No. 1294 also has plain stretchers except on the front and back where they are turned. The turnings of all of the legs are in a form resembling somewhat the turnings on the six–legged highboy No. 632 in the William and Mary style. About 1675–1700.

No. 1295 is another small table, resembling No. 1291 except in the leg turnings which are in the form of an elongated vase. The stretchers are plain and there are six legs with feet. About 1675–1700.

No. 1296 is a large table. The turnings on the side stretchers of the central portion are of two kinds; those in the centre are of the vase–and–ring type and those at the ends are in a ring form. On the six outer legs the turnings are of the vase–and–ring type with a ball foot below. The drawer of this table is seen on the left. About 1675–1700.

In No. 1297 the turnings of the front and back legs are in a form which is said to be found mainly in the South. The design of the stretchers in the gates is a pleasing variation from the vase–and–ring form. The legs of the gates are turned in a different manner from those of the front and back. The usual method of connecting the edges of the leaves to the edges of the top appears near the drawer; the hinges underneath are not visible, whether the leaves are up or down. See note 1, F in this section. About 1675–1700.

No. 1298 is a plainer gate–leg table than the others shown here and is small. The turnings of the legs are said to be in a Southern manner. The stretchers are all plain. The height is about twenty–seven inches, the length thirty–four inches and the width when open is thirty–seven inches. About 1675–1700.

No. 1299 may be regarded as a gate–leg table of an unusual kind. The framework on the left is triangular, with a half–round stationary top. The half–round drop–leaf on the right is attached by hinges to the top and is supported by the gate. The triangular portion has a stationary gate–like support in the front, and under the top is a drawer. The legs are turned and the stretchers are plain. Probably about 1725.

The next three illustrations, Nos. 1300–1302, are of folding gate–leg tables in which one part of the table folds into the other part, as will be seen in the examples. This folding and easily movable table is sometimes called a "tuckaway" gate–leg table.

No. 1300 is a form of folding table which shows a close relationship to the form of the gate–leg tables. Here, however, there is only one leg at each end, instead of the usual two, to support the top; and when the two gate–legs are folded in, the leaves drop down and the table would easily fall over except for the wide base stretcher with trestle feet. About 1675–1700.

In No. 1301 the usual two gates on the sides are made as one gate which swings as a whole on a pivot where there is a pointed ornament, and supports the top. There is no wide base stretcher such as is seen in the preceding piece, but the trestle feet prevent the table from falling. About 1675–1700.

No. 1302 is very similar to the preceding piece in construction, and is noticeable for the turned legs and stretchers and for the support by the double gate by which the leaves are held in a horizontal position. The legs at the ends are supported by trestle feet as in the previous pieces. About 1675–1700.

In addition to the types shown here there are simple folding tables which have a single gate on one side only; others with two gates swinging from the sides of the frame; others, of much later date, with folding legs and tilting top; others with a rectangular top; and others with various details of no special importance.

Section 156. Butterfly tables.

Section 156. Butterfly tables.—These tables, as well as those shown in the two preceding sections, are early tables, but are of such a different character and of such interest at present that they are considered in this separate section.

The butterfly table is doubtless an American development from the gate–leg tables. It acquired its modern name from the supposed resemblance of its brackets, or supports, which hold up the leaves, to the wings of butterflies. At the lower part of the table these brackets are attached to the side stretchers and above they are attached to the framework. With these two connections the brackets may be swung out to support the leaves.[1] A butterfly table is in fact a drop–leaf table in which the leaves are supported by a wing bracket and not by a gate–leg as in the tables shown in the previous section, nor by the usual kind of movable leg seen in the drop–leaf tables in section 162, nor by a small bracket as in the Pembroke tables shown in section 163 and in other tables. A necessary feature in true butter-

---

1. The tops of these tables were generally made of maple or cherry; the other parts were of various woods. There is usually a drawer, the bottom of which is wider than the top, because the sides slant in the same manner as the legs. On the drawer a small wooden knob was used. The stretchers are generally plain and straight, but "turned" ones are also found. The tops when opened are usually either oval or rectangular. The feet are of the small ball–foot kind, but there are variations of this pattern. Hinges of the type known as "butterfly" hinges, shown in section 42, are not named from butterfly tables, although they have been found on these tables. Butterfly tables are small, the height ranging from about twenty–five to twenty–seven inches.

A butterfly table with four wings, two on each side, is illustrated and discussed in "Antiques", August, 1924, frontispiece. The table is much larger than those with two wings, being three feet wide and five feet and six inches long.

The subject of butterfly tables suggests the matter of fakes. As with other furniture pieces, a counterfeit may be so well made by a skilful forger that only an equally skilful critic, familiar with all details by actual experience, can detect the fraud. In his book "Knowing, collecting and restoring early American antique furniture", 1930, page 152, Mr. Henry Hammond Taylor explains the methods of the faker; and Mr. Wallace Nutting in his "Furniture of the Pilgrim Century", Revised Edition, page 566, gives a warning to collectors and states that "it is a favorite trick of furniture forgers to place a butterfly top on the splayed–leg frame of a small tavern table." The high prices brought by genuine butterfly tables in fair condition make successful faking a very profitable operation.

Butterfly tables are seldom found in good condition, and a certain amount of restoration or replacement seems to be expected. For example, a replacement of one of the leaves may be regarded by a seller as only a slight defect. Just what restorations or replacements should be tolerated by a purchaser is a matter of individual opinion and taste. See "Restorations", section 10 and notes. An article entitled "New Wings for an Old Butterfly", in "Antiques", February, 1927, page 112, illustrates a table before and after restoration.

In "The Antiquarian", April, 1931, page 40, is a fully illustrated article, by Mr. Walter A. Dyer, entitled "Butterflies", meaning "Butterfly tables".

Butterfly tables are referred to as one of the few exclusively American tables in section 214, C.

fly tables is the slant outwards, or "splay", or "rake", of the legs, the top of the frame being narrower than the lower part; if the legs were exactly vertical, the wings, or brackets, would not be workable. These tables have been found in Connecticut and other States of New England; they are not known in England. They are all dated at about 1700–1725.

In No. 1303 we see the characteristic features of butterfly tables. The top is oval, the brackets supporting the leaves are cut in the form regarded as resembling the wings of a butterfly, the legs are slanting, and the stretchers are plain and straight. The usual and only ornamental effect is in the turnings of the legs. The small ball feet will also be noticed. About 1700–1725.

1303 Mrs. John S. Gibbs, Jr.   1304 Anonymous.

No. 1304 is very similar in its general appearance, but the wings are larger and in a more rounded pattern and are thus more conspicuous. The drawer is unusually deep, extending back to the end of the frame. The knob on the drawer should be a small wooden one. This table is somewhat larger than usual, being twenty–seven inches in height and about forty–two inches in length when the wings are opened, as in the illustration. About 1700–1725.

Section 157. Sideboard tables; dining tables.—The "sideboard table" is the ancestor of the modern sideboard as stated in the chapter on sideboards, where it is also said, in section 126, that these tables are not readily distinguishable from certain other tables.[1] The sideboard table was used in dining rooms as a serving table and was generally placed against the wall; but it is not to be regarded as merely a "side" table as we now use that term and as illustrated in section 166. Sideboard tables were apparently not made after the modern sideboard was developed.

In England these sideboard tables were often very elaborate, and frequently had tops of marble which would not be injured by hot dishes. In the time of

1. Section 166, entitled "Side tables; serving and hunters' ", may be examined in connection with this section.

Chippendale they reached their highest point of workmanship and design; and the designs of Robert Adam were also of much elegance.[2] Few, if any, sideboard tables of such excellence were made in our country and in fact not many sideboard tables of any kind seem to have survived; only three are illustrated here,[3] two of which, Nos. 1305 and 1307, appear through the courtesy of Mr. L. V. Lockwood.

No. 1305 is a walnut sideboard table with a white marble top. The legs and the Dutch, or club, feet place the table in the Queen Anne style. The legs are straight, not in the cabriole form. These straight legs with Dutch feet, said to be found chiefly in Rhode Island, are also shown in No. 1308 and are referred to in No. 1286 and in note 2, A in section 25. The tops of the legs are rounded. About 1720–1750.

No. 1306 is a mahogany sideboard table whose legs and feet indicate it to be in the Chippendale style; and the shaggy claw feet seem to place its origin in Philadelphia. The top is white marble. The skirt is cut in cyma curves and the knees are carved with leaves. This table is not a large piece, being twenty–nine inches high and four feet long. About 1750–1760.

No. 1307 is also in the Chippendale style, having the straight rectangular legs which are seen on so many of his chairs and other articles. The top is of wood. The brackets at the intersection of the legs and the "skirt" are a feature of the Chippendale style. This is a higher table than the previous ones. About 1760–1770.

Passing to the "dining tables", it is said that few tables in the Queen Anne or Chippendale style can be identified as dining tables exclusively. All which appear to be dining tables have drop–leaves, but may have been used in other rooms than the dining room. As mentioned in the third paragraph of section 155, gate–leg tables were often used as dining tables. It is said that there are no designs of dining tables in any of the books of the cabinet makers in the time of Chippendale. In Mr. Lockwood's "Colonial Furniture" are illustrations of several tables which he regards as dining tables of the two periods mentioned, and Nos. 1309 and 1310 are copied here.[4] See also section 214, J.

No. 1308 is a large walnut table in the Queen Anne style, about nine feet long and five feet wide across the open leaves. The eight legs are straight, a form of leg said to be found chiefly in Rhode Island, as mentioned in the comment on No. 1305. It is said that this table has always been in Southern Maryland until recently, and others with similar legs have been seen by the writer in Williamsburg, Virginia. The feet are of the Dutch, or club, type. The joints between the leaves and the central part of the top are faintly seen in the engraving. It is probable that this table was not made for a dining table; see "Antiques", July, 1933, page 12. About 1725–1740.

2. An Adam style sideboard table, with pedestals and urns on the side, is No. 948, A, in the chapter on sideboards.
3. These two are figures 197 and 201 in Mr. Lockwood's "Colonial Furniture", volume 1.
4. No. 719 in the second volume of Mr. Lockwood's "Colonial Furniture" is our No. 1309 and our No. 1310 is on his page 328.

No. 1309 is regarded as a walnut dining table, with a rectangular top and six cabriole legs having ball and claw feet. The outer four of these legs swing out and support the leaves and the two in the centre are stationary. About 1725–1750.

In No. 1310 the mahogany and the ornamental carving indicate the Chippendale style. As in the preceding table, there are on each side two legs which swing out and support the leaves, and the four legs under the frame, in the centre, are stationary. One of the two drawers is seen, under which is a carving and there is also carving on the knees of the legs. About 1760–1770.

We now examine the dining tables in the Hepplewhite style. These tables are chiefly found in the South, especially in Maryland. They are almost all of the same general character, having two rounded end parts which may be connected, thus forming a rounded or oval table, and frequently having one or more separate rectangular sections which may be placed within the end parts, thus forming a longer table. In some cases, as in No. 1313, a rectangular leaf is attached to one or both of the end parts, by means of which the table may be made longer without using a separate section. All of these dining tables are of mahogany.

The inlaid decorations of these tables are very pleasing. The places where decoration may be used are on the surface under the top, called the "skirt" or "apron" or "frieze", and on the legs, and at these places the inlaid forms of the Hepplewhite–Sheraton period are seen. The chief differences in the appearance of the tables here shown are in these decorations and the number of legs. Some of the dining tables in this style are without decoration of any kind, but the very plain ones are not shown here. The legs are square, straight and tapered as on the sideboards and card tables in the Hepplewhite style. About 1785–1800.

In No. 1311 only the two ends are used, making an almost round table. On each of these ends are four legs and some of these eight legs are perhaps too close together for the comfort of those seated at them, and in this respect the table may rival the gate–leg tables referred to at the end of the third paragraph of section 155. Under the top, on the "skirt", are inlaid designs of parallel lines with rounded ends, a form which has been previously referred to several times, as in note 6 in section 127 of the chapter on sideboards. The legs are tapered in the Hepplewhite manner and some are inlaid on more than one of the surfaces. Bands of satinwood are near the feet, which are supplied with casters. About 1785–1800.

No. 1312 is a wide table from which some of the inner leaves have been removed for the purpose of this illustration. It is supported by ten legs which terminate in brass feet with casters. The long inlaid oval in front, with corresponding ones at other places, the small ovals above the legs, the strings of flowers inlaid on the legs and the satinwood bands all contribute to the decorative design of this table. About 1785–1800.

In No. 1313 each of the ends has a drop–leaf so that the table may be enlarged by the use of one or both leaves which may be supported by one or both

1305 (Upper) Lockwood Col. Furn., Fig. 197.
1307 (Centre) Lockwood Col. Furn., Fig. 201.
1309 (Lower) Lockwood Col. Furn., Fig. 719.

1306 (Upper) Anonymous.
1308 (Centre) Georgetown University.
1310 (Lower) Mr. L. V. Lockwood.

of two legs which swing. Under the top are rectangular inlaid forms and oval medallions and on the eight legs are inlaid strings of flowers. Here also, as in No. 1311, the tapering legs are inlaid on more than one of the surfaces. About 1785–1800.

No. 1314 is a two–part table with an oval top, formed by having a central leaf between the two rounded ends. There are eight square and tapered legs, which are inlaid with lines on the front; and other inlaid forms are seen under the top. This table is fifty–three inches wide and six feet long. About 1790–1800.

No. 1315 is shown with the two ends forming almost a round table and with a fifth leg supporting the centre. With only five legs in all, there can be no discomfort to those seated at the table. As in many other pieces the inlay is pleasing, resembling No. 1311 in that respect. About 1785–1800.

In No. 1316 we see one end of a dining table to which a large rectangular leaf is attached. In this form it is not suitable for dining purposes but may serve well as a side table by removing the leaf. A feature of the table is the inlaid coat of arms of the Bosley family, of Maryland, one of which was the original possessor of the table and was an ancestor of the present owner. About 1785–1800.

No. 1317 is a three part table with sixteen legs. Each of the two ends with their drop leaves is supported by six legs and the central section has four legs. The edge of the top has lines of inlay and the outer legs are ornamented with an inlaid design. Under the top at the ends are oval medallions and three vertical lines of inlay of the same type as the six lines in the sideboard No. 955 and several other pieces. This dining table is almost fourteen feet long and its width is four feet. About 1785–1800.

In No. 1318 the ends are semi–circular, or nearly so. Fourteen legs support the ends and the extensions. The legs are rectangular and some are grooved, a form of ornamentation used in the Chippendale style and followed in that of Hepplewhite; other examples of grooving are in the Pembroke tables Nos. 1405 and 1409. About 1785–1800.

The next dining tables, Nos. 1319–1327 are in the Sheraton style. The principal features distinguishing the dining tables in this style from those in the Hepplewhite style are that the legs, if they are straight, are round and generally reeded; that in many cases the legs are not straight but curved, and support a platform or pedestal; and that inlay was not used, but carving was often used on the curved legs and on other parts. All of the tables are of mahogany, as in the Hepplewhite style.

No. 1319 is a dining table of the same general shape as the preceding one in the Hepplewhite style, but with rounded corners and twelve reeded legs. The edge of the top is also reeded. About 1810–1820.

Comparing No. 1320 with No. 1313 in the Hepplewhite style, we see that from each a drop–leaf hangs; and in each the legs are straight and tapering. In No. 1320, however, there is no inlay, the legs are round and reeded and the feet end in brass sockets fitted with casters. The edge of the top is also reeded. There are ten legs, two of which are swinging legs which hold up the leaves. The table

1311 (UPPER) MRS. C. P. ROGOW.   1312 (UPPER) MR. J. G. D'ARCY PAUL.
1313 (CENTRE) ANONYMOUS.   1314 (CENTRE) ANONYMOUS.
1315 (LOWER) MRS. A. ADGATE DUER.   1316 (LOWER) MR. GEORGE W. EVANS, JR.

1317 (Upper) Anonymous. 1318 (Next to Top) Dr. James Bordley, Jr.
1319 (Next to Lower) Mrs. Miles White, Jr.
1320 (Lower) Mr. J. Ramsey Speer. 1321 (Lower) Mrs. Wm. M. Roberts.

1322 (UPPER) DR. JAS. BORDLEY, JR.   1323 (NEXT TO TOP) ANONYMOUS.
1324 (NEXT TO LOWER) MET. MUS. OF ART.
1325 (LOWER) MET. MUS. OF ART.   1326 (LOWER) MET. MUS. OF ART.

is four feet wide and when a separate section and all the additional leaves which belong to it are in place it is fourteen feet long and has sixteen legs. The reeding on this table is of finer character than in some later pieces. About 1800–1815.

No. 1321 is of the same type but of somewhat later construction, as is shown by the less delicate reedings which project further outward. Here also are ten legs. In this and the preceding table there is a ring under the reeding on each leg and below the ring the leg continues in the round and tapering form seen on other articles of the Sheraton style, as in the chairs Nos. 276 and 277. About 1810–1820.

Six other dining tables, Nos. 1322–1327, have curved legs. Some of these tables have two or more pedestals and others have a platform on which are vertical columns supporting the top.

Nos. 1322 and 1323 are examples of the first kind, with two or more pedestals supporting the top. These follow the designs of the English examples of the Sheraton period and are said to have a great advantage in giving "free play to the sitter's knees", an agreeable feature not possessed by many other dining tables of earlier periods, "and on account of this virtue the patterns are sought after in America".[5] These tables were made with either three legs, in the tripod form, or with four legs, and in some pieces both types were used.

No. 1322 is composed of three parts. The top of each part is supported by a round "turned" pedestal which rests upon finely reeded concave legs sloping downward and outward. The legs terminate in brass cups with casters. There are three legs on each of the end sections and four legs on the central section, the latter being for extra stability. About 1800–1815.

No. 1323 is a two–part table. The central portion of the top is an extension leaf[6] supported by two swinging brackets which open from the pedestals. The edges of the top are reeded and on each pedestal is a reeded form of a vase. The legs are carved with acanthus leaves on the upper portion, below which they are reeded. This piece is in the style of Sheraton, and its ornamental reeding and carving suggest the workmanship of Duncan Phyfe. About 1810–1825.

The next three illustrations, Nos. 1324–1326, are of two dining tables made by Duncan Phyfe, which are now in the Metropolitan Museum of Art, through whose courtesy they are shown here. Nos. 1325 and 1326 are views of the same table.[7] These tables follow the Sheraton style which was in fashion during the

5.   As remarked by the English writer Mr. G. Owen Wheeler in his "Old English Furniture", third edition, pages 576–578, where an illustration is given of a Sheraton style dining table with two pedestals, each with three legs. See also a remark quoted in section 155, paragraph 3, in connection with gate–leg tables.

6.   The device by which tables may be extended and reduced in length by a telescopic arrangement immediately under the top was invented in 1800 by Robert Gillow, one of the celebrated firm of cabinet makers in London commonly called "Gillows". This was in the Sheraton period.

7.   The book "Furniture Masterpieces of Duncan Phyfe", by Mr. Charles Over Cornelius, published for the Metropolitan Museum of Art by Doubleday, Page & Company, 1922, contains fifty–six illustrations, including Nos. 1325 and 1326 here shown, which are on plate 39.

period of Phyfe's best work, about 1800–1820, and have some of the embellishments and fine workmanship which have made his furniture famous. They are, however, regarded as in the Sheraton style, not in a "Duncan Phyfe style", for the reasons mentioned in sections 20 and 171. In these tables the features are the platforms supported by the four curved legs, and the four columns which rest upon the platform and hold the top. A similar platform is seen on the table No. 1640.

No. 1324 is a long table consisting of two end tables and one central one. The top of each part is supported by four carved columns. The delicate carving on the columns and on the upper part of the legs, not well seen in a small engraving, is a decorative feature used by Phyfe. The form of the legs is not one of the best of the Phyfe designs. About 1800–1820.

Nos. 1325 and 1326 are two illustrations of another dining table by Phyfe, the first showing a side view and the second showing an end view. Here there are two platforms with carved columns and carved and curved legs which terminate in brass feet finished with casters. The graceful proportions of this table, especially when seen from the end as in No. 1326, and its decorative elegance, are much admired. About 1800–1820.

Table No. 1327 is of an unusual type and would be better understood if it had been photographed in the same position as the similar table No. 770 in volume 2 of Mr. Lockwood's "Colonial Furniture".[8] At each of the two ends is a group of three legs, two of which extend sideways as in No. 1326; the third leg is attached to the other two at a right angle. The groups may be turned inward as in the illustration, or outward if desired. Above the legs are inverted lyre-shaped supports to which the top is attached. About 1800–1820.

The next four dining tables, Nos. 1328–1331, are in the Empire style, which will be recognized by the heavily built pedestals which are used instead of the lighter and more graceful ones seen above, and also, in some places, by the animals' claw feet and other somewhat inelegant carvings.

In No. 1328 each of the heavy pedestals is supported by four legs which are not well seen and in form resemble those in No. 1322, with which this dining table may be compared. The top is partly supported by four swinging brackets. About 1815–1830.

In No. 1329 only the two ends of the table are shown. Here also are massive pedestals carved mainly with leaves. The heavy reeded legs end in animals' claw feet, and coarse leaf carvings are on the "skirt". About 1820-1830.

In No. 1330 the heavy pedestals are ornamented with a series of rings. The legs are in a form used in the Empire period; the upper portion of the legs is carved in a plain design and the lower portion is reeded. About 1820–1830.

No. 1331 is one end of an elaborately ornamented dining table which is now used as a side table. As in the previous Empire style pieces, we see the massive

8. An illustration of a similar dining table, with a comment, is in "Antiques", January, 1932, page 32.

1327 (Upper) Mr. C. W. L. Johnson.
1329 (Centre) Coll. of Late Mrs. J. Stabler.
1331 (Lower) Est. of Mrs. J. H. Whiteley.

1328 (Upper) Mr. J. L. G. Lee.
1330 (Centre) Mrs. F. G. Boyce, Jr.
1332 (Lower) Mrs. Joseph Whyte.

1333 (Upper) Mr. & Mrs. M. P. Morfit.
1335 (Centre) Anonymous.
1337 (Lower) Mrs. S. Johnson Poe.

1334 (Upper) Mr. John C. Toland.
1336 (Centre) Anonymous.
1338 (Lower) Miss Helen H. Carey.

carved pedestal under which is a heavy platform carved on the top. The grotesque legs are carved to represent those of animals. About 1820–1830.

No 1332 is a dining table in the late Empire style. It is not shown here as an antique in the strict sense of the word, but as an example of the last development of style before the Victorian style became the fashion. The heavy legs, "scrolled" in form, and the heavy base, very close to the feet of a sitter, are characteristic of the period in which massive size and great weight were the predominant features. The two columns in the centre were probably made to support an extension leaf. See "Furniture styles of 1840", in the Appendix, section 199. About 1835–1840.

Section 158. Rectangular tea tables.—Small tables made especially for tea service, and hence known as tea tables, were in two forms. In one form the table has four legs and a top which is rectangular, or nearly so, and in the other form there are three legs, making a tripod, and generally a round top. These tables were very popular for many years from about 1725, but in the time of Hepplewhite and Sheraton they were almost superseded for tea service by the Pembroke tables, such as some of those shown in section 163.

The rectangular tables may be recognized as tea tables by their small size and especially by having in most cases a rim,[1] or raised edge, which projects above the level of the top to prevent the cups and saucers and other articles from slipping off, and gives to the top the appearance of a tray.[2] Under the top in the earlier tables, such as Nos. 1333–1335, there is a plain surface three or four inches deep; in the three later tables, Nos. 1336–1338, about that much space was often taken by a drawer.

No. 1333 is a rectangular tea table in the Queen Anne style with cabriole legs terminating in pointed Dutch, or club, feet, a type of foot which is shown as figure 12 in illustration No. 11. A rim, or raised edge, is around the top and below is a plain surface under which is a small skirt which "flares", or slants, outward. About 1735–1750.

No. 1334 is also in the Queen Anne style, with cabriole legs ending in round Dutch, or club, feet with "shoes" underneath. Here the skirt is conspicuous and its flare is clearly seen. The knees at the top of the legs are carved in a shell pattern, and the fact that all four knees are carved, and not those on the front only, shows that the table was meant to be seen from all sides. About 1735–1750.

In No. 1335 the skirt is cut in a series of double cyma curves, as to which see section 23. The legs are long, slender and graceful and terminate in Dutch, or club, feet. This table is about twenty–eight inches high. About 1735–1750.

1.   It is said that counterfeits of these tables are made by adding a rim to an old rectangular table with a plain top.
2.   Tea trays were fitted with a rim for the same purpose.
      Eleven tea tables with four legs are shown in Mr. Lockwood's "Colonial Furniture", figures 729–739, dating from about 1725 to 1770.
      The three–legged, or tripod, tea tables are considered in the text and notes in section 159. Urn stands, used in connection with tea tables, are illustrated in section 175. Nests of tables, used for tea, are shown in section 174, Nos. 1623–1625.

No. 1336 is a mahogany tea table which became celebrated because it brought at auction the highest price ever paid for an American table.[3] It is in the Chippendale style, as shown by the legs and the ball and claw feet. The rim is cut in the same shape as that of the skirt, which is a modified form of the "block" work shown in the chapter on "Block–front furniture", sections 118–119. The skirt is deep and is not ornamented by carving; but the upper part of the legs is finely carved with leaves. The legs are angular, not round. The date is known to be 1763.

Nos. 1337 and 1338 are in a somewhat different form, each having an unusual kind of rim and also having a wide drawer.

No. 1337 has cabriole legs and Dutch, or club, feet. The corners of the rim project somewhat upward and outward in a curved form. A drawer in tea tables is not often seen, but is occasionally found. The handles on the drawers are of a later period. Perhaps about 1750–1775.

In No. 1338 the rim is somewhat higher than in the preceding piece and resembles the rim of the tripod table shown in No. 1389. The corners of the rim project upward and outward as in the preceding table. The drawer is concave in the upper portion and convex in the lower portion. The escutcheon and handles are in the Chippendale style. Perhaps about 1750–1775.

Section 159. Tripod tables.—This section includes almost all kinds of three-legged tables except the pie–crust tables and the tripod candle stands, the latter of which are merely a certain type of small tripod tables. For convenience the pie–crust tables and the candle stands are considered in separate sections, Nos. 160 and 161.

The tripod[1] form, generally regarded as popularized in England by Chippendale, became fashionable in that country about 1755, and shortly after that

3.   This tea table was sold at auction for $29,000. It is apparently the one referred to in certain correspondence of John Goddard, cabinet maker, of Newport, Rhode Island, in 1763, who is mentioned in section 114, note 3. It was in the collection of the late Philip Flayderman, of Boston, and was sold in January, 1930, at the American Art Association Anderson Galleries from whose catalogue the above engraving and information are copied.

The highest prices paid for articles of American antique furniture are mentioned in section 209 entitled "Auction sales and prices."

1.   A.   The word "tripod" as an adjective means "having three feet or legs"; as a noun it means "any object having three feet or legs as a three–legged stool"; Century Dictionary.

B.   In "English and American Furniture", by Cescinsky and Hunter, page 212, Mr. Cescinsky writes that "a definite idea is embodied in the tripod form. A table or other article supported on four legs will rock on an uneven floor; one with three only, (a tripod), will rest firmly anywhere." On the plainer type of tripod tables there is no carving and the pedestal is "turned" in a simple form. It is said that these pedestals are often "glorified" by carving them. Mr. Cescinsky mentions on page 214 that in England, by reason of this modern embellishment, the tables without carving are diminishing in number and the supply of ornate ones is increasing.

The words "pedestal", "pillar", "column" and perhaps other words have been used by writers as synonymous in descriptions, as in Mr. Lockwood's Colonial Furniture, page 213, and in "Furniture Masterpieces of Duncan Phyfe", by Mr. C. O. Cornelius, plate 27, and others.

(*Note 1 is continued on page 722.*)

date it became popular in our country. In the Chippendale period it was used for the legs of small round tables, candle stands, pole screens, wig stands and several other articles. In the Hepplewhite–Sheraton period, and later, it served the same purposes and was also used for the pedestals of dining tables and for certain other tables shown in this book. The tables in this section are arranged mainly according to their style and shape, not according to the purposes for which we may think the tables were to be used, because many tables were used for several purposes.

The tripod table is in three parts, the top, the pedestal and the three feet or legs which give the table its name. The top is generally made to tilt, frequently to revolve but often is stationary.

The principal differences in tripod tables of the same type are in their size and shape, the presence or absence of carving or inlay, and the character of the wood and workmanship. These tables were all made in the mahogany period and most of them were of that wood, although some may be of walnut, cherry or other woods. So many tripod tables are owned in private houses that it seems desirable to present a considerable number of them.[2]

The round tops of tripod tables may be divided into five types, known as plain tops, tray tops, (also called "dish" tops), pie–crust tops, plate tops and gallery tops. Almost all of the gallery top type are regarded as of English make and only one is shown here, No. 1343, which is octagonal. These names are fairly descriptive of the tops, as will be seen in the illustrations, and need not be explained here. In addition to the round tops there were also tops in other forms—square, oval and octagonal.

The sizes of these tables varied greatly. The large ones were generally for afternoon tea, with ample space for cups and saucers as well as for the kettle and other accessories.[3] Perhaps the smallest tables were those for holding candles,

(NOTE 1, continued)

C. The legs of many tripod tables are braced together with pieces of iron screwed into them on the under side where they join the pedestal. The purpose of this is to prevent the legs from breaking away from the pedestal, which would occur if the strain on them from the weight of the upper part and of any objects placed on the top was too great.

D. The shrinkage of the tops of round tables as an indication of age is referred to in connection with pie–crust tables in section 160, note 1, E.

E. A revival of fashion in England in about 1875–1885 led to the reproduction of tripod tables with fretted galleries in the style of No. 1343. In Mr. Cescinsky's "English Furniture", volume 2, page 209, it is said that there was no intention to deceive in making these reproductions, "the rage for the collection of antique furniture having hardly begun at this period"; but "it is frequently by no means easy to detect them from the originals." In order to strengthen the open frets, they were "laminated", that is, made up of three layers of veneer, the grain of the centre layer being placed at right angles to the grain of the other two layers.

2. Most of the tripod tables shown here are small and are fairly well seen in the small engravings. The writer thinks that the reader will prefer to have a large number of small but clear illustrations rather than a less number of large illustrations. Many of the tables are very similar.

3. In "English and American Furniture", by Cescinsky and Hunter, pages 222–224, Mr. Cescinsky makes some interesting remarks on "purpose–made furniture", such as tables made for card–playing and others made for afternoon tea. He mentions that "an accompanying piece was the urn

known as "candle stands". Between these large and small tables there were many of intermediate sizes which were useful for tea or candles or ornaments or any objects of small size. These medium sized tables are by far the most numerous, and it is often difficult or impossible to determine whether such a piece is a table or a stand; in fact, between a small tea table and a candle stand of the same character there is often no real difference. Section 161 on tripod candle stands and section 175 on stands of various types should be examined in connection with the present section.

The first group of tripod tables here shown, Nos. 1339–1344, has a type of foot often used on these tables, known as a "snake" or "snake head" foot, which is more clearly shown in figure 20 in illustration No. 11 in section 25. The principal difference in these tables is in the design of the top and of the pedestal supporting it. All have small tops averaging about sixteen inches in diameter. They are regarded as being in the Chippendale style.

No. 1339 has a rim around the top, giving to the top a resemblance to a tray, or dish, and hence is known as a "tray top", or "dish top", table. The tapering pedestal, although long and without any ornamental "turnings", except at the base, gives a graceful appearance to the table. The legs are in the usual form and terminate in snake feet. About 1760–1790.

No. 1340, also, has a tray top. A vase–shaped "turning" is on the lower part of the pedestal. About 1760–1790.

No. 1341 has a plain top, meaning one without ornamentation by a rim or otherwise. Under the top is an attachment, sometimes called a "birdcage", by which the top may be tilted or revolved or both, a device which is more fully illustrated in connection with the tripod table No. 1373. About 1760–1790.

No. 1342 is another tray top table, more ornamental than the previous ones, the pedestal being fluted and turned. The legs are pointed, not rounded, on the upper side. The height is twenty–two inches. About 1760–1790.

In No. 1343 the top is octagonal in shape and is ornamented with a fretwork "gallery" around the edge. The presence of a gallery is generally regarded as

(NOTE 3, *continued*)

table made to support the silver or plated hot water urns of the period. The water was heated before being placed in these urns and kept to a high temperature" by a certain device. "The secret of making tea with water absolutely boiling was unknown at this date (the Chippendale period) and is far from being general in America at the present day." An American urn stand is shown in "Antiques", April, 1930, page 330. An old saying is apropos here: "Except the kettle boiling be, filling the tea pot spoils the tea."

In "Antique Furniture", page 348, by Mr. F. W. Burgess, an English writer, it is said that tripod tea tables and coffee tables with cabriole legs were made from about 1760 when the fashion for drinking tea began and there were no tables for holding the fine china that was made for the new beverage. These tables were so useful for the purpose that long after the cabriole leg passed out of style in chairs and other furniture it remained in vogue in the tripod tea tables. Tripod tables with cabriole legs had, however, been made before the tea drinking fashion began, and were used as candle stands. Some of the little tripods were no doubt intended as stands for ornaments.

Urn stands used in connection with tea tables are shown in section 175.

indicating that the table is an English one, which is probably the case with this table as it was inherited with other furniture known to be English. A gallery of this type is called a "spindle" gallery because it is made with small spindles. A note on tables with fretwork galleries is numbered 1, E in this section. About 1760–1790.

In No. 1344 the top is tilted upward in order to show clearly its design. The round inner portion is composed of eight wedge–shaped pieces whose points unite at the centre somewhat in the manner of No. 1370. A circle of inlay separates the central portion from the outer one. The fine grain and color do not appear well in the engraving. About 1760–1790.

In the next group, Nos. 1345–1350, the cabriole legs and the ball and claw feet place the tripod tables in the full Chippendale style. Here also the tops average about sixteen inches in diameter.

No. 1345 has a plain round top under which is a "birdcage" attachment by which the top may be revolved and tilted, as in No. 1373. The pedestal is turned in a vase form. About 1760–1790.

No. 1346 has a tray top, and the pedestal is turned in a plain column under which is an enlarged turning known as a "bulb", which is also seen on No. 1347 and others. About 1760–1790.

No. 1347 is also a tray top table and has a "birdcage" as in No. 1373, under which is a pedestal having a form somewhat similar to that in the preceding table. About 1760–1790.

No. 1348 is an English table which is in the same ownership as No. 1343. The rim is finely carved and there is also carving on the pedestal. In the legs there is an opening which gives a lighter appearance to them. About 1760–1790.

No. 1349 appears with the top up, showing the rim to some extent. The pedestal is turned in a vase design under which is a bulb. The claws holding the balls are conspicuous, as in No. 1346. About 1760–1790.

No. 1350 is more ornate than the other tables in this group. Under the tray top is a "birdcage", below which the pedestal is turned for a few inches and then carved. The legs are carved with leaves. About 1760–1790.

The next eleven tables, Nos. 1351–1361 are in the Sheraton style. Here the cabriole legs seen above are superseded by other types of curved legs, the curves being either convex, as in most of the tables, or concave. The tops are without rims and are in a variety of forms, and the pedestals are in various designs. Tripod tables were apparently not made with straight tapering legs which are features of the Hepplewhite style.

No. 1351, shown with the top up, is a pleasing tripod table with an oval top, in the centre of which is an inlaid American eagle with a shield and arrows, but without the stars supposed to indicate the number of States in the Union as on the desks Nos. 803 and 805. A line of inlay is near the edge. The pedestal is turned in a manner resembling Nos. 1340 and 1354. About 1800–1810.

1339 (UPPER) MR. & MRS. B. TURN-
    BULL.
1342 (CENTRE) MISS M. C. PAINTER.
1345 (LOWER) MRS. T. J. PACKARD.

1340 (UPPER) MRS. HOWARD SILL.
1343 (CENTRE) MR. & MRS. E. H.
    MCKEON.
1346 (LOWER) MR. & MRS. B. TURN-
    BULL.

1341 (UPPER) MRS. A. MORRIS
    CAREY.
1344 (CENTRE) MR. & MRS. WM. M.
    ELLICOTT.
1347 (LOWER) MRS. JOS. WHYTE.

No. 1352 is more ornamental than many others, the top having a border of light wood, and an inlaid centrepiece which is in the same eight–sided form as the top itself. Bands of inlay are on the lower part of the legs. The convex form of legs of this and other tables is shown in Sheraton's "Drawing Book", plate 54 and others. The pedestal is turned with rings. About 1800–1810.

No. 1353, also shown with the top up, has a top with the corners cut in curves. The pedestal is turned in a vase and ring design. About 1800–1810.

No. 1354 has a plain top under which is a "birdcage" device as in several other pieces. The turning on the pedestal is a vase as in No. 1351 and others. Lines of inlay are on the legs. About 1800.

In No. 1355 the top, at the corners, is cut in curves. The pedestal has a vase pattern with other designs. About 1800–1810.

No. 1356 is a curly maple table which was photographed with a leaf screen and a candle stick which, however, do not indicate that the table is a candle stand. The top is round and the pedestal has a vase design. About 1800–1810.

No. 1357 has an octagonal top which is grooved on the edges. The turned pedestal has a vase over which is a plain column. The legs seem to be somewhat heavy for the other parts. About 1800–1810.

No. 1358 is a curly maple table with a top cut in a concave curve on each side and a convex curve at each corner. The pedestal is turned in a vase pattern with a plain section above. About 1800–1810.

No. 1359 has a top somewhat similar to that of No. 1355. The lower part of the pedestal is turned in a vase form and is reeded, an ornamental treatment which will be seen in No. 1367 and other tables of the finer sort. About 1800–1810.

In No. 1360 the curved legs are more nearly upright than in the previous tables, giving an appearance of greater height. The top is octagonal and has a line of inlay near the edge. About 1800–1810.

In No. 1361 also the top is octagonal. The pedestal has a heavy reeding, similar to that on the legs of the dining table No. 1321. The base of the pedestal is larger than in the preceding pieces. The legs are concave and heavily reeded, terminating in brass feet. About 1810–1820.

No. 1362 is in the early Empire style, as is indicated by the heavy base of the pedestal and the carved portion having the familiar pineapple design of the period, often seen, for example, on the posts of bedsteads, as on No. 1071. The top is rounded at the corners. About 1815–1830.

Nos. 1363–1365 are unusual tables. The first two are of the Sheraton period, but the third is earlier in date.

In No. 1363 the square top of light wood is decorated with delicate flowers in the centre, inlaid fans at the corners and inlaid lines around the sides. The upper portions of the legs are convex and are carved with leaves. The feet are grooved in the same manner as the bottoms of the supports on the dressing glass No. 1270. Probably about 1815–1820.

1348 (UPPER) MR. & MRS. E. H. McKEON.
1351 (CENTRE) HAMMOND–HARWOOD HOUSE.
1354 (LOWER) MRS. MILES WHITE, JR.

1349 (UPPER) MRS. PAUL H. MILLER.
1352 (CENTRE) MR. E. G. MILLER, JR.
1355 (LOWER) MISS M. C. PAINTER.

1350 (UPPER) ANONYMOUS.
1353 (CENTRE) MRS. T. J. LINDSAY.
1356 (LOWER) MR. & MRS. W. A. DIXON.

In No. 1364 the feature is the group of three slender turned columns, instead of one pedestal, supporting the top and resting upon a small platform. The columns may be compared with those on the Sheraton style card table No. 1550. The legs are carved at the top, and terminate in brass feet.[4] About 1820.

In No. 1365 there is the same kind of legs and snake feet as Nos. 1339–1344. At the position occupied in some other tables by pedestals or columns, supporting the top, there is a cabinet with a door upon which a shell is carved. This cabinet closely resembles in form the central compartments seen in so many desks in the Chippendale style, such as Nos. 791–794 and others. The square top has doubtless been substituted for an original round one.[5] About 1760–1780.

The next two tripod tables, Nos. 1366–1367, are examples of fine workmanship and elegant design.

No. 1366 is a side table, not a card table, as it has no folding top. The top has three curves in the so–called "clover–leaf" design which is seen also in the Sheraton style card tables Nos. 1548 and 1549. The upper portion of the pedestal is fluted and below is a vase carved with leaves. The upper parts of the concave legs are carved with leaves, under which are reedings. The brass feet are in the form of animals' claws, and have casters. About 1810–1820.

No. 1367 is a similar table made by Duncan Phyfe and now in the Metropolitan Museum of Art. The top is reeded on the edges and is in a series of curves. The upper portion of the pedestal is in a plain design, below which is a reeded vase. The concave legs are reeded and terminate in brass feet and casters. About 1810–1820.

In No. 1368 the rectangular top is plain on one side and on the other side is a board for chess and other games.[6] The drawer below is for the accessories of the games. The top is supported by a vertical sliding bar which holds the board at a desired height. The delicate reeding of the pedestal and of the concave legs will be noticed. About 1810–1820.

The next three tripod tables, Nos. 1369–1371, are in the Empire style, which is recognized by the heavy pedestals and the kind of platforms and feet.

In No. 1369 the base of the pedestal is fully but coarsely carved with leaves and other objects, and rests upon a large and heavy triangular platform with concave sides. The feet are carved and end in animals' paws. About 1820–1830.

In No. 1370 the finely veneered top is in twelve wedge–shaped parts which extend to a brass circle in the centre, a method which is also used in No. 1344. A carved form of vase is at the lower end of the pedestal, under which is a base in the form of a dish. The platform is of the same type as that in the preceding table. The feet are brass, in a scroll design. About 1820–1830.

4. In " Antiques" May, 1927, pages 364–365, two tables are shown which have four slender and fluted columns supporting large round tops.

5. In "Antiques", November, 1923, pages 224–225, is an article illustrating three tables of this type having large round tilting tops and larger compartments than the one here shown.

6. An article entitled "Backgammon tables of the Eighteenth Century", by Mr. Robert Tasker Evans, with many illustrations, is in "The Antiquarian", March, 1931, pages 33–37. The article of Mr. Evans is also referred to in section 169, note 2. The tables are not in the tripod form.

1357 (UPPER) MD. SOC. COL. DAMES. 1358 (UPPER) MRS. J. S. GIBBS, JR. 1359 (UPPER) MRS. F. T. REDWOOD.
1360 (CENTRE) MR. & MRS. M. P. 1361 (CENTRE) DR. H. J. BERKLEY. 1362 (CENTRE) DR. M. A. ABRAMS.
    MORFIT. 1364 (LOWER) ANONYMOUS. 1365 (LOWER) MR. MORRIS WHIT-
1363 (LOWER) MRS. F. P. GARVAN. RIDGE.

1366 (Upper) Mr. & Mrs. Bayard Turnbull.   1367 (Upper) Anonymous.
1368 (Centre) Mr. Edgar G. Miller, Jr.   1369 (Centre) Miss Helen H. Carey.
1370 (Lower) Mr. Edgar G. Miller, Jr.   1371 (Lower) Judge F. N. Parke.

1372 (Upper) Mrs. I. R. Trimble.
1374 (Centre) Coll. of Mrs. J. Stabler.
1376 (Lower) Md. Society of Colonial
     Dames.

1373 (Upper) Mrs. I. R. Trimble.
1375 (Centre) Chase House,
     Annapolis.
1377 (Lower) Anonymous.

No. 1371 shows the last type of the Empire style. The pedestal has lost its former shape and seems to represent a four–sided vase. The platform is round and is supported by three scroll feet which are in about the same shape as those on the sewing table No. 1580 and several feet shown in the Appendix, section 199 entitled "Furniture styles of 1840". About 1830–1840.

With No. 1372 we begin another type of tripod tables. Almost all of these have large round tops, often more than three feet in diameter, which may be tilted and frequently may be revolved. All of these tables were probably used as tea tables, although some have no rim around the top. The pie–crust tables belong to this group, but because of their distinctive character they are considered separately in the next section. The dates of all of these tables are probably about 1760–1780.

No. 1372 is the front view, and No. 1373 is the rear view, of the same table. The top has a rim and hence the table is called a tray–top table. The legs and snake feet are in the same style as those in Nos. 1339–1344. About 1760–1780.

In No. 1373 we see the construction of the "birdcage" by which the top may be tilted or revolved or both. First we notice the two long pieces of wood, called "cleats", which are screwed on the under side of the top and tend to prevent it from warping. The base of the "birdcage" consists of a square piece of wood resting on the round pedestal which extends loosely through a round opening in the base and permits it to revolve; and over the base are four small posts which connect the base with its top. The cleats are connected with the top of the base by pivots by means of which the top may be tilted. When the table top is down, the latch, seen between the cleats on the under side of the top, holds the top down until it is released by opening the latch. About 1760–1780.

No. 1374 is a tripod table with a large top, the edge of which is cut in a rope design. It will be noticed that the balls in the feet are flat, being only about one–half of a sphere, as also in No. 1378 and some other articles of the period. About 1770–1780.

No. 1375 has a large plain and square top which is attached to the pedestal in a position which gives an appearance of greater height and width than if its sides were upright and horizontal. This table and other articles of the period are on exhibition in the Chase House, at Annapolis; the house was built in 1770–1771. About 1770–1780.

No. 1376 has a top which was probably made of two boards instead of the usual one, as appears from a joint in the centre. The form is that of a square top cut in a manner to have rounded corners and serpentine sides, with cyma curves, as to which see section 23. About 1770–1780.

No. 1377 is a table in a form which was popular in England. It has been called a "plate–top" tripod table because of the curved spaces for plates or saucers.[7] Here there are eight spaces within the raised and scalloped rim and in

---

7. Tables of this type are illustrated in Mr. Lockwood's "Colonial Furniture", volume 2, figure 752, and in Mr. Cescinsky's "English Furniture", volume 2, figure 211.

the centre are elaborately carved leaves and figures. The legs are carved and the "snake" feet are of the same type as those seen in Nos. 1339–1341. Tables with a similar form of top, but without the eight spaces or the central carving, have been called "scalloped" tables and by other partially descriptive terms. This table is doubtless of English make. It has been regarded as an original table of the period, but the owner is of the opinion that the eight spaces and the carving in the centre are "glorifications" of later date than the date of its arrival in Charleston, South Carolina, where it was found. About 1760–1780.

Section 160. Pie–crust tables.—These are the most highly esteemed of the tripod tables. In their general form they follow the tables Nos. 1372–1374, having a large circular top made of a single piece of wood, usually mahogany; the top always tilts and generally revolves; and there is a pedestal which rests upon three wide–spreading cabriole legs with feet of the "snake", or the ball and claw, type, the latter generally birds' claws. The distinctive ornamental feature is that the raised edge of the top, instead of being plain, as in other tables, is carved in a series of curves which are supposed to resemble the edge of the crust of a pie.[1]

Mr. Lockwood, in his "Colonial Furniture", volume 2, page 213, mentions that the type of edge most frequently used consists of a combination of only three different curves which are repeated around the entire raised edge; and he points out that if these three curves vary in their relative sizes on different tables the tops have a different appearance, although they have the same curves. This feature

1. A. The pie–crust table is a development from the plain tripod tables, such as No. 1372, with the edge cut in curves and generally with carving on the pedestal, legs and feet.

B. The word "pie–crust", as applied to these tables, originated in England. The pie which is honored by the use of the form of its edge as an ornamental feature of these tables, was probably an English cold veal pie. Our American cabinet makers followed the design of the English pie–crust table, but our cooks fortunately abandoned the English cold veal pie.

C. Mr. Cescinsky, in "English and American Furniture", pages 213–214, states that the word pie–crust "expresses nothing in particular, and is copied, perhaps, from the small silver trays— 'waiters' as they are styled—of the period."

D. The high prices brought by these tables have led to much faking. A table with a plain top may be furnished with an applied edge cut in a pie–crust form. The wood of a plain top may be cut down in a manner to produce a raised rim, in which case the original thickness of the wood will be noticeably reduced. Plain pedestals and legs have been "glorified" by recent carving; see the previous section, note 1, B, and also No. 1377. These faking tricks may be discovered by an expert cabinet maker who knows the details of the making of antique furniture, but will seldom be noticed by an amateur.

E. The round top of any table will surely shrink *across* the grain, not *with* the grain, and the length across the grain will therefore be less than with the grain. If the top of an alleged antique pie–crust table is in a perfect circle, it is probably a fake. If a round top has been recently made of old wood which has already shrunk all it can, the top may be a perfect circle and the substitution may be apparent. In the small pie–crust table No. 1379, the shrinkage is three–eighths of an inch as mentioned in the comment.

F. An article entitled "A study of American Pie–crust Tables", by Mr. Wm. M. Hornor, Jr., is in the "International Studio", June, 1931, pages 38–40.

will be referred to in the comments. In some of the tables other forms of edges are seen, all of a character adapted to the round shape of the top.

In addition to the ornamental pie–crust edge, these tables are often decorated with fine carving on the pedestal and on the legs and feet. A flattened ball, or "bulb", on the lower part of the pedestal, as shown in No. 1388, is said to be an indication of the workmanship of Philadelphia, where the finest American pie–crust pieces were made. Only a few pie–crust tables were made in New England. These tables are all of the Chippendale period.

In all fine tripod tables much of the charm comes from the harmony of size between the top and the legs. This is particularly true in the case of pie–crust tables, which being elegant in workmanship require elegance in design. In all cases the size and diameter of the top should be in proper proportion to the spread of the legs. A table with a small top should not have wide–spreading legs, and vice versa. The eye of the trained observer, accustomed to the best, will discriminate between the perfect and the merely good.

In pie–crust tables the chief differences are in the combination of curves on the edge, the number of repetitions of that combination, the carving on the pedestal and legs, and the kind of feet. As the edge is the distinctive feature, the tables are shown with their tops up, hiding almost all of the pedestal; but in order that a fine pedestal may be seen in some detail, one is shown without the top in No. 1388. In Nos. 1378–1381 the same design on the edge appears six or more times on each table. This design was apparently the favorite one.

In No. 1378, at the centre of the top, we see a short projection which appears to be straight, but which is generally slightly curved, as it is a curve of the circumference of the round board from which the top was made. To the right of this circumference curve is a small half–round curve; next to the right is a long serpentine curve, to the right of which is another half–round curve. These four curves constitute one section of the pie–crust design of this table. This section appears eight times on the edge of the table. On the pedestal a carved bulb will be seen, and the legs are also carved, terminating in flat ball and claw feet. About 1760–1780.

In No. 1379 also there are eight sections on the edge, and the curves are the same as in the preceding table and are of almost the same relative size. Here the feet are in the snake form, as in Nos. 1339–1344 in the previous section. The top of this small table measures twenty–four inches with the grain and three–eighths of an inch less across the grain, probably indicating the shrinkage referred to in note 1, E. About 1760–1780.

In No. 1380 the relative sizes of the same three curves vary somewhat from those in the two preceding pieces, and the actual sizes of the curved parts are so much smaller that ten sections are required to fill the edge. The pedestal has a carved vase at its base and other carving is on the legs. The feet are in a ball and claw form. The top of this table is twenty–six inches in diameter. About 1760–1780.

1378 (Upper) Dr. Jas. Bordley, Jr.
1380 (Centre) Mr. & Mrs. H. L.
    Duer.
1382 (Lower) Mr. John C. Toland.

1379 (Upper) Mr. Edgar G. Miller, Jr.
1381 (Centre) Dr. M. A. Abrams.
1383 (Lower) Mr. & Mrs. J. Marsh
    Matthews.

No. 1381 has the same three curves, appearing six times; but the relative sizes of the curves are somewhat different, the lengths of the circumference curves and the serpentine curves being greater than in the preceding pieces. The upper portion of the leg is carved and the snake feet are also carved. Here there are six sections on the edge. About 1760–1780.

In No. 1382 we notice a variation from the preceding tables, there being no serpentine curves. The circumference curve and the two half–round portions are used twelve times. The legs are carved at the top, terminating in a kind of animals' feet. About 1760–1780.

In No. 1383 also there are no serpentine curves. The circumference curve is small, and it and the two half–round portions each appear twenty times on the edge. The base of the pedestal is carved, as are also the upper portions of the legs, and the feet are of the ball and claw pattern. About 1760–1780.

No. 1384 is another table which has only two kinds of curves, the circumference curve and the half–round one. This form is used eighteen times. The base of the pedestal is ringed. The legs are carved on the upper portion and the feet are of the ball and claw type. About 1760–1780.

No. 1385 has a different kind of rim. The circumference curve is at the top as usual, next to which on each side is a half–round, and then a double cyma curve and then another half–round. This section appears eight times. A carved form is at the base of the pedestal and carving is also on the legs which terminate in ball and claw feet. About 1760–1780.

In No. 1386 the carving on the top changes the appearance of the table, which has almost the same three curves in each section as No. 1378. Two of these curves, the circumference curve, which is not exactly at the top here, and the serpentine curve, are decorated with carving; the other curve, the half–round, is plain. Each section here appears eight times. The legs are carved and the feet are of the snake type. About 1760–1780.

No. 1387 is also a handsomely decorated table, not exactly of the pie–crust type, but resembling the type in some respects. Here the edge is cut in nine "C" curves, (as to which see the mirror No. 1103 and the comment), nine shells and eighteen other curves. The pedestal and legs are decorated with carving. About 1760–1780.

No. 1388 shows the pedestal and feet of a fine pie–crust table on a larger scale than in the preceding pieces in order that the carving may be more clearly seen. Under the "birdcage" is a fluted column, below which is a carved "flattened" ball or "bulb" which, as mentioned above, is said to be a clear indication of Philadelphia workmanship. The legs are carved and end in ball and claw feet. The carving is of a high quality, but cannot be fully appreciated in a small engraving. It may be mentioned that in all cases where there is carving, it is the "quality" which determines whether or not it adds to or detracts from the elegance of the piece.

In No. 1389 the top is not cut in the usual "pie–crust" form, but may be regarded as being a variation of that type of table. The rim is carved in a series of

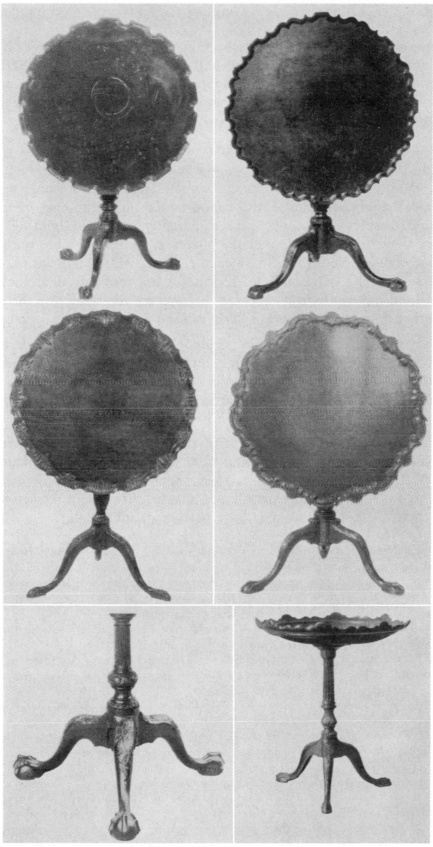

1384 (Upper) Mr. S. Johnson Foe.
1386 (Centre) Mr. & Mrs. E. H. McKeon.
1388 (Lower) Metropolitan Museum of Art.

1385 (Upper) Mrs. Alexander Armstrong.
1387 (Centre) Mrs. Maurice F. Rodgers.
1389 (Lower) Dr. Jas. Bordley, Jr.

double cyma curves, (as to which see section 23), which rise above the edge of the table, and between these curves are half–round prominences. There are certain points of resemblance between this top and that of the rectangular tea table No. 1338. The pedestal is fluted above and a vase below is carved. The legs are carved and the feet are of a claw type. About 1750–1775.

Section 161. Tripod candle stands.—The term "tripod candle stand" is often somewhat loosely applied to almost any tripod table with a small top; but in correct usage the term only applies to tripod tables which, because of their small tops or other distinctive features, were apparently made for holding a candlestick rather than for general household purposes. A tripod table with a top of medium size could serve for holding a candlestick as well as one with a small top, but in this section the tripod tables illustrated were probably made only for the purpose of holding candlesticks, because the tops are too small for the service of tea or for other domestic uses, except perhaps for a flower pot or a vase of flowers.[1]

A large number of plain candle stands in a variety of forms were made in our country throughout the eighteenth century. It is said that they come under the class of "folk furniture",[2] and not many have sufficient merit in design or workmanship to be illustrated here. Three examples of the better sort are shown, Nos. 1390–1392.

No. 1390 is regarded as the oldest of the first three. It is said that candle stands of this type were first made about 1700, and continued to be made for very many years thereafter. The top is sixteen inches square, resting on a turned pedestal which is supported by a cross base. The height is about twenty–six inches. This is in the style of 1700, but may have been made much later.

1.   A.   Tall candle stands, called "torchères", in pairs and ranging in height from about three feet to five feet, were made in England in the time of Chippendale, who published several designs of them in his "Director", as to which book see section 15. A few of these tall candle stands have been found, especially in some of the southern States. Several are shown in Mr. Wallace Nutting's "Furniture Treasury", Nos. 1322–1328. See Nos. 1397 and 1398 in this volume.

B.   These pieces are called "candle stands", not "candle tables". As to the distinction between a "table" and a "stand", see the remarks at the beginning of sections 173 and 175.

C.   In section 169 two card tables Nos. 1478 and 1479 have flat places at the corners for holding candles. These candle places were seldom constructed in card tables after the movable and more convenient candle stands came into fashion.

D.   An article entitled "Rare Windsor Candlestands", by Mr. Clarence W. Brazer, is in "Antiques", October, 1924, pages 190–194, with ten illustrations. These pieces have a large or small round top resting on three "turned" legs which, as also the stretchers, resemble those seen on certain Windsor chairs. They are plain, but are interesting on account of their use of the Windsor chair designs.

2.   As remarked by Mr. Wallace Nutting in his "Furniture Treasury", volume 1, at No. 1336. Mr. Nutting shows candle stands of this general character in his illustrations Nos. 1318–1393. At No. 1364 he remarks: "The variety of these wooden stands is endless. The author saw in one shop twelve different patterns, all of them new, all purporting to be old. Good patterns were rare and the demand always finds itself met by a certain sort of supply."

As to the word "pedestal" and others see the last note on page 721.

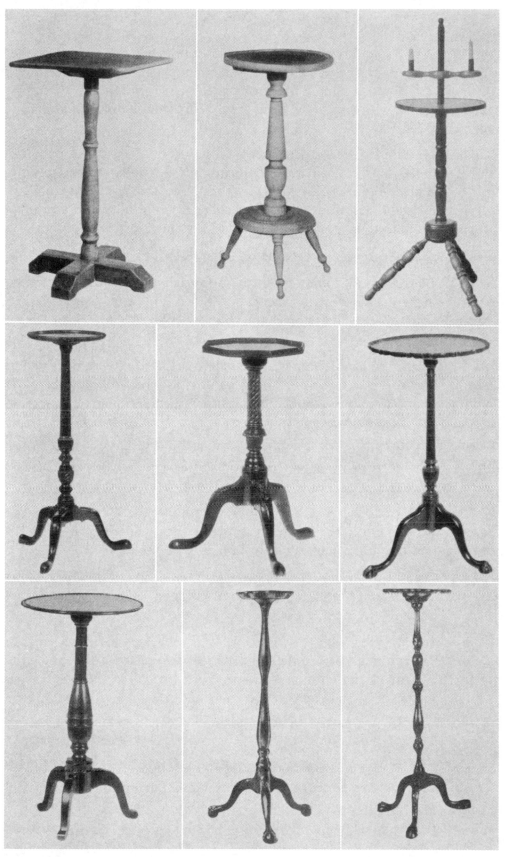

1390 (UPPER) MRS. FRANCIS P.
　　GARVAN.
1393 (CENTRE) MR. & MRS.
　　H. L. DUER.
1396 (LOWER) COLL. OF LATE
　　MRS. J. STABLER.

1391 (UPPER) MRS. FRANCIS P.
　　GARVAN.
1394 (CENTRE) MRS. J. S. GIBBS,
　　JR.
1397 (LOWER) ANONYMOUS.

1392 (UPPER) HAMMOND–
　　HARWOOD HOUSE.
1395 (CENTRE) MRS. HOWARD
　　SILL.
1398 (LOWER) ANONYMOUS.

No. 1391 has a round top, eleven inches in diameter, with a raised edge. The turnings of the column are more ornamental than those in the preceding piece. The column rests upon a round platform which is supported by three slanting, or "raked", legs, sometimes called "peg legs". The height is twenty–five inches. Perhaps about 1750–1775.

No. 1392 is often called a screw candle stand, because the round stand intended for candlesticks screws up and down on the pole, thus regulating the height. In this piece there is also an arm which holds two candles. Candle stands of this type were generally about three feet or more high, but were also made in a small form to be placed on a table or elsewhere. About 1725–1750.

Nos. 1393–1398 are candle stands of later date and finer quality.

No. 1393 has a small round tray top supported by a column of which the lower part is ornamented with a ring and vase design. The legs and the snake feet are similar to those of the tripod tables Nos. 1339–1344 in section 159. About 1760–1790.

No. 1394 is a small candle stand, or perhaps a tea kettle stand, only twenty–two inches high. The top is octagonal and has an upright rim. The upper portion of the column is carved in a spiral pattern, as to which see note 2 in section 155. The legs and feet resemble those in the preceding piece. About 1760–1790.

In No. 1395 the top is cut in a series of curves and is supported by a tapering column which has a turned vase at the base. The legs and feet are of the same type as in the tripod tables No. 1345–1350. About 1760–1790.

No. 1396 is a small table with a top in the tray form. The lower part of the column is in the shape of an elongated vase with rings. The legs and feet are of a later period than the other parts and are probably about 1820.

No. 1397 is a tall candle stand, thirty–six inches high. The top is about nine and one–half inches in diameter and has a raised edge. The legs end in ball and claw feet. This and the next piece are examples of "torchères", referred to in note 1, A in this section. About 1760–1780.

No. 1398 is another tall candle stand which differs from the preceding one mainly in the form of the column which is here turned in a series of graceful forms. The top is very small and the feet are of the ball and claw type. About 1760–1780.

Section 162. Certain drop–leaf tables.—The descriptive term "drop–leaf" applies of course to any table having leaves which drop; but certain kinds of drop–leaf tables, in which the drop–leaf is an essential but not the distinctive feature, are known by special names, such as gate–leg tables, butterfly tables, Pembroke tables, library tables, sofa tables and corner tables. Moreover many tables with drop–leaves were used for a special purpose from which they acquire their names, such as dining tables.[1] All of these special kinds of tables are shown in other sections, leaving for this section only a few drop–leaf tables having drop–leaves as their distinctive feature and having a utility value for almost any purpose for which a plain table is desired.

The leaves of these drop–leaf tables, like those of the gate–leg tables, were so made as to hang down on hinges from the sides of the central section when not in use, and when up they were held in position by legs which swing out. When both leaves were extended, the top of the table was sometimes round but usually oval, or rectangular.[2]

The points of difference in the form of these drop–leaf tables are the size and shape of the top, the type of legs, the kind of feet and the treatment of the ends of the central portion. In these features the styles of the Queen Anne period and the Chippendale period will be noticed. Drop–leaf tables of the type here shown passed out of fashion in the time of Hepplewhite and Sheraton.

No. 1399 is an oval drop–leaf table with six legs instead of the usual four. The centre section has four fixed legs and the other two legs swing out and support the leaves. This six–legged type is regarded as more elegant than the type with four legs. The Queen Anne style is indicated by the cabriole legs, here graceful and delicate, and by the Dutch, or club, feet. The end of the central section is cut in a double cyma curve, as to which see section 23. About 1740–1760.

In No. 1400 the leaves are rectangular and their inner edges are made in such a manner that the hinges are not seen, as referred to in note 2, and as in the gate–leg table No. 1297. There are four legs in the cabriole form and the feet are in the Dutch, or club, style with a large "shoe" or "cushion", even larger than those on some of the highboys, such as No. 636; see note 10 in section 85. The end of the centre section is cut in a semi–circular form. About 1740–1760.

No. 1401 is a somewhat smaller drop–leaf table in which the leaves are cut in pleasing curves in about the same design as in the Pembroke tables Nos. 1406–1408 in the next section. The cabriole legs terminate in Dutch three–pointed feet such as are seen on the lowboy No. 692; see figure 11 in illustration No. 11. The end of the centre section is cut in arched curves. About 1740–1760.

1. Many drop–leaf tables were used as dining tables and several of these were shown in section 157. In some cases it may be possible to distinguish those tables from drop–leaf tables which were not intended for dining purposes, but it is difficult to see any clear distinction between them. The larger ones were doubtless used for dining purposes. Gate–leg tables were also much used as dining tables; see section 155. Drop–leaf tables with square or rectangular tops could be coupled together and thus form one long table.

2. In his "English Furniture", volume 2, page 32, Mr. Cescinsky mentions that in England these drop–leaf tables were originally nearly always rectangular, but later the tops were generally cut to an oval form which was more convenient for the purpose of a dining or centre table.

The tops or leaves of these tables are frequently missing or in bad condition so that a restoration is necessary. In section 155 on gate–leg tables, note 1, E, are remarks as to the difficulty of determining whether a top is original or otherwise. The hinges connecting the leaves with the central section of the top were of the same type as those of the gate–leg tables, and the usual form of joint was so made as to conceal the hinges, as is well seen in No. 1400; see also note I, F, in section 155.

The wood is generally either walnut or mahogany.

No. 1402 is a round drop–leaf table with four almost straight legs ending in Dutch, or club, feet. The two side legs are swung out to support the two leaves. This is a small table about two feet high and with a diameter of twenty–nine inches across the top. The end of the central section is cut in a double cyma curve. The wood is mahogany. About 1740–1760.

No. 1403 has cabriole legs and ball and claw feet. The leaves are rectangular as in No. 1400 and may be connected with another similar table if a larger one is desired. The appearance of a single table of this kind is not as attractive as that of a table with oval or other curved leaves. About 1740–1760.

No. 1404 is an oval top table, with ball and claw feet as in the preceding piece. The upper part of each leg, called the "knee", is carved. The proportions of the leaves seem to be well adapted to the size and shape of the piece. About 1740–1760.

Section 163. Pembroke tables.—The small and attractive drop–leaf tables were apparently first made in the time of Chippendale, but the name "Pembroke" was given at a somewhat later period.[1] Their distinctive feature is that the drop–leaves are short and when open are supported by brackets which swing out under the leaves, instead of by swinging legs such as are seen in previous types of drop–leaf tables. They were popular during the Chippendale, Hepplewhite and Sheraton periods, extending from about 1760 to 1820.

The tables were made with tops of various forms. In the Chippendale period the tops were often in a square shape, but their leaves were as often in a serpentine form. In the Hepplewhite and Sheraton periods the tops are generally in an oval shape, but in some cases the leaves have other curved forms. There is generally one drawer. These tables are finished on all sides, as usual with tables which are meant to stand in the centre of a room, where all parts may be seen. They were often used as tea tables in our country in the Hepplewhite and Sheraton periods, superseding the tripod tables of the Chippendale style.

Nos. 1405–1408 are in the Chippendale style; Nos. 1409–1411 are in a transition[2] form, having features of both the Chippendale and the Hepplewhite styles; Nos. 1412–1414 are in the Hepplewhite style, and Nos. 1415 and 1416 are in the Sheraton style.

In No. 1405 the square legs are grooved in the manner seen in many chairs and other pieces of the Chippendale period. The inner edges of the legs are cut off somewhat, making the legs irregularly shaped and providing flat surfaces for

1.   Tables of this type were called "breakfast" tables by Chippendale in his "Directory". In Hepplewhite's "Guide", they are called "Pembroke" tables, and it is said that they "are the most useful of this species of furniture"; and elaborate inlaid designs of them are given. In the "Maryland Gazette", April 10, 1786, John Rutter, a cabinet maker of Baltimore, advertised "Pembroke tables". In Sheraton's "Drawing Book", it is said on page 337 of the edition of 1802 that "the use of this piece is for a gentleman or lady to breakfast on."

2.   As to "transition" pieces, see the chapter on chairs, section 51, notes 17 and 43.

1399 (Upper) Mr. Albert G. Towers.
1401 (Centre) Mrs. Thos. J. Lindsay.
1403 (Lower) Mrs. Arthur Hale.

1400 (Upper) Mr. Albert G. Towers.
1402 (Centre) Anonymous.
1404 (Lower) "Lock. Col. Furn.", Fig. 724.

the insertion of stretchers. The leaves are short and rectangular. Under the drawer is a molding in the form known as "godroon".[3] About 1760–1780.

No. 1406 is more ornate, the leaves being serpentine on the sides with rounded corners and concave ends. The stretchers are flat, pierced and crossed,[4] and at their intersection is a platform upon which a vase of flowers or other objects could be placed. As in the preceding table the inner edges of the grooved legs are cut off, making flat surfaces in which the stretchers are inserted. About 1760–1780.

No. 1407 has similar leaves and grooved legs. This is a somewhat plain form of the preceding tables, having no decoration or ornamental stretchers. About 1760–1780.

In No. 1408 the leaves are rounded at the corners, and have two concave curves on their sides and one on their ends. The front and back of the top of the central section are also cut in concave curves. The cross–stretchers are vertical and are in an openwork design. About 1760–1780.

Nos. 1409–1411, as mentioned, are transition tables, having features of both the Chippendale and the Hepplewhite styles. In No. 1409 the Chippendale style predominates, the table having square and grooved legs, four carved brackets at the junctions of the legs and the skirt, and convex and concave leaves. The features of the Hepplewhite style are the veneered drawer with inlay and the slight tapering of the legs on the inside, none of which details were used in the Chippendale style. The illustration is taken from the front, and in the rear we see that the table is finished with a similar veneered drawer front, but no drawer; this is called in England a "sham" drawer. In our country the less descriptive words "blind" or "dummy" are used, not implying, however, an intention to deceive.[5] About 1780–1790.

No. 1410 is a table resembling No. 1406 in having crossed stretchers and also in general form, but it has no ornamental features. The Hepplewhite style is seen in the tapering of the legs. About 1780–1790.

No. 1411 is a transition table in which the features of the Hepplewhite style are more noticeable than those of the style of Chippendale. The principal Chippendale feature is seen in the form of the leaves, which have a serpentine curve

3. This word, sometimes erroneously spelled "gadroon", is derived from the French word "godron", meaning ruffle or plait. As used here it means a curved ruffle or fluted ornament, of great variety in form, straight, concave or convex, used as a carved decoration on tables, chairs and other articles of furniture.

4. The stretchers on these tables are crossed and are known as "cross–stretchers", "X" stretchers or "saltire" stretchers, the latter word meaning the same as "saltier", that is, in the form of a St. Andrew's cross, which is X-shaped. See section 26, note 4.

5. In England, in the latter part of the eighteenth century, "sham" drawers, doors and some other parts were much used, the method being called "shamming". The purpose was to have a proper decorative balance and its use was regarded as a legitimate treatment.

Other examples are on the sideboard No. 953 and others, where two shallow drawers are apparently seen although there is merely one cupboard; on the highboy Nos. 646–647 where three apparently separate drawers are in reality one; on the Sheraton style desk No. 838 where there seem to be drawers at the ends; and on No. 1650 where one door appears to be four drawers. See "Shamming" in the Index.

1405 (UPPER) MRS. W. D. STEUART.
1407 (CENTRE) MR. J. G. WHITELY.
1409 (LOWER) MR. EDGAR G. MILLER, JR.

1406 (UPPER) DR. JAS. BORDLEY, JR.
1408 (CENTRE) COL. MRS. J. STABLER.
1410 (LOWER) MRS. M. S. HARTSHORNE.

on the sides and corners and a concave curve on the front, as in No. 1406 and others. The Hepplewhite features are the square tapering legs with spade feet, and the inlay on the legs, leaves and front. About 1780–1790.

Many pleasing Pembroke tables were made in the Hepplewhite style. The principal characteristics are the square legs, generally tapering on the inner sides, the spade feet, the oval form of the top and the abundance of inlay.

No. 1412 is wholly in the Hepplewhite style and is finely ornamented with inlay. The tapering legs are decorated with inlaid strings of flowers and over the legs are inlaid oval medallions with American eagles, without stars. A wide border of inlay is between the medallions. The top being oval, the front of the central section of the top is curved. The brackets which swing out and support the leaves are seen here. About 1785–1800.

No. 1413 is a handsome oval table, decorated with a fine inlay of flowers on the legs, and with a band of inlay near the bottom. The inlay on the drawer and the top will be noticed, and also the medallions on the front and side, the latter being partly visible even when the leaves are down. The height of this table is twenty–eight inches and the length when open is forty inches, which are about the usual dimensions of these tables. About 1785–1800.

No. 1414 is similar in form to the preceding table, but the inlaid decoration is less attractive. Above the legs are diamond–shaped designs in inlay. The small visible spaces on the sides of the frame are decorated with fan designs. Perhaps the inlaid fans were used in order to cover the vacancy caused by the short leaves, or perhaps the leaves were made short in order not to hide the inlaid fans. Here the height is thirty inches and the length when open is thirty–five inches. About 1785–1800.

No. 1415 is a Pembroke table in the Sheraton style, which is recognized by the familiar round and reeded tapering legs with "turned" feet. There is no inlay, but the leaves are rounded and are of a light wood, making a pleasing decorative contrast with the mahogany. About 1795–1810.

No. 1416 is a plain table, also in the Sheraton style. The front of the table is veneered and there are small veneered panels over the legs. The upper portion of the legs is turned in a ring form. About 1795–1810.

Section 164. Library tables.—Perhaps because there is no better name which can well be applied to them, the term "library tables" seems to be suitable for the drop–leaf tables shown in this section. In some cases these tables have been called "breakfast tables",[1] a term which implies the use of the table for a single purpose. The presence of drawers seems to indicate that the tables were not intended to be used for meals.

---

1. Other names given to these tables are "drop–leaf tables" and "centre tables". These terms apply equally well to several other kinds of tables and are too indefinite.

In "English and American Furniture", by Cescinsky and Hunter, pages 212–213, Mr. Cescinsky, referring to certain tripod tables of moderate size, states that they "are usually termed 'breakfast tables' on the principle that guests do not, as a rule, stay over night, and a smaller table

1411 (UPPER) MRS. JOHN S. GIBBS, JR. 1412 (UPPER) MRS. WM. M. ROBERTS.
1413 (CENTRE) ANONYMOUS. 1414 (CENTRE) ANONYMOUS.
1415 (LOWER) MRS. EDWIN B. NIVER. 1416 (LOWER) MR. EDGAR G. MILLER, JR.

The upper portion of these tables, that is, the top, the brackets and the frame and drawer, resembles in form and construction that of the Pembroke tables seen in the previous section; but often the lower portion, instead of having the four legs of the Pembroke tables, has one or more pedestals resting upon four curved legs, similar to those seen on some of the dining tables of the period, such as Nos. 1322–1326. These library tables are larger than the Pembroke tables shown in the preceding section, and are finished on all sides for use in the centre of a room, where all parts may be seen.

Tables of this type were chiefly made in the Sheraton period and style, about the year 1800, and they continued to be made in the early part of the Empire period. The wood is mahogany, generally of fine quality.

In No. 1417 the top of the central section is rectangular and the two drop-leaves are cut in a favorite pattern. The edge of the top is reeded. The drawer should be furnished with a "lion's–head and ring" handle or a brass knob, as in Nos. 1418 and 1419. A small drop or "pendant" hangs from each corner of the centre section, a detail seen on many of these library tables. The upper part of the pedestal is in the form of a vase carved with acanthus leaves, and the base is also carved. The four concave and wide–spread legs are tapered and are ornamented above with carved acanthus leaves and below with reeding, terminating in brass paw feet and casters. The height of tables of this type is generally about twenty-nine inches and the length when open about fifty inches. About 1810–1820.

No. 1418 is regarded as having been made by Duncan Phyfe in his late period, and is partly in the Empire style.[2] The upper portion is similar to that of the preceding table, except that the edge of the top is not reeded. The drawer is furnished with a brass "lion's–head and ring" handle of the period. Instead of a single pedestal seen in the preceding table, there are four carved columns which rest upon a heavy platform. This platform has concave sides, and is supported by heavy carved legs placed under it and terminating in large animals' paw feet; these features indicate the Empire style. Other somewhat similar columns and platforms are seen in the dining tables Nos. 1324–1326, the table No. 1640 and also in No. 1421. About 1815–1825.

No. 1419 is less ornate than the two preceding tables. The upper portion is in about the same form, but with somewhat longer drop–leaves than in No. 1417.

(NOTE 1, *continued*)

only is required in the morning than on the night before"; and he pleasantly continues: "It may be useful here to cite Earl Balfour's definition of a bore as 'one who, invited to tea, stays to dinner'. Presumably the tea–invited who remains to breakfast is a super–bore; certainly he may be a nuisance, which is much the same thing."

A table of a different type, called a library table, but without drop–leaves, was made by Duncan Phyfe. The table was finely made, but was apparently not popular. It is shown as No. 1644 in section 174. In England it is called a "Canterbury" table.

Three other tables which perhaps should be called "library tables" are shown in section 174, Nos. 1638–1640. They may have been made either for a library or a drawing room.

2. The Empire style in the furniture of Duncan Phyfe is mentioned in section 20.

1417 (UPPER) MISS ELEANOR S. COHEN.
1419 (CENTRE) MR. EDGAR G. MILLER, JR.
1421 (LOWER) DR. M. A. ABRAMS.

1418 (UPPER) MR. HOWARD MANSFIELD.
1420 (CENTRE) MR. F. HIGHLANDS BURNS.
1422 (LOWER) DR. M. A. ABRAMS.

The panel on each side of the drawer, the pendants under the panels, and the brass knob, will be noticed. The single pedestal has a spiral turning on a vase form. The legs are grooved. About 1810–1820.

No. 1420 is recognized as having features of the late Sheraton and early Empire styles by its less delicately reeded legs and its larger and heavier pedestal. The upper portion is similar in form to that of the preceding tables. The top is reeded all around, as in No. 1417. The drop handle on the drawer is not of the period. The brass animals' claw feet are furnished with casters, as was usual at the time. About 1815–1825.

No. 1421 is somewhat similar in form to No. 1418, but may be regarded as being in the Sheraton style. The upper portion is supported by four small and slender columns, called "colonnettes", which rest upon a platform. Other slender columns are in the tripod table No. 1364 and in No. 1424. This platform is supported by four reeded legs. The corners of the leaves are cut off, making the top different in form from the others. The round brass handles on the drawer drop from the top. About 1810–1820.

No. 1422 is different in some respects. The upper portion is supported by two large upright "standards" which rest upon the parallel legs and are connected by two horizontal bars or stretchers. At the ends of these bars are applied rosettes. The fine reeding on the legs is too delicate to be well seen, and the reeding is continued on the brass feet, a method which is mentioned in the comments on the sewing tables Nos. 1574 and 1589. About 1815–1825.

Section 165. Sofa tables.—The principal features of a sofa table such as No. 1423, compared with a library table such as No. 1421, are that the front of the sofa table has two drawers and is therefore wider, and that the legs, being further apart, require a stretcher. Nos. 1423 and 1424 are very graceful and elegant tables; Nos. 1425 and 1426 are of different types in later styles. It is said that in England these sofa tables are generally placed in front of a sofa where they are convenient for the use of persons sitting on the sofa, especially for ladies with needle–work and tea; in our country, however, they are often placed behind the sofa,[1] or in the centre of the room or in the hall or elsewhere, and are used for any purpose desired. Being seen from all sides they are generally finished on all sides. They were first made in the Sheraton period, about the year 1800, and continued in fashion until the end of the Empire period, about 1840.

No. 1423 is a handsome sofa table made by Duncan Phyfe in the Sheraton style, and now owned by the Metropolitan Museum of Art. The edge of the top is reeded and the drop–leaves are supported by brackets. The two drawers are bordered with a light veneer and are furnished with brass knobs. At the ends are graceful carved and reeded lyres which support the upper portion and rest

---

1.   It is said that the sofa table was often placed behind the sofa, for two reasons, that is, to hide the back of the sofa when the latter was in the centre of the room, and to hold a lamp to furnish light to one sitting on the sofa.

1423 (Upper) Metropolitan Museum of Art.
1425 (Lower) Lockwood Col. Furn., Fig. 797.

1424 (Upper) Metropolitan Museum of Art.
1426 (Lower) Mr. & Mrs. Wm. A. Dixon.

upon concave legs which are carved and reeded and are connected by a stretcher. The fine workmanship and design of this table and the next one are examples of the skill of Phyfe at his best period. About 1805–1815.

No. 1424 is also by Duncan Phyfe in the Sheraton style, and is equally fine.[2] The leaves are bordered with a light veneer, as in the preceding table, but the veneer is not well seen in the engraving. Each end is supported by two small columns, or "colonettes", under which are carved and reeded legs. The two delicate stretchers are reeded in the centre. About 1805–1815.

No. 1425 illustrates the decline of the sofa table from the style of Sheraton as interpreted by Phyfe to the style of the late Empire period. Here the lyre supports have no delicacy, the heavy stretcher is a shelf with lyre–shaped ends, and the feet are of the coarse animals' claw pattern seen in so many pieces of the period. About 1825–1835.

No. 1426 is probably a Victorian sofa table, with certain features more pleasing than those in the preceding Empire style. At this period there was a revival and mixture of many earlier forms as in the bureaus Nos. 767 and 768. Above the trestle are small moldings in an arched form. There is one large drawer with a curved front and three heavy upright supports on each end, but no stretchers. The mahogany veneer is of fine quality. About 1840.

Section 166. Side tables; serving and hunters' tables.—Almost all of the tables shown in previous sections may be called "centre tables", that is, tables which are intended to be placed in the centre or open spaces of a room or at least not against a wall, and are therefore finished on all four sides. "Side tables" are intended to stand against a wall and are not finished on the rear; these are shown in the present section and in later ones.[1] The side tables in this section are to be distinguished from the "sideboard" tables shown in section 157. The tables shown

2. In his "Furniture Masterpieces of Duncan Phyfe", page 77, Mr. Charles Over Cornelius remarks that these two sofa tables are "superb examples of absolutely finished workmanship."

1. Several side tables of a special character, and known by special names, are shown in other sections. A tripod side table is No. 1366. Card tables may be used as side tables when the folding leaf is down. The ends of dining tables in the Hepplewhite and Sheraton styles are sometimes used as side tables. Pier and console tables are also side tables; see section 174, Nos. 1647, 1648.

In the full page illustration of furniture in the Adam style, No. 4 in section 16, two side tables are illustrated in order to show some of the important features of that style, although such furniture was seldom if ever made in our country for the reasons mentioned in that section.

In the rectangular table at the upper left corner the skirt is fluted and in the centre is a panel with festoons of drapery tied with tassels, and at the ends are oval applied rosettes. The legs are straight, square and tapering, a form which was followed by Hepplewhite and to some extent by Sheraton.

In the half–round, or semi–circular, table the skirt is ornamented with a series of festoons of drapery, the legs are fluted, at the tops of the legs are applied rosettes and the feet are of the spade type. The top of the table is decorated with paintings.

These features were copied by later cabinet makers, but the original designs are those of Robert Adam. The illustrations are from Mr. Cescinsky's "English Furniture", volume 3, figures 14 and 18, and appear here through his courtesy. Both of these tables were about 1765–1780.

here were made for various purposes and therefore differ considerably in height and length and in other respects. The wood is usually mahogany.

First we see four side tables, Nos. 1427–1430, in the Chippendale style.

No. 1427 is a handsomely carved side table in the Chippendale style. On the "skirt", under the top, the carvings are in a variety of designs and on the upper part of the legs are carved leaves which at their ends take the shape of "C" curves. The legs are in the cabriole form and terminate in ball and claw feet, the ball being somewhat flattened. This table is thirty–one inches high and forty–two inches long. About 1760–1780.

No. 1428 is a plain table in the same style. Here the legs are square and straight, as in so many of the Chippendale style chairs and tables, and terminate in block feet, a type from which the spade feet were later developed by Adam and Hepplewhite. The upper portion is without ornament except that small brackets in a "C" form are at the junction of the legs and the skirt. About 1760–1780.

No. 1429 has a feature of the Adam style, that is, the "fluting" of the skirt, a decorative form explained in section 41. This feature is seen on the two tables shown on the page of Adam style furniture, illustration No. 4, mentioned in note 1. The Chippendale style appears in the brackets and in the square and straight grooved legs with the inner edges of the legs cut off, as in the Pembroke table No. 1405 and others. The height is thirty–eight inches and the length forty–four inches. About 1770–1780.

No. 1430 is said to be the most elaborate American side table now known. It is called the "Cadwalader" table from the name of the family in Philadelphia for which it was made. It is mainly in the French, rather than the English, style, and was originally gilded and had a marble top. This table is fully carved with "C" curves, such as those on the mirrors Nos. 1103–1106 and others, and with leaves and fanciful designs; and it has "French" feet such as those on the chairs Nos. 116 and 117, although the "shoes" or "cushions" under the feet are of English usage. It is of a special character, and although interesting, is not of importance to the amateur in the study of American styles. See also section 174 in connection with pier tables. About 1770.

In the next group of side tables, Nos. 1431–1436, several resemble a card table of the Hepplewhite style, but they do not have a folding leaf supported by a swinging leg which are seen on card tables. Because of their moderate size, these tables were probably suitable for general household purposes. It will be noticed that none of these tables have a drawer, mainly on account of the curved shape of the frames.

No. 1431 is a half–round or semi–circular side table, in the Hepplewhite style, sometimes erroneously referred to as a "pier table", or "console table", as to which see section 174 and Nos. 1647–1648. The skirt is inlaid with rectangular forms and panels and the tapering legs are decorated with inlaid flowers, such as those seen on the Hepplewhite style dining tables in section 157 and the sideboards in section 128. Because of the semi–circular form, the two front legs present two sides to the front view, as also in the next table, but here only one of the sides is decorated. About 1785–1800.

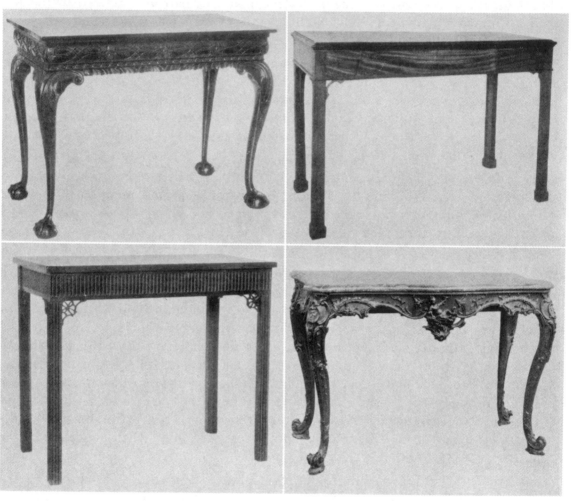

1427 (UPPER) HAMMOND–HARWOOD HOUSE. 1428 (UPPER) MRS. HOWARD SILL.
1429 (LOWER) HAMMOND–HARWOOD HOUSE. 1430 (LOWER) METROPOLITAN MUSEUM OF ART.

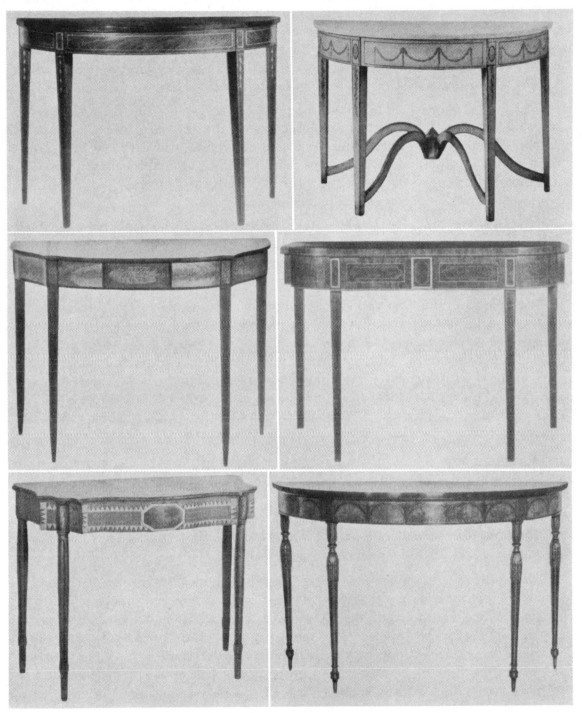

1431 (Upper) Mr. H. Oliver Thompson.
1433 (Centre) Anonymous.
1435 (Lower) Mr. John Ridgely, Jr.

1432 (Upper) Mr. & Mrs. E. L. R. Smith.
1434 (Centre) Miss Elisabeth H. Bartlett.
1436 (Lower) Hammond–Harwood House.

No. 1432 is also a half–round side table, painted white with graceful decorations. The festoons of flowers on the skirt, the oval medallions and the strings of leaves on the legs follow designs of Robert Adam which were copied by Hepplewhite. The curved stretchers are in a "dome" form used in the period; a somewhat similar design appears in the small table No. 1602. See also the companion chair No. 295 which has a similar decoration. About 1775–1790.

No. 1433 is another side table in the Hepplewhite style. The skirt is veneered with panels of finely grained and colored wood, the central panel enclosing an oval one. The legs have lines of inlay and are tapered to a smaller end than usual, almost pointed, a method occasionally seen, as in the card tables Nos. 1506–1507 and others. The top is in the same form as in the card tables Nos. 1505–1508. About 1785–1800.

No. 1434, in the Hepplewhite style, is also finely ornamented on the skirt with three small panels in front and with several rectangular forms enclosing other inlaid forms in which the corners are cut in a concave shape. Below the lines of inlay on the legs are strings of flowers. About 1785–1800.

No. 1435 is in the Sheraton style, as appears from the round and tapering legs which project forward from the line of the framework, a method seen in the bureaus and sideboards of that style and in the card tables Nos. 1521, 1522 and others. This is a painted table, with a landscape on the eight–sided panel in the centre of the skirt. The legs at the upper ends are decorated with a leaf design and below are inlaid with vertical lines of light wood, an ornamental feature also seen in the Baltimore tables Nos. 1436, 1441, 1442 and 1462. About 1800–1810.

No. 1436, also, is in the Sheraton style, as shown by the legs and the use of carving upon them. Under the almost half–round top the skirt is decorated with a series of applied arches under which are inlaid leaf designs. At the upper ends of the four legs are carved vases supporting the top, and below these vases the legs are carved for a short distance and are ornamented with vertical lines of inlay as in the preceding table. The height of this table is about thirty–five inches, and the length is about fifty–four inches. About 1800.

Side tables such as Nos. 1437–1442 are often called "serving tables", that is, primarily, tables used in the dining room for the service of meals; but their variety and fine character of their design, workmanship and materials seem to indicate that they were also used for other purposes. The presence of marble tops on the last two of this group may mark them as serving tables; but the others are so elegant that their place would seem to be in the best room of the house. The height of these tables is in most cases about thirty–eight inches or a little more.

No. 1437, a half–round satinwood side table, has a very pleasing appearance. As in Nos. 1431 and 1432, each of the two front legs, following the semi–circular line of the framework, exposes two sides to the view, and here these two sides are decorated with strings of flowers. Bands of dark wood are near the bottom, making an effective contrast with the light colored satinwood. This table is thirty–eight inches high. About 1800.

1437 (Upper) Mr. Arthur E. Cole.
1439 (Centre) Mr. & Mrs. H. L. Duer.
1441 (Lower) Mr. Chas. Morris Howard.

1438 (Upper) Mr. Arthur E. Cole.
1440 (Centre) Mr. J. F. H. Maginn.
1442 (Lower) Anonymous.

No. 1438, in the Hepplewhite style, has a serpentine front, and on the skirt are two large and one small rectangular inlaid panels. Decorative rectangular panels of this type will also be seen on Nos. 1441, 1442 and other pieces. The legs have lines of inlay and strings of flowers, with bands of light wood near the bottom. This table is thirty–seven inches high. About 1800.

No. 1439, in the Hepplewhite style, is of unusual distinction, having six legs on each of which is a wide inlay of satinwood extending more than half the length of the leg. This satinwood inlay is in turn inlaid with strings of darker wood terminating in tassels, and below the wide inlay are inlaid strings of flowers. A somewhat similar highly decorative treatment, said to be peculiar to Baltimore, will be seen in the Hepplewhite style card tables Nos. 1487–1490, and is referred to in the comments on those pieces. The skirt is ornamented with rectangular forms and in the centre is a panel of darker wood. Card tables with five or six legs are Nos. 1493–1497. About 1800.

In No. 1440 the front is in the form which, in sideboards, indicates the Hepplewhite style, that is, the ends are concave, not convex, as stated in section 128. On the front are three diamond–shaped inlaid designs in satinwood and on each of the tapering front legs are four small inlaid diamond–shaped designs in dark wood enclosed in inlaid forms. The front of No. 1495 is similar in shape. About 1800.

No. 1441 is in the Sheraton style for reasons mentioned in the comment on No. 1435. Here the marble top, cut in curves in the form of the woodwork, indicates that the table was probably intended as a serving table upon which hot dishes could be placed without injury. The legs are ornamented with inlaid vertical lines as in No. 1435 and others. The front skirt is painted in panels, the one in the centre enclosing a painting of musical instruments and the other two containing designs of painted leaves and flowers, which are repeated on the ends of the table. This is one of the "Baltimore Sheraton style painted" tables, another example of which is next shown. In this connection reference may be made to the Baltimore painted chairs Nos. 290 and 291. About 1800.

No. 1442, also, has a marble top, shaped in curves to fit the woodwork. The skirt is veneered with fine mahogany and in the centre is a glass panel decorated with a classic scene painted in gilt and blue. Particular interest attaches to the slender legs which are about the same as those in the corner table No. 1462; these two tables were probably made by the same Baltimore cabinet maker, at present not certainly known. The legs are said to be ornamented with inlaid lines as in the preceding table. The shelf is cut in the same general curves as the top and is attached to small square and decorated blocks. This serving, or mixing, table is thirty–seven inches high. About 1800.

The next eight tables, Nos. 1443–1450, also known as "serving tables", are somewhat different from the preceding ones in this section; and it is uncertain whether the term "serving table" should be applied to all of them.

No. 1443 is a small illustration of a large and high table in the Sheraton style as appears from the convex ends of the top which distinguish the sideboards

1443 (UPPER) METROPOLITAN MUSEUM OF ART.   1444 (UPPER) ANONYMOUS.
1445 (LOWER) ANONYMOUS.   1446 (LOWER) MR. & MRS. WM. A. DIXON.

759

in that style from those of the Hepplewhite style, the latter having concave ends; spade feet[2] were used in both styles. There are six tapering legs; the two central front ones are inlaid with lines and flowers on three sides. The six stretchers are concave. The three drawers are inlaid with panels of dark wood. About 1800–1810.

Nos. 1444 and 1445, in the Sheraton style, were probably made by Duncan Phyfe, and have been called "serving tables".[3] They are not as high as the preceding piece.

In No. 1444 there is one wide drawer and below is a concave shelf. The round legs project forward from the line of the front as in the card tables Nos. 1533 and 1534 and others, and are finely reeded from the top to the brass feet, except below the drawer and at the square blocks to which the shelf is attached. The handles are of the "lion's head and ring" type, which was a favorite with Phyfe. About 1800–1810.

No. 1445 is of the same general type, but differs from the preceding table in having three drawers, two small ones above a wide one, and in not having a shelf. The fronts of the drawers are finely veneered with a darker mahogany than that of the other framework. The delicacy and fine proportions of these two serving tables will be noticed. Their projecting and reeded legs follow the form of other pieces in the best Sheraton style, as in the card tables mentioned in the comment on the preceding piece. About 1800–1810.

No. 1446 is a somewhat later form of the same type of serving tables as the two preceding ones. Here we have the projecting legs and a shelf as in No. 1444, and three drawers as in No. 1445. The legs are in spiral forms, as to which see section 155, note 2; and other differing details will be noticed. The handles are of an unusual pattern. About 1810–1820.

The serving tables Nos. 1447–1449 are in the late Sheraton style and No. 1450 is in the Empire style.

No. 1447 is thirty–seven inches high, not counting the back board, and has thick tapering legs with coarse reeding, over which is a carved ring and vase. At the two ends of the skirt are panels with applied carvings. About 1815–1825.

No. 1448 is a small table with a marble top. On the skirt are two small panels at the ends and a larger one in the centre. The legs, with carved tops, are heavily reeded as on the preceding table. Under the legs are square plain blocks and ball feet, as in the sideboard No. 1014 and other pieces; see also figure 3 in illustration No. 11. About 1815–1825.

No. 1449 is a large serving table with six heavily reeded legs. The top has a low back board which extends over the ends. There are two small end drawers and a large one in the centre with brass lion–and–ring handles. About 1815–1825.

2.   See section 127 as to spade feet and also figure 17 in illustration No. 11.
          This table seems to be an American adaptation of a design in plate 4, dated 1793, in the Appendix to Sheraton's "Drawing Book", as to which see section 18; almost the same table appears in some of the English books.
3.   As in "Furniture Masterpieces of Duncan Phyfe", by Mr. Charles Over Cornelius, plates 48 and 50. Very similar tables have been called "dressing tables" by other writers.

1447 (UPPER) MR. JOHN C. TOLAND.
1449 (LOWER) MR. W. W. LANAHAN.

1448 (UPPER) MISS HELEN H. CAREY.
1450 (LOWER) MRS. I. R. TRIMBLE.

No. 1450 has a marble top, under which the skirt is decorated with fanciful carvings on the panels at the ends and still more fanciful carvings on the panel in the centre, showing scrolls and leaves. At the tops of the legs are vase–shaped forms carved with leaves and in a reversed position, as in No. 1472. The heavy spiral twists on the legs are such as were used in the early years of the Empire style, as on the posts of the bedsteads Nos. 1069–1070, which are mentioned in note 2 in section 155. The feet seem to have been removed. About 1815–1830.

The next six side tables, Nos. 1451–1456, are the so-called "hunters' tables", or "hunting tables" or "hunting boards". On these long and high tables, found chiefly in the South,[4] liquid and other refreshments were served before and after the hunt. The tables illustrated here are all in Maryland homes, where some of them have been for several generations. They are about thirty–seven to forty–two inches high by about five to six feet long. The first five tables, Nos. 1451–1455, are in the Hepplewhite style, with graceful serpentine fronts, and are very similar, the principal difference between them being in the inlaid ornamentation; the sixth example, No. 1456, is in the Sheraton style. All are made of mahogany and are of about the same date.

No. 1451 is more fully decorated than the other hunters' tables, almost the entire skirt being covered by rectangular inlaid panels. The legs have the usual strings of flowers used on tables in the Hepplewhite style and above the legs are other inlaid designs. In this table is clearly seen a feature of the Hepplewhite style, used also to some extent in the Sheraton style, that is, the tapering of the legs is made only on the inner side, not on both sides as generally in the Adam style; hence the outside of the leg is exactly vertical. This is also seen in the next piece. About 1800.

In No. 1452 the skirt is veneered with finely figured mahogany. Here also the skirt and the ends are decorated with oval medallions, and lines of inlay are on the legs. The serpentine form of the front is well seen in this engraving. About 1800.

No. 1453 is six feet long and about thirty–seven inches high, and the top at its widest point in the centre of the serpentine form is about two feet in depth. At each end a drawer is shown open. The inlay consists of lines on the edge of the top and on the skirt and legs. About 1800.

No. 1454 is forty–two inches high and sixty inches long. Its height, the shallow skirt and the long, slender and tapering legs give an unusual appearance to this "hunters' table". The inlay consists of three oval medallions on the skirt and the ends, and strings of flowers and bands on the legs. About 1800.

---

4.   Tables of the same or similar name were used in several of the Southern States, especially in South Carolina. Those tables, however, were of a different type from those shown here, being of small size, with cupboards or drawers, and with few or no decorative features, appearing in fact to be small sideboards. Several illustrations of this type of tables are in "Antiques", November, 1927, pages 378–379, and August, 1931, pages 83–85. Georgia "huntboards" are illustrated and discussed in the issue of September, 1932, page 105.

In "Southern Antiques", by Mr. Paul H. Burroughs, 1931, pages 61–67, a number of pieces regarded as "hunting boards" are illustrated. Most of these bear little or no resemblance to the handsome pieces shown in this section.

1451 (Upper) Mr. W. W. Lanahan.
1453 (Centre) Mr. & Mrs. J. M. Matthews.
1455 (Lower) Mrs. Miles White, Jr.

1452 (Upper) Mr. Albert G. Towers.
1454 (Centre) Mr. & Mrs. H. L. Duer.
1456 (Lower) Mr. & Mrs. Geo. Ward.

In No. 1455 the serpentine form is well seen. The two oval medallions above the legs are inlaid with American eagles, and inlaid strings of flowers are on both the front and rear legs. The height is thirty–eight inches and the length is about sixty–eight inches. The tapering legs terminate in spade feet. About 1800.

No. 1456 is in the Sheraton style as appears from the convex, not concave, ends, and also by the carving over the legs, which was not used on the tables in the Hepplewhite style. Square tapering legs with spade feet, such as those here, were used in both styles, as shown in section 128 in the chapter on sideboards. The brackets at the intersections of the skirt and the legs will be noticed. Two round ebony knobs, with ivory centres, are on the drawer; there are no drawers in the ends. This table is thirty–eight inches high and sixty–six inches long and is of mahogany. It may be English, but it has been in our country in the family of the present owners for several generations. About 1800.

Section 167. Corner tables.—The usual type of corner tables has a triangular frame with four legs, of which three are stationary and one swings out and supports a drop–leaf when it is raised. The stationary top over the frame, and also the drop–leaf, are triangular and of the same size, so that when the drop–leaf is up, the top is square; but when the drop–leaf is down, as in the first three illustrations, the top is triangular and the table may be placed in a corner of a room. This feature gives the table its name of "corner table", although whether square or triangular the table may well be used in other parts of a room. Nos. 1457–1459 are examples of this type. Many of them are small and plain. Other types are shown in Nos. 1460–1462.

In No. 1457 the drop–leaf is down and the table may be placed in a corner with the drop–leaf facing the centre of the room. The movable leg which swings out and supports the drop–leaf is the next to the last on the left. This table is in the Queen Anne style, as indicated by the shape of the legs and also by the feet which are in a modified form of the Dutch, or club, feet. About 1750–1760.

In No. 1458, in which also the drop–leaf is down, we see a similar corner table from another point of view. The sides, which were not visible in the preceding illustration, are seen here to be finished suitably for the centre of a room. The Queen Anne style is apparent from the legs and the Dutch, or club, feet which are protected by "shoes", as in the card table No. 1477 and others. About 1750–1770.

No. 1459 is a very small table. The square and straight legs are in the Chippendale style, as are so many on the chairs in that style, such as Nos. 98–100 and others. The inner corners of the legs are cut off, as in the Pembroke table No. 1405, making flat surfaces which here are not intended to hold stretchers. About 1760–1780.

The next three tables, which are without leaves, are more strictly "corner tables", because they can be well used only in a corner. In each table the frame has a curved front and four or more stationary legs. In appearance these tables are more attractive than those of the preceding type.

1457 (Upper) Mr. John C. Toland.
1459 (Centre) Mr. John S. McDaniel.
1461 (Lower) Mrs. Jas. W. Wilson.

1458 (Upper) Mrs. Miles White, Jr.
1460 (Centre) Mrs. Wilbur W. Hubbard.
1462 (Lower) Miss Eleanor S. Cohen.

No. 1460 is an example of a corner table with a curved front. This piece is in the Chippendale style, as appears from the straight and square rear leg and the three front legs which have a peculiar cabriole form and ball and claw feet. The skirt is cut in two sections of double cyma curves, as to which see section 23. Small corner tables of similar shape were also made in the Hepplewhite style. Three small stands of this type are Nos. 1669–1671 in section 175. About 1760–1780.

No. 1461 also was made to stand in a curved corner of a room. It is rounded in the rear, where it it supported by two legs. The front is serpentine and is well ornamented. The skirt has a border of inlay and the tapering legs with spade feet are decorated with strings of flowers over which are small inlaid panels, not clearly seen. This table is in the Hepplewhite style and its date is probably about 1790–1800.

No. 1462, said to have been made in Baltimore, is a corner table of an unusual type. The skirt is concave at the ends and is straight in the centre. The ends are inlaid with a design of parallel lines with rounded ends such as are mentioned in section 127, note 6. The glass panel in the central straight portion is painted with patriotic designs similar to those on the mirrors in Nos. 1171 and 1172. The upper portion of the legs is ornamented with inlaid lines in the same manner as on the serving table No. 1442; the lower portion of the legs is in dark wood. The short columns over the legs are painted with the same design of leaves as in No. 1442 and the feet are the same in both tables. The stretchers are "domed", as in Nos. 1432 and 1602, and at their junction there is a carved vase. A very similar table is owned by Dr. James Bordley, Jr., of Baltimore. About 1800.

Section 168. Dressing tables.—In his chapter on "Chests of Drawers" Mr. Lockwood applies the term "dressing tables" to the low chests of drawers which we know as "lowboys",[1] the term "dressing tables" being historically correct and also descriptive of their utility, whereas the term "lowboy" is merely a popular one. But as the word "lowboy" is in general use in our country, the dressing tables of that type are considered in this book separately in chapter 10, sections 88–92.

In addition to lowboys there was another kind of dressing tables, known as "knee–hole" dressing tables.[2] These knee–hole dressing tables are very similar in

1. "Colonial Furniture", volume 1, figure 55 and many others. See also the remarks in the present book on lowboys as dressing tables, section 119.
2. In Mr. Lockwood's book, volume 1, several articles of this type are illustrated; figures 113 and 123 are termed "knee–hole dressing table"; figure 253, a very similar piece, is termed a "knee–hole desk", because the top drawer has writing arrangements; figure 295 is termed a "knee–hole writing table" for the reason that it has a lid which falls over and rests upon pulls as in our secretary desks Nos. 800, 801 and others.
    When a dressing table of this kind was used for the purposes of the toilet, a movable dressing glass such as one of Nos. 1255–1259 was generally placed on the top. See also the comment on No. 1468.
    Mr. Lockwood states, page 114, that knee–hole tables were never popular in our country and that few were found "until the time of their revival in the block–front type in the third quarter of the eighteenth century"; as to which see section 119 in the present book.

1463 (Upper) Mrs. John S. Gibbs, Jr.
1465 (Lower) Dr. Jas. Bordley, Jr.

1464 (Upper) Dr. Jas. Bordley, Jr.
1466 (Lower) Chase House, Annapolis.

form to the knee–hole desk No. 832 and are also similar to the block–front knee–hole desks Nos. 904–907. Indeed these knee–hole dressing tables and the knee–hole desks are so similar that it may be difficult to distinguish easily the one from the other. This will be noticed by comparing the first four dressing tables with the knee–hole desk No. 832. Moreover, the knee–hole dressing tables were used as desks and the desks were used as dressing tables, each being suitable for both correspondence and the arts of the toilet. It is therefore possible that some of the knee–hole tables here presented as dressing tables may have been known and used as desks at the time they were made.

The four knee–hole dressing tables here shown are very similar in character. The wood is generally walnut or mahogany. It is suggested that section 119 in the chapter on "block–front furniture" be examined in connection with these dressing tables, and also the knee–hole desk No. 832 in the chapter on desks.

No. 1463 has one long drawer with an early type of handle such as No. 9 in illustration No. 13. The central portion below is called the "recessed portion", made to accommodate the knees of a person sitting at the table, but not wide enough to be comfortable. On each side of this recessed portion are three drawers, gradu-ated in depth, which are provided with locks, and at the rear is a large plain door within which is a cupboard. The feet are of the straight bracket type and are cut in curves. About 1760–1780.

No. 1464 is similar to the preceding dressing table, differing in some details. The door of the cupboard in the recessed portion is paneled in the arched form seen on the doors of many secretary–bookcases, such as Nos. 841 and 845; the skirt under the door is cut in a double cyma curve, as to which see section 23; the feet are of the straight bracket type cut in a modified form of a cyma curve; and the skirt at the top of the recessed portion, which is often the front of a small drawer, is cut in a series of cyma curves. About 1760–1780.

In No. 1465 the variations from the preceding dressing table consist of the plain door of the cupboard in the recessed portion, the plain skirt over that portion, and, more especially, the form of the two feet which are of the "ogee" bracket type, as to which see figure 9 in illustration No. 11. The absence of the two feet at the inner ends of the bottom drawers gives the front a somewhat un-finished and vacant appearance, as also in the sideboard No. 994 and the dressing tables Nos. 1467 and 1468. About 1760–1780.

No. 1466 is in the Chase House, at Annapolis, where it has probably been ever since the house was built in 1770–1771. Under the top is a slide which pulls out, and below is the usual long drawer, with handles in an open–work pattern. On each side there is a closed cupboard instead of drawers, and at the rear of the recessed portion there is the usual plain cupboard. The feet are of the straight bracket type, cut in cyma curves. About 1760–1780.

No. 1467 is a dressing table in the Hepplewhite style, resembling a small sideboard in some respects, such as No. 994. There is one long drawer in the centre and under it is a large arch which doubtless enables a person to sit com-fortably at the table with his knees under it. On each side of the arch are three small drawers. The legs are slightly tapered. Tables similar to this were also made in the Sheraton style, but with reeded legs. About 1790–1800.

No. 1468 is also in the Hepplewhite style, and is somewhat higher than the preceding piece. Here the small arch in the centre is for ornamental purposes, as it is of no service to one sitting at the table. Under the long drawer are two short ones at the ends and a small shallow one in the centre. Dressing glasses such as Nos. 1260–1263, shown in section 152 in the chapter on mirrors, were no doubt used on these two dressing tables. See note 2 in this section. About 1790–1800.

Nos. 1469 and 1470 are very different in appearance from the preceding two dressing tables in the Hepplewhite style, but they have about the same form of arched framework and drawers, evidently following the Hepplewhite and Sheraton styles in that respect. Under the framework, however, the parts are of the early Empire style, well made and with fine mahogany veneer. In both of these pieces the lyres are an important feature, as are also the heavy platforms and the feet with animals' paws. About 1810–1830.

In No. 1469 the framework, as mentioned, resembles to some extent that of Nos. 1467 and 1468, having a long drawer under which are two small drawers. The finely grained mahogany veneer and the oval brass handles hanging from the top of the plate will be noticed. The rear supports are wide and plain. The use of carved lyres as front supports for a dressing table is an unusual application of that favorite ornamental feature.[3] About 1820–1830.

In No. 1470, also, the framework is somewhat similar in form to Nos. 1467 and 1468, with one long and two small drawers, here with brass "lion–and–ring" handles. The rear supports are in the same form as in the preceding piece; the four front legs are round columns with brass caps at the top and bottom, similar in form to the columns on the Empire style table No. 1653 and the bureau No. 764. The feet are of the animals' paw type, with scrolls on the sides. The fact that the mirror is a structural part of this piece, not removable, may perhaps constitute the piece a bureau in the modern sense. It is interesting to examine this dressing table in connection with the bureaus Nos. 753–756. About 1820–1830.

No. 1471 is a plain dressing table in the late Sheraton style, the legs being heavily reeded as in the serving table No. 1449. Above the top are three drawers similar to those on the Sheraton style bureau No. 759, and over these is a back–board. Under the top is a slide which pulls out and below this is a long drawer. Wooden knobs of graduated size are on the drawers, the smaller knobs being on the smaller drawers. About 1810–1820.

No. 1472 is in the Empire style, as shown by the heavy spiral, or rope, legs, with a carved vase in a reversed position, as in the serving table No. 1450. On the top are two small drawers with a third drawer above them, and above the latter is a back–board in the same design as the tops of the fretwork mirrors No. 1128 and others. Large knobs are on the large drawer and smaller ones on the others. About 1820–1830.

---

3. Compare the card tables Nos. 1539–1542 in which the supports are lyres; also the sewing tables Nos. 1566–1571. A note on lyres is in section 171, note 7.

1467 (Upper) Mr. & Mrs. H. L. Duer.
1469 (Centre) Dr. J. Hall Pleasants.
1471 (Lower) Mrs. P. L. C. Fischer.

1468 (Upper) Dr. Jas. Bordley, Jr.
1470 (Centre) Mr. & Mrs. E. H. McKeon.
1472 (Lower) Md. Soc. Colonial Dames.

1473 (Upper) Mr. & Mrs. E. G. Gibson.
1475 (Lower) Mr. W. W. Lanahan.

1474 (Upper) Mr. & Mrs. H. L. Duer.
1476 (Lower) Mr. Herbert T. Tiffany.

The four dressing tables, Nos. 1473–1476, are of the type commonly called "Beau Brummell" dressing tables, a name given to them at one time in honor of the famous English leader of fashion.[4] They are fitted with mirrors, and their small drawers are for cosmetics and other aids to beauty, and also for the implements of the toilet.

No. 1473 is a "Beau Brummell" dressing table in the Hepplewhite–Sheraton period, following designs in the books of both Hepplewhite and Sheraton.[5] The two folding half–tops, opening sideways, are held in place by hinges and when in this position the attached mirror may be raised as in the illustration. On each side of the mirror are compartments for toilet accessories. Below are three drawers under which is a slide which pulls out. About 1800.

No. 1474 is a similar dressing table of the same period. The mirror may be lowered into a space in the back, vertically. This arrangement requires a deeper frame than that in the previous example, and the additional space is occupied by cupboards and a drawer, on which are lines of inlay. Folding half–tops are also seen in the washstand No. 1724 in section 179. About 1800.

No. 1475 is a dressing table resembling in form No. 1467, except that here there is a rectangular opening in front instead of an arch. The central portion of the top opens upward and on the top is an inlay of flowers and rectangular forms. The inlay on the front of the five drawers is in the same design as that in the lowboy No. 685. The legs, tapered on the inside, and the surfaces above, are grooved. About 1790–1800.

No. 1476 has a top in one piece, on the inner side of which is a large mirror which in the illustration reflects a marble surface upon which toilet accessories may be placed. When the top is down the table resembles the preceding piece in outline. The three drawers are bordered with brass moldings and the round and tapering legs have brass caps at the tops. This seems to be French. About 1800–1810.

4. Beau Brummell, 1778–1840, had a varied career, rising to the height of public interest, later sinking to the depths of poverty and ending his days in a charitable asylum. From his early years he paid great attention to his dress. At Eaton and Oxford he was known as a wit and a good story–teller, and was found so amusing by the Prince of Wales that the Prince became his patron and gave him a commission in his own regiment. In 1798 he inherited a considerable fortune. "His social success was instant and complete, his repartees were the talk of the town. . . Though he always dressed well, he was no mere fop. Lord Byron is credited with the remark that there was nothing remarkable about his dress, except 'a certain exquisite propriety'. For a time Brummell's sway was undisputed. But eventually gambling and extravagance exhausted his fortune, while his tongue proved too sharp for his royal patron." In 1816 he fled to France to avoid his English creditors. Later his French creditors had him imprisoned for a time. He and his predecessor "Beau Nash", (1674–1762) were bachelors. "Beau Nash" was the master of ceremonies at Bath, the celebrated English watering place. This information is condensed from the Encyclopædia Britannica.

It should be recalled that the word "Beau" as applied to Brummell and Nash does not mean a man who is attentive to a lady; the meaning is "one who is very neat and particular about his dress, and fond of ornaments and jewelry; a fop; a dandy; now most often said of a man of middle age or older"; Century Dictionary.

5. In the "Guide" of Hepplewhite and the Appendix to Sheraton's "Drawing–Book" are drawings of dressing tables almost the same in form as those here shown, including the mirror, slide and tapering legs, but decorated with a different style of inlay.

Section 169. Card tables; Queen Anne and Chippendale styles.—In England throughout the eighteenth century "the rage for play and for high stakes was a characteristic and fashionable vice", as remarked by Mr. Cescinsky,[1] particularly during the latter part of the period. "Card tables were indispensable articles of furniture in the drawing room and the salon, from six to twelve of a kind being no unusual number in one house among the wealthy" aristocracy of that period; and they seem to have been almost equally popular in America. The shapes of the card tables of the Queen Anne, Chippendale, Hepplewhite and Sheraton styles were about the same, but the details of their ornamentation, the forms of the legs and feet, and some minor features, were very different. In this section we see several card tables in the Queen Anne and Chippendale styles. The tops of the tables made in these two styles were often covered with cloth; but this was generally not used on the later tables in the styles of Hepplewhite and Sheraton, the folding top being finished so that it would look well when opened against a wall.

Nos. 1477–1480 are shown with the folding tops raised, in order that the shape and conveniences for play may be well seen. On each table one of the rear legs swings out and supports the folding top.

No. 1477 is in the Queen Anne style, as appears from the cabriole legs and the Dutch, or club, feet, which here are protected by "shoes" as in many other pieces, such as the corner table No. 1458. The four rectangular corners are enlarged in order to provide spaces for candlesticks. The four oval shaped cups, or wells, sunk below the surface, are to hold money or chips. There is no front drawer in this table. The skirt and the legs are plain. On the two rectangular plates are inscriptions as to the former ownership. About 1750–1770.

1.   A.   In "English Furniture", volume 2, page 164.

B.   In "The Homes of our Ancestors", by Halsey and Tower, page 112, it is said that "after supper, which was usually served at nine o'clock, it was time for some other form of amusement. Cards were a favorite pastime and certainly not a vice. In Washington's account book there are frequent entries of winnings or losings, without any apparent thought of the right or wrong of gambling. . . Indeed cards were even more necessary in colonial times than they are today, for books were scarcely written to entertain, even if the light for reading in the evening had been better."

C.   The distinctive feature of card tables is that the top is in two equal parts, one of which folds over upon the other. One part of the top is permanently "fixed" to the frame–work, and the other is attached to the fixed one at the rear ends, by hinges, in such a manner that it may fold over on the fixed part, or may stand upright if leaning against a wall, or may fall back horizontally, in the latter case the two parts making one top. In this latter position the folding part is supported by one or more swinging legs, in the manner shown in the drop–leaf tables in previous sections. Occasionally the whole top may revolve, the front moving to the sides. In some cases there are two folding tops, as in No. 1478. In certain fine English tables the back legs do not swing, but are attached to an extension under the frame and may be drawn backward to support the folding top in somewhat the manner mentioned in the comment on the card table No. 1642.

D.   A card table and a side table may be of about the same size, design and ornamentation, the chief difference being that the card table has a second top which folds over, as above stated, giving the appearance of a top with a double thickness, whereas a side table has only one top. Compare the top of the side table No. 1433 in the Hepplewhite style and that of the card table No. 1506 in the same style.

E.   The most elaborate American card table in the Chippendale style is that known as the "Cadwalader *card* table' which is illustrated in "Antiques", January, 1930, page 22. The "Cadwalader *side* table" is illustrated in this book in section 166, No. 1430.

No. 1478, in the Chippendale style, is a combined card and backgammon[2] table, known as a "triple–top" table, having one fixed and two folding tops. The enlarged rectangular corners of the fixed top and of the first folding one are slightly sunken for candlesticks, and there are four cups, as in the preceding table. The lower surface of the second folding top and the upper surface of the first folding one are inlaid in forms for backgammon. The skirt is molded in a "godroon"[3] design, the knees of the legs are carved in a shell design and the feet are of the ball and claw type. About 1760–1780.

In No. 1479, also in the Chippendale style, the enlarged corners of the fixed top are round, instead of rectangular as in the preceding pieces, and are slightly sunken. The folding top also is round at the corners, following the form of the frame. The legs are carved at the knees and terminate in ball and claw feet. This table has been in the possession of the present Maryland family, and on the same land, since about 1760. Here also there is a drawer in the skirt. About 1750–1770.

No. 1480 is a plain type of card table in the Chippendale style. The edge of the top is in a series of serpentine curves, and has a rim to prevent the chips from sliding off. The legs terminate in small ball and claw feet. There is one drawer in the front and a smaller one on the side, and under the front drawer is a carved ornamental design. This is probably a Dutch table. About 1760–1780.

Nos. 1481–1486 are shown with the folding tops down. Some of these tables have the same form of top as in the preceding examples, and in others the tops are rectangular.

No. 1481 is in the Queen Anne style and has the same type of plain legs with Dutch, or club, feet with a "shoe" as in No. 1477. The edges of the tops are carved in an unusual design and the corners are enlarged and rounded as in the two preceding tables. A drawer is in the skirt. About 1750–1770.

No. 1482 and the following card tables in this section are in the Chippendale style. This table resembles Nos. 1477 and 1478 in having enlarged rectangular corners for candlesticks. The skirt is plain but the upper portion of the legs, the "knees", are carved in a large leaf design. The feet are of the ball and claw type. About 1760–1780.

In No. 1483 the front of the top is in a serpentine curve and the corners are rectangular but are not enlarged sufficiently to hold candlesticks; this may indicate that the candlesticks were to be placed on candlestands, because when candlestands came into use the places on the card tables for candlesticks were no longer made. The edges of the top are carved with flowers and leaves. The base of the skirt and the edges of the front legs are carved in tiny beads. The legs are straight and square and are grooved, as on many chairs and tables of the Chippendale style. About 1760–1780.

2. An article entitled "Backgammon tables of the Eighteenth Century", by Mr. Robert Tasker Evans, with many illustrations, is in "The Antiquarian", March, 1931, pages 33–37. Some of the tables have also boards for chess and other games.

A chess–board table in the Sheraton style is shown in No. 1368.

3. This word is defined in section 119, note 3.

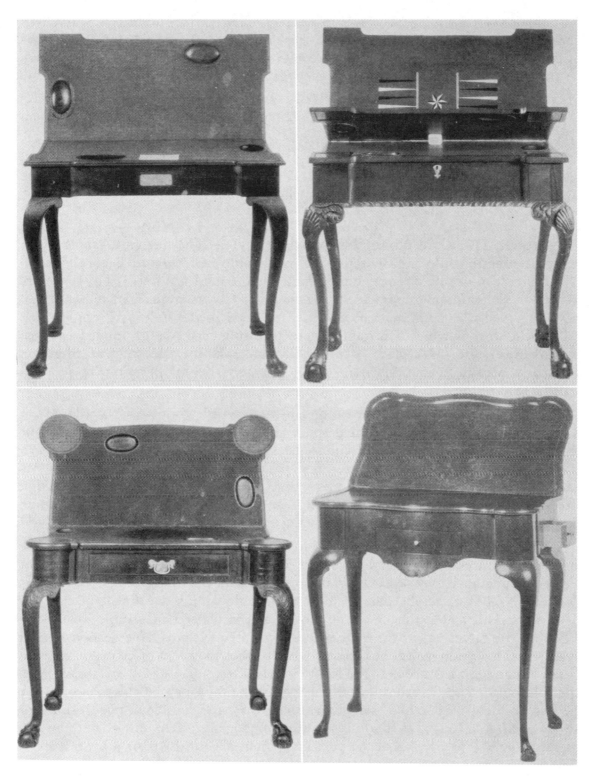

1477 (Upper) Md. Historical Society.
1479 (Lower) Family of Thos. Cradock.

1478 (Upper) Mr. John C. Toland.
1480 (Lower) Col. of Mrs. Jordan Stabler.

No. 1484 resembles No. 1479 in having round corners on the top and ball and claw feet. Here also the front is serpentine, and the bottom of the skirt is ornamented with "godroon" carving as in No. 1478. The knees, also, are carved. In this and the two preceding tables there is no drawer. About 1760–1780.

No. 1485 has a rectangular top. Under the drawer the skirt is cut in a series of cyma and other curves. The legs are plain and terminate in ball and claw feet. About 1760–1780.

No. 1486 is similar to the preceding card table in having a rectangular top and plain legs with ball and claw feet. Under the drawer and on the ends the skirt is carved in the "godroon" form. About 1760–1780.

Section 170. Card tables; Hepplewhite style.—The fine card tables in the styles of Hepplewhite and Sheraton are so pleasing in form and decoration that it is difficult to decide in one's mind which are the most attractive; but if we are guided by the opinions of our ancestors as indicated by the number of pieces which have survived, the palm must be awarded to those in the style of Hepplewhite. All of the Hepplewhite style tables were probably made before any decadence in furniture styles took place, whereas the tables in the late style of Sheraton gradually became somewhat coarse under the influence of the Empire style, as will be seen in the next section.

Of the large number of card tables in the Hepplewhite style[1] available for illustration in this book, the limited space allows only thirty–four examples to be shown, which have been selected chiefly because of their elegant appearance. All have certain characteristic features which the reader has already seen in the Hepplewhite style sideboards, dining tables, Pembroke tables, side tables and dressing tables. These features are mainly the straight and tapered legs sometimes ending in spade feet, and the inlaid ornamentation.

The tables illustrated here are arranged according to their special and conspicuous features, rather than by their supposed dates, in order that those of similar appearance may be easily compared. Thus in the first group, of six tables, Nos. 1487–1492, the noticeable features are the decorative treatment of the legs of the first four and the shape of the tops of all; in the second group, Nos. 1493–1498, all the tables have five or more legs; and other groups have certain special features. This arrangement has no importance other than that of convenience, and is not altogether satisfactory. The last ten tables, Nos. 1511–1520, are shown with the folding tops up, in order that the shapes of the tops may be clearly seen. The height of these card tables, sometimes made in pairs, is about twenty–nine or thirty inches. The wood is almost always mahogany, often inlaid with maple or satinwood. They are all of the period of about 1785 to 1800, or a little later.

1. In Hepplewhite's "Guide", as to which see section 17, only two designs of card tables are shown. In the edition of 1804 these are on plate 60. Both have straight and tapered legs and spade feet. The American cabinet makers used the general style of the drawings of Chippendale, Hepplewhite and Sheraton but often added or omitted details as they or their customers desired.

The distinctive feature of card tables is stated in note 1, C in the preceding section.

1481 (Upper) Mr. John C. Toland.
1483 (Centre) Mr. John C. Toland.
1485 (Lower) Mrs. Wilbur W. Hubbard.

1482 (Upper) Mr. Arthur E. Cole.
1484 (Centre) Mr. John C. Toland.
1486 (Lower) Mr. John C. Toland.

Nos. 1487–1490, four handsome tables in the first group of six, were doubtless made in Baltimore, as they have apparently been found only in or near that city. Each of these four tables is highly decorated in much the same style, which also appears in the serving table No. 1439. All of the six tables have the same form of top, the corners of which are rounded, a better illustration of which appears in No. 1511, in which the top is up, showing the corners and the straight front between them.

No. 1487 has the usual Hepplewhite style square and tapered legs, one of which swings out and supports the folding part of the top. The corners of this top are rounded, as mentioned. The sections of the skirt are banded with a light wood, and between them are inlaid oval medallions with leaves. The most notable feature is that the legs have a wide inlay of light wood for about half of their length and this inlay is itself inlaid with strings of flowers of a darker color. Further below is an inlaid string ending with a tassel. This table has been referred to by a learned critic as a "Baltimore card table that offers the most brilliant treatment of veneers and inlays of any American item" known to him and as "exemplifying the Southern taste for richness of ornament and restraint of line." About 1790–1800.

In No. 1488 the frame is in the same shape as in the preceding piece, and the wide inlay on the legs, and the oval medallions above them, are similar. The skirt is inlaid with forms which have concave corners as in the next table; and the edge of the skirt is bordered with inlay. The illustrations of this and the three other tables of this character cannot do justice to their elegance. About 1790–1800.

No. 1489 is even more fully decorated than the others in this group. The wide inlay of light wood on the legs extends almost to the bands of similar wood near the bottom. The skirt in front is ornamented with two large inlaid ovals, between which is an inlaid design with concave corners as in the preceding table. Over the legs are medallions and on the curved portion of the skirt are other inlaid designs. The inlaid lines on the edges of the fixed and the folding top will be noticed and also the bright bands of inlay within the line of the top. About 1790–1800.

In No. 1490 the long inlay on the legs tapers gradually to a point. Above the front legs are inlaid oval medallions. The tapering of the legs on the inside is noticeable, as in many other tables in the Hepplewhite style. About 1790–1800.

In Nos. 1491 and 1492 the top is in the same form as in the preceding tables, but there is not the same ornamental treatment of the legs. In No. 1491 the edges of the top are veneered with a light wood which is also used around the panels in the skirt and the ends, and also on the small panels above the legs. Each of the four legs is decorated with inlaid lines and strings of flowers. About 1790–1800.

No. 1492 is ornamented with inlaid lines on the edges of the top. On the skirt are long parallel lines of inlay with rounded ends, as also in No. 1499, a design which is referred to in section 127, note 6, and section 96, note 1, C; and on the edge is a delicate border of light wood. In the small ovals above the legs are inlaid urns, and on all the legs are decorations similar to those in the preceding table. About 1790–1800.

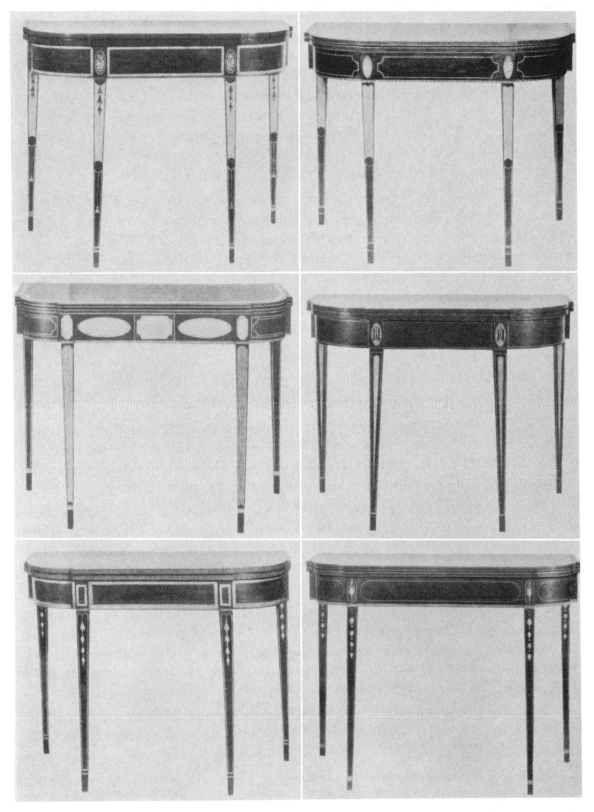

1487 (UPPER) MR. & MRS. B. TURNBULL.
1489 (CENTRE) MR. A. E. COLE.
1491 (LOWER) MR. ARTHUR E. COLE.

1488 (UPPER) MR. JOHN C. TOLAND.
1490 (CENTRE) DR. GEORGE E. HARDY.
1492 (LOWER) MRS. EDWARD SHOEMAKER.

In the next group of six tables, Nos. 1493–1498, each of the tables has five or six legs four of which are stationary and the other one or two swing out and support the folding lid. The side table No. 1439, also, has six legs, and several card tables in the Sheraton style have more than four, such as Nos. 1527 and 1535. The use of more than four legs is not confined to any particular type of card table in the Hepplewhite style and seems to have no significance except as a variation from the usual form. Other than the number of legs, the principal differences in these six tables are in the inlay and the shapes. About 1790–1800.

No. 1493, with six legs, is shown with the folding lid in use, supported by the two swinging legs in the rear. The top is eight–sided as shown here, and six–sided, including the back, when the folding top lies on the "fixed" one. The edges of the two front legs face the front, thus presenting two inlaid sides to the view. The inlaid forms on the skirt are rectangular, with the exception of the diamond–shaped panel in light wood, and the inlaid oval medallions at the corners. About 1790–1800.

In No. 1494, with five legs, the corners of the top are in the same rounded form as those in the tables Nos. 1487–1492 and 1511; between the corners the top is straight. The skirt is ornamented with a series of rectangular inlaid forms, and the legs have interlacing lines of inlay. About 1790–1800.

No. 1495 has five legs all of which are ornamented with inlaid flowers. The ends are concave, between which the front is straight, as in the serving table No. 1440. On the skirt are rectangular inlaid forms and on the lower edge is a band of inlay. About 1790–1800.

In No. 1496 the top is rounded at the front corners; this form of top appears also in the Sheraton style card table No. 1531 and others. Above the two front legs are rectangular panels, and in the centre of the skirt is an inlaid panel of light wood in which there is an inlaid centre of dark wood. Here also are five legs. About 1790–1800.

No. 1497, also with five legs, has a bowed or swell front, in this respect resembling No. 1519. The skirt is ornamented with inlays of dark and light wood. The two large dark inlaid panels have the same form as in No. 1488, with corners in a concave form; and between these panels is a third one, with an oval design in light wood. The legs are tapered to an unusual degree. About 1790–1800.

No. 1498 is a round card table which might be mistaken for a round dining table, such as No. 1315. In the illustration the folding top is supported by the leg in the rear which swings back when not needed. About 1790–1800.

The next group is of six card tables, Nos. 1499–1504, which are round when open and half–round when the folding top rests upon the fixed one. As in the two preceding groups, the principal difference between these tables is in the ornamentation. In these tables the two front legs, being attached to a curved skirt, are in a position which shows two sides.

1493 (Upper) Hammond–Harwood House.
1495 (Centre) Mr. & Mrs. Ralph Robinson.
1497 (Lower) Mr. Albert G. Towers.

1494 (Upper) Mr. J. F. H. Maginn.
1496 (Centre) Miss Elisabeth H. Bartlett.
1498 (Lower) Mrs. C. E. Henderson.

In No. 1499 the edges of the top are veneered with a light wood, as in No. 1491. On the skirt are three long parallel forms of inlay in light wood with rounded ends, as are also seen and referred to in No. 1492, and two small panels of the same wood are over the legs. About 1790–1800.

In No. 1500 the skirt is ornamented with long ovals in dark wood, between which are two small panels with designs in light wood on a dark background. The legs have lines of inlay and strings of flowers. About 1790–1800.

No. 1501 is more fully decorated, having in the skirt inlaid forms with concave corners, between which are two ovals with figures of an eagle clutching a snake. On the front legs are inlaid designs, apparently of flowers. About 1790–1800.

In No. 1502 the front and ends have inlaid horizontal strings of flowers tied in the centre and at each end. In the panels over the front legs are inlaid shells under which, on the legs, are other shell designs. About 1790–1800.

No. 1503 is shown with the half–round folding top in a vertical position as though it were leaning against a wall. The top is bordered with a light wood which is also seen on the panels in the skirt. Oval medallions are over the front legs, and all the four legs are inlaid with strings of flowers. About 1790–1800.

No. 1504 is shown from the rear in order to see the inlaid semi–circle which is at the rear of the folding top. When this folding top is resting flat upon the fixed top, and the table is closely in front of a low mirror, the folding top, with its inlaid semi–circle, is reflected and makes a complete circle. This reflection is also mentioned in connection with pier tables in section 174, note 1. When the folding top falls back upon the swinging leg, the inlaid semi–circle is on the under side and is not visible. About 1790–1800.

In the next four tables, Nos. 1505–1508, the top is in a different form from those seen above. The front is curved in a bow, or swell, form, and the ends are in cyma curves, as to which see section 23. The shape of the top is more clearly seen in No. 1512. When the folding top is in use, the fixed and folding tops together form curves on the sides.

No. 1505 is shown from the side in order that the end may be well seen. All the legs are inlaid with strings of flowers on two sides, and over the legs are oval medallions with inlaid leaves and flowers. The skirt has inlaid rectangular panels with wide borders. The cyma curve of the ends will be noticed. About 1790–1800.

No. 1506 is in the same form with more abundant decoration. The skirt has five panels, the one in the centre enclosing an oval which is veneered with dark wood; and four small panels are over the legs which terminate in pointed feet. About 1790–1800.

No. 1507 is similar to the preceding table, especially in having five panels on the skirt and in having pointed feet. The oval in the central panel is veneered with light wood with a finely figured grain, and the other panels on the front and ends are also of fine wood. About 1790–1800.

1499 (UPPER) MR. C. EDWARD SNYDER.
1501 (CENTRE) MRS. J. P. PLEASANTS.
1503 (LOWER) MRS. S. S. BUZBY.

1500 (UPPER) MRS. C. P. ROGOW.
1502 (CENTRE) MR. & MRS. JAS. CAREY, JR.
1504 (LOWER) MISS HELEN H. CAREY.

No. 1508 has an unusual type of bright inlay on the edge of the skirt and on the small panels over the legs; and on the skirt are rectangular designs in line inlay. On the legs are the usual flowers. About 1790–1800.

Nos. 1509 and 1510 are similar in having rounded ends with a concave centre, a form of which is also seen in No. 1514, in which the top is up. This type of card table was apparently not very often made, perhaps because the concave front was not so well adapted to sit at as the straight or convex fronts. A similar card table in the Sheraton style with reeded legs is seen as No. 1527.

In No. 1509 the skirt has inlaid designs of parallel lines with rounded ends, within each of which is another inlaid design of parallel lines with pointed ends. Medallions of inlaid leaves and flowers are over the legs which end in tapered feet. About 1790–1800.

In No. 1510, which belongs to the same owner as the preceding table, the lines of inlay on the skirt may be seen but are difficult to describe. Over the legs are small panels of light wood within which are diamond–shaped panels of dark wood. About 1790–1800.

The remaining ten illustrations of card tables in the Hepplewhite style, Nos. 1511–1520, were taken with the folding tops up in order that their shapes might be well seen. The fixed top and the folding top of a card table are of course exactly of the same shape and size.

Nos. 1511 and 1512 are handsome card tables belonging to the same owner. They are similar in having in the centre of the skirt an inlaid American eagle with a shield, above which are eighteen stars. These stars may represent the number of States in the Union at the time the tables were made,[2] and if so the date would be between the year 1812, in which the eighteenth State, Louisiana, was admitted to the Union, and the year 1816, in which the nineteenth State, Indiana, was admitted. This date seems to be late for the Hepplewhite style. Other similar features are the inlaid urns in medallions over the front legs, and the almost pointed feet.

In No. 1511 the top is in the same shape as in Nos. 1487–1492 and 1494, having rounded ends and a straight front. The skirt has brilliant mahogany veneer, matched.[3] The inlaid eagle and stars are referred to in the preceding paragraph. Lines of inlay are on the front legs, but not on the rear ones. The legs taper sharply at the bottom. Assuming that the date is indicated by the number of stars, it is about 1812–1816.

In No. 1512 the top is in the same shape as in Nos. 1505–1508, the ends being in curves and the front being in a bow, or swell, form. The panels on the front and the ends are of curly maple. Delicate lines of inlay are on the front legs. The finely grained mahogany of the folding top will be noticed. About 1812–1816.

2. Other articles of which the dates are shown in this manner are the desks Nos. 803 and 805, and the mirror No. 1160. See note 5 in section 145; and also section 208 in the Appendix for the list of States in the order of their admission to the Union.

3. This word "matched", as used here, is explained in section 32, note 2. Other examples are in Nos. 1610 and 1616.

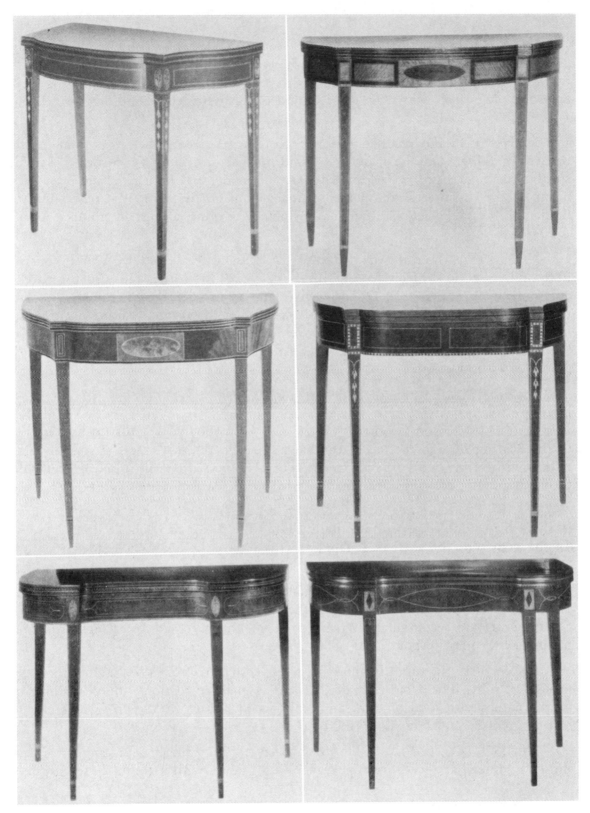

1505 (Upper) Mr. Herbert T. Tiffany.   1506 (Upper) Hammond–Harwood House.
1507 (Centre) Mr. J. Gilman D'Arcy Paul.   1508 (Centre) Mr. & Mrs. J. M. Matthews.
1509 (Lower) Mrs. I. R. Trimble.   1510 (Lower) Mrs. I. R. Trimble.

In Nos. 1513 and 1514 the tops are almost in the same form as in Nos. 1509 and 1510, having a concave portion in the centre, making the front recessed. On the skirt of No. 1513 are inlaid forms with concave corners, and strings of flowers are on the legs, over which are small inlaid panels with leaves and flowers. About 1790–1800.

In No. 1514 the recessed concave portion of the top is larger than in the preceding table. On the skirt are inlaid forms with concave corners, a small similar form enclosing a six–pointed star, and oval medallions over the legs. The usual strings of flowers are on the front legs and on these and the rear ones are lines of inlay. The legs are unusually delicate, ending almost in points. About 1790–1800.

In No. 1515 the top is in the so–called "clover–leaf" pattern, which consists here of five sections of circles of different sizes. This form, and also the three–curve one, was a favorite of Duncan Phyfe and appears on the Sheraton style card table No. 1535. The line of the top follows that of the frame, making an interesting shape, although probably not a convenient one for the card players. The skirt is ornamented with inlay and the usual medallions and flowers are on the legs. About 1790–1800.

In No. 1516 the top resembles somewhat that in Nos. 1487–1492 and 1494, having curved corners; here, however, the centre of the front is not straight but is in a graceful serpentine curve. A band of satinwood surrounds the under side of the folding lid and the top of the fixed one. On the skirt are four rectangular panels with satinwood borders. In the centre of the skirt is an inlaid griffin, said to be chained.[4] The tops are covered with green baize. About 1790–1800.

No. 1517 has another form of top, with rounded ends and a serpentine curve in the centre. The edges of both the fixed and the folding tops have lines of inlay. In the centre of the skirt is a panel of curly maple and on each side are other inlaid designs. About 1790–1800.

In No. 1518 the top is very similar in form to that of the preceding table. A pleasing feature is that the edges of the folding and fixed tops are finely reeded. On the skirt are rectangular inlaid forms, and the rear and front legs are ornamented with inlay. About 1790–1800.

In No. 1519 the top is in the same form as that of No. 1497, having a bowed, or swell, front. The front part of the skirt is in three sections, the centre one of which encloses an oval of dark and light wood. Here the tapering legs extend into pointed feet. About 1790–1800.

No. 1520 is an ordinary Hepplewhite style card table in a rectangular form, but of a somewhat agreeable appearance. This table, with little inlay, seems plain

4.   A design of a similar character, with the griffin holding a string of flowers, appears on plate 56 in the 1802 edition of Sheraton's "Drawing Book", (as to which see section 18), between pages 352 and 353, where it is termed an "Ornament for a frieze or tablet". Figures of griffins are also seen on the mantel mirror No. 1229 and on other articles referred to in the comments on that mirror; and see also the Index and the Sheraton style card table No. 1553 and note 11 in section 171.

1511 (Upper) Mrs. Francis P. Garvan. 1512 (Upper) Mrs. Francis P. Garvan.
1513 (Centre) Mr. Morris Whitridge. 1514 (Centre) Col. of Mrs. Jordan
1515 (Lower) Mrs. A. Morris Carey.   Stabler.
                                      1516 (Lower) Mrs. Francis P. Garvan.

in comparison with the previous pieces with their abundant inlay, curved tops and decorated skirts. Here there are three drawers, with oval brass handles of the period. About 1790–1800.

Section 171. Card tables; Sheraton and Empire styles.—In this section are thirty–six illustrations of card tables, many of which are in the early and finer style of Sheraton;[1] others are of the later and less desirable type which also bears his name, and a few are in the still later Empire style.

Many of the card tables in the Sheraton style differ from those in the Hepplewhite style chiefly in having round and reeded tapering legs instead of the square, inlaid and tapering legs of the Hepplewhite style; several tables will be seen in which this is the only noticeable difference.

The style of Sheraton was the fashionable one in our country from about 1795 to 1815, or later, as mentioned in section 18, and it was in this period that Duncan Phyfe made his best furniture and became the leading cabinet maker in New York. It was natural, of course, that Phyfe should work in that style in those years, and that his card tables and other articles of furniture should be made in that style. We may regret that Phyfe did not often use the Hepplewhite style also, but the fact that he did not do so is an indication that his work was done at a time when that style was not the most fashionable one. The main features of his card tables are in the Sheraton style, to which Phyfe added various embellishments of carving and other details which contributed to the elegance of his furniture. His work seems to have been copied by other cabinet makers, but not with all of his details. We may repeat what has been stated in substance in other sections, namely, there was and is no "Duncan Phyfe style" of furniture[2] in the sense that there was a Hepplewhite style or a Sheraton style.

The height of these card tables, as of those in the Hepplewhite style, is about twenty–nine inches, and the wood is almost always solid or veneered mahogany, often veneered also with maple or satinwood. The dates are from 1795 to 1825.

The straight and reeded legs of the card tables in the Sheraton style are very similar to the legs on several other articles made in that style; this will be seen, for example, in the illustrations of the dining tables Nos. 1319–1321 and the sideboard No. 996. Some of the legs project beyond the line of the frame, as in the Sheraton style bureau No. 745 and others, and in the sideboard No. 992 and others. In the first group, Nos. 1521–1538, the legs are attached directly to the frame of the table, as in the Hepplewhite style tables, not to a lyre or platform or pedestal as in others in this section.

1. Two designs of card tables are shown on plate 11 in the Appendix to Sheraton's "Drawing Book", edition of 1802, as to which see section 18. On the plate are the words "Published by T. Sheraton, April 30, 1793". One of these designs, with projecting legs, is evidently the model for tables in the form of No. 1521. The other design has not apparently been exactly copied by the American cabinet makers.

The distinctive feature of card tables is stated in note 1, C in section 169.

2. See "The Duncan Phyfe furniture", section 20, and "The American Directory style", section 19.

1517 (UPPER) MR. EDGAR G. MILLER, JR.
1519 (LOWER) ANONYMOUS.

1518 (UPPER) RT. REV. & MRS. E. T. HELFENSTEIN.
1520 (LOWER) DR. JAS. BORDLEY, JR.

In No. 1521 the skirt and top are in a bowed, or swell, shape except a small straight portion at each end. The skirt is finely veneered with a light wood which extends over the rounded corners to the back. The tapered legs are reeded and at the bottom are "turned" feet, as to which see section 35. The projection of the legs beyond the line of the frame will be noticed. Card tables of this type are said to be of New England origin. About 1800–1815.

In No. 1522 the top and the skirt are in a serpentine curve. In the centre of the skirt is a large oval of veneered light wood. Here also, as in the preceding table, the front corners are rounded, below which are carved rings over the projecting reeded and tapered legs which end in turned feet. About 1800–1815.

In No. 1523 the top is bowed, or swelled, with rectangular corners. The front of the skirt has three panels of finely figured veneer and at each end is a small panel over the leg. The fixed and the folding top are each ornamented with two lines of inlay. The form of the top of this table resembles that of the Hepplewhite style card table No. 1519. About 1800–1815.

No. 1524 has the same shape of top as the Hepplewhite style tables Nos. 1505–1508, the front being curved in a bow, or swell, form. The shape of this kind of top is clearly seen in the Hepplewhite style table No. 1512, which it resembles also in having on the skirt four panels of satinwood, and between the front ones is a panel of dark wood enclosing an inlaid oval. About 1800–1815.

No. 1525 is similar in shape to No. 1522, having a serpentine front with rounded corners. Here the veneer on the front is carried around the corners and on the ends as in No. 1521. The legs are in a different form from the usual one, being without reeding but turned with several rings. About 1800–1815.

No. 1526 resembles somewhat No. 1493 in the Hepplewhite style, having a top which is six–sided, including the back, when the folding top lies upon the fixed top, and becomes eight–sided when it is supported by a swinging leg. The four legs are ornamented with somewhat heavy reeding which indicates a later date than that in the preceding examples. About 1810–1820.

No. 1527 resembles the Hepplewhite style card tables Nos. 1509–1510, which belong to the same owner, in having a top and skirt with rounded ends and a concave centre in the manner of No. 1514. The edges are finely reeded and also the five legs, but are not distinct in the engraving. In this piece and in several others, especially those of Duncan Phyfe, there is no decoration with inlay of different colors; the fine effects are secured by the harmonious proportions, the quality of the mahogany, either solid or veneer, and the elegance of the carving. About 1800–1815.

No. 1528, with a form resembling that of the preceding table, is fully and finely decorated with paintings of a character similar to those on the chairs Nos. 290 and 291. In the concave portion of the skirt is an eight–sided panel with a painting of a large building, and on the ends are similar panels with paintings of musical instruments. The edges of the top are painted in the same style as the borders of the rectangular panels. The legs, instead of being reeded, are inlaid

1521 (UPPER) MR. EDGAR G. MILLER, JR.
1522 (UPPER) MR. EDGAR G. MILLER, JR.
1523 (CENTRE) HAMMOND–HARWOOD HOUSE.
1524 (CENTRE) MR. ARTHUR E. COLE.
1525 (LOWER) HAMMOND–HARWOOD HOUSE.
1526 (LOWER) MR. & MRS. H. L. DUER.

in the same manner as in the Baltimore corner table No. 1462 and the serving tables Nos. 1441 and 1442. This table was made by Robert Fisher,[3] a Baltimore cabinet maker. About 1800–1815.

No. 1529 has about the same form and workmanship as certain tables known to have been made by Duncan Phyfe, but in the absence of definite proof it cannot be said to be a product of his shop. The skirt is veneered with mahogany, and four small panels are above the legs, which terminate in round brass feet. The fifth leg is the inner one on the rear left. About 1800–1815.

No. 1530 is known to be a product of Duncan Phyfe. With the folding top down, the top is six–sided, including the back, and is eight–sided when it is in use. The skirt is ornamented in the centre with a panel carved with a festoon of drapery, and over the legs with smaller panels. The upper portions of the curved legs are carved with acanthus leaves, below which the legs are plain and terminate in animals' claw feet—a combination which has not been admired by all collectors.[4] About 1815–1825.

No. 1531 is in the form of a card table although its width of forty–four inches is greater than usual. The edges of the tops are grooved and the folding top when in use is supported by a swinging leg in the usual manner. The legs are ringed at the top, and below are reeded in the heavy form which is seen in other pieces in the late Sheraton style, such as the dining table No. 1321. In form this table resembles No. 1496 in the Hepplewhite style, having rounded corners and straight front and ends. About 1810–1820.

No. 1532 is in the Empire style, as indicated by the kind of carving on the legs and the skirt; the feet, however, are of the Sheraton type. Instead of being ornamented with reeding, the legs are carved with large leaves which twine around them. Above the legs are small panels carved with leaves, and in the centre of the skirt is a panel in which there is a carved eagle with outspread wings. The form of the top is very similar to that in the preceding table. About 1810–1820.

The next six card tables in the Sheraton style, Nos. 1533–1538, are shown with their folding tops up in order that the shapes may be well seen, as with several tables in the Hepplewhite style in the previous section. The fixed tops are of course exactly the same in shape as the folding tops.

3. Robert Fisher has been identified by labels on furniture and by the city directories as a cabinet maker of Baltimore. He used paintings on several pieces known to have been made by him, such as the "fancy" chair No. 291, the settee No. 516 and the window seat No. 536, all of which are now the property of the same owner. Fisher's name appears in the Baltimore City directories from 1800 to 1812 as a chairmaker. He is mentioned in section 20, note 1, in connection with Lachlan Phyfe.

4. By one experienced writer this design has been called "highly dramatic and stimulating"; by another it is regarded as an example of the beginning of the decline of Phyfe's style. But all agree that the table is of the finest material and workmanship. Similar combinations were used by Phyfe on some of his chairs, not illustrated in this book.

1527 (Upper) Mrs. I. R. Trimble.
1529 (Centre) Miss Margaret C. Painter.
1531 (Lower) Mrs. Rignal W. Baldwin.

1528 (Upper) Mrs. Miles White, Jr.
1530 (Centre) Mrs. Francis P. Garvan.
1532 (Lower) Mr. J. Ramsay Speer.

No. 1533 is a handsome table which in form resembles No. 1521, having a skirt which is bowed or swelled in the centre, but with straight ends, and also with rounded corners and reeded, tapering and turned legs projecting beyond the lines of the frame. On the edges of the fixed and folding tops are small bands of inlay in a "checker" pattern, that is, having small blocks of wood of alternate dark and light color, as on a checker board. The oval and rectangular panels are veneered with satinwood. The folding top appears less shapely in the upright position; it may be compared with the top of the table in the Chippendale style with rounded corners, No. 1479. About 1800–1815.

In No. 1534 the curves of the folding top are somewhat more graceful than in the preceding table, although the corners are not pleasing when seen in a vertical position. The skirt is similar to that in No. 1524, having four veneered panels of satinwood, with an inlaid oval in the mahogany central panel. As in the preceding table, there are ringed columns over the legs. About 1800–1815.

In No. 1535 the top is in the so–called "clover–leaf" pattern, with five curves, similar to those in No. 1547 and in the Hepplewhite style card table No. 1515. This table follows a design of Duncan Phyfe in having no inlay, relying upon the fine proportions of the piece, with carving in some instances. The five legs are finely reeded and terminate in round brass feet, differing in these respects from the Hepplewhite table. About 1800–1815.

In No. 1536 the centre of the top is recessed in a serpentine curve, which is more graceful than that in the Hepplewhite style table No. 1514. There is no decorative inlay, but the edges of the tops, the legs and the small panels over them are finely reeded. About 1800–1815.

In No. 1537 the top is in the same form as that in No. 1534 and the edges are finely reeded; but the reeding of the legs, and of the columns above them, as well as the carving of leaves between, are of a less elegant character, indicating the change from the early to the later Sheraton style. About 1810–1820.

No. 1538 has a clover–leaf design of three curves. The legs are carved in the heavy spiral form which was much used in the Empire period, and the table must be regarded as having features of the Empire style and therefore as of that period.[5] About 1820–1830.

The next group of card tables in the Sheraton style, Nos. 1539–1546, are known as "lyre" card tables because the top is supported by two lyres, or lyre-shaped pieces, which are called the "standards"[6] of the table. The lyre form was

5.   This is in accordance with the principle that the date of the latest feature determines the date of the piece, as mentioned in section 6.

6.   The word "standard" as applied to tables means the upright part which supports the frame and top of the table. In these lyre card tables the lyres are the standards.

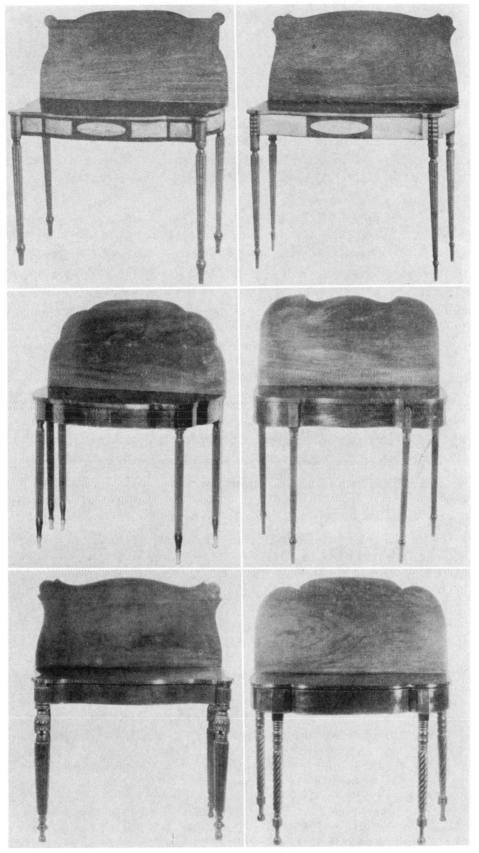

1533 (UPPER) ANONYMOUS.   1534 (UPPER) ANONYMOUS.
1535 (CENTRE) MRS. M. S. HARTSHORNE.   1536 (CENTRE) DR. M. A. ABRAMS.
1537 (LOWER) MR. S. JOHNSON POE.   1538 (LOWER) MRS. A. MORRIS CAREY.

a favorite of Sheraton[7] and was copied by Duncan Phyfe[8] in his furniture in the Sheraton style, as in the chair No. 326, the sofa No. 574 and the sofa table No. 1423. In these card tables and others the top revolves to a position in which the folding portion when open is supported by the frame, as shown in No. 1541. The strings on the lyre are almost always made of brass, but sometimes whalebone was used. The eight illustrations exhibit the gradual change from the delicate forms of the early Sheraton style to the heavy form of the late Empire period. The lyre sewing tables, Nos. 1566–1571, may be examined in connection with these card tables.

No. 1539 is a fine example of lyre card tables and was probably made by Duncan Phyfe. The slanting position in which the photograph was taken gives to the carved panel in the skirt the appearance of not being in the centre. The lyres and the legs are carved with acanthus leaves and the platform on which the lyres rest is fluted. The four legs are attached to the platform and are in concave curves and end in brass claw feet with casters, as in the Sheraton style dining table No. 1326 and the library table No. 1421. This table, like No. 1493 in the Hepplewhite style and No. 1526 in the Sheraton style, has eight sides when the folding top is in use and six sides when the folding top lies upon the fixed one. Very few of these tables have been found. About 1810–1815.

No. 1540 is known to be by Duncan Phyfe. Here the two lyres are "crossed", not parallel as in the preceding table, and the strings are attached to crossed bars at the top. In some tables of this type the strings are omitted and an ornamental pineapple is placed at the base. The arms of the lyres are carved with acanthus leaves and a small rope design. The platform is plain, but the legs have a carved rope design similar to that on the arms. The concave legs are wide–spreading as in the preceding piece, but are not quite as long. About 1810–1815.

No. 1541 is shown with the top open and turned around. As with No. 1539, this table was photographed in a slanting position, causing the joint between the fixed and folding top to appear off the centre. Instead of two lyres with strings, there is only one, the other standard being a solid piece of wood in the lyre shape,

---

7.   In Sheraton's "Drawing Book", (as to which see section 18), edition of 1802, in its Appendix, plate 13, a fire screen is shown with an elaborate lyre on the screen portion; on plate 26, dated September, 1793, is a "ladies work table" with lyre standards at the ends; on plate 29 a lyre is at the top of the case of a grandfather clock; and on plate 36, dated August, 1792, it is in a chair back. On plate 4 of the "Accompaniment" to the "Drawing Book", dated November, 1793, a lyre is in a painted panel on a wall; in plate 9, January, 1794, it is on the top of a table leg; on plate 12, February, 1794, it is on a window cornice. See also the chair No. 13 in the full page illustration No. 234. Other examples might be cited, showing the frequent use of the lyre as a decorative feature in the book of Sheraton which is known to have been used, but not precisely followed, by the American cabinet makers of the period. Our cabinet makers also derived their designs from the English furniture which they imported. See the paragraph entitled "The lyre as an ornament" in section 44.

8.   The idea that the lyre form in furniture was introduced by Phyfe, or that almost any article of furniture with a lyre was in the manner of Phyfe, instead of Sheraton, is of course erroneous.

    In a letter written in 1794 by an English visitor, before Phyfe had become a prominent cabinet maker, reference is made to the English chairs in a Philadelphia drawing room with "the backs in form of a lyre". This appears in an article by Mr. William M. Hornor, Jr., in the "International Studio", March, 1931, page 47.

1539 (UPPER) DR. JAS. BORDLEY, JR.
1541 (LOWER) DR. M. A. ABRAMS.

1540 (UPPER) MRS. FRANCIS P. GARVAN.
1542 (LOWER) DR. J. HALL PLEASANTS.

797

as also in Nos. 1566 and 1567. This less elegant treatment, not as expensive as the other, was sometimes extended to both lyres, as in No. 1543. The legs are in the form of cyma curves, as to which see section 23, and are grooved, terminating in brass claw feet. About 1815–1820.

In No. 1542 two parallel lyres with strings support the frame above. The front of the skirt is ornamented with a brass design and with two panels of figured maple, all of which are repeated on the platform below. On the arms of the lyre and at its base are other brass ornaments. The concave legs are in a different form from those seen on previous card tables, being rectangular and without carving as also in the tables Nos. 1568 and 1586. The use of the metal mounts and the form of the table place it in the early Empire style, which is here seen at its best.[9] About 1810–1820.

No. 1543 has a curved top which is supported by two solid standards in the lyre form. At the upper ends of the standards are two small applied rosettes and two larger ones are near the base. The legs are in the form of cyma curves, and are grooved, as in the table No. 1541. About 1810–1820.

Nos. 1544–1546 are in the Empire style, the first two being in an early form of that style and the third in the last form.

In No. 1544 the two parallel lyre standards are in the graceful form of the earlier tables, and have strings as in No. 1539; but the awkward legs, placed under the heavy platform, not attached to the sides, are coarsely carved and end in the claw feet seen on other pieces of the period, illustrating an important departure from the Sheraton style. About 1820–1830.

No. 1545 is a rendition in the Empire style of the Sheraton style card table No. 1540, with "crossed" lyres which here have only two strings each. The lyre–shaped standards are without ornamentation and rest upon a large and heavy platform. As in the preceding table, the legs, which are placed under the plat-form, are coarsely carved, here with an unusual type of feet. About 1815–1825.

In No. 1546 we see one of the last forms of the Empire style card tables, from which the charm of the Sheraton style has wholly disappeared. The moldings on the skirt and on the base suggest the Victorian style. The top is supported by one lyre–shaped standard, of massive proportions and without strings, which rests upon a large and heavy base with an applied molding. Under the base are scroll feet.[10] The top is in a serpentine form with rounded corners. In spite of its form this table must be admired for its fine mahogany, both solid and veneered. We also notice the four applied rosettes on the lyre, as in No. 1543. About 1830–1840.

Each of the three fine Sheraton style card tables, Nos. 1547–1549, have a pedestal and three legs. These tables are without inlay.

9.   See section 38 entitled "Applied decorations; mounts".

10.   In connection with this table, the illustrations in the Appendix, section 199, entitled "Furniture styles of 1840", will be found interesting.

1543 (Upper) Mr. Blanchard Randall.
1545 (Lower) Mr. & Mrs. E. H. McKeon.

1544 (Upper) Mr. John C. Toland.
1546 (Lower) Mrs. G. Frank Baily.

In No. 1547 we recognize the five–curve clover–leaf top which appears also on the table No. 1515 in the Hepplewhite style and on No. 1535 in the Sheraton style. This table was made by Duncan Phyfe, who is said to have been the only cabinet maker who made a card table without a skirt, as here. The top is bordered with veneer, is covered with baize and is supported by a pedestal with a reeded vase similar to those on the tripod tables Nos. 1366 and 1367. The concave legs are carved above with acanthus leaves, below which they are reeded, terminating in brass claw feet. About 1810–1820.

No. 1548, also by Phyfe, has a three–curve clover–leaf top, and a veneered skirt. The pedestal has a vase–shaped portion, below which is a round carved portion. The legs are carved with acanthus leaves which extend almost to the brass feet. In this table, as explained in the comment on the next one, the side legs may be made to swing back and thus give greater stability. About 1810–1820.

No. 1549 is a somewhat plainer table of the same type as the two preceding ones. The top is in a three–curve clover–leaf form and the edges are reeded. The pedestal is in the shape of a large vase and the legs are in the form of cyma curves. On the base of the skirt are small carved panels under which are drops. An interesting feature of this and the two preceding tables is that in the rear of the frame there are two brackets which swing out and support the folding top when it is opened flat, and the movement of these brackets, by an ingenious mechanism, moves the two side legs backwards and thus gives the table a firmer support. About 1810–1820.

In No. 1550, also, the top is in a three–curve form as in the two preceding pieces. The supports are four slender columns, or colonnettes, which are reeded at the top, with rings and acanthus leaves below. These columns may be compared with those on the tripod table No. 1364. Under the columns is a small platform from which four concave legs extend, ornamented with acanthus leaves and reeding. About 1810–1820.

The next four card tables, Nos. 1551–1554, have features of the late Sheraton style; the last two, Nos. 1555–1556, are in the Empire style.

In No. 1551 the top has rounded front corners resembling those in the next table and in No. 1531. The edges of the top are reeded, as are also the concave legs, but not finely. The pedestal has a vase–shaped portion which is reeded, below which is a ringed design. About 1800–1820.

In No. 1552 the top is in the same form as in the preceding table, with reeded edges. The skirt is made of a light wood and is ornamented with inlaid panels of dark wood, an example of contrasting colors which was a favorite decorative feature. The pedestal is ringed and is in a vase shape. The legs are convex and reeded above and are concave below, somewhat in the form on the dining table No. 1330 and the tripod table No. 1363. On the corners of the platform are four small applied horizontal and cylindrical forms which are also seen in No. 1646 and are mentioned in the comment on the sewing table No. 1568. About 1810–1820.

1547 (Upper) Anonymous.
1549 (Lower) Anonymous.

1548 (Upper) Mrs. Francis P. Garvan.
1550 (Lower) Mr. Albert G. Towers.

No. 1553 is one of a type of rectangular and painted card tables which have been found in Maryland and Virginia. This table presents an interesting study of several features, as stated in the note.[11] About 1820-1830.

No. 1554, also a painted card table, is similar in general form to the preceding table, except that the legs are of the concave type and the round and ringed pedestal is without a vase. The skirt is decorated at each end with a wreath enclosing a star, and in the centre with a sword and a wreath, as in the chair No. 329 belonging to the same owner. At the base of the pedestal is another "anthemion", or honeysuckle, design, mentioned in note 11. About 1820–1830.

No. 1555 is in the early Empire style, as shown by the character of the carving and the rounded skirt which latter resembles in form the rounded fronts of the drawers in the sewing tables Nos. 1578–1580. The top is six–sided when closed, as here, and eight–sided when open. The pedestal is carved in three sections. The legs are carved on the upper surface with acanthus leaves and on the sides down to the feet with small lines supposed to represent the hair[12] on the legs which here terminate in animals' claw feet. About 1820–1830.

No. 1556, a card table with a folding top, is a monstrosity in the Empire style. The tops revolve, and rest on the skirt when they are open as in No. 1541. Two fierce–looking creatures of the ocean serve as legs and supports of the top; these represent dolphins[13] which in England at certain periods were favorite decorative features on tables and were also seen on girandole mirrors, as in No. 1242. Under the legs are platforms connected by a horizontal carved stretcher supported by animals' claw feet, making a kind of trestle base in a form such as appears on some of the early tables, as Nos. 1300–1302. The time and skill spent on the carving on this card table were worthy of a better style, especially on the carving of the scales, of the shells under the skirt, and of the leaves over the feet, the latter being also seen in No. 1577. About 1820–1830.

11.   The skirt is decorated with small griffins and large floral designs as in the Adam style mirror No. 1147, the Hepplewhite style card table No. 1516, the Sheraton style mantel mirror No. 1229, and the Empire style chair No. 328. The pedestal is round, with rings and a vase which is painted with leaves. These leaves seem to be a form of the "palmette", a small palm leaf, which appears on the knees of the chair No. 342 and on other pieces of the period. The horizontal legs include "corbel" forms illustrated in connection with the French mantel mirror No. 1231 and the French table No. 1656.

On the base of the pedestal is a Grecian "anthemion", or honeysuckle, a design which is mentioned in note 48 in section 51. It is also an important architectural decoration of the cornice and other exterior parts of the new "Enoch Pratt Free Library" of Baltimore, which was opened in January, 1933. The designs at the ends of the skirt consist of wings, arrows and another object.

The vertical feet are in the general form used in several designs by Sheraton in his "Drawing Book", and copied by Duncan Phyfe on a sewing table shown in plate 33 in "Furniture Masterpieces of Duncan Phyfe" by Mr. Charles Over Cornelius; simpler forms are on the Sheraton style sewing table No. 1594 and the pole screen No. 1684.

12.   It is said in reference to a certain dog's–foot design used by Duncan Phyfe that "the hair on the leg is suggested by small, irregular, curved grooves"; by Mr. Charles Over Cornelius in his "Masterpieces of Duncan Phyfe", page 54.

13.   Dolphins on sofas are in No. 585 and in Mr. Lockwood's "Colonial Furniture", volume 2, figures 667 and 669. See also note 5 in section 174 in the present book.

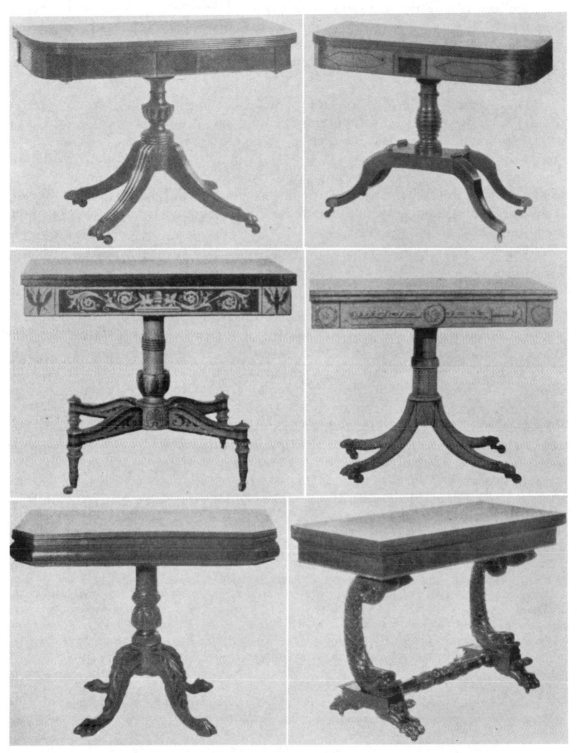

1551 (Upper) Mr. C. Edward Snyder.
1553 (Centre) Mr. Alexander Brown.
1555 (Lower) Mr. Daniel R. Randall.

1552 (Upper) Mrs. Edwin B. Niver.
1554 (Centre) Mr. & Mrs. J. M. Harris.
1556 (Lower) Anonymous.

Section 172. Sewing tables.—Perhaps no other minor articles of antique furniture have survived in such numbers as the small tables, and of these the most important are the sewing tables, or "work tables" as they are often called in the books. This is doubtless because the sewing tables sustained almost no weight and were used only by gentlewomen.[1]

These sewing tables were made to some extent in the Hepplewhite style,[2] but the great majority of them were in the Sheraton and Empire styles. Certain kinds of sewing tables were made in each of these three styles; and in order that a comparison may be easily made of the tables of the same kind, but of different styles, the illustrations are given in groups. One group is of the so-called "Martha Washington" tables, which were made in the Hepplewhite, Sheraton and Empire styles; another group is that in which the upper portion is supported by lyres; and similarly with other kinds.

The wood of these tables is almost always mahogany, often finely veneered in parts with maple or satinwood; the height is generally about twenty-eight to thirty-one inches; the dates range from about 1800 to as late as 1840.

Nos. 1557–1565, and also No. 1566 in the next group, are sewing tables of the type commonly called "Martha Washington", a name based upon the tradition that the lady used one of this kind of sewing table at Mt. Vernon, as also the "Martha Washington" chair No. 419. This type of table was apparently not copied from England. The distinctive feature is that the upper portion is in an oval form, or nearly so, having rounded or angular ends which serve as boxes. The tops are either in one piece which lifts up from the rear, or are in three parts, the central one of which does not lift up, and two others, over the boxes at the ends, which do lift up. The upper portion is supported either by a pedestal or by four legs, or by lyre standards. These tables seldom have a silk bag. In all cases the interior is fitted with arrangements for sewing accessories, and in some cases with a mirror or a writing board.

No. 1557, in the Sheraton style, is a sewing table of elegant appearance and fine wood and workmanship. The top, reeded on the edges, is in one piece and

---

1. A silk bag, generally used as a screen to hide a wooden box inside, but sometimes used merely as a bag without a box, will be seen on many sewing tables. This bag could not be expected to survive the usage of a century or more, and hence a modern bag has often been substituted for the original one, or both the bag and the box have been removed; in the latter case some of the tables may not be easily distinguishable from certain other small tables with drawers, such as some of those shown in the next chapter.

2. In Hepplewhite's "Guide", (as to which see section 17), there are no designs of sewing tables, but the cabinet makers working in the Hepplewhite style had no difficulty in adapting that style to the requirements of a sewing table, as in the Martha Washington table No. 1559. There are no designs of these tables in Chippendale's book.

In the "Appendix" to Sheraton's "Drawing Book", (as to which see section 18), page 403, plate 26, dated September, 1793, are two designs of "work tables" which have not been exactly followed by our cabinet makers. The silk bags were ornamented with drapery.

The illustrations in this section are small, as the writer thinks that the reader will prefer a large number of small, but clear, illustrations, rather than a smaller number of larger ones, as remarked in connection with several other articles.

1557 (UPPER) MR. H. T. TIFFANY.
1560 (CENTRE) MR. & MRS. JAS. CAREY, JR.
1563 (LOWER) MR. B. RANDALL.

1558 (UPPER) MRS. WM. M. ROBERTS.
1561 (CENTRE) MR. A. G. TOWERS.
1564 (LOWER) MR. A. G. TOWERS.

1559 (UPPER) MR. A. McLANAHAN.
1562 (CENTRE) ANONYMOUS.
1565 (LOWER) MR. & MRS. W. M. ELLICOTT.

lifts up from the rear. Under the top is a wide veneered band of finely grained light wood, below which the entire frame is in delicate "tambour" work, such as is seen on the desks Nos. 815–824 in the Sheraton style. The plain pedestal is vase–shaped, the four concave legs are veneered on the upper surface with the same light wood as used on the wide band under the top, and the feet are brass, with casters. Under the single drawer is a compartment which opens from the side. A duplicate of this table descended from the same ancestor to Miss Mary Leigh Brown, of Baltimore. About 1800–1810.

In No. 1558, also in the Sheraton style, the top is in three parts, the central one and the two end ones. There are three drawers, each with replaced handles, and the usual two end boxes which are in one continuous curve, not in several sections as in the next table and others. The pedestal is in a vase–shaped and reeded form and the concave legs, also reeded, terminate in animals' wooden claw feet. About 1800–1810.

No. 1559 is in the Hepplewhite style, as indicated by the tapering and inlaid legs, and the use of several inlaid designs on the central portion. Here the ends of the sewing table are not in one continuous curve, but are each in seven sections, which is an easier form of construction. There are two large drawers and two small square ones, all of which are veneered with dark wood. Between the two small drawers there is a small arch, as also in the small table No. 1608. About 1790–1810.

No. 1560, a plain sewing table, is in the Sheraton style, as shown by the round, "turned" and tapering legs. The ends are in a continuous curve and there are three drawers with round wooden knobs. The legs are in about the same form as in the next table. About 1800–1810.

No. 1561 is one of a pair of sewing tables of curly maple. The ends are in five sections of the type of those in No. 1559. The three drawers have glass knobs. The round legs have an unusual turning near the bottom, and end in round feet. About 1800–1810.

No. 1562 is even more clearly in the Sheraton style, having reeded legs, above which are reeded panels. The edge of the top is also reeded. The three drawers have small glass knobs. The ends are in a continuous curve. About 1800–1810.

In No. 1563 the top is in one piece which lifts up from the rear as in No. 1557. There is a drawer at the base with a brass lion–and–ring handle, above which is a large panel which does not open. The keyhole at the top is for a lock for the top. The legs are reeded, as are also the panels above. The ends are in a series of sections and are furnished with brass handles. About 1800–1810.

In No. 1564, also, the top is in one piece. It is in the Hepplewhite style, with inlay on the skirt and on the square and tapered legs. Below the skirt the frame is covered with silk in four sections. The ends are in a continuous curve. This sewing table is of a somewhat unusual type. About 1800-1810.

In No. 1565 the top is similar in form to several of the preceding pieces, being in three parts. The pedestal and the base, however, are of a later form than in the preceding tables. The reeding of the pedestal is of a heavy type of the late

Sheraton style and the platform upon which it rests is in a triangular form seen on other tables in the Empire period, such as Nos. 1369, 1592 and others. About 1820–1830.

Nos. 1566–1570, in the Sheraton style, have lyres or lyre–shaped pieces as supports, or standards, upon which the upper portion rests. They may be compared with the lyre card tables Nos. 1539–1546.

No. 1566 is a so–called Martha Washington sewing table with two lyre standards, one being a lyre with strings and the other a solid piece in the lyre shape, as also in the next table and in the Sheraton style card table No. 1541. The top is in three parts and the ends are in several sections as in No. 1559 and others. In the centre are one shallow and one deep drawer, on each side of which is a reeded panel with a drop ornament. The front of the lyre with strings is carved with leaves as are the upper portions of the concave legs. About 1800–1810.

In No. 1567 the lower portion is almost the same as in the preceding piece. The upper portion is of a different type, being rectangular, with reeded and projecting columns at the four corners, a favorite form in the Sheraton style as will be seen from other tables below. Three horizontal bands of lighter wood form a contrast with the color of the drawers. The handles are of the lion–and–ring pattern. About 1800–1810.

No. 1568 has two parallel lyres resting upon a platform which is supported by concave legs, as in the Sheraton style card table No. 1542. At the top of the legs, as also on the card tables Nos. 1542 and 1552, and more clearly in No. 1646, are small horizontal cylindrical forms, a frequent ornamental detail of the period. The upper portion is in about the same form as in the preceding table, with projecting columns which are ringed instead of reeded. Brass knobs are on the two drawers. About 1800–1810.

No. 1569 resembles the preceding piece in the form of the upper portion. The two drawers are inlaid and banded with light wood and the projecting columns are turned in a ring–and–spool design. The two lyres are in a less attractive form than the others. The legs are concave, in a form sometimes called a "C" curve, resembling the curves of that name much used in the Chippendale period, as mentioned in the comment on the mirror No. 1103 and others. About 1810–1820.

No. 1570 has at the corners large and plain round projecting columns instead of reeded or ringed ones, and the entire fronts of the two drawers are veneered in a light wood, making a pronounced contrast in color. The legs are reeded, but not delicately, and are somewhat heavy for a table of the size, as is also the platform upon which the lyres rest; these features and the corner columns indicate a change towards the Empire style. About 1815–1825.

No. 1571 is a lyre sewing table constructed in a form to hold a bag. Here the two lyres, with their ends towards the front, are attached to a heavy Empire style platform, and support a deep box with a lid. Below the box is a shallow drawer, under which is a frame which holds the silk bag and may be pulled outward. Excepting the two lyres and the bag, this table shows no features of the Sheraton style, and is therefore regarded as being in the Empire style, in which the lyre continued to be popular as an ornamental detail. About 1825–1835.

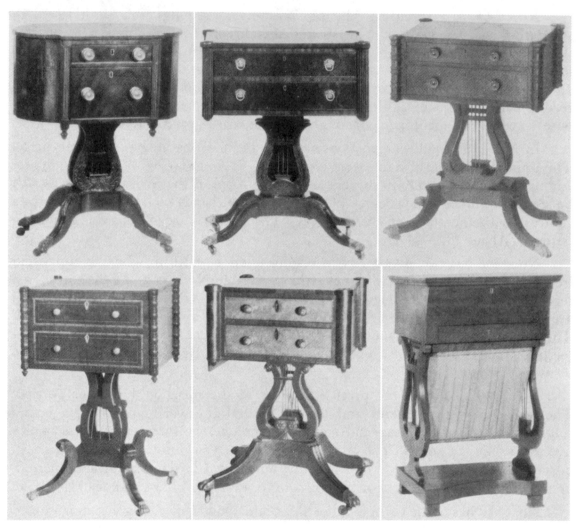

1566 (UPPER) DR. M. A. ABRAMS.   1567 (UPPER) MR. W. W. LANAHAN.   1568 (UPPER) DR. WM. P. E. WYSE.
1569 (LOWER) MR. B. C. HOWARD.   1570 (LOWER) MR. H. T. TIFFANY.   1571 (LOWER) MR. & MRS. J. CAREY,
                                                                                                     JR.

1572 (Upper) Mr. A. G. Towers.　1573 (Upper) Mr. C. E. Snyder.　1574 (Upper) Mr. H. O. Thompson.
1575 (Centre) Mrs. John Stokes.　1576 (Centre) Mr. J. C. Toland.　1577 (Centre) Miss E. M. Miller.
1578 (Lower) Miss Mary K. Hink-　1579 (Lower) Mr. S. Johnson Poe.　1580 (Lower) Mrs. R. W. Baldwin.
　　　ley.

In the next group of nine tables, Nos. 1572–1580, the upper portions are rectangular and are supported by a pedestal, in which respect these tables are similar in their general form, and illustrate both the Sheraton and the Empire styles. The first three may be regarded as in the late Sheraton style; the other six, Nos. 1575–1580, show the change from the early to the late Empire style. Rectangular upper portions supported by pedestals are also seen in other groups in this chapter.

No. 1572 is of mahogany and bird's–eye maple. The two small upper drawers and the large one below form a pleasing contrast in color to the dark pedestal and legs, in which respect it may be compared with the small table No. 1606 in the next section. The legs are concave and end in a "C" curve, as in No. 1569. About 1810–1820.

In No. 1573 the upper portion is ornamented with broad bands of curly maple around the two drawers, upon which are large cut glass knobs. At the corners are round columns with turned rings, and drops below. The lower portion has carving upon the vase–shaped pedestal, the round platform and the upper part of the legs, below which they are grooved, ending in brass claw feet. About 1810–1820.

In No. 1574 the columns at the corners are turned in rings and other forms. The pedestal is reeded above and carved below. The legs have a higher curve than usual and are carved with leaves at the top and reeded below. The reeding on the legs does not stop at the feet but continues into them, a method referred to in the comments on Nos. 1422 and 1589. This method was also used by Duncan Phyfe on card tables. About 1810–1820.

No. 1575 has ringed columns at the corners. The oval brass handles upon the two drawers are of an earlier style than the table. The pedestal has the spiral carvings which were a feature of the Empire style, and the concave legs are grooved and end in brass feet. About 1810–1820.

No. 1576, also in the Empire style, has a straight upper drawer overhanging in part the two curved lower ones. The top is in two equal parts, or lids, which are on hinges on the sides. Near the top of each side is a small and not well seen "pull" which when drawn out may support the lids when open, in the manner of Nos. 1473–1474. The small columns at the corners are fully carved, as are also the lower part of the pedestal and the grotesque legs which are attached to the bottom of the platform and end in animals' claw feet. About 1820–1830.

In No. 1577, in the Empire style, the upper portion is ornamented with four painted designs, the two on the drawers being on a dark background. The panels within the lines of inlay on these drawers project forward slightly as the top does in No. 1591. The knobs are of wood. The carved pedestal is in a vase–shaped design and rests upon a large platform with concave sides. The legs are carved and are attached to the bottom of the platform, as in the preceding table. Over each of the feet is a leaf which projects forward in the manner of those in No. 1556. About 1820–1830.

No. 1578, in the Empire style, has two rounded drawers in the upper portion and ringed columns at the corners. The pedestal is carved in the central portion and on the base. As in the preceding piece the platform has concave sides. The winged legs and the animals' claw feet are under the platform. About 1820–1830.

In No. 1579 the rounded overhanging upper drawer is prominent; the two small columns at the corners, one of the last surviving features of the late Sheraton style, become smaller; the former round and carved pedestal gives way to a heavy and plain one; the platform of the Empire style continues, and the Empire style scroll feet supersede the carved ones. About 1830–1840.

No. 1580 is wholly in the late Empire style. The columns at the corners have disappeared; the pedestal is plain and has another shape. Scrolled feet of this type are only seen on the furniture of the late Empire period, as in the tripod table No. 1371 and others. In this connection section 199 in the Appendix, entitled "Furniture styles of 1840", will be interesting. The drop–leaves on the sides of the upper portion, when raised, are supported by small brackets, as in No. 1576. About 1840.

In the next group, Nos. 1581–1592, are twelve sewing tables, each with a silk bag which generally conceals a box for sewing materials. In most of the tables of this type the bag and box are attached to a slide, under the drawers, which pulls out and gives access to the interior, as shown in No. 1595. In some cases, as in No. 1564, silk coverings are placed in sections between the legs around the entire frame. Each of these tables is in a different design.

No. 1581 is a curly maple sewing table in the Hepplewhite style, the legs being square and tapered. There is one drawer, below which is a slide which pulls out and to which the bag is attached. About 1790–1810.

No. 1582, also, is in the Hepplewhite style, in a form not often seen in American pieces. The oval top is in one piece and opens from the rear as in the "Martha Washington" table No. 1557 and others. The slender tapering legs are square, curving outward at the lower end, as in one of Hepplewhite's designs, and are braced by cross–stretchers with a shelf, as also in No. 1600 in the next section. About 1790–1810.

No. 1583, also in the Hepplewhite style, has an eight–sided top which is decorated with inlay. The legs are square and tapered, with a slight curve at the bottom, and are attached to the centre of the corner sections. About 1790–1800.

No. 1584, in curly maple, is in the Sheraton style, as indicated by the legs which are square and reeded above the stretchers and round below them. The top is eight–sided, with brass handles at the ends. About 1800–1810.

No. 1585, also of fine maple, is in the Sheraton style, having the same familiar projecting, rounded and tapered legs as the tables Nos. 1521, 1533 and others. There are two drawers with brass lion–and–ring handles. About 1800–1810.

In No. 1586 the edges of the top and its two drop–leaves are grooved, and the four supporting columns and the stretcher are reeded. Under the two drawers with glass knobs is the slide with the bag attached. The two reeded columns at each end rest upon the two connected concave legs; this trestle method may also be seen on the table No. 1644 and others. About 1800–1810.

1581 (UPPER) MR. & MRS. H. L. DUER. 1582 (UPPER) MRS. A. ARMSTRONG. 1583 (UPPER) HAMMOND—HARWOOD HOUSE.
1584 (CENTRE) MRS. JOHN S. GIBBS, JR. 1585 (CENTRE) MRS. P. H. MILLER. 1588 (LOWER) MRS. E. N. DUNHAM. 1586 (CENTRE) ANONYMOUS.
1587 (LOWER) ANONYMOUS. 1589 (LOWER) MRS. E. N. DUNHAM.

1590 (UPPER) MR. W. W. LANAHAN. 1591 (UPPER) MRS. J. S. GIBBS, JR. 1592 (UPPER) MISS H. H. CAREY.
1593 (LOWER) HAMMOND–HARWOOD 1594 (LOWER) MR. B. RANDALL. 1595 (LOWER) MRS. F. G. BOYCE, JR.
    HOUSE.

No. 1587 is a finely decorated mahogany table in about the same form as No. 1585. The edges of the top are reeded, and the columns over the reeded legs are carved, probably by Samuel McIntire,[3] with pineapples and leaves. One of the two drawers is for writing and underneath is the pull–out frame to which the bag is attached. About 1800–1810.

In No. 1588 the twist of the legs is a change from the Sheraton to the Empire style. The other parts of the sewing table, however, with the drawers, slide and wooden knobs, follow the designs of preceding pieces in the Sheraton style. About 1815–1825.

No. 1589 more fully shows the Empire style. The fronts of the three drawers are rounded, the supporting columns are round and plain, the platform with concave sides is large and heavy and the feet are in the shape of scrolls; some of these features resemble those in Nos. 1579 and 1580. The feet are not connected with legs, but are reeded as though their reeding were a continuation of reeding on legs, a method seen in Nos. 1422 and 1574. About 1820–1840.

Nos. 1590–1592 are three unusual sewing tables on which there are bags. In the first two of these tables the upper portion rests upon a form of "curule"[4] support, and in the third the support is of a somewhat similar character. They are in the late Sheraton or early Empire style, and are of about the same date.

In No. 1590 the two drawers are bordered on the edges with maple, as is also the slide below, to which the silk bag is attached. The supports have a short pedestal which rests upon a small platform to which concave legs are attached. These legs are plain and terminate in brass animals' claw feet. About 1810–1820.

In No. 1591 the top opens from the rear and has a raised panel in the centre in about the same form as on the drawers of No. 1577. Small round columns are at the four corners, as in No. 1578. The concave pedestal rests upon a heavy platform with concave sides as in Nos. 1577–1580 and others. The feet are reeded. About 1810–1820.

In No. 1592, which is shown on a more reduced scale, the upper portion is square and when the top is open, as here, it is held in position by a metal support. The bag and box are within four curved arms which rest upon a small round platform which is supported by a short, reeded and gilded pedestal. The lower platform is triangular and under it the brass feet are attached. About 1810–1820.

No. 1593 resembles a sewing table from which a bag has been removed. The top is in the shape of a Martha Washington table, but is not as deep as others of

3.   The fine carving on this sewing table is now regarded as being the work of Samuel McIntire of Salem, Massachusetts. Careful investigation has shown that McIntire was not a cabinet maker, but that he was a skillful carver in addition to being an architect. The subject is more fully mentioned in section 72, notes 5 and 6. See also "Antiques", December, 1933, page 218.

4.   As to the "curule" form see the comment on chair No. 490 and see also the Index under "Curule".

A sewing table of this type is illustrated in an advertisement of Beach and Loveland, cabinet makers, on August 22, 1820, in a newspaper of Northampton, Mass.; and two somewhat similar tables are shown in Mr. Wallace Nutting's "Furniture Treasury", Nos. 1009 and 1187.

that type shown in Nos. 1557–1565, having only two shallow drawers, with small boxes at the ends. The long and slender legs are very delicately reeded in the Sheraton style. About 1800–1810.

No. 1594 is an unusual sewing table having a round top with a raised rim, as on the tripod tray–top tables Nos. 1339, 1350 and others. Under the top is a round box with a drawer. The pedestal is long and plain, and rests upon three legs in the form of cyma curves, as to which see section 23. The feet are somewhat in the shape of those on Nos. 1553 and 1684. About 1815–1825.

No. 1595 is presented here in order to show the slide to which the bag and box of many of these sewing tables were attached. Here the slide, without the bag and box, is pulled out a short distance. If the slide were not seen, it might be difficult to decide from the photograph whether this table is a sewing table or merely a small table or stand. This piece is in the Hepplewhite style and has cross–stretchers with a small shelf in the centre as in No. 1582. About 1790–1800.

Section 173. Other small tables.—In this section are illustrations of twenty–seven small tables, some of which may apparently be called either "tables" or "stands". These words in connection with furniture appear to have almost the same meaning in some cases; thus the terms "sewing table" and "sewing stand" seem to be equally appropriate.[1] On the other hand, the word "candle–stand", not "candle–table", is used when speaking of a small table made to hold a candle-stick. According to the dictionaries a "stand" is a small table, and the word "table" thus includes the small table called a "stand".[2] Whether certain of the small tables shown in this section should be called "tables" or "stands" may be a question of individual choice, and not worthy of debate; but it is clear that the small tables shown in section 175 should be called "stands".

Another question is whether some of the small tables are "sewing tables" or merely "tables". In some cases the interior fittings or other evidence, not visible in the illustrations, may show that a table was made as a sewing table; and even

1.   As mentioned in section 153, note 1, the word "table" in the Century Dictionary is defined as "an article of furniture consisting of a flat top (the table proper) of wood, stone or other solid material, resting on legs or on a pillar; . . as a dining–table, writing–table, work–table", etc. A stand is defined as "a table, set of shelves or the like, upon which articles may be placed . . specifically, a small light table, such as is moved easily from place to place."

Mr. Lockwood, in his "Colonial Furniture", applies the word "stand" to small tables made to hold candlesticks and to one small oval table like No. 1599.

Mr. Cornelius, in his "Masterpieces of Duncan Phyfe" does not use the words "sewing table", preferring "sewing stand".

Mr. Nutting, in his "Furniture Treasury", at No. 1214, remarks: "The reader will be lenient with us in the matter of classification (of certain tables and stands). . . The greatest difficulty seems to occur with stands. . . The division must . . be arbitrarily made."

2.   In "The Dictionary of English Furniture" by Macquoid and Edwards, volume 3, page 140, it is said that "the term 'stand', used in a very comprehensive sense, implies almost any kind of support, either forming a distinct object, as a candle stand, or in connection with another piece of furniture, as a stand for a cabinet. . . The many purposes to which they could be applied preclude an exhaustive classification."

if a table was not made as a sewing table, it may have acquired that name from long usage as such a table. Judging from their appearance, however, almost all of the small tables shown in this section may be regarded merely as small tables suitable for any domestic purposes. If intended to be seen on all sides, a table is always finished on all sides.

These tables are arranged in the Hepplewhite, Sheraton and Empire styles; they are generally of mahogany or maple; and their dates range from about 1790 to 1840.

Nos. 1596–1604 form a group of nine small tables in the Hepplewhite style. As in other tables in that style, the legs are square and tapering, in some cases slightly curved at the lower end. Some of these tables may have been made as sewing tables. Only brief comments are made, as the general features are familiar to the reader who has examined other tables in the Hepplewhite style.

No. 1596 has a rectangular top whose edges are lined with inlay. The single drawer is banded with inlay, as also is the bottom of the skirt. The slender legs are inlaid with the usual lines and strings of flowers and near the lower ends are inlaid bands. About 1790–1810.

No. 1597 is unusual in having three drawers with inlaid edges, on each side of which is a long inlaid panel. The tapering of the legs is on the inside as usual. About 1790–1810.

No. 1598 is an oval table with a top which lifts up from the rear as in the next table and in the oval sewing table No. 1557. The two wide drawers are bordered with inlay, and similar inlaid decorations are on the sides and back. The four legs are inlaid on more than one side. About 1790–1810.

No. 1599 also is oval and is shown with the top partly raised. The skirt is ornamented with parallel lines of inlay with rounded ends, a design which is seen also in No. 1492 and is referred to more fully in section 127, note 6, and in section 96, note 1, C. The legs are slender and graceful and over them are inlaid satinwood panels. About 1790–1800.

No. 1600 is decorated with an inlaid border on the skirt. The legs are slightly curved at the lower end as in one of Hepplewhite's designs and as in the sewing table No. 1582. The crossed stretchers form a small shelf. About 1790–1810.

No. 1601 is a different form of table. The top is provided with two small drop–leaves which, when open, are supported by brackets, and form serpentine curves on all sides, with rounded corners, as is also seen in the Pembroke table No. 1406. There is one drawer and below is a shelf with a rim which is cut in a series of curves or scallops. There is no inlay on this table. See also No. 1610. About 1790–1810.

No. 1602 has a rectangular top with edges lined with inlay, as is also the edge of the skirt. The legs are ornamented with the usual inlay. The crossed stretchers are of the type called "domed" because of the dome–like shape, as in Nos. 1432 and 1462. About 1790–1810.

1596 (UPPER) MR. & MRS. R. ROBIN-
SON.
1599 (CENTRE) MR. A. E. COLE.
1602 (LOWER) MR. & MRS. J. CAREY,
JR.

1597 (UPPER) MR. J. S. MCDANIEL.
1600 (CENTRE) MR. B. RANDALL.
1603 (LOWER) MRS. MILES WHITE,
JR.

1598 (UPPER) MR. & MRS. B. TURN-
BULL.
1601 (CENTRE) MRS. M. WHITE, JR.
1604 (LOWER) MR. A. G. TOWERS.

In No. 1603 the top and the drawers are recessed in concave curves, as in the Hepplewhite style card table No. 1514. The two drawers have oval handles of the period. As in No. 1601 there is no inlay. The height is about twenty–four inches. About 1790–1810.

No. 1604 is a rectangular table, plain in shape but pleasing in appearance and unusual in having inlay on curly maple. Small panels of darker wood are inlaid on the upper portions of the legs, and below these panels are lines of inlay with an inlaid flower suspended in the centre. About 1790–1810.

The next group of small tables, Nos. 1605–1613, are in the Sheraton style, as appears from the round and tapered legs, some of which are reeded, and the "turned" feet. Several of these tables, as in the previous group in the Hepplewhite style, may perhaps be regarded as sewing tables.

No. 1605 is of curly maple. The corners are cut out and the projecting columns above the legs are inserted in the recess. The round and tapered legs end in small ball feet. In the centre of the drawer is a panel of darker wood. About 1800–1820.

No. 1606 is of curly maple and mahogany. Above and on the sides of the two drawers are panels of the lighter wood; the legs below are of mahogany. The oval handles will also be noticed. About 1800–1820.

No. 1607, also chiefly of maple, differs from the preceding table in having the legs of the light wood and the panels above of dark wood. The two drawers have glass knobs. About 1800–1820.

In No. 1608 the front resembles the central portion of the "Martha Washington" sewing table No. 1559, having two wide drawers above two small square ones, with a small arch in the centre. Two drop–leaves are on the sides. The knob on the upper drawer is missing. The round and tapering legs, and the panels above, are reeded. The feet are larger at the lower end than above, a form occasionally seen, resembling a vase as also in No. 1620 and in the corner chairs Nos. 429 and 435. About 1800–1820.

No. 1609 is a plain table, distinctly in the Sheraton style as shown by the round legs, here not so gracefully tapering as in some other cases, but ending in small round feet. About 1800–1820.

No. 1610 has the characteristic projecting legs of the Sheraton style, with rings on the upper portion, as in No. 1521 and others, but without reeding. The tapering begins below the shelf, which has a raised rim cut in curves, or scalloped, as in the Hepplewhite style table No. 1601 which has also drop leaves. The two drawers have finely grained and "matched"[3] mahogany veneer, with brass ring handles. About 1800–1820.

No. 1611 is a table with drop leaves. The edges of the top and the leaves are reeded, as are also the tapering legs, and the two drawers have glass knobs. About 1800–1820.

3.   This method is explained in section 32, note 2.

1605 (Upper) Hammond–Harwood House. **1606** (Upper) Rev. & Mrs. A. C. Powell. **1607** (Upper) Mr. & Mrs. W. A. Dixon.
1608 (Centre) Miss H. R. Chew. **1609** (Centre) Mr. & Mrs. W. A. Dixon. **1610** (Centre) Miss E. S. Cohen.
1611 (Lower) Miss E. S. Cohen. **1612** (Lower) Mr. & Mrs. R. L. Cary. **1613** (Lower) Mrs. J. V. Wagner.

In No. 1612 the top is bowed, or swelled, following the form of the two drawers, resembling the front of a bureau. The edges of the top are reeded, and also the legs. About 1800–1820.

In No. 1613 we again see the legs projecting beyond the corners of the frame of the table, and finely reeded above and below. The legs do not extend above the top, but in the tables Nos. 1615–1617 they seem to extend slightly above perhaps by an applied ornament. About 1800–1820.

The next seven tables, Nos. 1614–1620, resemble in general form the Sheraton style tables here shown and might be regarded as being in the late Sheraton style; but they also exhibit certain features of the still later Empire style and therefore should be called by that name, for the reason mentioned in section 6 at note 4. These features are chiefly seen in the legs, leaves, spiral twists, rings or other forms, all of which compare somewhat unfavorably with the previous features in elegance of carving and design. Nos. 1621 and 1622 are in the early Victorian style for the reasons mentioned in the comments.

In No. 1614 the legs are carved with large acanthus leaves and above them are other leaves carved somewhat coarsely. The two large drawers are fitted with glass knobs. About 1810–1825.

In No. 1615 the corners are cut out and the projecting legs are placed in the recess and extend slightly above the top, as also in the next two tables. The legs have thick rings above and a large spiral form below. The fronts of the two drawers are of finely grained and "matched" mahogany veneer, as in No. 1610. The handles are of later date. About 1815–1825.

No. 1616 is a similar table in which the legs have become heavy and ungraceful and the carving is not delicate. The feet may have been partly cut off. The front of the drawers is finely veneered and "matched" and the legs extend above the top, as in the preceding table. About 1815–1830.

No. 1617 presents a different form of ornamentation of the legs, consisting of turnings of spools, rings and vases, with ball feet. The rings have the appearance of horizontal reedings. The drawers are veneered with curly maple and have wooden knobs. About 1815–1830.

No. 1618 has three drawers with finely veneered fronts and large glass knobs. The legs are elaborately turned with more than twenty rings in the central portion. A plain shelf is supported on square blocks. About 1815–1830.

In No. 1619 the legs are carved in a design which is suggestive of a pineapple, the emblem of hospitality. The shelf is cut in a double cyma curve. The upper portion, like that in the preceding table, is in a plain design. About 1815–1830.

In No. 1620 there is an upper rounded drawer as in the Empire style sewing table No. 1579 and others; the entire front of this top drawer is of curly maple, making a very strong contrast with the mahogany. On the legs are carved square blocks of the type seen on the bed–post No. 1070. Below these blocks are large carved acanthus leaves. The feet are in the form seen in No. 1608. About 1825–1835.

1614 (UPPER) MRS. M. F. RODGERS.   1615 (UPPER) MR. M. WHITRIDGE.   1616 (UPPER) MRS. E. N. DUNHAM.
1617 (CENTRE) MRS. E. N. DUN-   1618 (CENTRE) MRS. JOS. WHYTE.   1619 (CENTRE) MRS. F. G. BOYCE,
    HAM.   1621 (LOWER) MISS H. H. CAREY.   JR.
1620 (LOWER) MRS. C. E. HENDER-   1622 (LOWER) MR. & MRS. J. CAREY,
    SON.   JR.

Nos. 1621 and 1622, although having legs with the Empire style turnings called "spool" or "ring", are regarded as of the Victorian era because of the moldings around the drawers. It is said that moldings of this type, resembling somewhat those on the table No. 1632, were made by a machine which was invented after 1840. A marble top is on No. 1622. About 1840–1860.

Section 174. Miscellaneous tables.—In this last section on tables are illustrations of several types which differ in form and purpose from those seen in the preceding sections.

In the first group are three nests of tables, Nos. 1623–1625. This type of tables may have been originated by Sheraton, who published a design of them in his "Drawing Book", as to which see section 18, and who called them "quartetto" tables because they were made in nests of four. They are small and light, are made in different sizes in order that the smaller ones may be enclosed within the largest, require but little room and are easily separated. They were used mainly as tea or coffee tables.

No. 1623 is shown with a front view. Each table has a stretcher which is concave when seen from the front. These tables are lacquered and are ornamented on the ends and the front with floral and other designs. The top is supported by standards in the form of lyres without strings, which rest upon an arched base with concave legs and claw feet. Perhaps about 1820–1830.

No. 1624 is a very similar table, shown from the side in order to have a clear view of the pleasing decorations. The form of the standards is seen here to better advantage than in the preceding illustration. The lacquer and the style of decoration suggest that these two nests of tables were made in China or at least in the Chinese manner. Perhaps about 1820–1830.

No. 1625 is a plainer nest of tables with slender legs supporting the top. In the illustration some of the legs are so close together in the line of vision that they are not seen as separate legs. Three of the stretchers are missing. In England legs of this type are called "spindle legs" or "spider legs", which are referred to in note 1, C, in section 155. About 1800–1810.

Nos. 1626–1628 are three "drum" tables which have acquired their name from the resemblance of the form of their upper portions to the form of a drum. They were popular in England at about the beginning of the nineteenth century, and most of those found here are of English origin. The distinctive features are the single pedestal, the round upper portion, which in some cases revolved, and the skirt of sufficient depth to contain one or two rows of drawers. Because of the round form of the upper portion the drawers could not be of the usual rectangular shape. Parts of the skirt were often paneled to imitate drawers and were furnished with handles, making "sham" drawers, a term which is referred to in the comment on the Pembroke table No. 1409. The wood was mahogany in almost all cases.

No. 1626, in the Sheraton style, has a revolving top with drawers which are lined with mahogany and maple. The pedestal is carved in a so–called pineapple

1623 (UPPER) MISS H. H. CAREY.   1624 (UPPER) MRS. J. S. GIBBS, JR.   1625 (UPPER) DR. H. M. FITZHUGH.
1626 (LOWER) ANONYMOUS.   1627 (LOWER) COL. MRS. J. STABLER.   1628 (LOWER) MRS. R. W. PETRE.

pattern and the four concave legs are reeded, and terminate in brass claw feet. The diameter of this table is about twenty–four inches and the height about thirty–one inches. About 1810–1820.

No. 1627 has a deeper skirt containing two drawers, one above the other. The pedestal is vase–shaped and reeded, and carved on the base. The legs are carved on the upper portion and reeded below, and terminate in animals' claw feet. The lower portion resembles that of the Sheraton style sewing table No. 1573 and others. About 1810–1820.

No. 1628 may be regarded as being in the Empire style as is shown by the form of the legs and the carving, which is of a somewhat coarse character. This table may be compared with the French Empire style table No. 1656. On each side of the drawer in the centre is a "sham" drawer. The legs and feet may be compared with those on the sewing table No. 1576 and others. About 1820–1830.

Nos. 1629–1633 are oval tables which were meant to stand in the centre of a room, but apparently not for any special purpose. The first three and the fifth are in the Hepplewhite style, are graceful in form and pleasing in decoration, and although similar in appearance are all worthy of examination. The wood is mahogany.

No. 1629 is the largest in size and has more than the usual overhang at the ends. The skirt is inlaid with rectangular forms and with small panels over the legs which have the usual lines of inlay, strings of flowers, and bands near the lower ends. Lines of inlay are also on the edges of the top and on the bottom of the skirt. About 1790–1800.

No. 1630 is a very small table and is similar in form to the small table No. 1599, in which latter, however, the top opens from the rear, whereas in this table the top does not open and there is a drawer. The inlay here is on the skirt and the legs. About 1790–1800.

No. 1631 is less in size than No. 1629, but is not a small table, being forty–seven inches long and thirty–three inches wide. The inlay on the skirt consists of lines on the base and oval panels over the legs, and on the legs are the usual lines and flowers. About 1790–1800.

No. 1632 is a small oval table, far removed in style and date from the preceding three pieces in the period of Hepplewhite. Here the Victorian style, as to which see section 22, is seen in the moldings around the edge of the top and the skirt, somewhat similar to the moldings on the small table No. 1621; and also the style is seen in the "trestle" form of the feet. About 1840–1850.

No. 1633, in the Hepplewhite style, approaches a circular form, the length of the table being less in proportion to the width than in Nos. 1629 and 1631. The inlaid ornamentation on the legs resembles somewhat that on the two preceding tables. About 1790–1800.

In No. 1634 the top is six–sided as in the sewing tables Nos. 1583 and 1584. The pedestal is triangular and concave, as is also the too small tripod base which

1629 (Upper) Rev. & Mrs. A. C. Powell.
1631 (Centre) Bishop Edward T. Helfenstein.
1633 (Lower) Dr. Henry J. Berkley.

1630 (Upper) Estate of Mrs. J. H. Whiteley.
1632 (Centre) Miss Mary S. Schenck.
1634 (Lower) Mr. Herbert T. Tiffany.

in part resembles that in the sewing table No. 1565. The paintings on the skirt and the base will be noticed. This table seems to have indications of both the Empire and the Victorian styles, but may be French. About 1840–1850.

The next group, Nos. 1635–1637, is known as "architects'" tables or "drawing" tables, the former name being preferable. Architects' tables were made in the styles of Chippendale, Hepplewhite and Sheraton. They are fitted with various devices, such as an adjustable and hinged top which may be raised and sloped, and with compartments for drawing implements and materials used by architects. The wood of these tables is mahogany.

No. 1635 is an English architects' table and is in the Chippendale style, as is shown by the plain square legs, the brackets at the junctions of the legs and the skirt, and the fretwork of the skirt. The top may be raised to any angle desired or may be laid flat on the frame. About 1760–1780.

No. 1636 is in the Hepplewhite style, as is indicated by the tapering of the straight and square legs. Here also the top is attached to a movable frame in such a manner that it may be held at any angle. The leaves are in a serpentine form and are supported by brackets, giving to this table, when the top also is flat, the appearance of a Pembroke table such as those in section 163. This table was probably made in the West Indies. About 1785–1800.

No. 1637 is in the Sheraton style, as is shown by the round, reeded and tapering legs, of which there are five. The top, here in a vertical position, may be folded back upon the fifth leg, which is the inner one of the two close together in the rear right. The sloping board, covered with baize, may be adjusted as desired. About 1800–1810.

Nos. 1638–1640 should perhaps have appeared in section 164 with the library tables, but they differ from the latter in having one large top without drop leaves or drawers. In these tables there are devices under the top by which the latter may be easily removed or tilted to an upright position, as otherwise the large tops would prevent their passage through a door of the usual size. These tables are not often seen. They are in the Sheraton style, are made of mahogany and are of about the same date.

No. 1638 has a plain round pedestal, supported by concave legs which are carved with acanthus leaves on the upper portion and are reeded below, terminating in brass feet and casters. About 1800–1820.

In No. 1639 the edge of the top is reeded, and two of the sides are in a serpentine form, the other two sides being straight with rounded corners. The vase–shaped pedestal and the curved legs are reeded. The form of the legs is much the same as that in the small tripod tables Nos. 1354–1356. This table is of South Carolina origin. About 1800–1820.

No. 1640 is a larger table, fifty–five inches in length and forty inches in width. Four spiral and carved columns support the top and rest upon a platform below, as in the dining tables Nos. 1324–1326. The concave legs are reeded and end in brass feet and casters. About 1800–1820.

1635 (Upper) Mr. & Mrs. Henry L. Duer.
1636 (Upper) Mr. Austin McLanahan.
1637 (Centre) Anonymous.
1638 (Centre) Mr. C. Edward Snyder.
1639 (Lower) Mr. Benjamin H. Read.
1640 (Lower) Mr. Edgar G. Miller, Jr.

Nos. 1641–1646 form a group which is truly "miscellaneous", each table being of a different type from the others in the group and in most cases different from any others illustrated in this chapter.

No. 1641, at first sight, resembles a corner table such as those shown in section 167; but it is evident that it would not fit in a corner because the back is straight. The semi–circular folding lid turns back and in that position, making a round table, is supported by one of the rear legs which swings out. If the fixed top be lifted a compartment within the skirt is seen, furnished with a lock. The legs are round and almost straight, ending in Dutch, or club, feet and shoes, resembling the legs in the table No. 1308 and others. The upper ends of the legs continue round to the top. About 1740–1760.

No. 1642 also at first glance resembles a corner table, but the rear line of the top is straight and could not be placed in a corner. It is in reality a card table in which the folding top may be folded back, making the table square. The particular feature is that the central rear leg, which supports the folding top when it is open, does not swing out, but pulls out from the back like a desk pull which is pulled out to support the lid. This method is referred to in section 169, note 1, C. About 1800–1810.

No. 1643 is a well–known table belonging to the Metropolitan Museum of Art. It is called a "mixing" table because the two compartments with knobs are for bottles and the flat surface under the curved tambour top is of marble. This covered table is generally shown with the tambour top up in order to show the table open, but here the tambour top is down, because the chief interest is in the design as a whole. The elegant satinwood inlay on the tapering legs resembles the inlay on the Baltimore card tables Nos. 1487–1490. This table is in the Hepplewhite style, with some features suggesting the Sheraton style especially the ornamental features. About 1800–1810.

It is said that No. 1644, also the property of the same Museum, was made by Duncan Phyfe and called a "library" table. In England it would be called a "Canterbury" table, meaning a small table with drawer and shelves. It is referred to in section 164 on library tables, note 1. The upper portion has a large drawer, with lion–and–ring handles, and is supported at each end by two carved columns which rest upon trestle feet similar in form to those in the sofa table No. 1424 and others. The two shelves have reeded edges. About 1800–1810.

No. 1645 is called a "book" table because when both drop–leaves are down it is in the shape of a book with a narrow back above and leaves below. The two large drop–leaves are attached to a round horizontal piece about four inches in diameter which is the only "top" of the table when the leaves are down. Under each leaf are two swinging brackets which support the leaf when raised. A solid pedestal in a lyre form supports the upper portion and rests upon a platform with four short legs. The Empire style will be recognized in the pedestal, the carving and the legs. About 1825–1835.

No. 1646 is a table in the late Empire style. The large curved drawer is finely veneered and the corners of the skirt are rounded as in the bureau No. 768

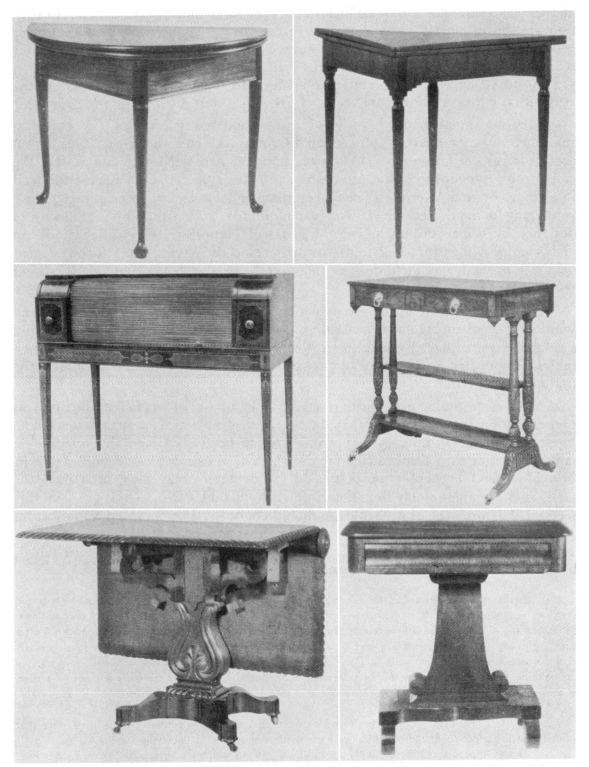

1641 (Upper) Mr. & Mrs. Richard L. Cary.   **1642** (Upper) Mr. & Mrs. Edward H. McKeon.
1643 (Centre) Metropolitan Museum of Art.   **1644** (Centre) Metropolitan Museum of Art.
1645 (Lower) Mrs. J. P. Pleasants.   **1646** (Lower) Mr. H. Oliver Thompson.

and the bookcase No. 875. The pedestal is very large and heavy. In this illustration are shown clearly two cylindrical forms, reeded at the ends, near the lower end of the pedestal, which are of the same character as those shown on a smaller scale on the card tables Nos. 1542 and 1552. The feet are of the trestle type as on the music stand No. 1675, and similar feet are shown in section 199 in the Appendix, entitled "Furniture styles of 1840". About 1830–1840.

Mention should be made of "pier tables"[1] and "console tables". As stated in reference to "pier mirrors", in section 139, near the end, the word "pier" is an architectural one meaning a wall space between two windows; and it was the fashion throughout the eighteenth century to place a "pier table" against the wall in a "pier", with a "pier glass" behind it, the pier table and the pier glass together producing a handsome effect. Large and highly ornamental pier tables were designed by Robert Adam, and in the books of Hepplewhite[2] and Sheraton[3] are elaborate drawings for these tables in their respective styles, often to be painted on the top. Some of these designs show semi–circular tables and others almost rectangular ones.

In our country the use of pier tables and pier mirrors in combination between windows was of course not as general as in England;[4] but in many cases, no doubt, side tables were placed under mirrors and were called "pier tables"; but such tables do not often appear to be of any special elegance nor made particularly for use under a mirror.

Many side tables have been referred to in books and magazine articles as pier tables on the supposition that they were made or used as such tables. The finest American example now known is said to be the Philadelphia–made side table known as the "Cadwalader table" which is illustrated as a "side" table in No. 1430; and perhaps some of the other side tables may have been made or used as pier tables, including the Empire style tables Nos. 1651–1653 in this section. The presence of a marble top should not of itself be regarded as indicating a pier table, because a marble top was often used, for example, on serving tables, as in Nos. 1441 and 1442. The English pier tables were taller than card tables, being about thirty–eight inches in height.

1. A pier table is defined in the Century Dictionary as "an ornamental table intended to stand between two windows. . . It is often combined with a pier–glass and the glass is sometimes carried down below the top of the table and between its uprights." Mr. Cescinsky in "English and American Furniture", glossary, page 295, defines a pier glass as "a wall mirror hanging between windows, usually above a semi–circular or pier table." These mirrors were often very tall and extended below the top of the table, in which case the top of the table was reflected in the mirror. If the table was semi–circular, it and its reflection produced the appearance of a round table. See the comment on the card table No. 1504.

2. In Hepplewhite's "Guide", (as to which see section 17), third edition, page 12, it is said that "pier tables are made to fit the pier and rise level with or above the dado of the room."

3. In the Appendix to Sheraton's "Drawing Book", (as to which see section 18), plate 4, page 371, it is said "as pier tables are merely for ornament under a glass, they are generally made very light, and the style of finishing them is rich and elegant. Sometimes the tops are solid marble, but most commonly veneered in rich satinwood."

4. In Mr. Lockwood's "Colonial Furniture", volume 2, a marble top table is illustrated, page 224, which resembles to some extent the table mentioned in the text above, and it is said that "a few specimens are found in this country".

In connection with pier tables, reference should be made to console tables, two of which, Nos. 1647 and 1648, are copied from English authorities. These console tables are of a very different type from pier tables, but the two terms, "pier tables" and "console tables", are sometimes used as synonymous in our country, and the term "console table" is thus applied to tables which have no resemblance to the console type. The word "console" is French and means a "bracket", and a console table is called by that name because it is constructed, and fixed against a wall, like a bracket. In the definitions in the note[5] it appears that a console table is one which has legs in front only and is made stable by being fixed against a wall.

No. 1649 is a Victorian drop–leaf table which follows in some respects the mechanism of the gate–leg table No. 1291 and others. Here each of the two side leaves when in use is supported by a straight swinging bracket which is connected with a curved and swinging bracket below. An upright bar with a spool turning connects the upper and the lower bracket. The two supports at the ends of the table are on curved trestle feet and are cut in fanciful designs. The casters are of white china. A somewhat similar table is illustrated and discussed in "Antiques", October, 1931, page 248. About 1850–1860.

No. 1650 is out of place. The door is partly open so that the stand may be better understood. When the front is closed it appears to be a cabinet with four drawers, but when opened it is seen to be a stand with shelves, a form of "shamming" mentioned in connection with the Pembroke table No. 1409. The fine round drop handles on the front and the handles on the sides will be noticed. The feet are in

---

5. In the Century Dictionary the term "console table" is defined as "a table which, instead of straight or nearly straight legs, has consoles or legs so curved as to resemble them, and is therefore usually set against the wall from which it appears to project as a sort of bracket." Mr. Cescinsky in "English and American Furniture", page 196, refers to tables of "the console type where the framing of the top is supported on front legs only, being secured at the back" to a wall. The same meaning is given in Macquoid and Edwards' "Dictionary of English Furniture", volume 3, page 254, in the Encyclopædia Britannica and in Murray's Dictionary.

The reader may have noticed a tendency in this book to be over–particular in regard to the exact meaning of various words; but the writer thinks that this caution may be helpful in avoiding confusion of thought and a misunderstanding of the subject. For example, we should surely know the exact difference between a "pier table" and a "console table", as established by the authorities on the English language. Calling a semi–circular table with four legs a "console table", as is often done, is obviously erroneous, although it may be a common usage.

An article entitled "English Eagle and Dolphin Console Tables", by Mr. R. W. Symonds, a prominent English writer, is in "Antiques", October, 1930, pages 304–307. The six illustrations are of a form of console tables in which the table supports, instead of being two front legs, are the two wings of an eagle or the tails of two dolphins. These are dated about 1725–1750. Dolphins are also seen on the later Empire style card table No. 1556, and on the girandole mirror No. 1242. At various times dolphins have been popular ornamental features. The early English lantern clocks Nos. 1745 and 1747 have dolphins; see section 185, note 9.

In the same magazine, November, 1931, pages 272–273, are illustrations of three other eagle tables, with editorial comment to the effect that these eagles were probably made for other purposes than to support the tops of tables; that the tops are later additions; and that it is very difficult to determine whether the eagles were made in America, England or Continental Europe. See also the same magazine, May, 1936, page 191.

1647 (Upper) Anonymous.
1649 (Lower) Mr. Edgar G. Miller, Jr.

1648 (Upper) Anonymous.
1650 (Lower) Miss Margaret L. Myers.

1651 (UPPER) MISS HELEN H. CAREY.
1653 (CENTRE) MRS. ARTHUR HALE.
1655 (LOWER) MR. & MRS. CHARLES H. WYATT.

1652 (UPPER) MRS. W. D. STEUART.
1654 (CENTRE) MRS. WM. DEFORD.
1656 (LOWER) MISS MARY LEIGH BROWN.

the French bracket type which is seen on so many bureaus and desks in the Hepplewhite style. There is documentary evidence indicating that this piece was a gift from George Washington to an ancestor of the present owner. About 1785–1795.

The next three tables, Nos. 1651–1653, are in the French Empire style, which is shown by the rounded front of the skirt, the round columns serving as legs, the heavy shelves, and the large animals' brass or gilded claw feet—the latter being the only objectionable feature of these dignified and well proportioned pieces. These tables are side tables, made to stand against a wall,[6] either in a room or in a hallway, as are the side tables in section 166. The wood is mahogany.

No. 1651 is apparently the table on the right in the signed and dated Edouart silhouette of a family in section 200 in the Appendix. The Empire style is here seen in all parts of the table—the rounded skirt, the large round columns, the large claw feet and the somewhat coarse carving. About 1810–1830.

No. 1652 is very similar to the preceding table, except that it has a heavy recessed platform or shelf and a marble top. In the Empire period many tables were made with marble tops and their presence does not indicate that the table was made as a serving table or as a pier table. The columns taper upwards and terminate in scrolls with carved and gilded leaves. About 1810–1830.

In No. 1653, also with a marble top, the two rounded columns have brass caps on the upper ends and smaller ones on the base. A shelf, with brackets under the ends, is set back from the line of the front, and a mirror is at the rear in a wooden frame. About 1810–1830.

Nos. 1654–1656 are also French tables of a type which was popular in our country in the early part of the nineteenth century. These tables are made of fine mahogany. The first two are decorated with brass designs, and the third is painted on the top as well as on the lower portion.

No. 1654 is a round table with a top supported by four pairs of round columns which rest upon a heavy platform with concave sides. Each of the four feet is in the form of the Egyptian sphinx, a favorite design following the conquest of Egypt by Napoleon in 1798, an interesting feature of which is referred to in section 64, note 1. About 1810–1820.

No. 1655 is an elaborate table, in much the same general form as No. 1653. The upper portion is supported by two large white marble columns, with brass capitals, resting upon a concave platform, or shelf, under which are large brass decorations of scrolls and flowers. The feet, also, are of brass. In the rear is a large mirror with a small one on each side. About 1810–1820.

6. If a mirror were above the table, each table would probably be known as a "pier table", but this name would not be strictly appropriate unless the table was to be placed in a "pier" between two windows, as previously mentioned in the text. Nor can they be properly called "console tables", which have only two legs.

A table in the French Empire style, similar to No. 1653, made by a French cabinet maker in New York named Honoré Lannuier, is shown in "Antiques", June, 1933, page 224.

These tables were very popular in our country and many have been carefully kept.

In No. 1656 the round top is fully decorated with paintings, those in the centre being surrounded by a circle of flowers. On other parts, especially in the base, are several forms and designs which have been seen on other pieces, such as the card table No. 1553. The designs on these two tables include the favorite Grecian "anthemion", or honeysuckle, which appears on the centre of the base of the pedestal, and also the several forms resembling "corbels" which we have seen in illustration No. 1231. This table may be compared with No. 1628, a drum table. About 1810–1820.

Several other less important types of tables are mentioned in the note,[7] without illustrations.

Section 175. Stands.—In the first paragraph of section 173, it appears that it is difficult to determine whether certain articles should be called "tables" or "stands", and that according to the dictionaries a "stand" is a "small table"; but it is said that it was clear that the "small tables" shown in the present section should be called "stands". Tripod candle stands are treated separately in section 161 and several early stands or small tables are shown in section 154. The woods used in the stands here illustrated are of walnut, mahogany, cherry and perhaps others. The dates range from about 1785 to 1830.

No. 1657 is a stand in the Queen Anne style, with a square top, very slender cabriole legs and Dutch, or club, feet. There is no carving or other ornamentation on this stand. About 1750–1770.

No. 1658 is also in the Queen Anne style with the same type of legs and feet, but of heavier construction. The legs are carved on the knees. The drawer is furnished with a bail handle. About 1750–1770.

The most attractive stands are the "urn stands" in the style of Hepplewhite, of which six designs, dated 1787, are given in the 1794 edition of his book called the "Guide", as to which see section 17. Each of his designs has four square and tapering legs which are "raked", or "splayed", meaning "slanting outwards"; these give stability to the stands, as they do to the Windsor chairs shown in section 62; but there are no stretchers although they appear in American tables. Around the

7. A. Kidney tables. Quoting the words of Sheraton in his "Drawing Book", third edition, 1802, plate 58, page 310, "This piece is called a kidney table on account of its resemblance to that intestine part of animals so called." His drawing is for a curved table four feet in length and two feet in width. Kidney tables were not very popular in our country, but many of them were made in England and are illustrated in the English books. They were intended for use in the library as writing tables, having a tier of drawers on each side of a central open space where the writer sat.

B. Papier mâché tables. These were made in England and were popular in our country for some years until about 1860. Many were highly decorated with painted flowers and with mother-of-pearl. The form of the table was often oval and in the style of the period. A chair-back made with this material is No. 493. An illustrated article on the subject is in "Antiques", March, 1929, pages 205–208. See also the next to the last paragraph in section 44.

C. Reading tables. The flat top of a reading table could be raised and tilted to an angle convenient for reading. A design, dated 1792, of a combined reading and writing table is shown in Sheraton's "Drawing Book", third edition, 1802, plate 44. A reading table with a tilting top, designed by Thomas Jefferson, is at Monticello, and is illustrated in "Antiques", April, 1928, page 294.

top is a rim and there is also a little pull–out slide to hold a tea–pot or coffee–pot. On the top was placed one of the large silver urns with boiling water which were at that time almost always a part of the tea service. These designs were not always copied exactly by our cabinet makers, but were followed in their general form. Urn stands were also used in the time of Chippendale, but in the "Drawing Book" of Sheraton, which is mentioned in section 18, they do not appear.

No. 1659 is an example of an urn stand in the Hepplewhite style and is almost exactly like one shown in Hepplewhite's book. The top is round, with a low raised rim, under which is the skirt in a serpentine curve and a slide which is here pulled out a few inches. The very slender inlaid legs are raked, or splayed, and are connected by cross–stretchers. About 1790–1800.

No. 1660 is similar to the preceding urn stand, differing mainly in having a higher rim and in not having stretchers. Lines of inlay are on the legs and within these lines are wide inlays of light wood which bring to mind the similar treatment of the legs of the Hepplewhite style card tables made in Baltimore, Nos. 1487–1490 in section 170. About 1790–1800.

No. 1661 is not an urn stand in the style of the two preceding pieces, as it does not follow the Hepplewhite designs; it is, however, in the same general form except that the top is in a different shape, and there is no rim. The skirt is in concave curves which are edged with a light wood. Here, too, are cross–stretchers. About 1790–1800.

No. 1662, also, is not an urn stand. The octagonal top has a lid which opens from the rear as in several sewing stands, such as No. 1584 and others. At the top of the legs is a bracket on each side and at the lower ends the slender legs curve slightly outward as in the sewing table No. 1582 and the small table No. 1600. The height is about twenty–seven inches. About 1790–1800.

In No. 1663 the top is in the form seen in the "Martha Washington" sewing tables Nos. 1557–1566. A line of inlay is on the edge of the top, and the lower edge of the skirt is bordered with a band of inlay. The square legs are slightly curved at the lower ends as in the preceding piece. About 1790–1800.

In No. 1664 the slightly tapering square legs are fluted, an ornamental treatment much used by Robert Adam and sometimes adopted by the cabinet makers working in the style of Hepplewhite. This stand is about twenty–four inches high. About 1785–1800.

No. 1665, in the Hepplewhite style, is a stand to the top of which a cabinet is attached. The front of the cabinet opens forward, on hinges, from the bottom and rests upon the two pulls whose knobs are seen. The lines of inlay on the cabinet and on the skirt of the stand, and the inlaid strings of flowers on the legs, are seen in the engraving. Somewhat similar stands with a bottle cabinet above, but not attached, have been found. Here the cabinet is fitted with shallow drawers, perhaps for a coin collection. About 1790–1800.

Nos. 1666–1668 are plain stands with square, tapering and splayed legs which may perhaps place them in the Hepplewhite style, although they have no other features which are distinctively in that style.

1657 (Upper) Mr. & Mrs. E. H. McKeon.
1658 (Upper) Dr. Jas. Bordley, Jr.
1659 (Upper) Mr. & Mrs. J. M. Matthews.
1660 (Centre) Est. of Mrs. Whiteley.
1661 (Centre) Mrs. J. S. Gibbs, Jr.
1662 (Centre) Mrs. Miles White, Jr.
1663 (Lower) Mrs. Miles White, Jr.
1664 (Lower) Mrs. Miles White, Jr.
1665 (Lower) Mr. J. F. H. Maginn.

No. 1666 has a round top which considerably overhangs the frame of the stand. There is one drawer and the legs are of the typical style. About 1790–1810.

No. 1667 has a square top and the usual type of legs. The stretchers are often called "H stretchers" because of their resemblance to that letter in form when seen from the front or rear, as mentioned in section 26, note 4. About 1790–1810.

No. 1668 is a small stand with a rim which suggests that it was for the service of tea. With this protective rim and with the widely raked, or splayed, legs to hold the table steady, the safety of the china was almost assured. About 1790–1810.

Nos. 1669–1671 are unusual corner, or bed room, stands of pleasing appearance. Each stand is curved in front, and has straight sides which form an angle in the rear. A compartment in the nature of a cupboard is the principal receptacle, with one or more small drawers in two of the pieces. The corner table No. 1460 in section 167 may be compared with these stands in form. No. 1672 is another type of bed room stands, or tables.

In No. 1669, in which several features suggest the Adam style, we notice under the top the "anthemion", or honeysuckle, designs, and between them the favorite bell–flowers; we also see the fluting, instead of reeding, on the round legs. The tambour slide is more often seen in the Hepplewhite and Sheraton styles. There are three legs, the rear one in the corner being square and plain. This stand is probably of English make. About 1775–1790.

In No. 1670, in the Hepplewhite style, under the drawer in the centre, are two doors similar in shape and inlaid ornament to the doors on the Hepplewhite sideboard No. 963. There is a double cyma curve on the skirt and the legs are slightly curved at the lower end as in No. 1663 and others. This also was probably made in England. About 1785–1800.

No. 1671 is of the same general form as the preceding stand, except that there is an additional leg in the front. Under the central cupboard with the keyhole there is a drawer, and on each side of the drawer is a panel which resembles a drawer; two of the knobs are missing. About 1785–1800.

Not all of the next six illustrations are of tables or stands, strictly speaking, but are shown here because no other place was available. See also No. 1650.

No. 1672 is closely copied from a design dated 1787 in Hepplewhite's "Guide", where it is termed a "night table". The upper portion of the veneered front, with brass handles in the large inlaid oval, appears to be the front of a deep drawer, but in reality it is attached to the top by hinges and rises with the top when the latter is raised. The lower portion of the front is a compartment with two inlaid doors. The feet are of the French bracket type. About 1790–1800.

No. 1673, in the Hepplewhite style, is a stand for a candle or a vase with flowers or for other purposes. In part it resembles a washstand, such as No. 1724, without the folding tops. A bracket in the "C" form is in each of the eight corners formed by the legs and the skirt. A shelf and a drawer are in the centre, and below are crossed stretchers forming a shelf. About 1780–1800.

1666 (Upper) Mr. & Mrs. W. M.
ELLICOTT.
1669 (Lower) Mr. & Mrs. E. H.
McKeon.

1667 (Upper) Hammond–Harwood
House.
1670 (Lower) Mrs. T. J. Lindsay.

1668 (Upper) Mr. J. S. McDaniel.
1671 (Lower) Mr. Blanchard
Randall.

No. 1674 is a low music stand or rack with three divisions in which music books may be placed. The plan of this rack resembles that of the upper portion of the next piece, having narrow upright divisions. There is also a drawer on which there are ring handles. About 1810–1830.

No. 1675 is a music stand, in which the lyre is appropriately the conspicuous feature. The ends of the upper portion are lyres with strings, the ends of the lower portion are in a lyre shape, reversed, and the solid partitions between the five divisions for music books are in the lyre form. The drawer is for sheet music, and there is a shelf below. The feet are in a trestle form such as several in "Furniture styles of 1840" in section 199. About 1830–1840.

The word "dumb–waiter" is more familiar to us as meaning a small elevator running from one floor to another than as a stand for holding food, with two or three revolving trays or tops. As far back as 1767, in the time of Chippendale, they were made in our country.[1]

The usual form of the dumb–waiter is that of a tripod table with the pedestal extending up through the table and supporting two other smaller ones at convenient distances apart, all with tray–tops, or rims, to prevent the dishes from slipping off. At present the principal use is for the display of china, glass or other articles.

In No. 1676 the cabriole legs terminate in ball and claw feet, the balls apparently more closely approaching perfect spheres than any others in this volume, even such as No. 1290. The bulb over the legs is reeded, the three trays, or tops, are graduated in size, and a well carved pineapple, the emblem of hospitality, is at the top of the pedestal. About 1765–1795.

No. 1677 is an interesting so–called "wig stand" of the days when wigs were worn by almost all men of the upper classes, and not, as now, chiefly by judges and lawyers of England and elsewhere and by those who vainly seek to hide the vagaries of nature. The term "wig stand" is misleading, as the stand was not made to hold wigs, but was a basin stand placed in front of a mirror before which wigs

1.　In the Maryland Gazette, April 9, 1767, Gerrard Hopkins, of Baltimore, "cabinet and chair maker from Philadelphia", advertised that he "makes and sells candle stands, tea kettle stands, dumb–waiters, tea boards", etc.

In an article by Marie Kimball, entitled "Thomas Jefferson's French Furniture", in "Antiques", February, 1929, pages 123–128, it is said that according to John Trumbull, the painter, who was a guest of Jefferson in Paris in 1786, one dumb–waiter was "placed between each two guests at the table and the servants were dismissed for the remainder of that course"; and when Jefferson became president in 1801 he introduced the custom "at the White House where it caused no little comment". On page 126 is a sketch by Jefferson showing a dumb–waiter similar in form to No. 1676.

The dumb–waiter here shown is of course very different from the small waiters with revolving round shelves, now occasionally used in the centre of a table, which may be reached and turned by the sitters, making unnecessary the services of an attendant. This latter kind of dumb–waiter was perhaps referred to by Dickens in "Little Dorrit", published in 1855–1857, volume 1, chapter 16, where Mr. Meagles "gave a turn to the dumb–waiter on his right hand to twirl the sugar towards himself. . . Besides his dumb–waiter, Mr. Meagles had two other not dumb waiters, in the persons of two parlour–maids . . who were a highly ornamental part of the table decorations."

1672 (Upper) Mrs. Miles White,
    Jr.
1675 (Lower) Anonymous.

1673 (Upper) Mrs. John Stokes.
1676 (Lower) Mr. & Mrs. B. Turn-
    bull.

1674 (Upper) Mrs. F. T. Redwood.
1677 (Lower) Mrs. Miles White,
    Jr.

could be adjusted.[2] The round top is merely a hollow frame in which a small water basin was placed, and below is the lower part of a round powder box. Two small drawers are in the triangular space between the three upright columns and below is a platform with a sunken place for a small pitcher. From this it appears that the term "powdering stand" or "basin stand" is more descriptive of the piece than the term "wig stand". The three legs are in cyma curves and terminate in snake feet. About 1760–1780.

2. "The wearing of wigs and powder for men" went out of fashion about 1780. "George the Third was the recipient of a memorial from the wig makers of London, praying that he would lend his august patronage and example to the renewal of the fashion, and pleading that since gentlemen had taken to wearing their own hair the trade of the wig maker had declined to the point of ruin. Another petition, in derision of the first, was also presented to royalty, showing that the trade of the maker of artificial limbs was also in a moribund condition and beseeching that the King would lend his royal favor to the introduction of wooden legs in the court circle"; Cescinsky, "English Furniture", volume 3, pages 290, 293.

In volume 2, page 215, Mr. Cescinsky remarks that stands of this type are often regarded as washingstands "and our ancestors have been credited with performing their ablutions in a bowl but little larger than a tea cup." The powdering of the wig was "the office of the lacquey and was performed on a block, but writers of this period frequently refer to gentlemen, principally beaus of middle age and sober aspect, who wore their own hair and powder, and to these the small basin stands must have been a great convenience. With the change of fashion they are now generally used to hold potpourri bowls." A potpourri is "a mixture of the dried petals of rose leaves or other flowers with spices and perfumes"; Century Dictionary. See also the remarks of Mr. Cescinsky, quoted in note 2 of section 179, in connection with washstands.

CHAPTER XIX

POLE SCREENS; STOOLS; WARDROBES; WASHSTANDS

Section 176. Pole screens.—The two principal types of screens used as a protection from the heat of a fire were called, in the eighteenth century, "fire screens" (or "pole screens") and "horse fire screens".[1] With the latter we are not concerned, as they were seldom, if ever, made in our country; but many "fire screens" were produced by our cabinet makers, and as all of them were made with a pole to support the screen, they are commonly called "pole screens". The screen was attached to the pole in such a manner that it could be raised or lowered to any height desired. In the Chippendale, Hepplewhite and Sheraton periods the most usual type of pole screen was that with three legs, above which was a carved or "turned" column to which the pole was attached.

Pole screens were especially popular in our country in the periods when the furniture styles of Hepplewhite and Sheraton were in vogue. The designs in the books of these two masters are mentioned in the note.[2] The pieces as made by the cabinet makers of England and America, however, did not follow these designs

---

1.   These "horse fire screens" were large screens supported by two upright columns on the sides in a form somewhat similar to that of the dressing glass No. 1268 in section 152. Sheraton in his "Drawing Book", 1802, page 380, states that they were about three feet six inches in height and about nineteen inches in breadth. The word "horse" indicates a large object, as mentioned in connection with dressing glasses in note 7 in section 152 above cited. Screens of a somewhat similar form, but of a later date, are shown in Mr. Wallace Nutting's "Furniture Treasury", Nos. 1402–1404.

"Folding screens" to protect against drafts, or to hide a portion of a room, were made with hinged frames of two or more sections, similar to those now used. They were often decorated with Chinese designs.

"Fire screen desks" are shown in Nos. 829–831. These are not "pole screens".

The "banner" type of fire screen had a piece of velvet or other material, often with tassels, suspended from a cross–bar on the pole. This was of later date than the other types here mentioned.

2.   In the three designs in Hepplewhite's "Guide", plate 93, the frames are in three shapes, round, oval and rectangular. The round and oval frames have round bases, without feet; the rectangular frame has three legs with snake feet, such as those on the tripod tables Nos. 1339–1344 and on the pole screens Nos. 1680–1683.

In Sheraton's "Drawing Book", plate 38, the frames are also in three shapes. One is in the form of a shield resembling somewhat those in the shield backs of the chairs of Hepplewhite; another is in an oval form but with the edges cut in concave curves, as in No. 1683; and the third is rectangular. In each there are three legs, and the feet are vertical, such as those on the card table No. 1553 and the pole screens Nos. 1684 and 1685.

precisely, so that it may be uncertain in some cases whether a particular piece should be regarded as being in one style or the other. The form of the frame is not to be relied upon to determine the style, as many of the frames have no resemblance to those in the books and their form depended upon the taste of the cabinet maker or his customer. The feature which most clearly indicates the style is the kind of legs, those in the Sheraton style being in either concave or convex curves, as in the tables and candle stands shown in sections 159–161. In the Empire period a round or triangular base with scroll feet was generally used; and it is said that in the frames of that period the horizontal dimension was generally longer than the vertical one.

In our pole screens the ornamentation within the frame consisted chiefly of needlework and paintings of flowers, sometimes covered with a protective glass. Petit point was the most highly esteemed of the needlework.[3] Of course a pole screen is of little use "as a protection to the face from the heat of the fire. Its popularity was more probably due to the fact that the panels were used to display the feminine skill with the needle."[4] It was certainly not a very useful piece of furniture, but was a decidedly ornamental object in a drawing room.

The pole screens shown here are examples of the styles from the time of Chippendale to the Victorian period. There is so much similarity in these screens that in order to avoid repetition of details the comments are very brief. The "style" of a piece refers to the style of the legs, as above mentioned, and of the feet and the column; it does not necessarily refer to the frame or its needlework or other decoration, as some of these are doubtless substitutions for the originals.

No. 1678 is an English tripod pole screen in the Chippendale style, having a type of claw feet, with carving on the knees of the legs. The column has four spiral carvings. The frame is square and encloses a variety of designs, with flowers in the centre. This illustration is copied by permission of Mr. Cescinsky from figure 229 in the second volume of his "English Furniture". About 1760.

In No. 1679, in the Chippendale style, the legs and feet resemble those in the preceding piece. The lower part of the column is carved and turned in a design of a vase. The frame is rectangular and encloses a later needlepoint picture of a child and a dog. About 1760–1780.

3.   "Petit point" and "gros point" are mentioned in section 43.

4.   In Mr. Wheeler's "Old English Furniture", pages 351–354, it is said that "the interest and value of the fire screen are largely contingent upon the quality of the needlework which it displays. The age and period of this needlework do not of necessity correspond with that of the woodwork. . . Each family possessed its needlewoman and we find exquisite or mediocre panels as the women folk were skilled or less proficient in the art." Mr. Wheeler also remarks that because of the frequent removal of panels from one frame to another, in the course of years, "it is probable that only half of the examples (of needlework) now extant" are the original ones; and that in many cases "the needlework which appears was not intended for its present position and probably not for a screen of any kind."

It is said that it is not difficult to produce a pole fire screen from parts of other pieces. The column (which may be carved if originally plain) of a small tripod table which lacks a good top may be used to support a pole, a rectangular frame of a broken dressing glass may be added, the needlework or other ornamentation supplied, and the mixture may appear to the amateur collector to be a genuine pole screen of the eighteenth century.

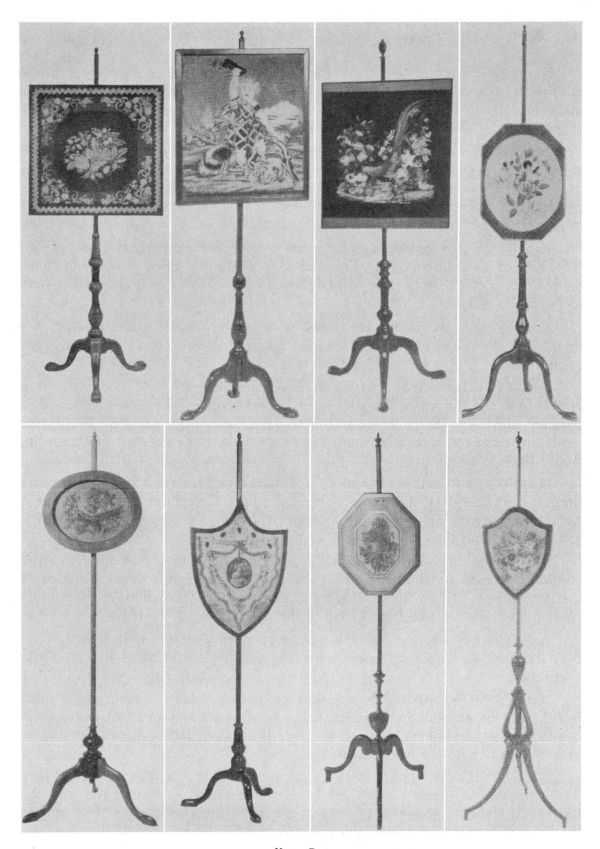

UPPER ROW
1678 ANONYMOUS.   1679 MR. W. W. LANA-   1680 MRS. MILES WHITE,   1681 MR. A. E. COLE.
HAN.   JR.

LOWER ROW.
1682 MRS. J. S. GIBBS, JR.   1683 DR. M. A. ABRAMS.   1684 EST. OF MRS. WHITE-   1685 MR. & MRS. E. H.
LEY.   MCKEON.
845

In the frame of No. 1680 there is a finely colored design of a bird in a cluster of flowers. The column has spiral carvings. The legs are plain and terminate in snake feet which are of the same type as those shown in one of the designs in Hepplewhite's "Guide", mentioned in note 2. About 1785–1800.

No. 1681 has the same type of legs and feet. The column has a carved vase and several rings. The frame is eight–sided, enclosing an oval with flowers, in these features closely resembling the Sheraton style frame in No. 335 in volume 3 of "English Furniture", by Mr. Cescinsky. This is an example of a Sheraton style frame with some other parts in the Hepplewhite style. About 1785–1800.

In No. 1682, in maple, the oval frame is hung horizontally, and encloses an embroidered bird and flowers. The pole extends almost down to the legs, there being no column except a turned and flattened ball. This piece is about fifty–four inches high. About 1785–1800.

In No. 1683, also in the Hepplewhite style, the frame is in the shape of a shield, and the design within it follows the lines of the frame to some extent. This form of shield is also seen on the dressing glass No. 1261. About 1785–1800.

No. 1684 is the first of six pole screens in the Sheraton style. The three legs are concave and the small feet are vertical as are those in Sheraton's book and in the card table No. 1553. A vase and several rings are on the column. The frame is six–sided and the decoration in the centre is enclosed in a panel of similar form. About 1795–1810.

No. 1685 also has concave legs terminating in vertical feet. Over the legs are three curved upright pieces and over these is a vase. The frame is in the shape of a shield, a design which seems to have been the common property of Hepplewhite and Sheraton and the cabinet makers of the period. About 1795–1810.

In No. 1686 the concave legs are reeded and small balls serve as feet. The column is carved and turned. The frame is in the form of a shield which is of the same type as is seen in the dressing glass No. 1260. The embroidery shows a woman and bird. A vase is at the top of the pole. About 1795–1810.

No. 1687 has a type of convex legs seen on the Sheraton style tripod tables Nos. 1353–1356. The rectangular frame encloses a piece of embroidery. About 1800–1820.

No. 1688 is a combined pole screen and candle stand. A plain eight–sided board takes the place of an ornamental frame and at the bottom of the board there is a small shelf to hold a candlestick. Over the convex legs a turned vase serves as a column to hold the pole. About 1800–1820.

No. 1689 is in the late Sheraton style, as shown by the type of curved legs. The column is "turned" in several forms. The frame is rectangular and the horizontal length is greater than the vertical one, a form which was often used in the Empire style, as mentioned above in this section. About 1810–1830.

No. 1690 and the following three pole screens are in the Empire style. The distinguishing feature in each is the triangular or tripod base which is seen on many of the tables in that style, as in Nos. 1369, 1592 and others. No. 1690 is well

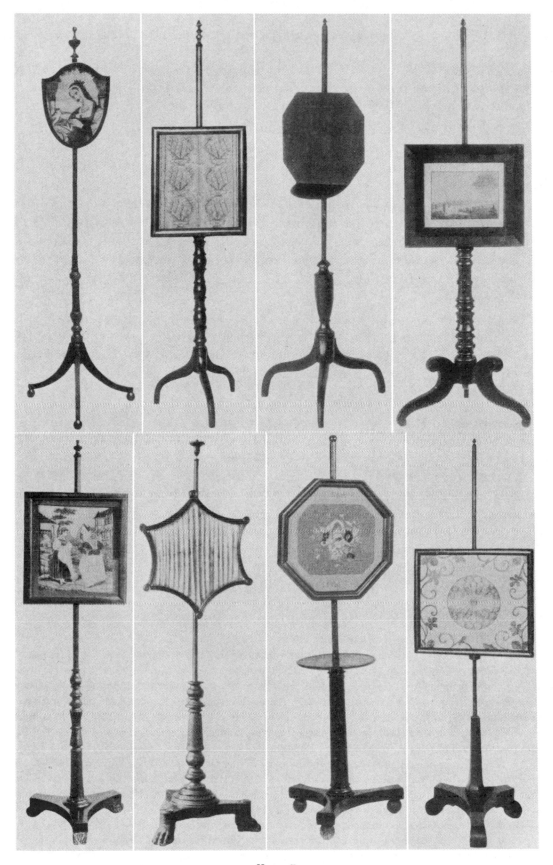

1686 Mrs. Miles White, Jr.   **1687** Miss H. H. Carey.   **1688** Mrs. Arthur Hale.   **1689** Mrs. I. R. Trimble.

LOWER ROW.

1690 Mrs. Miles White, Jr.   **1691** Courtesy of Mr. Morris Barroll.   **1692** Mr. B. Randall.   **1693** Miss H. H. Carey.

shown, with the three concave parts and the short feet which are carved with leaves. The column is turned in several designs. The frame is rectangular and is ornamented with embroidery. About 1820–1830.

In No. 1691 six reeded concave sections make a frame of pleasing form. The column is elaborately turned and the base is triangular as in the other pieces of the group of four pole screens. The short feet are carved in animals' claws. About 1820–1830.

In No. 1692 the base is supported by ball feet as in several other articles in the Empire style, such as the sewing table No. 1565 and the bureau No. 763. The column is plain and heavy and above it a small round shelf with a raised rim has been added, as seen in the tripod table No. 1339 and others. The frame is eight–sided and contains needlework of recent date; the other parts are about 1820–1830.

No. 1693 has a similar base, but with scroll feet, such as are seen in No. 1717 and in illustrations in section 199 in the Appendix entitled "Furniture styles of 1840". The width of the frame is greater than the height, which is characteristic of the period as mentioned in the comment on No. 1689. About 1830–1840.

Section 177. Stools.—The usual definition of a stool—"a seat without arms or back, for one person"—is sufficient for the purpose of this section if it be understood that foot–stools and piano–stools are included. In England the stool and the bench constituted the seating equipment of the household until the chairs were no longer reserved for superior persons[1] and came into general use. After that time the stool was gradually superseded by the chair as an important article of furniture. In our country a plain type of stool known as a "joint" stool was the earliest one worthy of study, and this was followed by other types in the successive furniture styles.

Nos. 1694 and 1695, the property of the Metropolitan Museum of Art, are "joint" stools, the word "joint" meaning that the stool was made of parts joined[2]

1.   As to this, see the chapter on chairs, section 45, note 3, B.

One form of stool not apparently used in our country was known as a "gouty stool". This was so constructed that the seat could, in the words of Hepplewhite, be "easily raised or lowered at either end", a feature "particularly useful to the afflicted", as his leg could thus be supported at any height or position desired. It is said that in the eighteenth century the gout was a fashionable complaint and was regarded as a sure indication of a fine pedigree. The raising and lowering of the seat was accomplished in much the same manner as with the tops of the architects' tables shown in section 174, Nos. 1635–1636. A design of a similar stool is in the book of Sheraton.

2.   The joining of one part with another was by a "mortise and tenon". The "mortise" is a hole, opening or socket cut into a piece of wood, such as a stool seat; the "tenon" is a projecting end of another piece of wood, such as the leg of a stool. The tenon is inserted into the mortise, making a joint. This ancient method is in common use today. It is mentioned in the twenty–sixth chapter of Exodus, verse nineteen, where directions are given for making the tabernacle.

In Mr. Wallace Nutting's "Furniture of the Pilgrim Century", Revised Edition, page 388, it is stated that the English joint stools are "common enough, especially in their spurious imitations which flood the country." In his "Furniture Treasury" joint stools are shown in No. 2706 and others.

These stools are also referred to in section 45, note 3, A.

(*Note 2 is continued on page 850.*)

1694 (Upper) Met. Mus. of Art.   1695 (Upper) Met. Mus. of Art.   1696 (Upper) Hammond–Harwood
1697 (Centre) Mr. & Mrs. E. H.   1698 (Centre) Mr. & Mrs. H. L.   House.
    McKeon.   Duer.   1699 (Centre) Mr. & Mrs. B. Turn-
                                                                                    bull.
         1700 (Lower) Mr. & Mrs. H. L. Duer.   1701 (Lower) Mrs. John S. Gibbs, Jr.

together by a "joiner", the English word for a certain skilled type of wood–worker, as distinguished from plain and roughly made stools of the period. These joint stools were about twenty–two inches high. The top was generally made of pine and the lower part of oak or maple. The legs are usually "raked" or "splayed", that is, they slant outwards, as shown also in the Windsor chairs in section 62; in some cases only two legs slanted, the other two being vertical. The four sturdy stretchers and the turnings on the legs may be compared with some of the turnings on the contemporaneous gate–leg tables Nos. 1296 and 1297. The date is from about 1670 to 1700.

No. 1696 is a stool somewhat later in date, and with a recently upholstered seat. There are five turned stretchers; the three in the H form are below and the other two are above. The turnings of these stretchers are of about the same type as those on the gate–leg table No. 1292. About 1690–1710.

No. 1697 is in the Queen Anne style, having cabriole legs and Dutch, or club, feet as in the chairs, tables and other pieces in that style. The knees are carved. These pieces, and in fact all stools, were apparently made to match the other furniture on which people sat or reclined. About 1730–1750.

No. 1698 is an elaborately carved English stool in the Chippendale style, as shown by the cabriole legs and the ball and claw feet. The knees of the legs are carved with shells, and also with "C" curves which are not well seen in the engraving; these curves were much used on articles in the Chippendale style, as mentioned in connection with the mirror No. 1103 and others. About 1760–1780.

No. 1699 is a plain stool in the Hepplewhite style, which is recognized in the characteristic square and straight tapering legs. The stretchers are in the H form. About 1785–1800.

No. 1700 is a long stool for more than one person, in the Chippendale style, as it has cabriole legs and ball and claw feet. The knees are carved. There are no stretchers as these were generally regarded as unsuitable for legs in the cabriole form. About 1760–1780.

No. 1701 is also a long stool in the Chippendale style, but having the straight and square legs, not tapered, which are seen on so many of the chairs and tables in that style. The upholstery is secured by numerous nails with brass heads, as in many chairs and sofas of the period. At each end is a short stretcher and these two are connected by a long one, all three being in harmony with the shape of the legs. About 1760–1780.

(NOTE 2, *continued*)

An illustrated article entitled "Joint Stool and Candlestick", by Mr. Malcolm A. Norton, is in "Antiques", May, 1924, pages 226–227.

The next five stools, Nos. 1702–1706, have legs in the "curule" form[3] or in a similar form derived from it. This form was much used in the Sheraton and Empire periods on several articles of furniture. The stools shown here are regarded as being in the Empire style.

No. 1702 is a plain and strong example of a curule stool, as seen from one end. The curule form consists of two legs at each end, which are connected by a turned stretcher, as in stools of this type. The two legs together form two semi-circles, somewhat resembling the letter X. In this stool and No. 1705 the legs are on the short sides of the stool; in the three other pieces the legs are on the long sides. About 1800–1820.

In No. 1703 the legs are of a similar form, but are not exactly semi-circular. The seat rails and the legs are ornamented with painted lines, and at the junction of the legs are painted leaves in a diamond-shaped form. The stretchers in this and the preceding piece are in a similar form. About 1800–1820.

In No. 1704 the legs are more nearly in a semi-circular shape and the upper and lower portions are braced with small stretchers in addition to the usual one. At the top of the legs and at their junction are large applied rosettes. About 1810–1830.

In No. 1705 the legs are rounded and the lower portions are curved under, forming feet. The seat rails also are rounded. The legs are on the short sides, as mentioned in connection with No. 1702. About 1800–1820.

In No. 1706 the legs have lost their semi-circular shape and each resembles two elongated forms of the letter "C", which is mentioned in the comment on No. 1698. Rosettes are freely used on the legs. The seat is concave in the manner seen in many chairs in the Chippendale and Hepplewhite styles, as in Nos. 176 and 196. The legs are about the same as those in the stool numbered 158 in "Furniture styles of 1840", section 199. About 1820–1830.

Nos. 1707–1714 are foot-stools. It is said that these articles were made to furnish a better and more elegant method of protecting one's feet from drafts of cold air than by resting the feet on the stretchers of chairs or tables. Foot-stools are of course not important articles of antique furniture, and very little attention is given to them in the books; but as they were made in the Chippendale and later styles, it is well to examine them. The principal difference between foot-stools and seating stools is in their height, which depends chiefly upon the length of the legs; and even with this difference in mind it is not in all cases easy to distinguish them in photographs taken on different scales. Perhaps some of these so-called foot-stools were intended as seating stools for small children.

No. 1707 is in the Chippendale style, having cabriole legs and ball and claw feet. If the legs were longer, and if the seat were enlarged in proportion, this foot-stool would be similar in general form to the seating stool No. 1698. The seat rail is larger than appears necessary for the duty of supporting two feet. About 1760–1780.

---

3. As to the "Curule" design see note 9 in section 52 and also the chairs Nos. 490 and 491, and the Index under the word "Curule".

1702 (Upper) Mrs. M. S. Harts-
       horne.
1705 (Centre) Mrs. Wm. A. Dixon.
1708 (Lower) Dr. M. A. Abrams.

1703 (Upper) Mr. & Mrs. L. Birck-
       head.
1706 (Centre) Mr. J. C. Toland.
1709 (Lower) Mr. John S.
       McDaniel.

1704 (Upper) Miss E. H. Bartlett.
1707 (Centre) Mr. & Mrs. Wm. M.
       Ellicott.
1710 (Lower) Mrs. Wm. A. Dixon.

1711 (Upper) Mr. & Mrs. Jas. Carey, Jr.

1712 (Upper) Mrs. W. D. Poultney.

1713 (Upper) Mrs. F. T. Redwood.

1714 (Centre) Mr. John Ridgely, Jr.

1715 (Lower) Mr. E. G. Miller, Jr.

1716 (Lower) Mr. J. C. Toland.

1717 (Lower) Miss E. S. Cohen.

No. 1708 also is in the Chippendale style, with legs and feet as in the preceding piece. The short legs and flattened feet are suggestive of those on some of the bureaus and desks in the Chippendale style, such as the bureau No. 716 and the desk No. 786 and others. The seat rail is grooved. About 1760–1780.

No. 1709 has inlaid lines on the seat rail and these lines might indicate the Hepplewhite style and period, but the feet are not in the Hepplewhite style. Foot–stools do not appear in the designs of Hepplewhite's book. This piece may be regarded as a transitional one of about 1785–1800.

No. 1710 is in the Sheraton style which is seen in the reeding of the seat rail and the round and tapering legs. As with the cabinet makers working in the Hepplewhite style, the cabinet makers working in the Sheraton style could easily produce a foot–stool in the Sheraton style by using the characteristic reeding and the tapering legs seen in this piece. About 1795–1815.

In No. 1711, which is in the Empire style, the seat rail is in a convex curve above and a concave curve below, making a cyma curve, which is seen at the corners and is described in section 23. The heavy scroll feet are of the same type as those seen in many tables and other pieces in the Empire style and in section 199 entitled "Furniture styles of 1840". About 1830–1840.

No. 1712 has a similar seat rail, but the feet seem to place it in the early Victorian period in which designs of earlier periods were often combined without regard to their lack of harmony. Here the feet are in the curved bracket type as in the foot–stool No. 1709, to which are added branches or wings of peculiar form. About 1840–1850.

In No. 1713, in the Victorian style, the seat rail is again of the same type, with convex and concave curves. The feet resemble bracket feet with the sides cut off and at the bottom is a form resembling a "spade foot" as seen in many feet on the chairs and other pieces in the Hepplewhite style. About 1840–1850.

No. 1714 is a long foot–stool, somewhat lower than the three preceding pieces. It was used in front of a sofa or settee, but is not as long as those articles. The inlay on the legs and on the seat rail is of the fanciful type sometimes seen on chairs, sofas and settees in the Empire period. About 1820–1830.

Nos. 1715–1717 are piano stools of the Empire period. In each of these pieces the lower portion, under the seat, resembles the corresponding portion of some of the tables of the period. The chair portion revolves with a metal screw and may be raised or lowered as desired.

The lyre in No. 1715 is an appropriate ornament for a piano stool. The curve of the back is graceful, resembling the curves of the back of the chair No. 326 in the Directory style. The column has a series of rings and the legs and claw feet are coarsely carved. A detail which does not clearly appear in the engraving is that the sides of the legs are cut in small lines, representing hair on animals' legs, as in the card table No. 1555. About 1820–1830.

In No. 1716 the column is heavier than in the preceding stool and is ornamented with a vase form with reeding, as in the table No. 1627. The legs are
carved on the sides and have carved acanthus leaves on the upper portion and
animals' claw feet. Under the feet are wooden "cushions", or "shoes", to protect
the feet. About 1820–1830.

No. 1717 is in the late Empire style with a heavy triangular base and scroll
feet, as in the pole screen No. 1693, and in various tables and other articles of the
period shown in previous chapters and in section 199 in the Appendix, entitled
"Furniture styles of 1840". About 1830–1840.

An interesting piano stool appears as chair No. 492 in section 64 in the chapter
on chairs.

Section 178. Wardrobes.—These articles, as we now know them, with doors
extending to the base, were apparently made in our country as far back as about
1725–1750; but only one of that period, shown here as No. 1718, seems to be now
known. Later, in the time of Hepplewhite and Sheraton, they were made in two
parts, as in Nos. 1719 and 1720, the lower part having several drawers and the
upper part consisting of a cupboard; this type is commonly called a "clothes
press".[1] In the Sheraton period the wardrobes of this latter type were often very
wide and high, with three sections, and were generally ornamented with inlay, as
in Nos. 1720 and 1721. Still later, in the Empire period, the early form with doors
extending to the base, as in Nos. 1722 and 1723, again became the fashion and this
construction continued with variations throughout the Victorian period. Wardrobes of the periods before the Empire style are not often seen in our American
homes, "probably because the houses had ample closet room", as remarked by
Mr. Lockwood.

No. 1718 is shown here through the courtesy of Mr. Lockwood, in whose
"Colonial Furniture", vol. 1, it appears as figure 179. Mr. Lockwood regards
this wardrobe as of the period of about 1725–1750, as is shown by the details of

1. The term "clothes press", often loosely used as synonymous with wardrobes with shelves, is
defined as a chest of drawers with a cupboard over them to hold clothes, a definition which describes
Nos. 1719 and 1720. An earlier type of clothes press was in the form of a chest, often with short legs,
which is shown in the "Director" of Chippendale, as to which see section 15. See also "Cupboards",
section 121, in which a "Kas" is shown, No. 910. Certain wardrobes of local character, such as those
of the country districts of Pennsylvania, are not illustrated here; several may be seen in Mr. Wallace
Nutting's "Furniture Treasury", Nos. 506, 577–579.

In the English books the term "hanging" wardrobe is often used, meaning a wardrobe in
which clothing could be hung as distinguished from pieces in which clothes were placed flat in drawers
or on shelves. In the Appendix to Sheraton's "Drawing Book", plate No. 8, coat hangers are shown on
a cross–bar as now used. Mr. Cescinsky, in his "English Furniture", volume 3, page 279, states that
"the hanging wardrobe, made to accommodate the hooped and flaring dresses of the ladies of the period,
was an introduction of the Sheraton school, Hepplewhite confining himself" to the type with sliding
shelves above and drawers below; and that the doors often opened only to a right angle.

It may be assumed that the wardrobes here shown have the usual hanging portions or the
sliding shelves or both, so that it is not necessary to refer to them in the comments; but in some cases the
original interior arrangements have been removed and new ones substituted.

the moldings, the scroll top and the long beveled panels in the doors, all of which are of the period mentioned. Mr. Lockwood mentions that "this is the only wardrobe of this period which has come under the writer's observation." Here there are long doors reaching to the base, a method which was not in fashion in the period of Chippendale or Hepplewhite, but appeared only in the Sheraton and Empire periods as shown in Nos. 1721–1723. About 1725–1750, or perhaps later.

No. 1719, in the Hepplewhite style, is made in two parts, the upper one having two large doors with a recessed panel in each. Under the cornice is a molding and a series of flutings and rosettes which follow the Adam designs, as in illustrations Nos. 4 and 181. The lower portion has two drawers under which is one large one. The feet are in the bracket type. This closely resembles several designs in Hepplewhite's "Guide", as to which see section 17. About 1785–1800.

No. 1720 is an English wardrobe in the Sheraton style, copied by permission of Mr. Cescinsky from his "English Furniture", volume 3, figure 302; on page 279 it is said that this "is the more usual type of wardrobe of this period, a cupboard with two doors superimposed upon a chest of drawers." A resemblance of several designs of this wardrobe to designs on several secretary–desks will be noticed, as in No. 868, where the oval panels are conspicuous. About 1795–1815.

No. 1721 is a large wardrobe in the Sheraton style. There are three sections, the central one projecting forward from the two wings, as in the bookcases No. 869–871. The four doors extend to the base, and on the upper and lower portion of each door is a large inlaid oval panel of satinwood, the oval being a favorite form of decoration in the period. The wardrobe rests upon the floor without feet, as in the bookcases above cited. The inner section here would by itself be a fair–sized wardrobe. About 1800–1810.

No. 1722 is in the early Empire style, which is indicated by the ball feet and the heavy base and also by the overhanging cornice; but the four applied and reeded columns with carved tops are survivals of the reeding seen on so many tables and other pieces in the Sheraton style. The finely "matched" veneer on the two central doors will be noticed, a method which is described in section 32, note 2. About 1815–1830.

No. 1723 is entirely in the Empire style, as appears from the wide cornice, the two large columns supporting the upper portion, the heavy base and especially the animals' claw feet. Columns or feet of the same character are seen in the tables Nos. 1651–1653. About 1820–1830.

Section 179. Washstands.—Well–to–do families of the eighteenth century were provided with many comforts of home life, but in the matter of heating, lighting and plumbing even the houses of royalty would now be thought unbearable, particularly in the matter of plumbing. Bathrooms were almost unknown,

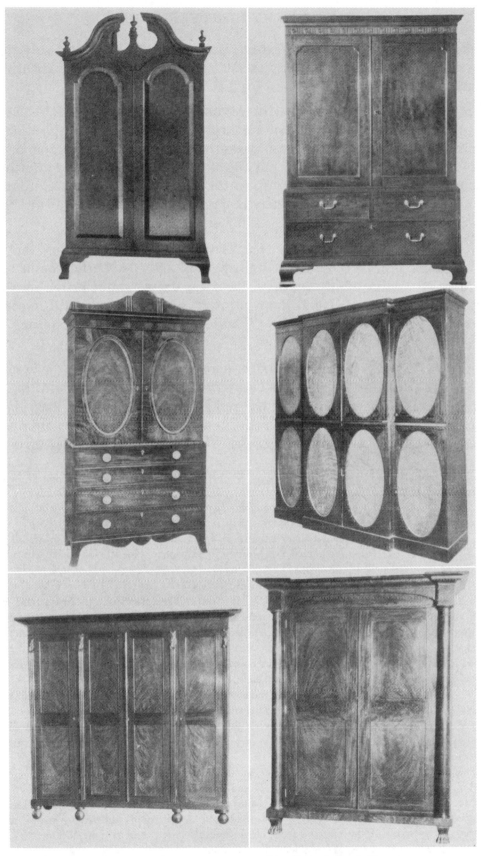

1718 (Upper) Lock. Col. Furn., Fig. 179.   1719 (Upper) Dr. J. Hall Pleasants.
1720 (Centre) Cescinsky, Eng. Furn. 302.   1721 (Centre) Mr. Blanchard Randall.
1722 (Lower) Mr. Edgar G. Miller, Jr.   1723 (Lower) Anonymous.

and washstands[1] of even modest capacity were not developed.[2] Small tables or lowboys or dressing tables, with a pitcher, a small bowl and a soap dish furnished the washing equipment.

It seems that washstands with folding half–tops, as in No. 1724, were made in England with characteristic features of the style of Chippendale, but no examples in that style of American make have apparently been found. In our country the washstand first became an object of elegance in the Hepplewhite style and continued in a very similar form in the style of Sheraton, so similar in fact that in some cases the washstands may be properly referred to as of the "Hepplewhite–Sheraton" period.[3]

No. 1724 is a washstand in the Hepplewhite style. The folding "half–tops"[4] are of the same type as those in the dressing table No. 1474. The basin rests in a round opening under which appear to be three drawers, but in reality there are only two, the upper one being a "sham" drawer, a method mentioned in connection with the Pembroke table No. 1409. The legs are slender and tapering. About 1785–1800.

No. 1725 is in the form which Hepplewhite referred to[5] as "a design for a new one on a triangular plan. This is a very useful shape as it stands in a corner out of the way." The front is rounded and at the top is a raised back–board intended to prevent splashing of the wall by a careless user. This "splash–board" is cut in curves and has two openings by which the piece may be carried. The

1. The term "basin stand" also was used in the sense of "washstand" in the books of Hepplewhite and Sheraton.

A "wig–stand", so–called, is sometimes classed as a "washstand", but, as indicated in connection with No. 1677 in the previous chapter, it is not a "washstand" in the usual sense.

An illustrated article entitled "English Basin–stands and American Washstands", by Mr. Walter A. Dyer is in "The Antiquarian", January, 1931, pages 48–50. In this article the word "splash–board" is used for the raised board at the top.

2. Mr. Cescinsky, in his "English Furniture", volume 3, page 279, in referring to bedroom furniture of the Sheraton period, about 1790–1805 in England, remarks that "the washstand was nearly always a very insignificant piece of furniture, sometimes made to stand in a corner and cut for a basin of the dimensions of a modern salad bowl. Considering that bathrooms were practically unknown and that washstands capable of holding basins of the size usual at the present day do not appear to have been made, one is lost in wonder as to how our eighteenth century ancestors managed to keep themselves even decently clean." See also the remarks of Mr. Cescinsky quoted in note 2 in section 175.

An examination of the designs in the books of Hepplewhite and Sheraton and of the designs of Shearer seems to indicate that the triangular form of washstand was first designed by Shearer, from whom both Hepplewhite and Sheraton apparently derived their models, as they did in the case of sideboards, as mentioned in section 127. This also appears in the book "English Furniture", etc., by Mr. T. A. Strange, pages 269, 270 and 310.

3. As to this period see the remarks in regard to sideboards in section 127.

4. These folding half–tops on washstands and on the dressing tables Nos. 1473–1474 when not opened, gave to the articles the appearance of being tables and they were used as such. These articles were placed in rooms which in the period were used both as bed rooms and sitting rooms, and by this device the real purpose of the piece was disguised. See also note 3 in section 133 in the chapter on bedsteads, in regard to the use of bed rooms for receptions.

5. In the "Guide", edition of 1794, plate 83; see section 17 as to this book.

1724 (Upper) Mr. & Mrs. L. Birck-   1725 (Upper) Hammond–Harwood   1726 (Upper) Mrs. Miles White,
     head.   House.   Jr.
1727 (Centre) Mr. B. Randall.   1728 (Centre) Sheppard & Enoch   1729 (Centre) Mrs. Daniel Miller.
1730 (Lower) Mrs. E. P. Brundige.   Pratt Hospital.   1732 (Lower) Md. Soc. Col. Dames.
     1731 (Lower) Metropolitan Mu-
     seum of Art.

skirt is cut in double cyma curves, as to which see section 23, as in many pieces in the Hepplewhite style. Two small drawers, apparently, are under the shelf, and pierced brackets are at the junctions of the legs and the framework. Here there are four legs, all of which are round above and square below and all extend up to the skirt. About 1785–1800.

No. 1726 follows substantially the designs of Shearer, Hepplewhite and Sheraton, and may be said to be of the Hepplewhite–Sheraton period, as mentioned.[6] The splash–board is cut on each side in two cyma curves, as to which see section 23, with a section of a circle at the top. The cross–stretchers support an oval platform. As in the preceding piece there are four[7] legs, one of which in this piece does not extend above the shelf, which is thus not obstructed in front. Two small wooden cups for soap are faintly seen on the top. As in No. 1724 the basins and pitchers give a pleasing appearance. About 1785–1800.

No. 1727 is very similar in form, but has several different details; a small shelf is near the top of the splash–board; there are three legs which are turned in a vase shape above, and below are round and tapering and are connected by a shelf. In the engraving a part of the rear leg is reflected on this shelf. About 1785–1800.

In No. 1728 there are three square legs which are curved outward at the lower end as in No. 1726. There is no opening in the upper portion to hold a basin, the surface being solid as is sometimes seen in these pieces; nor are there any stretchers. About 1785–1800.

No. 1729 is of curly maple and is a good example of the Sheraton style as developed by our cabinet makers. The splash–board is somewhat similar to that in No. 1726, having two cyma curves on each side; and at the top the wood is cut in a curved form resembling that on the fretwork mirror No. 1128. A small shelf is near the top, but there are no cups for soap as in No. 1726 and others. The skirt is cut in double cyma curves. There are four legs which are turned in about the same manner as in No. 1727. This washstand is a part of a bedroom set of curly maple, three other articles of which are the highboy No. 644, the lowboy No. 694 and the bedstead No. 1067. About 1800–1820.

No. 1730 is another curly maple washstand, very much like the preceding piece. The chief differences are that the splash–board is cut in a fanciful form and that portions of the legs are turned in an unusual, almost cylindrical, shape, not tapering. About 1800–1820.

No. 1731 is a square washstand of the same period and has the Sheraton style of legs and feet. Although perhaps not as graceful as the triangular pieces it was doubtless more useful and convenient. The sides of the splash–board are cut in

6.   In the books of Hepplewhite and Sheraton the legs are square, and in the Sheraton design the lower ends are slightly curved outward, as in No. 1728; this appears in Sheraton's "Drawing Book", third edition, 1802, on plate 42, dated November, 1792; but in our American pieces in the Sheraton style the legs are usually round and are sometimes reeded in the usual Sheraton manner. With us, square legs are generally regarded as typical of the Hepplewhite style.

7.   The English designs have only three legs, not having a half–length leg in the centre of the front.

curves but the back is plain and has a wide shelf. The four legs are reeded in a vase form and a drawer with lion–and–ring handles is under the shelf. About 1800–1820.

No. 1732 is a later form of the triangular type and illustrates the decline which took place in furniture styles after about 1820. The splash–board is in about the same form as that in No. 1728, but the other parts are not pleasing. The shelf with the drawer is lowered almost to the floor. The upper portion and the shelf project forward in a sharper curve than in the preceding pieces. About 1825–1835.

Chapter XX

CLOCKS

Section 180. General remarks.—So many of the clocks[1] in our homes and museums are of English, French or other foreign origin that in this chapter it seems proper to illustrate a considerable number of them in addition to our American pieces, although in doing so we go beyond the scope of the title of this

---

1. The original meaning of the word "clock" was a machine which measured the passing of time by striking the hours on a bell. The French word "cloche" and the German word "glocke" mean "bell". It is said that many early clocks had a bell but no dial and the word "clock" was thus appropriate, and it continued in use after a dial was added. The word therefore now properly means a machine which measures time on a dial and strikes a bell at the hours or oftener. Strictly speaking, a time-measuring machine without a bell is a "timepiece", which is the word used, for example, by Simon Willard and others for a clock of that kind, as mentioned in section 194, note 1.

Mr. Eben Howard Gay, in an article entitled "Four Typical Colonial Clocks", in "Antiques", January, 1923, page 27, writes: "An especial fascination attaches to the acquisition of old clocks, apart from their time-telling function. * * Unlike other antiques, the clock is peculiarly *alive,* its friendly face, peaceful tick and faithful record of the hours over generations of time serving to create a vital bond between past and present. Indeed, the clock collector may find ample justification for his hobby in the words of Froissart, a celebrated French chronicler, 1337-1410, penned five centuries ago: 'If it be but rightly considered, the clock is a machine most comely and of good repute; pleasant also, and profitable. For day and night it sheweth us the hours, its subtilty being in no wise diminished in the absence even of the sun, on which account it should be held in more esteem than those lesser instruments which do not so, however cunningly they be made.' " The clocks made before 1410, when Froissart died, were mainly of the type of the German and French clocks referred to in section 197, note 1.

book.[2] Moreover, the purpose is to present briefly, with numerous illustrations, an outline of the whole subject of domestic[3] clocks from the point of view of an amateur collector who desires to know the principal features of the American and foreign[4] clocks of the various periods, and also their dates and nationalities.

Almost all domestic clocks have two parts; first, the mechanical part, called the "mechanism", or "movement", or "works", which is the timekeeping part; and, second, the "case",[5] within which the timekeeping part is enclosed. On some

2.   In order to save space in an unsuccessful effort to print this book in one volume instead of two, it became necessary that much of this chapter should be printed in small type in the notes instead of in the large type of the text. This method is used in the "Encyclopædia Britannica" and in the "Century Dictionary" and other publications.

3.   The clocks here shown are those of the types found in homes or museums, no examples being given of clocks in churches or in spires, towers or public buildings, or of clocks made mainly for astronomical purposes.

Domestic clocks are generally regarded by the courts as "furniture" in the interpretation of wills; see the last note in section 1.

4.   Especially French clocks. In very many of the one hundred and forty-eight homes visited by the writer in preparing this book there were French mantel clocks which had been in the possession of the families of the owners for several generations.

5.   Some clocks have no cases; examples are the skeleton clocks Nos. 2004-2012, whose only protection from dust is a glass covering, separate from the clock; the so called "wag on the wall" clocks, mentioned at the end of section 195, were also without cases.

The word "clock", as commonly used, means a clock movement, or works, in a case; but in the books it is often used to mean the "works" as distinguished from the case. Thus it may be said that a certain "clock was made in 1750 but the case is of a later date". This double meaning of the word does not create any confusion if the context is clear.

The learned and versatile editor of "Antiques", January, 1923, page 27, in a note, remarks: "The clock is pretty generally recognized as offering to the collector more dangerous pitfalls than does any other article of old time which may captivate his enamored fancy. For a clock consists of two parts,— an outward, visible and accessible case, and an inward, mainly invisible, and far from accessible, mechanism. One may be permitted to pride himself upon the certitude of his judgments as to the age and proper attribution of cabinet work, perhaps even of a dial, perhaps of the glass painting, when that occurs. But to be so familiar with the aspect of the master workman's touch on the mysterious vitals of a timepiece as to speak with authority concerning their genuineness is to have spent painstaking years in the task of dismemberment and rehabilitation."

Books on Clocks. The principal books on antique furniture contain chapters on antique clocks; the English books naturally deal only or mainly with English clocks; the American books do not treat the subject as a whole. The leading books are now mentioned, from each one of which the writer has derived information in preparing this chapter.

A.   "Old Clocks and Watches and their Makers", by F. J. Britten, fifth edition, 1922, published by Spon, London. This is a leading English work on the general subject, with 841 illustrations of English, French and other clocks and watches, and a vast amount of information. The subject of clocks is treated with particular reference to makers of clocks and watches, without special reference to furniture styles or dates. A very valuable feature is the list of nearly twelve thousand makers, mainly English.

B.   "English Domestic Clocks", by Herbert Cescinsky and Malcolm R. Webster, 1913, published by George Routledge and Sons, London. This valuable book was written, as stated in the preface, to supplement Mr. Cescinsky's "English Furniture", (so often quoted herein), in which chapters 14-21 of volume 1 were devoted to grandfather and mantel, or "bracket", clocks in connection with the English furniture types of the periods. In "English Domestic Clocks" there are 407 fine illustrations. The subject is treated in a more analytical and historical method than in Britten. This book is indis-

of these cases we will notice designs which resemble those seen on articles of furniture shown in previous chapters, and we will thus occasionally recognize the style of Chippendale and of other great designers of the eighteenth century, and also the style of the Empire period. Because of their various forms, the

(Note 5, *continued*)

pensable to every one who desires a scholarly knowledge of English clocks, especially of the grandfather clocks which were copied by our American clock makers. The present writer gratefully acknowledges his indebtedness to this book for numerous illustrations and much authoritative information.

C. "Time and Timekeepers", by Prof. Willis I. Milham, Field Memorial Professor of Astronomy in Williams College, published by The Macmillan Co., New York, 1923, is a book of more than 600 pages, with 339 illustrations of clocks, watches, makers and mechanisms. The great amount of research and work expended upon this book has produced a notable contribution to the subject. It treats of the scientific principles of timekeeping and the practical methods of the clock maker, from the earliest dates to the present time, all written in an easy and agreeable style. It does not consider the cases of clocks from the standpoint of the collector of antiques, but it illustrates and explains many antique cases of English and American make. Appendix V is a bibliography of publications connected with the subject of clocks and watches; this is the largest and most satisfactory list published.

D. "The Old Clock Book", by Mrs. N. Hudson Moore, first published by F. A. Stokes Co., New York, in 1911, is a small book with 104 illustrations. It treats of English and American clocks, the latter being in groups according to the locality of their makers. Brief biographical sketches are given. Two lists of clock makers occupy the latter half of the book. The American list seems to include dealers whose names appear in advertisements and directories of the periods as "clock makers", as to which see the last paragraph of this section.

E. "The Clock Book", by Wallace Nutting, published by Old America Company, Framingham, Mass., 1924, has 250 illustrations of clocks made in various countries, with very brief items regarding them. There is a list of English clock makers, taken from Britten, and also a list of American "clock makers" which doubtless includes many who were merely "dealers".

F. In the "Furniture Treasury" of Mr. Nutting, volume 2, published by Old America Company, 1928, are 324 illustrations of clocks, most of which appeared in his "The Clock Book". Volume 3, published in 1933, contains much additional information and a large list of American clock makers and dealers.

G. "Chats on Old Clocks", by Arthur Hayden, not dated, published in America by F. A. Stokes Co., New York, is a small English book of 302 pages with about 65 illustrations of representative English clocks and watches.

H. "Connecticut Clockmakers of the Eighteenth Century", by Mr. Penrose R. Hoopes, 1930, has 56 illustrations and much biographical information regarding seventy-nine clock makers of Connecticut.

I. "Watchmakers and Clockmakers of the World", by G. H. Baillie, published by Methuen & Co., London, 1929, an immense compilation in one medium sized volume, is especially valuable in respect to the dates of English and French makers. In reference to this book it is said that "the list comprises the names and dates of twenty-five thousand makers. * * The records of the Clockmakers Company, (of London), thoroughly sifted for the first time, have yielded an accurate list of London makers, and a long research among the manuscripts of the 'Bibliotheque Nationale', (of Paris), has brought to light a mass of information about the makers of Paris". Mr. Baillie's volume has been of much help to the writer, especially in the preparation of section 193 on French mantel clocks.

J. Chauncey Jerome, one of the leading Connecticut clock makers, published in 1860 a small book entitled "History of the American clock business for the past sixty years". This is a source of much information and has often been quoted by later writers. See section 191, note 6.

K. Henry Terry, of Waterbury, Conn., published in 1872 a pamphlet of twenty-four pages, entitled "American Clock Making: its early history". This pamphlet refers to less than its title implies, treating chiefly of some of the Connecticut makers.

cases are generally of more interest than the works to those interested in antique furniture.

It must not be assumed, however, that the style of the English cases at a given date followed the style of the furniture of the same period. The records of the Clockmakers Company[6] and other evidence make it possible to fix the dates of many English clocks with accuracy, and it appears that after about 1735 the style and wood of the cases were often those which were used in the furniture made twenty or thirty years previously; for example, clock cases were made of walnut many years after mahogany became the fashionable wood.[7]

(Note 5, *continued*)

L. A paper was written by Mr. D. F. Magee, of Lancaster County, Pa., entitled "Grandfather clocks: their making and their makers in Lancaster County". This paper, read before the Lancaster County Historical Society in April, 1917, was published in pamphlet form in the same year.

M. "The Lure of the Clock", by Dr. D. W. Hering, is "an account of the James Arthur Collection of clocks and watches at New York University". This book deals mainly with the mechanical features of the clocks and watches in the collection, of which there are eighty-nine illustrations. Published in 1932 by the New York University Press, New York.

N. The book "Simon Willard and his clocks" is mentioned in section 187 at note 20.

O. A notable French book on antique clocks other than domestic ones is "Les Horloges Astronomiques et Monumentales les plus remarquables de l'Antiquité jusqu'à nos jours". This book is by Alfred Ungerer, and was published by him in Strasburg in 1931. It contains 514 pages and 458 illustrations, most of which are of clocks on churches and public buildings in France, Germany, England, Italy and other countries.

P. Another book, in French, is "L'Horloge", by Mathieu Planchon, published in 1923, which is mentioned in connection with illustrations Nos. 1960, 2002 and 2094.

6. The "Worshipful Company of Clockmakers of the City of London", commonly known as the "Clockmakers Company", was organized in 1631. It was a guild for the protection of its members. In its records the dates appear at which clock makers were admitted to its membership. If a man's name is not in the list of members it does not mean that he was not a good clock maker; it merely indicates that he did not join the Company. In 1704 it is recorded in the proceedings of the Company that "certain persons at Amsterdam (Holland) are in the habit of putting the names * * of well-known (London) makers on their works and selling them as English"; as to which Mr. Britten remarks, page 628, that "it is to be feared that some English makers were not free from suspicion of similar misdeeds both then and since". To prevent this practice the Company doubtless exercised its right to prevent "making, buying, selling, transporting and importing any bad, deceitful or insufficient clocks, watches, larums, sundials", etc. The "C. C." is still in existence.

A book entitled "Some account of the Worshipful Company of Clockmakers of the City of London" was privately printed in London in 1881. This book contains much interesting information about the Company.

Another guild, formed prior to the Clockmakers Company, was the "Blacksmiths Company", members of which made, among other things, certain kinds of large clocks. The term "Blacksmiths' clock" has occasionally been applied to the "lantern clocks" which are shown in section 185.

English clocks have always had a high reputation as timekeepers, not only in England and America, but also in other parts of the world. In China mantel clocks are found made in the manner of the eighteenth century English types, as in No. 2087; clocks were made for the Turkish market with numerals of the kind used in Turkey, as in No. 1894; on clocks made for the Spanish market, such as No. 1895, Spanish words were used; and many old English clocks are seen in Italian shops.

The "golden age" of English clocks is regarded as being from about 1670 to 1770, and in the early part of that period many clocks of the best character were made.

7. See section 186, note 15, and section 189, note 5, E. (*Note 7 continued on next page.*)

When it is said that an English or American antique clock was made by a certain clock maker it is understood that only the works were made by the clock maker. The case was always made by a cabinet maker;[8] the dial was made by a dial maker;[9] any engraving on the dial was done by an engraver; any painted decoration was done by an artist,[10] and the hands were generally cut out by a worker in metal. But although these parts were made by different persons it was the clock maker who controlled the form and appearance of the completed clock; and in almost every instance the case was made to fit the clock.

A convenient classification of the great majority of antique domestic clocks is in three classes, depending upon the position which the clock occupies in a dwelling, namely, floor clocks, mantel clocks and wall clocks;[11] but there are a

(Note 7, *continued*)

As remarked by Mr. Hayden in his "Chats on Old Clocks", pages 147-148, "in the case of provincial made furniture, whole districts carried on fashions for a quarter of a century or longer after they had been forgotten in London, and the clock case is no exception". This may be important in considering the dates of English clocks made elsewhere than in London, of which several are shown in later sections.

8.   Both in England and our country the clock-making craft was entirely distinct from that of the cabinet maker. Mr. Cescinsky, in his "English Furniture", volume 1, page 242, states that the clock maker was the important person in the combination of trades. "If he did not exactly dictate the style of the case, he certainly commissioned the work and to a large extent regulated the size. * * He was the one who actually sold the clock in its case." And on page 250 it is said that to show the evolution of clocks by types of case work is often misleading, as the clock makers generally consulted their own particular fancy with regard to the cases and often chose cases of a previous fashion. Given a clock and its case made at the same time, the clock is a much more certain index of date than the case.

Many American cabinet makers advertised that they made clock cases. In the "Maryland Gazette", October 21, 1746, John Anderson "late from Liverpool" advertised that he "makes chairs, tables * * clock cases and all kinds of furniture * * in the neatest, cheapest and newest modes". In the same newspaper, June 1, 1769, William Slicer "makes and sells" clock cases. These examples are from an article by Dr. Henry J. Berkley in the "Maryland Historical Magazine", March, 1930, pages 6 and 7.

In the two volumes entitled "The Arts and Crafts in Philadelphia, Maryland and South Carolina", published by "The Walpole Society", other examples are given.

The names are known of several of the American cabinet makers who made clock cases of fine character. For example the cases of many grandfather clocks of the Willard family were made by John Doggett, a cabinet maker of Boston; see "Antiques", March, 1929, page 196, and section 187, note 22.

9.   See section 183 as to dials.

10.   For example the paintings on the glass fronts of many of Simon Willard's banjo clocks were done by an unknown Englishman and by a Charles Bullard, as mentioned in section 194, note 6.

11.   The floor clocks are the "grandfather" clocks and the smaller ones of the same type known as "grandmother" clocks. The term "grandfather" clock is of course merely a colloquial one, not descriptive of its character, but is so familiar that it is preferred to the terms "long" or "tall" or "hall", which are often used, especially in English books. See the origin of the name "grandfather" in section 186, note 2.

The clocks shown in sections 189-191, entitled "Mantel clocks", are called "mantel" clocks in this book in preference to the terms "shelf", "bracket" or "table", for the reason that at the present time such clocks are almost always placed upon a mantel and not upon a shelf or bracket or table.

The "wall" clocks are, of course, those which are hung on a wall, such as the banjo and lyre clocks, and some others.

few which are not included in this classification, such as clocks intended to be placed upon a table, and others which are shown in section 197 in this chapter.

The name on the dial of an antique clock in our country is often misleading. The name may be that of the maker of the works of the clock, placed on the dial by him or for him, or it may be the name of an American dealer in clocks who had it for sale,[12] or it may be a wilful forgery;[13] or the name of a well-known maker may be used merely to indicate a style.[14] It is probable that in a large number of the grandfather clocks found in our country, bearing an American name and address, the person named was a merchant or dealer who imported the works from an English maker, had his own name placed on the dial and had the case made by an American cabinet maker.[15]

Section 181. Early timekeepers.—The timekeepers mentioned in this section are not clocks in a proper sense, and are considered here very briefly and merely as a matter of interest. The principal early timekeepers were sun-dials and water clocks.

Sun-dials have been made in many forms from an uncertain date of antiquity to the present time. They are all based upon the fact that the shadow of a vertical object, such as a pole, moves as the sun apparently proceeds across the sky. When the sun is lowest in the sky, at sunrise and sunset, the shadow is longest; when

(Note 11, *continued*)

Clocks are also classified, in a descriptive manner, as "weight driven" clocks and "spring driven" clocks, indicating the method by which the power to drive the clock is furnished. As to "spring" clocks, see section 189, note 2.

12. Many "clock makers" advertised English clocks for sale. In the "Maryland Journal", November 16, 1784, Gilbert Bigger, "watch and clock maker", advertised that "he has for sale a few elegant house clocks, just arrived in the 'Arethusa' from London; amongst which is a musical clock", etc. Many instances of the importation of English clocks by American "clock makers" are found in advertisements. In England the clocks were sold by the makers, not by dealers.

Many French clocks made by manufacturers have only the words "a Paris" on the dial, leaving a space above in which a Parisian dealer could insert his name; see note 13 to No. 1974.

In a few instances in England the name of the owner appears on the dial; and in some clocks the name of the maker appears twice on the dial, as mentioned in the comment on No. 1788.

In several instances English makers placed a fictitious name on their clocks and watches in order to conceal their identity for purposes of their own. One example is "Yeldrae Notron" which is the name of a well-known London maker, "Eardley Norton", spelled backwards. Another is "Notyap" which is the reversed spelling of William "Payton". Clocks with these names have been found in Holland and France.

13. This is sometimes discovered. The writer knows of a case where an artist was asked to paint on a dial the name of "Robert Roskell", an English maker, in place of the name then on the dial. The artist declined to be a party to the deception.

14. As in certain banjo clocks bearing the name of Aaron Willard. As stated in note 12 in section 194, a Boston firm of good standing thought it not improper to paint that name on the dials of their unnamed banjo clocks if the clocks appeared to be in the style of Aaron Willard. Another dealer now offers for sale new dials with the name of Aaron Willard painted on. These methods overstep the limits of propriety, even if there be no intention to mislead. Another advertiser offers for sale "Simon Willard movements reproduced".

15. See also note 5 in section 186.

the sun is highest in the sky the shadow is shortest, and at that moment the time is called twelve o'clock, noon. The time thus indicated is based entirely upon the sun and its position in the sky,[1] and is called "solar" time. It is not proper to say that the sun is highest at twelve o'clock, noon; we should say that when the sun is highest, the time is twelve o'clock, noon.

Sun-dials are mentioned in the Bible, (Isaiah 38, 8), and other ancient writings. Both the horizontal and vertical types were used in the Middle Ages, the latter especially on the walls of churches and public buildings of Europe. In our country, in China and perhaps other countries they are even now made in small wooden cases which may be carried in the pocket; and sun-dials are often seen in our gardens and parks. No other scientific instrument has continued in use for such a long period as the sun-dial.

The water clock is often called by its historical Grecian name of "clepsydra", meaning "steal water", but it seems entitled to its name of "clock" because it sometimes had a dial, especially in its late form, as in illustrations Nos. 1734-1736. These water clocks were all constructed in much the same manner, consisting of a vessel which was filled with water and had a small hole at the bottom through which the water could run out, the time being measured by the amount of water running out. These clocks had one great advantage over the sun-dial in that they could be used at night and at other times when the sun did not shine. In the note[2] it appears that they were used in Athens about four hundred years

1.   The details of a sun-dial cannot be stated here, and even if stated they are somewhat difficult to understand, but it should be said that the sun-dial in its simplest form, with a vertical pole, is not a good timekeeper. Although the *shadow* is always in the same *position* at noon, when the sun is highest, it is not always correct at other hours because the position of the sun is not the same in winter as in summer. But if the pole, instead of being vertical is inclined so that it points to the North Star, parallel to the axis of the earth, the shadow will be in the same position at a given hour throughout the year. Instead of an inclined pole, a pointer, generally triangular, will be seen on the sun-dials now used in gardens and other open places.

It is said that in many American farm houses, until recently, a substitute for a sun-dial was used, called a "noon-mark", which was painted on a window sill of a room facing the south, and sometimes a mark was also in the kitchen.

2.   In a law suit in Baltimore in November, 1932, one of the attorneys complained that the Court did not allow him sufficient time to conduct the case. In considering this point the Court, Judge Eugene O'Dunne, referred to the practice in the courts of Athens as stated by Aristotle, the Greek philosopher, (B. C. 384-322), in his monograph on the "Government of Athens", as set forth in Professor Wigmore's book entitled "A Panorama of the World's Legal Systems", volume 1, page 298. Aristotle wrote that "water clocks are provided, having small supply tubes, into which the water is poured by which the length of pleadings is regulated. Ten gallons are allowed for a case in which an amount of more than five thousand drachmas is involved". Judge O'Dunne held that "measured even by the foregoing standard, counsel was not hampered". A similar method of checking the loquacity of counsel was used in ancient Rome; and even the length of the speeches in the Roman Senate was similarly regulated—sometimes no doubt to prevent what is now known in legislative halls as a "filibuster".

Another ancient Greek writer, Æschines, mentions that "the first water was given to the accuser, the second to the accused and the third to the judges". This custom, said another Greek writer, "was to prevent babbling, that such as spake should be brief in their speeches". When a person was allowed to speak for a certain length of time it was said that he was allowed so much "water".

Other timekeepers were the "sand-glasses", in which sand in glass containers ran out slowly, the amount of sand being such as would require an hour or other period of time to pass out.

before the Christian era. They continued in use throughout the centuries and gradually took on various wheels and other mechanical devices until they were superseded by the early weight-driven clocks; and if the date on No. 1736 is correct[3] they were made in England as late as about 1690.

Illustration No. 1733 shows a water clock with a dial ring. From a container on the left, not seen in the engraving, the water comes through the pipe H to the conical vessel A from which it falls through a pipe, drop by drop, into the large cylinder below. In order to control the volume of water flowing into the

1733 ANONYMOUS.   1734 ANONYMOUS.   1735 ANONYMOUS.   1736 MR. J. S. McDANIEL.

vessel A there is a conical stopper which may be raised or lowered by the cogged rod D. Any overflow in the vessel A runs out through the pipe I. The water in the large cylinder gradually rises and the float and the rod E rise with it, and the cogs on the rod E move the wheel G to which the hand is attached. The hand moves around the dial which has two sets of numbers, 1-12, making twenty-four

(Note 2, *continued*)

Other less important devices were candles marked with notches between which the candle would burn in an hour or other period; still another device was a lamp of small diameter with oil, a wick and an hour scale, the number of hours being indicated by the amount of oil consumed as shown by the scale.

3. It is not likely that these clocks are genuine. Clocks of this type are now made in Birmingham, England, and may be purchased from importers in New York. These reproductions are well made and look old. Compare the remarks in section 185, note 7, in regard to lantern clocks.

hours of equal duration, in about which time the cylinder becomes full and must be emptied. The speed of this clock obviously depends upon the rate of flow of the water into the cylinder. It is said that this general form of water clock was used in Egypt about 300 B. C. This illustration is copied from Britten's "Old Clocks and Watches", page 10; it does not represent an actual clock, being merely a drawing made to show the working of a water clock.

Nos. 1734 and 1735 are illustrations of the same clock, closed and open. This type of clock is centuries later than No. 1733. On the curved plate near the bottom are the words "Jonathan Bentley of ye towne Chester Anno Dom 1643". The dial at the top is elaborately chased with rays of the sun and with Roman hour numerals from 1 to 24, outside of which are the words "I showe ye fleeting houres of daye as one by one they passeth awaye". The lower brass portion is engraved with dolphins. The operation of this clock is stated in the note.[3] This clock is probably a reproduction.

No. 1736 is of the same type, with the same method of operation. Here there is no enclosing frame and perhaps there never was one. The dial is square, with winged cherubs engraved in the corners, as on many of the early dials, as mentioned in section 183. The hand is long and somewhat similar to the hand in the preceding water clock. The hours are divided into half-hours and the hour numerals are in the Arabic form. The opening in the dial shows the wheel to which the hand is attached. On the curved plate above the water container are the words "Robert Smeaton Fecit of ye towne Salisbury Anno Dom 1692". The height is thirty-three inches.

Section 182. Mechanism of clocks.

—Although this section may be ignored by many or most readers, it will well repay those who take the time to examine it, or at least the text. The technicalities of the subject are omitted and the few essential parts of the works are much easier to understand than are those, for example, of an automobile.[1]

3.   The longer part of the hand extends to the outer line of the circle in which the hours are divided into quarters. Behind the centre of the dial, and connected with the hand, is a small wheel with teeth on which the chain catches, and at the other end of the chain is a hollow metal float which is not seen in the engraving as it is inside the metal tank. This tank holds the water, upon which the float rests. Under the door is a small faucet through which, when opened a little, the water comes, drop by drop, and falls into the container below, which is removable. As the water in the tank falls, the float and the chain fall also, and the chain pulls the wheel behind the hand, moving the hand forward. The speed of the hand thus depends upon the speed at which the water in the tank falls, and this in turn depends upon the rate of flow of the water through the faucet which depends upon the extent to which the faucet is opened. The tank holds enough water to move the hand around the dial about three times, or 72 hours. The height is 35 inches.

1.   In the first section of this book it is said that technical words are omitted so far as possible, and in this chapter the remark applies particularly to the mechanism of clocks.

Mr. Willis I. Milham, Field Memorial Professor of Astronomy in Williams College, Williamstown, Massachusetts, the author of the valuable book "Time and Timekeepers", which is

A clock is said to "keep" time, by which we mean that it "measures the passage" of time, and by the statement that a clock "keeps good time" we mean that it "measures the passage of time" correctly, or nearly so.

There are four essential parts of the mechanism by which a clock keeps time. The first is the "driving" part which furnishes the power which gives motion to the wheels and other moving parts; this driving part is either a weight, as in grandfather clocks, or a spring as in mantel clocks. The second is the transmitting part, consisting of a series of wheels which transmit the motion to the regulating part. The third is the regulating part, generally a pendulum and its connections which control the speed at which the other parts move. The fourth part consists of the hands which, if the clock is working at the proper speed, indicate the passage of time in hours and minutes. There are often other parts in antique clocks, such as a striking mechanism, but the above four parts are the only essential ones.

The most interesting of these four parts is the regulating part, which controls the speed of the clock. Since about the year 1658 this part has generally consisted of a pendulum and the connecting mechanism which together are sometimes loosely called the "escapement", a technical word which means the regulating part. Before that date other less accurate methods of regulating the speed of a clock were used, and although those methods are of no practical importance now, it is worth while to mention them. The principal one is known as the "foliot" (a French word) balance which is shown in illustration No. 1737; this has a horizontal cross-bar which swings to and fro, regulating the timekeeping.[2] This method was never used in England or America, but is seen on the Japanese[3]

(Note 1, *continued*)

mentioned in section 180, note 5, has very kindly read this section at the request of the writer with the desire to keep the technical details as correct as possible.

2. This engraving and Nos. 1740 and 1742 are copied from "English Domestic Clocks", by Cescinsky and Webster, figures 8, 9, 10. The heavy weights, not seen in the engraving, operating through several wheels, also not seen, cause the vertical wheel C, called a "crown" wheel from its resemblance to a crown, with which the hand of the clock is indirectly connected, to try to revolve; but this wheel cannot revolve any faster than is allowed by the two small pieces called "pallets", which project from the vertical revolving rod. These two revolving pallets alternately stop the wheel C momentarily by catching a tooth of the wheel and then letting it move again. The speed of the wheel and the pallets is controlled by the cross-bar A which swings to and fro, and the speed of the cross-bar is controlled by the position of the small weights, B and B; the nearer these small weights are to the centre, the faster the cross-bar swings. The speed of all the wheels is thus controlled to such an extent that the hands may measure the hours and minutes. This description of the foliot balance is not complete, but it perhaps makes the engraving easy to understand.

This method is used in the first mechanical clock known, called De Vick's clock from the name of the maker, which was made about 1360 and is now on a wall of the Palais de Justice in Paris; the clock had originally no minute hand and it did not keep time within two hours a day.

The heavy weights, and the small weights on the cross-bar, must of course be of such a weight as will be found sufficient, neither too heavy nor too light, as in all clocks driven by weights.

3. This clock is also shown as No. 2083 in section 197 where it is more fully explained.

clock No. 1738, and the wooden clock No. 1739, the latter being one of a large number made at the time of the World's Fair at Chicago in 1893.[4]

The next method of regulation, shown in No. 1740, is based upon almost the same principle as the "foliot" balance,[5] but instead of a horizontal cross-bar there is a horizontal "balance wheel" at the top which turns to and fro; a

1737 (Upper) Cescinsky & Webster.   1738 (Upper) Mr. Edgar G.   1739 (Upper) Mr. Edgar G. Miller,
1740 (Lower) Cescinsky & Webster.   Miller, Jr.   Jr.
                                    1741 (Lower) Anonymous.   1742 (Lower) Cescinsky & Webster.

4. Some readers may recall that this Exposition was in commemoration of the four hundredth anniversary of the discovery of America by Christopher Columbus in 1492. For this reason the head of Columbus is at the top of the frame with the name "Columbus" under it, and below is the inscription "Anno 1492". The clock is made entirely of wood, except the small weights and the pins and screws which hold the parts together. On the dial the hour numerals are in Arabic form and are all vertical, as to which see section 187, note 32. Some persons, seeing figures "1492", have imagined that these clocks were made in that year!

5. Here we again see the vertical rod with the two pallets E and E and the crown wheel "D", as in No. 1737. The chief difference between this and No. 1737 is that here a cross-bar is not used, its function being performed by the horizontal "balance wheel" at the top, marked B; this method of control of speed is therefore called a "balance wheel escapement".

somewhat similar wheel, shown in No. 1741, belongs to the Japanese[6] clocks Nos. 2063 and 2064. The next illustration, No. 1742, shows the first form in which a pendulum was used.[7]

None of the above methods of regulating the speed of a clock were satisfactory and they were all superseded by the pendulum,[8] which when applied to clocks about the year 1658 made possible an accurate measurement of time.[9] The pendulum was used in almost all clocks made after that date, and its superiority over previous regulating devices was such that the latter were often removed from older clocks and a pendulum was substituted.[10]

In grandfather clocks the pendulum is usually made in such manner that it may swing one way in one second.[11] The pendulum is the device which marks the passage of time, and the time is recorded on the seconds dial. The time of the swing depends upon the length of the pendulum. If the pendulum rod is made of metal it will expand and become somewhat longer if the temperature rises,

6. In this illustration we see two small round movable weights which influence the oscillations of the "balance wheel" as similar weights influence the "foliot" cross-bar in No. 1737. There is also a hairspring to assist in controlling the speed. In this very interesting little Japanese clock the striking mechanism serves as a weight to furnish the power which runs the clock; see the comment on Nos. 2063 and 2064.

7. Here there is a change in the positions of the "crown" wheel and the rod with the two pallets, both are horizontal and the rod is supported at each end, and at the rear end, (the left), the pendulum was attached to it. The crown wheel pushes the pallets to and fro and the rod turns and its speed is controlled by the pendulum. This form of escapement was not suitable for grandfather clocks but was used in many English mantel clocks until about 1800.

8. When the youthful Galileo, in 1581, watching a lamp swinging in the cathedral at Pisa, observed that whether the swings were long or short they always took the same time, he could not foresee that this fact would be the basis for the pendulum clocks of the world. Whatever the length of a given pendulum, and whatever the weight, each swing to and fro of that pendulum takes the same length of time whether the swing is long or short. The longer the pendulum is, the longer the time taken by a swing, and the clock therefore goes slower; the shorter the pendulum, the shorter the time of the swing, and the clock goes faster; hence raising the weight makes the clock go faster, and lowering the weight makes the clock go slower; for which purposes a movable nut or other device is used on the rod to support the weight at the point where the speed of the pendulum is the correct one for that particular clock.

The weight at the bottom of a pendulum of a grandfather clock is a round thin disk, having a shape whose swing is not much impeded by the resistance of the air; a pendulum with this kind of weight is called a "disk pendulum". In mantel clocks either the disk weight or a rounded weight, called a "bob", was used. The word "bob" is also used to mean a weight of any shape at the bottom of a pendulum.

9. The honor of its application seems to belong to the Dutch scientist Christian Huygens and the honor of its introduction into England belongs to the Dutchman Fromanteel who was a clock maker in London.

10. In "The Homes of Our Ancestors", by Halsey and Tower, page 14, an advertisement in the "Boston News Letter", October 6, 1707, is quoted. The advertiser stated that "if any person or persons hath any occasion for New Clocks; or, to have old Ones turn'd into Pendulums", etc.

11. In some English grandfather clocks very long pendulums, reaching almost to the bottom of the case, were used. In these the swing one way was made in one and one-quarter seconds, or more. These " admitted of closer regulation and more exact timekeeping"; Cescinsky and Webster, "English Domestic Clocks", pages 113 and 119.

and if the temperature falls the pendulum will become shorter, making a slight difference in keeping time;[12] and in order to reduce or overcome this variation the pendulum is sometimes made of two or more metals which counteract each other in changes of temperature or of some wood which is very slightly affected by a change in temperature; or other methods are used which accomplish the same result.[13]

Although the winding keys of clocks are not parts of the mechanism, it seems proper to present a page of illustrations, No. 1743, of several of the more usual types of keys, most of which belong to clocks illustrated in this chapter.[14] The

12. A pendulum which swings one way in one second makes 60 swings in a minute, 3600 in an hour, 86,400 in a day, 604,800 in a week; and if it varies one ten-thousandth of a second in each swing, the clock in a week will be about one minute and five-tenths of a second faster or slower.

13. Most of these are "compensating" devices and the pendulum is called a "compensated pendulum". In one method the pendulum contains mercury in a glass or iron vessel; if the temperature rises the mercury expands upwards, while the metal rod lengthens downward, being fastened at the top, so that the rise of the mercury "compensates" for the lengthening of the rod. This method is frequently seen in clock makers' and jewelers' shops. In another method, equally familiar, the pendulum is made of alternate parallel rods of two different metals which expand differently, such as steel and brass; these compensate each other, and maintain the pendulum at a fixed length. By experiment the lengths of these rods may be made such as will overcome the influence of changes of temperature. This type is called a "gridiron" pendulum because of its shape. It is often seen on French mantel clocks, such as Nos. 1975 and 1990. In some instances this type of pendulum is merely for ornament.

In a few clocks the pendulum is in front of the dial, but this position has no advantage except as a curiosity. Examples are in the Terry mantel clock No. 1930 and the wall clocks Nos. 2057 and 2058.

The French word for a domestic clock was formerly "horloge", but after the introduction of the pendulum the word "pendule" was adopted and has since been used.

In clocks driven by weights the driving power is constant, with no variation in the power. In a clock driven by a spring, the spring loses power as it runs down and the clock may become slow. This irregularity is overcome in many clocks by the "fusee", which is seen in the skeleton clock Nos. 2004-2005 and is described in the comments.

Although other parts of the mechanism are interesting and important, especially the striking part, the limitation of space prevents further consideration of the subject.

14. Of the six keys on the upper line, those marked "a"—"e" belong to English and American grandfather clocks; the similar key marked "f" belongs to the American grandmother clock No. 1868. These six keys are plain and strong and are very similar in design; three have wooden knobs. The key "d", which belongs to the English grandfather clock No. 1766, has a long shank, that is, the vertical part between the handle below and the keyhole part above. This clock has a very heavy striking weight and the shank was made long because to wind a clock with a key having a long shank is easier than to wind the same clock with a key having a short shank. Keys of these types are also used with English mantel clocks.

In the second line are five keys, "g"—"k", which are keys of French mantel clocks shown in section 193. The first four, "g"—"j", are of the same design, with an oval handle, the almost universal form used on these clocks. On the shank of each of these four keys a number is stamped near the handle, indicating the size of the key; this system of numbering is also used in the modern American keys of this and other types. The key "k" belongs to the French revolving band mantel clock No. 1970 for which a long key is needed.

In the third line, with six keys, the first five, "l"—"p", are German. The key "l" belongs to the two-faced clock Nos. 2080 and 2081. The keys "o" and "p" have an extension at the top for turning the rod which moves the regulating device by which the speed of the clock is controlled. The

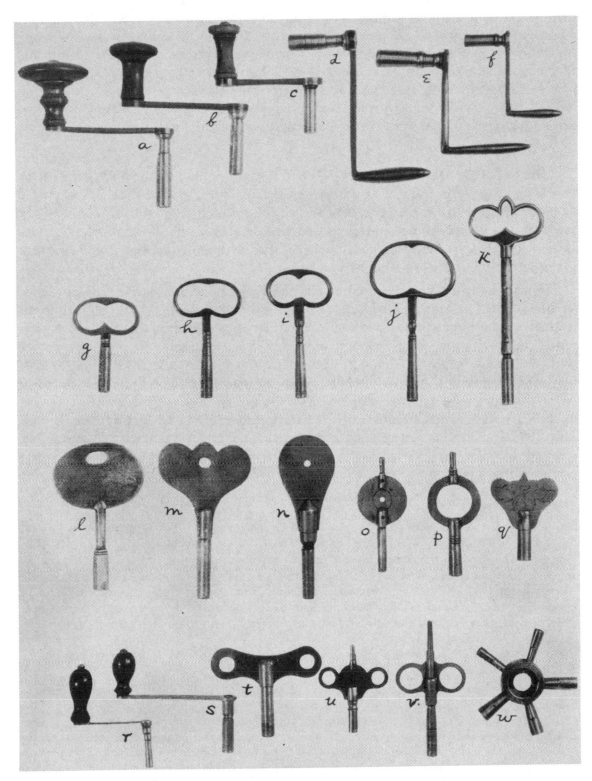

1743 VARIETIES OF CLOCK KEYS.

original keys of a great number of antique clocks are missing, especially the keys of mantel clocks which are generally moved to different positions more frequently than others; in many instances the keys used are modern; and often an old key taken from another type of clock is seen. The twenty-three keys here shown do not, of course, include all types, but they are sufficiently representative to give an idea of what should be used with the principal kinds of clocks. The illustrations are somewhat less than one-half of the actual size of the keys.

Section 183. Dials of clocks.—The dials and the hands, the only parts of the timekeeping portion usually visible, are of special interest; and dials are regarded as more reliable in fixing dates than the cases in which they are seen. All of the features of dials mentioned in this section will be seen in the illustrations of grandfather clocks, and many of them are seen also in mantel clocks. The dates here given apply primarily to English clocks.

Until about the year 1770, almost all English and American dials were made of brass with an attached silvered circle, or "ring", upon which the numerals indicating the hours were engraved. The open space within the circle was generally "matted", that is, pitted or punched with small dents,[1] or was ornamented with engraved designs. About the year mentioned a less expensive type of dial began to supersede the brass one. This was an iron plate which was enameled or painted white, with painted numerals for the hours, and with decorative designs at the corners.[2] Dials silvered all over were also made; and in the mantel clock No. 1895 the dial is entirely of brass, with no "ring" attached. About 1795, painted wooden dials were used on the American clocks with wooden works made in the Terry style, and after about 1837 the dial degenerated into a thin

(Note 14, *continued*)

key "q" belongs to the modern Chinese clock No. 2087 and is chased with designs similar to those on the back plate of that clock. The key "m" belongs to a modern German clock.

The keys on the bottom line are modern American. The first two, marked "r" and "s", are of the same general form as "a"—"f" on the first line, and have a revolving knob on the handle. The next three, "t"—"v", have wide handles and are used on mantel clocks, two of these have the extension at the top seen on "o" and "p" in the line above. The last key has five arms of different sizes which will fit many domestic clocks; it is known as a "bench" key, because it is used by men working on clocks while sitting at the bench.

Several of the American clock companies have keys of their special design; for example, "t" and "v" are designs of the Seth Thomas Clock Company.

1.   Matted surfaces are also seen on other articles, such as certain sofas of Samuel McIntire, of Salem, Mass., as mentioned in section 72 at note 6.

2.   In "Antiques", September, 1931, page 166, is an illustrated article, by Mr. Penrose R. Hoopes, entitled "Osborne and Wilson, Dial makers", in which it is stated that on a plate behind many painted iron dials are the names "Osborne and Wilson", or one of them, of Birmingham, England. The names refer to the dial, not to the works. The dates of these dial makers are from about 1772 to 1815. In an advertisement in 1772 Osborne and Wilson described themselves as "manufacturers of white clock dials in imitation of enamel". The name "Osborne" is on a plate behind the dial on the grandfather clocks Nos. 1820 and 1835, and others; and on No. 1827 the name "Wilson" is in a similar position, and on the back of the moon attachment is "Wilson Birm", the latter meaning Birmingham, England.

piece of painted metal in the clocks made with sheet brass, such as those shown in section 192.

The form of the dial changed at various periods, as will be seen in the illustrations. In the earlier grandfather and mantel clocks the dial was square, ranging in size from ten to twelve inches. This shape continued in general use until about the year 1725 when an arched top, behind which the bell was placed, came into fashion and continued in use until about 1800. In this arched portion of the dial was the maker's name, or a strike-and-silent hand, or a moving ship or figure, or one or more small dials, or a round convex plate called a "boss",[3] or some kind of decoration, or a revolving moon attachment, the latter feature being in fashion from about 1760 until after 1800. Other forms of dials, especially round ones and a few oval[4] ones, were made about 1800 and later, and about the same time there was a revival of the square form. All of these forms are shown in the illustrations and are mentioned in the comments.

At the four corners of the brass dial, outside of the silvered ring, are triangular spaces, known by the architectural name "spandrels", which on brass dials are occupied by ornamental brass pieces which also are called "spandrels", or preferably "corner pieces". Similar ornamental pieces are seen on the arched portion of many dials. The early corner pieces had a cherub's head in the centre with flowers and fanciful designs on the sides, but various other designs were used later. The design of a corner piece is said to be a "doubtful indication of the date of a clock, excepting in a general way", as many replacements were made with later designs and a design was often used long after it passed out of fashion. On painted dials the corners are generally ornamented with painted decorations.[5]

The numerals indicating the hours are almost always in the Roman form, but in some clocks the Arabic form was used; as to the latter see note 32 in section 187. An interesting matter in connection with Roman numerals is that the four o'clock numeral is almost always IIII instead of IV, the probable reason being that IIII balances the VIII on the opposite side of the dial and makes the dial symmetrical. The bottoms of the Roman numerals are always toward the centre, an obvious fact which is seldom noticed, even though the clock has been looked at for a lifetime.

Minute marks or numerals were not used on the early clocks which had no minute hand; the time, however, could be approximately estimated by the division of the spaces between the hour numerals into four parts, indicating the quarters of an hour, with an engraved design at the half-hour, as seen in No.

3. On the "boss" the name of the maker or the warning words "Tempus fugit" were often engraved, but in some cases it was blank. It was in use at intervals from about 1725 to 1780. Examples are in Nos. 1773-1775, 1785, 1788, 1807, 1864 and 1865.

4. An oval dial is in the grandfather clock No. 1778 and the mantel clock No. 2099.

5. In "English Domestic Clocks", pages 92-98, are forty-five illustrations of "spandrels" or "corner pieces". It is said that the early pieces were skillfully made but that after about the middle of the eighteenth century the former high standard was rarely maintained.

1752 in section 186, and in very many others. These divisions into quarters of an hour and the engraved designs were of no practical value after the minute hand was used,[6] but they continued to appear occasionally until about 1800, perhaps for their decorative effect.

The moon attachment seen on so many grandfather clocks, and sometimes on mantel clocks, was apparently first used in England about 1740; it became popular about 1760 and continued in style until about 1820. This device is intended to indicate the age of the moon, counting by days from the day of the new moon.[7] The usual form is a circular sheet of metal, with the face of a moon painted on each of two halves of its front surface. This sheet makes one complete revolution in about two months, showing each painted half in about one month. Emerging from behind a disk on the left, one of the moons revolves and finally sinks behind a similar disk on the right, and the other moon then appears on the left and takes the same course, in which they show the "phases", that is, the apparent forms of the moon's illuminated surface. Other forms of moon attachments are in Nos. 1791, 1803 and 1810. Other matters concerning dials are mentioned in the note.[8]

6.   When the minute hand was introduced, minute marks were placed on the outer edge of the hour circle, outside the hour numerals; and twelve Arabic numerals for the minutes, 5 to 60, were afterwards added on the extreme edge of the dial, some appearing to be very large, as in No. 1756 in section 186; these large outside minute numerals continued to be used until about 1820. Other changes in position are sometimes seen.

7.   The average time from new moon to new moon is twenty-nine and one-half days, and this number is often seen cut on small disks on the sides, probably as a reminder that the actual number of days in a month is not always the same as those of the clock and as a warning that an adjustment should be made. The moon attachment is now of little use, is often out of order and is seldom in harmony with the moon itself unless it is adjusted monthly. But although almost useless in these days, like the barometers shown in the Appendix, section 201, it is ornamental and interesting.

The two metal disks behind which the moons appear and disappear are generally ornamented in the English clocks with engraved designs. On many American grandfather clocks from about 1800, and on some of the English ones, the disks are painted with maps of the eastern and western hemispheres, using the names then applied to the oceans and land. For example, the name "New Holland", which is the English equivalent of the former Dutch name of Australia, appears as the name of that continent on the English clock No. 1778 and the American clock No. 1850 and others. These names may indicate the approximate dates of the dials, unless the makers were not particular about their geography. See illustration No. 1863, in section 187, and the comment.

8.   A.   Several small dials are often in the main dial of many antique grandfather and mantel clocks, the principal one being a dial in which a second hand revolves, known as the "seconds dial". Another dial, called "strike-silent", has a hand which controls the striking mechanism, and a similar one turns on or off any chimes or musical attachments.

B.   The openings in the dial are for various purposes. There are of course two round openings for the key which winds the two parts—time and striking—or one opening if there is no striking part; these are called "winding holes". In clocks from about 1700 to 1740 the holes were often surrounded by "rings", perhaps in order to protect the dial from being scratched by careless handling of the key. Such scratches, often seen on painted dials, are sometimes regarded as an indication of great age, but they may be easily given to a new dial. A third winding hole is necessary if another weight or spring is to be wound up, as for chimes or musical attachments, as in No. 1825.

Section 184. Hands of clocks.—The earliest English domestic clocks had no minute hand, as will be seen in the illustrations in the next section which treats of the "lantern", or "bird cage", and the "hooded" clocks.[1] From the time of those early clocks to the clocks of the present day, the hands have been made in a series of designs by which the approximate dates of the clocks may in many cases be known.[2] As the American antique clocks followed the English styles, they were generally fitted with the kind of hands used on the English clocks; but some of the late American clocks, such as those in the Terry and other styles, not being copied from English models, had hands of different designs.

(Note 8, *continued*)

      C.   Another opening shows the day of the month; this is generally rectangular and placed over the six o'clock numeral. A circular disk, marked with the figures 1 to 31, revolves behind the opening, a new figure appearing each day, or preferably during each night.

      D.   In some clocks, chiefly the mantel ones from about 1725 to 1790, a curved opening two or three inches long with rounded ends, appears over the centre, behind which a disk moves to and fro with the swing of the pendulum, to the top of which it is attached. An example is in No. 1883.

      E.   In clocks made for special purposes, as for astronomical use, the dial sometimes has twenty-four hour divisions. A dial similarly divided is on the water clock No. 1736. This form of dial is said to be preferable for railroad and scientific purposes.

      F.   A small round alarm attachment, (spelled "alarum" in the English books), was occasionally placed in the centre of the dial, under the hands, as in the "hooded" clocks Nos. 1748 and 1749, until about 1780, and also in late American mantel clocks such as No. 1952 and others. In some clocks this attachment has been removed because it was difficult to keep in order.

      G.   Other useful or ornamental features are occasionally seen in dials. In the Rittenhouse clock No. 1839 are various astronomical features, and also in No. 1790. In No. 1789 the times of high and low water at the seaport town of Bristol, England, are shown. In the clocks shown in "English Domestic Clocks" are many dials with finely engraved designs. In English clocks made for the Turkish and Spanish markets the dials have distinctive details, as in Nos. 1894 and 1895.

      H.   As to the maker's name on the dial, see section 186 in the paragraph beginning "The name of the maker" on page 888.

      I.   A Dutch dial, not illustrated here, which might be mistaken for an English one, has near the edge a line which is straight over the Roman hour numerals but is curved over the spaces between them. Over the hour numerals are large Arabic minute numerals. An example is in figure 692 in Britten's "Old Clocks and Watches". These dials were made about 1750-1800.

      1.   In the previous section the quarter-hour divisions on the dial are referred to in connection with the early clocks which had only an hour hand.

      2.   Provided, of course, the hands are the original ones belonging to the clock. Perhaps no parts of clocks have suffered so much from breakage as the hands. The minute hand on account of its length being more fragile than the hour hand, and more often moved carelessly in setting the clock to the correct time, was especially liable to be broken; and when broken its place was often taken by a hand of a different type and period. An original hour hand and a substituted minute hand of a later style are very frequently seen, but the error is seldom known to the owner.

      Even if the hands are the original ones, their style cannot be relied on in all cases to determine the date when they were made, because the clock makers were not obliged to use a particular type at a particular time and there was often an overlapping of styles.

      The length of the hour hand should be about enough to touch the hour numerals, and the length of the minute hand should be about enough to touch the minute marks; if the hands are much longer or shorter they are likely to be substitutes for the original ones. After about 1800 the English clock makers were sometimes not careful about the length of the hands; and many of the American makers were not more particular.

In illustration No. 1744 eighteen representative forms of hands[3] on English clocks from about the year 1705 are shown.[4] Some of the clocks are of the lantern and grandfather types and others are mantel clocks. The dates given in the note[5] are those of the period in which the forms of the hands came into fashion in London. In every case the date is merely approximate; and many types of hands were used for years after a new type became popular. No American hands are shown here; but many of them are well seen in the engravings in later sections.

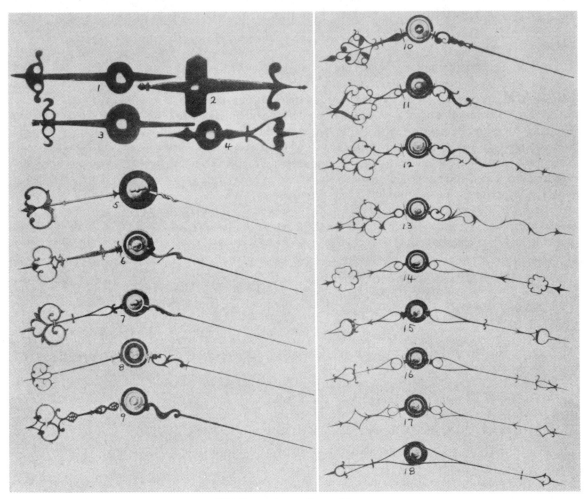

1744 Varieties of Clock Hands.

Section 185. Lantern and hooded clocks.—The brass "lantern" clock was the first type of domestic clock made in England and was the predecessor of the grandfather and mantel clocks. The name "lantern" was given to it because its

3. An almost infinite number of variations of the hands here shown are found in both English and American clocks of the grandfather and the mantel types. For example, the finely pierced hands Nos. 10 and 12, used on both types of clocks, were made in great numbers, often in less elaborate forms.

An interesting matter is that until about 1790 the hour and minute hands differed from each other greatly in shape, the hour hand being wide and often elaborately cut out and the minute hand being a plain one with a decorative form at the inner end; but in many of the later grandfather and

shape resembled a lantern of the period.[1] It was made to hang on the wall or to stand on a bracket attached to the wall. At the top is a large dome-shaped bell, under which are the works. On the front and the sides, over the dial, are three "frets", cut out of brass in various designs.[2] The dial is circular and at first had only an hour hand, and as there was no minute hand there were no minute marks; but the spaces between the hour numerals were divided into quarters, with an engraved design at the half-hour mark.[3] Later, minute hands were sometimes used. The power was furnished by one or two weights on ropes or chains which were pulled up by hand, not by a key, and were long enough to operate the time and striking works for about thirty hours.[4] The earliest lantern clocks were con-

(Note 3, *continued*)

mantel clocks after about 1790 the forms of the two hands became in many cases almost the same, although of course different in length, as in Nos. 14-18.

Clock hands were filed out of a piece of steel by hand, and it is said that unless one pair was copied from another no two pairs of hands were ever exactly alike.

The usual form of the small "seconds" hand was generally plain, and the insecure method of attaching it was such that it is often missing. The "sweep-second", or "centre second", hand is of a different type, being about as long as the minute hand. It is connected with the mechanism at the same point as the hour and minute hands and sweeps around the dial in sixty seconds. Although of no particular value for household timekeeping, it is full of action and interest as it passes the hour and minute hands every minute. Examples are in the grandfather clocks Nos. 1812 and 1825. A "pointer", a kind of hand, pointing to a circular row of figures under the hour numerals, indicating the days of the month, is occasionally seen, as in the same clocks.

4. These illustrations are a few of those shown in Cescinsky and Webster's "English Domestic Clocks". They include the more important of the English types of various periods in chronological order. Mr. Cescinsky states in regard to his illustrations that the examples are instructive as they show "the relating design of the minute hand to the hour hand"; page 89.

In Mr. Wallace Nutting's "Furniture Treasury", volume 3, pages 469-486, are illustrations of 277 hands.

5. Nos. 1, 2, 3 and 4 are hands of lantern clocks such as Nos. 1745-1747. The other hands are of English grandfather and mantel clocks. Nos. 5, 6, 7, 8, 9 are about 1670 to 1690.   Nos. 10 and 11 are about 1725.   Nos. 12 and 13 are about 1750-1760.   No. 14 is about 1775.   Nos. 15, 16, 17 and 18 are from about 1790 to 1850.

In connection with these illustrations the English dials Nos. 1785-1793 may be examined, in some of which one or both of the original hands have been replaced, as in Nos. 1788 and 1789. See also the American dials Nos. 1853-1861.

1. This clock is also called a "bird cage" clock because of its resemblance to the bird cages seen in some of the paintings of the period. It is sometimes called a "chamber" clock; and the term "blacksmiths' clock" has also been used; see section 180, note 6, paragraph 3.

2. The pattern of the frets is said to be some indication of the date, but not a conclusive one. Certain forms prevailed at various times, but not exclusively. The form with dolphins was a favorite one; see note 9. The purpose of the frets was to conceal the bell and to add to the ornamental appearance.

3. See section 183 on "Dials" at note 6. This is an interesting feature in many grandfather and mantel clocks from a very early date until the latter part of the eighteenth century. It is well seen in No. 1747, and is often referred to in section 186.

4. Visitors to Monticello will recall Thomas Jefferson's clock with two faces, one inside the house and the other outside, and with chains running through the floor into the cellar, sufficiently long to keep the clock going for a week. The weights are Revolutionary cannon balls.

trolled by balance wheels,[5] but later the pendulum was used, either a short one swinging rapidly to and fro,[6] or a long one which led to the development of the grandfather clock. The dates and other matters are mentioned in the note[7] and in the comments.

Many reproductions of lantern clocks have been made in England and widely sold in our country, because of which the subject is mentioned here somewhat fully. In the illustrations, the brackets upon which the clocks were placed, the weights and the chains have been omitted. Clocks of this type were apparently not made in America.

No. 1745 is one of the earliest English clocks known,[8] having on the movement the date 1618, which is doubtless the year in which it was made. This has the "balance wheel" type of regulation, shown in No. 1740, which is under the large and sonorous bell. Almost under the lower edge of the bell, on the front and sides of the clock, are the "frets", in the central portion of which are two dolphins with their heads at the bottom, a favorite design but not indicative of an exact date.[9] There is only one hand, the hour hand. The open space within the hour circle is ornamented with chased designs. The hour circle, better seen in No. 1747, is divided into quarters of an hour with an engraved design at the half-hour, as mentioned above at note 3. About 1618.

5.   As to these see section 182, Nos. 1740 and 1741.

6.   On some clocks the swing of the pendulum was so wide that it could be seen from the front. In order to hide this mechanical feature, extensions called "wings" were placed on the sides.

7.   These lantern clocks were made as far back as 1618, which is the date of No. 1745. Although they were the first domestic clocks made in England, they were not always early in date, as they were "produced, especially in country districts, until well into the nineteenth" century; and it is said that Birmingham, England, has turned out thousands of imitations of them to meet the demand of the antique market. They may be purchased now in quantity, with an old maker's name on the dial, from a Birmingham factory. See also the remarks in section 181, note 3, in regard to reproductions of water clocks.

On the sides and back of the clock are brass doors. For the purpose of showing the works, one or more of these doors are often removed when a photograph is taken; and in many instances they are broken off.

Small round alarm dials, (spelled "alarum" in the English books), are on many of these clocks, placed in the centre of the dial under the hands. Similar alarm dials are on other types of clocks, as in the "hooded" clocks shown in this section; see also section 183, note 8 F.

Almost all original lantern clocks have been changed in the course of years, with substitutions of new parts which improve the accuracy of the timekeeping. The remains of one are shown in No. 1750, which has been changed into a nondescript piece, but still runs and keeps good time; see the comment on this "Warning Clock".

These clocks are generally about sixteen inches high and about six inches wide; but a miniature one, about eight inches high, striking the hours, is illustrated in the English books.

8.   This illustration and the next two are copied from "English Domestic Clocks", by Cescinsky and Webster, figures 24, 33, 36.

9.   As mentioned in note 2. Dolphins continued to be popular designs until late in the Empire period; see the card table No. 1556, and the girandole mirror No. 1242; also note 5 in section 174 in regard to console tables about 1725-1750.

1745 (UPPER) CESCINSKY & WEBSTER, FIG. 24.
1748 (LOWER) CESCINSKY & WEBSTER, FIG. 393.
1746 (UPPER) CESCINSKY & WEBSTER, FIG. 33.
1749 (LOWER) CESCINSKY & WEBSTER, FIG. 395.
1747 (UPPER) CESCINSKY & WEBSTER, FIG. 36.
1750 (LOWER) MR. EDGAR G. MILLER, JR.

In No. 1746 the dark object under the bell is a group of four small chiming bells. The open space within the hour circle is faintly seen to be ornamented, or at least occupied, by three skeletons which address Latin mottoes to the observer informing him that "what I am you will be". The frets here are in a heraldic design somewhat resembling the royal arms. About 1630.

No. 1747 is much later in date, as appears from the name and address of the maker under the fret, not visible in the engraving. The dolphin fret is again seen. The open space in the centre of the dial is engraved with flowers and leaves, and the half-hour marks on the hour circle are well seen. As in the previous examples there is no minute hand and therefore there are no minute marks. About 1675.

Another English type of clock made to hang on a wall and having only an hour hand is the "hooded" clock, of which two illustrations[10] are shown, Nos. 1748 and 1749. The early clocks of this kind may be regarded as transition pieces, indicating the process of development of the late lantern clocks, which had a pendulum but no protecting cover, into the grandfather clocks with a long pendulum and with a case enclosing all the parts. These "hooded" clocks were all of the same general character, consisting of works enclosed in a hood such as those on grandfather clocks, but with the chains and weights exposed. Almost all hooded clocks ran for thirty hours, as the lantern clocks did, and had an alarm attachment in the centre of the dial under the hand.

No. 1748 is an English hooded clock, with an hour hand of an early type and with an alarm attachment in the centre of the dial. The half-hour marks resemble those in the lantern clock No. 1747. The spiral columns are similar to those seen on the clocks Nos. 1753 and 1880, and on several early tables and chairs of about the same period, such as Nos. 35 and 1279. About 1690.

In No. 1749 the case is made of mahogany, and this fact, the inlaid design of flowers, the circular dial and the date of a certain clock maker under the alarm attachment indicate a much later date than that of the preceding piece; but the clock follows the old form in having only an hour hand. About 1800.

Perhaps No. 1750 should not appear in this book, but to the writer it serves as a valuable "warning clock" showing how easily one may be misled if details are not noticed. The rear portion is that of a lantern clock with a short pendulum, to which extent it is without reproach, except that the iron doors on the sides are missing; the rest of the story is in the note.[11]

10.   These are copied from "English Domestic Clocks" by Cescinsky and Webster, figures 393 and 395.

It is said that this type of clocks originated in Holland. Other types of Dutch wall clocks, having two hands and with the works protected, are shown as Nos. 2060-2062 in section 196, in which a number of wall clocks of different styles and dates are illustrated.

11.   Several features in this partly "lantern clock" may be noticed. First, the dial is arched, a form not used on lantern clocks. Second, there are no winding holes in the dial, although English clocks with arched dials were wound by a key, not by chains. Third, there are no divisions or marks for minutes, and therefore the minute hand does not belong to the dial. Fourth, the pattern of the hands is of about 1800 or later, and was not used on lantern clocks. Fifth, the "boss", a round plate at the top, bears the name "John Wallis, London", a maker who worked from about 1825 to 1840, as appears in Britten's

Section 186. Grandfather clocks; English and other foreign.—In this section the illustrations present a series of English grandfather[1] clocks and enlarged dials which show the important changes from the earliest type to the latest of those which may be called "antique"; and several examples of French and Dutch clocks of the grandfather type are also shown. Only a very few of the early English clocks are seen in our country, except in museums, but without them the reader would have an incomplete picture of the clocks from which our American ones were derived.[2] Before examining the illustrations, however, a number of preliminary matters should be mentioned.

(Note 11, *continued*)

"Old Clocks and Watches", page 796, too late for lantern clocks. Sixth, a round plate of this kind passed out of style in London before the days of John Wallis. Perhaps the only parts which may be regarded as the work of John Wallis, or made in his time, are his name and address and the hands. Nevertheless this mongrel clock still runs and keeps good time.

1. The clock now commonly called a "grandfather" clock is also called a "tall" clock or a "long case" clock in the English books. These two latter terms are of course more descriptive of the case of the clock than the merely fanciful name "grandfather", but this name is now so widely used in both England and our country, and is so well understood, that it seems proper to use it. Examples of other names of popular origin are "highboy" and "lowboy" which in our country have supplanted the former descriptive English names, as mentioned in the chapters on those articles.

2. In considering grandfather clocks we must examine those of English make if we wish to understand our American pieces, and therefore a considerable number of them are illustrated; in this respect a discussion of clocks requires a method of treatment different from that used in the chapters on American furniture, in which English pieces were not often shown.

In the English books the grandfather and other clocks referred to are understood to have been made in London unless otherwise stated, and all other English clocks are called "provincial". The provincial makers generally followed the London styles, but often clung to styles for a long time after they had gone out of fashion in London, making it difficult to fix the dates. For example, as mentioned in the previous section, note 7, the lantern clocks were made in country districts for many years after they were discontinued in London. In certain counties in England various distinctive styles were popular and became known by the name of the county, such as the "Yorkshire" clocks Nos. 1771 and 1772. Clocks made in Wales, Scotland and Ireland are also distinguished from the London pieces. The dial of a Scotch clock is shown here, No. 1792.

A fine grandfather clock has a dignity and character which make it important in any household. Its location should be carefully selected so that the whole clock may be clearly seen, and particularly the dial which often has features of special interest. If possible the front of the clock, not the side, should be visible to those entering the house. It should not be crowded into a narrow place, but should have a space on each side. Sometimes the clock stands at the head of a staircase where it may be seen from both the first and second floors, but this position is not often desirable, as the clock does not show to advantage when seen either from above or below. Moreover a grandfather clock should be viewed from a minimum distance of somewhat more than its height, in order that we may see it as a whole and thus determine whether its proportions are harmonious; if viewed at a very short distance the proportions are not well seen.

In many families the grandfather clock is the most highly prized of inherited furniture. Serving several generations, the old clock has for a century or more, almost without interruption, been important in the family life of the ancestors of the owner. The clock deserves all the praise that has been given to it in prose and homely poems, the latter almost exhausting the list of words rhyming with "tick" and "clock".

It is said that the name "grandfather" clock came from an American song, written about 1880, which in the words of an English writer "carried the United States and our country by storm".

(*Continued on next page*)

The English grandfather clocks were developed from lantern and hooded clocks, as mentioned in the previous section. When a long pendulum was placed on a hooded clock, not a pleasing combination, it became desirable to enclose it and the weights and chains in a cover, or case, and when this was done the hooded clock became a grandfather clock. As stated on page 884, in the text, this was about 1670, and in the next one hundred and eighty years, until about 1850, when it is said to have passed out of fashion, the grandfather clock continued to be made without any great change in the general form of the case.[3]

The case of a grandfather clock is in three parts which have appropriate names. The upper part, in which the dial and the works are enclosed, is known as the "hood"; this part, without the two other parts below it, would be similar to the case of a hooded clock, such as Nos. 1748 and 1749. Under the hood is the long and somewhat narrower part in which the weights hang and the pendulum

(Note 2, *continued*)

The title of the song is "My Grandfather's Clock" and the author was Henry Clay Work, of Connecticut, (1832-1884), a writer of popular songs. It is printed, with the music, on page 161 of "The Book of a Thousand Songs", edited by Albert E. Wier and published in 1918 by the Mumil Publishing Co., New York. The rule against quoting poetry in a book on antique furniture has already been broken in this book, in section 11, note 1, and another infraction of the rule may be excused. The song is as follows:

1. My grandfather's clock was too large for the shelf,
        So it stood ninety years on the floor;
    It was taller by half than the old man himself
        Though it weighed not a pennyweight more.
    It was bought on the morn of the day he was born
        And was always his treasure and pride,
    But it stopped short, never to go again,
        When the old man died.

2. In watching the pendulum swing to and fro
        Many hours had he spent while a boy,
    And in childhood and manhood the clock seemed to know
        And to share both his grief and his joy;
    For it struck twenty-four when he entered the door
        With a blooming and beautiful bride,
    But it stopped short, never to go again
        When the old man died.

CHORUS

Ninety years without slumbering, tick tock, tick tock,
    His life seconds numbering, tick tock, tick tock,
It stopped short never to go again
    When the old man died.

3. Only in the modern adaptations has there been a substantial change in the form of the case, converting it into an ill-proportioned box with a glass front which discloses several chains and weights and a large brass pendulum disk which is perhaps the most conspicuous object in the case, except the gaudy dial.

swings; this is called the "waist".[4] Under the waist is the "base", which is partly for the weights and partly ornamental. These three parts, in a proper combination, give a dignified appearance to the case as a whole and place the dial at a convenient height to be seen. The relative sizes of these three parts determine whether the case of the clock as a whole is well proportioned or ungainly.[5]

In the "Director" of Chippendale and the "Drawing Book" of Sheraton, as to which see chapter 3, sections 15 and 18, are several designs of clock cases. Those of Chippendale are of grandfather and mantel clocks and those of Sheraton are only of the grandfather type. No clocks have been found in England with cases of the exact character of any of these designs, and it is thought that none were ever made, the probable reason being that the designs were not suitable for the works. The influence of the Chippendale school is often seen, however, in the use of a "scrolled" top on grandfather clocks, as in No. 1767 and many others, or fretwork or other characteristic features of that style;[6] and the influence of

4. In the back of the upper part of the waist of many grandfather clocks are small holes made by screws which fastened the clock to the wall. These fastenings were intended to keep the clock in the proper position if the floor was warped and also to keep the clock from falling forward if too strong a pull were made in that direction, as in removing the hood. A grandfather clock with a heavy hood may be somewhat top-heavy, especially if the weights are high up, raising the centre of gravity. Screws were also used on wall clocks which are liable to slide from an exactly vertical position while being wound up, as mentioned in connection with banjo and lyre clocks in section 194, note 10, and section 195, note 4.

The length of the catgut or chain supporting the weights in a grandfather clock having the usual mechanism determines the length of time the clock will run after being wound. This time is generally about eight days. By the addition of certain extra wheels and attachments the time may be extended as, for example, in No. 1766 which runs for four weeks. Clocks running for one year have occasionally been made.

5. Extremes of elegance and the opposite in form, not in decoration, may be seen in the cases of the four early English clocks Nos. 1758, 1760, 1762 and 1764 and in the two clocks Nos. 1771 and 1839, the former of these two being an English Yorkshire case and the latter an American case made to enclose a notable clock by David Rittenhouse of Philadelphia.

In this and the next section the question may arise whether a particular grandfather clock found in our country is English or American. Whenever an English name and address appear on the original dial, it is certain that the works are English, unless the name and address are forgeries, which are not unknown; but the case may be American, as works were often imported without a case, the latter being made in our country. If however a dial bears an American name, it does not follow that the works are American, because on many English works without a name, imported for sale, the American clock makers and dealers put their own names on the dials, as mentioned in section 180 at notes 12-15.

But when no name or address appears, the question for the amateur collector often is whether the works and the case, or either of them, are English or American. In some instances the case is clearly American, as when the wood is an American wood or there is some feature of obvious American origin, as in No. 1805 and others where there is a carved shell of American design on the top of the lower door. If, however, there is no plain evidence of origin, as in many clocks of standardized types, we arbitrarily assume in this book, for the purpose of classification, that both the works and the cases were made in America. Certainly there were many American clock makers and cabinet makers, some trained in English shops, who were capable of doing fine work. Such clocks will therefore appear in "American grandfather clocks" in the next section; but of course this classification may be erroneous in some instances. The French and Dutch grandfather clocks Nos. 1794-1799 are not included in these remarks.

6. See Nos. 1767-1776 and the comments and notes.

Hepplewhite and Sheraton may be noticed in inlaid designs of shells and ornamental forms. Several of these features are referred to in the comments.

In presenting the English grandfather clocks found in our homes it should be
remarked that in some of them the original dials or hands or other parts may
have been removed and new ones substituted, or the works may have been placed
in cases not originally made for them.[7] These substitutions are occasionally found
in some of the finest English specimens shown in the books or offered at auction
sales or in the shops. It is not often possible for an amateur to detect these
changes. Moreover many parts which may appear to be substitutions may in fact
be the original ones put on by makers who did not keep up with the changing
styles, or whose customers may have preferred an old style of case or dial or
hands or other parts.

The name of the maker does not always appear on the English clocks, but
fortunately the custom, at certain periods required by law, was to display his
name and place of business on the dial. In the earliest grandfather clocks the name
was in a straight line along the bottom of the square dial; about 1700, it was generally engraved in a curved line in the two spaces between the numerals VII and V,
a method which continued in some clocks until about 1770. After the arched top
came into use, about 1725, a round convex plate called a "boss", (mentioned in
section 183), was often attached to it, with or without the maker's name or some
inscription, as in No. 1785 and others referred to in note 3 of that section; this
also continued in use for many years, perhaps until about 1775. Another method,
beginning about 1700 and continuing until about 1800, was to engrave the
maker's name on a small metal plate which was fastened on the dial, as in No.
1791 and others. After about 1770 the maker's name was at various places, and
in some instances it was a very conspicuous advertisement. The dates mentioned
above are only approximate, and moreover the methods, depending upon the
ideas of the maker or dealer, overlapped each other to such an extent that the
position of the name is not convincing evidence of the date of the clock.

In regard to the dates of English grandfather clocks it must be realized
that the forms of the cases and dials overlapped to an extent not seen in our
American pieces. An extreme example, mentioned by Mr. Cescinsky[8] in connection with the cases of clocks of the type shown below as Nos. 1774-1776, is that
"although the form of these cases is late—from 1775 to about 1810—it is not
unusual to find them fitted with dials of the fashion from 1730 to 1750".

7.   In his "Chats on Old Clocks" Mr. Hayden remarks, page 83, that "it sometimes happens that
a clock maker, as the differences in size of many of these clocks are not great, found an earlier case to
his hand, or a client desired a particular style of decoration, and he accordingly put his new clock into a
case twenty years earlier. * * These are the conundrums left as a heritage to the collector, who now
comes two hundred years later." And in "English Domestic Clocks", page 8, it is said that "there is no
doubt that many of the long case clocks which are met with are not in their original cases"—a remark
which also applies to many of our American pieces.

8.   "English Domestic Clocks", page 216. Here it is said that two conspicuous features of the
dials of the earlier period may be found in clocks of the later period. These features, when seen in the
later clocks, will naturally mislead the amateur collector into thinking that such clocks are about fifty
or sixty years older than they really are. See the comments on Nos. 1774-1776.

Forty-three illustrations[9] of English grandfather clocks and of enlarged dials of such clocks are shown in this section. The clocks of the types shown in the first eight illustrations are the most highly esteemed of the English grandfather pieces because of their age, their fine design and cabinet work and their superior timekeeping quality.

For the purpose of classification the English grandfather clocks are said to be in four periods, the first of which, from about 1670 to 1720, is known as the period of "marquetry",[10] for the reason that in those years the cases were ornamented with that form of inlay. In the second period, about 1720-1740, many fine clocks were made with burl[11] walnut veneer. The third period, from about 1740 to 1760, is that of "lacquer",[12] which was decorated with various designs, generally of a Chinese or Japanese character. The fourth period, from about 1760 to 1800, was, for clocks, the period of mahogany; in the latter part of this fourth period the designs of grandfather clocks in England began to decline, although in our country the period was that of some of the best of these clocks, as will be seen in the next section. In the present section, illustrations[13] are given of English grandfather clocks in the order above mentioned, so that their gradual development may be seen.[14] The woods used are mentioned in the note.[15]

9.   The illustrations of the first eight clocks and the six enlarged dials are copied, by permission, from "English Domestic Clocks", a book gratefully referred to in section 180, note 5, B.

In order to illustrate some of the dials on a larger scale, without taking too much space, the engravings of the dials of six clocks are placed under those clocks; but the space is not sufficient for more than three dials on a page. Nine other enlarged dials, Nos. 1785-1793, are on a separate page at the end of this section.

10.   Marquetry is mentioned in section 33, note 1.

11.   Burl walnut is mentioned in section 28, note 3.

12.   Lacquer is mentioned in section 31.

13.   For many of these illustrations the writer is indebted to "English Domestic Clocks", which should be in the library of everyone interested in the subject. As far as possible the illustrations in this section follow the order of those in the English book.

14.   It should be understood that this division into periods does not mean that in any one period only one kind of grandfather clock was made. On the contrary many clocks made, for example, in the fourth period may have been made in the style of earlier periods, especially by clock makers living in the country districts who were not so particular about changes in styles as the makers in London. Therefore the dates given for the clocks here shown are often merely approximate, although some of them may be accurate, such as those of clocks made by members of the Clockmakers Company whose dates are recorded in the books of that organization. In Britten's "Old Clocks and Watches", and in Baillie's "Watchmakers and Clockmakers of the World", the names and dates of the members may be found.

15.   The wood used in the cases of grandfather clocks may be mentioned. In the marquetry cases the wood was generally oak, veneered with walnut and inlaid with some light-colored wood. The burl walnut cases were veneered on oak. The lacquered clocks were of oak. Mahogany was generally veneered on oak, solid mahogany being seldom used in English cases.

The years in which walnut and mahogany were used in England for grandfather clock cases did not coincide with the years in which those woods were used for other articles of domestic furniture. Walnut was not generally used until about 1735, when its use had ceased to be in fashion in other articles in England. Mahogany was not generally used until about 1760, although it was the favorite wood for furniture after about 1730. See also section 189, note 5, E and section 180, at note 7.

No. 1751 is said by Mr. Cescinsky to be "perhaps the earliest example of a long case clock which was ever made". The form of the case, with its rectangular panels on the door, was a favorite one until about 1690. The pointed top and the square dial will be found revived in No. 1781, which was made about 1825. The maker was "Johannes Fromanteel", "Londini", one of the family regarded as the first to introduce the pendulum into England. About 1670-1675.

No. 1752 is an enlarged dial of the preceding clock. An important feature is that there are no minute marks because there is no minute hand, but on the inner edge of the silvered ring, between the hour numerals, are four division marks which indicate the quarters of an hour; and at the half-hour mark is a design which shows the half-hour more prominently; this division into quarters of an hour, mentioned also in section 183, continued to be generally used until about 1750, but is also seen as late as about 1800. The corners of the dial are not occupied by ornamental "spandrels", or "corner pieces", which are mentioned in section 183 at note 5. The dial is about nine inches square. About 1670–1675.

No. 1753 is a highly decorated marquetry[16] clock, said by Mr. Cescinsky to be "a true type of the period to which it belongs". As in many of the early clocks, the hood is removed by lifting it upwards instead of sliding it forwards. The dial is square, as in the preceding clock and the next five. The top of the hood is flat, and the fret-work under it is of stamped brass. An opening in the door in the waist has a convex glass, called a "bull's-eye". On the hood of this and the next clock are spiral columns such as are seen on the legs of tables and chairs of the period, as mentioned in the comment on No. 1748. The dial is eleven inches square. About 1700-1705.

No. 1754 is an enlarged dial of the same clock. Here there are two hands, a seconds dial, and a small opening in which the day of the month appears. The two keyholes are "ringed", perhaps as a protection against scratching by the key, as mentioned in section 183, note 8, B, and as seen in the American dial No. 1854. Quarter-hour divisions and half-hour designs are on the inner edge of the silvered ring. At the corners are brass "spandrels". The photograph of the dial was not taken at the same hour as that of the clock. About 1700-1705.

In No. 1755 the hood has a high top and spiral columns. The marquetry on the waist, in three sections, is in very minute detail, as is also that on the base. There are no feet, as was customary in the cases of this period. About 1710-1715.

No. 1756 is the dial of the preceding clock. One of the three keyholes is for a chime on eight bells. The minute numerals, on the outer edge of the silvered ring, are much larger than those on the preceding dial. The name of the maker is in a curved line on the bottom of the dial, between the hour numerals V and VII, the usual position in the clocks of the period. About 1710-1715.

No. 1757 is said by Mr. Cescinsky to be a "very good example of the last years of the reign of Anne", 1702-1714, except that the base is modern. The

---

16. In Mr. Symonds' "Old English Walnut and Lacquer Furniture", pages 110, 171, warning is given to the amateur collector as to numerous clock cases with spurious marquetry and lacquer.

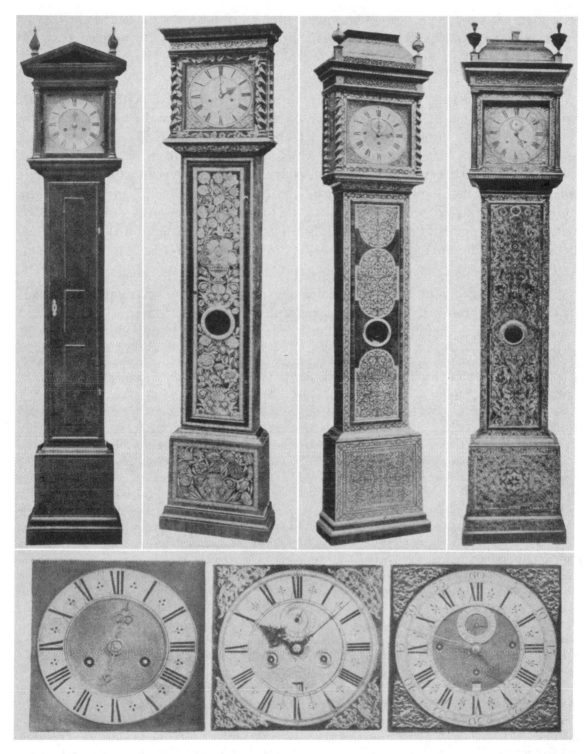

1751 (Upper) Ces. & Web.,   1753 (Upper) Ces. & Web.,   1755 (Upper) Ces. & Web.,   1757 (Upper) Ces. & Web.,
   Fig. 75.   Fig. 122.   Fig. 149.   Fig. 153.
1752 (Lower) Ces. & Web., Fig. 76.   1754 (Lower) Ces. & Web., Fig. 123.   1756 (Lower) Ces. & Web., Fig. 150.

marquetry is very elaborate. The square dial continues in style and there is fret-work over the dial as in the two preceding clocks. It will be noticed that the top of the door in these clocks is straight, not arched, harmonizing with the rectangular forms of the hood and dial. About 1710-1714.

In No. 1758 the case is veneered with burl walnut, inlaid with walnut bands and lines. This clock, which runs for a month, was made by the famous Thomas Tompion,[17] "the father of English watchmaking", 1638-1713, and is also of special interest in having two devices which are occasionally seen in later clocks; one is the "pull-repeater", by which the last hour or quarter-hour or half-hour is made to strike again when a string on the outside is pulled;[18] the other is the "maintaining power" device described in the note,[19] the only visible parts of which are the pieces of metal, called "shutters", which are behind the keyhole, as better seen in the enlarged dial, No. 1759, of this clock and in No. 1763. About 1705-1710.

The enlarged dial No. 1759 shows the shutters of the "maintaining power" device referred to in the preceding paragraph and note 19. There is also a second hand and an opening showing the day of the month. The four elaborate "span-

17.   "He left English watches and clocks the finest in the world and the admiration of his fellow artists. * * In the Grand Pump Room (at Bath, the English watering place) there is a splendid example of his later work, which he gave to the city in 1709"; Britten, "Old Clocks and Watches", pages 279, 286. Bath is also referred to in section 168, note 4, in connection with "Beau Nash". A mantel clock by Tompion is No. 1882.

18.   It is said that before lucifer matches were invented this device was useful if one wished to know the time at night in a dark room when the hands on the dial could not be seen. On pulling the string or pressing a knob the clock again strikes the last hour, or quarter-hour, the pull or the pressing doing what the clock machinery does at each hour or quarter. Perhaps this device was more of a curiosity than one of actual usefulness. If the occupant of the room is in bed and the room is dark he must first find his way to the clock in the darkness, at the risk of a collision with a chair or table. Moreover the hour struck is the same whether the time is one minute after, say, three o'clock, or a few minutes before four o'clock—not a very exact time. The repeater was invented in 1676 and con-tinued in use until about 1830. This device is more frequently seen on mantel clocks, as shown in section 189, than on grandfather ones, and is generally operated by pulling a string rather than by pressing a knob.

19.   This device is clearly described by Mr. Cescinsky in "English Domestic Clocks", page 67, and also in a catalogue by him, in the latter as follows: "The power which drives a long-case clock is the fall of a weight, and when the clock is wound, the weight is lifted by the winding key. While the act of winding is in operation, the falling of the weight is stopped, and the driving power removed. The fraction of inaccuracy, in consequence, is very trifling, but it is an error, and, in the early clocks, this was corrected by the maintaining-power device." The winding holes are closed by shutters on the inside and to open the holes for the purpose of winding the clock a string must be pulled, or a lever depressed, and this puts a spring in action, which drives the clock for about a minute while the clock is being wound. The purpose of the shutters is to prevent the key being inserted and the clock wound up without providing power to drive the clock during the winding. The left hand shutter, on the striking side, is not necessary and is merely for symmetry. After the clock is wound and the key with-drawn, the shutters are closed by the swing of the pendulum. In the American grandfather clock No. 1815, bearing the name of a Baltimore maker, about 1785-1795, the shutters are held open by a small lever on the right hand side of the dial.

1758 (Upper) Ces. & Web.,   1760 (Upper) Ces. & Web.,   1762 (Upper) Ces. & Web.,   1764 (Upper) Ces. & Web.,
Fig. 159.   Fig. 174.   Fig. 198.   Fig. 203.
1759 (Lower) Ces. & Web., Fig. 160.   1761 (Lower) Ces. & Web., Fig. 175.   1763 (Lower) Ces. & Web., Fig. 199.

drels" or "corner pieces" are too small to be well seen in this or other dials; they are mentioned in the text in section 183 which treats of dials. About 1705-1710.

No. 1760 is veneered on the front with burl walnut which is "matched", a process described in section 32, note 2; the effect is faintly seen on the waist where two designs resembling the letter "C" are in the upper portion, the design on the right facing the right and that on the left facing the left. This decorative form was much used many years later on flat surfaces, such as the mahogany doors and drawer fronts in No. 728 and No. 1723. The base is cut in two cyma curves. About 1710.

No. 1761 is the enlarged dial of the clock last referred to. It has about the same features as those on the preceding dial, except that there are no "shutters" behind the keyholes. About 1710.

No. 1762 is the first of two clocks decorated with "lacquer", a treatment mentioned in section 31. This clock must have presented a gorgeous appearance when it was new, being, in the words of Mr. Cescinsky, "decorated with silver and coloured Chinese ornament on a lacquered ground of a beautiful powdered blue. The caps and bases of the columns (on the hood), and the spires, are also silvered to correspond." About 1700-1705.

No. 1763 is an enlargement of the square dial of the preceding clock. A feature here is an oval plate under the centre, in which is the name of the maker, "George Allett", of London; a similar plate is in No. 1791. Back of the keyholes are the shutters of the "maintaining power" device explained in note 19. About 1700-1705.

In No. 1764, also a lacquered clock, we see the first illustration of an arched dial instead of a square one. This arched form of dial, mentioned in the text of section 183, came into general use about 1725 and continued in fashion until after 1800. In the arch of the dial is a convex "boss" on which is the name of the maker. The top of the door in the waist is arched, harmonizing with the arch in the dial. On the waist and the base are Chinese scenes. This clock is said by Mr. Cescinsky to be "a rare example of a fine green lacquered ground. The ornament is beautifully executed and in pure gold leaf and powder." The elaborate hood is a study in itself. About 1730.

Having examined the above examples of fine early English grandfather clocks, which are seldom seen in our country but are important to us if we wish to understand the later ones and our American clocks, we proceed with illustrations of twenty later English clocks found in our homes, Nos. 1765-1784. With a few exceptions, all of these clocks have arched dials and hence are of later date than about 1725.

No. 1765 has an arched dial with a flat top on the hood. In the arch is a small "boss" bearing the words "John Burgess de Wigan"; the latter word is the name of a town near Liverpool. The important feature is the dark oak case, the entire front of which is carved.[20] The figures on the lower door represent St. George and the Dragon. The top of the lower door is arched to correspond with the arch of the dial, as in the preceding clock. The spiral columns resemble those of the earlier clocks Nos. 1753 and 1755. The dates of Burgess, the maker, are given as 1690-1740, and the date of the clock may be near the latter year.

No. 1766 has a burl walnut case. At the top is a box-like superstructure resembling that on the block front chests on chests Nos. 880 and 881, a form seen also on the clock No. 1764 and others. The corners of the waist and the base are cut off, or "chamfered", as in the bureau No. 714 and others; a round opening in the waist, with glass, called a "bull's-eye", discloses the pendulum weight; the door in the waist is "arched", corresponding with the arch of the dial. The ornaments which were on the top of the hood are missing.[21] An enlarged dial of this clock is shown as No. 1787. About 1740-1760.

We next examine a group of ten English grandfather clocks, Nos. 1767-1776, in cases which are commonly said to be in the Chippendale[22] style. These cases are easily recognized by the form of the upper part of the hoods, often called the "pediment", an architectural term. The forms of the pediments are of two kinds. One kind has two scrolls, between which there is usually a short pedestal on which is placed an ornamental brass or carved wood ornament, such as a vase or a flame, and at the inner ends of the scrolls are applied rosettes; these features are seen in Nos. 1767-1773. This form of pediment is sometimes called a "swan-neck pediment". It was in fashion in England from about 1770 to 1810. The other and somewhat earlier kind, called by Mr. Cescinsky the "hollowed pediment", is shown and explained below in connection with Nos. 1774-1776.

20. In Britten's "Old Clocks and Watches", figure 721, a somewhat similar clock is illustrated and it is said that "dark oak cases carved in high relief do not seem to have been the fashion of any particular period, but the result rather of occasional efforts by enthusiastic artists in wood, and then in most instances they appear to have been made to enclose existing clocks in substitution for existing or worn-out coverings."

21. Other features of this clock may be mentioned. The dial has the quarter-hour divisions and the usual design at the half-hours; a moon attachment is in the arch, with brass hemispheres on the sides; a small seconds dial and an opening showing the days of the month are on the dial. This clock runs for four weeks, the extra wheels requiring the winding to be to the left; there are two bells, one of which is struck on the hour and the other on the half-hour, the latter striking the next hour. The names, "Clarke & Dunster" of London, are within the minute marks at the bottom of the dial between the hour numerals V and VII, as in other clocks of the period.

22. Mr. Britten, in his "Old Clocks and Watches", page 548, remarks that it is not easy to define exactly what constitutes a Chippendale case, nor why it should be ascribed to Chippendale. Mr. Cescinsky in "English Domestic Clocks", page 207, states that the clocks with scrolled tops exhibit some influence of the great cabinet maker's style. Mr. Wheeler in his "Old English Furniture", page 380, states that many clocks are "christened 'Chippendale' because it is not possible to father them on any other designer or because they take on an added lustre through the parentage implied." See also this section at note 6.

     The scroll top is seen in various articles of furniture. Among them are highboys, as in Nos. 657-668; secretary-bookcases, as in Nos. 847-850; and especially in mirrors, as in Nos. 1107, 1138, 1159 and others. Many of the Terry mantel clocks have the scroll top, as in Nos. 1928-1935.

Other features of the so-called Chippendale style case are the two columns at the front corners of the waist; these columns are often fluted or reeded and are generally ornamented at the top and bottom with brass caps and bases;[23] and another feature is the use of fretwork[24] as a decoration which may be either "applied" or cut out of the solid wood.

No. 1767 is a handsome clock showing the phases of the moon in the arched portion of the dial.[25] The so-called "Chippendale style" is indicated by the scrolls on the pediment, the fretwork over the lower door and on the lower part of the wide waist and on the base, the fluted columns on the waist and other less important features. There are no quarter-hour divisions on the inner edge of the dial as there were on many of the earlier dials. A panel is on the base. On the dial is the name "Barnish", with the word "Cockermouth", a town in the north of England. About 1770.

No. 1768 is also a handsome clock, whose inlaid ovals and corner pieces on the waist and base are in the Hepplewhite style. Here the fluted columns on the hood, those on the two front corners of the waist, and the somewhat unusual ones on the corners of the base, have brass caps in the Corinthian form and the usual base pieces. Above the arched top of the door in the waist is a horizontal line of fluting, suggestive of the Adam style of decoration. Below the keyholes is a curved opening in which the days of the month appear, under which is an attached plate bearing the words "Robert Roskell, Liverpool". About 1790-1800.

No. 1769 is also decorated with inlay, having designs on the top of the hood, and on the somewhat wide waist, and with two "fan" inlays on the base. The hood is unusual in having the space between the two scrolls entirely filled in; a similar treatment is shown in Nos. 1771 and 1772 and in Nos. 217-220 in "English Domestic Clocks", by Cescinsky and Webster, in which the clocks are classified as of provincial make. The top of the door in the wide waist is shaped in a

23.   The columns are often called "quarter-round columns"; if a round column, or a round lead pencil, is cut lengthwise into four equal parts, each part will be a "quarter-round" column.

In the Chippendale period in our country the caps and bases of the columns of clocks were of wood, as in Nos. 1805, 1808 and 1809, as were also the columns in the highboy No. 660 and the lowboys Nos. 711-712; later, in the grandfather clocks in the Willard style, as in No. 1840, the caps and bases were of brass.

In writing of the similarity of the cases of these grandfather clocks made from about 1760 to 1810, it is said in "English Domestic Clocks", pages 241 and 244, that it is only necessary to select one hundred examples at random to see the resemblance of them all. "The same arch-headed upper and lower doors, the cornices straight or following the arches, the shaped pediments either scrolled or hollowed, with two or three pinnacles of brass in the centre and the corners, will be found in nearly all. Out of five hundred mahogany grandfather clocks from 1765 to 1810, chosen at random, how many would be found with the fluted or reeded columns with brass caps and bases on either side of the hood? Certainly ninety-nine per cent."

24.   A fretwork, or fret, is an ornamental piece of metal or wood cut in an interlaced or trelliswork form. One kind is perforated, or pierced, and shows through, as on the top of many grandfather clocks made by the Willards or in their style; and another kind is applied on a background, as is well seen over the dial in No. 1840 by Simon Willard. On some grandfather clocks both forms were used, as in No. 1850.

25.   As to this see section 183 on "Dials".

kind of Gothic arch. On the top of the arch of the dial are the words "Shake-shaft, Preston", the latter being a town in Lancashire. About 1820.

In No. 1770 the wide waist and the base are similar in form and inlay to those in the preceding clock, but the upper portion is of a different form, having a "pediment top" of the style shown in the American clocks Nos. 1826-1833. The painted dial is square, not arched, a revival of the early shape seen in Nos. 1751-1762. At the bottom of the dial are the name and address "A. Coates, Wigan", the latter being the name of a town near Liverpool. About 1790-1800.

Nos. 1771 and 1772 are examples of "Yorkshire" clocks, made about 1790-1810, which are said by Mr. Cescinsky in "English Domestic Clocks", pages 235, 239, to "stand in a class by themselves. The cases, hardly without exception, are gigantic—almost elephantine—and although often veneered with choice curl mahogany, and inlaid with satinwood or ivory, they can only commend them-selves to those who prefer quantity to quality." These remarks do not refer to the workmanship nor to the earlier clocks made in Yorkshire. In each of these two clocks the top of the hood resembles that in No. 1769.

In No. 1771 the dial is arched and over the moon attachment are the words "As the hours pass, so passes the life of man". On the round painted dial are four small dials; the one at the top is for the time, with a sweep-seconds hand; and of the other three that on the left is for the day of the week, that on the right is for the day of the month, and the lower one is for the month, and has the words "Eli Bentley, Liverpool". The waist, with its columns, is short and very wide, with a small arched door. The bracket feet are very small, and the base is cut in curves. About 1800-1810.

In No. 1772 the case is over-decorated with wide inlay on the top, the waist and the base. The columns on the hood and the waist are not fluted, but are "turned" with rings. At the rear sides of the hood the back-board is extended beyond the usual point, a feature also seen in the American clock No. 1831. On the arched dial the corners are decorated with figures which perhaps represent the four continents, and the two hemispheres are painted with maps of the world. On the dial are the words "Cottrell, Handsworth". The bracket feet are very small, as in the preceding piece. About 1800-1810.

No. 1773 has a more elegant form of case than those of the two preceding clocks and is the last English one shown here with a scroll top. The inlay on the waist and base is rectangular, except at the top of the lower door where it is arched, conforming with the door. The "boss" in the arched portion of the dial is marked "Thomas Wagstaffe, London",[26] who was also the maker of No. 1776. About 1770-1790.

26. In Britten's "Old Clocks and Watches", page 795, Thomas Wagstaffe, 33 Gracechurch Street, London, is listed as a clock maker from about 1766 to 1794, and it is said that "there are a number of long-case clocks by him in America, generally in the possession of Quakers and their descendants. I learn from Dr. Walter Mendelson, of New York, that Wagstaffe was a Quaker and that members of the Society of Friends, when visiting London, were accustomed to lodge at Wagstaffe's house, and on their return frequently took one of his clocks with them."

(*Note continued on page 900.*)

1765 (Upper) Mr. Leigh Bonsal.
1769 (Lower) Mrs. F. G. Boyce, Jr.

1766 (Upper) Mr. Edgar G. Miller, Jr.
1770 (Lower) Mr. A. G. Towers.

1767 (Upper) Mr. A. E. Cole.
1771 (Lower) Mrs. T. J. Lindsay.

1768 (Upper) Eutaw Savings Bank.
1772 (Lower) Mr. J. S. McDaniel.

898

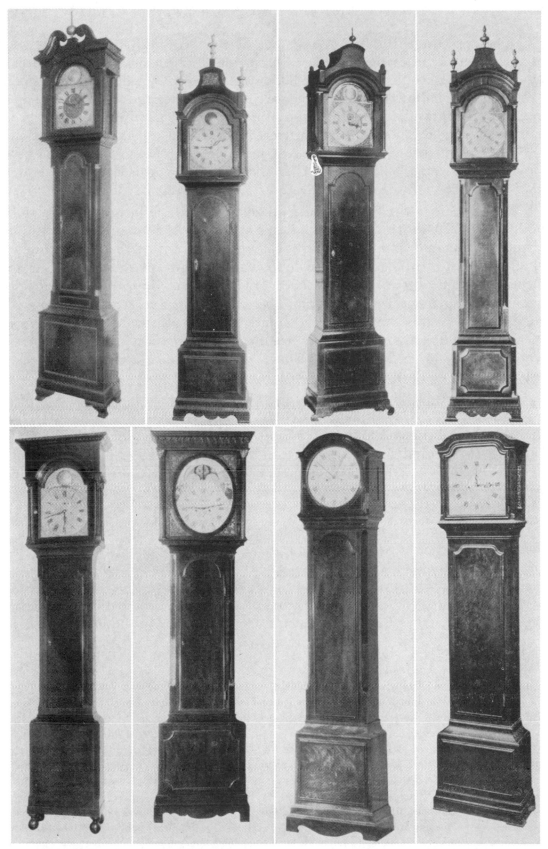

1773 (Upper) Mr. B. RANDALL.

1774 (Upper) Chase House, Annapolis.

1775 (Upper) The Kenmore Asso.

1776 (Upper) Dr. J. Bordley, Jr.

1777 (Lower) Mr. B. C. Howard.

1778 (Lower) Mr. Edgar G. Miller, Jr.

1779 (Lower) Mr. J. G. D'A. Paul.

1780 (Lower) Ces. & Web., Fig. 255.

The next three English grandfather clocks, Nos. 1774-1776, are examples of the second type of the so-called Chippendale style clocks. These are called by Mr. Cescinsky "clocks with a hollowed pediment", which means that the "pediment" is hollowed out, or concave, in the manner shown in several of the designs of Chippendale, although apparently not original with him. This type of case was first made about 1750 on lacquered clocks, and was in fashion until about 1810. As mentioned at note 8 in the text above, in reference to the dates of certain English grandfather clocks, Mr. Cescinsky states that it is not unusual to find clocks of this type fitted with two features[27] of the dials of 1730-1750.

No. 1774 is in the Chase House in Annapolis, a fine historic brick dwelling built about 1770, in which the clock seems to have marked the passage of time for about one hundred and sixty years. The concave sides of the top, forming the "hollowed pediment", are in the style shown in designs of Chippendale, as above mentioned. The three carved wooden ornaments are apparently original, and under the upper one is a fretwork. There is no inscription on the "boss". An enlarged dial of this clock is No. 1786, in which the quarter-hour marks are seen. Near the bottom of the dial, between the hour numerals V and VII, are the words "Jona'n Wych, London"; this name does not appear as of this period in the lists of Britten or Baillie. About 1770-1780.

No. 1775 is also in a historic house, "Kenmore", the home of George Washington's sister, Bettie Washington Lewis, at Fredericksburg, Virginia. It is said that this clock belonged to the mother of Washington, who died in 1789. It will be noticed, as an indication of date, that there are no quarter-hour marks on the dial, or half-hour designs, as were usual on earlier clocks. The scroll feet are doubtless substitutions for the original bracket feet. On the "boss" are the words "Joseph Barnes, London". This name does not appear in the books. About 1780.

The handsome case of No. 1776 has fretwork at the top and in a curve over the upper door. The wooden ornaments at the top resemble those in No. 1774. In the arch of the dial is a small "strike-silent" dial with a movable hand by which the striking mechanism may be controlled; this is well seen on the enlarged dial of this clock, No. 1793. The three pairs of columns, at the corners of the hood, the waist and the base, have small decorative brass rods in the lower ends of the

(Note 26, *continued*)

A letter written by Wagstaffe, dated "16th. 8 mo. 1764", in regard to a clock shipped by him to the Pennsylvania Hospital in Philadelphia is in the possession of the owner of this clock.

Several Wagstaffe clocks have been found in Maryland, and also in Philadelphia in which city there were many Quakers. No. 1892 is a mantel clock by this maker and No. 2055 is a wall clock by him.

27. The first of the two features mentioned by Mr. Cescinsky is the use of quarter-hour marks on the inner edge of the silvered ring with a design at the half-hour point, as mentioned in the comment on dial No. 1752; the second feature is the early custom of placing a small strike-silent dial in the arch of the dial, as in No. 1776.

It seems that very few clocks of this type were made in America; one, No. 1834, bears an American name and address, which may be that of either a dealer or a maker. Several are shown in "Connecticut Clockmakers of the Eighteenth Century", by Mr. Penrose R. Hoopes; see Nos. 33, 34, 35, 40 and others in that book, all dated from about 1750 to the end of the century.

fluting. The molding on the lower door and on the base will also be noticed. On the enlarged dial we see the name "Thomas Wagstaffe", who is referred to in note 26. About 1770-1790.

The next five clocks, Nos. 1777-1781, are examples of several other English types. No. 1777 has an arched dial with a flat top, a combination seen on the much earlier clock No. 1765, on No. 1778 and on the American clock No. 1835. The dial has quarter-hour marks on the silvered ring with a design indicating the half-hour divisions, as in the earlier enlarged dials Nos. 1752-1756 and 1785-1788. On the "boss" in the arched portion of the dial are the words "Wm. Allam, London", who was in business about 1780-1800. The ball feet are probably substitutes for the original bracket feet. About 1790-1800.

No. 1778 is a handsome English grandfather clock with a flat top and an oval dial, the latter a feature seen also in the mantel clock No. 2099. On the four corners of the upper door are pierced designs in fretwork with silk behind them. Under the cornice is a carved "acorn" or "pear drop" design, forming arches, seen also on various articles of furniture such as the secretary-bookcase No. 855. The fluted columns on the hood and the waist have brass rods at their lower ends, as in No. 1776, and the base is paneled in the same style as in that clock. Over the moon attachment are the words "Husband—London". About 1800-1810.

In No. 1779 the distinctive features are the round dial and the curved hood. In "English Domestic Clocks", figure 245 is almost a duplicate and is dated about 1785, and this clock might be regarded as of the same date except for the fact that on this dial are the words "Barraud's,[28] Cornhill, London" and in Britten's list it is stated that the Cornhill location began in 1796. The date may be uncertain, but is apparently after 1796.

No. 1780 illustrates a square type of dial which was popular about the beginning of the nineteenth century. This form of dial is a revival of the earliest English clocks shown here and was generally used for the very exact "regulator" clocks. A very similar case is the subject of an interesting error made by reliance upon tradition.[29] About 1800.

28. The absence of the first name or partnership names makes uncertain the exact date. In Britten's list there are three persons or firms of the name of "Barraud", in Cornhill, London, working from 1796 to 1842.

The use of a surname only is also seen on French clocks. The business of several prominent makers passed from father to son and sometimes to others who used the same business name. An example is "Le Roy, a Paris". The first prominent Le Roy, Julien, died in 1759; his son Pierre, "the most eminent of French horologists", died in 1785; Charles Le Roy and Theodore Le Roy were others. It is said that all of these men used merely the name "Le Roy, a Paris" on their clocks. In estimating the date of their clocks reliance must be placed upon the style and mechanism.

See note 23 to the Simon Willard grandfather clock No. 1840, in which the date of the label is closely fixed by the exact firm name of the printers and their location on "Quaker Lane" in Boston.

29. In the Admiralty Office in London is a clock in a case very closely resembling that of No. 1780. As told by Mr. Cescinsky, in "English Domestic Clocks", pages 175-177, the cornice of the hood has a brass plate affixed, engraved with the words "Presented by Queen Anne", who reigned from 1702 to

(Note continued on page 902.)

In No. 1781 there is a revival of an early form of hood, the top being similar to that in the first English grandfather clock here shown, No. 1751. This top resembles somewhat the gable end of a building and the hood is sometimes called

1781 Ces. & Web., Fig. 252.   1782 Mr. & Mrs. E. H.   1783 Mr. & Mrs. H. L.   1784 Mrs. E. Shoemaker.
McKeon.   Duer.

a "gabled" hood and the top a "portico" top. The dial is silvered all over, without an attached ring for the hour numerals. About 1825.

The next three clocks, Nos. 1782-1784, are called "miniature" grandfather clocks in the English books because of their small size compared with that of

(Note 29, *continued*)

1714. The case is veneered with curl mahogany. Mr. Cescinsky remarks that "Queen Anne could not possibly have presented a clock case veneered with curl mahogany, as the wood was utterly unknown in England at the date of her death." As to dating furniture by family tradition see section 6 at note 16.

many other grandfather clocks. They are sometimes called by the more appealing name of "grandmother" clocks, but the American "grandmother" clocks are so much smaller than these, and the style of the cases is so different, that the name may be confusing to us if applied to the English ones. Several English clocks more nearly the size of the small American ones are shown in section 188 as "grandmother" clocks. The average height of the three clocks here shown is between five and six feet and the width of the waist is about seven or eight inches. In some of these clocks the narrow waist prevented the use of a long pendulum with its wide swing, and therefore a short pendulum, like those on mantel clocks, was often used. They were made in the styles of about 1700 to 1775.

No. 1782 has the features seen in the early grandfather clocks. The square dial, the fretwork over the dial, the flat top and the spiral columns of the hood are all similar to those in the grandfather clock No. 1753. The height is sixty-four inches. Because of the long period in which clocks of this type were made, and the absence of the name of the maker, it is not possible to fix its date with certainty; but the style of the case and the works seems to be about 1700-1715.

In No. 1783 the hood and dial are of about the same type as in the preceding clock. A noticeable feature is the line inlay on the waist and the base, which is associated with the later periods of Hepplewhite and Sheraton, but is not unknown on clocks of this period and type, as in No. 86 in "English Domestic Clocks". On the dial are the words "Eduardus Hooper, London, fecit". Style of about 1715.

No. 1784 is of much later date, as indicated by the molding at the top of the hood, by the design of the columns on the hood, and by the curves at the top of the lower door, none of which are seen in the two preceding clocks. What appears to be a light inlay at the top is merely a reflection of the molding. The height is sixty-nine inches. Although the date is uncertain the style appears to be about 1780.

The next nine illustrations, Nos. 1785-1793, all on one page, are of dials of grandfather clocks on a somewhat larger scale than those in the clocks already seen. The brief comments on these dials may in some cases duplicate what has already been said. These illustrations are not in exact chronological order.

No. 1785 is an example of an early square dial to which an arch has been added by riveting it on to the square dial from behind. This addition was often made when the arch dial became the fashion. As in some other early clocks the minute marks are on the outer edge of the "ring" on which the hour numerals are placed. On the inner edge of the ring are marks for the quarter-hours. At the half-hour marks are designs as on the enlarged dial No. 1756 and others, and also on four others in this group. The convex "boss" on the arch bears the words "Windmills and Bennett, London". About 1720-1730.

No. 1786 is the dial of No. 1774, in the Chase House, Annapolis. Protective rings around the keyholes may be seen, as in No. 1754. The minute marks are not on the outer edge of the ring, as they are in the preceding dial; on the outer edge are large minute numerals; and the quarter-hour marks and the half-hour designs are also seen. This dial has a "boss" in the arch, but there is no inscription upon it, the name and address of the maker being near the bottom, as mentioned in the comment on the clock. About 1770-1780.

No. 1787 is the dial of No. 1766. Here there is a moon attachment, first used about 1740, with brass hemispheres. The rings around the keyholes are faintly seen. The hour and minute hands are of exactly the correct length, just reaching the quarter-hour and the minute marks. In the centre, under the hands, is an alarm attachment. About 1740-1760.

In No. 1788 what appear to be rings around the boss and the dial are merely unoccupied spaces of the brass dial. The hour hand is too long and is a substitution. On the boss are the words "Jona'n Beake, Crutched Fryars, London"; and another name "John Lupton", is at the bottom between the hour numerals V and VII. A peculiar custom of marking the maker's name on the dial twice or three times is mentioned by Mr. Cescinsky in "English Domestic Clocks", pages 181, 184; but here there are two different names, the reason for which is not apparent. The name of John Lupton is given the date 1825 in Britten's "Old Clocks and Watches", and in Baillie's "Watchmakers and Clockmakers of the World" Jonathan Beake is dated 1724-1745.

In No. 1789 the dial is of a type which was popular at seaport towns where the rise and fall of the tides or of a tidal river were matters of importance. This dial bears the words "Henry Lane, Bristol"[30] at the bottom of the hour ring, and at the top of the arch are the words "High water at Bristol Key", under which are half-circles with the hours of the day and the days of the month. The hands are substitutions, being later than the dial and too long and not mates. Britten gives the date as about 1780.

In No. 1790 the arch of the dial is of an astronomical character. At the **top** is the name "Willm. Wilkinson, Leeds", England, under which are several semi-circular divisions showing the time of the rising and setting of the sun and various other matters. A hand points upward to numerous figures. The centre of the dial is ornamented with engraved designs. About 1780-1800.

---

30.   This clock, made in Bristol, England, brings to mind the large number of English, Welsh, Scotch and Irish people who came to America from that port in the period of about 1654 to 1679. In the book entitled "Bristol and America", published in London in 1929, a list is given of about ten thousand "servants to foreign plantations", most of whom went to New England, Maryland and Virginia. These persons were "indentured immigrants" under contracts by which they agreed to serve for a certain number of years, and at the end of their term of service they were to receive land or other compensation. Many of these were cabinet makers, carpenters and other artisans. Remarks on "Indentured servants" are in the Appendix, section 207; and see note 7 in section 187.

The names of these emigrants from Bristol were written in ledgers by official clerks who spelled the names in any way they thought best. At that time the owners of the names were not particular about the spelling. Even a century later the spelling of the name "Hepplewhite" was not the same in different editions of his book, the "Guide"; see section 17, note 1. The name of Sir Walter Raleigh was spelled by him in three different ways.

The names of many clock makers, especially the French, were spelled in two or more ways.

As to middle names, see section 17, note 1, above cited.

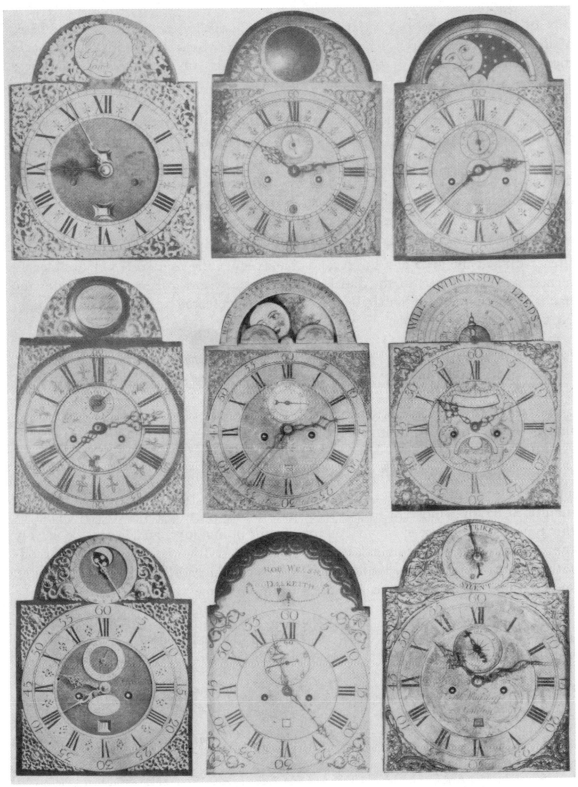

1785 (Upper) Cescinsky & Webster, Fig. 180.
1788 (Centre) Mrs. E. N. Dunham.
1791 (Lower) Cescinsky & Webster, Fig. 230.

1786 (Upper) Chase House, Annapolis.
1789 (Centre) Judge F. N. Parke.
1792 (Lower) Miss Mary Leigh Brown.

1787 (Upper) Mr. Edgar G. Miller, Jr.
1790 (Centre) Mr. C. W. L. Johnson.
1793 (Lower) Dr. James Bordley, Jr.

In No. 1791 the particular feature is the attachment showing the phases of the moon. In the arch is a dial engraved with two circles divided into spaces marked with the days of the month and the hours of the day. Within these circles is a disk on which the moon and the sky are shown, the pointer indicating the age of the moon. Another form of moon in a circle was a globe which rotated, as in the American clocks Nos. 1803 and 1810. The name of the maker, "John Carter", of London, is on an oval plate, as in No. 1763. About 1775.

No. 1792 is a provincial dial, made in Dalkeith, a town near Edinburgh. A decorative design is on the top of the arch of the painted dial and the name of the maker is below, with festoons underneath. At the four corners are painted designs. Britten gives the date of the maker, Rob. Welsh, as about 1790.

No. 1793 is an enlarged illustration of the dial of No. 1776. Here the "strike-silent" dial in the arch and the seconds hand under the numeral XII are clearly seen. The central part of the dial is finely chased with scroll designs. Under the hands is the name of Thomas Wagstaffe, who is referred to in the comments on Nos. 1773 and 1776. About 1770-1790.

The next four clocks, Nos. 1794-1797, are in the French style. Their forms are very different from those of the "grandfather" clocks of English and American types; these clocks, however, are regarded as the French equivalent of the English grandfather clock. Many of them are so handsome and of such distinctive types that it seems proper to illustrate several examples even in a book on "American Antique Furniture".

The design of the English grandfather clock was never popular in France,[31] and the case of the French grandfather clock generally resembles the English case mainly in having sufficient length to contain a long pendulum. French clocks of this type are seldom seen in our country except in museums and in this book only four, illustrating the principal styles, are shown. Although few French grandfather clocks were imported into America, great numbers of French mantel clocks, such as those shown in section 193, are seen in our homes.

31.   It is said that "French and English cabinet makers have especially excelled, although in entirely different ways, in the making of clock cases. The English aimed at comely utility, often made actually beautiful by fit proportion and the employment of finely grained woods; the French sought a bold and dazzling splendor in which ornaments overlay material. * * French love of applied ornament was generally inimical to the rather uncompromising squareness of the English case, and the great Louis the Fifteenth and Louis the Sixteenth cabinet makers made some magnificent and monumental long (grandfather) clocks, many of which were 'long' only as regards the case, the pendulum being comparatively short, while sometimes the case acted merely as a pedestal for a bracket (mantel) clock fixed on the top. These pieces were usually mounted very elaborately in gilt bronze, (ormolu), cast and chased"; from the Encyclopædia Britannica, eleventh edition, pages 552-553.

In Mr. Arthur Hayden's "Chats on Old Clocks", pages 197-198, it is said that "the French craftsman realized the possibilities of his subject. His cases are elaborate and imaginative in conception. His fertility of invention is remarkable. On the whole it must be admitted that the case is the weakest part of the English clock. * * There is a stability and a solid, almost stolid, soberness that might have been lightened, so one thinks at times."

1794 (Upper) Anony-
    mous.
1797 (Lower) Anony-
    mous.

1795 (Upper) Wallace
    Collection, Lon-
    don.
1798 (Lower) Mr. Jos.
    K. Hubbard.

1796 (Upper) Anony-
    mous.
1799 (Lower) Balti-
    more Museum
    of Art.

Many tall, or grandfather, clocks of French design have the appearance of a clock placed upon a pedestal, and because of the pedestal they are sometimes called "pedestal" clocks, which may be a better name for them than "grandfather" clocks. In some examples the clock and the pedestal are made as one piece, as in No. 1794; in others a mantel clock, with a short pendulum, is placed upon a pedestal, as in No. 1795. These clocks and pedestals are handsomely decorated in the French styles of the various periods.[32]

Another form of the French grandfather type is that in which the case is "bulbous", or "swelling", near the base, as in No. 1796; and still another form is of a provincial French character, as in No. 1797.

In No. 1794 the opening in the lower half of the case, and the greater width of the case at this point, indicate that a long pendulum swings within, although it is not seen in the engraving. The pedestal and the upper part enclosing the works are made as an entirety, not as two separate parts. Applied ornaments and inlaid decorations are lavishly used, covering almost the whole front surface. The dial is in the form generally seen on fine clocks of the period of Louis the Fourteenth, with the hour numerals on separate porcelain blocks, similar to those on the French mantel clocks No. 1955 and others in section 193. About 1675-1700.

No. 1795 is a clock placed on a separate pedestal. This clock, having a short pendulum, could be placed upon a mantel, or bracket, or table. It is in the late style of the period of Louis the Fourteenth, in which the straight line was a characteristic feature. The clock and pedestal are finely decorated with "Boulle" work, which is mentioned in section 193, note 3; here the metal is inlaid in tortoise shell. The mounts and figures are of ormolu. This illustration appears here through the courtesy of the officers of the "Wallace Collection" in London. About 1700.

No. 1796 is an example of a French grandfather clock with a "bulbous" or "swelling" feature in the lower portion. The dial is white porcelain; over the dial is the figure of a cock; the case is ornamented with ormolu; in the bulbous portion is a large opening with glass, behind which the pendulum swings; and the feet will also be noticed. The case bears the date 1779.

No. 1797 is said to be in a French provincial style, made in Normandy. The upper portion is very pleasing, with a basket of flowers at the top and fruits and flowers at the sides, all delicately carved in wood. Below is another carved wooden basket. The lower portion of the case is plain. This clock is almost eight feet high. About 1760-1790.

The next two grandfather clocks are in the Dutch style. The Dutch clocks have much the same form as the English ones, but are frequently more ornamental. The base is often in a swelling shape somewhat resembling the "bombé" form seen on the bureau No. 724 or in some other swelling form. These clocks are generally almost ten feet high.

---

32.   The French periods are stated in section 193, note 2.

In No. 1798 the figure at the top represents Atlas supporting the world and on each side is another allegorical figure. The arched dial has a pointer which indicates the twelve tunes which are played, as in the American clock No. 1825; and two small dials are at the corners. Above the dial are carved scrolls and fretwork. The door in the waist has an opening with a brass design, as also in the Dutch wall clock No. 2062. The base is in a swelling shape somewhat resembling the bombé form mentioned above. Probably about 1750–1775.

No. 1799 is even more elaborately decorated. The figures at the top are missing. Over the arched dial is carved fretwork. Within the hour circle on the dial are a seconds dial and three other devices. Under the dial is painted a country scene, a feature often seen in these Dutch clocks. The door in the waist has an opening as in the preceding piece and is inlaid with flowers. The base, inlaid with curved lines, instead of being in the "bombé" form, has projections which swell out. Probably about 1750–1775.

Section 187. Grandfather clocks; American.—In considering English grandfather clocks in the previous section, certain preliminary remarks on the general subject were made which are also applicable to our American grandfather clocks. As those remarks are not repeated in this section the reader is requested to examine the previous section at least as far as the comment on No. 1751, in connection with these American clocks.

In a general way the American clock makers followed the English models,[1] as is shown not only by the clocks themselves but also by the advertisements of clock makers in the newspapers of the time.[2] The "works", the mechanical parts of clocks, were often, if not generally, imported from England or were made by English artisans who came to our country, sometimes as "indentured" men;[3] but the cases, in which we are especially interested, were almost always made in this country. Although the American cases at first followed closely the English cases, some of them were later ornamented with carvings in an American style, as on the block front lower door in No. 1805 and others, and with the inlaid decorations, patriotic and otherwise, which were used on other articles of American furniture.

When the "scroll top" style of grandfather clock cases, shown as Nos. 1767–1773, came into fashion in England and our country, about 1770, it superseded

1. So far as is known, no grandfather clocks were made in America of the English marquetry type shown in Nos. 1753–1757, and few if any of the lacquered type, Nos. 1762–1764. One American clock of the burl walnut type is shown as No. 1802, made by William Claggett, of Newport, Rhode Island. The making of grandfather clocks in considerable numbers apparently began about 1775 when the "scroll top" type became the fashion.

2. Many advertisements of American clock makers and clock dealers, the latter calling themselves then as now "clock makers", are in the two volumes issued by "The Walpole Society" entitled "The Arts and Crafts in Philadelphia, Maryland and South Carolina. Gleanings from Newspapers. Collected by Alfred Coxe Prime", 1929 and 1932. In volume 1, covering the period 1721–1785, pages 227–273 are devoted to clock and watch makers; in volume 2, pages 238–273 cover the years 1786–1800.

3. As to "Indentured servants" see the Appendix, section 207; also section 186, note 30 and section 187, note 7.

the previous types of American grandfather cases and continued in vogue until the grandfather clock itself ceased to be popular about 1850. In this period the form and ornamentation of the American cases show the influence of the Chippendale, Hepplewhite and Sheraton styles of furniture designs. The great similarity in the form of the cases of this period, as also in England,[4] continued for such a long period because no form more suitable could be designed, not even by Chippendale or Sheraton;[5] perhaps the chief substantial change was the use of fretwork at the top of the grandfather clocks of the Willards and their associates, a change which may not be regarded as an improvement.

As mentioned in the previous section, in note 5, any grandfather clock shown in this section without an English or American name or address, or other indication of origin, is regarded in this book, for the purpose of classification, as an American clock although this may be erroneous in some instances.

In No. 1800 the case recalls the tall and slender English clocks Nos. 1782-1784, with small square dials; but here the dial is arched, a form which was first used about 1725, as mentioned in section 183. The dial is six inches wide and has quarter-hour marks and half-hour designs, but no minute marks, showing that it did not originally have a minute hand. The case is made of pine and is about seven feet in height. The base is in two parts as also in No. 1803. A long pendulum was used at one time, as shown by parts of the inner sides of the case which were hol-

4.   See the remarks of Mr. Cescinsky quoted in the third paragraph of note 23 in section 186.

5.   See section 186 at note 6.

A.   A great number of grandfather clocks of very plain and originally inexpensive types, both in the works and the cases, were made in our country, especially in the smaller towns and rural districts. The cases, made of local woods by local carpenters, are not interesting. In Pennsylvania, for example, hundreds of grandfather clocks running about thirty hours were wound by pulling a chain, not by a key. In New England, especially Connecticut, large numbers of grandfather clocks with wooden works were made. Unimportant clocks such as these are not illustrated in this book.

B.   It is more difficult to fix the dates of our American grandfather clocks than of most of the English ones for the reason that the great majority of English clocks were made by London makers who were members of the "Worshipful Company of Clockmakers of the City of London", the guild mentioned in section 180, note 6, of this chapter. The records of this Company give the dates at which the members were admitted, and as the names of the makers almost always appear on the dials, it is possible to fix the dates of their clocks with some certainty. In our country the advertisements in the newspapers, the records of the courts in which the estates of deceased makers were settled, and other contemporary mention, are generally the only authentic evidence. The least reliable information as to the date of any kind of antique household furniture is that of family tradition, as mentioned in section 6 in chapter II.

C.   Detailed articles on the business careers, family relationship and personal characteristics of a number of American clock makers have been published in books, magazines and newspapers. Some of these articles are interesting and valuable contributions to the history of American clock-making. In this chapter, however, the available space is not sufficient to present more than brief statements regarding a few of the more important makers, such as the Willards.

D.   In New York and the States south of Maryland only a few grandfather clocks seem to have been made, judging from the small number of advertisements and surviving examples. Most of the good clocks in the South are said to be of English make.

lowed out, thus giving a wider space for the swings of the pendulum; and a short pendulum has been substituted. In the arch are the words "Thomas Jackson, Portsmouth", (New Hampshire); see also No. 1852 and note 31. The style is probably about 1730-1750.

No. 1801 is now in the "Home of Mary Washington", the mother of George Washington, in Fredericksburg, Va., and is shown here through the courtesy of the "Gallery of Fine Arts, Yale University", to which it was presented as a part of the "Mabel Brady Garvan Collection". The dial is square, but there are no quarter-hour marks on the inner edge of the circle, or "ring", nor half-hour designs, such as are commonly seen on early clocks with square dials. The centre of the dial is ornamented with a large star, not visible in the engraving, similar to that in the enlarged arched dial No. 1853. In a curved plate over the numeral VI are the words " Jacob Godschalk, Towamenoin", the latter being probably the town "Towamensing" in Carbon County, Pennsylvania. The top is in an early form; the arched top of the lower door is ornamented with a shell carving, not similar to the fine one in No. 1805 and others; "H" hinges have been placed on the outside of the door; and the base has a rectangular sunken panel and bracket feet. The date of the maker is said to be about 1780.

No. 1802 is a handsome clock bearing the name "William Claggett", of Newport, Rhode Island, one of the best of the early American clock makers, who died in 1749. The top is high and in an unusual form. The dial is square and has quarter-hour marks and half-hour designs, and the keyholes are "ringed" as in No. 1754. The burl walnut veneer on the lower door is "matched" as in No. 1760, and the panel in the base is also veneered. This clock, both works and case, is in the best English style. Several clocks by this maker are shown in Mr. Lockwood's "Colonial Furniture", figures 839-843, and on page 337. About 1740.

No. 1803 is another fine clock by the same maker, William Claggett. Here the dial is arched, and in the arch is a dial with a small opening behind which the moon appears, (see also Nos. 1791 and 1810), and a pointer which indicates the days of the month. Under the hour numeral XII is a seconds dial, and below is a plate on which the name of the maker appears, as in No. 1791. Quarter-hour marks and half-hour designs are on the inner edge of the silvered ring. The lower door has brass hinges on the outside and is ornamented with a brass design with a figure of a cupid. The top of the hood is arched and has cut-out designs somewhat resembling those in No. 1852. About 1740.

In No. 1804 and the next two clocks the top of the hood is arched to follow the arch of the dial, as in the preceding clock. Usually the top of the lower door is also arched in order to correspond with the arches above, but here the top is straight. A "strike-silent" dial, with a star in the centre, is in the arched portion, and a seconds dial and an opening showing the day of the month are below. Quarter-hour marks and half-hour designs are seen, as in the preceding clock and in the English grandfather clock dial No. 1756 and many others. The feet are in a form of the ball type. A triangular plate bears the words "Samuel Bagnall, Boston". About 1740-1760.

No. 1805 is particularly interesting for the reason that it illustrates the statement, several times made in this chapter, that English works, without cases, were imported by American dealers or clock makers who employed local cabinet makers to make cases for the works. The name "William Tomlinson", of London, 1699-1750, appears on the round "boss" on the arch of the dial as the maker of the works, and a printed label inside the case bears the name of the maker of the case, "John Townsend" of Newport, Rhode Island, who is referred to in connection with a cousin in law John Goddard, in the chapter on "Block front furniture", section 114. The blocked lower door, with a shell design, is characteristic of Townsend and Goddard,[6] whose furniture at the present writing is perhaps the most highly esteemed of any made in our country. This illustration is the first in this section in which there are fluted quarter-round "corner columns", mentioned in note 23 in the previous section No. 186 on English grandfather clocks; here the ornaments on the columns are of wood, not brass. The works may be dated about 1740-1750 and the case perhaps about 1760-1770.

In No. 1806, also, the "blocked" lower door has a shell design at the arched top. Instead of fluted corner columns, as in the preceding clock, there are fluted "pilasters", meaning flat columns. The ornaments at the top are of wood, as in the preceding clock. The dial is painted white and is decorated with flowers and other designs. Painted dials were first commonly used about 1770, as mentioned in section 183. There is no name on this clock, nor is its place of origin known, but its case follows in some respects the Townsend case in the preceding clock. About 1780-1790.

No. 1807 has a high top which is cut in curves. The brass dial is of the same general character as that of No. 1805. On the "boss" in the arched portion are the words "Isaac Pearson,[7] Burlington, fecit", and on the oval plate under the hands are the words "Tempus Fugit". An enlarged view of the dial is shown below as No. 1854. About 1750-1760.

The next twenty-six clocks, Nos. 1808-1833, have "scroll tops" which, with other features, have given to similar English clocks the name "Chippendale style", as mentioned in the previous section, No. 186 at note 22, which the reader is requested to examine. The general form of these American clocks resembles that of the English pieces, differing chiefly in the decorative treatment. There are probably more American grandfather clocks of this type than of all other types combined. All of the dials are arched and almost all are painted white, only a

6.   Several block front cases made by John Goddard or his associates for grandfather clocks are illustrated and described in "Antiques", July, 1933, pages 3-4 and frontispiece.

7.   In the "Family Edition" of the "Life of Samuel J. Levick" of Philadelphia, published by W. H. Pile's Sons, 1896, pages 441-444, the clocks made by Pearson are described and it is stated that only four grandfather clocks were made by him and that all of them were known. In a letter published in this book, a certain William Morely, who came to America about 1726 as an "indentured man", writes: "I was sold for eleven pounds to one Mr. Isaac Pearson, a man of Humanity, by trade a smith, clockmaker and goldsmith, living at Burlington, New Jersey. He was a Quaker, but a wet one." As to "Indentured servants" see the Appendix, section 207, and note 30 in section 186.

1800 (Upper) Balti-
    more Museum
    of Art.
1804 (Lower) Metro-
    politan Muse-
    um of Art.

1801 (Upper) Yale Uni-
    versity.
1805 (Lower) Metro-
    politan Museum
    of Art.

1802 (Upper) Mr. H. T.
    Tiffany.
1806 (Lower) Anony-
    mous.

1803 (Upper) Anony-
    mous.
1807 (Lower) Mrs.
    Daniel Miller.

few being of brass. As painted dials[8] and "scroll" tops came into fashion in England about 1770, our American clocks with these features were all doubtless not earlier than that year, continuing to be made until grandfather clocks went out of fashion and ceased to be made, which it is said was about 1850.

Nos. 1808 and 1809 are scroll top clocks with carved shells on the "blocked" lower door, in the manner of the Rhode Island cabinet makers, Townsend and Goddard, mentioned in the comment on No. 1805. In each of these clocks the arched dial is painted white, the former being ornamented with floral designs and the latter having a moon attachment. The wooden ornaments at the top of the hood of each are carved; applied rosettes are at the inner ends of the scrolls; quarter-round columns, with carved wooden caps and bases, are at the corners of the waist; and the corners of the bases are cut off, or "chamfered", as in No. 1766. The feet are of the bracket type.

In No. 1808 the scrolls at the top are somewhat low, distinguishing them from the higher scrolls generally made. On the top is a box-like superstructure which may be a survival of the box seen on the English grandfather clock No. 1766 and mentioned in the comment on that clock. About 1770-1780.

In No. 1809 the scrolls are of about the usual height. The box behind the scrolls is somewhat different from that in the preceding clock. The "blocking" of the lower door is made from a single piece of mahogany as in the preceding blocked clocks, and is not a separate applied piece, although in some instances such false blocking has been made. About 1770-1780.

Nos. 1810-1812 have over their dials a form of ornamentation which we have seen on the highboys in the Philadelphia style in section 87, that is, carved and applied scrolls of fantastic but graceful designs in the rococo style of the period. No. 1810 is the most elegant of these three clocks.[9] Between the two scrolls at the top is a carved wooden ornament, called a "cartouche" in the description of the highboy No. 660. About 1770.

In No. 1811 the scroll designs above the painted dial are of much the same character as in the preceding clock. Between the two scrolls at the top is a wooden flame, and two similar ones are at the ends. The dial has vertical Arabic hour numerals, as to which see note 32 in this section, and two smaller dials, one for the day of the month and the other for the seconds. A moon attachment of the usual type is in the arch. At the corners of the waist and base are fluted quarter-columns; the lower door is arched; and the feet and the projection between them are similar to those in the preceding clock. On the dial are the words "C. & D. Farrar, Lampeter, Pa." About 1770-1780.

8.   See "Dials", section 183.

9.   In the arched portion of the brass dial is a rotating sphere showing the phases of the moon; see also Nos. 1791 and 1803. At the bottom of the dial, between the hour numerals V and VII, is the inscription "E. Duffield, Philada." Duffield was a well-known clock maker and a friend and executor of Benjamin Franklin. The height of this clock is more than nine feet. The abbreviation "Philada." is also seen in Nos. 1831, 1915 and 2044.

In No. 1812 the wooden ornaments which were at the top are missing. The scroll designs over the dial are less elegant than those in the two preceding clocks. The proportions of the applewood case are not altogether pleasing, the waist being somewhat narrow, as is often noticed in Pennsylvania cases, and the base is too high. There are four hands on the dial, the vertical one at the hour numeral VI being a "sweep-second" one. The words "Martin Schreiner, Lancaster", indicate a date about 1790-1800.

The next twenty-one American grandfather clocks with scroll tops, Nos. 1813-1833, are not arranged with special reference to their dates or their works or their cases. In fact, some of the works and cases, now united, probably started their careers as unrelated members of the clock family. Each clock, however, is interesting because of its form, or inlay, or other feature briefly mentioned in the comments. There is some uncertainty in fixing the probable dates of several of these clocks, especially if no name appears.

No. 1813, by mistake, is out of place in this section on American grandfather clocks, as on the bottom of the dial is the name "W. Young", and the address "Dundee", Scotland. For several generations this clock has been in the possession of a Baltimore family, including the present owner. The two columns on the corners of the waist are decorated with a light inlay for about two-thirds of the length of the columns, below which the columns are not decorated. The inlay is also seen on the columns on the hood. This form of decoration is also seen in the columns on the hood in the American clock No. 1825 and on the legs of the Baltimore tables Nos. 1441 and 1442. It is probable that the works were imported from Scotland without a case and that the case was made by a Baltimore cabinet maker; see also the comment on No. 1805. The round brass "boss" in the arched portion of the dial has no inscription or design, as also in the English clock No. 1774. In Baillie's "Watchmakers and Clockmakers of the World", "William Young, Dundee", is dated 1805-1843. This clock was probably made about 1805-1820.

In No. 1814 the plain walnut case has high and somewhat ungraceful scrolls at the top, as in No. 1820. The dial is of brass and the hour ring was originally silvered. The phases of the moon are in the arched portion of the dial; a sweep-second hand points to the hour numeral IV; and a plate between the keyholes bears the words "Jacob Mohler, Baltimore, No. 23". Mohler died a young man in 1773 and the unfinished clocks mentioned in the inventory of his estate in the court show that he was a maker; a copy of one of his advertisements is in the Appendix, section 207. About 1770.

In No. 1815 the three dials are in the form of those in the very exact English "regulator" clocks which were used by clock makers for the adjustment of clocks and watches. An enlarged engraving of the dial is shown as No. 1856. In the arched top are the words "George Levely, Baltimore". Levely, prominent in his business, led the jewelers' and clock makers' section of a parade held in Baltimore in July, 1788, in celebration of the ratification of the Constitution of the United

1808 (UPPER) MRS. F. P. GARVAN.
1812 (LOWER) ANONYMOUS.

1809 (UPPER) ANONYMOUS.
1813 (LOWER) MR. M. WHITRIDGE.

1810 (UPPER) ANONYMOUS.
1814 (LOWER) ANONYMOUS.

1811 (UPPER) ANONYMOUS.
1815 (LOWER) MR. EDGAR G. MILLER, JR.

1816 (Upper) Anony-
MOUS.
1820 (Lower) Mr. Edgar
G. Miller, Jr.

1817 (Upper) Metro-
POLITAN   MUSEUM
OF ART.
1821 (Lower) Anony-
MOUS.

1818 (Upper) Anony-
MOUS.
1822 (Lower) Mrs. Paul
H. Miller.

1819 (Upper) Anony-
MOUS.
1823 (Lower) Miss H. H.
CAREY.

States. He died in 1796. The large dial is for the minutes, the lower small one for the hours and the upper small one for the seconds. On the right hand side of the dial is a lever, not seen in the engravings, which is a part of the "maintaining power" device explained in note 19 in section 186 in connection with the English grandfather clock No. 1758. The brass ornaments at the top are not original. About 1785-1795.

No. 1816, with a brass dial, has a plain scroll top, with the original wooden urns. On the arched door in the waist is an applied molding with an arched top. The wooden ball feet may not be the original ones. On a plate on the dial are the words "John Wood, Philadelphia". Wood was a well-known maker whose advertisements were in the Philadelphia newspapers from 1768 to 1790. About 1780-1790.

Nos. 1817-1833, the remaining clocks of the "scroll top" kind shown here, are, except No. 1824, ornamented with inlaid designs in the styles of Hepplewhite or Sheraton or both. The period in which these clocks were made includes the early years of the young American republic, in which patriotic feelings were sometimes expressed by inlaid eagles and stars on the cases of clocks and on other articles of furniture and by paintings on mirrors.[10]

Nos. 1817-1820 are grouped together because each has a similar form of inlaid decoration, that is, an oval on the waist and a circle on the base. It is obvious that on the long and narrow surface of the waist the oval form is suitable, and that on the almost square base the circle is appropriate. Each of these clocks is handsome and interesting.[11]

No. 1817 is of curly maple, not well shown in the engraving. In the centre of the oval on the waist is a small oval enclosing an eagle, and in the circle on the base is an eight-pointed star; and other inlaid forms will be noticed. The feet seem to have been cut off somewhat. This clock bears the name of "N. Storrs", of Utica, New York. About 1800-1810.

No. 1818 is not so finely decorated as the preceding clock, but it has an inlaid American eagle and shield over the lower door; and at the four corners of the base are fan inlays. The third hand, pointing downwards, indicates the day of the month. On the dial is the name of "Joseph Doll", whose name and address do not appear in the books. About 1800-1810.

In No. 1819 there is no moon attachment, but the arch is decorated with painted designs. Above the lower door is an inlaid panel and below the door is a rectangular inlay, the spaces occupied by them causing the door to be shortened. An inlaid shell is in the lower door and an inlaid rosette in the base. The name "Thomas N. Bolles" appears as maker, but is not in the books. About 1800-1810.

10.   Examples of such mirrors are in Nos. 1168-1173 and others.

11.   Several clocks of very similar designs are illustrated and discussed in "Antiques", March, 1931, pages 232, 234; December, 1931, page 384; May, 1933, page 173. It seems that clocks of this type were made in New Jersey.

No. 1820 has the oval and circle inlays as in the preceding three clocks. The scrolls at the top seem to be too high, as in No. 1814, and the hood seems to be too large. As in the preceding clock the lower door is shortened. The hour numerals are in Arabic form. On a plate behind the dial, and not seen unless the hood is removed, is the name "Osborne", an English dial maker referred to in note 2 in section 183. The name of the maker of the clock does not appear. About 1800-1810.

No. 1821 is a plain clock, the case being ornamented merely by a five-pointed star on the hood and a similar one on the base, and by two small three-cornered inlays above the columns on the hood. On the arched portion of the dial flowers are painted, with a large white rose in the centre. There is no seconds dial nor are the days of the month shown. The corners of the waist have no columns. About 1800-1820.

No. 1822 is well ornamented, having two rectangular inlays under the hood, a long design with fans in the corners on the lower door and a square design with fans in the base. An unusual and pleasing touch of decoration in the waist and base is given by small ovals, within each of which is a figure in a foreign peasant costume in colored woods. The hour numerals on the dial are in Arabic form. The three brass ornaments are not original. The name of the maker is not known. About 1800-1820.

In No. 1823 the inlaid designs under the scrolls on the top are very similar to those in the English clock No. 1769. Around the upper door, under the hood, and on the lower door and the base are lines of inlay. The hour numerals are in Arabic form, as in the preceding clock. On the dial are the words "John M. Weidemeyer, Fredericksburg", Virginia. About 1800-1820.

No. 1824 has a fine brass dial on which there are four hands, not well seen in the engraving, one for the hour, one for the minutes, one for the day of the month and a sweep-second one. The waist is slender and somewhat longer than usual and the escutcheon on the door is of an earlier design. On the base is an elaborately curved panel. The three brass urns at the top are similar to those on the next clock. On the dial are the words "Wood and Hudson, Mount Holly", New Jersey. About 1790-1800.

No. 1825 is a handsome clock with two inlaid ovals, one at the top and the other in the base, each enclosing an American eagle and sixteen stars. These stars are supposed to indicate the number of States in the Union at the time the clock was made, as is stated in connection with the desks Nos. 803-806. The sixteenth State, Tennessee, was admitted in 1796 and Ohio, the seventeenth, in 1803, so that the date represented by the sixteen stars was between 1796 and 1803. Other details, including the names of the eight tunes played, are in the note.[12] About 1796-1803.

12.   The painted dial has four hands, as in the preceding clock. The sweep-second hand is a series of circles similar to those on the Curtis banjo clock No. 2033. In the semi-circle at the top are the names of eight tunes, with a pointer to indicate the tune being played. These tunes have English, Irish, Scotch and American names, spelled as follows: "Federal"; "Padywhack"; "Irishvalteer"; "Fish's hornpipe";

The next eight clocks, Nos. 1826-1833, differ from those seen above in having a horizontal molding, or cornice, which separates the top from the hood below. The part above the molding is called the " pediment", an architectural term as mentioned above. The pediments on these clocks, because they have scrolls instead of other forms such as in No. 1838, are called "scrolled pediments", and in England "swan-neck pediments", as mentioned in section 186 at note 22. Very similar pediments were used on certain highboys, such as No. 666, on secretary-bookcases, such as No. 853, and on mirrors Nos. 1107-1112.

No. 1826 has a scrolled pediment with a pedestal between the scrolls on which there is a brass eagle upon a brass urn. Inlay is used on all parts of the case. In the arched portion of the dial is a "rocking vessel" which swings to and fro with the motion of the pendulum, a feature popular in seaport towns. The dial is decorated with painted flowers and bears the words "John J. Parry, Philadelphia". About 1795-1810.

In No. 1827 the high scrolled pediment is ornamented with fretwork and the hood below is inlaid with vines and leaves. The waist and base have the usual lines of inlay and over the lower door is a graceful inlaid design. On the dial is the name "Charles Tinges", Baltimore, who appears in the newspapers and city directories from 1787 to 1816 as a watch and clock maker. Some of the men who have cleaned or repaired this clock have scratched on the works their names or initials and date of repairing, the first date being 1812. On a plate behind the dial is the name "Wilson" of Birmingham, England, who is referred to in note 2 in section 183. About 1800-1810.

No. 1828 also has fretwork in the pediment. In the four corners of the dial are paintings of allegorical figures. On the hood, the waist and the base are borders which enclose panels of darker wood. The hour numerals on the dial are in the vertical Arabic form and the brass hands are finely formed. The name of the maker does not appear. About 1800-1810.

No. 1829 is a third clock with fretwork in the scrolled pediment. Here the designs of inlay on the waist and base are similar to some of those on the preceding clocks. In the corners of the dial are allegorical paintings of women. The feet are of a bracket type. The name of the maker is not given. About 1800-1810.

No. 1830 is of the same general form as the preceding clocks with scrolled pediments, but the short waist is wide in proportion to the other parts and the hood is somewhat high. In other respects, however, this clock is handsome, the mahogany being brilliant, the inlay sufficient and the dial interesting with paint-

(Note 12, *continued*)

"Washwoman"; "Trip to Bath"; "Nagls hornpipe"; "Free from envy". These tunes are not played on bells but by a music box attachment which has lost any musical tones which it might have possessed when the clock was made. The columns on the hood are ornamented with vertical lines of inlay, as on the legs of the tables Nos. 1441 and 1442 and others, and on the clock No. 1813. On the dial are the words "George Long, Hanover", the supposed maker or dealer, who has not been located by the writer in any town of that name in any of our States. A very heavy weight furnishes the power to drive the musical attachment.

ings in the arched portion and at the four corners. The maker's name does not appear, but if English he was probably a provincial, not a Londoner. About 1810-1820.

No. 1831 has a line of inlay under the scrolled pediment and another of the same design is over the lower door. The rear board of the hood projects on the sides, and is cut in curves, a treatment seen also on the English clock No. 1772. The top corners of the lower door are cut in concave curves as are also the corners of the inner inlay on the base, in these respects resembling No. 1826. The caps and bases of the columns on the hood are of brass and those on the columns on the waist are of wood. On the dial is the name "Robert Shearman" and the abbreviation "Philada.", as in No. 1810 and others. About 1800-1810.

Nos. 1832 and 1833 are Canadian clocks with scrolled pediments of somewhat low form. These clocks are of similar design, differing mainly in their inlaid decorations which are more abundant than on the clocks made in our country. The principal inlaid decorations in each consist of an oval design on the pedestal between the scrolls, a band under the cornice, horizontal lines of inlay under the hood, a rectangular form enclosing an oval design on the lower door, another rectangular form under the lower door and a border of inlay enclosing an urn on the base. In the arched portion of the dial of each is a moon attachment, and in the corners below are painted designs. On each dial the name "G. S. H. Bellerose" appears and the words "Three Rivers", which is a town between Montreal and Quebec. The wood is walnut. The dates are said to be about 1790-1800.

The next three clocks are of different types and after them are three clocks by David Rittenhouse, of Philadelphia.

No. 1834, a musical clock, has a "hollowed pediment" similar to those on the English grandfather clocks Nos. 1774-1776, in the preceding section. In the comments on those clocks it is said that apparently very few of this type were made in America except in Connecticut, and that the present clock bears an American name and address, which may be that of either a maker or dealer. Here the dial is painted white and in the arch is a pointer which indicates the tune being played, as in No. 1825. The names of the five tunes are "Bunker Hill", "Banks of the Dee", "Washington Re", "Nancy Dawson" and "Rakes of Marlow"—a repertoire of which two tunes seem to be American and three are apparently English. The three wooden ornaments on the top resemble those on two of the English grandfather clocks above mentioned. On the dial are the names "Leslie and Williams" and the address "New Brunswick", New Jersey.[13] About 1780-1790.

No. 1835 has a flat top and an arched dial, a combination also seen in Nos. 1765, 1777 and 1778. The usual quarter-round columns are on the corners of the waist and the base, all with wooden caps and bases instead of brass. The dial is

13. In "Antiques", November, 1928, page 417, is an article by Mr. W. M. Hornor, Jr., in which another musical clock bearing the names "Leslie and Williams" is shown.

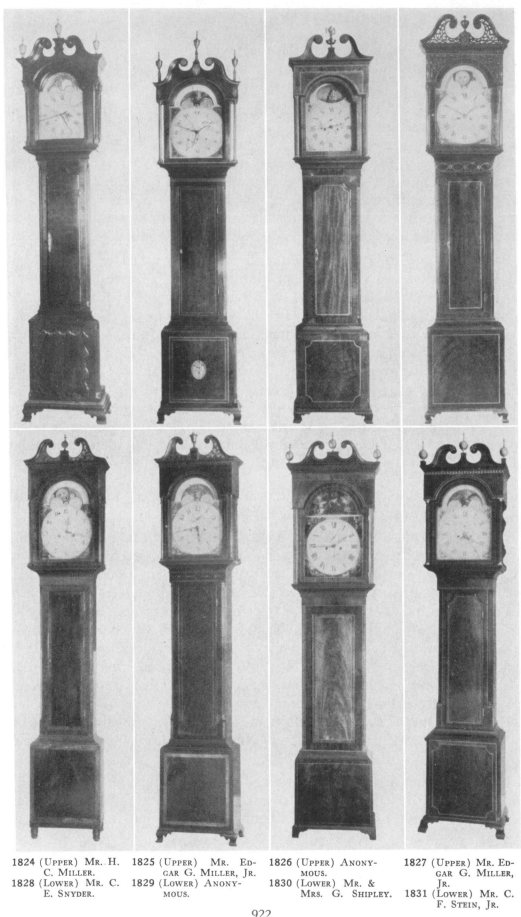

1824 (UPPER) MR. H. C. MILLER.
1825 (UPPER) MR. EDGAR G. MILLER, JR.
1826 (UPPER) ANONYMOUS.
1827 (UPPER) MR. EDGAR G. MILLER, JR.
1828 (LOWER) MR. C. E. SNYDER.
1829 (LOWER) ANONYMOUS.
1830 (LOWER) MR. & MRS. G. SHIPLEY.
1831 (LOWER) MR. C. F. STEIN, JR.

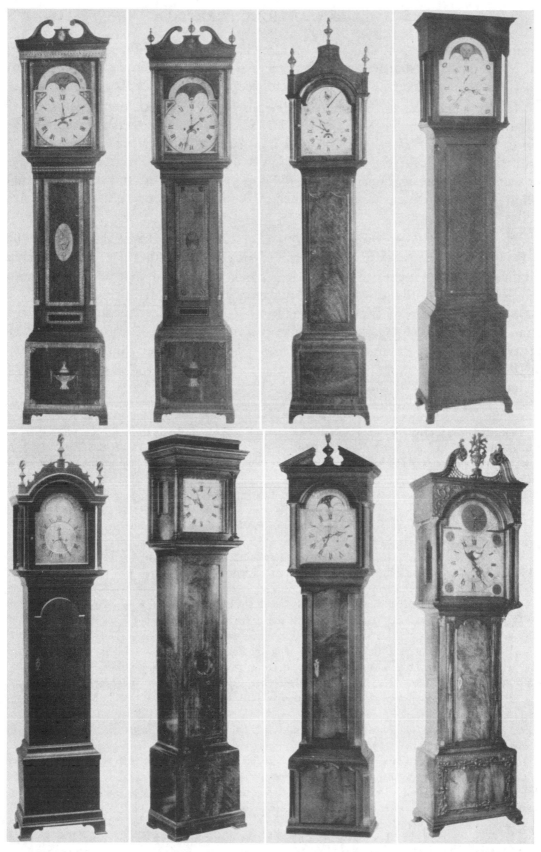

1832 (Upper) Anonymous.

1836 (Lower) Metropolitan Museum of Art.

1833 (Upper) Anonymous.

1837 (Lower) Mr. J. Ambler Williams.

1834 (Upper) Anonymous.

1838 (Lower) Mr. J. F. Stokes.

1835 (Upper) Mr. Edgar G. Miller, Jr.

1839 (Lower) Drexel Institute, Phila.

painted white, with oval and scroll designs in the corners. On a plate behind the dial is the name "Osborne", which is referred to in note 2 in section 183. On the dial is the name "Peter Little", of Baltimore. About 1800-1810.

In No. 1836 the top is cut in a design, partly pierced, of a type somewhat similar to the designs in Nos. 1803 and 1852. In other respects the case is plain, having no inlay or carving. The dial has the usual moon attachment, and two small dials in the centre portion. The lower door is arched, the base is plain and the feet are of the bracket type. At the top of the arch of the dial is the name "Thomas Harland", a prominent maker of Norwich, Connecticut.[14] About 1780-1800.

Nos. 1837-1839 are three grandfather clocks, the works of which were made by David Rittenhouse,[15] of Philadelphia, an eminent American astronomer and scientist and also a maker of grandfather clocks. It is said that he made not more than about seventy-five clocks, of which only a few are definitely known.[16] The cases of his clocks were apparently made by various cabinet makers who in many instances doubtless followed the directions of Rittenhouse as to size and suitability for the works; and this may account for certain peculiarities in the styles and designs of the cases, in which we are more interested than in the special mechanical features of the works.[17]

14.   In "Connecticut Clockmakers of the Eighteenth Century", by Mr. Penrose R. Hoopes, it is said, pages 10, 83-87, that Thomas Harland came from England, where he learned his trade, to Norwich, Connecticut, in 1773, and that he was the most skillful maker of clocks in the trade. His "clocks were superior in workmanship and were made in larger numbers than those of any of his contemporaries." He continued in business until his death in 1807.

15.   David Rittenhouse was born in 1732 and died in 1796. He is remembered chiefly as a maker of instruments of precision for astronomical purposes and for his clocks. He was also a surveyor, and in 1763 he laid the corner stone for the Mason and Dixon line which marks the boundary between Pennsylvania and Maryland. He held several positions of public trust and at the University of Pennsylvania was professor of astronomy. In April, 1932, the two-hundredth anniversary of his birth was celebrated in Philadelphia, with an exhibition of his clocks and scientific instruments. His brother Benjamin was also a clock maker.

The Rittenhouse "orrery", the most important of his creations, is an astronomical instrument which showed the course of the movements of the earth and moon, and the other planets and their satellites, around the sun. This was sheltered in a large cabinet resembling in general form a bookcase with three sections, as in Nos. 869-871, finely made by Philadelphia cabinet makers in the Chippendale style, with a broken arch top, standing on eight legs decorated with fretwork. This is now in the new "Benjamin Franklin Memorial" in Philadelphia, one of the most interesting museums in our country. An orrery owned by Harvard University is illustrated in "Antiques", March, 1937, pages 113-115.

16.   It is said that plates bearing the name of David Rittenhouse have been fraudulently made for the purpose of being placed on old clocks.

17.   No lack of appreciation of these clocks is indicated by the remark that from the standpoint of the collector of American antique furniture some of these cases, made to fit unusual works, are of inferior design. For example, in No. 1839, the most important of the clocks, the case, although finely ornamented, is ungainly, suggesting the clumsy Yorkshire case No. 1771.

Two illustrated articles by Mr. George H. Eckhardt, entitled "David Rittenhouse—his clocks", are in "Antiques", May and June, 1932. In the latter article it is said, page 278, that " occasionally an example is offered for sale; but it will seldom be one that has not suffered from undesirable tampering"; and that Rittenhouse made for his brother-in-law, a Tory clergyman at Lancaster, Pa., a

In No. 1837 the plain case is the earliest in style, and probably in date, of those here shown. The dial is in the early square form, as in No. 1802 and others. The top of the hood is also in an early form. In the door of the waist is an opening through which the pendulum could be seen, as in No. 1766 and earlier pieces. There are no winding holes on the dial, thus probably indicating that the clock was a one day clock which was wound by pulling a chain. Probably about 1760.

In No. 1838 the works and the case are of later types. The dial is arched and has a moon attachment and also four hands which show the hours, minutes, seconds and days of the month. The feature of the case, seldom seen on clocks, is the "broken pediment" above the cornice, with an ornament in the centre; this is in the same form as that on the secretary-desk No. 851 and several other objects. The curves on the top of the panel on the base follow the design of those on the top of the door in the waist. The feet are missing. Probably about 1770.

No. 1839, with a "scrolled top" pediment, is perhaps the most important grandfather clock and case made in our country in workmanship and in mechanical features, although not in elegance of design as mentioned in note 17. The scrolls on the top with the carved designs on the inner ends, the carved vase and flowers in the centre, and the applied designs over the arch were doubtless adapted from the elaborate highboys made in Philadelphia, such as that shown in the highboy No. 660. The ornamental applied designs on the base, the finely reeded columns on the hood and the other details of the cabinet work are of the best Philadelphia type. The dials are mentioned in the note.[18] About 1770.

The next group, twelve American grandfather clocks, Nos. 1840-1851, consists of clocks made by Simon Willard, Aaron Willard, Ephraim Willard, Aaron Willard, Jr., and other makers working in the Willard style.

Simon Willard[19] is generally regarded as the leading American clock maker, having made many grandfather clocks of the finest workmanship, and having

(Note 17, *continued*)

clock upon whose dial was inscribed the message "Tempus fugit, Mind Your Own Business", the latter part of which sounds like a maxim of Benjamin Franklin; also, page 276, it is said that many of the clocks bear the date 1769.

18.   On the arched dial in the usual form are five subsidiary dials. At the top is a dial which shows the position of the sun and the planets, called a "planetarium", and to some extent operates as an "orrery", mentioned above in note 15. It is said that one of the four small dials at the corners indicates the position of some of the stars, another shows the position of the constellations, another shows the length of each day and another divides the day into tenths. The phases of the moon are under the hour numeral XII. There is also a musical attachment with sixteen sets of chimes. The clock is nine feet high and two feet wide. See the remarks in note 17 above. This clock belongs to the Drexel Institute, Philadelphia. It is not in working order.

19.   Simon Willard, a son of Benjamin Willard, a clock maker, was born in Grafton, Mass., in 1753, and died in Boston in 1848, aged 95 years. At an early age he learned clock-making and made a number of clocks which are marked "Simon Willard, Grafton". Examples are the wall clock No. 2041 and the grandmother clock No. 1872. About 1780 he went into business in the town of Roxbury, now a part of Boston, where he opened a shop in a house which he continued to occupy until he retired from business in 1839. During his long career he had the highest reputation for making superior clocks of almost all kinds for household use and for public buildings and churches. One in Statuary Hall in the Capitol at Washington was made by him at the age of eighty-five.

invented the "banjo" clock, the most popular of any of the clocks made to hang on a wall, as is mentioned in section 194, and having also invented a clock known as a "shelf", or "mantel", clock which is the subject of section 190.

In a book entitled "A History of Simon Willard, Inventor and Clock Maker", also entitled "Simon Willard and his clocks", by Mr. John Ware Willard, a great-grandson, published in 1911, examples of clocks made by Simon Willard, Aaron Willard and others, are illustrated, and some of their distinctive features are stated.[20] From that book, now out of print, several illustrations have been copied and much information has been obtained, some of which appears in the note,[21] with references to the pages in Mr. Willard's book which has no index.

20.   Since the publication of Mr. Willard's book in 1911, other matters have been discovered in regard to Simon Willard and his clocks; but the principal statements in his book have not been questioned. Much of the information contained in various books, magazines and newspapers has been copied from Mr. Willard's book without quotation marks or other acknowledgment.

21.   A.   Simon Willard's reputation was so high that other clock makers put the name "Willard" on their clocks very much as the Dutch clock makers put the names of celebrated English clock makers on their dials, as mentioned in section 180, note 6. Mr. Willard remarks that he "has found several instances of this kind. Simon Willard clocks, both hall and timepieces, have been counterfeited innumerable times"; pages 58-59. As to counterfeits of banjo clocks, see section 194, note 4.

B.   Many of the grandfather clocks made by Simon Willard and Aaron Willard and their followers are so similar that their origin can be distinguished by the amateur buyer only by a genuine printed label in the case, or a genuine painted name on the dial. Certainty can only be secured by an examination made by experts, such as a clock maker and a cabinet maker experienced in handling clocks and cases of the period. Moreover, the label should be examined by one familiar with old paper and type and the painted name by one experienced in antique painting and lettering. Of course the works and the case must belong together. See also section 194, note 5, F.

C.   Simon Willard allowed his apprentices, and apparently the other clock makers of his time, to copy his "Patent Timepiece", (the banjo clock), or anything he invented, and seemingly never thought of prosecuting them for infringing on his patent; page 35. Upon his retirement in 1839, Elnathan Taber, his best apprentice, bought most of his tools and the good will of his business and received permission to put the name "Simon Willard" on the dials of the clocks he made. As Taber made an excellent clock, Simon Willard, Jr., took all he could make and sold them at his (Simon Jr.'s) store, and all clocks sold from there had the name "Simon Willard, Boston" or "Simon Willard and Son, Boston", on the dial. All this has resulted in many people thinking that they had a Simon Willard, Sr., timepiece when it was really one of Taber's; page 58. See also note 30 as to Taber.

D.   Simon Willard, Jr., son of Simon Willard, was born in 1795. For about two years, 1824-1826, he was in partnership with his father and later went into the chronometer and watch business. About 1832 he made a fine astronomical clock which is in Harvard University.

E.   Distant cousins of Simon Willard, named Philander J. Willard, 1772-1840, and Alexander T. Willard, 1774-1850, brothers, living at Ashby, Mass., were also clock makers. The Simon Willard book, pages 120-128, and an illustrated article entitled "The clock makers of Ashby, Mass.", in "Antiques", May, 1933, page 178, give information regarding them. An unusual clock by Philander J. Willard is No. 2048.

F.   The more important clock makers having the name "Willard" are as follows, with the dates of their births and deaths. Four brothers, sons of Benjamin Willard; Benjamin, 1743-1803; Simon, 1753-1848; Ephraim, 1755—perhaps about 1835; Aaron, 1757-1844. Simon Willard's sons, Simon, Jr., 1795-1874, and Benjamin F., 1803-1847. Aaron, Jr., son of Aaron, 1783-1864. As to Philander J. and Alexander T., see note above.

G.   It is said that Simon Willard and his brothers "always" made clocks with brass works, "never" using wooden works. The words "always" and "never" are dangerous.

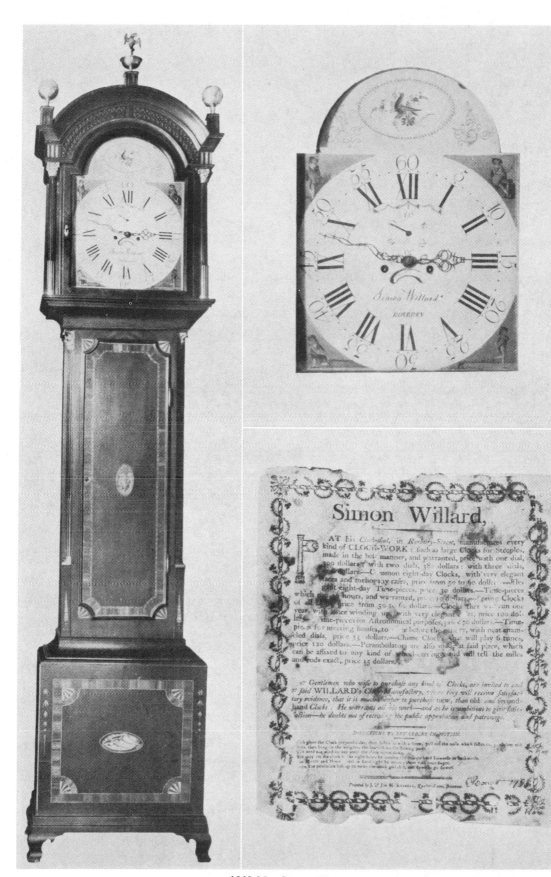

1840 Mr. George Ward.

No. 1840 is one of the few illustrations large enough to present a clock in the detail to which many other clocks are also entitled. This clock, by Simon Willard, has been owned by ancestors of the present owner for several generations. Here we see the clock itself, the enlarged dial and the original label of the maker.

The very handsome mahogany case is nine and one-half feet in height, the product of a skillful cabinet maker.[22] The top is arched, with brass ornaments above and carved fretwork below. The arched portion of the dial and the corners below are decorated with paintings. A seconds dial, a day of the month opening and the words "Simon Willard, Roxbury" are well seen on the enlarged dial. The abundant inlaid decorations on the case, in the Hepplewhite style, are similar to those seen on many tables and larger articles in previous chapters; among these decorations are two ovals and eight fans. Around the lower door is a border of lighter wood and on the base is a rectangular band of the same wood, on the sides of which are strings of flowers. The usual fluted columns are on the corners of the waist and hood, with small brass rods at the lower ends, and brass caps and bases at the top and bottom. Features of the label are mentioned in the note.[23] A very similar clock by the same maker is No. 3287 in Mr. Nutting's "Furniture Treasury". About 1795-1800.

(Note 21, *continued*)

H. In their early days Simon Willard, Aaron Willard and Eli Terry were peddlers of their clocks. Simon went from door to door on the "North Shore" near Boston and Aaron went down the "South Shore". Eli Terry with his clocks with wooden works rode around the country-side in Connecticut. The peddling customs of the time may have suggested the sketches which were collected in book form and published under the name of "The Clockmaker; or, the Sayings and Doings of Samuel Slick of Slickville", by T. C. Haliburton. This humorous book was published in 1836 and republished several times. Editions were also published in London.

I. See also section 194 for other information about the Willards in connection with banjo clocks.

22. An illustrated article entitled "The man who made Simon Willard's Clock Cases", by Mabel M. Swan, is in "Antiques", March, 1929, pages 196-200. The man was John Doggett, of Roxbury, and the information came from Doggett's ledger, covering the period 1802-1809. In this ledger are entries showing that Doggett not only made cases of grandfather clocks for Simon and Aaron Willard and other clock makers of the period but also gilded the brass ornaments at the top of banjo clocks, called "timepieces", the frames holding the glass doors, the wooden eagles which were sometimes used by Simon Willard and later by other makers, and other parts. On page 200 is an illustration of two pages of Doggett's ledger in his handwriting.

An article entitled "The man who made brass works for Willard clocks", by the same writer, is in the same magazine, June, 1930, page 524.

23. In this label is Simon Willard's sign, a two-faced dial in front of his shop on Roxbury Street, in Roxbury, near Boston. The use of a dial as an advertisement was a custom of clock makers. The "perambulators" mentioned in the label were not family carriages for infants, but devices for measuring distances, which "can be affixed to any kind of wheel-carriage and will tell the miles and rods exact, price 15 dollars". At the bottom the printers' name and address are given—"Printed by J. and Jos. N. Russell, Quaker Lane, Boston". An examination of the Boston directories indicates that this firm was in business at the location given for several years before 1798, but not after that date. At the lower right hand corner is written in ink "Bought 1796". See the label of Aaron Willard which was also used by Aaron Willard, Jr., No. 1862.

No. 1841 and some others made by Simon Willard, when compared with the preceding clock, seem somewhat plain; and in fact the average household clock must have been of a much less expensive type. In this clock, for example, the only inlaid ornamental features are ovals on the lower door and the base. The illustration is copied from Mr. John Ware Willard's book above mentioned, plate 18, and the clock is said by him to be "in absolutely perfect condition with all the original parts even to the wooden pendulum rod". The fretwork at the top is less fully developed than on many other clocks. The arched portion of the dial and the four corners below are decorated with painted designs. About 1800.

No. 1842 was presented by Simon Willard to Harvard College and is now in the Faculty Room in University Hall. On the dial is an inscription in Latin which may be freely translated as follows: "Simon Willard made it for the use of the President of Harvard College and his Overseers". This translation and the facts connected with the clock have been furnished by Mr. Frederick B. Robinson, of Harvard University, of which the original Harvard College is a part. With the exception of a few minor repairs and changes this clock is in its original condition. Short brass rods are at the bottom of the fluted columns, as in the preceding clock. The brass eagle at the top is a substitute for an original ornament. The illustration of this clock in the book of Mr. John Ware Willard, plate 11, is incorrect in several particulars. Another clock given by Willard to the same institution is the "regulator" wall clock No. 2035 on which also he displayed his knowledge of the Latin language. About 1800-1820.

In No. 1843 the top is cut in a simple design and is pierced with small narrow openings which are barely seen in the engraving. The moon attachment, the brass fittings on the bottom of the fluted columns on the hood and the waist, the arched door in the waist, the fine grain of the mahogany and the inlay on the base all contribute to an ornamental appearance. The name of Simon Willard is on the dial, under the curved opening in which the day of the month appears. About 1800-1825.

Next to Simon Willard in importance as a maker of grandfather clocks in this period was his younger brother, Aaron Willard, 1757-1844, who began business in Grafton, Mass., and moved to Roxbury, now a part of Boston, about 1780, and retired in 1823. Aaron followed the style of Simon in the manufacture of grandfather and other clocks, was an excellent maker and also a successful business man.[24] His output of clocks was much larger than that of Simon Willard, which accounts for the greater number which have survived. Many of the cases of his grandfather clocks are so similar to those of Simon Willard that only the name on the dial distinguishes his pieces to the eye of the amateur from those

24. In this latter respect Aaron Willard was more fortunate than Simon, whose talents did not include the art of money making. Simon, the inventor and the most esteemed clock maker of his time, retired from business, after almost seventy years of work, with about five hundred dollars, and died a poor man. Aaron, however, was keen in business and doubtless realized that the only way to make money in the clock business was to make clocks in quantity. He established a factory in Boston about 1790 adjoining his house, and at one time employed from twenty to thirty men.

of his brother and of several other makers of the period, especially William Cummens[25] and Elnathan Taber,[26] who were apprentices of Simon Willard.

No. 1844 is the first of the four grandfather clocks shown here made by Aaron Willard. As mentioned above, these clocks are very similar to those made by his brother Simon Willard. The moon attachment, the dial, the columns on the hood and the waist, and the arched door in the waist are all about the same in design as those in the preceding clock. In this one, however, the fretwork has no vertical lines and is wholly composed of curves. The name is under the curved opening in which the day of the month appears. As Aaron Willard retired from business in 1823, the date is probably between 1800 and 1823.

In No. 1845 the fretwork at the top is similar to that in the Simon Willard clock No. 1841. On the moon attachment a ship is painted between the two moons. Instead of the bracket feet seen in the preceding clocks the feet here are of the ball type, as in No. 1816, and are probably restorations. There is no inlay. On the dial is the name of Aaron Willard. About 1800-1823.

In No. 1846, in the arched portion of the dial, there is a "rocking ship" which every two seconds approaches, but never reaches, the shore of a harbor. This ship is attached to an extension upward of the pendulum and swings to and fro with it. Around the hour circle there is a gilded line which is somewhat heavy and conspicuous. The lower door is smaller than usual. As in the two preceding clocks, there is no inlay. The feet appear to be too high and may be restorations. The name of Aaron Willard is on the dial. About 1810-1823.

In No. 1847 the unusual divisions of the parts of the dial, at the points where the arched portion begins, changes the form of the upper "spandrels", or corner pieces. On the waist and the base are inlaid rectangular designs, with concave corners. On a label within the case is the name of Aaron Willard. The other features are similar to those in the other clocks. About 1810-1823.

On the dial of No. 1848 are the words "Aaron Willard, Jr.,[27] Boston". The label shown as No. 1862, found in this clock, is the label of his father Aaron Willard, after whose name is written in ink the abbreviation "Jr.", which no doubt indicates the use of his father's label for a time after the latter retired from business in 1823. The case resembles those used by Aaron Willard, Senior, except that on the top there are now no brass ornaments or fretwork. The fine grain of the mahogany case and the dark bands on the base will be noticed. About 1823-1830.

25.   See the comment and note on No. 1850.
26.   See the comment and note on No. 1851.
27.   Aaron Willard, Jr., was in the clock-making business with his father Aaron until 1823 when the latter retired, after which date Aaron, Jr., carried on the same work alone and in his own name. He had a large business, making grandfather clocks, banjo clocks, then called "timepieces", and other kinds. He invented the lyre clocks, as mentioned in section 195, and made a great number of them. It is not likely that his name appeared on any clocks until he took over his father's business in 1823. This information is from "Simon Willard and his clocks", pages 94-97.

1841 (Upper) Anony-
    mous.
1845 (Lower) Mrs. F.
    T. Redwood.

1842 (Upper) Harvard
    University.
1846 (Lower) Anony-
    mous.

1843 (Upper) Anony-
    mous.
1847 (Lower) Anony-
    mous.

1844 (Upper) Anony-
    mous.
1848 (Lower) Col.
    W. Bowie, Jr.

No. 1849 is by Ephraim Willard,[28] brother of Simon and Aaron, whose name and address, "E. Willard, Boston", appears on the enlarged dial, No. 1860, of this clock. For more than a century this clock has served the Orphans Court of Balti-

1849 ORPHANS COURT, BALTIMORE.   1850 BALTIMORE MUSEUM OF ART.   1851 ANONYMOUS.   1852 MR. & MRS. C. E. McLANE.

more in its administration of the estates of deceased persons and the care of the property of minors. A small brass plate over the door in the waist states that the clock was presented to the Court before 1810 by William Buchanan who was

28. Little has been found concerning the career of Ephraim Willard. He was a younger brother of Simon and Aaron; he was born in Grafton, Mass., in 1755; in 1777 he became a clock maker in Medford, Mass.; in 1798 he lived in Roxbury; in 1801 he moved to Boston and some years later went to New York and from there to other places. Only a very few clocks by him are known. From "Simon Willard and his clocks", pages 100-103.

Register of Wills of Baltimore County from 1779 to 1824. The turned columns on the hood are of a different type from those on other clocks in the Willard style, and the original base has suffered damage which has been made worse by the restoration. About 1800-1809.

No. 1850 is by William Cummens[29] who learned his trade as an apprentice of Simon Willard. The handsome case is ornamented with bands of dark woods on the lower door and the base, and with inlaid fan designs. The corner columns on the hood and base have brass rods at the lower ends. Perforated fretwork is at the top and applied fretwork is over the dial, but is not well seen in the engraving. The very small size of the brass ornaments on the top indicates that they are substitutes. The two hemispheres in the arch of the dial appear on an enlarged scale in No. 1863, with a comment stating the reason why the name "New Holland" on the continent of Australia probably establishes the date as being before 1817. About 1805-1815.

No. 1851 was made by Elnathan Taber,[30] another, and said to be the best, apprentice of Simon Willard. The arched portion of the dial has a country scene instead of a moon attachment, and on the four corners below designs of uncertain meaning are painted. As in the preceding clock the lower door is ornamented with dark bands. On the dial are the words "Warranted by E. Taber". About 1800-1820.

No. 1852 is not a clock by one of the Willards or by one of their apprentices. It bears in the arch the words "Thomas Jackson, Preston",[31] a name which also appears on the tall and slender clock No. 1800 in this section, but with the address "Portsmouth". The case is of curly maple. The dial is of brass without an attached circle or hour ring, as also in the English mantel clock No. 1895. The four corners

29.   William Cummens was born about 1768 and died in 1834. He lived in Roxbury and it is said that he made all of his clocks at his home and generally marked upon the dial "Warranted by Wm. (or William) Cummens". Although it is said that good specimens of his work are not often found, the writer has two of his clocks, one a grandfather clock and the other a banjo clock, and has seen several others in Baltimore homes. His clocks, both in the works and cases, generally resemble very closely those of Simon and Aaron Willard.

30.   Elnathan Taber was born in 1768 and died in 1854. He was a favorite of Simon Willard and when the latter retired from business in 1839 Taber bought the good-will of Willard's business and most of his tools, and received permission to put the name "Simon Willard" on the dials of his clocks. Mr. John Ware Willard in his book, page 108, states that Taber made "a most excellent clock, fully as good as Simon Willard". His clocks are not often seen; they generally bear on the dials the inscription "E. Taber". Reference to him is also made in note 21, C in this section.

31.   In the list of clock makers in the English book, "Old Clocks and Watches", by Britten, appears "Jackson, Thomas, Preston, 1760". "Preston" is the name of a city in England, and the writer, examining Britten's book, thought that the maker of this clock was the English maker referred to by him. The owner, however, states that he purchased the clock near Preston, Connecticut, and that Thomas Jackson was known to have been a clock maker of that town. The name of an American "Thomas Jackson, Preston" does not appear in the American lists. A curly maple clock with the name "Preston" in Mr. Nutting's "Furniture Treasury", No. 3324, is regarded as English. Since the above was written, an article by Mr. Penrose R. Hoopes has appeared in "Antiques", September, 1935, page 105, in which the name of a "Thomas Jackson of Preston (and Boston)", is mentioned. A book by Mr. Hoopes, published in 1930, is entitled "Connecticut Clockmakers of the Eighteenth Century".

of the dial are ornamented with scroll designs. The work on the top is of a different type from that on the clocks in the Willard style above, but resembles somewhat that on the earlier William Claggett clock No. 1803. About 1780-1800.

Nos. 1853-1861, all on one page, are enlarged dials of nine American grandfather clocks, several of the dials belonging to clocks shown above. These dials have been selected for enlargement because each one has some particular feature of interest. The first and second dials are of brass and the other seven are painted.

In No. 1853, as in No. 1846, the dial has a "rocking ship", one of the oscillating devices which began to be used in England about 1770. On an attached curved plate are the words "George Miller, Germantown"; this form of plate may also be seen on the dial of the American clock No. 1801 in the "Home of Mary Washington"; and within the hour circle, or "ring", is a large twelve-pointed star, referred to in the comment on the same clock. About 1770-1790.

In No. 1854 the "rings" around the keyhole, mentioned in the comments on the English dial No. 1754, are clearly seen. Here there are the familiar quarter-hour marks and half-hour designs on the inner edge of the hour circle. This is the dial of No. 1807. The inscription "Tempus Fugit" on the oval plate was evidently done by an amateur. About 1750-1760.

In No. 1855 the dial is painted white. In the arched portion the inscription seems to indicate that the maker, David Evans, understood the Latin language. The painting shows country people at work, illustrating the inscription that "such is the life of man". The dial has suffered the loss of the second hand and the two lower "spandrels", or "corner pieces". The minute hand is in a different style and is of a later date than the hour hand, and the word "Baltimore" seems to have been the work of a less skillful artist than the one who painted the name of the maker. An advertisement of David Evans is shown in the Appendix, No. 2113 About 1775-1795.

No. 1856 is the dial of No. 1815 and is sufficiently described in the comment on that clock; but attention may be called to the delicacy of the work in the arched portion. About 1785-1795.

No. 1857 has a country scene in the arched portion between the moons, and painted roses are at the four corners. Under the day of the curved month opening are the names and address of the makers or dealers, "D. Beard & C. Weaver, Appoquinimink"; the latter word is the name of a village in Newcastle County, Delaware, a name of Indian origin, as the writer is informed through the courtesy of the Historical Society of Delaware. About 1780-1790.

In No. 1858 the arched portion of the dial has a painting of two houses and a large tree, and two children playing "see-saw" on a plank. The second hand is in an unusual form. The name is "Peter Ford", under which is the address "York Town", which is probably the Pennsylvania town, not the Virginia one of Revolutionary fame. The case, not illustrated, is slender and its height is six feet and three inches. Probably about 1800-1810.

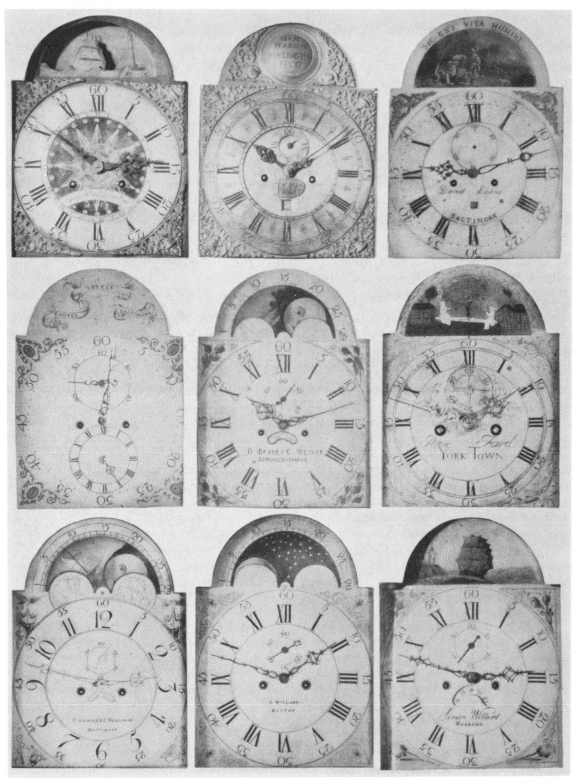

1853 (UPPER) MR. WM. M. ELLI-
    COTT.
1856 (CENTRE) MR. EDGAR G.
    MILLER, JR.
1859 (LOWER) MR. & MRS. WM. A.
    DIXON.

1854 (UPPER) MRS. DANIEL MILLER.
1857 (CENTRE) MR. & MRS. M. P.
    MORFIT.
1860 (LOWER) ORPHANS COURT, BAL-
    TIMORE.

1855 (UPPER) MRS. J. P. PLEASANTS.
1858 (CENTRE) MR. W. W. LANA-
    HAN.
1861 (LOWER) MRS. J. S. GIBBS, JR.

No. 1859 has a moon attachment, too dark in the engraving, with the usual hemispheres on which the more important lands and seas appear. The hour numerals are Arabic in form, in regard to which certain details are mentioned in the note;[32] on this dial the only exactly vertical hour numerals are 12 and 6. The hands are graceful in form. The names "Chandlee and Holloway", of Baltimore, are under the day-of-the-month opening. This firm was in business from about 1819 to 1823.

No. 1860 is the dial of clock No. 1849 and bears the name "E. Willard, Boston"; No. 1861 is the dial of a "Simon Willard, Roxbury", clock. These dials are well designed and well executed, but except for the names of their makers are not of much greater interest than many others seen in this section. About 1800-1820.

No. 1862 is an original label of Aaron Willard, pasted on the inside of the case of No. 1848 and referred to in the comment on that clock. The name of Willard is well engraved with large flourishes and the abbreviation "Jr." is added in handwriting, the letters "Jr." thus appearing on the dial and label. The engraved border, largely composed of "C curves", may be compared with that of the more elaborate and much earlier label of Benjamin Randolph, of Philadelphia, shown as No. 1 in this book. Aaron Willard, Jr., went into business in his own name in 1823, as mentioned in note 27. Several interesting details of this label are referred to in the note.[33] About 1823-1830.

32.   Arabic numerals designating the hours seem to have been more popular in our country than in England. The earliest shown in this book are on the American grandfather clock No. 1811, dated about 1770, in which all of the numerals are Arabic and are in a vertical position except "7"; other examples of this vertical Arabic type are in No. 1828 and in several of the mantel clocks in the Terry style in section 191. In many of the clocks having Arabic numerals the figures 12 and 6 are the only exactly vertical ones, the others being at various angles, as in Nos. 1820, 1823 and others; we also notice that the tops of the Arabic hour numerals 4-8 are towards the centre of the dial, but that Roman numerals are in a reversed position, the bottom always being towards the centre of the dial, as in the next dial, No. 1860. Other examples of Arabic numerals are in the "grandmother" clocks Nos. 1868-1870 in the next section. These matters are not important, but may be interesting to some readers, serving to test one's observation of details seen daily for years. Other matters concerning hour numerals are in section 183 on "Dials".

33.   At the top of the label is an English mantel, or shelf, clock on a shelf attached to a wall. The arched dial has a large moon attachment. In front of the word "Boston" is written "No. 4", which may refer to the size or type of clock to which the label was attached. Under "Boston" is a written dollar mark and the letters "r b", which were perhaps code symbols for the price, just as letters of the ten-letter word "Cumberland" are now often used by dealers, the letter "C" meaning in dollars "one", the letter "u" meaning "two", and so on; in this case "$rb" would mean $64. The letter "s" appears in both the long and the short form, the long form too similar to the letter "f", as in the words "for setting" after the word "Directions".

        The long form of the letter "s", as in the word "setting", in italics or otherwise, was the usual form of that letter in England until about 1775, except at the end of a word, as in the word "constructions" over the words "Aaron Willard". This long form of letter went out of style in the London newspapers about 1805, but about twenty years prior to that date Benjamin Franklin, who was himself a printer, wrote from London that "the Round 's' begins to be made and in nice printing the Long 's' is rejected entirely". The abolition of the long "s" is said to be due to a leading London publisher, John Bell, who discarded it about 1775. Readers interested in this and other matters of

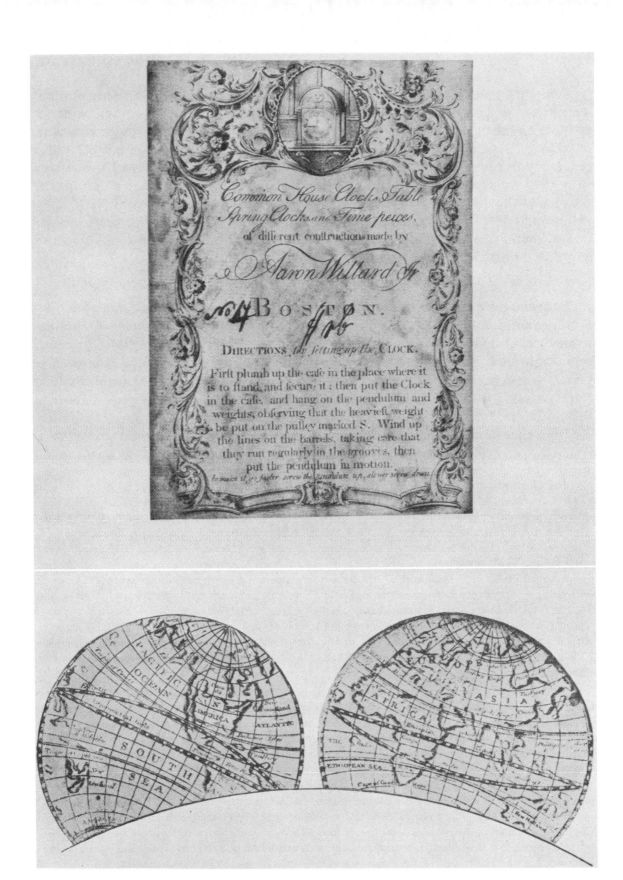

1862 (Upper) Col. Washington Bowie, Jr.
1863 (Lower) Baltimore Museum of Art.

No. 1863 shows in detail an example of the hemispheres which are so often seen in the arched portion of the dials of grandfather clocks. These hemispheres are those on the clock No. 1850, made by William Cummens, and are in almost the actual size. As mentioned in section 183, on "Dials", note 7, the names of the oceans and lands on the hemispheres are assumed to be the names in use at the time the clock was made. In this illustration the continent of Australia appears as "New Holland" which was the English version of the name given by the Dutch settlers in 1664. In 1817, this name was changed to "Australia" by the English. It may therefore be assumed, unless the dial maker was not up-to-date in his geography, that the clock was made before 1817.

Section 188. Grandmother clocks.—The term "grandmother"[1] as applied to certain small clocks is an American one, as is the term "grandfather" as applied to tall clocks. The words "miniature grandfather clock" are more descriptive of their origin and small size, but are formal and less interesting. A "grandmother clock", properly speaking, is a small[2] floor clock in the grandfather form, that is, with the case in three parts—the hood above, the base below and the waist between, with a door. The term is sometimes loosely applied to any floor clock of smaller size than that of the usual grandfather clock, such as the slender English clocks

(Note 33, *continued*)

types and forms of letters should see the book "John Bell" by Stanley Morrison, page 105, published in 1930 at Cambridge, England, by the University Press; also "Printing Types", by Daniel B. Updike, volume 2, page 229, published in 1922 by the Harvard University Press. These sources of information have been found for the writer by Mr. Samuel E. Lafferty, of the Peabody Institute Library in Baltimore. Dr. J. Hall Pleasants in his handsome and exhaustive volume entitled "Maryland Silversmiths, 1715-1830", published in 1930, refers to Mr. Lafferty as one who "possesses a flair, quite uncanny, for putting his hand on book and page where something one needs lies concealed"; in which enconium the writer gratefully concurs, and also expresses his thanks to Mr. Henry J. Fickus and Mr. Harry C. Kaufmann of the same library.

  See the copies of advertisements in Maryland newspapers shown in the "Appendix", sections 207 and 210. In section 207 two of the advertisements appeared in 1773; those in section 210 were in 1819. The change in the form of the letter "s" as used in these struggling newspapers will be noticed.

  1. Unlike the grandfather clocks which have inspired many poetical efforts, one of which is quoted in section 186, note 2, the grandmother clocks are, in poetry at least, "unhonored and unsung". Perhaps a reason is that the poets, in their verses on grandfather clocks, have exhausted the words which rhyme with "tick" and "tock". Many of these grandmother clocks are highly esteemed for their quaint and homelike character and often for their excellence in workmanship and timekeeping.

  The term "grandmother" clocks is also used in England. In "Old English Walnut and Lacquer Furniture", by Mr. R. W. Symonds, 1923, page 111, it is said that "genuine long case clocks of this small size, especially of the walnut period are few and far between"; that "the spurious grandmother clocks generally have modern movements, faked to give them an appearance of age." Moreover "sometimes old movements obtained from the hood or wall clocks, which have small dials, are used."

  2. No exact height has been agreed upon as distinguishing a grandmother clock from a grandfather clock. The height of No. 1864 is sixty-one inches, of No. 1868 forty-six inches; No. 1872, by Simon Willard, is only about twenty-four inches high.

  In several of the cases of these clocks certain peculiarities or crudities suggest the work of country cabinet makers who were not close followers of the styles prevailing in the large cities.

Nos. 1782-1784 and the similar American one No. 1800; and some of the American mantel, or shelf, clocks in the Willard style, Nos. 1916-1927, in section 190, have been mistaken for grandmother clocks.

In No. 1864 the top has scrolls with ornaments at the sides as on grandfather clocks from about 1770, as mentioned in section 186 in connection with Nos. 1767-1773, and Nos. 1808-1833. In the arch over the dial is a round and convex metal "boss"[3] on which is engraved "Thomas Clagett, Newport", Rhode Island, whose dates are somewhat uncertain. The base is in two parts, the lower one being larger, a form seen also in the American grandfather clocks Nos. 1800 and 1803. As mentioned in note 2 this clock is taller than many others, its height being sixty-one inches, the extreme height for a grandmother clock. About 1770-1780.

In No. 1865 the hood is of the same general type as in the preceding clock, but with higher scrolls. On the arched dial a "boss" is seen. On the corners of the waist are fluted columns. The corners of the base are cut off, or "chamfered", as in Nos. 1766 and 1809. There is no name on this clock, but on the boss are the warning words "Time is flying". The feet are of the bracket type, as in several others of these clocks. About 1770-1780.

No. 1866 has a scroll top of good form, with the usual rosettes on the inner ends of the scrolls and an arched dial as in the two preceding pieces. In a curved opening on the dial a disk moves from side to side with the swinging of the pendulum. A tiny door is in the very short waist, as in No. 1876. Lines of inlay around the upper door and at other places indicate the period of the Hepplewhite-Sheraton styles. About 1800-1810.

In No. 1867 the plate upon which the dial is painted is circular, a form seen in several other grandmother clocks shown here and in the English grandfather clock No. 1779 and others. There are no columns on the hood. The dial is somewhat large and the waist somewhat wide for the small size of the clock, which is thirty-eight inches high. The case is veneered with crotch mahogany and is inlaid. About 1800-1810.

No. 1868 is a plain clock, forty-six inches in height. The scrolls at the top are not ornamented with rosettes at the inner ends and there are no columns on the corners of the hood. In the lower door is a glass opening through which the pendulum weight is seen. On the dial are the words "Noah Ranlet, Gilmanton", New Hampshire. The hour numerals are in the Arabic form. The skirt under the base is cut in curves in the same form as in the next clock. About 1800-1820.

Nos. 1869 and 1870 have variations of the "bell top" form seen in the English mantel clocks Nos. 1883-1885 and others, and as in the Willard style mantel clocks Nos. 1916-1918. Each has an arched dial with a painting on the arch, a third hand pointing to the day of the month, Arabic numerals, wide waist and curved skirt. The names on these clocks are almost worn off, but seem to be "Joshua Wilder" of Hingham, Mass. About 1790-1800.

3.   As to a "boss", see section 183, on "Dials", note 3.

1864 (Upper) Metropoli-
    tan Museum of
    Art.
1868 (Lower) Anonymous.

1865 (Upper) Mrs. S. C.
    Rowland.
1869 (Lower) Mrs. Miles
    White, Jr.

1866 (Upper) Dr. Jas. Bord-
    ley, Jr.
1870 (Lower) Anonymous.

1867 (Upper) Anony-
    mous.
1871 (Lower) Metro-
    politan Museum
    of Art.

1872 (UPPER) ANONY-
    MOUS.
1876 (LOWER) ANONY-
    MOUS.

1873 (UPPER) ANONYMOUS.
1877 (LOWER) MRS. J. S.
    GIBBS, JR.

1874 (UPPER) ANONY-
    MOUS.
1878 (LOWER) ANONY-
    MOUS.

1875 (UPPER) ANONY-
    MOUS.
1879 (LOWER) MR. &
    MRS. H. L. DUER.

In No. 1871 the arched dial has two small dials, for the seconds and days of the month respectively. This clock is forty-seven inches high. At the top of the arched dial are the words "Caleb Leach, Plymouth", Massachusetts; the business dates of this maker are said to be 1776-1790.

No. 1872 is a grandmother clock about twenty-four inches high, as mentioned in note 2, bearing on the brass dial the words "Simon Willard, Grafton", Massachusetts, where Simon Willard worked in the early part of his career.[4] The round dial is surrounded by a square veneered mahogany door; the fretwork at the top is in a different form from others seen on Simon Willard's clocks; the feet are high and awkward—a detail which seems to indicate a substitution or an early experimental stage in Simon Willard's career. This clock, with its very small seconds dial, may be compared with Simon and Aaron Willard's wall clocks Nos. 2041 and 2042. About 1770-1780.

Nos. 1873, 1874 and 1875 form a group of three grandmother clocks with cases of plain character, which are probably the work of country cabinet makers. They range from forty-four to forty-eight inches in height. Each has a different fretwork at the top and the ornaments which may have been on the pedestals are missing. The dials are painted.

In No. 1873 the left column has a white appearance, owing to a reflection. The arched dial is decorated with floral and other designs. Under the centre of the dial are the words "Reuben Tower, Hanover", Massachusetts. The waist is too wide, giving a bulky appearance to the case. The wood is cherry stained to imitate mahogany. About 1810-1820.

In No. 1874 the arched portion of the dial is too small. The top is flat, not arched, as is sometimes seen on clocks with arched dials, as in Nos. 1777 and 1835. Here also the wood is cherry stained to imitate mahogany. About 1800-1820.

In No. 1875 the round dial and the surrounding square frame-work are of the same character as in No. 1872, although here the dial itself is larger. Reeded columns are on the waist. The wood is mahogany. About 1800-1820.

In No. 1876 the case is somewhat of a curiosity, certainly not a work of art. The top, with its two scrolls and three ornaments, is of a normal character. The decorated arch of the dial, which may have been made for a different case, is partly hidden behind the arch of the upper door. The short and narrow waist with a tiny door, as in No. 1866, is in a form said to have been a favorite in country districts in Pennsylvania. The base has two panels. The bracket feet, however, are in good form. About 1800-1820.

No. 1877 is a small clock, twenty-nine inches in height, which in some respects resembles the preceding piece, having a hood of the usual grandfather type and a slender waist, here decorated with a painting of a woman. On each side of the waist is a figure in peasant costume, and on the very wide base is a painting of a

---

4.   See the remarks on Simon Willard in section 187, note 19.

The illustration here is copied from Mr. John Ware Willard's book "Simon Willard", plate 17 and pages 39-40, where Mr. Willard states that this clock is in "absolutely perfect condition".

house and grounds. The skirt of the base is cut in the same manner as in the Terry style mantel clock No. 1928 and many others; from which we may infer that the date is about 1810-1820.

No. 1878 is an English grandmother clock which has on the top a box-like structure of the type well seen on the English grandfather clock No. 1766. On the arched top of the dial is a convex "boss" with the familiar words "Tempus fugit". The height is about five feet. There is only one keyhole, indicating that the clock does not strike. In the centre of the dial is an alarm disk. This clock bears the words "S. Collier, Eccles", the latter being a town in Lancashire, showing that it is a provincial clock, not made in London. About 1770-1780.

No. 1879 is also an English clock. The hood and the top of the door in the waist are arched; and "Tempus fugit" again appears on the "boss". The height is about four feet. In this and the preceding clock the cases are examples of good design and workmanship. Here there is no name or minute hand. About 1770-1780.

Section 189. Mantel clocks; English styles.—These clocks[1] were first made in England at about the same time as the grandfather clocks, that is, about the year 1670. Apart from their size and shape, they differ from the grandfather type mainly in three respects, that is, they are driven by a coiled spring[2] instead of by weights, they have a short pendulum instead of a long one,[3] and they have a different form of ornamentation.[4] Several similarities, however, will be noticed between

1. The term "bracket", although generally applied in England to this type of clocks, is declared by English writers to be a misnomer now. The word is properly applied to a clock which rests upon a bracket or shelf attached to a wall—a necessary position for a lantern or hooded clock such as Nos. 1745 and 1749, each with its weight and chain, and a safe, but not the most desirable, position for any other clocks which are now placed upon a mantel. In England and France it was the custom to place these clocks on brackets, and the cabinet makers made attractive designs for the purpose. The term "table" clock is also inappropriate at the present time for the reason that these clocks are seldom placed upon a table and then only on a table which stands against a wall; if the table is in the centre of a room the back of the clock, not always attractive, is generally as conspicuous as the front. In this connection see the ornamental "back plates", Nos. 1910-1912.

    In his "Chats on Old Clocks", page 180, Mr. Hayden pleasantly refers to a clock of this kind as standing on "the mantelpiece, a place it can almost claim as its own in the English home by tradition".

2. The spring is a narrow strip of steel which is coiled in a "barrel-shaped" receptacle. The struggle of the spring to uncoil itself furnishes the power which drives the clock. In this connection see the "fusee", illustrated and explained in the comment on the clock Nos. 2004-2005.

    The use of a spring, instead of the weights which were used on lantern and grandfather clocks, made it possible to place a clock on a table, a shelf, or a mantel; and of course the mantel clock is easily movable.

3. As to pendulums see section 182, at note 8.

4. For example, the fine marquetry and lacquer work on the cases of the early grandfather clocks, as in Nos. 1753, 1762 and others, was rarely used on the mantel clocks of the same period; and the elaborate "basket-tops" of the early mantel clocks were not used on the grandfather clocks. Other ornaments on the mantel clocks are referred to in the comments on the illustrations.

the cases and dials of the mantel clocks and the hoods and dials of the grand-father clocks of the same period; for example, the square dial was used on both types of the early period; the arched dial and the painted dial were adopted on both at about the same time; the form of the hands was of the same general char-acter, and the four brass ornamental spandrels in the corners of the dial were of similar designs. About the beginning of the nineteenth century the form of the cases and the style of ornamentation of the mantel clocks changed greatly, as will be seen in the illustrations. Several matters of interest regarding these mantel clocks are in the note.[5]

As mentioned below, in connection with Nos. 1913-1915, few if any mantel clocks of this type were made in our country, but very many English ones are found in our homes.

5. A. The furniture styles at several periods influenced to some extent the shape and decoration of the cases of mantel clocks. Mr. Cescinsky in "English Domestic Clocks", page 250, summarizes the subject as follows: the "broken-arch" top may be described as the Hepplewhite type; the "arch top" is the Sheraton style, alternating with the "balloon" form of clock; the "lancet" is the latest of the eighteenth century patterns. These types of mantel clocks are shown in the illustrations. The Chippen-dale style seen in the grandfather clock cases is referred to in section 186 at note 22. The Empire style French mantel clocks are shown in section 193.

B. Handles were perhaps always placed on mantel clocks. Whether a handle was placed at the top, or at the sides, depended largely upon whether the top was in a form suitable for a handle. In a general way, however, it may be said that until about 1790 only one handle was commonly used and this was at the top. In some of our illustrations the handle at the top is shown, but it is usually omitted for the reason that if it were shown the space available for the case would be reduced. After about 1790 two handles were generally used, one on each side, near the top. If the clock is carried by two handles the danger of breakage is much less than if by one, but a careful owner would now never carry a clock even by two handles; and carrying it by one handle at the top would invite disaster, as the wood work of the top of the case, after more than a century, is not in a condition to sustain the heavy weight of the brass works.

C. As a person winding the spring of a mantel clock does not always know just how many times to turn the key, and may wind the spring to a sudden stop and break it, a cautionary device is sometimes used which gives notice that the spring is nearly wound up. This "caution" is felt and heard by the person winding. In grandfather clocks the weights are, or may be, seen and there is no need of a "caution". Modern clocks and watches have devices which serve the same purpose.

D. Many mantel clocks have a string which extends outside the case and connects with a spring inside, and when the string is pulled the spring causes the striking mechanism to repeat the last strike. This is more fully referred to in connection with English grandfather clocks, section 186, note 18, with a query as to its usefulness. In some of the earlier mantel clocks, with only one keyhole, the striking mechanism was operated by a string attached to a spring, as in No. 301 in "English Domestic Clocks" as stated on page 283 of that book; see also No. 1882 in this section.

E. The woods used in the cases of mantel clocks may be mentioned. In many of the early clocks, such as Nos. 1881-1883, the case is veneered with ebony; walnut was used from about 1735 to 1760; after 1760 mahogany was almost always used; but ebony and walnut cases were sometimes made as late as 1790. Other woods were occasionally used, as in the satinwood clock No. 1898. The kind of wood is not to be relied on in fixing the dates. See sections 186, note 15, and 180 at note 7.

F. Seconds hands are not seen in mantel clocks unless the clocks were for astronomical or other special purposes. The pendulum is necessarily short and each swing is made in less than one second.

Nos. 1880-1888 are illustrations of English mantel clocks which, with others, have been copied, by permission, from "English Domestic Clocks". These illustrations present a view of the changes in style of representative English mantel clocks from about 1670 to 1800. The next twenty-one illustrations, Nos. 1889-1909, with one exception, are of English mantel clocks owned in our country and photographed for this book; Nos. 1910-1912 are finely engraved back plates; and Nos. 1913-1915 are mantel clocks in the English style on whose dials are painted the names and addresses of American clock makers or dealers. Two other English mantel clocks, photographed too late for inclusion in this section, are Nos. 2093 and 2099 in section 197.

Examining the first group, Nos. 1880-1888, we see that the forms of the case and the square dial of No. 1880 are similar to those of the hood and dial of the grandfather clock No. 1753 in section 186, which is of about the same period. The two spiral columns are similar in form to the legs of the table and chair Nos. 1279 and 35, as mentioned in the comment on No. 1748, which are also of about the same date. In this very early clock the hands are fine and delicate and there is a seconds dial and an opening showing the day of the month. The keyholes are closed by a maintaining power device which is explained in the comment and note on No. 1758. The case is of walnut, except that the spiral columns are stained to resemble ebony. The four brass "spandrels", or "corner pieces", have cherub heads, which also appear in many other clocks. Brass ornaments on the top were apparently not used at this time. About 1675-1700.

In No. 1881 we see on the top a decorative feature of early mantel clocks, that is, a brass openwork ornament, formed and pierced somewhat like a basket and called "basket work", which gives to clocks having this work the name of "basket top" clocks. The term is also applied to wooden tops without the brass basket work, but of the same general form as the basket tops. This ornamental top was used from about 1680 to 1705 on cases having square dials. On some clocks there is a small basket above a large one. Division marks indicate the quarters of the hour and a design shows the half-hour, as in the early grandfather clock dial No. 1756 and many others. The handles on these clocks are often interesting. The small dial under the hands shows the day of the month. The case is veneered with ebony. Another basket top clock is shown below, No. 1889. About 1680.

No. 1882, also, has a square dial and a "basket top", which in this clock is of wood, mounted with pierced brass. The front is ornamented with four brass mounts, two of which are keyhole escutcheons, that on the right being apparently to give a symmetrical appearance. There is no winding keyhole here for striking the hour, but there is a "pull repeater" by which the hour may be struck, as explained in note 5, D. On the plate at the back of this clock is the name of the celebrated Thomas Tompion, the "Father of English Clockmaking", who died in 1713; one of his grandfather clocks is No. 1758. About 1700.

In the next two clocks, Nos. 1883 and 1884, the dials are not square as in the previous three pieces, but are arched. In section 183, on the subject of dials, it is mentioned that arch dials were in fashion from about 1725 to 1800. The tops of these two clocks are in one of the forms known as "bell tops",[6] as mentioned in the comments. These tops are found chiefly on clocks with arch dials. In a mantel clock with a bell top and an arch dial, as here, the door has two "spandrels", or "corner pieces", at the top.

In No. 1883 the arch has a small dial with the words "strike" and "silent" and a hand which controls the striking mechanism, as seen also on the dial No. 1793 on a grandfather clock. Large minute numbers are on the outer edge of the hour ring. In the centre is an opening in which there is an oscillating disk which is attached to the pendulum and moves from side to side. The top is in one of the forms known as "bell" top. The handle has been omitted. The case is ebony. About 1730.

No. 1884, also with an arch dial, has a moon attachment, a device not often seen on mantel clocks, which is explained in section 183 at note 7. Another clock of this type is No. 1913. On a plate under the hour figure XII the name of the maker appears on an attached plate, as was a fashion of the period. A "bell top" form is also seen on this clock. The case is mahogany. About 1765.

In No. 1885 the top is of the same "bell" form as in the preceding clock. Here the dial is round, and is enameled white, with very large minute figures on the outer edge. At the four corners of the door are brass fretwork ornaments corresponding to the spandrels in the previous pieces. The four pineapples on the top were a favorite form of ornament. This clock may be compared with No. 1914. About 1790.

Nos. 1886 and 1887 show the "broken arch" type of clock case, which became popular about 1765. In connection with mantel clocks a "broken arch" does not mean a pointed top cut apart in the centre, as in the grandfather clock No. 1838, but an arched top whose ends do not extend to the full width of the case, as seen in the illustrations. Several other clocks of this type are shown below. In No. 1886 a string is seen at the rear on the right hand side; when this is pulled the striking mechanism repeats the last stroke, as also in No. 1889 and others. In No. 1887 the round dial is enameled and on the front and side the brass fretwork is seen, the two pieces on the front being survivals of the lower spandrels seen in previous clocks. The brass frame holding the glass is a part of the door and opens with it. A very similar clock, No. 1901, is shown below. Nos. 1886 and 1887 are dated at about 1770-1785.

6. Two types of "bell tops" are recognized by Mr. Cescinsky. The first type in date, beginning about 1715 and continuing in use throughout the whole of the eighteenth century, is that in Nos. 1883 and 1891-1895; these tops are known as "inverted bell tops". The second, beginning about 1760 and continuing until the middle of the nineteenth century, is that in Nos. 1884, 1885 and 1896, which is called a "true bell top". The difference between the two forms seems to be that in the "inverted bell top" a concave curve is above and a convex curve is below; and in the "true bell top" the concave curve is below and the convex one is above, more closely resembling a bell. This distinction may be of assistance in fixing the dates of some clocks; but, as with several other designs, the earlier type continued in use after the later one began. For our purposes the term "bell top" is sufficiently descriptive for both types.

1880 (Upper) Ces. & Web., Fig. 275. 1881 (Upper) Ces. & Web., Fig. 277. 1882 (Upper) Ces. & Web., Fig. 297.
1883 (Centre) Ces. & Web., Fig. 306. 1884 (Centre) Ces. & Web., Fig. 328. 1885 (Centre) Ces. & Web., Fig. 335.
1886 (Lower) Ces. & Web., Fig. 341. 1887 (Lower) Ces. & Web., Fig. 342. 1888 (Lower) Ces. & Web., Fig. 363.

No. 1888 has a round enameled dial and a plain arch top. The mahogany case is inlaid with lines of holly, and the triangular inlays under the dial and the oval inlays below are of satinwood. The feet are brass balls, which were often used in the period. About 1800.

The next twenty illustrations, Nos. 1889-1908, are of English mantel clocks owned in our country.

No. 1889 is a "basket top" clock similar in some respects to No. 1881. It has pierced brass basket-work at the top, a square dial and brass cherub heads in the corners. Division marks for the quarter-hour and half-hour are between the hour numerals, as in Nos. 1881 and 1882. There is only one keyhole, which is for winding; but a striking mechanism operates when the string at the bottom on the left hand side is pulled. The feet are of a type seen in this period. The name "Benja. Meryman", (London), is on a plate attached to the back plate; his business dates are given as 1682-1734. About 1700.

No. 1890 is a plain form of the type of No. 1882, with no brass mounts on the top or front, although there was doubtless one in the long horizontal opening above the door and perhaps others. There are three keyholes, for the time, the strike and a chime, respectively. The day of the month appears in the small rectangular opening, which is almost invisible in the engraving. Over the figure XII is the word "noon". The brass bracket feet are of a later style. This clock is about eleven inches high. Between the hour numerals V and VII are the words "Jonat Puller, London". About 1700.

No. 1891 and the next five mantel clocks have bell tops and arch dials and in some other respects have similar forms. In the arch is a small dial with a hand pointing to the day of the month, and on each side is a brass allegorical figure. The curved opening in which there was probably an oscillating disk, as in No. 1883, has been closed. There is a ringed keyhole for winding the clock but none for striking, and below is an attached plate for the name. About 1770-1780.

No. 1892 is similar in form to the preceding example. In the arch is a small "strike-silent" dial with a hand which controls the striking mechanism. Under the hour numeral XII is a plate with the name "Thomas Wagstaffe", London, who is referred to in the comments on the grandfather clocks Nos. 1773 and 1776. A wall clock by this maker is No. 2055. About 1770-1790.

In No. 1893 the third keyhole indicates that there is a chime attachment, this playing at the quarter-hours. As in No. 1890 the position of this keyhole required the opening showing the day of the month to be under the hour numeral XII instead of being in the usual position over the hour numeral VI. The "strike-silent" dial in the arch is conspicuous. Between the hour numerals V and VII are the words "Green and Bentley", London, who were in business about 1790-1800.

No. 1894 was acquired by the present owner in Constantinople. The general form is similar to that of the three preceding clocks, but the ornamental features were made for the Turkish market. The entire front and sides are decorated with paintings of flowers and with ormolu mounts finely chased. On the bell top is a silvered design of uncertain meaning and at the four corners are ormolu figures. On the dial the hour numerals are in Turkish figures, and in the arch are two small dials on one of which are the words "A Jigg" and "A Dance", eighteenth century compositions which are played on bells; on the other small dial are the words "Chime" and "Not Chime". Between these two small dials is a plate bearing the name "Benj. Barber", London, who was in business about 1785-1795.

No. 1895 is a clock made for the Spanish market. The dial is brass, without an attached hour circle or "corner pieces", and in the arch is a small dial with the Spanish words "Tocar" and "Silencio", the Spanish equivalent to "Strike" and "Silent". The clock strikes the hours and half-hours. The case is decorated with designs, in lacquer, of flowers and leaves on a red background. On the dial are the names of the makers, "Higgs y Evans", and the word "Londres". About 1785-1795.

In No. 1896 the bell-top is in a different form from that seen in the preceding clock, the upper portion here being in a convex curve and the lower portion in a concave curve; in the preceding form the concave curve is at the top and the convex curve below. This matter is mentioned in note 6. In addition to the "strike-silent" dial in the arch, there is a dial showing the days of the month. The name of the maker, "Benjamin Taylor", of London, is too faint to be seen in the engraving. About 1790-1800.

No. 1897 has a "broken arch" case, a form which is shown in Nos. 1886 and 1887; as is said in the comment on those two clocks, a "broken arch" in connection with mantel clocks means an arched top whose ends do not extend to the full width of the case. Here the dial is of brass, but in the next four clocks of this type the dials are enameled white. In the arch is the familiar "strike-silent" dial and on the oval plate between the hands are the names "Wightwick and Moss", of London. About 1790-1800.

In No. 1898 the dial is of enamel with brass "spandrels", or "corner pieces". In the arch are two small enameled dials, one for "strike-silent" and the other for the adjustment of the pendulum. The case is of satinwood. On the large dial are the words "James Tregent, Watchmaker to the Prince of Wales, London". The hands are probably substitutes, being too plain for a clock of this fine appearance. About 1780-1790.

No. 1899 has an arched dial in the usual form, painted white, with a "strike-silent" dial in the arch and a day of the month dial below. This clock has a "caution" device giving notice to the person winding the clock that the spring is nearly wound up, as mentioned in note 5, paragraph C. The case and dial are plain and the clock was probably not expensive; there are perhaps more of this type in our country than of any other type. On the dial is the name "John Field", London. About 1795-1810.

No. 1900 differs in several respects from those seen above. Over the dial is an ornamental brass fretwork in a crescent-shaped form and below are two brass

1889 (UPPER) DR. J. HALL PLEAS-
 ANTS.
1892 (CENTRE) MR. EDGAR G.
 MILLER, JR.
1895 (LOWER) MR. EDGAR G. MILLER,
 JR.

1890 (UPPER) BALTIMORE MUSEUM
 OF ART.
1893 (CENTRE) ANONYMOUS.
1896 (LOWER) MR. ALBERT G. TOW-
 ERS.

1891 (UPPER) MR. & MRS. E. H.
 McKEON.
1894 (CENTRE) MR. EDGAR G.
 MILLER, JR.
1897 (LOWER) MR. J. G. D'ARCY
 PAUL.

1898 (Upper) Anonymous.
1901 (Centre) Anonymous.
1904 (Lower) Mr. Edgar G. Miller, Jr.

1899 (Upper) Anonymous.
1902 (Centre) Mr. & Mrs. E. H. McKeon.
1905 (Lower) Mr. John Glenn, Jr.

1900 (Upper) Mr. John C. Toland.
1903 (Centre) Anonymous.
1906 (Lower) Mr. J. G. D'Arcy Paul.

"spandrels", or "corner pieces". On the front corners are fluted columns with brass caps above and brass rods at the bottom, as seen on so many grandfather clocks and on No. 1905. The dial is round and is painted white. The hands are not mates. The brass feet will also be noticed. A clock with similar brass ornamentation is No. 2099, which should have appeared here. About 1810-1820.

No. 1901 is similar in form to the preceding clock, but is not so fully ornamented with brass fretwork. The brass frame holding the convex glass is a part of the door and opens with it. On the right hand side is one of the two side openings fitted with brass fretwork, seen also on No. 1905 and others; this is an ornamental treatment often found in mantel clocks at this period. The two brass fretwork spandrels on the lower corners of the front are survivals of the four spandrels which began with the first mantel clocks, as also in No. 1887. The hands are too long and are probably substitutes. About 1820-1830.

No. 1902 is of the same type as No. 1888, but is less ornamental. The lower portion has only lines of inlay to relieve the plain surface of the mahogany. The brass frame holding the convex glass—the "bezel"—is supported by a hinge on the left and is not a part of the door which was the method in the preceding clock. On the dial are the words "Wightman, St. Martin's Lane, London". About 1800-1815.

No. 1903 is a "lancet top" or "lancet" clock, so called because of the resemblance of the form of the top to a surgeon's instrument. The top is also suggestive of a pointed Gothic arch. These lancet clocks are almost always ornamented with an inlay of brass designs, and brass ball feet are generally used. The ring handle and the brass fretwork on the side may be seen. This type of clock was popular from about 1800 to 1850 but in the later part of the period it was debased in its decoration. On the dial are the words "John Bentley, Maker, London", and the figures "2507", the latter probably indicating the shop number of the clock. Another lancet clock, photographed too late to appear in this section, is No. 2093. About 1810-1820.

No. 1904 is a handsome "balloon" clock inlaid with finely grained decorative woods. This type of case was a favorite from about 1790 to 1835, in the latter part of which period it suffered a decline. The band of dark wood around the dial and the base, the circle of inlaid wood in the base and the brass feet in the French style will be noticed. On the dial are the words "Jabez Smith, Fenchurch Street, London". About 1785-1795.

No. 1905 should follow No. 1900 as it is in part an elaboration of the design of that clock. Over the arch is an ornamental addition with fretwork; on the corners are fluted columns with brass rods at the bottom; inlaid designs, instead of brass fretwork and spandrels, ornament the front; and the corners of the base are cut off, or "chamfered". An interesting incident, in which this clock continued to chime and strike when it should have been silent, is mentioned in the note.[7] The initials of the first American owner are in the panel of light wood over the dial. About 1810-1820.

No. 1906 may be regarded as an elaboration of the design of the lancet clock No. 1903. On a platform at the top of the pointed arch is the British lion; at the front corners are Egyptian figures instead of fluted columns; and on the base is a creature of the Nile—a combination which suggests the victory of the British fleet of Nelson over that of Napoleon in the battle of the Nile in 1798. On the dial is the name "Brockbank", of London. About 1800.

Nos. 1907-1909 are in a later and a different style from the preceding mantel clocks. The cases are mainly rectangular and are ornamented with applied moldings and brass "lion's-head-and-ring" handles. The glass convex doors, with brass frames, or "bezels", are attached to the front by one hinge which often breaks the wood of the frame because of the weight when the door is open. The brass feet are of the ball type.

In No. 1907 are four sunken panels, almost triangular in form, and with brass pieces on the sides, recalling the spandrels of so many of the earlier clocks. These panels are said to show the influence of Thomas Hope,[8] an English collector who published a book entitled "Household Furniture" in 1807. At the top and above the base are moldings which extend across the front; these were made in quantity, and, in the words of Mr. Cescinsky, were adopted "as a cheap and more or less effective substitute for carving". On the dial are the words "James Murray, Royal Exchange, London". The location at the "Royal Exchange" indicates that this clock was made between 1824 and 1838, because in those years his shop was in that building.

No. 1908 has two horizontal moldings similar to those mentioned in the preceding comment, and other moldings almost cover the front. The top is arched, with pointed moldings at the sides. The dials of this and the preceding clock are large in proportion to the size of the case and the time is easily seen at a distance. The name "Tobias Livett", of London, is on the dial; Livitt, (or Levitt), was a

7. In the riots in Baltimore in 1835, following the closing of the Bank of Maryland, the mob attacked the homes of several of the directors, including that of John Glenn, whose initials are on the panel of light wood. Mr. Glenn had left the city, after putting in barrels his most precious household belongings, including this clock. The barrels were hidden in a coal bin in the cellar under a pile of coal and were not discovered by the rioters; but just as they were leaving, this dutiful but indiscreet clock began to chime and then struck the hour, betraying the location of itself and the other valuables. The clock was carried off by the mob and was not recovered until several years afterwards when it was found in a pawn shop. It is now the property of a descendant of Mr. Glenn.

8. Thomas Hope, (1770-1831), was an English art collector and writer. His book, "Household Furniture", had considerable influence on furniture and interior decoration. His designs were in the so-called "English Empire" style and were a mixture of Egyptian and Roman forms. Mr. Cescinsky remarks that "it was reserved to Thomas Hope to show to what depths of degradation the rage for the classical could be dragged", and that his influence permeated the trade of the clock-maker almost as much as that of the cabinet maker. In an article in "Antiques", January, 1934, pages 20-23, several designs by Hope are illustrated.

nephew, and at one time a partner, of Morris Tobias, (about 1794-1840), whose watches were popular in our country.[9] About 1830-1840.

No. 1909 has an arched top which is decorated with applied moldings and has a superstructure in a terraced form, also a Thomas Hope feature, on which was a brass pineapple. The four triangular corner pieces are sunken as in No. 1907 and in the base is a sunken panel in rectangular form. The brass fretwork on the side is well seen. The words on the dial are "Thomas Gostling, Diss", the latter a small town in Norfolk, England. About 1845.

Nos. 1910-1912 are illustrations of back plates of mantel clocks. Until about the end of the eighteenth century it was the fashion to ornament the back plates with elaborately engraved designs, and in order that the plates might be seen the clock cases were made with a glass door. The name and address of the maker were often engraved on the plate. The illustrations are copied, by permission, from "English Domestic Clocks", by Cescinsky and Webster. Many of the mantel clocks shown in this section have engraved back plates, but the plates shown here are perhaps of finer design and workmanship than those on later clocks. A finely engraved back plate adds interest to a mantel clock and a purchaser should always look for this feature.

In No. 1910 the bell is seen at the top as also in the next two illustrations, and below, to the left, is an ornamental and finely pierced brass piece, called a "cock", which protects the mechanism which moves the pendulum. A smaller piece, of the same name, was used in old watches, often delicately pierced and engraved, and a few years ago many were taken from watches and used for bracelets, necklaces and other articles of adornment. The pendulum is held in a hook to prevent it swinging when the clock is being moved. The brass pieces at the bottom of the plate are for ornament as well as for the mechanism. The plate is finely engraved with curved designs, and the maker's name is near the centre, hardly visible. A pulling string for repeating the striking is on the left side. About 1700.

No. 1911 is a back plate finely engraved with flowers and with the name of the maker in the lower portion. The illustration includes two bells at the top, the large one for the hours and the smaller for the quarter-hours. A part of the pull repeater string is at the right hand lower corner. About 1700.

No. 1912 is elaborately chased with fanciful curves and with a basket of flowers in the centre. It has fewer attachments than the two preceding back plates.

9. Another Baltimore incident, in addition to that in note 7, may perhaps be pardoned. Three friends of the writer were chatting one evening in a club, and when one of them said that it was time to go home, Mr. B looked at his watch and said that it was exactly right, stating that it was a "Tobias", which came to him from an ancestor. Mr. L then produced his watch, also a "Tobias", which had belonged to his grandfather, and was a good timekeeper; whereupon Mr. R drew from his pocket his watch, also a "Tobias", which had descended to him from a relative and was a fine timepiece. The meeting of these three watches, after almost one hundred years of service to three families, was not only an interesting coincidence, but also a tribute to the quality of the watches and the care given to them by several generations of owners. A song should be written to the watch as a companion piece to "My Grandfather's Clock" which appears in note 2 of section 186.

1907 (UPPER) ANONYMOUS.
1910 (CENTRE) CES. & WEB., FIG. 295.
1913 (LOWER) MR. A. E. COLE.

1908 (UPPER) ANONYMOUS.
1911 (CENTRE) CES. & WEB., FIG. 290.
1914 (LOWER) BALTIMORE MUSEUM
OF ART.

1909 (UPPER) CES. & WEB., FIG. 370.
1912 (CENTRE) CES. & WEB., FIG. 310.
1915 (LOWER) ANONYMOUS.

Instead of a handsome "cock" at the top as in the first back plate, there is a simple shield which is engraved in harmony with the plate. About 1730.

This section on mantel clocks in the English style closes[10] with three, Nos. 1913-1915, which are of the same design as certain English clocks shown in this section, but bear the names and addresses of American makers or dealers. These clocks may or may not have been made in our country, and except for the names painted on them they would be regarded as English pieces. It is probable that they are in fact English clocks and that the names on them are those of American dealers who imported foreign clocks. If many clocks such as these had been made in our country it is likely that more would have survived than the few which have been found. The three clocks here shown, being of doubtful origin, are classified merely as being in the English style.

No. 1913 has a bell top, an arched dial and the usual two spandrels at the upper corners of the doors of bell top cases with arched dials, as in Nos. 1891-1896. The moon attachment is an. unusual feature in mantel clocks, only two being shown in "English Domestic Clocks", one of which is No. 1884 in this section. The day of the month dial is above the hour numeral VI. The plain hands are of brass and four brass pineapples are on the top. On the painted dial are the words "Abraham Stein", Philadelphia, whose name appears in Baillie's "Watchmakers and Clockmakers of the World" with the dates 1796-1825, and the remark "Probably only a dealer". If these dates are correct, this clock must be given the late date of about 1796-1810.

In No. 1914 the bell top differs from that in the preceding clock and is in the form of that in No. 1883, having a concave curve above and a convex curve below, as referred to in note 6. At the four corners of the front are nearly triangular fretwork designs, the two lower being well seen because of the white paper placed behind them for the photograph. The round brass door swings on a hinge at the right, as in No. 1909 and others. The hands are of an unusual type. On the dial is the name "Thos. Parker", of Philadelphia, a watch and clock maker of prominence, who was in business from 1783 to about 1833, as appears in a book of the Walpole Society entitled "The Arts and Crafts in Philadelphia", etc., series 2, pages 263-264, where Parker's advertisements of his own work and of his imported clocks are quoted.[11] Probably about 1790-1800.

No. 1915 is a broken arch clock similar in form to No. 1899. The dial is painted white and is decorated with paintings of flowers on the arch and the corners. On the right hand side is one of two oval openings, over which are "lion's-head-and-ring" handles. On the dial are the words " John Child, Philada.".[12] The brass feet are in the ball pattern. About 1810-1820.

10. Reference may be made again to two English mantel clocks, photographed too late for inclusion in this section, a lancet clock, No. 2093, and a clock, No. 2099, having an oval dial, as in the English grandfather clock No. 1778.

11. In Mr. Nutting's "Furniture Treasury", No. 3517, a broken arch clock with Parker's name is shown and it is said that whether his name "means that he imported it or not does not appear. But dealers had their names placed on the clocks, as was probably the case here".

12. This form of abbreviation is also on the clocks Nos. 1810, 1831 and 2044.

Section 190. Mantel clocks; Willard style.—The clocks illustrated in this section are sometimes called "Massachusetts shelf clocks" for the reason that they were chiefly made in that State, and also in order to distinguish them from the Terry style mantel clocks made in Connecticut; but as Simon and Aaron Willard were apparently the first to make the type of clocks here shown, it seems better to refer to them as mantel clocks in the "Willard style".[1]

It is said that these clocks were made to stand on a shelf, as were the Terry style clocks shown in the next section; but as shelves are now seldom used and as the clocks are almost always placed on a mantel, or sometimes on a table, they are here referred to as "mantel clocks". They were also known as "half clocks" at the time they were made.

These clocks are doubtless a development from the earlier wall clocks of Simon and Aaron Willard shown as Nos. 2041 and 2042 in section 195, in which the upper portion was made almost as a separate piece, with feet resting upon a base in which the pendulum swung. If the feet on those wall clocks were removed from the upper portion and were placed on the lower portion, the form of those clocks would be practically the same as that of the mantel clocks here shown. No. 1926, by Aaron Willard, illustrates the process of change from the wall type to the mantel type.

No. 1916 is a good mantel clock in the Willard style. The top is a variation of a "bell" top and is in about the same form as that on the grandmother clock No. 1870; as to bell tops, see section 189 at note 6. In the oval under the painted dial are the words "Daniel Munroe, Concord". The inner outlines of the door follow the lines of the metal plate of the dial and are in the form called "kidney-shaped".

---

1.   In many of these Willard style clocks, as in No. 1916, the dial plate and door are in a form commonly known as "kidney-shaped", because of a supposed resemblance to that organ. This form may have been copied from some of the French mantel clocks, such as Nos. 1957-1959 in section 193. This form was also occasionally used in English mantel clocks. In Cescinsky and Webster's "English Domestic Clocks" kidney-shaped dials are illustrated, as in figure 360. See also the Willard wall clocks Nos. 2041 and 2042.

The round dial on these clocks is often concave, and if so is sometimes called a "dish" dial, as in No. 1923 and others.

Some of these clocks have a door in the base, as in No. 1920, but generally the base has no door and is ornamented with a simple inlay or a painted design. Sometimes both the upper portion and the base were decorated with paintings on glass as in Nos. 1922-1924.

Most of these clocks are from about thirty to thirty-six inches in height. They are arranged here with reference to form rather than date. All of them were apparently made within the period of about 1780 to 1830. The cases are generally of mahogany.

The question is sometimes asked "What became of the large number of clocks made by the Willards and other makers during a long period of years". As expressed by Mrs. N. H. Moore in her book "The Old Clock Book", page 104, the mystery is "where different kinds of clocks which were made by the thousand have disappeared to". As to these Willard style mantel clocks, which in the old days were placed on a shelf, the answer probably is that they "were always getting knocked off and getting smashed", as said by Mr. John Ware Willard in his book "Simon Willard and his Clocks", page 13. On page 91 Mr. Willard states that Aaron Willard made these clocks in great numbers and in the greatest variety of styles.

The upper portion, with the door, slides forward, exposing the works. The lower portion is somewhat wider than the upper one and is without a door such as is seen in several other of these clocks, as No. 1920. On the lower portion are lines of inlay, and the "skirt" below is cut in scrolls. The feet are in a form of the French bracket type. The date is about 1800-1808, in which latter year Daniel Munroe, the maker, moved to Boston.

In No. 1917, as in the preceding clock, the skirt is curved in the manner of the period, the feet are of a French bracket type, and lines of inlay are on the lower portion. The two round columns at the corners of the door frame, adapted from the columns seen on many of the grandfather clocks, are unusual. An extra space between the door and the lower portion is seen, as also in No. 1925. In an oval under the dial are the words "David Wood", of Newburyport, Mass., who died in 1824. About 1800-1820.

In No. 1918, at the corners of the upper portion, are fluted columns in the style of those on grandfather clocks, with small brass rods at their lower ends. Inlay is liberally used, there being lines on the door and four inlaid fans and an oval with leaves on the lower portion. The feet, awkward in appearance, are of the bracket type seen on many articles of furniture of an earlier period. On the plate under the dial is the inscription "A. Willard, Boston". As Aaron Willard retired from business in 1823 this clock must be dated before that year; more definitely, judging from the features mentioned, about 1800-1810.

In No. 1919 the top is in the form seen on the secretary-desk No. 864 and others in the style of Sheraton, having two concave curves with three pedestals to hold ornaments. Below the dial are floral designs between which, in the oval, is painted "S. Ham", whose first name was "Supply", and who is listed as a clockmaker in Portsmouth, New Hampshire. On the base is a large panel of finely grained mahogany. The feet are of the French bracket type. About 1800-1820.

In No. 1920 the width of the upper and lower parts is the same, the dial is arched and a door is in the lower portion. This clock at first sight might be thought to be a "grandmother" clock, such as some of those shown in section 188; but those clocks, like the grandfather clocks, are always in three parts, the hood, the waist and the base. The fretwork at the top will be noticed; the ornaments on the two ends are missing. On the dial is the name "David Wood", of Newburyport, Mass., who was also the maker of No. 1917. About 1800-1820.

In No. 1921 the dial is arched, as in the preceding clock, and in the arch is a country scene. At the top is a fretwork and three pedestals with their ornaments. The lower portion has a door, and on each corner is a fluted column with brass ornaments as in grandfather clocks, that on the left appearing almost white by reflection. The skirt is curved and the feet are in the French bracket type. About 1800-1820.

The next three clocks, Nos. 1922-1924, are of a different type. The fronts are of glass decorated with painted designs. Under the dial is a painted panel, generally with the name of the maker. At the bottom of each is a heavy rounded piece, suggestive of the Empire style, as frequently seen on the furniture of the period, and also seen on the base of the lyre clock No. 2037. These three clocks should be compared with the Willard style wall clocks Nos. 2043 and 2044 in section 195, as they are all practically the same, except that these three are made with feet and will stand on a mantel or shelf or table and the two others referred to are made to hang on a wall. It is said that clocks with glass fronts were first made by Simon Willard and were soon copied by other makers.

No. 1922 is by "Aaron Willard, Boston", as appears in the oval below the dial. An agreeable decorative effect is produced by the various colors of the case and the glass. At the top the pineapple and the balls form an unusual combination; a similar pineapple is in No. 2027. Four lyres are around the dial. About 1800-1820.

No. 1923 has a scroll top resembling somewhat the tops of the mantel clocks in the Terry style shown in the next section. Four lyres surround the dial as in the preceding piece. There is no name in the oval under the dial. On the lower glass is a painting of Mt. Vernon. About 1800-1820.

In No. 1924 the glass is decorated with many flowers, and above and below the dial are leaves. In the rectangular panel in the base is a wayside scene in the country. On the top is a peculiar form of pierced wooden ornament and three pedestals and brass pieces. About 1800-1820.

No. 1925 has an arched dial on which the hour numerals are in the Arabic form, which is referred to in note 32 in section 187. Under the dial and around the door in the lower portion are wide bands of satinwood. The feet are of the French bracket type and the skirt is curved. The space between the upper door and the lower portion is unusual, as in No. 1917. The central ornament at the top is missing. About 1800-1820.

No. 1926 is apparently in a transitional form between the early wall clock No. 2042, referred to in the third paragraph of the text above, and the Willard style mantel clocks shown in this section. Both of the two clocks mentioned were made by Aaron Willard and in both the upper portion has feet which rest upon the lower portion; the difference is that No. 1926 has a base with feet and was plainly intended to be placed on a shelf or mantel, but No. 2042 has no such base or feet and was intended to hang upon a wall. No. 1926 is the only clock shown here which has the entire upper portion in a "kidney-shaped" form, not merely the dial plate and the inner lines of the door. The base has lines of inlay, indicating the Hepplewhite style; the hour numerals are Arabic as in the preceding clock; and "A. Willard—Boston" is in the centre of the dial. About 1790-1800.

In No. 1927 the upper portion, with its small round metal dial and its kidney-shaped glass door resembles somewhat the corresponding parts of the Willard wall clocks above mentioned, Nos. 2041 and 2042 in section 195; and this upper portion rests upon feet, as in the preceding clock. The two triangular designs at the top of the door suggest the "spandrels", or "corner pieces", seen on many grandfather and mantel clocks. Except for the long fluted flat columns, the lower portion is plain. The words "Simon Willard, Roxbury" are engraved on the metal plate which supports the dial. About 1790-1800.

1916 (Upper) Mrs. J. S. Gibbs, Jr.
1919 (Lower) Mrs. Miles White, Jr.

1917 (Upper) Mrs. S. C. Rowland.
1920 (Lower) Mrs. Miles White, Jr.

1918 (Upper) Anonymous.
1921 (Lower) Dr. Jas. Bordley, Jr.

1922 (UPPER) MRS. MILES
    WHITE, JR.
1925 (LOWER) MRS. E. N. DUN-
    HAM.

1923 (UPPER) MR. A. G. TOW-
    ERS.
1926 (LOWER) METROPOLITAN
    MUSEUM OF ART.

1924 (UPPER) ANONYMOUS.
1927 (LOWER) MRS. MILES
    WHITE, JR.

Section 191. Mantel clocks; Terry styles.—The number of mantel clocks made by Eli Terry[1] and his firm and family probably exceeds the combined total of all other antique mantel clocks made in our country. For many years they were lightly esteemed, but at the present time they are regarded as interesting, even if not very valuable, examples of the progress of clock making in America. They were especially for the farm house and the small dwelling, and being made in quantity, and generally with wooden works instead of brass ones, they were sold for a sum which placed them within the reach of persons who could not pay the price for the more elegant clocks of the Willards and other makers. Whether made by Terry himself or by members of his family, or copied by other makers, especially by Seth Thomas who purchased the right to do so, the "Terry style clocks" continued to be the favorite clocks of the people at large until the new era of machine-made American clocks with sheet brass works began about the year 1837, as mentioned in the next section.

Nos. 1928-1935 are the "Terry style" scroll top clocks described in the second paragraph of note 1; the later clocks Nos. 1936-1938 have the same kind of works but a different form of case. Almost all of these clocks have suffered injuries

---

1. The story of Eli Terry has been told in many books, magazines and newspapers, some of which may be found in almost every public library. He was born in 1772 and died in 1852. In 1792 he began his career as a clock maker at New Windsor, Connecticut, and in 1794 he moved to Plymouth in the same State. At the age of twenty-five he secured a patent for an invention of "an improvement in clocks, time keepers and watches", said to be the first patent on clocks issued in this country. He made a number of clocks of various kinds in his early period, but his efforts were directed chiefly to making cheap clocks with wooden works and in this he was so successful that in 1808 he was able to secure a contract to make and deliver within three years four thousand wooden works clocks at four dollars each, without the cases.

    With this experience he developed, and apparently patented, a new type of wooden works clocks which were not too large to put upon a shelf or mantel, ran thirty hours, had a scroll-top case with small round pillars at the sides about twenty-one inches long, a wooden dial about eleven inches square painted white and a painted glass below, four very small feet, with running and striking power furnished by two weights, one on each side—the "Terry style clock" as now called. The price of the complete clock and case was fifteen dollars. The success of these clocks was immediate and made a fortune for Terry. After 1815 Terry took his two sons Eli, Jr., and Henry, into his business under the firm name of "Eli Terry and Sons", a firm name which appears on a majority of the Terry labels. The labels of "Eli and Samuel Terry" and "Eli Terry, Jr." are also found, as mentioned below in the comments.

    Mr. Albert L. Partridge, secretary of the "Clock Club", in Boston, stated at a meeting of the Club held on March 17, 1934, that the records of the Patent Office in Washington show that Eli Terry secured seven patents for improvements in his clocks between the years 1797-1826.

    Both types of clocks were copied by other clock makers, as stated above, and except for the labels it would not be possible in many cases to distinguish such clocks from those of Eli Terry and his family.

    Very few of the clocks made by Terry before about 1815 have been found. Most of his clocks shown here are probably after that date.

    The reader will notice that the scrolls on the tops of these clocks resemble those on the hoods of the grandfather scroll top clocks Nos. 1826-1833; and also that one or both of the hands of many of these Terry clocks are too long or too short, indicating that they are substitutes for the originals.

requiring replacements of lost or broken parts. Wooden works, with weights at the sides, were originally in all of these clocks illustrated here.[2]

Inside No. 1928 is the label shown as No. 1929, which reads "Patent. Invented, made and sold by Eli Terry, Plymouth, Con.". The engraved label seems to be in the earliest form, with an abundance of decorative curves and with an oval enclosing the most important of the words; the later labels were plain printed ones. The Arabic hour numerals are vertical, as to which see note 32 in section 187; the hands are variations of a favorite type; the dial is ornamented with scrolls at the four corners, adapted from the "spandrels", or "corner pieces", in the grandfather and grandmother clocks. Several large circular designs are in the centre. The "skirt" at the bottom is cut in "cyma" curves, as to which see section 23. The slender feet seem to be too fragile and small for the size and weight of the clock. The top with its scrolls is a simple adaptation of the scroll tops on grandfather clocks. The style of building painted on the lower glass, perhaps Chinese, was frequently used. As is apparent from the label, this clock was made by Eli Terry alone, before he took his sons into business with him under the firm name of Eli Terry and Sons about 1815, and the date was therefore probably about 1810-1815.

In No. 1930 the door is open in order to show the label, which is the same as No. 1929, and to illustrate the method of furnishing power by the two weights, which have run down. The weight on the right furnishes power for the time-keeping movement and that on the left for the striking movement. The pendulum is in front of the dial, a method which Eli Terry soon discontinued as unsatisfactory; the small brass escape wheel connected with the pendulum will be noticed. The hands are too short and are probably substitutes for the originals. The hour numerals are of the Roman type. The paper containing the label has also a two-part calendar, too small to be well seen, that on the left from January to the end of June and that on the right from July to the end of December; but unfortunately the year does not appear. This clock, like No. 1928, and for the same reason, may be dated about 1810-1815.

No. 1931 and the next four are of about the same outward appearance, differing mainly in the new paintings on the glass, and in the hands; but in each clock the label is different. Here the label is printed, not engraved, in plain type as follows: "Patent clocks made and sold at Plymouth, Connecticut, by Eli Terry,

---

2.   In many of these clocks the wooden works, running for thirty hours, have been removed and new brass works running eight days have been substituted as a practical convenience, without changing the outward appearance. In numerous instances one or both of the hands are not the original ones, especially the minute hands which are often broken by carelessly moving them. The scroll tops and the small and delicate feet are frequently broken off and new ones substituted. The painting on the lower glass panel is seldom found in its original condition. Fortunately the printed form pasted on the back-board behind the pendulum is often in place, sometimes containing a calendar or the figures of a census together with the name of the maker, and directions as to the usage and care of the clock. The wood is almost always mahogany veneer.

A change from thirty hour wooden works driven by weights to eight day brass works driven by a spring generally requires a change in the position of the keyholes. In such cases the old keyholes are usually plugged up and painted over; but the paint often cracks off and reveals that the existing keyholes are not the original ones.

1928 (Upper) Anonymous.
1931 (Centre) Anonymous.
1934 (Lower) Anonymous.

1929 (Upper) Mr. Edgar G.
    Miller, Jr.
1932 (Centre) Anonymous.
1935 (Lower) Mrs. John S.
    Gibbs, Jr.

1930 (Upper) Dr. John Collin-
    son.
1933 (Centre) Anonymous.
1936 (Lower) Anonymous.

1937 (UPPER) ANONYMOUS.
1940 (LOWER) BALTIMORE MUSEUM
    OF ART.

1938 (UPPER) ANONYMOUS.
1941 (LOWER) MR. JOHN J. SCHWARZ.

1939 (UPPER) BALTIMORE MUSEUM
    OF ART.
1942 (LOWER) MR. DUDLEY S. IN-
    GRAHAM.

Inventor and Patentee. Warranted if well used." The painting is almost the same as that in No. 1928. The hands are of good design, and the hour numerals are vertical. About 1810-1815.

In No. 1932 the label is as follows: "Patent clocks. Invented by Eli Terry. Made and sold at Plymouth, Connecticut, by Eli and Samuel Terry." Samuel was a brother of Eli and it is said that he was in business as a clock maker in Bristol, another town in Connecticut, from about 1820 to 1835. The painting is of Mt. Vernon. The date of this clock may be before 1820.

In No. 1933 is the label of the firm of Eli Terry and his sons Eli, Jr., and Henry, as follows: "Patent clocks. Invented by Eli Terry. Made and sold at Plymouth, Connecticut, by E. Terry and Sons." As remarked in note 1, the name of this firm appears on a majority of the Terry labels which have been found. About 1815-1830.

No. 1934 is probably one of the clocks which Seth Thomas[3] made after he purchased from Eli Terry the right to make the Terry style clocks, as also No. 1938. The label reads "Patent clocks made and sold by Seth Thomas". An unusual feature is that the pendulum is not hung in the centre and therefore the opening in the glass door is not in the centre. This was doubtless a new method which was not followed later. The hour numerals, as also in No. 1928 and others, are vertical. About 1815-1835.

No. 1935 is a somewhat smaller clock than the preceding ones, being about thirteen inches wide and twenty-three high. It bears the name of Mark Leavenworth, of Waterbury, Connecticut, who, it is said, was in business from about 1810 to 1830. This clock follows closely the original Terry design, the principal differences being in the dial, on which the Arabic numerals are small and are in a smaller circle than in others, and also in the lower glass panel which is larger than others. About 1820-1830.

Nos. 1936-1938 illustrate another type of "Terry style" clocks. These were apparently made at a somewhat later date than certain of those shown above, but differ from them mainly in the cases.[4]

No. 1936 is decorated with a stenciled eagle and basket of fruit at the top, all faded in color, and with other designs on the half-round columns. The hour

3.   The name of Seth Thomas, (1785-1859), is perhaps more widely known by the public at large than that of any other American clock maker not only because of his early clocks which are now desired as antiques, but especially because the corporation which has succeeded to his business has continued to use his name.

4.   The square wooden dial continues to be of about the same size, and the glass door with a painting is not materially different; but the scroll top with ornaments is superseded by a top whose curves are somewhat similar in design to those on the bottom of the scroll top clocks, but in a reversed position; and the top is decorated in stencil. Instead of slender columns at the sides, these later clocks have the half of a larger column applied to the case, as in the Empire style mirrors Nos. 1203-1205, and decorated with stencil work. The feet, or at least the front ones, are of the carved animals' claw or other similar types seen on many articles, such as the bureau No. 761 and others. These changes from the earlier style indicate the influence of the Empire style upon the designs of clocks.

numerals are Arabic, but not vertical. On the lower glass is a painting of a naval battle. The carved feet are in a design seen also on several of the following clocks.[5] On the label are these words: "Patent clocks. Invented by Eli Terry. Made and sold at Plymouth, Connecticut, by Eli Terry and Sons." About 1815-1830.

In No. 1937 a change in form is seen, the painted glass occupying the larger part of the front. The stencil designs have faded. The painting is of a church with columns and a high steeple. The label reads: "Patent clocks. Invented by Eli Terry. Made and sold at Terryville, Connecticut, by Eli Terry, Jr." Terryville was named after this Terry. He was a son of Eli Terry, and one of his partners. In 1824 he went into business for himself. He died in 1841. 1824-1841.

No. 1938 has stenciled fruits and flowers on the top and on the half-columns are stenciled leaves; the hour numerals are Roman; the painting is of a large country house and a tree. Here the label reads: "Patent clocks. Invented by Eli Terry. Made and sold at Plymouth, Connecticut, by Seth Thomas." About 1815-1835.

Four other later clocks, Nos. 1939-1942, are next shown which are not exactly in the Terry style, but whose general form was evidently developed from the three preceding Terry clocks; and as they were apparently made during the period when the Terry clock was the outstanding one it seems proper to present them in connection with the Terry style. The names of the makers appear on the labels in these clocks, but exact information in regard to their dates is not at hand.

No. 1939 is similar to the preceding clock in general form, the principal difference being in the carved and gilded wooden eagle facing the left, and the use of gilding and painting on the columns which here are in sections resembling those on certain mirrors in the Empire style such as No. 1204. On the door is a painting of a naval battle, probably between the ever popular American "Constitution" and the English "Guerriere", and below is a fanciful design. The round wooden feet are gilded. On the label are the words: "Manufactured and sold by Philip Barnes & Co., Bristol, Conn." The height is thirty-four inches. About 1825-1840.

No. 1940 resembles the preceding piece in style, but some of the details are different. Here the carved wooden eagle, facing the right, is not gilded; the front is in three sections, the upper one being a door, the central one a glass panel with a country scene and the lower one a glass door with another country scene. The side columns are in three sections, the central one of which is gilded all over; the hour numerals are Arabic. The height is thirty-seven inches. The words "Barnes, Bartholomew & Co., Bristol, Conn." are on the label. About 1830-1840.

In No. 1941 the columns at the corners are carved instead of being gilded as in the preceding two clocks. The door is in three sections, the dial, a central section, here without the usual painting, and a small lower glass decorated with a dish of fruit. The label contains the words "Jerome and Darrow, Bristol, Con-

---

5. A somewhat similar, but well carved, clock is No. 2097 in section 197, which is out of place because the photograph was received after this section was completed.

necticut, * * eight day clocks". In the note[6] the career of Chauncey Jerome is mentioned. It is said that this firm was in existence from 1824 to 1831.

No. 1942 is an unusual clock which bears several points of resemblance to the wall clock No. 2046 in section 195. Here there are scrolls on the top and a large square dial as in the Terry clocks; instead of the half-round or round columns seen on the preceding clocks in this section there are fluted flat columns similar to those on certain articles of furniture in the Sheraton style, such as the sideboard No. 1006 and the bureau No. 751 and other pieces; under the dial is a house and a water scene, below which is a glass panel with several stars and other designs. This piece does not appear to have been originally a wall clock such as the clock above mentioned. It is about thirty-five inches high and sixteen inches wide. On the label is the firm name "Jerome, Darrow and Co.", of Bristol, Connecticut. About 1831-1840.

Section 192. Mantel clocks; later American.

—In this section are illustrations of twelve clocks with brass works which were made about and after the year 1837, when the use of sheet brass for making all the works caused a reduction in the cost of manufacture and produced a better timepiece than was possible with wooden works.[1] These clocks are not yet regarded as "antiques" and most of them do not possess a sufficient degree of elegance to entitle them to much consideration; but they illustrate the development of American timekeepers and some of them are of pleasing appearance. Moreover such a large number are found in our households and so many inquiries in regard to their dates are made by their owners that it is proper to present a few of the more interesting types. It is, however, impossible in many cases to determine their dates except as may be indicated by the period in which their makers were in business.[2]

6.   Chauncey Jerome was one of the leading clock makers of Connecticut. He was born in 1793, and went to work with Eli Terry in 1816 but soon started in business for himself and moved to Bristol, Connecticut, in 1821, and formed the firm of Jerome and Darrow about 1824. One popular clock invented by Jerome in 1825 was called by him a " bronze looking glass clock ", which at first had a large looking glass in a panel under the dial; later a third panel with decorations was often used and the position of the looking glass was changed. These clocks were copied by other clock makers. In 1838 Jerome invented the first one-day brass clock, which soon superseded the wooden works clock. He was very prosperous for some years but in 1855 he became bankrupt and died a few years later. A book by him is referred to in section 180, note 5, J.

1.   So many different types of inexpensive clocks were made in the period of about 1837 to 1870 that the group of illustrations here shown might be greatly enlarged; but those shown here are among the most familiar and interesting.

2.   The custom of pasting in the clocks printed advertising labels giving the names and addresses of the makers was almost universal. It is fortunate that the names on the labels are those of the makers, not of the dealers, thus avoiding a confusion often referred to in this chapter.

It will be noticed that all of the clocks here shown were made by factories in Connecticut where the business of making clocks with brass works began and became one of the principal industries of the State and where it is even now most extensively carried on. The business of the original individual maker has in some cases been incorporated under his name and has been continued under that name; as for example, the business of Seth Thomas, (1785-1859), Elias Ingraham, (1805-1885), and William L. Gilbert, (1823-1866). Chauncey Jerome, (1793- about 1855), was another important clock maker whose products are frequently seen; see also note 6 on this page.

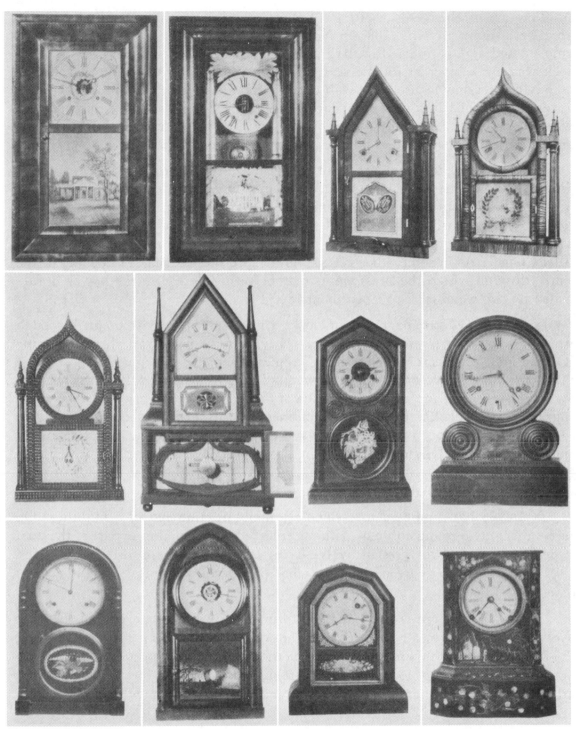

1943 (UPPER) MR. FRED. FUCHS.
1944 (UPPER) ANONY-MOUS.
1945 (UPPER) THE E. IN-GRAHAM CO.
1946 (UPPER) THE E. IN-GRAHAM CO.
1947 (CENTRE) THE E. INGRAHAM CO.
1948 (CENTRE) ANONY-MOUS.
1949 (CENTRE) MR. FRED. FUCHS.
1950 (CENTRE) MR. FRED. FUCHS.
1951 (LOWER) NEW HA-VEN CLOCK CO.
1952 (LOWER) ANONY-MOUS.
1953 (LOWER) ANONY-MOUS.
1954 (LOWER) ANONYMOUS.

The case of No. 1943 is brilliantly veneered and its form is similar to that of the mirror shown in No. 1208; in fact if the works and door of the clock were removed and a glass inserted in the frame, there would be a mirror. This type of clock was made in great numbers. It was doubtless made as a mantel clock, but not having feet may be used as a wall clock. The minute hand is a substitute. The power is furnished by two weights as in No. 1930. The label bears the name of "Waterbury Clock Company, Waterbury, Conn.". The picture apparently represents Monticello, the home of Thomas Jefferson. Probably about 1840-1850.

No. 1944 is of the same type, but within the case are ornaments consisting of gilded leaves at the top and a gilded column on each side, behind which are mirrors which from some points of view reflect the column in front. Under the picture are the words "Merchants Exchange, Philadelphia". The words on the label are "Brass eight day clocks made and sold by Hills, Goodrich & Co., Plainville, Conn.". As in some other clocks shown here the dial has an opening in the centre through which the brass works may be seen. Here also the power is furnished by two weights. Probably about 1840-1850.

Nos. 1945-1947 are examples of clocks whose tops, often with pointed wooden ornaments somewhat resembling steeples, have given to some of them the name "Gothic arch" clocks, or, if they have steeples, the name "steeple clocks". These clocks are driven by springs, not by weights. Their general form was invented by Elias Ingraham, and the name on each of them is that of his firm, "Brewster and Ingraham, Bristol, Ct. U. S.". The business of this firm was carried on from 1843 to 1848, and since by Elias Ingraham, who died in 1885, and his descendants, one of whom, Mr. Dudley S. Ingraham, has furnished the writer with the photographs. The dates of these clocks is fixed at 1843-1848 because the firm of the above name was in existence only during those years.

No. 1945 has a pointed top which resembles a gable end of a building. On each side are two round columns with "steeples" above. The lower part of the door is decorated with two lyres in ovals. Lyres as ornaments are also seen in Nos. 1922 and 1923. There are no feet, the clock being well supported by a heavy flat base. 1843-1848.

In No. 1946 there is a variation in form, the top being curved and the glass over the dial being in a round frame. The wreath of leaves on the lower part of the door, recalling the wreath of laurel on the brow of Napoleon, the lyres on the door of the preceding clock, and the heart-shaped wreath on the following clock, all seem to indicate that the artist was French or fond of French designs. 1843-1848.

No. 1947 is almost the same as the preceding clock in form, but its appearance is changed by the molding covering the entire front woodwork except the columns. Moldings of this kind were made by hand to some extent, but about 1840-1845 a machine was invented by which they were made at small expense; similar moldings are on the table No. 1621. The wreath in the shape of a heart is mentioned in the preceding paragraph. 1843-1848.

No. 1948 also is a steeple clock and the design of the upper portion is almost the same as that of No. 1945. In the engraving the two front steeples hide the rear ones. The feature of this clock is the "wagon spring", which is explained below.[3] On the label are these words: "Patent accelerating lever spring eight day brass clocks made * * by Birge and Fuller, Bristol, Conn." Probably about 1830-1840.

In No. 1949 the top is pointed, but in a wider angle than in No. 1945. The entire front opens as a door with two round glasses. Under the dial glass are two applied rosettes under which is another round glass decorated with grapes. The circular metal piece in the centre of the dial is the alarm attachment, as also in No. 1952. On the label are the words "E. Ingraham & Co., Bristol, Conn. 1871".

In No. 1950 the round upper portion follows the form of certain English mantel clocks of a much earlier date, such as No. 371 in Cescinsky and Webster's "English Domestic Clocks". The dial is larger than is usual in small clocks. The two applied rosettes under the dial furnish the only decoration. The base is heavy and plain. On the label is the name of the same firm as in the preceding clock and the date "1862".

No. 1951 is another small clock with a rounded top, a form doubtless copied from that of certain English mantel clocks, such as No. 1902. Under the dial is a round glass door with an oval in which there is a painted eagle with outstretched wings and several stars, but not enough to indicate the number of States in the Union as in No. 1825 and others. On the sides and over the top is an applied molding. This clock was made by the New Haven Clock Co. and is in an exhibit of their clocks in the United States National Museum in Washington. About 1860-1870.

No. 1952 is somewhat in the form of an English "lancet" clock such as Nos. 1903 and 2093. Under the round door in front of the dial is a rectangular door which is decorated with a water scene with trees in the foreground. An alarm attachment is in the centre of the dial, as in No. 1949. The label within this clock has the name "Jerome & Co., New Haven, Conn.", and on the outside of the back is a label with the words "J. S. Turner's patent eight day alarm clock". This clock is about eighteen inches high. The two keyholes are at the bottom of the dial as in No. 1948 and others. About 1845-1850.

No. 1953 is only eleven inches high and is a friendly little clock with a busy pendulum, a loud tick and pleasing decorations of flowers. Under the dial at the corners are painted "spandrels", or "corner pieces", which are not often seen on these later American clocks. The frame of the door is gilded. The label contains the words "Wm. L. Gilbert Clock Co., Winsted, Conn., makers of brass clocks". Said to be about 1870.

3.   Instead of the coiled spring used in almost all spring driven clocks, here the two ends of small springs, of a type similar to those on a wagon or automobile, are pulled up by winding-chains. The struggle of these springs to unbend to their natural straight position furnishes the power to the works. These clocks were not very successful, as the power of the bent springs diminished too much as they straightened and in some other respects the mechanism was not satisfactory. The keyholes are at the bottom of the dial.

No. 1954 is a clock of a type which is said to have been popular from about 1850 to 1870. The case is of iron, painted black, and is decorated with painted designs and with inlaid pieces of mother-of-pearl. The corners are cut off, or "chamfered", as in the grandfather clock No. 1766 and others. Although this clock is far removed from the types which are esteemed today, it is not unpleasing. The flat top was perhaps intended to hold a vase or an ornament. The name and address on this clock are "Bristol Brass and Clock Co. Depot, 3 Courtland St., New York". The date may be between the years mentioned above.

Section 193. Mantel clocks; French.—The reader may be surprised to find in this book on "American Antique Furniture" more illustrations of French mantel clocks than of any other single type of clocks except the "grandfather". One reason for their being shown is that in very many American homes there are one or more French mantel clocks and the owners are interested in knowing something about them; and another reason is that in variety of form, and in elegance and artistic design, many of these clocks far surpass the English and American mantel clocks,[1] and to omit them would be to ignore some of our most esteemed household possessions.

In this section are illustrations of several French mantel and shelf clocks of the periods of Louis the Fourteenth and Fifteenth, but the great majority are of the time of Louis the Sixteenth and the French Empire.[2] No attempt is made, how-

1.   See note 31 in section 186, in reference to the elegance of French clock cases.

When the name of the maker appears on a clock shown in this section the date has generally been obtained from Mr. Baillie's "Watchmakers and Clockmakers of the World", which is mentioned in section 180, note 5, I.

"Ormolu" is often mentioned in the comments on French mantel clocks. It is a metal made to resemble gold by the addition of copper and zinc to brass. The golden color was partly obtained by the use of acids and gold lacquer. The mounts on clocks are generally of ormolu, and "bronze gilt" mounts are often called "ormolu".

In many French mantel clocks, as in No. 2007, the pendulum is suspended by a silken cord instead of being connected directly with a metal piece. This method has a certain advantage, but is not found in English or American clocks.

Almost all of the French mantel clocks shown here run for two weeks.

In Britten's "Old Clocks and Watches", pages 451-452, it is said that "from the middle to the end of the eighteenth century the shops of leading horologists in Paris were a great attraction to visitors. * * Louis the Sixteenth had from a youth a liking for the mechanical parts of timekeepers and Marie Antoinette possessed a large number of choice specimens, but there are in existence clocks and watches purporting to have belonged to her and having thereon 'M. A.' interlaced which were really made between about 1818 and 1830, when enthusiasm at the restoration of the French monarchy induced people to pay high prices for anything connected with the Court of Louis the Sixteenth". See also the comment on No. 2011.

2.   The dates of the principal French periods are as follows: period of Louis the Thirteenth, 1610-1643; Louis the Fourteenth, 1643-1715; the Regency, during the minority of Louis the Fifteenth, 1715-1723; Louis the Fifteenth, 1723-1774; Louis the Sixteenth, 1774-1793; the Directory and Empire periods, 1793 until about 1830.

A brief statement of the principal characteristics of the styles of the clocks of these periods may be useful; see the continuation of this note on the next page.

ever, to present all of these latter clocks in strict order either as to periods or styles, and the dates given are only approximate.

No. 1955 is a French mantel clock of the time of Louis the Fourteenth, as appears from the straight lines of the sides and the "Boulle work"[3] on the lower part of the top. Each of the twelve hour numerals is on white enamel on a separate copper plate, a method which continued in later periods. The shape of the top is somewhat similar to that of the "bell top" seen in many English clocks, such as No. 1883. This illustration is copied from Mr. Britten's "Old Clocks and Watches", figure 553. About 1680-1700.

No. 1956 is a reproduction[4] of another type of clock of the period of Louis the Fourteenth. The case and dial are almost the same as in Figure 549 in Mr. Britten's book. Here the "Boulle work" is clearly seen on the top and the door. Special features are the brass openwork railing over the door, the dark cloth within and

(Note 2, *continued*)

In the long reign of Louis the Fourteenth, 1643-1715, the furniture styles, including those of clocks, were as a rule characterized by straight lines, vertical or horizontal; but this characteristic feature was not used in all cases, as the designs of the latter years of the previous reign (Louis the Thirteenth) and those of the early years of the next reign (Louis the Fifteenth) overlapped to some extent the designs of the period of Louis the Fourteenth.

In the periods of the Regency and Louis the Fifteenth, 1715-1774, the straight lines were generally superseded by curved ones—"the flowing curves of Louis the Fifteenth"—with many scrolls and fantastic ornaments. Examples are illustrated in this section and in section 196.

In the reign of Louis the Sixteenth, 1774-1793, straight lines somewhat similar to those of the period of Louis the Fourteenth were again largely used. In mantel clocks, for example, the straight lines are constantly seen, especially in those shown in this section. The decorations were generally ormolu mounts in a great variety of forms with elegant workmanship.

In the Empire period, 1793-1830, the most noticeable feature of style in clocks is the use of chased ormolu mounts as decorations, chiefly claw feet, acanthus leaves, pineapples, pillars, cornucopias, "anthemions" and animals of various kinds, all of which are seen on the clocks illustrated in this section. A wreath enclosing the letter "N", for Napoleon, the Egyptian animals and various classic designs were also frequently used. The large and heavy features seen in other furniture in the Empire style were not often conspicuous in clocks, although mantel clocks with large and heavy bases were made about 1830-1840 as mentioned in connection with No. 1987.

The Directory style, 1793-1804, is commonly included in the Empire style; see section 19.

3.   On the next clock the "Boulle work" is better seen.

This much admired work was apparently invented, and certainly perfected, by Andre Charles Boulle and is properly called by his name which was often corrupted in England to "Buhl". He was born in Paris in 1642 and in 1673 was allotted a room in the Palace of Versailles by Louis the Fourteenth as his cabinet maker. He died in 1732. "Boulle work" was either an inlay of brass or other metal in a layer of tortoise shell or ivory veneered on a surface, or, reversing the method, an inlay of tortoise shell or ivory in a layer of brass or other metal veneered on the surface. This work continued popular in France throughout the eighteenth century. It is also mentioned in this book in section 33, note 1.

It may be mentioned for the information of any reader who may purchase a "Boulle work" clock that some of the brass and tortoise shell falls off in our climate and heated houses, at least in Baltimore.

4.   This chapter on clocks is perhaps the only one in which reproductions, instead of original pieces, are allowable. If these reproductions were not shown in this book, of course stated to be reproductions, the reader would not have the pleasure of seeing a number of handsome and representative clocks in the French styles.

under the dial and the two columns of deep blue stone resembling lapis-lazuli. Under the dial is a fanciful design in the centre of which is the maker's name "Gribelin", with "a Paris" as one word. About 1690-1710.

Nos. 1957 and 1958 are said to be in the style of the Regency, 1715-1723, in which the straight lines of the preceding period have disappeared. They are shown here on brackets, but without the brackets they would doubtless be placed upon a mantel. It is not easy for the amateur collector to distinguish the Regency designs from the somewhat similar designs in the style of Louis the Fifteenth.

No. 1957 has an enameled dial in a case painted with flowers, not clearly seen in the engraving, and has pierced and chased ormolu mounts. Over the dial and on the lower portion and bracket are "C" curves, similar to those seen so frequently on various articles of furniture, such as on the mirror No. 1105. This and the next clock bear the names of the Parisian makers on the movements, not on the dials. About 1715.

No. 1958 is an even more elaborately decorated and more graceful clock than the preceding one. The ormolu mounts above and below the dial represent the hunt, with figures of hunters and wild animals. The bracket is also gracefully decorated with applied ormolu mounts. The height of this clock and bracket is forty-one inches. In this and the preceding and following clock the glass door is in the so-called "kidney" shape, which was seldom seen on English clocks but is well known to us from its frequent use in the Willard style mantel clocks such as No. 1916 and others. About 1715.

No. 1959 is a reproduction of a handsome clock in the style of Louis the Fifteenth, 1723-1774. The "Boulle work" which was on the first two clocks in this section, made in the period of Louis the Fourteenth, is again seen here; and "the flowing curves of Louis the Fifteenth" are numerous. About 1730-1750.

No. 1960, also in the style of Louis the Fifteenth, is copied from illustration No. 65 in the book "L'Horloge", by Mr. Mathieu Planchon, mentioned in the last paragraph of note 5 in section 180, and in the comment on No. 2094. The case of this clock is of gilt bronze. This type of curves is referred to by Mr. Planchon as being "carried sometimes to exaggeration". About 1740-1760.

The styles of the period of Louis the Sixteenth, 1774-1793, and of the Directory and Empire periods, 1793-1830, are seen in the other clocks in this section. Almost all of the clocks in our homes are of one or the other of these two periods.

The next seven illustrations, Nos. 1961-1967, except No. 1966, are of clocks known as "Washington clocks" because their distinctive feature is a figure of George Washington. They were made shortly after the death of Washington in 1799 by several makers in Paris. Four of these clocks bear the name and address "Dubuc, Rue Michel-le-Comte, No. 33, a Paris". All of these Washington clocks are highly esteemed because of their patriotic interest and their excellent design and workmanship.

1955 (UPPER) ANONYMOUS.
1958 (LOWER) ANONYMOUS.

1956 (UPPER) MR. EDGAR G. MILLER,
JR.
1959 (LOWER) ANONYMOUS.

1957 (UPPER) ANONYMOUS.
1960 (LOWER) ANONYMOUS.

In some of these clocks made by Dubuc[5] the famous expression of Colonel Henry (Light-Horse Harry) Lee[6] in regard to Washington is incorrectly quoted as follows: "First in war, first in peace, and *in his countrymen's hearts."* This error was corrected in other clocks which were presumably made later.

Nos. 1961, 1962, 1963 and 1965 are by Dubuc, the second one by inference. In each of the first three there is a figure of General George Washington in uniform, standing, with his left hand resting on his sword and his right hand holding a document. Over the dial is an American eagle, under which are the words "E Pluribus Unum"; and under the dial is a banner with the words "Washington. First in war", etc. These clocks are of fine ormolu and are ornamented on the front and sides with applied designs. Several differences in details may be noticed.

No. 1961 is one of the earlier clocks bearing the name and address of Dubuc and having the incorrect words, "in his countrymen's hearts", referred to above. At the upper corners are applied "anthemions",[7] which are more clearly seen on the base of No. 1964, where they are horizontal. The height is about sixteen inches and the width about ten inches. About 1800-1810.

In No. 1962 the words of Light-Horse Harry Lee in his eulogy of Washington are correctly given, in a different style of lettering. In several other details this clock is not the same as the preceding one, among which we notice that the face of Washington looks more to the front, that the decorations are different and that the feet are in another form. On this clock the name "Dubuc" does not appear, the only lettering being "a Paris",[8] but it is regarded by the owner as being his work. About 1800-1810.

No. 1963 is larger, being almost twenty inches high by fourteen inches wide. The words "First in war", etc., are correct and are in the same type as in No.

5. In "The Old Clock Book", by Mrs. N. Hudson Moore, page 86, it is said that "a small number of very choice French gilt clocks made by Dubuc, Paris, were sent to this country in 1805. They were consigned to John Shaw, a merchant of Annapolis, Maryland, and sold by him". Mrs. Moore's illustration is of a clock similar to No. 1962. Diligent search of records and newspapers has failed to verify the reference to Shaw, but the statement that most of these clocks were sent to Annapolis is probably correct for the reason that more of them have been found in homes in Maryland than in any other State.

6. The expression "First in war, first in peace and first in the hearts of his countrymen" was originated by Colonel Henry Lee. In a resolution prepared by him on the death of Washington, and presented to the House of Representatives by John Marshall in the absence of Lee, the words "fellow-citizens" were used, but in a eulogy by Lee a week later the words "fellow-countrymen" were used.

The eulogy appears in the Appendix, pages or columns 1305-1311, to the "Debates and Proceedings in the Congress of the United States", Sixth Congress, December, 1799–March, 1801. Reprint published in 1851.

Interesting matters in this connection may be found in Marshall's "Life of Washington", volume 5, page 766; in General Robert E. Lee's "Life of Henry Lee", 1869, prefixed to his son Henry Lee's "Memoirs of the War of the Revolution", pages 51 and 52; and in "Light-Horse Harry Lee", by Thomas Boyd, 1931, pages 255-256.

7. As to these see note 48 in section 51; also the Index.

8. This is referred to in note 13.

1961. On the base is a panel on which a left-handed figure representing Washington, as appears from the uniform, delivers his sword to a seated figure in the garments of classic Rome.[9] About 1800-1810.

No. 1964 presents Washington in a different position and with a different appearance from that seen in the preceding illustrations. The open book under his outstretched arm is marked "American Independence". The case is ornamented with eagles on the fluted columns. On the base is an eagle with a shield and outspread wings surrounded by four flags and at the ends are applied horizontal "anthemions". About 1800-1810.

No. 1965 is more elaborate than the preceding Washington clocks and also somewhat larger. The name "Dubuc" is on the brass dial. On one side is the figure of Washington and on the other is a pedestal upon which is a globe representing the earth. A telescope is leaning against the pedestal. Under the eagle are thirteen stars. On the two tablets, or pages, are the date, July 4, 1776, and the words "The birthday of liberty, America, the asylum of the oppressed". The words "First in war", etc., are in the correct form. The panel on the base is the same as that in No. 1963; and on each side of the panel is an applied ornament very similar to those on that clock. About 1800-1810.

No. 1966 is not a clock, but is inserted here because it is a somewhat similar tribute to the memory of George Washington. The figure of Washington, the eagle and the correct inscription on the banner are about the same as those seen on the clocks; and the round and fluted white marble column on the white marble base gives a pleasing effect. The base is ornamented with ormolu borders, claw feet and a panel with classical figures and with "anthemions" on the sides. About 1800-1810.

In No. 1967 a bust of George Washington, in military uniform, is on a pedestal in which the clock is enclosed. On the rectangular support under the bust are the words "First in War", etc., in the correct form. Under the dial is an eagle with outstretched wings surrounded by rays. The eighteen small stars, not visible in the engraving, may indicate the eighteen States in the Union at the time the clock was made, and if so the date would be between 1812 and 1816 as ascertained in the manner shown in the comment on the American grandfather clock No. 1825.

Two other examples of French ormolu clocks of the same general design as some of the Washington clocks are in Nos. 1968 and 1969.

In No. 1968 is an allegorical figure of a woman said to represent "Thought", and on the base are figures of Cupid and Psyche representing "Love". The ormolu case of the clock is rounded at the top and under the dial it is ornamented with

---

9. This clock was too fine and expensive to have an unsuitable or erroneous scene shown in connection with Washington; but the meaning of the scene is not clear. It has been interpreted to represent Cincinnatus, (in modern uniform), surrendering his sword; as Washington presenting his sword to Congress, (in togas and other Roman costumes); and as Congress delivering the sword of command to Washington who receives it in his left hand, his right hand holding his hat. The figures at each side appear to be in sorrow. The engraving is small but these details may be seen with a magnifying glass. A similar and clearer panel is in No. 1965.

classic designs. Above the dial is a small streamer bearing the words "De Près, de Loin" and to the right are objects said to be trophies. About 1805-1815.

In No. 1969 is the manly form of Adraste, a legendary Greek hero, whose name is on the shield. Over the front are designs of military objects, with quivers and arrows under the dial and various other articles on the base. The feet of this and the preceding clock will be noticed; similar ones are in Nos. 1990 and 1997. About 1810-1830.

The next three illustrations, Nos. 1970-1972, are of French "revolving band" clocks, a type which includes some of the handsomest examples of clock-making. In these clocks there are at the top two stationary parts, one above the other, with a small horizontal space between them, in which space are two horizontal white bands which revolve. The upper band, the minute one, has minute numerals, 1 to 60, and makes one revolution every hour; and the lower band, the hour one, marked with hour numerals, 1 to 12, revolves once every twelve hours. A stationary pointer points to the bands and indicates the time. Earlier clocks operating in the same or a similar manner are Nos. 2084 and 2085 in section 197.

In No. 1970 the case, bearing the Sevres factory mark, is made of porcelain decorated with paintings and delicate designs in enamel. The stationary portion at the top is in two parts, between which are the two horizontal revolving bands, above which the pointer may be seen. The cupid and the two graceful figures, with strings of flowers, are pleasing. This clock, which is probably a reproduction, is finished on the back as well as in front, indicating that it might stand on a mantel in front of a mirror or on a table where it would be seen from all sides. The name on the bottom plate is "Baltazar", of Paris, a well-known family of clock makers. The clock is wound under the base where two wheels are seen, one being a part of the striking mechanism. About 1775-1800.

No. 1971 is in the form of a classic temple with a dome and a white marble base and columns. Under the dome is an ormolu figure said to represent "Time". Over the dome is the clock with a cupid holding a pointer. On the roof of the dome are stars and other celestial bodies. The height is twenty-eight inches. The name of the maker does not appear. About 1780-1800.

No. 1972 is a fine example of the "revolving band" type. Within the urn is the mechanism which causes the two bands to revolve from right to left. The time is twelve minutes after five o'clock, as shown by the pointing hand of the cupid. The marble urn and pedestal, the ormolu decorations and the life-like cupid all unite to make a very pleasing picture, only the four serpents on the sides being unlovely. The style of this clock and the inscription "Lepaute, a Paris", not seen in the engraving, indicates that the date is about 1775-1800.

The next six clocks, Nos. 1973-1978, except No. 1975, are of a particular type which was popular in France from about 1760, in the period of Louis the Sixteenth, to well into the nineteenth century. The feature of these clocks is that the dial is suspended between two marble columns which rest upon a marble base. The decorations consist mainly of applied mounts of ormolu and various figures, all finely made and interesting.

Nos. 1973 and 1974 are similar in their general design, but different in some of the decorative details which are displayed over the entire fronts. Each is about twenty-five inches in height and is ornamented at the top with a French eagle with outspread wings. On the outer sides of the supporting marble columns are other marble pieces with a scroll at the bottom, on which there is a small ormolu vase with flowers. On the base is an ormolu panel with tiny figures in the style of those in the wall paintings at Pompeii. In each clock the pendulum is interesting.[10]

In No. 1973 two black metal cupids are above the white marble supporting columns. On the front of these columns are female heads in ormolu on dark marble pedestals. One of the keyholes is lower than the other, as also in No. 1993 and others. The dial bears the maker's name, "Thiery", above the centre and the words "a Paris" below. About 1775-1800.

On No. 1974, a reproduction, are two black metal figures said to represent winged sphinxes, which became popular decorations after the conquest of Egypt by Napoleon[11] in 1798, and which are not to be mistaken for the winged griffins[12] of Robert Adam. The two ormolu female figures, with feet resting upon black marble supports and with leaves in front, are also suggestive of Egyptian designs. The maker's name does not appear on the dial or elsewhere, but below the centre are the words "a Paris" which are often seen without a name on French clocks of this period.[13] About 1800.

No. 1975 is a reproduction of another interesting clock having some of the same Egyptian features as the two preceding ones, for which reason it is shown here although it is not one of the suspended dial type. At the top are two birds with long necks representing the sacred bird of Egypt, the "ibis". The dial is open in the centre, disclosing the works.[14] Style of about 1800.

10.   A clock of similar type appears in the photograph of the music room at Mt. Vernon, opposite page 98, in the book "Mount Vernon" by Mr. Paul Wilstach, published by Doubleday, Page and Company, 1916. The clock was not at Mt. Vernon during the life of Washington.

11.   See note 1 in section 64 in regard to Napoleon's "learned men and asses" in his Egyptian campaign.

12.   These are seen on the mirror in the Adam style, No. 1147, and on the mantel mirror No. 1229.
        The usual design of a winged sphinx has the head of a woman, the body of a lion and the wings of an eagle. A griffin has the head and wings of an eagle, with the body and feet of a lion. Other examples of a sphinx are in Nos. 1981 and 2092.

13.   It is thought that some French manufacturers marked the dials with the words "a Paris" for Parisian dealers, leaving a blank space for a dealer's name to be painted on when purchased by him. This clock, in the style of about 1800, was bought from a Parisian maker about 1840-1850, and bears on the back of the works the words "J. E. Caldwell & Co., Philadelphia. Made in France". See also No. 1962.

14.   On each side of the dial is a winged sphinx, with urns; a rail around the platform recalls the one on No. 1956 in the style of Louis the Fourteenth; supporting the upper platform are six marble figures in Egyptian form, with ormolu heads and decorations, as in the preceding clock; the "gridiron" pendulum, (as to which see section 182, note 13), perhaps only for ornament, holds a sunburst weight with sixteen projections. The marble base, rounded at the ends, is adorned with leaves of laurel. The words "Fd. Berthoud—a Paris", an eminent maker who died in 1807, are between the hour numerals V and VII; and on the back of the works are the words "Made in France", indicating that it is modern reproduction.

1961 (UPPER) MR. EDGAR G. MILLER, JR.
1964 (CENTRE) METROPOLITAN MUSEUM OF ART.
1967 (LOWER) MR. HENRY F. DU PONT.

1962 (UPPER) METROPOLITAN MUSEUM OF ART.
1965 (CENTRE) ANONYMOUS.
1968 (LOWER) ANONYMOUS.

1963 (UPPER) MR. EDGAR G. MILLER, JR.
1966 (CENTRE) ANONYMOUS.
1969 (LOWER) ANONYMOUS.

1970 (Upper) Mr. Edgar G. Mil-
    ler, Jr.
1973 (Centre) Anonymous.
1976 (Lower) Anonymous.

1971 (Upper) Anonymous.
1974 (Centre) Mr. Edgar G. Miller,
    Jr.
1977 (Lower) Mr. Leigh Bonsal.

1972 (Upper) Metropolitan Muse-
    um of Art.
1975 (Centre) Anonymous.
1978 (Lower) Anonymous.

No. 1976 is a white marble clock with the dial and works suspended between two columns.[15] Above the dial is an ormolu figure of Minerva, the goddess of war, with a helmet, a spear and her shield on which is the head of the mythological Medusa whose hair was turned into snakes and whose face was so terrifying that all who looked upon it were turned into stone. At the base of the columns are military objects. About 1790-1800.

No. 1977 has a similar design, but without warlike features. Over the dial is a white figure of a man, not well seen on the white page; the gray marble columns are ornamented with ormolu caps; and around the marble base is a railing within which are festoons of chains. The frequent use of festoons of chains on clocks of this period recalls the festoons of inlay on the furniture designs of Robert Adam and Hepplewhite. On the dial are the words "Pochon a Paris". About 1790-1800.

No. 1978 is a small clock in which several features of the two preceding clocks may be seen, such as the supporting columns, the base and the use of chains, here attached to ormolu lyres on the tops of the columns. The words "Piolaine a Paris" are on the dial. About 1800-1820.

The next nine illustrations, Nos. 1979-1988, are of clocks of a miscellaneous character without any special features in common.

No. 1979, probably a reproduction, illustrates a fantastic type which was in favor in the latter part of the eighteenth century, having an animal carrying a clock as the important feature. Here an elephant is provided with Asiatic trappings and the clock is perched upon its back. On the top of the clock is a bearded man, apparently Chinese, riding sideways. The elephant is standing in a tray, the feet of which doubtless provide a more even foothold than would those of the animal. On the dial are the words "Le Roy—a Paris", the name being that of a family of prominent clock makers whose firm is still in existence, and is referred to in note 28 in section 186. The style is probably about 1770-1790.

No. 1980 is said to be of the period of the French Directory, 1793-1804, which is mentioned in section 19 and in note 2 in this section. The case is made of a black metal with ormolu mounts. At the top are four revolving rings and in the centre is a ball representing the earth, all of which are enclosed within three stationary rings, suggesting an astronomical clock. The maker's name does not appear. About 1795-1800.

No. 1981 is a marble clock in the Empire style. The dial is on a pedestal; the two wingless sphinxes are not similar to those in Nos. 1974 and 1975. On the top are birds and below the dial is a lion's head. The base is decorated with a diamond-shaped design and two rosettes, all in ormolu. The purpose of the vase under the lion's head on the pedestal is not apparent. On the dial are the words "Folin a Paris". About 1800-1810.

15. A clock of this type, but plainer and of black marble, was designed by Thomas Jefferson for his home, Monticello. In a letter to his representative in Paris Jefferson enclosed the sketch and gave directions in regard to it, and stated that "this was the form of the little clock which was stolen from the chimney of my study". This is stated in an article entitled "Thomas Jefferson's French Furniture", by Marie Kimball, in "Antiques", February, 1929, pages 125-126.

No. 1982 is perhaps emblematic of the conquest of Egypt by Napoleon in 1798, as were also Nos. 1974 and 1975 to a certain extent. Here the dark figure of a native woman is seated upon the works; beside her is a palm tree and below her is an alligator or crocodile, all of which are seen in Egypt. On the base, rounded at the ends, are festoons of leaves, and the knots are formed of snakes. The woman holds a spear, on her back is a quiver and arrows, and she is adorned with head gear, a necklace, bracelets and anklets. On the dial is merely "a Paris", as in No. 1974. About 1800-1810.

No. 1983 is a handsome clock in brilliant ormolu, also probably emblematic of a victory in the Egyptian campaign of Napoleon. The dial is on a wheel of a chariot with two prancing horses driven by a cupid holding a palm leaf in his hand. A denizen of the Nile is on the rear of the chariot. On the unusual form of base is a triumphal procession in which there is a chariot with four horses. The works are in a case between the wheels of the chariot. This clock is much larger than is indicated by the small engraving. On the dial are the words "Gentilhomme, Palais Royal a Paris". About 1800-1820.

No. 1984 is an interesting clock with varied designs in ormolu. On the top are rose leaves and a large rose within which is a tiny figure of a child. The works are carried by two children facing in opposite directions, and below the dial is the pendulum formed of two hearts pierced with an arrow. The base, supported by four swans, is decorated with quivers and torches, between which are two figures. There is no name on this clock. About 1790-1810.

In No. 1985 the marble scrolls on the sides are similar to those on Nos. 1973 and 1974. The seated figure at the top holds a laurel wreath. The dial is unusual in having an oval painting above the centre, and below is another oval in which are the words "Courvoisier a Paris". The base is decorated with a panel of cupids and also with rosettes. About 1800-1820.

In No. 1986 the dark figures are of a woman and a cupid. At the four corners of the square dial are "spandrels", or "corner pieces", such as are seen on so many English and American grandfather and mantel clocks. The ends of the base are rounded and on the front is a panel with ormolu designs. One of the keyholes is lower than the other, as also in No. 1973 and others. On the dial are the words "Cachard a Paris". About 1790-1800.

No. 1987 is a later clock than the others here shown, having a very high base with heavy mounts. Many examples of this less desirable late Empire type are seen in our homes. The spirited figure at the top apparently represents a leader in costume urging his followers. The name of the maker seldom appears on clocks of this type. About 1830-1840.

No. 1988 is a pleasing example of a clock within a round and fluted pedestal of white marble. The significance of the cupid at the top is not apparent in connection with the bearded head and the globe in a frame. The column is ornamented with ormolu festoons of flowers and with a band on which are small figures of the type better seen in No. 1974. On the dial is the name "Festeau Le Jeune", of Paris. About 1780-1790.

1979 (Upper) Anonymous.
1982 (Centre) Mr. & Mrs. L. Birck-
    head.
1985 (Lower) Mrs. J. W. Wilson.

1980 (Upper) Anonymous.
1983 (Centre) Mrs. E. G. Gibson.
1986 (Lower) Mr. A. E. Cole.

1981 (Upper) Anonymous.
1984 (Centre) Mr. H. T. Tiffany.
1987 (Lower) Miss H. R. Chew.

1988 (Upper) Metropolitan Museum of Art. 1989 (Upper) Mr. Edgar G. Miller, Jr. 1990 (Upper) Metropolitan Museum of Art. 1991 (Upper) Anonymous.

1992 (Centre) Mr. J. J. Schwarz. 1993 (Centre) Mrs. L. W. Cottman. 1994 (Centre) Baltimore Museum of Art.

1995 (Lower) Anonymous. 1996 (Lower) Anonymous. 1997 (Lower) Anonymous.

The next three clocks, Nos. 1989-1991, are French mantel clocks in the form of a lyre, an instrument which is said to have been a favorite of Marie Antoinette. The lyre-shaped clocks are regarded by some writers as being "among the most elegant conceptions of the period of Louis Sixteenth". Three types of these clocks are shown here. American wall clocks in the lyre form are shown in section 195, Nos. 2037-2040.

In No. 1989 the frame is of marble and is in the form of a lyre resting upon a marble base. All parts of this frame are decorated with ormolu mounts consisting mainly of festoons of flowers, a wreath and leaves. The dial is stationary and around it, but not touching it, is a ring of brilliants which is attached by a rod to the pendulum in the rear, so that when the pendulum swings the ring swings also, and the movement of the brilliants to and fro creates a pleasing effect. On the dial are the words "Le Roy, Paris", whose name is also mentioned in the comment on No. 1979. This clock is a reproduction of an original made about 1780-1790.

In No. 1990 the frame, in the shape of a lyre, is of mahogany decorated with ormolu mounts in the form of leaves and, at the top, with a woman's face. The curved cross-bar at the top holds the pendulum, which is of the "gridiron" type as in No. 1975. At the lower end of the pendulum is the dial, behind which are the works of the clock. The dial and the works, being a part of the pendulum, swing to and fro. On the dial is the name "Delaunay" and, in French, the words "pupil of Breguet", an eminent French maker who died in 1823. The feet are in the same form as in Nos. 1969 and 1997. About 1800-1820.

In No. 1991, a reproduction, the design is attractive although the mahogany frame may be too wide. On each side of the dial is an ormolu cornucopia with fruits and leaves. The pendulum is suspended from the cross-bar at the top and above is an ormolu decoration. Four upright bars, representing the strings of a lyre, extend from the cross-bar down to the platform over the dial. About 1800-1820.

No. 1992 is a clock much in the style of the Washington clocks Nos. 1961-1963 in this section, but with a lyre at the top instead of an eagle. The figure at the right is playing the flute. The ormolu mounts under the dial are interesting and of an unusual character, consisting of two lighted candles, a festoon of leaves and a basket of fruit. The mounts on the base are well designed. The significance of the upright rod at the left is not clear to the writer. About 1800-1810.

In No. 1993 the dial and works are supported by a rectangular black marble column with an ormolu mount which seems to be a variation of the usual form of "anthemion" seen on No. 1964. On the sides are two curved arms resting on black marble bases with rosettes and with birds' heads holding tassels at the top. Ribbons of ormolu are around the dial and under the white marble vase at the top. The keyholes are on different levels, as in No. 1973 and others. A similar clock is No. 594 in Britten's "Old Clocks and Watches". On the dial is the name "Cronier", a Parisian maker. About 1800-1810.

No. 1994 presents the design of a dial and works, with a woman's figure above, supported by two birds with ruffed and chained necks, a fanciful conceit of

French designers of the period of Louis the Sixteenth. The dial has fine hands and also a pointer which indicates the day of the month. The hour numerals are in the Arabic form. The stands upon which the birds rest, and the base rounded at the ends, are finely decorated. On the dial are the words "Le Jeune a Paris". About 1780-1790.

No. 1995 is an example of a clock inserted in a vase. Here the vase is of porcelain and is decorated with a variety of designs, including cameos and white leaves. The handles are the heads of eagles. The dial is open in the centre, except for a star, in this respect resembling No. 1975. Several forms of vases with clocks were made in the period, some of much elegance. Two "anthemions" appear on the ends of the ornament on the base. The name "Angevin", of Paris, is on the dial. About 1815-1825.

No. 1996 is regarded as being in the style of the First Consulate of Napoleon, 1799-1802. The conquest of Egypt is recalled by the two ormolu figures of sphinxes which resemble to some extent the famous one at the Pyramids. The triangular forms around the dial suggest the "spandrels", or "corner pieces", of the English grandfather and mantel clocks. The hour numerals are in the Arabic form. The name "Perret Gentil" appears on the dial. About 1800.

No. 1997 is a bronze clock, said to be in the style of the First Empire, 1804-1814. The top is arched in the manner seen in the English mantel clock No. 1902. The dial is enclosed in a decorated ring of the same type as that seen in the pillar clock No. 2000. In the ormolu mount under the dial are two profiles, probably those of Napoleon and the Empress Josephine; and below is a mount at the sloping top of the base. The ormolu feet resemble those in Nos. 1969 and 1990. There is no name on this clock. About 1804-1809, in which years Josephine was Empress.

The next four clocks, Nos. 1998-2001, are commonly called "pillar clocks" because of their four pillars or columns. They were very popular in our country and more of them are found than of any other kind of French clocks. Their features are the pillars, which rest upon a rectangular base and support the top; the dial and works which are generally attached to the top by a screw; the decorated rim around the dial; and the pendulum of the gridiron type with a round weight which has an applied embossed front, often of fine workmanship. The pillars and frame were made of marble, wood, glass, alabaster or brass, those of white marble being perhaps the most elegant. They were often placed on oval wooden bases which have a groove cut in to hold a glass cover. They are all in the Empire style, which is indicated by their classic pillars and architectural design. These clocks were made in quantity for the American market from about 1820 to 1840. The name of the maker seldom appears.

No. 1998 is a white marble pillar clock with a silvered dial surrounded by a finely chased ormolu rim. At the top and bottom of each column is a brass piece, as in all clocks of this type. The base is without decoration, but in some clocks of this character there is an applied ormolu design. About 1820-1840.

No. 1999 is a wooden clock which has inlaid decorations on the top and the base and also on the upper surface of the base. The pillars are inlaid with vertical lines. The centre of the dial is of chased ormolu and is surrounded by a white enameled ring on which are the hour numerals. The feet are missing. About 1820-1840.

Nos. 2000 and 2001 are of wood and are so similar in construction that either of them would apparently serve as a sufficient example of the type; but as the first is ornamented with ormolu mounts and the second is not, and as the dials are not

1998 (Upper) Mr. Edgar G.   1999 (Upper) Anonymous.   2000 (Upper) Mr. & Mrs.   2001 (Upper) Anonymous.
     Miller, Jr.   J. M. Berry.
          2002 (Lower) Planchon's Book.   2003 (Lower) Planchon's Book.

the same, they present a different appearance. The skill of the French artists in designing ormolu mounts has been noticed in many clocks and articles of furniture; see section 38. About 1820-1840.

Nos. 2002 and 2003 are copies of two pictures of Parisian clock makers' shops, figure 114 in Mr. Mathieu Planchon's "L'Horloge", a book also mentioned in the comment on No. 2094 in section 197, and in section 180, note 5, P. Under the pictures in the book is a note in French which reads as follows: "Original design representing the manufacture of clocks about 1830."

No. 2002 shows a salesman receiving visitors. On the counter is a pillar clock such as those shown here, with a glass cover. The costumes and attitudes of the visitors and the salesman are interesting. No. 2003 shows the workshop, in which the seated worker is apparently engaged in putting one of the pillars in its place.

Nos. 2004-2012 are "skeleton" clocks, most of which are of French origin. This term is applied to them because, like skeletons, they have nothing in the way of a body, or frame, around them. The French term for clocks of this kind is "squelette", which means "skeleton". They are intended to be kept under a glass cover in order to protect them from dust, but the covers are omitted here, except in No. 2007, for the reason that the reflections on the glass would interfere with the photographs.

No. 2004 presents a front view of a skeleton clock of a type which is occasionally seen in our country, several examples being in the Essex Institute in Salem, Mass. No. 2005, described below, shows a part of its mechanism. The question of the nationality of this clock, and of others of this type, has caused a difference of opinion, but Mr. Herbert Cescinsky, the leading English authority, has informed the writer that the clock is English, in the French style, and was made about 1850. It is therefore not French or strictly antique. The French style is seen in the base, the feet and the arms supporting the dial, all of which are similar to others seen in French clocks in this section. A brief description is in the note.[16]

No. 2005 gives a view of the operation of the "fusee" of No. 2004, an interesting part of the mechanism of many English and French mantel clocks and others driven by a spring. In this skeleton clock the "fusee" is seen so much better than in a clock having a case around it, that an illustration has been postponed until this point. Looking at the illustration, the lower object is a round "barrel" containing the spring which here is partly run down, as seen from the appearance of the wire cord; the grooved object above, in the form of a cone, with the other part of the wire cord around it, is the "fusee", which is explained by Mr. Cescinsky.[17]

No. 2006 is an interesting example of French ingenuity. All of the mechanism is "attached to a sheet of plate glass, (not seen in the engraving), giving the appearance of a clock floating in the air". The movement is of much delicacy and

16. The silvered dial is open in the centre, showing parts of the mechanism. At the top is a bell which is struck, one stroke every hour, by the spear-head. The works rest upon two curved brass arms which rest upon two short supports. The marble base is rounded at the ends and has three marble feet. A clock very similar to this appears on the title page of an English book entitled "Treatise on Clock and Watch making", by Thomas Reid, published by Blackie and Son, Glasgow, 1857. Compare the French mantel clocks Nos. 1993 and 1994.

17. In "English Domestic Clocks", pages 49-50, from which the following is partly taken. In a grandfather clock the weight is suspended on a cord or catgut and the downward pull of the weight is about the same whether the clock is wound up or almost run down. But in a clock driven by a spring, the power is greater when the spring is wound up than when it is almost run down. Now we must realize that it requires a greater pull to keep the works in motion when the cord is at the small end of the fusee than at the large end—which may appear strange, but is true. By this fusee method, when the spring is wound up and its power is greatest, the cord is on the small end of the fusee where the greatest power is needed; and as the spring runs down and its power is lessened the cord is on the larger end of the fusee where less power is needed.

the large wheel has a great number of tiny teeth. The spring is in the round dark case above the top of the pendulum weight. The base is of marble, and the height is nineteen inches. Only two or three of these clocks seem to be known.[18] The height of the sheet of glass is seventeen inches. About 1800.

No. 2007 is a small clock, its height being seven inches. There are three dials; the upper one shows the time, the lower one on the right shows the days of the month and the lower one on the left is for the alarm. The escapement is at the top with a small knob above by which the cord which holds the pendulum may be raised or lowered, as mentioned in note 1 in this section. About 1800-1810.

No. 2008 is about twenty-five inches in height. On the large dial the signs of the zodiac are painted, and in the centre are two small dials; below is a dial with the phases of the moon; and another dial is at the top under an ormolu basket with flowers. On the sides are two figures with bows and arrows. The dark supporting piece and the animals' feet on the marble base are the only unattractive parts. About 1810-1820.

In No. 2009 two small wheels are at the top and below them is a large wheel, and in front of these three wheels is a white dial showing the time. In the high oval base, made of walnut, is the striking and chiming mechanism, and in front is a dial within an ormolu wreath. The cord, or chain, of the barrel and fusee may be seen, as in No. 2005. About 1810-1820.

No. 2010 is regarded by Mr. Cescinsky as an English clock in the French style. It has an oval wooden base, a silvered lyre design in the centre and a large dial with an open centre. At the top is the escapement, in the manner of a watch, with a hair-spring. On the two round surfaces under the ends of the half circle at the top are letters, on the left, "S", for "slow", and on the right, "F", for "fast". The dial is seven inches in diameter. As a timekeeper this clock is a failure, as it races as it runs down; but as an interesting curiosity it is decidedly a success. About 1850-1860.

No. 2011 is an interesting small French clock, fourteen inches high, with the words "Wm. Carpenter, St. Martin's Court, London" on the enameled dial. It has somewhat the same design as No. 2009, but with an open base. The marble columns with scroll ends, (compare No. 1985), support a platform upon which the clock is placed. A large wheel with small teeth is connected with a barrel and fusee, as in No. 2005. On the front of the pendulum are the letters "M A" and "Born Nov. 2, 1755" and "Died Oct. 16, 1793", indicating Marie Antoinette; see note 1 in this section. Festoons originally on the front and sides are missing. About 1795.

No. 2012 bears the name "Simon Willard" on the lower part of the dial. The similarity in principle between this clock and that by the French clock maker Lepine, shown in No. 2095, is referred to in the comments on the latter. The two

18. In addition to the clock illustrated here there is one, or a very similar one, shown opposite page 38 in the book entitled "The Lure of the Clock: an account of the James Arthur Collection of Clocks and Watches at New York University", New York, 1932, by Dr. D. W. Hering, Curator. A similar clock is in Britten's "Old Clocks and Watches", No. 599. Another interesting clock on glass is the "Mystery Clock", No. 2088.

2004 (UPPER) MR. EDGAR G. MILLER, JR.
2007 (CENTRE) ANONYMOUS.
2010 (LOWER) ANONYMOUS.

2005 (UPPER) MR. EDGAR G. MIL-LER, JR.
2008 (CENTRE) ANONYMOUS.
2011 (LOWER) MR. EDGAR G. MIL-LER, JR.

2006 (UPPER) ANONYMOUS.
2009 (CENTRE) ANONYMOUS.
2012 (LOWER) ANONYMOUS.

suspended weights bring to mind the similar ones in the Eli Terry mantel clock No. 1930. The large curved bar at the top supports a brass eagle on a globe. Below the dial is a thermometer. The base, in the French form, is decorated with inlaid designs. No clock made by Simon Willard in this style has apparently been illustrated or mentioned in the books or magazines. About 1800.

Section 194. Wall clocks; banjo.—The clock which we know as the "banjo" clock[1] was invented by Simon Willard[2] as appears from a patent[3] issued to him in 1802 when he was living in Roxbury, Mass. It is thought that no other kind of antique clocks, except those of the grandfather type and the Terry mantel clocks, have been so popular in our country and have been made in such numbers; and it may also be said that no other clocks have been so frequently tampered with and counterfeited.

The experience of the writer has been that only a very few banjo clocks have survived in their original condition and that very many which are called "antiques" are wholly or largely modern. Moreover, there is perhaps no other important article of antique furniture so easy to counterfeit;[4] and it is very difficult for an amateur collector to distinguish, in whole or in part, between an original clock and a clever "fake". In the note several of the more common substitutions and replacements of parts are mentioned.[5] The amateur collector should espe-

1. The name "banjo" is a modern one which was applied to these clocks because of a certain similarity to a banjo in form. In the schedule attached to the patent the clock is called a "timepiece", a word which was used to indicate a "time keeper" only, thus excluding a striking mechanism.

    The making of banjo clocks by various makers continued from the time of its invention until about 1870. In the latter portion of this period the workmanship, especially of the paintings on the panels, declined greatly in character.

2. As to the career of Simon Willard see notes 19-21 in section 187 which treat of Willard's grandfather clocks and several matters in connection with the Willard clock makers and their clocks.

3. The patent, dated February 8, 1802, was signed by Thomas Jefferson, President, James Madison, Secretary of State and Levi Lincoln, Attorney-General. The schedule filed with the application for a patent describes both the works and the case, including the painting of the glass on the lower door.

    In the book of Mr. John Ware Willard, mentioned in section 187 at note 20, it is said, page 15, that there is good reason to think that Simon Willard made these clocks for several years before he patented them. See the comment on No. 2013.

4. An expert clock repairer in Philadelphia told the writer several years ago that he knew of over five hundred Howard wall clocks which had been changed into the shape of antique banjo clocks, were gilded and supplied with painted panels, were sold to the trade and were then passed off on collectors as original banjo clocks. The Howard movements were used because they resembled those of the Willard type. In Mr. John Ware Willard's book it is said, page 59, that these counterfeits were often made. The Howard clocks were extensively used in stations of the Pennsylvania Railroad some years ago. An example of the banjo clocks made by the Howard Company is No. 2036.

5. A. The two original glass panels, decorated with paintings, are of course fragile and easily broken, especially the panel on the door which has probably been opened many hundreds of times in the course of a century; therefore it is to be expected that the glass panels are not often the original ones. There are many artists who can make excellent reproductions of the original painted panels, as in the banjo clocks Nos. 2023 and 2024 and others; and an antique appearance may easily be obtained.

    B. The enamel paint on the dial has often become cracked to such an extent that the dial must be repainted. New dials, painted with an antique finish, may be purchased from supply firms. New dials bearing the name of "Aaron Willard" may be had in quantity. In some instances a dial does not

cially bear in mind that the name of a noted maker on a dial is not proof that the clock was made by that maker, as more fully mentioned in the last paragraph of the text in section 180.

We are so accustomed to seeing banjo clocks with paintings on the glass panels,[6] a case with a gilded front,[7] a brass eagle[8] on the top and a gilded base[9] under the lower door, that these decorations are often regarded as being in the

(Note 5, *continued*)

exactly fit the form of the round part of the case to which it is attached, indicating that it was made for another clock of a different size.

C.   The works of the clock, especially the pendulum and its rod, may have been worn or broken to such an extent that they had to be replaced. Advertisements in the magazines offer for sale "Willard movements", made exactly like the originals. See also note 12.

D.   The hands are often not mates. In such cases the minute hand is generally the wrong one, probably because it has been carelessly moved backwards or forwards more frequently than the hour hand. In some cases the hands are obviously in different designs or designs of later styles. Often the hands are too long or too short, indicating that they are not the original ones. The hands of a finely made banjo clock are of precisely the correct length, that is, the hour hand extends exactly to the bottom of the hour numerals, and the minute hand extends exactly to the circular line with minute marks, as in No. 2020 and others. These matters are seldom noticed by the owner. Many styles of hands, made in quantity, are advertised for sale. See also section 184, note 3.

E.   A clock in the banjo form without the two brass curved side arms appears to become what stiff and angular in design, as in No. 2025; but with the side arms such an appearance is avoided and the clock presents a pleasing combination of curves and straight lines. These side arms seem to have been original with Simon Willard. They are now made in quantity.

F.   It may be asked "how can I be sure that the banjo clock is all original or almost all original?" The answer is that no one but a clock repairer or expert, who knows the mechanism of antique banjo clocks, can give a correct answer as to the works; and that no one but an experienced gilder can surely know whether the gilding is old or modern; and that no one but a cabinet maker or expert can know whether the case is entirely old. Mr. John Ware Willard, in his book mentioned above says, page 59, that Simon Willard clocks, both of the grandfather and banjo types, "have been counterfeited innumerable times and it requires a thorough knowledge of the peculiarities of his workmanship to detect the fraud". See also section 187, note 21, B.

6.   It is said that Simon Willard never used any painting of a landscape or naval battle on the glass panel of the lower door, nor an American flag, such as were used by Aaron Willard and others on their timepiece clocks. The favorite painting on the Simon Willard timepiece was an ornamental design, such as those in Nos. 2017-2020. In some cases when the glass doors were broken, the owners had new glasses inserted with other designs. Simon Willard's painted designs are very pleasing, and it is said that they were made by an Englishman whose name is not known and by Charles Bullard, a Boston artist. On the upper glass panel a design of flowers was often used. From Mr. Willard's book, pages 57-58. In No. 2014 the painting on the lower glass panel is a mythological one.

7.   It is said that neither Simon nor Aaron Willard covered all of the front wooden parts of their ordinary clocks with gilding and that the gilding now seen on banjo clocks is almost always modern. Mr. John Ware Willard's father, a clock maker in Boston from 1840 to 1870, repaired hundreds of these clocks, and stated that he never saw a Willard timepiece, or any other old ones, covered with gilding; pages 59-60. These statements may be too broad.

8.   Brass eagles were not used on Simon Willard's timepieces; the usual ornament at the top was a brass or wooden acorn-shaped piece or a ball with leaves. Brass eagles were imported in great numbers and when an original ornament was lost or broken, a brass eagle was generally substituted. From Mr. Willard's book, page 58. It seems likely, however, that gilded wooden eagles were sometimes used.

9.   A base piece under the lower door was never used by Simon Willard except on his "presentation" timepieces, but was generally used by Aaron Willard and others, imitating the presentation pieces. From Mr. Willard's book, pages 96-97.

Concerning several statements in notes 7-9 see "Antiques", March, 1929, page 196.

usual style of Simon Willard; but it is said that these features were not used by him except on a very few clocks which were specially made as "presentation" pieces, generally to be given by his customers as wedding presents, and bearing his name as maker.[10] It seems likely that it became the fashion for other clock makers to decorate all their fine banjo clocks in almost the same manner that Simon Willard did in his "presentation" clocks; and many of his plainer clocks have been "glorified" by later decoration.

The illustrations of banjo clocks begin with eight, Nos. 2013-2020, which are regarded as having been made by Simon Willard; next are three bearing the name of Aaron Willard, Nos. 2021-2023, which are followed by nine examples, Nos. 2024-2032, by various clock makers of the period and later; Nos. 2033 and 2034 illustrate a type of handsome banjo clocks known as "Curtis clocks" from the name of the maker, Lemuel Curtis; No. 2035 is a "regulator" clock by Simon Willard, which is much in the style of a banjo clock, and No. 2036 is a Howard clock of similar design.

Beginning with No. 2013 we now examine eight banjo clocks which are regarded as having been made by Simon Willard, six of which are copied from the book[11] of Mr. John Ware Willard, mentioned frequently in this section. Mr.

(Note 9, *continued*)

Illustrated articles on the subject of banjo clocks and other clocks made by the Willards are in "Antiques" as follows: "The man who made Simon Willard's clock cases; John Doggett of Roxbury", March, 1929, page 196, by Mabel M. Swan; "The man who made brass works for Willard clocks", June, 1930, page 524, also by Mabel M. Swan; "The clocks of Simon Willard; the improved timepiece", February, 1922, page 69, by Daniel J. Steele.

10. Simon Willard's ordinary banjo clocks apparently did not have his name on the dial; but on the lower glass door he generally placed the words "S. Willard's Patent", or "Willard's Patent", in a running hand or capital letters in gold leaf. This was imitated by other clock makers, but probably because they did not dare to imitate too closely, they rarely put the words on the glass door but put it on the narrow glass panel and used merely the words "Willard's Patent"; from Mr. Willard's book, page 57.

Simon Willard never used a wooden frame for the glass door over the dial; this frame, called a "bezel", was always made of brass; Mr. Willard's book, page 96.

Reproductions of painted glass doors bearing the inscription "S. Willard's Patent" may be obtained from dealers; see also note 12, second paragraph.

A wall clock, unless it is screwed to the wall, or otherwise attached firmly to it, will of course not keep its position when it is being wound. Old screw holes are very often seen in banjo clocks, and also in lyre clocks and other wall clocks. Similar remarks in connection with other clocks are in section 195, note 4, and in section 186, note 4. In a label of Aaron Willard, Jr., the directions include one to screw the back of the clock to the wall with two screws; see also the label No. 1862.

An original mechanical feature of importance in Simon Willard's banjo clocks was the placing of the pendulum in front of the weight, "by which means the pendulum may be made longer and will therefore vibrate more accurately" than if it were in the space behind the weight. The banjo clocks run for about eight days.

11. It is here said, page 13, that Simon Willard's banjo clock was "an instant and complete success, coming at once into public favor. It was a perfect timekeeper and beautifully simple in construction". Moreover, "not the slightest improvement has been made upon them". Their simple but graceful design and their pleasing decorative features, combined with their excellent timekeeping ability, have obtained for them an enduring position in our households. Recently their popularity has induced the leading American clock manufacturers to make reproductions which generally depart from the designs of the originals to some extent.

Willard states, page 49, that No. 2013 is the nearest approach to a "presentation" clock, mentioned above at note 10, that he has found, and that it was made for a customer to be used as a wedding gift. The brass eagle with outspread wings is not original and the upright glass panel is a reproduction. We notice that the hands are of exactly the correct lengths; the hour numerals are in the Roman form; the glass in the upright panel and in the door frame below is decorated with delicate designs; there is no name on the dial, but in the door frame below is the inscription "S. Willard's Patent"; under the door is a base-piece which Simon Willard used only on his "presentation" clocks, but is now used on almost all clocks of the banjo type; and the entire woodwork of the front is covered with gold leaf, as was Willard's method in these fine pieces. The date is said to be 1797, which is prior to the date of the granting of Willard's patent referred to above in note 3.

No. 2014 is said to be in its original state. The painting in the rectangular frame is supposed to represent Aurora; somewhat similar designs are in Nos. 2021, 2027, 2029 and 2034. On the upper panel is the name of Simon Willard, but is not visible in the engraving. The hour numerals are in the Arabic form. The brass eagle is not original. The extreme height is about forty inches. About 1800-1820.

No. 2015 has no base-piece, nor is there one in any of the following examples of Simon Willard's banjo clocks, these being of the ordinary type, not presentation pieces. The brass urn at the top is probably a substitute for the original. The paintings on the glasses are in designs with square and diamond shaped open-work. At the bottom of the upper panel a classic head in gold leaf is faintly seen. About 1800-1820.

Nos. 2016-2019 illustrate various forms of decoration of the glass panels. In each there is an opening in the lower panel through which the pendulum may be seen, and above and below the openings are the words "S. Willard's Patent", mentioned in note 10. In Mr. John Ware Willard's book the paintings and brass side arms of these clocks are in colors, which cannot be well reproduced in the engravings. In each of these four clocks the decorations are different, but they have a certain similarity in the lower panels, all of which have rectangular outlines. The slenderness of the upright panels and their frames should be noticed, these being much more graceful than those having a wider form, as in Nos. 2027, 2029 and others; and the size and proportions of the lower panels are more pleasing than those in some other banjo clocks. The variety of ornaments at the top should be noticed, that in No. 2018 being perhaps the only original one, for the reasons stated in note 8. It is not possible to distinguish between the dates of these four clocks, but it may be safe to regard them all as about 1800-1820.

In No. 2020 the inscription "S. Willard's Patent" and a painted and gilded design are on the glass panel of the door, with a similar design on the upright panel above. At the top is a brass ornament supposed to be a pheasant, a bird which is seen on many mirrors of an earlier period, as in No. 1110 and others. About 1800-1820.

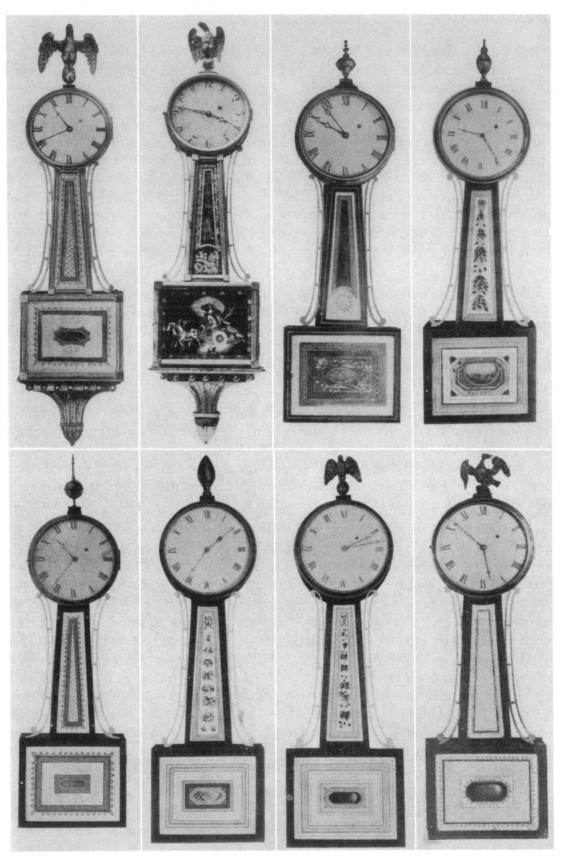

2013 (Upper) Anony
    mous.
2017 (Lower) Anony
    mous.

2014 (Upper) Anony
    mous.
2018 (Lower) Anony
    mous.

2015 (Upper) Anony
    mous.
2019 (Lower) Anony
    mous.

2016 (Upper) Anony
    mous.
2020 (Lower) Anony
    mous.

2021 (Upper) Anony-
    mous.
2025 (Lower) Anony-
    mous.

2022 (Upper) Anony-
    mous.
2026 (Lower) Anony-
    mous.

2023 (Upper) Anony-
    mous.
2027 (Lower) Anony-
    mous.

2024 (Upper) Anony-
    mous.
2028 (Lower) Anony-
    mous.

The next three banjo clocks, Nos. 2021-2023, are believed to be the work of Aaron Willard, whose career is briefly mentioned in section 187, at note 24. Aaron generally put his name on the dials. He did not ornament the lower glass panel with delicate designs as his brother Simon did, but generally had them painted with scenes of various kinds, one of which, shown on the lower panel of No. 2021, was a favorite. Aaron's clocks were often provided with a gilded base, and with an acorn at the top, or a ball and spike, and sometimes with an eagle. They are good timepieces, but in workmanship and accuracy they are not so highly regarded as those of Simon Willard. The dates of Aaron's banjo clocks are between 1802 and 1823; he retired from business in the latter year and was succeeded by his son Aaron Willard, Jr.

The remarks upon counterfeiting, at the beginning of this section, are particularly applicable to banjo clocks bearing the name of Aaron Willard.[12]

No. 2021 is regarded as a fair example of the banjo clocks made by Aaron Willard. The engraving is copied from an illustration in Mr. John Ware Willard's book and is not very clear. At the top of the mahogany case is the original gilded ornament; and at the bottom is a plain base-piece. The painting on the glass door, not clear, is said to have been a favorite one, and that in the panel above is also frequently seen, with variations. The narrow beaded moldings around the glass door and the panel above are gilded, as in the Simon Willard clock No. 2013 and in most of the banjo clocks made by others. About 1802-1823.

In No. 2022 the glass door is ornamented with a painting of several buildings, below which are the words "Harvard College"; and above are the words "Presented to H. J. Ripley", who graduated from Harvard in 1816. On the dial are the words "Aaron Willard, Boston", and on the upright glass panel below is a gilded shield and an American eagle, and also the word "Patent"—which seems peculiar in view of the fact that the patent for this type of clock belonged to Simon Willard, as mentioned above. About 1816.

No. 2023 has a gilded eagle at the top and on the dial below the name "Aaron Willard" faintly appears. The narrow vertical panel has a gilded shield and an American eagle, as in the preceding clock, and other designs. On the glass door the painting, a replacement, shows a naval battle of the War of 1812, a subject very popular also on the mirrors of the period, as in Nos. 1162-1167. About 1815-1823.

12.   Several years ago, in Boston, the writer noticed a group of banjo clocks bearing the name of Aaron Willard in the shop of an apparently reliable jeweler and clock dealer, and remarked to the salesman that he was fortunate in securing so many by Aaron Willard. The salesman replied that these clocks had no name on them when purchased, but as they had the same movement as those of Aaron Willard, and in other ways resembled them, the jeweler felt justified in putting Willard's name on the dials. This feeling is apparently shared by some others. Moreover it is not difficult to substitute the name of Simon or Aaron Willard on dials bearing some other name.

In a certain catalogue of supplies are illustrations of new banjo clock dials for sale bearing the name of Aaron Willard; and in advertisements in the magazines are offerings of new Willard movements of banjo clocks. These are not intended to mislead, but they may obviously have the same effect as if they were so intended. Few amateur collectors can tell the difference between the old and the new if the latter are properly "aged".

The nine banjo clocks in the next group, Nos. 2024-2032, illustrate the work of various other clock makers. There is much sameness in these clocks and therefore the comments are brief.

On No. 2024 the dial bears the words "Warranted by Wm. Cummens", (1768-1834), an apprentice of Simon Willard, whose name also appears on the grandfather clock No. 1850; see note 29 in section 187. The decoration on the glass panels is new and is mainly copied from the Simon Willard banjo clock No. 2013, omitting the inscription "S. Willard's patent". About 1810-1830.

No. 2025 is by Elnathan Taber,[13] also an apprentice of Simon Willard. The inscription on the dial is "E. Taber, Roxbury, March, 1840". This is a plain clock of a type made in great numbers to be sold at a low price. There is no gilding and there are no side arms; the paintings are simple; and there is no base-piece. Dated 1840.

No. 2026 is by William King Lemist, (1791-1820), another apprentice of Simon Willard. Lemist had a short life and probably made only a few clocks. On the dial is the inscription "Made by William Lemist, 1812", at which date he was only twenty-one years of age. See also the wall clock No. 2044 made by "Lemist and Tappan".

No. 2027 is a striking as well as a timekeeping banjo clock, bearing the name "E. Jones", of Boston, on the panel under the dial. The striking attachment is not visible but its presence is indicated by the keyhole on the left hand side of the dial. A floral design is painted on the upper panel, and on the glass door below is a painting of a mythological character as in No. 2021. A carved and gilded pineapple is at the top, as in No. 1922. The hour hand is too long and is apparently a careless substitution, and the vertical central panel is wider than in the best examples. About 1810-1820.

No. 2028 is one of the large number of banjo clocks made in the Willard style by makers who did not put their names on their clocks. It has no features of an unusual character, but is a pleasing example. The central upright portion is slender, and the painted design resembles those in Nos. 2013 and 2024. On the lower door is a patriotic painting of a naval encounter, probably in the War of 1812. About 1815-1820.

No. 2029 has original paintings on the glass fronts, the lower one said to represent Neptune in a chariot; the upper one is of flowers, below which appears the inscription "R. W. Drown, Newburyport" in capital letters. The case is made of light mahogany and has a brass urn at the top. The width of the central vertical portion detracts somewhat from the appearance of this clock. About 1810-1820.

13. Elnathan Taber, (1768-1854), mentioned in section 187, note 21, paragraph C, and in note 30 of the same section, was "Simon Willard's best apprentice. * * Taber made a most excellent clock, fully as good as Simon Willard's. * * After Simon Willard retired from business in 1839, Elnathan Taber * * received permission to put the name 'Simon Willard' on the dials of the clocks he made"; from Mr. John Ware Willard's book, pages 58, 110. No. 1851 is a grandfather clock by Taber.

No. 2030 has an interesting painting on the glass front of the lower door, representing Liberty crowning with a wreath an American eagle which holds a shield. Somewhat similar patriotic designs are on the upper panels of many mirrors of about the same period, as in Nos. 1168-1173. On the dial is a faint inscription "Smith, New York"—which is thought to refer to "Smith's Clock Establishment" of New York. About 1810-1820.

No. 2031 has a thermometer on the central glass panel, instead of the usual flowers or designs. Under the thermometer is the word "Patent", as to which see the comment on No. 2022. The glass in the door below is painted with a naval scene, perhaps representing a victory of the "Constitution" in the War of 1812. A too large gilded eagle is at the top. The name of the maker does not appear on this clock. About 1815-1825.

In No. 2032 the special feature is an alarm attachment. The alarm keyhole is on the dial between the Roman numerals XI and XII. The hand pointing to VII indicates that the alarm is set for that hour. The weight operating the alarm hangs in the central section to the left of the weight operating the timekeeping works. The case is of mahogany, without gilding, and the two glass panels are ornamented in a simple manner. No name appears on this clock. About 1810-1830.

Nos. 2033 and 2034 are by Lemuel Curtis.[14] These clocks are regarded as a form of banjo clock and they differ from the Willard banjo clocks chiefly in having a round lower frame within which the pendulum weight swings, instead of the rectangular frame in the Willard style; and below the round frame is a base-piece with acanthus leaves instead of the usual form. In these clocks the entire front is very ornamental. The convex glass in the lower door frame is decorated with a painting of a mythological, patriotic or other scene and the glass panel above is generally adorned with a scroll design or an eagle and shield and sometimes with a thermometer. On the frame around the dial,—called the "bezel"—, and also on the lower frame, is a series of gilded wooden or brass balls, in some clocks as many as thirty-five on the lower frame; a similar decorative treatment is seen on the girandole mirror No. 1239 and others. All of the

14. Lemuel Curtis, 1790-1857, worked in Concord, Mass., from 1814 to 1818, and afterwards in Burlington, Vermont, until he died. At one period he was associated with a clock maker named Dunning. He made several kinds of clocks, but those of the type shown here are the most important, and the term "Curtis clocks" is generally used to refer only to them. Except as to the paintings on the glasses, they are all very similar, making it difficult to determine their dates. The clocks here shown are given the approximate date of 1810-1830, in which period the general style of decoration was of a character similar to that of the girandole mirrors cited in the text. The works are of a superior quality. The height is about forty-five inches. The case is generally of mahogany, but pine was used for the base-piece and panels. Curtis also made other types of clocks, some of which were very ugly.

An illustrated article entitled "The Clocks of Lemuel Curtis", by Walter H. Durfee, is in "Antiques", December, 1923, page 281. A warning is there given to the amateur collector: "now that their beauty is appreciated, they command prices high enough to make their faking profitable. In buying a clock of presumable Curtis make, therefore—especially if the purchase be made from a general shop—the collector should take all possible pains to have the specimen well authenticated."

2029 (Upper) Anony-
    mous.
2033 (Lower) Metropoli-
    tan Museum of
    Art.

2030 (Upper) Anony-
    mous.
2034 (Lower) Anony-
    mous.

2031 (Upper) Anony-
    mous.
2035 (Lower) Harvard
    University.

2032 (Upper) Mr. Edgar G.
    Miller, Jr.
2036 (Lower) E. Howard
    Clock Co.

wood is gilded; the side arms are in a somewhat different form from those on the Willard clocks; at the top is an eagle with folded or outspread wings; and on the dial is painted "L. Curtis", and generally the word "Patent". Although their proportions are not altogether harmonious, these clocks are the handsomest wall clocks made in our country, and are highly esteemed, and it is unfortunate that there are so very few of them.

In No. 2033 all of the features above mentioned are present, although the engraving is not large enough to show the details well. The hands on the dial are in the form of a series of circles or loops, as in the second hand in the American grandfather clock No. 1825, and the hands on the mantel clocks Nos. 1996 and 2093. Arabic hour numerals, as to which see note 32 in section 187, are used on the dial. The lower convex glass is decorated with a water scene with small sailing vessels. About 1810-1830.

No. 2034 resembles closely the preceding clock except that here the wings of the gilded eagle are folded and the restored painting on the lower glass represents a mythological female figure, probably "Aurora", driving a chariot, with the sun in the background. This painting is somewhat similar to that on the Simon Willard clock No. 2014 and others. The dial has the words "L. Curtis, Patent". The plain hands are probably substitutes. About 1810-1830.

No. 2035, a "regulator" clock of the banjo type, was presented to Harvard College by Simon Willard in 1829, as appears from the Latin inscription[15] on the lower glass door. The general form follows the usual type of Willard's banjo clocks, but there is a change, not for the better, in the appearance of the case. Instead of graceful brass side arms there are applied wooden ones, and instead of a rectangular lower door with painted designs there is a door with bulging sides. The pendulum weight and rod are too conspicuous. The form of clock was probably the model for clocks such as No. 2036. See also note 7 in the next section.

No. 2036 is a popular form of clock made from about 1867 by E. Howard & Co., of Boston, and their successor, "The E. Howard Clock Co.", of Waltham, Mass., which has kindly furnished a photograph and information for this book. In 1880 clocks of this type were made and sold by the Howard Company at the rate of about fifty a week. The similarity is apparent between this clock and the preceding one made by Simon Willard, indicating the adoption of the Willard form, but without side arms or an ornament at the top or a base-piece below. Clocks of this type are those referred to in note 4 of this section. Prior to about 1867 the Howard clocks were made with a rectangular base.

Section 195. Wall clocks; lyre and other American.—The most important and numerous of the American wall clocks are, of course, the banjo clocks which are considered in the previous section; but lyre clocks and several other types are

15. Freely translated by a Harvard scholar, Mr. Frederick B. Robinson, the inscription is as follows: "To Harvard College to the library of the President for his use. Simon Willard who made it gives it through the gratefulness of his spirit. In the year of Our Lord, August 17th, 1829." No. 1842 is a grandfather clock presented to Harvard College by Simon Willard.

of interest and are presented in this section. In the next section are examples of foreign wall clocks.

It is said by Mr. John Ware Willard in his book entitled "Simon Willard and his Clocks",[1] page 97, that the lyre clock was originated[2] by Aaron Willard, Jr.,[3] who made them in great variety and number after he took over the clock business of his father Aaron Willard in 1823; and that they were imitated by other clock makers.

These American lyre clocks were generally made of mahogany, somewhat coarsely carved with acanthus leaves on the front, with a base-piece below and an ornamental figure on the top. The more important forms appear in the illustrations. The lyre design, like that of the banjo, is well adapted to the requirements of a clock with a somewhat long pendulum. The few surviving original glass fronts are seldom found in good condition.

In No. 2037 the lyre-shaped portion of the front somewhat resembles the supporting lyres on the fine card tables shown in Nos. 1539-1542 and others. The carving represents a form of acanthus leaves and the vertical gilded lines on the repainted glass panel represent the strings of a lyre. The base under the lyre is of a different form from that on the banjo clocks, and has a somewhat heavy rounded portion. At the top is a gilded ornament. On the dial is the inscription "William Grant, Boston". This clock is pleasing in its proportions and decoration.[4] About 1825-1835.

1. This book is referred to and quoted frequently in connection with clocks of the Willard family; see section 187 at note 20 and section 194.

2. Other clock makers in Boston have been given the credit for originating this type of clock; perhaps the considerable number of these clocks bearing the name of other makers may have led to the belief.

These lyre clocks, of course, are entirely different from the French mantel clocks having the form of a lyre, as Nos. 1989-1991 in section 193.

The lyre as a decorative form in various articles of furniture, especially in tables in the Sheraton style, is referred to in section 171 note 7, and in section 44 in chapter 4.

3. Aaron Willard, Jr., son of Aaron Willard, was born in 1783 and died in 1864. In 1823 his father retired from business and the son took over the business and conducted it until he retired about 1850. After 1823 his name appears on many clocks.

See illustration No. 1862, in which "Jr.", is written on an engraved label of his father Aaron Willard, and the comment on No. 1848.

4. Some lyre clocks are gilded in whole or in part; but large gilded surfaces do not add to the appearance, and gilding on a small portion of the case does not harmonize with the other parts. It is probable that gilding was added later, as on the banjo clocks, as mentioned in section 194, note 7. In some cases the door at the bottom is furnished with a mirror, perhaps a substitute for a broken painted glass.

In order to start the pendulum of the lyre clocks which have no door below, such as No. 2037, it is necessary to take off the front with its painted glass. It is not very easy to do this, as the door of the dial must first be opened, then the front is to be raised slightly, disconnecting the bottom part of the front and enabling it to be lifted out. This operation requires the use of two hands. Replacing the front is also an awkward proceeding.

As with all wall clocks, the clock should be held firmly in place on the wall in order to prevent it from sliding. This is generally done by two screws, the holes of which are often seen in the backs of old wall clocks, as mentioned in connection with banjo clocks, section 194, note 10, and also in connection with grandfather clocks in section 186, note 4.

In No. 2038 a feature is the striking attachment, the winding hole of which appears on the left of the dial. There are two weights, one for the timekeeping mechanism and the other for the striking mechanism. The front of the rectangular frame over the base is a door which gives easy access to the pendulum; but this door, although ornamental, is not an improvement upon the graceful design of the preceding clock. The paintings are new. About 1825-1835.

No. 2039 is a plainer type of lyre clock, having a wooden panel instead of a glass one with lyre strings; and the wooden door below is without decoration. The frame enclosing the glass over the dial—the bezel—is of wood. At the top is a carved design resembling plumes and at the bottom is a small bracket. About 1825-1835.

In No. 2040 the lyre panel is of wood, with carvings of acanthus leaves, under which is a door with a glass panel upon which is painted an elaborate naval scene. On the central portion of the dial is a small painted circle of flowers, a form of decoration seen also on the Terry style mantel clocks Nos. 1935 and 1936. The base is fully carved with leaves, and terminates in a wooden ornament. About 1830-1840.

Nos. 2041 and 2042 are wall clocks made by Simon Willard and Aaron Willard, respectively, in the early part of their careers while living at Grafton, Mass. Each of these clocks is about twenty inches high. The upper portion, having a kidney-shaped[5] glass door and scroll feet, is placed upon a hollow base in which the pendulum swings and into which the single heavy weight falls. The rounded form of the base-pieces shows that the clocks were not made to stand on a mantel or shelf. If they had feet at the bottom, instead of a rounded base, their form would resemble that of certain mantel clocks of a later date in the Willard style, as stated in section 190. In each clock the small round dial is silvered and bears the engraved name of the maker. In No. 2041 the name is "Willard, Grafton" and in No. 2042 it is "Aaron Willard". The bell is seen above the dial, a conspicuous feature seldom found and which does not add to the appearance. Each of these two clocks has ornamental woodwork at the top. The form of these clocks seems to have led to that of the next two clocks here shown, and also to the design of some of the Willard mantel clocks referred to above. About 1770-1780.

Nos. 2043 and 2044 resemble the mantel clocks Nos. 1923 and 1924 in section 190, but were made to hang on a wall as they are without feet and have brackets, or base-pieces, similar to those on the lyre clock No. 2037. The glasses on the upper and lower portions are covered with paintings of flowers and country scenes, with the exception of the lower part of the upper glasses where the name and address of the makers appear in ovals. On No. 2043 the inscription is "Aaron Willard, Boston", and on No. 2044 is "Lemist[6] & Tappan, Philada."; this abbre-

    5.   The kidney-shaped dial and door are referred to in note 1 in section 190 which treats of mantel clocks in the Willard style.
    6.   William King Lemist was an apprentice of Simon Willard, as mentioned in connection with No. 2026. He died in 1820. The Lemist whose name is on this clock may be the same person.

2037 (Upper) Mr. E. G. Miller, Jr.

2041 (Centre) Metropolitan Museum of Art.

2045 (Lower) Mr. E. G. Miller, Jr.

2038 (Upper) Anonymous.

2042 (Centre) Metropolitan Museum of Art.

2046 (Lower) Anonymous.

2039 (Upper) Mr. C. E. Snyder.

2043 (Centre) Mr. J. G. D'A. Paul.

2047 (Lower) Anonymous.

2040 (Upper) Mrs. Robert Taylor, Jr.

2044 (Centre) Anonymous.

2048 (Lower) Anonymous.

1005

viation of "Philadelphia" was apparently usual at the period, and is also seen in the clock No. 1915 and others. In No. 2044 the dial is concave, or, as it is sometimes called, "dished", a fancy of the period. The upper front portion of these clocks slides off to the front. The date is about 1800-1820.

No. 2045 is an example of an eight day type of clock made by Aaron Willard and also by Aaron Willard, Jr. It is sometimes called a "regulator clock", although the movement does not seem to be of the very fine character required in a "regulator".[7] Because of its form, a clock of this type has also been called an "Act of Parliament clock", an erroneous term, as the latter clock is a very large English one for use in public rooms, as stated in the comment on a clock of that type, No. 2056. Here the dial is about thirteen inches in diameter and the height of the clock is thirty inches. The lower portion is wide enough for the swing of the pendulum and is furnished with a door. The bottom is curved inward. About 1810-1830.

No. 2046 is a very small illustration of a large eight day wall clock, about sixty-eight inches high and twenty inches wide. The top is in the form of the Terry style mantel clock No. 1928 and others, and the power is furnished by two heavy weights as in the Terry clock No. 1930. The entire front is a door, in three parts, extending from the top to the bracket, or base-piece, below, with hinges on the left side. The dial is about seven inches in diameter. On each side is a long reeded column, suggesting the style of the Sheraton period, and over these are curved supports, called "corbels", as in the mantel mirror No. 1231. This clock should be compared with No. 1942 in section 191 which treats of the mantel clocks in the Terry style. About 1820-1830.

No. 2047 has a gilded front in the same general form as the Empire style mirror No. 1203. The entire front is a door and the dial is seen through a glass in the upper panel, and below is a mirror. This clock might perhaps be used on a mantel, but it would be insecure, as the weight of the door when open would tilt the clock forward unless it were screwed to the wall. It is thirty-one inches high and eighteen inches wide. The power comes from a wide heavy weight. About 1820-1830.

No. 2048 is a wall clock made by Philander J. Willard, (1772-1840), who is referred to in section 187, note 21, E. Both as a timepiece and as an agreeable object to gaze upon it was a failure. The crude top with a brass urn recalls the scroll tops of many grandfather clocks, and the brass side arms remind us of the banjo clocks. This clock has no weights, spring or pendulum, and its own weight, pulling down on a vertical rod with teeth, not seen from the front, furnishes the power to move the hands. Illustration No. 2098 shows a modern clock operating upon the same principle. About 1800.

This section on "wall clocks" would be incomplete unless mention were made of an American "wag-on-the-wall" clock. It seems that a "wag-on-the-wall" con-

7. The word "regulator" as used by clock makers at the present time indicates a wall clock in a shape somewhat similar to this one, and does not mean a finely constructed clock, or "regulator", such as is used in clock shops as an exact timekeeper by which watches and other clocks are set.

sisted of a dial and works intended to be put in a grandfather clock case, but which was denied that protection from dust and was hung on a wall with its works exposed.[8] It is said that some American examples have survived, but that almost all of them became useless and were thrown away, or were put into grandfather clock cases. Their quaint name, however, is still used, and their place has been taken by a great number of cheap German clocks of similar appearance which have been imported as substitutes. In the language of the shops almost any clock which may hang on the wall with its works exposed is a "wag-on-the-wall".

Section 196. Wall clocks; foreign.—Two English clocks of the hooded type, Nos. 1748 and 1749, made to hang on a wall, are illustrated in section 185, entitled "Lantern and hooded clocks", for the reason that they are more closely connected with lantern clocks than with later ones. In this section several representative wall clocks[1] of French and other foreign types are shown.

No. 2049 is a French wall clock in the style of Louis the Fourteenth, 1643-1715, and has characteristic straight lines and the "Boulle work" which is described in note 3 in section 193. The "Boulle work", consisting of tortoise shell inlaid with brass, is seen on the front, and, through the glass, on the back. The numerals on the dial, as in No. 1955, are on enamel on separate copper plates. This clock is a reproduction and is shown here to illustrate the important style of about 1700.

No. 2050 is said to be in the style of the Regency, during the minority of Louis the Fifteenth, 1715-1723. Here the taste of the times is shown in the fantastic and overloaded decorations of cupids, leaves, flowers and scrolls with

8.   In Mrs. N. Hudson Moore's "Old Clocks and Watches", page 104, the authoress mentions that she had written forty-two letters trying to find a "wag-on-the-wall" clock made in America, and "when I add that they were made in quantities till about 1830, you can imagine my chagrin when I could not find one". Fortunately, when her book was almost completed, her industry resulted in a happy discovery. Her illustration of the clock shows a painted arch dial, with subsidiary dials for the seconds and the days of the month; all the parts were of wood, and the pendulum was thirty-eight inches long— a clock, one would suppose, too good for wilful exposure to the dust.

In "Time and Timekeepers", by Prof. Willis I. Milham, page 345, it is said that in America "some hang-up clocks or wag-on-the walls were also made. These looked like the works of a grandfather clock without the case. In fact many of them were simply that. It was often the custom to purchase the works from some clockmaker in a city and then to have a local cabinet maker construct the case. After the works were purchased they were often hung on the wall without having the case made and thus became wag-on-the-walls".

The writer has a wooden works and dial almost precisely the same as that shown by Mrs. Moore, and therefore qualified to pass as a rare wag-on-the-wall; but unfortunately it is now in a grandfather clock case and is thereby reduced to a less unusual class of timekeepers!

1.   This type of clock is known in France as a "cartel clock". The cases were sometimes made of wood, but more often of gilded bronze which at first was extremely brilliant, but later became more agreeable to the eye. They were made during the period of Louis the Fourteenth and his successors until about 1800. In clocks of this type the works and dial are usually inserted from the front.

The dates and characteristics of the principal French periods are briefly stated in section 193, note 2.

2049 (Upper) Anonymous.
2052 (Centre) Metropoli-
    tan Museum of Art.
2055 (Lower) Mr. J. G.
    D'A. Paul.

2050 (Upper) Wallace
    Collection, London.
2053 (Centre) Anony-
    mous.
2056 (Lower) Ces. & Web.,
    Fig. 400.

2051 (Upper) Museum of
    Fine Arts, Boston.
2054 (Centre) Anony-
    mous.
2057 (Lower) Anony-
    mous.

2058 (UPPER) ANONYMOUS.   2059 (UPPER) MR. EDGAR G. MILLER,   2060 (UPPER) ANONYMOUS.
                                                        JR.

2061 (LOWER) ANONYMOUS.   2062 (LOWER) ANONYMOUS.   2063 (LOWER) MR. E.   2064 (LOWER) MR. E.
                                                              G. MILLER, JR.   G. MILLER, JR.

gilded rocks at the bottom. The dial is enameled and the hour numerals are painted. This clock is in the "Wallace Collection" in London.[2] About 1720.

No. 2051, in the style of Louis the Fifteenth, 1723-1774, is also somewhat fanciful in its decorations, but is more restrained in its treatment. The "flowing curves of Louis the Fifteenth" are graceful and not too crowded. A Chinese figure at the top recalls the "Chinese style" of Chippendale. This clock appears here through the courtesy of the Museum of Fine Arts, Boston. About 1770.

No. 2052 is another wall clock in the style of Louis the Fifteenth. Here there is an abundance of branches, leaves and flowers, together with several "C curves" such as are seen on the Chippendale style mirror No. 1105 and others. On the top a young man is playing a flute and the seated damsel is apparently enjoying the music. On the dial are the words "Barat a Paris". About 1770.

No. 2053 is a reproduction of a French wall clock in the style of Louis the Sixteenth, as is shown by the dial with festoons of flowers, the cornucopias with fruits and by the shape and decoration of the clock as a whole. The pendulum weight is seen through the glass. Style about 1790.

The next three clocks, Nos. 2054-2056, are English. No. 2054 has a silvered dial, ten inches in diameter, on which are the words "Robt. Philpe, London". In the curved opening above the centre, not well seen in the engraving, a disk moves with the swing of the pendulum. Around the clock are carved wood branches with leaves and flowers. Two "C curves", suggesting the Chippendale style, are on the upper sides. About 1780-1790.

No. 2055 is a larger wall clock, with decorations in carved wood, similar in style to the preceding clock. Here also are two large "C curves", in this instance on the lower sides. On the top is a large eagle with outspread wings of the type seen on the girandole mirror No. 1239 and others. On the dial are the words "Thomas Wagstaffe, London"; other clocks by this maker are the grandfather clocks Nos. 1773 and 1776, and the mantel clock No. 1892. About 1770-1790.

No. 2056 is an "Act of Parliament" clock, a name sometimes erroneously applied to clocks of somewhat similar design but of much smaller size. Two theories as to the origin of the name are mentioned in the note.[3] This clock is

2. This engraving is copied from the book "The Wallace Collection" by Mr. A. L. Baldry, page 200.

The terms "rococo", "rocaille" and "baroque" are applied to this style of decoration, the latter term being given to the most extreme development of mixed and meaningless features. This style was popular in England during the Chippendale period and may be seen in the mirrors Nos. 1104-1106 in section 142.

Gilded rocks as ornaments are also seen on the girandole mirrors Nos. 1239 and 1245.

3. In "A Glossary of English Furniture" by Penderel-Brodhurst and Layton, published in America by Robert M. McBride & Co., New York, 1925, it is said in substance, on pages 1-2, that the origin of the name has never been satisfactorily settled. "It has been suggested that inn-keepers adopted this style of clock for the convenience of their customers when an Act (of Parliament) of 1797 imposed a duty of five shillings per annum upon every timepiece, in spite of the fact that clocks of this type were made long before that date." Another suggestion is that all inns were required by law to keep a clock in a public room, but there is no record of such requirement.

fifty-five inches high and the dial is twenty-four inches in diameter, which is about the average size of these clocks. The case is black and is lacquered with Chinese designs. There is no glass over the dial. The words on the dial are "Mattw. Hill, Devonshire Street". This illustration is copied from "English Domestic Clocks", by Cescinsky and Webster, figure 400. About 1790.

In No. 2057 all of the front surrounding the dial is of silvered metal hammered in designs of scrolls and flowers. The pendulum is in front of the dial as in the next clock, and in the Terry style mantel clock No. 1930. Very few clocks were made with the pendulum in this position, probably for the reason that it is much more liable to disturbance than when suspended inside the case. This clock is said to be of early French origin. The date is uncertain.

The next two clocks, Nos. 2058 and 2059, are regarded as Italian. No. 2058 has an iron door on each side, and an iron top, enclosing the works, indicating that it was probably not intended to be put in a case. The front is made of a soft metal and is stamped with various designs, including numerous "C scrolls". Above the centre of the crudely repainted dial is a figure of an ecclesiastic and a child. The pendulum is in front, as in the preceding clock. Behind the arch top are two bells upon which the hours and quarters are struck. Three weights furnish the power. The height is about fourteen inches. The date is probably in the middle of the eighteenth century.

In No. 2059 the upper part represents a stage with the curtains drawn to the sides. On this stage are five monks who strike the five bells, the upper monk striking the hours and the lower ones the quarters. As was the custom in parts of Italy in the latter half of the eighteenth century, the hours are struck from one to six o'clock and at seven o'clock they again strike one to six, dividing the twenty-four hours into four groups of six each. The dial has been repainted. There are three weights as in the preceding piece. The height is about twenty-two inches. This clock resembles some of the old clocks in Venice. Probably about the latter part of the eighteenth century.

The next three clocks, Nos. 2060-2062, were made in Holland, and represent types which are distinctively Dutch. Both the time and the striking parts are driven by one weight. Clocks of this type have been made over a long period of time and it is not possible to name a date with certainty.

No. 2060 is known as a "Zaandam clock" because it is in the style of clocks made in that town in Holland. The clock is attached to a wooden frame which has an opening in the lower part through which the pendulum is seen. A figure of Justice with a sword and a scale is at the top, below which is a large and loud bell for the hours and a smaller one with softer tones for the quarters. On the front and sides of the top are metal designs. Spiral columns are on the sides of

(Note 3, *continued*)

The term "Act of Parliament" has been wrongly applied to the somewhat similar "regulator" clock No. 2045, and to certain English clocks of small size. It is said that in the southern counties of England these large clocks are even now found in inns.

the square dial, as in the hooded clock No. 1748. The dial has a black cloth as a background. Spandrels with cherub heads, as in English clocks, are on the corners of the dial, and an alarm attachment is in the centre. The height is about thirty-one inches. Clocks of this type are still in common use in Holland and the date is therefore uncertain, but was probably in the latter part of the eighteenth century.

No. 2061 is a "Friesland" clock, so called from the name of the northern section of Holland in which it was made. A large design in soft metal is at the top and under it is a heraldic design with two lions, recalling one on the English lantern clock No. 1746. On each side is a faded painted figure supposed to represent a mermaid. In the centre of the repainted square dial is a country scene. The minute hand is missing. The round light-colored object in the centre is an alarm dial. The height is about twenty-nine inches. The date is probably about the latter part of the eighteenth century, as is the preceding clock.

No. 2062 seems to be generally known simply as a "Dutch wall clock". The upper portion slides off to the front and is in the form of the hood of a grandfather clock. The weight is in front of the long board which extends from the hood to the bottom and slides down when the small projecting pin on the right is removed; behind the board is the long pendulum, whose weight is seen through the oval opening, and in the rear is the back board. The centre and the arch of the painted dial are decorated. The height is about four feet. As with the two preceding clocks the date is uncertain, but is probably in the same period.

Nos. 2063 and 2064 are two views of an interesting Japanese clock, the escapement of which is shown in No. 1741 in section 182. In No. 2063 we see the complete clock, and in No. 2064 the hood and the long vertical dial in front are removed. A not-too-clear description is in the note.[4]

Section 197. Other types of clocks.—In this section are illustrations of thirty-five American and foreign clocks, many of which cannot be classified as being in any of the styles shown in the preceding sections and are shown together here without regard to nationality, style or date. Many other interesting clocks

4.   The hood is a rectangular box which slides off from the front. The time mechanism is within the hood and its front is ornamented with delicately carved brasswork. Attached to the time mechanism is a cord which extends downwards and holds the striking mechanism which serves as a weight to drive the time mechanism, as is shown in No. 2064. On this striking mechanism, to the left, is a pointer which descends with the weight, through a slit, and points to the horizontal brass pieces which represent the hours and half hours according to the complicated Japanese system of time. By a little device, not easily explained, the bell strikes as it passes these horizontal pieces. A keyhole is under the hood and when the clock is wound the combined striking mechanism and weight are drawn up. The height is about twenty inches. This type of clock is of special interest to those familiar with technical details. Illustrations and explanations are in Dr. D. W. Hering's "The Lure of the Clock", pages 65-68, mentioned also in the note to No. 2006.

        Other clocks in which their own weight is the motive power are: No. 2048, by Philander J. Willard; No. 2084, a falling ball clock; No. 2089, an inclined plane clock; No. 2098, a modern English clock.

        Another interesting Japanese clock is No. 2083, also shown in No. 1738.

could be illustrated if space permitted.[1] One example of each kind is generally sufficient to illustrate the type. Several are reproductions or clearly modern pieces; and some are mere curiosities.

We begin with three American clocks of plain character, which have been given fanciful names by some writers. These clocks cannot be regarded as grandmother clocks, such as those in section 188, for the reason that they are not in the form of those clocks; nor are they in the form of mantel clocks of the Willard type shown in section 190. Clocks of this kind have a certain interest as quaint examples of efforts of our clock makers to produce inexpensive clocks of an unusual character.

No. 2065 is about forty-five inches high and eleven inches wide. The kidney-shaped opening in front of the dial, which rests upon a support, is in a form somewhat similar to that in the Aaron Willard mantel clock No. 1918. The lower part of the case, long and ill-proportioned, is ornamented with two inlaid ovals and with inlaid lines as a border. The feet are of the bracket type. About 1800-1820.

No. 2066 is a plainer example of the same type, bearing the words "Joshua Wilder, Hingham", painted on the dial; two grandmother clocks by Wilder are Nos. 1869 and 1870. The height is about thirty-two inches. The case is made of pine, without ornamentation. Near the bottom is an oval opening through which the pendulum weight may be seen. About 1800-1820.

In No. 2067 are works which are engraved with the words "A. Willard, Boston". The front of the case is all in one piece and is as plain as it was possible to make it. At the top is a brass urn with an eagle on a reeded support, and also two curved pieces on the sides. Perhaps the case was an inexpensive substitute for one of the grandmother type shown in section 188, into which the Aaron Willard works of another clock were fitted and on which the top ornaments were placed. About 1800-1820.

No. 2068 is commonly called an "acorn" clock because the upper portion, enclosing the dial, somewhat resembles an acorn in shape. The side-arms and the front edges of the frame-work are not single pieces of wood bent into a form to fit the clock, but consist of several thin layers of different woods glued together,

---

1. Especially the elaborate and often intricate German and French clocks of about the sixteenth century, frequently architectural in design. Some of these may be seen in several books, particularly in Britten's "Old Clocks and Watches", Nos. 82-123; also in Mr. Wallace Nutting's "Clock Book", Nos. 220-225 and others, and his "Furniture Treasury", Nos. 3532-3535, 3545-3548.

Two examples of the style of these early clocks are the French table clock No. 2073 and the German "falling ball clock" No. 2084.

Certain clocks of uncertain age but of some little interest as curiosities are omitted as not being of the representative character desired. An example is a framed painting of a town with a church steeple or a high tower in which there is a clock; the painting has no artistic value and the clock is of no interest. A clock of this kind is illustrated in "Antiques", May, 1930, page 468.

The writer is unable to ascertain definitely the origin or date of several of the clocks here shown, and will be pleased to receive information in regard to them; among these are Nos. 2074, 2077, 2078 and 2079.

a method which tends to prevent warping. The height is twenty-four inches. The name and address on the dial is "Forestville Mfg. Co. Bristol, Ct. U. S. A." About 1825-1835.

No. 2069, known as an "Eddystone Lighthouse" clock and said to be modeled upon the English lighthouse of that name, was an invention of Simon Willard. Because of mechanical difficulties, clocks of this kind were not successful, and very few were made. They were all apparently of the same general design, although the base portion, here eight-sided, was made in several different forms. In this clock the brass frame around the dial—called the "bezel"—is decorated with grapes and leaves, and over the dial is the bell. The works are protected by a glass case. Because of their rarity, and the fact that they were made by Simon Willard, these clocks are valuable, although they are neither good timepieces nor of artistic appearance.[2] About 1800-1824.

Nos. 2070, 2071 and 2072 are interesting because of their unusual character, not because of any value as antiques. No. 2070 is a cheap late American piece on a china stand, and is protected by a glass cover. It is a lively little piece, ingeniously contrived, but not a fine timekeeper. Instead of a hanging pendulum there is a hairspring, and three weights at the ends of bars, somewhat in the style of the movement of the Japanese clock No. 1741 in section 182. The winding keyhole is at the back. The height to the top of the glass is about ten inches. On the back plate are the words "Terryville Manufacturing Company, Terryville, Conn. Patented October 5, 1852". About 1852-1860.

No. 2071 is a French marble clock with a brass cupid at the top, holding, at the end of a thread, a brass ball; the thread and the ball act as a pendulum and move in circles when the small horizontal wire below is made to revolve by a revolving vertical rod which is connected with the wheels of the clock. The ball pendulum controls the speed of the wheels of this clock in somewhat the same manner as the usual form of pendulum controls the speed of the wheels of other clocks, as explained in section 182, note 8. The mechanism is better seen in the next illustration. About 1840.

2. In the book entitled "Simon Willard and his Clocks", by Mr. John Ware Willard, it is said, page 52, that "These clocks are mentioned simply to show how inventors incline to complicated machinery".

Four of these clocks, differing mainly in the portions under the dial, are illustrated in Mr. Lockwood's "Colonial Furniture", third edition, 1926, pages 342-343. On two of these are the words "Simon Willard & Son Patent", which indicate for those two clocks a later date than that of the others, as the partnership was from 1824 to 1826, as mentioned in section 187, note 21, D.

This clock is an example of an antique article which is "rare", but not because it was especially difficult to make or very elegant or expensive. These lighthouse clocks are indeed "rare", as only a few were made; but the reason that only a few were made is that there was not much demand for them because they were not good timekeepers; and certainly the lighthouse is not a work of artistic elegance. In the opinion of the writer, this kind of "rarity" adds little to the value of a clock, even if the maker is famous. Even certain bad furniture of our Duncan Phyfe is not in demand. See the remarks in the note to No. 2086, and in section 209 in the Appendix, entitled "Auction sales and prices".

A modern German "lighthouse" clock, with nine dials, is No. 2082 in this section.

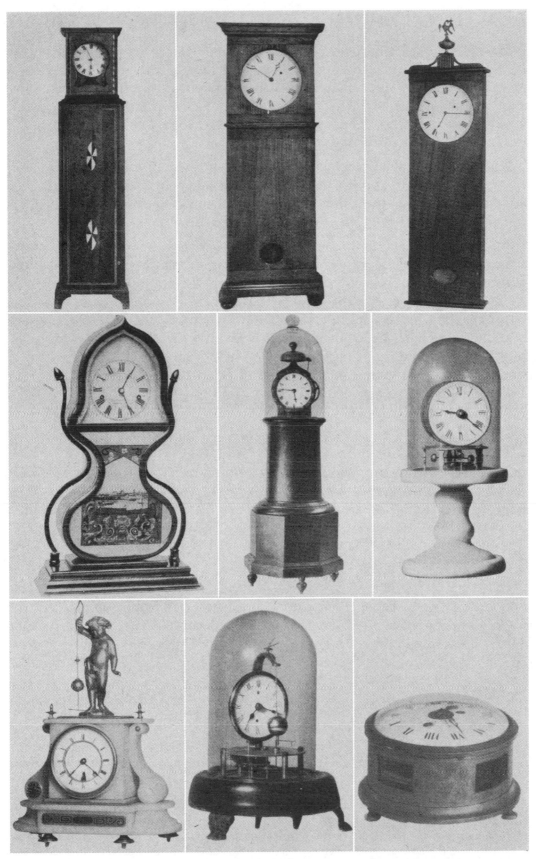

2065 (Upper) Metropolitan Mu-
     seum of Art.
2068 (Centre) Anonymous.
2071 (Lower) Mr. Fred. Fuchs.

2066 (Upper) Anonymous.
2069 (Centre) Metropolitan
     Museum of Art.
2072 (Lower) Anonymous.

2067 (Upper) Anonymous.
2070 (Centre) Anonymous.
2073 (Lower) Mr. E. G. Miller,
     Jr.

No. 2072 is an American clock. It has the same kind of pendulum as the preceding piece. The revolving wire may be seen at the right, under the ball. Under the bottom of the wooden base, which stands on three metal feet, is an attachment in the nature of a wheel, by which the clock is wound instead of by a key. The height is six inches. There is no name. This clock was probably made about the same time as No. 2070, about 1850-1860.

No. 2073 is the old French round table clock referred to in note 1 above. The term "table" clock is appropriate because the horizontal dial can only be seen from above and hence the clock was placed on a table, not on a mantel or shelf.[3] Probably about 1650-1700, if not a modern reproduction.

In No. 2074 the parchment dial is not opaque and when the candlestick attachment behind it is supplied with a lighted candle the hour and minute hands may be well seen in the dark; from which we may infer that the clock was made as a night-clock. On the dial the letters of the favorite words on clocks—"Tempus fugit"—serve as eleven of the hour numerals. The sixteen arches around the dial, the shape of the hands and the spears, and the other ornamental features suggest a German origin. The movement is new. Only a guess can be made as to the date, but the frame may be in designs of about 1850.

No. 2075 is an interesting modern English "revolving globe" clock, representing the earth and showing the time at any point on its surface. The mechanism is within the globe and runs one week. The clock is wound up by a forked key which is put into two holes at the South Pole. Instead of a dial there is a revolving circular brass band having two sets of hour numerals from 1 to 12, in the manner of the three French "revolving band" mantel clocks Nos. 1970-1972. The stationary pointer points to the correct time shown on the revolving band, here 11.30 A. M., and indicates the various places on the surface of the earth where that is the correct time. The globe and the revolving band revolve together and make one complete revolution every twenty-four hours. The time at any place may be found by a simple calculation.

No. 2076 is a German clock with four alabaster[4] columns on a black wooden base. These columns support the top, which is decorated with designs in mother-of-pearl. One of the winding keyholes is for the timekeeping, one for the hour strike and the other for the quarter-hour strike. This clock runs for about thirty

---

3. There are three winding holes, one for the alarm, one for the time and the third for the strike. The case is brass and the dial is porcelain. The works are seen through four rectangular glass panels, between which are chased designs of vases and flowers. On the bottom is a brass door which opens downward on a hinge, and in the door is an opening through which a bell projected. In Britten's "Old Clocks and Watches" a similar table clock is shown, figure 102, the date of which is given merely as the seventeenth century. Other somewhat similar table clocks are shown in Mr. Nutting's books mentioned in note 1 above.

4. Alabaster is a soft marble-like mineral which can easily be cut into forms as desired, ranging from large pieces for the walls of churches and houses to small pieces for vases, figures, clock cases and columns and other small objects. By a certain treatment it may be made to resemble marble very closely. The alabaster of the ancients was much harder than that used in modern times. The ancient kind is mentioned in the Bible in several places.

2074 (Upper) Anonymous.   2075 (Upper) Anonymous.   2076 (Upper) Anonymous.
2077 (Centre) Anonymous.   2078 (Centre) Anonymous.   2079 (Centre) Mr. E. G. Mil-
2080 (Lower) Anonymous.   2081 (Lower) Anonymous.   ler, Jr.
                                                           2082 (Lower) Mr. Edgar G.
                                                              Miller, Jr.

1018 AMERICAN ANTIQUE FURNITURE SECTION 197

hours. The date is not definitely known; but is probably about the same as the date of the somewhat similar French pillar clocks Nos. 1998-2001, that is, about 1820-1840.

No. 2077 has very elaborate cabinet work. Without mentioning too many details[5] it may be said that every part resembling inlay is in fact inlay. The dial resembles that of a watch, but the movement is that of a very small clock and has a pendulum. The maker and date are not known, but the style of ornamentation indicates that the date is probably about 1800-1810.

No. 2078 is probably of German origin, having two carved wooden figures which apparently represent characters in one of Wagner's operas. The dial, over which a large wreath falls, is placed in a wooden structure somewhat similar to a tower, with an opening through which the pendulum is seen. At the top, and on the base behind the figures, are wooden ornaments. The date is not known.

In No. 2079 the hands of the female figure point to the hour and minute numerals on the curved pieces on each side. The numerals on the left, from 1 to 12, indicate the hours, and the numerals on the right, from 5 to 60, indicate the minutes.[6] This clock is probably a German one. There is no name on any part and the date is not known, but judging from the base and the style of decoration it may be about 1820.

Nos. 2080 and 2081 show the front and back respectively of a German "table" clock, which has two dials on the front and one on the back, all of which could not be seen if the clock were placed against a wall or on a mantel.[7] Neither a name nor a date appears on this clock, but its decorative style may be of a period in or following the Empire style, about 1820-1840, although, being of German make, it may be of another period.

5. On a white bone plate over the dial are the Latin words "Tempus edax rerum" which may be freely translated as "Time the consumer of all things". Over these words is a small molding with arches and acorns similar to those on the grandfather clock No. 1778. The top is ornamented with a dome resting upon small white bone columns; carved ornaments are at the corners and four designs in mother-of-pearl will be noticed below. The sides and back are also fully ornamented, with brass figures on the sides.

6. In one hour the mechanism raises the hour arm on the left from one hour numeral to the next. In the same time the minute arm on the right is raised from the bottom to the top, that is, to 60, whereupon it falls back. At 12 o'clock, when the hour arm reaches 12 and the minute hand reaches 60, both arms drop to the bottom and begin again their journey upward. This clock runs for a week and is wound from the rear of the base. The base is of dark marble, the frame around the figure is brass and the background behind the figure is blue enamel inlaid with brass designs. On the arch at the top are eight brass ornaments resembling "anthemions", a design so often seen as a decorative feature, as on the French mantel clock No. 1964 and others, and the mirror No. 1149; see the Index. On the base is a brass design not well seen on the marble background.

7. Below the large dial on the front, with Arabic numerals, is a smaller dial with three pointers of unequal lengths; the longer one indicates the days of the month on the outer circle; the next in length points to the days of the week, in German words, on the centre circle; the short one points to the month, in the inner circle. On the rear is a larger dial, with Roman numerals, whose hands move with the hands of the front dial. The case is black and on the front is ornamented with applied gilt designs in wood, including those of butterflies, torches and swans. On the top is a gilded sleeping cupid and on the sides are other gilded forms.

No. 2082 is an ingenious modern German clock which shows the time at various places around the world. It is made in a lighthouse design, and has a main dial below and eight small revolving dials above. On each small dial is the name of a country or city, and the hands, when adjusted, show the time at those places when it is, for example, twelve o'clock, noon, in Baltimore. A vertical rod inside the lighthouse connects with the mechanism of the main dial and extends up to the top where it causes the small dials to revolve as one group. Each of these small dials moves separately and freely on a centre pin and has in the rear at the bottom a small weight which keeps the dial in a vertical position.[8]

No. 2083 is a Japanese clock which was also shown in No. 1738 in connection with the "foliot" balance which was used in early timepieces as a means of regulating the speed of a clock, before the pendulum was invented. The two crossbars are so adjusted that one runs for a certain number of hours when it stops and the other one begins and continues for the same period.[9]

No. 2084 is a German "falling ball" timekeeper, about three and one-half inches in diameter, and is one of the objects referred to in note 1 in this section. The sphere consists of an upper and lower part with a revolving band in the centre marked with Roman hour numerals, and may be suspended from a bracket or from the ceiling by a cord.[10] The date is said to be about 1650.

8. The uppermost small dial is marked "Baltimore" and the others are marked with the names of seven other places which might be visited in a cruise around the world, going east from Baltimore to Europe, to Asia, across the Pacific Ocean to Honolulu and then to California. The times at these places as shown on the small dials are as follows when it is twelve o'clock noon in Baltimore:

1. Baltimore, 12 o'clock, noon, Monday.	2. London, 5 P. M. Monday.
3. Cairo, Egypt, 7 P. M. Monday.	4. Bombay, India, 10.30 P. M. Monday.
5. Hongkong, China, 1 A. M. Tuesday.	6. Japan, 2 A. M. Tuesday.
7. Honolulu, 6 A. M. Monday.	8. California, 9 A. M. Monday.

The change from Monday to Tuesday at Hongkong and then back to Monday at Honolulu will be noticed.

The traveler across the Pacific Ocean is mystified by this change of date upon crossing the imaginary north and south line known as the "International Date Line", where by international agreement the date is set back or set ahead twenty-four hours. If the Line is crossed going from the United States to Japan, Monday noon becomes Tuesday noon; and if crossed going from Japan to the United States, Tuesday noon becomes Monday noon.

The names of any other places may be painted on the small dials as desired and the times at such places will be accurately shown when the simple adjustments are made.

This digression from "Antique clocks" may perhaps be justified by the fact that the subject relates to "time". If our clocks had a twenty-four hour dial the matter would be more easily understood.

9. This clock is placed on a shelf because the two weights require a means of falling, one operating the timekeeping works and the other the striking. Such clocks were often placed upon a stand with openings through which the cords passed. The dial is stationary and has one hand; in some clocks of this kind the dial revolves and the hand is stationary. The hood, or cover, is missing. The length of time which the clock runs depends upon the distance which the weights can fall. The Japanese system of dividing time is too complicated to describe here. It is said that these clocks are reproduced in England and also that they are still made in Japan.

10. The cord is coiled around a "drum" within the sphere, the "drum" connects with other parts of the mechanism, the weight of the clock supplies the power to move the band around and the time is

In No. 2085, also a German clock, the sphere has a revolving band with hour numerals, as in the preceding clock, but the power is obtained by a spring which is wound by a key. The design represents Atlas holding the world, and his hand points to the hour. The sphere is decorated with the signs of the zodiac and with certain constellations, not well seen in the engraving. This clock was probably made in the seventeenth century if it is not a reproduction.

No. 2086 is forty-two inches high, and is peculiar in having the upper portion in the form of a hood and dial of a grandfather clock and the base in a form somewhat resembling that of a base of a highboy, as in No. 662, but without drawers, and with a shell on the "apron" and on the ill-formed cabriole legs terminating in ball and claw feet. Other details and remarks are in the note.[11] About 1770-1800.

No. 2087 is a modern Chinese mantel clock of interesting character. The black wooden base and the front are recognized as being Chinese in style. The sixteen designs in mother-of-pearl on the frame are Chinese emblems, some, it is said, meaning "good health", "happiness" or "best wishes". The movement is a close copy of an English mantel clock, with a "fusee", such as that shown in No. 2005. It is not known whether the works were made in China or England. Other remarks are in the note.[12]

No. 2088 is a well-known French "Mystery clock" in the Franklin Institute, Philadelphia. Here we see a metal base and upon it a clear glass tube; at the top

(Note 10, *continued*)

indicated by the pointer as in the French revolving band clocks referred to in the comment on No. 2075. The clock is wound by lifting it, in which process the cord is again wound around the "drum" with the aid of a spring. This may be compared with the modern English inclined plane clock No. 2089. On the clock are the words "Lorenz Rehfus, Breslau", the latter word being the name of a city in Germany.

This clock, which was sold at auction for $4900., is mentioned in the Appendix, section 209 entitled "Auction sales and prices".

11. This clock is in the Chippendale style, having a scroll top as in the grandfather clocks Nos. 1767, 1811 and others. There are three urns with flames. On the front corners are quarter-columns which in grandfather clocks are on the waist—the central part of the case—not on the hood. The hands are of a later type than those used in the Chippendale period, as appears on the page of hands, No. 1744. The base is a novelty in clock construction; in fact the entire clock may properly be called a "freak", although it has more courteously been termed a "rarity", a term referred to in the note to No. 2069. Perhaps its chief claim to importance is the fact that at the auction sale of the Reifsnyder collection in the "boom" year 1929 it brought the sum of $3600., as to which see the Appendix, section 209, entitled "Auction sales and prices". The name and address on the dial is "Daniel Frost, Reading", probably Massachusetts, about whom no information is at hand. A very similar clock, by an unnamed maker, is No. 3415 in Mr. Wallace Nutting's "Furniture Treasury" and No. 215 in his "Clock Book", in the latter being termed a "shelf" clock.

12. The porcelain dial, with Roman numerals, is similar in design to the English and American dials. The form of the hour and second hand, and the presence of a sweep-second hand, are also noticed. There is no hinged door on the front or back, but the glass frames at the front and back may be lifted out. The dial is set in a brass plate which is fully chased. There are no keyholes in front and the winding is done at the back, requiring the clock to be turned around when being wound, and the winding is to the left. On the back plate there is much chased work, including, in Chinese characters, the name "Wu Hung Ta, Tsao" which a young woman Chinese student at the Johns Hopkins University interprets as the name of the maker, whose address is Nanking, China.

of this tube is a brass bracket supporting a round brass frame enclosing a glass dial; on the dial is an hour hand. A winding hole is in the base, but there is no visible connection between the movement in the base and the hour hand on the dial. The mystery, of course, is—"What makes the hour hand move and keep time?" For fear that the reader may not solve the mystery, the answer is given in the note.[13] About 1780-1785.

No. 2089 is a modern English "inclined plane" clock. The clock is entirely separate from the inclined plane and will work as well on any other smooth surface having the proper inclination, which is found by experiment. The motive power is derived from the tendency of the clock to roll down the plane rapidly, but a too rapid motion is prevented by an escapement somewhat similar to that in a watch and also by a weight inside which is so connected with the wheels that when they are working they are burdened with lifting the weight. This clock is based upon the principle of a clock made about 1660 which is illustrated and described in Britten's "Old Clocks and Watches", pages 465-467.

No. 2090 is another mystery clock, whose working is based upon the principle of the "inclined plane" clock. The ring is divided into hour and five minute spaces. The large disk contains the spring and wheels and a weight; the small disk is merely to balance the larger one. The pointer, or hand, revolves once in twelve hours.[14]

No. 2091 is an iron clock, about sixteen inches high, which indicates the time in the usual manner but in an unusual place. This comical timekeeper may have been a prized possession in a village tavern, but it does not equal a Mid-Victorian clock shown in an "Exhibition of Bad Taste" held in New York some years ago in which a statue of the Venus de Milo was supplied with a clock in her abdomen.[15] This little-man clock was made by a Connecticut firm about 1860.

13. The clear glass tube appears to be one tube, but within it there is a smaller clear glass tube which is not visible to the eye. This inner tube is connected with a mechanism in the base which causes it to revolve within the outer tube. The dial appears to be one piece of clear glass, but in reality there are two glasses, one in front of the other. The hour numerals are on the front glass, which remains stationary; but the rear glass, to which the hand is attached through the front glass, is made to revolve, having on its edge cogs which are hidden in the round brass frame; these cogs connect with a mechanism which is within the brass frame and is moved by the revolution of the inner tube. This description is not very clear, leaving some details to the imagination. It is said that this clock was presented to Benjamin Franklin while he was in France as American Ambassador, 1776-1785.

14. This illustration is copied from Britten's "Old Clocks and Watches", pages 467-468, where it is said that "this device has been several times re-invented, but never, I think, in so elegant a form as the original" which was invented by one John Schmidt, a Danish watchmaker, who secured a patent in England in 1808. A similar clock is No. 3563 in Mr. Wallace Nutting's "Furniture Treasury", and No. 130 in his "Clock Book".

15. A "drawing room" clock illustrated in "Antiques", January, 1934, page 20, No. 10, should be mentioned. On the back of a prancing mule, whose hind feet are encased in boots, a rider with a mule's head carries on his shoulder a clock dial with one hand pointing to the minutes; the hour hand is formed by the extremity of the mule's long tail which is curved upward and forward to the dial. The article is entitled "Foolish furniture in contemporary caricature" and is based upon one published in a magazine in London in 1807.

2083 (UPPER) MR. E. G. MILLER,   2084 (UPPER) ANONYMOUS.   2085 (UPPER) ANONYMOUS.
      JR.   2087 (CENTRE) ANONYMOUS.   2088 (CENTRE) BENJ. FRANKLIN
2086 (CENTRE) ANONYMOUS.   INSTITUTE, PHILADELPHIA.
          2089 (LOWER) ANONYMOUS.   2090 (LOWER) ANONYMOUS.

2091 (Upper) Anonymous.
2094 (Centre) Planchon's Book.
2097 (Lower) Mrs. M. P. Smith.

2092 (Upper) Wallace Collection, London.
2095 (Centre) Anonymous.
2098 (Lower) Anonymous.

2093 (Upper) Anonymous.
2096 (Centre) Anonymous.
2099 (Lower) Cescinsky & Webster, Fig. 348.

No. 2092 is a very small illustration of a finely ornamented mantel clock in gilt bronze in the style of Louis XVI made by the French maker Lepaute, who died in 1780. This clock is in the Wallace Collection, in London, and the illustration is copied from a book entitled "The Wallace Collection" by Mr. A. L. Baldry, page 212. Every part of the detail of the case is of elegant character, especially the work on the base. This illustration should have appeared with other French mantel clocks in section 193. The sphinx is also seen as an ornament on the French mantel clocks Nos. 1974, 1981 and others. About 1780-1789.

No. 2093 is a large English lancet clock, similar in form to No. 1903, but more handsome in appearance. The brass openwork above and below, and the brass columns at the sides, will be noticed. This clock is twenty-three inches high, and has quarter-hour chimes on eight bells. It bears the name "John Bowen, London". This clock was received too late to secure its proper place. About 1820.

No. 2094 is an amusing cartoon copied from a book entitled "L'Horloge, son histoire retrospective pittoresque et artistique", figure 105, by Mathieu Planchon, a well-known clock maker of Paris, published in 1923, and referred to several times in this chapter. The object over the head of the damsel is a dial in a clock frame, and below is a clock bracket or shelf. In the lower part is a dial with one hand. The curves in the lower portion may be compared with those in the mantel clock No. 1960. The trees in the background are grouped in a formal French manner.

No. 2095 is a clock by Lepine, a celebrated French maker who died in 1814. Its style recalls the skeleton clock bearing the name of Simon Willard, shown in No. 2012; and perhaps a similar one suggested to Eli Terry his method of hanging the weights on the side, as in No. 1930. The works are exposed, but were covered by a glass, as were all skeleton clocks, such as No. 2007. The clock is wound from the back. About 1790-1800.

No. 2096 might be taken for an English mantel clock, but the form of the case and the moldings on the lower part indicate that it is Dutch. The dome and the ball above it and the arches on the sides will be noticed. About 1800-1810.

No. 2097 is referred to in the note to No. 1936 which it resembles in some respects. The wooden works are driven by weights on the sides as in the Terry style mantel clock No. 1930 and others. At the top are a stenciled eagle and two carved ornaments. The columns at the sides and the feet are fully carved with leaves and other designs. On a label are the words "Hopkins and Alfred, Harwinton, Conn." It is said that these makers were in business at Harwinton about 1820.

No. 2098 is a modern English clock which may be called a "gravity" clock, the weight of the clock itself furnishing the motive power. It operates on the same principle as No. 2048 and others mentioned in the note to the Japanese clock No. 2063. There is no spring or key. The clock would fall to the bottom at once but for very small notches, which cannot be seen in the engraving, on the right hand upright post under the dial. These notches connect with the mechanism

ROMA - Le ore di Raffaello

Per ogni ora che passa, un ricordo.
Per ogni ora che batte, una felicità.
Per ogni ora che viene, una speranza.

2100 RAPHAEL'S HOURS.

which moves the wheels. The speed is controlled by the pendulum which consists of a swinging bar with a round weight at the top and bottom, like a dumbbell. The beat of this pendulum is one per second. In the illustration the lower weight is seen behind the hour numeral 6, but the upper weight is not clearly visible. When the clock almost reaches the bottom it must be pushed up to the top and then it begins to fall again. This clock is about ten inches in height, runs for about thirty hours and keeps fairly good time.

No. 2099 is an English mantel clock with an oval dial, a form which was not uncommon, but is now seldom seen; an English grandfather clock with an oval dial is No. 1778. It is a striking and musical clock, playing five tunes on twelve bells, one of the tunes being a favorite of the clock makers of the period, the Hundredth Psalm, the first verse of which begins "Make a joyful noise unto the Lord". The small dial with a pointer is for the change of the tunes. This clock resembles Nos. 1900 and 1905 in certain respects. It is copied from Cescinsky and Webster's "English Domestic Clocks", No. 348. The clock is dated 1801.

No. 2100. As the final illustration, closing this chapter on clocks, we present the famous "Hours", often but perhaps erroneously regarded as the work of Raphael, the greatest painter of all time, whose brief life extended only from 1483 to 1520. The twelve figures surrounding the dial represent the "hours", and these constituted the entire original painting, which is known to us only from engravings which have survived. The dial and all the other designs are inventions of a modern Italian artist who was employed to give a setting to the "hours" for reproduction. It is not surely known where the painting was, but it is thought by some that it formed a portion of the decoration of the ceiling of the Salon Borgia in the Vatican. The words, in Italian, under the painting, express a friendly greeting to the reader, wishing him

> "For every hour that passes, a remembrance;
> For every hour that strikes, a happiness;
> For every hour that comes, a hope."

APPENDIX

Section 198. Concerning these sections.—The purpose of this Appendix is to present to the reader a number of brief sections on certain subjects which the writer encountered in preparing this book on American Antique Furniture. In the search of eighteenth century newspapers[1] for advertisements of cabinet makers, chair makers and clock makers, many interesting items were seen, some of which are shown in this Appendix. Several of these subjects, such as "English Hall Marks", have no connection with furniture; others are difficult to locate except in encyclopædias; and perhaps some others ought not to appear in this book; but the writer thinks that the reader will be interested in all of them.

Section 199. Furniture styles of 1840.—"The Cabinet Makers' Assistant" is the title of an illustrated book of furniture designs published by John Hall,[1] of Baltimore, who refers to himself as "Architect and Draftsman".[2] The book was

1. A large number of old advertisements are copied in two books published by the Walpole Society. The first book is entitled "The Arts and Crafts in Philadelphia, Maryland and South Carolina, 1721–1785. Gleanings from newspapers. Collected by Alfred Coxe Prime." The second volume has the same title, except that the dates are 1786–1800. These books are also referred to in the chapter on chairs, in note 5, A in section 45.

1. The name of John Hall appears in the Baltimore City directories from 1835 to 1848 and in these years he is termed "draftsman", and "architect".

2. In this respect the occupation of John Hall resembled that of Robert Adam, who was an architect and also designed, but did not make, the furniture for the fine houses which he planned, as mentioned in section 16. But what a difference in their designs!

Fig. 147

Fig. 188

Fig. 189

Fig. 142

Fig. 158

Fig. 86

Fig. 171

Fig. 151

Fig. 152

Fig. 154

2101. FURNITURE STYLES OF 1840.

2102. FURNITURE STYLES OF 1840.

printed by John Murphy, of Baltimore, and is dated 1840. At least two American books on furniture without illustrations were published before this date;[3] but the book by Hall is thought by librarians to be the first illustrated one published in our country.[4] Unfortunately the year 1840 was in the worst period of the American Empire style, and the illustrations are in the style of that year and show designs which are painful when compared with the fine furniture of previous periods. The book is, however, interesting because it presents illustrations of articles which are still seen in many homes and are often fondly regarded on account of past associations. These pieces and others of their type are commonly called "Colonial" by those who are not familiar with American history.[5]

Perhaps the most conspicuous feature of many of the articles shown in the eighteen drawings copied from Hall's book in the full page illustrations Nos. 2101 and 2102, is the number of heavy and ungainly scrolls, which are seen especially in the feet. These scrolls are particularly referred to in the preface, where "the great variety of scrolls" is mentioned. In some of the pieces, almost the only objectionable features are these large scrolls and the extreme bulk of certain parts whose great size and weight seem to be entirely unnecessary for the use of the pieces; see especially the tables, figures 86, 156, 113 and 112.

It will be noticed that several characteristic features of the earlier Empire style were out of fashion in 1840. The round columns on bureaus, tables, wardrobes and other pieces were not used; nor were the claw or paw or ball feet in fashion. In almost all of the pieces we recognize a similarity in certain other respects to the previous Empire examples, or even to earlier forms; but most of the designs of 1840 were of a debased character. In one respect, however, praise must be given to the furniture of this period, that is, the workmanship and materials were generally good, the mahogany, whether solid or veneer, often being of very fine quality.

It is easy to see how greatly the articles in Hall's book had changed for the worse if we compare them with corresponding articles in the previous styles of Sheraton or the Early Empire. For convenience in making this painful com-

---

3. A "Book of Prices", without illustrations, was published in Philadelphia in 1795 entitled "Philadelphia cabinet and chair makers book of prices". In 1796 a similar book was published in New York.

4. The title page is as follows: "The Cabinet Makers' Assistant, embracing the most modern style of cabinet furniture: exemplified in new designs, practically arranged on forty–four plates containing one hundred and ninety–eight figures: to which is prefixed a short treatise on linear perspective, for the use of practical men. By John Hall, Architect and Draftsman. Baltimore: Printed by John Murphy, 146 Market Street, 1840." The book is about five by nine inches.

In the preface Hall writes: "Novelty, simplicity and practicability, are blended with the present designs, in which originality mostly prevails; a few of those designs have been taken from work previously executed, in consequence of their being highly approved. As far as possible, the style of the United States is blended with European taste, and a graceful outline and simplicity of parts are depicted in all the objects."

The only complete copy of the book thus far known is the property of Mr. R. T. H. Halsey, who kindly lent it to the writer for the purpose of copying the designs here shown.

5. See section 1, note 1, A.

parison, reference is made, for example, to the figure 86 and to the table No. 1655 which is of an earlier style; and other examples are also referred to.[6]

Section 200. Silhouettes with furniture.—In illustrations Nos. 2103–2105 are three silhouettes made by Augustin Edouart, a Frenchman who arrived in our country in 1839 and succeeded in getting a large amount of work.[1] These silhouettes are interesting not only because of the figures and the clothing of the persons who are portrayed but also because of the furniture shown in the rooms. Many of the tables and other articles appearing in these silhouettes are still in use in the homes of descendants of the original owners, and some of the articles are separately illustrated in this book. Each of these three silhouettes is original and is dated by Edouart.

No. 2103, dated 1840, is a profile portrait of seven members of the family of an ancestor of the present owner. A study of the clothing, and especially of the sharp–pointed shoes, is not within the scope of this book, but the furniture may be referred to. The table at the wall on the right is apparently the table which appears as No. 1651 in section 174; the white marble clock with a glass cover is about the same as No. 1998 in section 193; and the chair upon which the lady with the cap is sitting is much like No. 316 in the chapter on chairs. The late Empire style is seen in the heavy columns and the cross–piece of the mantel.

6. Figure 147, an arm chair. The lines of the back resemble somewhat those of the chairs in the Directory style; see section 56. The round front legs and also those in figure 151 resemble somewhat those in the Sheraton style chairs Nos. 330 and 332. Large "C" scrolls support the arms. This is at least a chair in which one might be comfortable.

    Figure 188, a piano stool, is a later form of No. 1715.
    Figure 142, a footstool, may be compared with No. 1711.
    Figure 158, also a footstool, may be compared with No. 1706.
    Figure 86, a table; compare with No. 1653.
    Figure 171, a bureau, may be compared with No. 774.
    Figure 152, a sewing table, may be compared with No. 1579.
    Figure 154, also a sewing table, may be compared with No. 1586.
    Figure 144, a sofa, follows some of the lines of No. 584.
    Figure 156, a square top table, may be compared with No. 1646.
    Figure 174 is a massive wardrobe; compare with No. 1723.
    Figure 173 is a bureau with a glass; the lower portion is the same as in figure 171; compare with No. 764.

1. The subject of silhouettes of American profiles is interestingly considered and illustrated in the book entitled "The Shades of Our Ancestors", by the late Alice Van Lear Carrick, published in 1928. In her book the work and career of Edouart is treated in chapter 11, pages 138–149.

    "Silhouette", meaning a profile portrait in black, was the name of "a French minister of finance in 1759, whose rigid public economy caused his name to be applied to things cheap", referring to the cheapness of a silhouette in comparison with the cost of a portrait. The word applies to "any opaque portrait, design or image in profile"; Century Dictionary.

    An article entitled "Silhouette Technique", by Mrs. F. Neville Jackson, is in "Antiques", May, 1927, page 375.

    Unfortunately the available space is not sufficient to show fully the window frames, the slat shades and the festooned hangings.

    White silhouettes in the dark backgrounds of chair backs are referred to in section 50, note 6, paragraph 3.

No. 2104, dated 1841, shows the members of the family of the present owner's ancestor, with three of the children. The old lady, holding her spectacles, is sitting upon a rocking chair without arms. Above the table is a large mirror on the wall between two windows.

In No. 2105, dated 1843, the little girl is "jumping rope" in the parlor, while the larger one is beating time for her, with a music score in one hand. Here the chair with its curved legs is similar to those seen in the two preceding illustrations. The piano with its massive reeded legs is in the late Empire style. This silhouette, as the others, is owned by a descendant of the family. Once again we must call attention to the sharp–pointed shoes—and be thankful!

Section 201. Barometers.—In the homes of our forefathers in the eighteenth century and the early nineteenth, before the newspapers furnished daily forecasts of the weather, mercury barometers[1] were important instruments in the household and were especially useful to farmers and other persons living in the country; but nowadays they are used chiefly as ornamental articles. Few of the present–day owners regard a barometer as a forecaster of the weather and probably even less than a few understand the principles, not at all technical, upon which a barometer operates and which are referred to in the comments and notes below. The general form of all the barometers shown here, except the last two, is about the same,

1. The word "barometer" is derived from two Greek words, "baros", meaning "pressure", and "metron", meaning "measure", the combined words meaning "measure of the pressure" of the atmosphere. We recall that the air has weight, and presses upon the earth, and that its weight and pressure at any point at sea level is greater than at a higher point, as on a mountain near by.

The barometers here shown are "mercury barometers", in which mercury in a long tube rises and falls with changes in the atmospheric pressure. An "aneroid", (meaning "without fluid"), barometer works on a different principle which need not be described here. The aneroid barometer, being less liable to breakage, movable without danger, and only a few inches in diameter, is more satisfactory for general use. It is said that barometers should be kept inside the house, rather than on the outside where the temperature may be more variable.

Most of the barometers here shown are of English make. Some of them bear the names of Italians who worked in England or Scotland. The frames are all of mahogany, except the last two. Reproductions of several barometers such as those shown here are made by the Taylor Instrument Companies, Rochester, New York.

Fine barometers are decorative and interesting in the household, but they vary considerably in their attractiveness. Some are not well–proportioned, especially if the dial is too large.

In purchasing a barometer the condition of the operating part should be carefully examined, as only a few persons, even in the large cities, are sufficiently familiar with the subject to put a damaged barometer in good order. Mechanics working with clocks and watches are sometimes able to make restorations and repairs, and factories making ships' barometers or optical instruments may do so. Although a barometer is used chiefly for its decorative effect, it is not desirable to get an instrument which will not work.

The eleven engravings of barometers are not numbered separately in illustration No. 2106, but are easily distinguished by the descriptive comments. The names of the owners are mentioned in a group, as are the names of the owners of the twenty–two boxes and tea–caddies shown in the next section. The owners of the barometers are Messrs. William M. Ellicott, Lennox Birckhead, James Carey, Jr., Henry Lay Duer and the writer.

2103 (Upper) Miss Helen H. Carey.   2104 (Centre) Mr. James Dixon.
2105 (Lower) Mr. George Ward.

differing chiefly in the decorations and in certain details. Almost all of these barometers are regarded as being in the style of Sheraton and are dated from about 1795 to 1820.

On the dials[2] of the barometers here shown, except the last two, are the figures 28 at the bottom on the left and the figure 31 at the bottom on the right with the figures 29 and 30 between. These figures indicate the height of the mercury column in inches, the rise and fall of the column in atmospheric changes being the controlling feature of the barometer. Around the dial, beginning at 31 and counting upwards are the words "Very Dry", etc., ending at 28 at the word "Stormy". As these words are descriptive of kinds of weather it is natural to suppose that when the hand points to the word "Fair", for example, "fair" weather is indicated. But the mercury in the barometer has no connection with these words. It is only the rise or fall of the mercury, caused by a change in the pressure of the atmosphere, which indicates a coming change in the weather, a *rise* of the mercury generally indicating the coming of fair weather and a *fall* of the mercury generally indicating the coming of rain or stormy weather. Thus if the hand points to figure 31, "Very Dry", and moves quickly to "30, Fair", the *fall* of the mercury from 31 to 30 inches in height would probably indicate a coming rain or storm instead of fair weather; or if the hand points to "28, Stormy" and rises to "29, Rain", the *rise* of the mercury probably means that there will be fair weather, instead of rain. Moreover, if a barometer at sea level stands at "30, Fair", and is taken up about nine hundred feet above sea level, the hand will at once fall to "29, Rain", for the reason that the elevation of about nine hundred feet causes a reduction of air pressure on the mercury. The words on the dial are thus practically meaningless; but the movement of the hand indicates the air pressure which affects the character of the weather.

The comments on the barometers are in note 3 and are perhaps too much in detail.

2. The dial is silvered and has a hand and a pointer. The pointer has no connection with the mechanism and may be moved around by the knob below the dial. Its purpose is to record the place on the dial at which the hand stood at the previous time when the barometer was read, instead of trusting to one's memory. The hand is moved by the mechanism behind the dial as shown in the second piece, in which white paper has been inserted by the writer in order that the glass parts may be more clearly seen.

The hands are generally finely made and graceful. They often follow to some extent the form of the hands on the clocks of the period. The hand extends beyond the centre of the dial and this extension serves as a counter–weight to balance the hand in any position. The hand in the fifth illustration is balanced by a duplicate of itself.

3. A. The first and second illustrations present the front and rear views of the first barometer, which is a "clock barometer", so–called because a clock is placed in the barometer case. The clock has no connection with the operation of the barometer and serves only as a ready means of knowing the time at which the reading of the barometer is made. In the rear view, the long and narrow door is open, showing a glass tube with its column of mercury and illustrating the method by which a rise of the column causes the hand on the dial to move forward, and a fall of the column causes the hand to move backward.

B. The top of the barometer is ornamented with two scrolls, between which is a small brass urn; this form of top resembles those on many grandfather clocks and other articles, and is referred

(*Continued on page 1036.*)

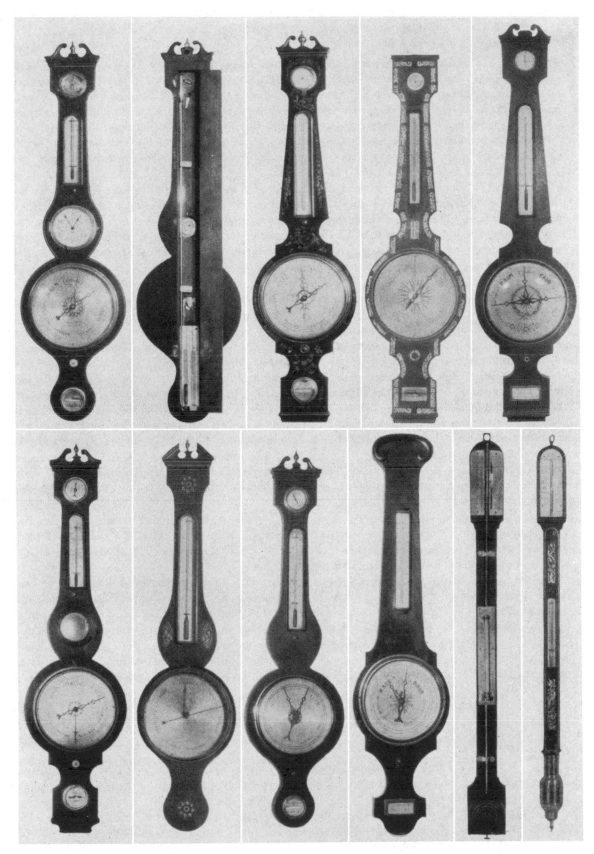

2106. Barometers.

1035

(NOTE 3, *continued from page 1034*)

to in section 186, at note 22. Next below is a small round opening, covered by a convex glass, in which is a pointer made of wood which is, or was, very sensitive to a change in the moisture in the atmosphere, and moves to the right, marked "damp", or to the left marked "dry", as it is affected by the changes in moisture. Next below is a thermometer which has no connection with the working of the barometer. Below the thermometer is the clock and underneath is the barometer's dial which, with its mechanism, is referred to previously in this note. At the bottom is a round opening, also with a convex glass, in which there is a spirit level by the aid of which the instrument may be hung exactly vertically. An Italian name is on the dial. About 1800–1820.

C. Examining the open rear of the barometer we see a long glass tube which is closed at the top and at the bottom is curved upward a few inches where it is open and exposed to the weight of the air. When the tube is filled with mercury, the mercury does not all run out of the open end, but falls from the top only to a point at which the weight of the air and of the mercury in the open curved part is equal to the weight of the mercury in the long tube, bearing in mind that at the empty top of the long tube there is a vacuum and no air pressure.

D. The next matter is the mechanism by which the hand on the dial moves from place to place with the changes in the air pressure. To describe properly this mechanism requires more space than is available here, but it can be easily understood by examining the barometer itself. It is sufficient to say that when the pressure of the air on the mercury in the open end of the tube increases, which generally indicates the coming of fair weather, the mercury in the open tube is pressed down by the air, and the column of mercury in the long part of the tube is forced up, that is, the barometer rises; and when the pressure of the air diminishes, the column of mercury in the long part of the tube falls, indicating rain or stormy weather, that is, the barometer falls. The change in height is the indication of a change in atmospheric conditions, that is, a change in the weather. The change in the weather may occur as long as twenty–four hours after the change in the height of the barometer; in other words, the barometer may predict the weather twenty–four hours in advance, subject to changes in air pressure.

E. In the barometer in the third illustration the case is decorated with raised lacquer work, a popular form of ornamentation in the period, as mentioned in section 31 in this book. Other examples of this work are seen on the English mantel clock No. 1895 and the Act of Parliament clock No. 2506. About 1795–1800.

F. In the next barometer the top is flat and a wide inlay extends around the entire case. On the dial is a finely chased design representing the rays of the sun. In this barometer, and in the preceding one and in others, the case, above and below the dial, is cut in a concave curve on each side, and the bottom portion is rectangular. About 1800–1820.

G. The fifth illustration is similar in form to the preceding one and, like it, has a finely chased design in the centre of the dial. The balanced hand is of an unusual type. The printed words on a paper in the lower opening for the spirit level are "114 John St., New York", probably the address of a dealer, the paper occupying the place of a spirit level which may have been broken. About 1800–1820.

H. In the sixth illustration, under the thermometer, the case swells out in a rounded form, and in the enlarged surface is a convex mirror enclosed within a series of rings. The pointer has accidentally become loose and has fallen. Here also is an Italian name above the spirit level. About 1800–1820.

I. The seventh illustration shows at the top a "broken arch", not with scrolls. The case above and below the dial is curved, and on the spaces thus provided are inlays of shells and flowers. There is no spirit level at the bottom, nor a piece of sensitive wood at the top as in other pieces. About 1800–1820.

J. The eighth illustration presents a plain example, having no clock, mirror or decoration except a thin line of inlay around the case. Above and below the spirit level are the words "Warranted correct". About 1800–1820.

K. In the ninth illustration the case lacks the pleasing curves and proportions which contribute to the graceful appearance of the preceding barometers. At the top is a heavy horizontal "C" curve in the form seen on many mirrors, as on No. 1103 and others. An Italian name is over the spirit level. About 1820–1830.

Section 202. Tea–caddies and small boxes.—The twenty–two engravings in this section are not numbered separately, but, as in the previous section, are all shown in one illustration, No. 2107. Some of the articles are tea–caddies and others are merely small objects.[1] In certain cases it is difficult to decide from the outside appearance whether the article is a tea–caddy or merely a box.

It is said that a tea–caddy was a box or chest in which were usually two finely made wooden boxes, lined with tin foil, for black and green tea. Very often there was a space filled with a basin for sugar and also provision was made for a little silver spoon. The caddy was made in the style which was in vogue at the time, beginning with the designs of the Chippendale style, continuing with the style of Hepplewhite, ending with the Sheraton period, and reviving in the Victorian period. The English writers mention that in the eighteenth century the caddy was kept under lock and key, and that the only means of access was in the hands of the house–wife who at tea–time blended the leaves of Chinese and Ceylon teas, which were very expensive, often "a guinea a pound".

(NOTE 3, *continued*)

L. The last two illustrations are of more recent barometers and are of a different type from the preceding ones. In the first of the two barometers the glass tube containing the mercury may be seen in the narrow frame, except behind the thermometer. The lower end of the barometer tube is open and is in a receptacle containing mercury which is exposed to the pressure of the air. Instead of having a round dial with a hand and a pointer, as in the preceding barometers, this one has a scale at the top divided into inches and fractions of an inch, and the rise and fall of the mercury is measured on the scale, as the temperature is measured on a thermometer. A small piece of metal on the left side of the scale may be moved in a slot, and serves as a pointer to make a record of the position of the mercury. At the bottom is a small screw by which adjustments may be made. This type of barometer was of course less expensive than the others shown here, and was often made in our country. On the thermometer are the names "F. W. & R. King", a Baltimore firm which was in business from 1855 to 1875.

M. In the last illustration an ornamental treatment is given to a barometer of the same type as the preceding one. The frame encloses the glass tube and is finely decorated with inlay, the receptacle at the bottom is of polished metal, and the top is arched. The scale is marked with the words "Fair, Rain", etc. as in the preceding piece. Perhaps about 1795–1800.

1. The word "caddy" means a box for keeping tea when in use. It is said to be a corruption of the word "catty" which is a Chinese measure of weight.

"Boxes" are referred to in sections 101 and 102 in connection with desks.

Illustrated articles on tea–caddies and small decorated boxes are in "Antiques" of May, 1923, pages 210–211; June, 1927, pages 464–465; May, 1935, pages 184–185, "Pennsylvania decorated boxes".

The owners of the tea–caddies and boxes here shown are Miss Helen H. Carey; Miss Harriett R. Chew; Mr. Wm. A. Dixon; Mrs. John S. Gibbs, Jr.; Mrs. M. S. Hartshorne; Mr. John S. McDaniel; Mr. J. G. D'Arcy Paul; Dr. J. Hall Pleasants; Mrs. Francis T. Redwood; Mr. & Mrs. Bayard Turnbull; Mr. & Mrs. George Ward.

The dates of almost all of these tea–caddies and small boxes are probably in the period of about 1785 to 1815, the years in which the styles of Hepplewhite and Sheraton were successively in fashion. The pleasing designs of some pieces, the fine satinwood of others, the inlay and the delicate paintings should be noticed. The box in the shape of an apple is a pleasing variation in form. Perhaps several pieces are Victorian.

These articles were often made of papier maché; see section 44, note 5.

2107. TEA–CADDIES AND SMALL BOXES.

Section 203. Furniture worms.—Having seen many articles of antique furniture which had been ravaged by furniture worms, but never having seen any of the worms, dead or alive, the writer offered a prize to a cabinet maker who had for many years lived and worked with old furniture if he would find and exhibit one or more of the furniture worms, alive. After several months the cabinet maker, working with some pieces of antique furniture, won the prize, and the writer met the sights which are shown in the three illustrations in No. 2108, the most interesting feature to him being that the holes are exit holes, not entrance holes.[1]

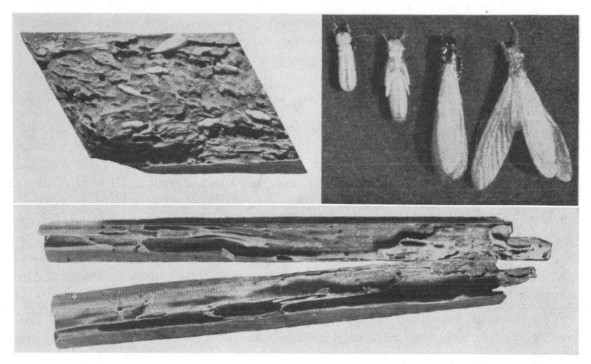

2108. FURNITURE WORMS.

In the illustration at the upper left corner the small white objects are on the inside of the wood of a piece of furniture. These are live worms in their early state, except the larger one with wings at the top.

1. In the "Dictionary of English Furniture", by Macquoid and Edwards, volume 3, page 339, information is given, in substance as follows: "The so-called furniture worm, the larva, or grub, is the insect which more commonly attacks furniture, panelling and small wooden articles. The eggs are laid by the insect, usually in June, in cracks or crevices in the wood. The larva, or grub, emerges in about three weeks and tunnels inwards, and when full size alters its course in the wood and comes near to the surface. Here it passes from the larval to the pupal stage, and, after an interval, the adult emerges from the chrysalis and bores its way through the thin wall of wood. The holes made by the insect are commonly known as 'worm–holes'." They are termed "exit holes of the furniture beetle" in figure 2 in the Dictionary above mentioned.

It may be mentioned that the word "grub" means about the same as the word "larva", both being the first stage of an insect after leaving the egg. The word "pupal" represents the next stage of the insect, which undergoes a change, as of a butterfly. The "chrysalis" is the pupa enclosed in a shell from which the fully developed insect comes out. "Beetles" are insects which have front wings which fit over the hind wings. (*Note continued on page 1040.*)

The next illustration, at the upper right corner, shows four beetles, much enlarged, all of which were alive, the smaller ones at the left being the younger. The background is black in order to show the insect clearly.

The lower illustration shows the inside of a piece of wood as ruined. The long channels were made by the worms, weakening the wood, and making it unsafe for use. The small round holes are the exit holes. This illustration is on a much reduced scale.

Section 204.   A Wax Portrait.—This is the story of a wax portrait sold at a "Sale of American Antiques" in an auction room in New York City in the year 1925. Here is an illustration of the wax portrait and also the description in the catalogue:

"RARE WAX PORTRAIT OF GENERAL GEORGE WASHINGTON. Dated 1797."

"An unusually large wax portrait of George Washington in bas relief, a profile facing left, after the Savage type. Washington is shown here with powdered wig and queue in Colonial military costume, and white lace jabot which is pierced and very daintily worked. The portrait is signed 'G. Rouse, Sculpt. General George Washington 1797'. In the original frame. Height 12½ inches; width 11½ inches. The artist George Rouse, a wax portrait artist of the eighteenth century, did many portraits of prominent people in England from 1780 to 1810. There is very little likelihood that this portrait was done from life, but in all probability the subject was selected from the Savage portrait in mezzotint." The portrait brought $250. at the auction.

In the same year Mr. Alexander J. Wall, Librarian of the New York Historical Society, who was interested in the subject, noticed that there were for sale a number of wax portraits of George Washington, dated 1797, by a hitherto unknown artist named "G. Rouse". Mr. Wall made an investigation and published an interesting article on "Wax Portraiture" in the April, 1925, Bulletin of the Society, pages 3–26.

In 1928 the writer of this book, visiting several of the Philadelphia antique shops, saw for the first time two of these "G. Rouse 1797" portraits, and, admiring

(NOTE 1, *continued*)

   Much information may be had upon application by letter to the "Bureau of Entomology", (the bureau of insects), in the United States Department of Agriculture, Washington, D. C. The bureau issues free pamphlets and also advises as to the best method of getting rid of the insects.

   We have all heard the story of the woman who testified in an English court that her husband worked in an antique furniture factory, and that his business was making worm holes in furniture by firing bird shot into the wood. When it became known that worm holes were made in that way, the purchaser also learned that the artificial holes went straight in the wood without turning, but that live worms turn their course and bore through the wood with the grain of the wood. The latest style of worm holes is said to be made by augers with lead shafts which turn like the worm.

   It will be seen in the lower illustration that channels are not bored on the outside. All the boring is on the inside. The only noticeable outside indications of the work of the worms are the exit holes.

their fine workmanship and signs of age, purchased both—one for $30. and the other for $40.—total $70., not dear compared with the auction price of $250. for one.

And now for the truth. The name "G. Rouse" was fictitious—there was no such person; the date "1797" was false—the wax portrait was made in 1924, by a

2109. A WAX PORTRAIT.

person named Grey, who was then living in Liverpool, England; and last, but not least, the coloring of George Washington's coat and even of George Washington's hair–ribbons, had been painted on the wax only a few days before the auction sale.[1]

1. Under the heading "Danger! Fraudulent Antiques" in the magazine "Antiques", June, 1933, page 232, the following warning is given:

"To any readers of this column, or their friends, who may chance to encounter a silhouette portrait of one of their Revolutionary ancestors that has miraculously turned up, all neatly labeled,

Beware of a wax portrait of George Washington, even if, like the auction one, it is "in the original frame"!

The most important American artist in wax work was Mrs. Patience Wright, 1725–1785. She made wax profiles of Washington and Benjamin Franklin, and many others. She met with great success in England. Her career is stated in an article by Mr. Wall in the April, 1925, Bulletin of the New York Historical Society, previously mentioned.

Section 205. English Hall Marks.—The subject of hall marks is of course entirely beyond the scope of this book on "American antique furniture"; but in his visits to the homes of the owners of antique furniture the writer has so often been asked for information in regard to inherited silver that it seems proper, as a convenience to some of the readers, to refer to the "hall marks"[1] of English pieces made

(NOTE 1, *continued*)

dated, and otherwise conveniently and convincingly identified—and happily for sale—I suggest the exercise of supreme caution. The portrait may, of course, be genuine. Bear in mind, however, that it is wiser, as well as easier, to investigate such objects fully and thoroughly in advance of purchase, than, in the face of subsequent doubts, to prove their lack of authenticity and to compel a refund of money paid."

"Nothing is simpler than to make a study of genealogical records and historical sources and to rig up quite convincing heirlooms of various kinds calculated to appeal to some scion of an old stock, or even to an unsuspecting dealer. Indeed, certain of the English portrait waxes, of late generously imported into the United States, may be relabeled to fit individual prides and prejudices. Not a few of these waxes, I regret to note, betray evidence of having been pressed in plaster molds taken directly from comparatively unfamiliar eighteenth–century portrait medallions."

An illustrated article entitled "Wax Portraiture" by Mrs. Elma A. Weil is in the "Antiquarian", March, 1928, page 49. On page 51 it is said that most of the wax portraits were in profile because they were more easily made and also because full and three–quarters faces are not as pleasing; and that finishing touches were mainly in colored wax.

A life–size bust of Benjamin Franklin by Mrs. Wright is referred to in "Antiques", October, 1931, pages 207–208. See also the same magazine of December, 1932, pages 221–223; also June, 1927, page 478, and references.

1. It is said that because of these marks the available information regarding old English silver is more definite and exact than that regarding any other article of an antique type.

Mr. Jackson in his book, page 49, referred to in the seventh paragraph in this note, states that the marks were required "solely with the object of preventing fraud and detecting the offenders in case of fraud being practiced; but by reason of the changes which were annually made in one of these marks (the date mark) we are in fact enabled to determine the exact year when a fully-marked example of London plate was assayed."

It may be noted here that another and a more recent kind of fraud is in use, such as the changing of the date mark to an earlier date, the change of the maker's mark to that of a more noted maker, and the change of the other marks as necessary to complete the fraud. An amateur collector runs a great risk in purchasing so–called "old English hall–marked silver" without expert advice, or from a dealer well informed and of unquestioned character.

In England the penalty for counterfeiting the marks of gold and silver has always been very severe. In our country, however, there is no general criminal law on the subject, and hence such counterfeiting is not a criminal offence; a few years ago an extensive fraud was discovered, in which a large set of silver was falsely marked with the initials of a celebrated English maker.

See "An American Consul's Report" on page 1059.

in London[2] during two centuries, from 1658 to 1856.

From about the year 1300 the English law has required articles of gold[3] or silver manufactured in London and elsewhere in England to be assayed, that is, tested; and if they were found to be of the legal standard of fineness, the articles, if made in London, were marked, or stamped, with a letter within a shield, by an official at "Goldsmiths' Hall", in that city, and because of this the marks were called "hall marks".[4] The letter was changed every year and thus each letter indicated a different year.

The letters and shields shown in illustration No. 2110 are London "date marks" and indicate the dates of the assays at Goldsmith's Hall; these date marks were used, a different one in each year, from 1658–1659 to 1755–1756. Similarly the letters and shields shown in illustration No. 2111 are also London "date marks";

(NOTE 1, *continued*)

      Illustrations of these marks may be found in many books, including Britten's "Old Clocks and Watches". Those shown here are copied from "Chaffers' Handbook to Hall Marks on Gold and Silver Plate", fifth edition, by Mr. C. A. Markham, published in London by Reeves and Turner, 1924. This is a small book, containing illustrations of the marks of the English assay offices, with sufficient information for the amateur collector.

      A larger English book, edited by Mr. Markham, is "Hall Marks on Gold and Silver Plate", by Mr. William Chaffers, tenth edition, issued by the same publishers in 1922.

      Another book, regarded as the leading one, is "English Goldsmiths and their Marks", by Sir Charles James Jackson, Barrister at Law, published by Macmillan & Co., London, 1921, containing a full account of the history of old English silver and reproductions of all the known marks.

      An illustrated article, entitled "Hall Marks: The Heraldry of English Silver", by Virginia Warren Allen, is in "Antiques", August, 1932, page 60.

      A recent book by Mr. Edward Wenham, entitled "Domestic Silver of Great Britain and Ireland", presents numerous illustrations. In "The Antiquarian", November, 1927, is an illustrated article entitled "The identifying of London silver", by Mr. Wenham.

    2. It is said that probably ninety–nine per cent of the silver pieces were made and assayed in London, and for this reason the marks of the other assay offices are not shown here, but the principal ones may be mentioned: the mark of Birmingham was an anchor; of Chester, a sword; of Edinburgh, a castle with three towers; of Sheffield, a crown; of Glasgow, a tree, fish, bird and bell; of Dublin, a harp crowned. The marks of other less important assay offices and also the letters indicating the dates may be found in the books above referred to.

    3. In the English books the term "goldsmith" is understood to include "silversmith"; the word "English" includes Scotland, Ireland and Wales; the word "plate" applies to both gold and silver, although "plate", strictly speaking, refers only to silver.

      Of course this meaning of the word "plate" will not be confused with its secondary meaning—"plated ware"—which is a name given to articles of base metal coated or plated with gold or silver, as distinguished from "plate"; Century Dictionary, under the word "plated". "Sheffield plate" is a form of "plate" in this secondary sense.

      The word "puncheon", or "punch", means a tool by which a mark may be stamped into the silver, and a "punch mark" is a mark made by the punch. All of the marks mentioned here are "punch marks".

    4. In our country, Baltimore is the only city which has had an assay office. A law passed in 1814 "created the position of an official assayer of silver plate for Baltimore . . and directed that certain official marks, in addition to the maker's initials or name, be stamped on all silver. This had as its result, that for a period of sixteen years silver made or sold in Baltimore bore marks or symbols showing that it was of standard purity, and indicating its place or origin and the year of manufacture." This quotation is from "Maryland Silversmiths, 1715–1830", page 25, published in 1930, a very handsome volume containing an exhaustive study of the subject by Dr. J. Hall Pleasants and Howard Sill.

2110. London "Date" Marks. 1658–1755.

Letter	Year	Letter	Year	Letter	Year	Letter	Year	Letter	Year
A	1756–7	a	1776–7	A	1796–7	a	1816–7	A	1836–7
B	1757–8	b	1777–8	B	1797–8	b	1817–8	B	1837–8 Victoria.
C	1758–9	c	1778–9	C	1798–9	c	1818–9	C	1838–9
D	1759–60	d	1779–80	D	1799–00	d	1819–20	D	1839–40
E	1760–1 George III.	e	1780–1	E	1800–1	e	1820–1 George IV.	E	1840–1
F	1761–2	f	1781–2	F	1801–2	f	1821–2	F	1841–2
G	1762–3	g	1782–3	G	1802–3	g	1822–3	G	1842–3
H	1763–4	h	1783–4	H	1803–4	h	1823–4	H	1843–4
I	1764–5	i	*1784–5	I	1804–5	i	1824–5	I	1844–5
K	1765–6	k	1785–6	K	1805–6	k	1825–6	K	1845–6
L	1766–7	l	1786–7	L	1806–7	l	1826–7	L	1846–7
M	1767–8	m	1787–8	M	1807–8	m	1827–8	M	1847–8
N	1768–9	n	1788–9	N	1808–9	n	1828–9	N	1848–9
O	1769–70	o	1789–90	O	1809–10	o	1829–30	O	1849–50
P	1770–1	p	1790–1	P	1810–1	p	1830–1 William IV.	P	1850–1
Q	1771–2	q	1791–2	Q	1811–2	q	1831–2	Q	1851–2
R	1772–3	r	1792–3	R	1812–3	r	1832–3	R	1852–3
S	1773–4	s	1793–4	S	1813–4	s	1833–4	S	1853–4
T	1774–5	t	1794–5	T	1814–5	t	1834–5	T	1854–5
U	1775–6	u	1795–6	U	1815–6	u	1835–6	U	1855–6

2111. LONDON "DATE" MARKS. 1756–1855.

they were used, a different one in each year, from 1756–1757 to 1855–1856. These dates, printed on the right of the date marks, are, of course, not parts of the date marks; they are printed in the books of modern writers in order to give ready reference to the date of each date mark. The mark was stamped on the silver by the London official assayer.[5] The style of the letter and of the shield was changed every twenty years, as appears in the illustrations. Each assay office had its own list of letters indicating the dates. In London the six letters, J, V, W, X, Y, Z were not used. The assay years began on May 30, not on January 1.

Another mark, not shown here, indicates that the silver is of the required standard. It is called the "standard mark", or "quality mark" and has been used for almost four hundred years, with an intermission from 1697 to 1720. It consists of the "lion passant", that is, a lion walking, facing the left, with the right forepaw raised.

Another of the marks indicates the hall or office at which the assay was made, whether in London or elsewhere. In London the mark was and is a "leopard's head", which had a crown before 1823, and is within a circle or other outline. This head bears but a slight resemblance, if any, to that of a leopard. Between 1697 and 1720 a lion's head was used.

Another mark is the "maker's mark", showing the name of the maker of the article by the initial letters of his first name and surname. This was stamped on the article by the maker.

Still another mark, used from 1784 to 1890, is the head in profile of the reigning English sovereign. This mark indicated that the duty on the article had been paid. From 1837 to 1890 the head of Queen Victoria was used.

In some cases a small mark is near the maker's mark, indicating the workman who was the actual maker.

The marks are seldom stamped in a straight line and some of them may be upside down; in many cases they have become indistinct.

Section 206. The tradition of English bricks.—The tradition still lingers that a large number of the old houses and churches now standing in Maryland and Virginia and several other States were built of bricks brought from England; but careful study has shown that this belief in most cases is erroneous. It is true that there is evidence to show that in the earliest years of the settlement of Maryland, bricks and other building supplies were imported, as at St. Mary's Town in

---

5.   In Mr. Jackson's "English Goldsmiths and their Marks", it is said, page 49, that the marks which are, or ought to be, found on plate assayed in London are in their chronological order as follows: 1. The leopard's head—the mark of the London assay office. 2. The maker's or worker's mark. 3. The annual letter—the date mark. 4. The lion passant—the standard or quality mark. 5. The lion's head erased and the figure of Britannia—when the standard for silver was raised in the years 1697–1720. 6. The Sovereign's Head, indicating the payment of the duty.

The subject of London hall marks is difficult, and the subject of hall marks in numerous other cities is more so.

St. Mary's County; but as early as the year 1694 reference is made, in the proceedings of the Maryland Assembly, to "brick clay of good quality having been discovered near Annapolis".

In a paper prepared by Dr. Henry J. Berkley, published in the Maryland Historical Magazine, March, 1924, pages 1–10, the subject of Colonial brickwork is fully considered, and it is said on pages 7–8, "That these bricks were made entirely out of local clays, and not brought from England as is often alleged, is shown by their microscopic examination, which shows clay corresponding to neighboring, never to English, clay. Furthermore there were gangs of brickmakers, who, on demand, went from place to place, and made bricks for any building about to be constructed. This custom obtained both in Maryland and Virginia. . . The bricks were fashioned after the English mould. This pattern lasted until the time of the Revolutionary War. Then this model was gradually replaced by another having the same width and length, but not the same thickness. This was the so-called Dutch pattern."

One of the finest and largest old houses in the South is the historic Miles Brewton House, built about 1770, and now called the Pringle House, in Charleston, S. C. This building has been carefully studied and measured, and in the "History of South Carolina" by Mr. Edward McCrady, the tradition that all of the bricks or any part of them were brought from England is carefully examined. The records of the United States Custom House do not show such importation, nor do the local newspapers of the period refer to it or carry any advertisements of foreign brick. Mr. McCrady considers that the erroneous tradition arose from the fact that, as mentioned above, two sizes of brick were then used, the larger one called "English" and the smaller one called "Dutch", and the term "English" brick referred to the size and not to the place of manufacture. We all know that in our restaurants an "English chop" does not mean a piece of meat from England!

The same conclusion has been reached by others who have studied the matter. In the letter column of the Baltimore "Sun", July 17, 1927, Dr. James Bordley, Jr., refers particularly to the search of the shipping records of England, to the small size and carrying capacity of the ships, and to the old brick moulds, made of English wood, found in our country. In the same column of the "Sun" a few days later Mr. James S. Shepherd, of Cambridge, Md., writes of his efforts to discover some evidence of the truth of the tradition, but the facts all indicated its falsity, especially the early records of imports in the Land Office in Annapolis, Md., which contain no reference to the import of bricks. Moreover, Mr. Lyon G. Tyler, President of William and Mary College, Williamsburg, Va., in a letter published in the "Century Magazine", February, 1896, pages 636–637, writes that "there is not a case to be found in the annals of Virginia of bricks imported from England. . . It was easier to import brickmakers than bricks." Mr. Tyler concludes: "How then did the idea of houses made of imported brick become so firmly fixed in the popular fancy? I conceive that the impression arose from mistaking the meaning of 'English brick'. Houses in Maryland and Virginia were, it is true, made of 'English brick', but that did not mean imported brick." The author is indebted to Mr. L. H. Dielman, Librarian of the Peabody Institute and the Maryland Historical Society, for a reference to this letter of Mr. Tyler. In the magazine of the Historical Society of Pennsylvania, January, 1929, there is an article on early brickmakers of Philadelphia, by Mr. Harrold E. Gillingham, of that city, who writes that he has "failed to find any evidence whatever here of any importation of bricks during the 17th or 18th centuries".

Section 207. Indentured servants; apprentices.—A considerable amount of literature in regard to indentured servants in the American Colonies, and especially in Maryland, may be found in the large libraries in our country. The subject is mentioned here for the reason that persons examining the newspapers of the period will find many references to it.

Until about the beginning of the Federal period it was a common practice for English men and women and young persons who wished to emigrate to the American Colonies, but were not financially able to do so,[1] to pay the "master" of the ship, also called the "captain", for their ocean passage by selling their services for several years to an American employer. For example, in the Maryland Gazette of March 8, 1759, is an advertisement of John Inch, a silversmith, stating that there was "to be disposed of by the said Inch, the Time of a Dutch Servant man, that has above six years to serve", etc.; and on March 11, 1762, he advertised that he "has also for sale a convict–servant Woman's Time, lately imported, who is a good Stay–maker."

In the Maryland Gazette, February 24, 1774, is the following advertisement: "Indented servants. Just imported, from London, and to be sold by the Subscriber, A Parcel of healthy indented servants, among which are valuable tradesmen consisting of carpenters, cabinet makers, sawyers, shoe makers, blacksmiths, tailors, gunsmiths, bricklayers, hatters, butchers, farmers, labourers and a few servant women; also a quantity of the powder blue, wig powder and black pins for hair."

In the Pennsylvania Packet, March 6, 1775, is an advertisement offering for sale "a strong healthy servant girl, has two years and eight months to serve; two servant men, one a good taylor of a good disposition, has two years and four months to serve."

Several of the advertisements quoted in this section appear in the book entitled "Arts and Crafts in Philadelphia, Maryland and South Carolina, 1721–1785", which is mentioned in note 8 in section 6.

These persons were called "Indentured Servants". They usually signed contracts, also called "indentures", with the master of a ship and upon their arrival they were disposed of by the master by private sale or at auction.

A redemptioner was a person who could redeem himself from debt to the master of the ship by a certain number of years work or by payment to the master.

1. Much of the above information was taken from "Maryland Silversmiths", 1715–1830, by Dr. J. Hall Pleasants and Howard Sill, published in 1930.
    See also section 186, note 30, and section 187, note 7.

FIVE CENTS REWARD.

Ranaway from the subscriber living near Ellicott's Patapsco Mills, on Tuesday 24th of October last, a bright Mulatto Boy about 19 years of age, named GERARD BARTON, an Apprentice to the Coopering Business.—He is about 5 feet high, slender made, and looks pleasant when spoken to. He frequently gets intoxicated—His clothing not recollected. The above reward will be given if brought home, and no charges paid.

THOS. GIBBINS.

jan 11   th&s4tf

SIX CENTS REWARD.

Ranaway from the Subscriber on ths 6th inst. an Apprentice Boy to the Sail Making business, named John Christopher Columbus Thomas Jefferson James Madison Bonparte League —about 15 years of age. Had on when he went away, a blue cloth roundabout jacket and trowsers : a yellow waistcoat, and tarpaulin hat— The above reward will be given if brought home.

I forwarn all persons from harboring or carrying off said boy, at the utmost peril of the law.   JOHN KENNEDY.

feb 7   d4t*

50 Cents Reward.

Ran away from the subscriber on the 19th inst. a white girl named Patty Linch ; she is of dark complexion, dark hair, a good looking face, very ugly feet, and has a very large scar on her right foot ; had on when she went off a light home made frock, a purple silk bonnet, blue yarn stockings, and a pair of men's shoes ; she is 13 or 14 years old, about 5 feet high— she stole a buff calico frock, a twilled dark cotton shawl, a pair of common shoes, and a pair of white cotton stockings ; she attempted to steal my pocket book the night before, from which she got some money, to what amount not known, as there was in the book between 4 and 500 dollars. The above reward will be given for the said apprentice.

ANTOINY NOBLET.

N. B.—I forwarn all persons from harboring and hiring her, under the penalty of the law, as it will be strictly enforced.

jan 20   d3t

Six Cents Reward.

Ranaway from the subscriber on Sunday last, 10th March, an apprentice girl named Eliza M'Dowall, about 12 years of age, hvs a scald or breaking out in her head, and was taking medicine for the Eras Ipulus. The above eeward will be paid for bringing her back, but no expences, and all persons are hereby forwarned from harboring, her as they will be prosecuted according to law.

HENRY S. KEATINGE,
No. 126 Green St. O. T.

mar 12   d4t

CAUTION.

Whereas my wife. Jane Handlen, hath in a clandestine manner left my house in Strawberry Alley, P. P. in my absence, and as several articles of my property are taken away, I expect that my wife, or some assistant of hers, have taken the same—I hereby forwarn all persons trusting my said wife on my account for board or other necessary, as I am determined to pay no debt of her contracting.

PATRICK HANDLON.

jan 2   d4t

To the Eitords of the American—

With no less grief than indignation, I observed in your paper of yesterday a publication giving a caution not to credit me on account of my husband, Patrick Handlon—and I would wish, through the medium of your paper to avail myself of no more than what the law prescribes ; and unwilling to bring to public view his conduct, I wish only to say, that from conjugal attachment I submitted as long as the frailty of human nature could bear, to ill treatment, and by ties to an affectionate family I was compelled to resort to the house of an affectionate brother, well known for his benevolence and munificence to strangers, where I have met with a friendly reception from the rude treatment of an unfeeling husband, who has heretofore had no reason to complain of debts of my contracting, as from my application and industry and frugality he must acknowledge the duties I have performed, not having received any support from him for five years.   JANE HANDLON

jan 4   4.

No. 2112.

1049

No. 2113.

Under the apprentice system young boys were bound by their parents, by a written agreement, to work for an employer, or master, for a term of years, often for seven years or until arrival at the age of twenty–one. The boy was termed an "apprentice" in the agreement in which the master agreed to teach the apprentice "in the same art which he (the master) employeth, finding unto his said apprentice meat, drink, apparel, lodging and all other necessaries." It is not strange that many boys found their master and their master's work to be unbearable and sought relief by running away; whereupon the master often inserted an advertisement in the local newspaper offering a reward for the capture and return of the runaway. The amount of the reward ranged upward in some cases from one penny to five or six cents. One advertisement in a Baltimore newspaper in 1786 reads as follows: "Ran away from the subscriber about two weeks ago, an apprentice lad, named John Taylor, about 13 years old, fair complexion. Had on a black hat and white shirt and trousers. Whoever takes up the said apprentice and will bring him to his master, shall receive the above reward."

In illustrations Nos. 2112 and 2113 are several advertisements for the return of runaway apprentices, stating some conspicuous features of clothing or personal appearance or other means of identification. Thus the five cents reward for the boy Gerard Barton mentions that the boy "looks pleasant when spoken to" and that "he frequently gets intoxicated".

The next advertisement below is for six cents for the capture of a fifteen year old runaway who was blessed with nine names, the list including Christopher Columbus, Thomas Jefferson and James Madison.

Fifty cents reward is offered in the next advertisement for a white girl named Patty Linch whose features include "a good–looking face, very ugly feet and a very large scar on her right foot."

Six cents reward is offered in the next advertisement for a girl about twelve years of age who was taking medicine for the "Eras Ipulus", which words may be a phonetic rendering of "erysipelas".

The next two advertisements in No. 2112 are examples of trials of matrimonial difficulties in the newspapers. Here the wife states that she has not "received any support from him for five years."

Two other advertisements in the next illustration No. 2113 offer larger rewards for runaways. In the upper advertisement on the left "A genteel–looking Runaway" is minutely described and is shown running rapidly. His vocal powers include "can sing a good song". Here the reward is eight dollars. The date is October 20, 1788.

In the next advertisement the reward of six dollars is for a young man with a staff and walking with a pleasant smile. He is called an Irish Servant Man.

The next two advertisements on the same page are from a Baltimore newspaper dated August 18, 1773. They are not in reference to "Indentured Servants" but are interesting.

The advertisement of "David Evans, Clock and Watch–maker, from Philadelphia" states that he "makes musical, horizontal, repeating and plain clocks in the neatest manner." See the clock dial No. 1855, bearing the name of this advertiser.

"Jacob Mohler, clock and watch–maker", in his advertisement points out that "An apprentice is wanted who can be well recommended." A grandfather clock by this Mohler is shown as No. 1814. He died in 1773.

Section 208. Admission of States into the Union.—Many times in this book reference has been made to the dates of certain articles of furniture as indicated by the number of stars inlaid or painted on the article, the number of stars representing the number of States at the time the article was made. For example, on the desks Nos. 803 and 805 we see inlaid marks or stars, and on the mirror No. 1160 and others in section 146 we see similar designs. For the convenience of the reader the dates at which the first thirteen States were admitted to the Union are given here and also the dates of the next twelve States.

The dates at which the first thirteen States were admitted:	The dates at which the next twelve States were admitted:
1—1787—Delaware	14—1791—Vermont
2— " —Pennsylvania	15—1792—Kentucky
3— " —New Jersey	16—1796—Tennessee
4—1788—Georgia	17—1803—Ohio
5— " —Connecticut	18—1812—Louisiana
6— " —Massachusetts	19—1816—Indiana
7— " —Maryland	20—1817—Mississippi
8— " —South Carolina	21—1818—Illinois
9— " —New Hampshire	22—1819—Alabama
10— " —Virginia	23—1820—Maine
11— " —New York	24—1821—Missouri
12—1789—North Carolina	25—1836—Arkansas
13—1790—Rhode Island	

In some cases the marks or stars are thought not to refer to the number of States then in the Union but to be merely decorative designs to avoid a vacant space. One is inclined, however, to ascribe a patriotic motive in the early years of the young Republic. For various instances see the Index under the word "Stars".

Section 209. Auction sales and prices.—Many pages have been written on the subjects of this section, interesting to experienced collectors as well as to amateurs; but here we mention briefly the more important matters.

Auction prices,[1] whether very high or very low, should not and do not always establish prices inside or outside the auction room. A high price paid for an

1. As remarked in "Antiques", May, 1932, page 236, "In days of prosperity, competition among half a dozen wealthy collectors is sufficient to raise a unique or exceptionally rare item to quite staggering figures. When in a period of reverses this thin margin of competitive support is withdrawn, the temporary drop in valuation is likely to be correspondingly great."

article at one auction does not mean that an exact duplicate will sell for as much at the next auction. A high bid for a certain article may have been reached because each of two or more persons of means was determined to buy the article. If the purchaser some time later wished to sell the article and offered it at auction and two bidders of means, each determined to buy it, were not present, the bid would probably be less than the price formerly paid.

(NOTE 1, *continued*)

In England an Act of Parliament passed in 1867 provided that a sale at auction would be rendered void if the price was bid up by a person secretly employed by the seller to do so. The person so employed is known as a "puffer", or "bye–bidder". In our country the Supreme Court of the United States in the case of Veazie vs. Williams, decided in 1850 and reported in 8 Howard Reports, page 134, held that the employment of a puffer operated as a fraud upon the real bidders.

In the case of Edmunds vs. Gwynn, 159 Southeastern Reporter, page 205, the Supreme Court of Virginia decided in 1931 that the general rule in the American courts is that unless the seller plainly reserves the right to bid, a fictitious bidding by the auctioneer or by any other person acting on behalf of the seller is a fraud on bona fide bidders. But if the bye–bidding had no effect or influence upon the purchaser's bid the purchaser cannot avoid the contract.

In a "Dutch auction" property is offered at a price known to be in excess of the market value and is then successively offered at lower prices until one is accepted.

In Mr. Nobili's "The gentle art of faking", page 29, an incident is told of an auction sale held by the Emperor Caligula in Rome. Not only was the Emperor present, but he put prices on the various objects, bidding on them as well. An old official, Saturninus, by name, who had made bids by nodding his head, became sleepy during the sale and in dozing he kept on nodding his head. The Emperor noticed this and told the auctioneer not to lose sight of that buyer and to put up the price each time the old official nodded his head. When the old man finally awoke he found that without knowing it he had bought about eighty thousand pounds worth of goods.

In "The Antiquarian", June, 1927, page 37, Mr. Charles Messer Stow, the editor, wrote that he "has sat in many an auction sale and has watched the bidding carry the price of an article away beyond its value. He has sat in others and has seen things sell for a fraction of what they ought to bring. He has come to the conclusion that an auction sale is a gamble, and his conclusion is backed by the word both of dealers and auctioneers themselves. In New York during one season an unusual number of auction sales was held. At some of them the results were all that the consignors hoped for. At others the prices realized brought huge disappointment. Apparently there was no outward reason why one day should have brought high prices and the next low ones, no reason, that is to say, other than the fickleness of the goddess who presides over the fortunes of the auction block."

Of course it would be folly for any amateur collector, and even for an experienced collector, to bid at an auction sale of furniture said to be antique, without having carefully examined the objects in which he may be interested. No careful person would buy antique objects in an antique shop without examining them carefully, and at an auction sale, where there is no guarantee of the objects, there is need for even more careful inspection. Of course in almost all auction sales an opportunity for inspection before the sale is provided.

The "knock out" is the English term for an arrangement among a small syndicate of dealers who combine to purchase articles at an auction sale and to keep other persons from bidding. The dealers appoint one member of the syndicate to do the bidding against the other persons at the sale and thus avoid the appearance of competition and of many bidders. If the articles are purchased at a low price by the bidder for the syndicate, a meeting of all the members of the syndicate is held later at which a private auction between them is held, and the dealer making the highest bid gets the articles. Then all the members, by a peculiar arrangement among themselves, divide the profits, which at times were considerable. This scheme was not regarded as illegal, but public criticism was unfavorable and it is said that the "knock out" has been abandoned. A good account of the proceeding is in "The Antiquarian", October, 1928, page 60, etc.

The five articles of American antique furniture which have brought the highest prices at public auction sales to this date are here mentioned.[2]

1. The Reifsnyder highboy. Sold for $44,000; April, 1929, illustrated in this book as No. 668; see section 87 and note 1.

(NOTE 1, *continued*)

Discussions have arisen as to whether it is better for the amateur collector to buy a particular article from a dealer or at an auction sale. The questions are concerned chiefly with the antiquity of the articles sold and the guarantee of the antiquity if desired. It is said in regard to sales at auction that there is no guarantee that the article is genuine in all respects; that many auction sales consist largely of articles which dealers have been unable to sell at their sales room; that the auctioneer may exaggerate the good points and may omit mention of the defects; that the excitement of the sales room may impair the judgment of the purchaser. These and other arguments are said to be especially important in auction sales in country places, when the "contents of an old house" are offered for sale—when in fact the house may be crowded with undesirable articles which have passed through other sales without finding a purchaser.

A remark in "Antiques", March, 1925, page 142, is that "One thing cannot be too much and too often emphasized is that a high price paid at auction for a certain object does not apply to all objects in the same field. This must be remembered in season and out of season. At an auction only two rival bidders are required to run prices up. Often the payment may represent the joy of conquest more than the rarity of the purchase."

On the other hand it has been said that the purchaser from dealers is liable to pay an excessive price, caused partly by the need of employees and by high rentals; that the dealer must pay high prices for his goods, especially as the newspapers publish auction sales at high prices but do not report the sales at low prices; that there are no standard prices for many articles of similar character and the dealer may fix his price according to the means of the customer.

If it is necessary that a collection of antique furniture outside of New York City should be sold, the question may arise whether it would be better to sell at auction sale in New York, which is the largest and wealthiest market, or to sell at a local auction. This question may be difficult to decide, as the comparative financial results are of course impossible to foresee. Several sales of furniture of some importance, which had been sent to New York and were well catalogued, well advertised and well attended, have had unfortunate results, mainly owing to the expenses which were large in proportion to the proceeds of sales. This matter is one of the subjects of an article by the editor of "Antiques" in the issue of October, 1931, pages 232–234.

In Mr. Nobili's book entitled "The gentle art of faking", on page 151, is a story of an English dealer who "realized large profits on Meissen china by the artful way he put before the public an article apparently out of fashion with collectors. For two or three years he bought all the fine Meissen ware within reach until he accumulated a large quantity at extremely low prices." Then he began sending his pieces to auction sales to be sold and also sent his agents to run the prices up and to buy the pieces. This trick gradually built up a reputation for Meissen ware and it became the rage and the dealer got rid of his stock at a large profit.

2. Interesting remarks in regard to the above mentioned auction sales are quoted from "Antiques".

In "Antiques", June, 1929, page 508, Mr. Homer Eaton Keyes, the editor, remarks: "Let me warn the reader not to make the grievous mistake of assuming that the sums realized at the Reifsnyder sale are applicable as a measure of value for his own belongings. Mr. Reifsnyder's collection enjoyed an extraordinary prestige. In many instances it was for this prestige, rather than for the objects themselves, that wealthy buyers paid high prices at the auction. In January, for example, a bureau with mirror, by Jonathan Gostelowe of Philadelphia, sold in New York for $1,100. Yet it was one of the rarest pieces in America. Had it belonged to Mr. Reifsnyder, it would have brought many times the figure quoted. . . As for the unique pieces in this collection, they, of course, offer no criteria for judging anything else."

In the same magazine, February, 1930, pages 154–158, it is said that "Mr. Reifsnyder's furniture, for the most part, had to speak for itself: that is to say, comparatively little of it was specifically

2. The Reifsnyder wing chair. Sold for $33,000; April, 1929, illustrated in this book as No. 406; see section 59 and note 7.

3. The Philip Flayderman tambour secretary. Sold for $30,000; January, 1930; illustrated in this book as No. 824; see section 106, note 3.

4. The Philip Flayderman tea table. Sold for $29,000; January, 1930; illustrated in this book as No. 1336; see section 158, note 3.

5. A Reifsnyder "sample" side chair. Sold for $15,000; April, 1929; illustrated in this book as No. 116.

It must be remembered that the above sales were made at a time when a wild speculation in real estate, stocks and other securities helped to raise the prices

(NOTE 2, *continued*)

documented or pedigreed. Enough that it was representative of the most brilliantly ornate achievements of American cabinetmakers in the richest and most luxurious Colonial city of the Revolutionary period. The Flayderman collection, on the other hand, bespoke the greater austerity of the New England style, an austerity, however, which, during the closing years of the 1700's, took on the habiliments of suavity and elegance. An unusual number of its items, furthermore, were either marked with the maker's label, or else were accompanied by well-attested statements of distinguished ownership and association. There were, too, several sets of chairs, which gained materially in group value because of the exceptional number of their units."

"To the man in the street, perhaps, the newspaper accounts of the sale might suggest that the collecting public had gone mad. With a few exceptions, the articles which brought high prices were literally priceless rarities, some of them beyond hope of duplication."

"I emphasize these instances in the hope of preventing owners of antiques from being seized with delusions of grandeur induced by reading casual summaries of the Flayderman sale. I could recite pathetic instances of family hopes which have been enormously inflated by acceptance of headline reports, only to be subsequently shattered by encounter with hard facts. So I urge my more inexperienced readers to bear in mind that, among the hundreds of carefully selected items in such a group as the Flayderman collection, only a relatively small number—the cream of the cream—bring the prices chronicled by the press; and that these prices are seldom paid except upon the advice of experts."

"The success of the Flayderman sale was due to the high quality of the items offered and to clever and courageous advertising, which awakened widespread interest and curiosity and brought together an extraordinary representation of collectors and dealers."

"Speaking of pedigreed pieces, most readers of 'Antiques' doubtless saw the newspaper account of the sale of the rocking-chair in which President Lincoln was seated in Ford's Theatre, Washington, at the time of his assassination. A picture of this chair was published on page 68 of 'Antiques' for February, 1925. If an uglier piece of furniture was ever achieved by the imagination of man, I have yet to see it. Surely one of many exactly similar chairs turned out from the same factory, it could probably be duplicated in a second hand shop for an insignificant sum. Stained as it was, however, with the blood of a murdered President, and haunted by the ghosts of turmoil and national distress, it fetched, at auction, the sum of $2,400. Evidently an object which has no worth whatsoever as an antique, may achieve value as a relic."

At the Reifsnyder sale a clock which is shown in this book as No. 2086 was sold for $3,600. As remarked in note 11 in section 197, this clock may be regarded merely as a freak. It was advertised as "one of the rarest types of clocks in America", which was doubtless true because of its ill-proportioned form. At another sale a clock, No. 2084, called a German "falling ball" clock, about three and one-half inches in diameter, said to have been made about 1650, was sold at auction for $4,900. See also the comment on the Simon Willard clock No. 2069, where it is said that "because of their rarity and the fact that they were made by Simon Willard, these clocks are valuable although they are neither good timepieces nor of artistic appearance."

of antique furniture to figures which had never before been reached or even imagined. In the years of the depression which ensued, the prices for antique furniture followed the decline in securities—a decline which some readers may sadly recall, not only in securities but also in antiques.

Illustrations of several other fine pieces of furniture which were sold at the Reifsnyder auction sale at very high prices, are shown in the following articles in "Antiques"; November, 1925, pages 272–275, by Mr. Herbert Cescinsky, chairs; May, 1927, pages 366–371, by Mr. S. W. Woodhouse, Jr., chairs; April, 1930, pages 328–331, by Mr. Homer Eaton Keyes.

Section 210. Lotteries.—In looking over old newspapers, searching for matters concerning antique furniture, many advertisements of lotteries were found, some of which, although not connected with the subject of this book, may be of interest to the reader.

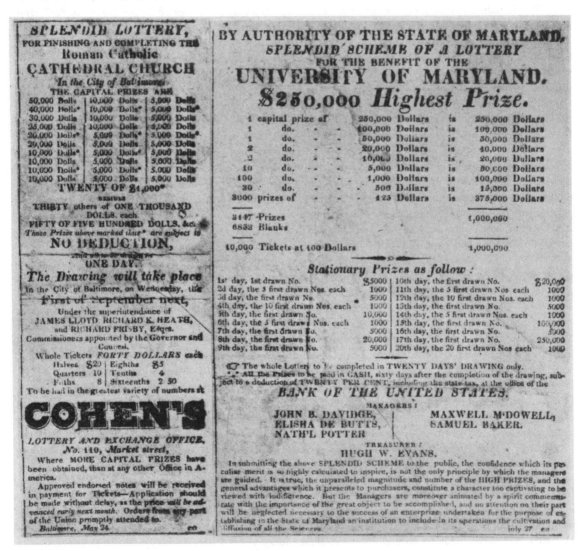

No. 2114.

In illustration No. 2114 are two advertisements of lotteries in a Baltimore newspaper of 1819. The lottery on the left was "for finishing and completing the Roman Catholic Cathedral Church in the city of Baltimore. . . (Tickets) to be had in the greatest variety of numbers at Cohen's Lottery and Exchange Office, No. 110, Market street, Where more capital prizes have been obtained than at any other office in America."

The raising of money by lotteries had been a favorite financial plan of several other churches. The year 1789 was the banner one in Baltimore, during which, it is said, "the inhabitants of the town had recourse to lotteries on every occasion to raise money for private and public improvements." At that date the lawful money was in pounds, not dollars. Among the lotteries for church enterprises were those for the Episcopal Parsonage house, 2000 pounds; the German Parsonage house, 1750; the German Reformed Church, 637; the Presbyterian Church, 2780.

The other advertisement in illustration No. 2114 offered a "splendid scheme of a lottery[1] for the benefit of the University of Maryland, $250,000 highest prize."

An interesting lottery authorized in 1825 by the legislatures of Virginia and Maryland was for the benefit of Thomas Jefferson in order to assist him in paying his debts and to save Monticello and his other estates. Jefferson wrote that the lottery "will offend no moral principle and expose none to risk but the willing and those wishing to be permitted to take the chance of gain." Unfortunately the lottery was not successful. Jefferson died July 4, 1826.

Section 211. An American Consul's Report.—The following article appeared in the United States Daily Consular and Trade Reports, November 24, 1909, No. 3644. A small part of this report is copied in section 8, note 1, in volume 1, and is also printed here for the convenience of the reader. The part referred to is headed here "Clever Ruse of Antique Furniture Dealer".

1.   An interesting article on the subject of lotteries, by Mr. George H. Sargent, is in the magazine "Antiques", March, 1923, pages 128–130. Several lottery tickets, issued about 1820 are illustrated; one was much older, entitled "Faneuil Hall Lottery No. Two, Oct. 1762", for rebuilding Faneuil Hall.

Mr. Sargent remarks that if the authorities of various States were powerless to suppress the lotteries, "a changing public sentiment and the lotteries themselves did it. When the lottery was no longer utilized for a public purpose . . but was known to be a private enterprise conducted solely for profit, it became honeycombed with fraud. In some cases it was discovered that the numbers which won the capital prizes were never printed. The economic situation created by the diverting of a multitude of small sums from the hands of the poorer classes into the hands of a few rascals became unsupportable."

The American Congress of 1776 instituted a national lottery, and most of the States at that time authorized lotteries for public purposes. The last legal lottery in the United States was the Louisiana State lottery, the charter of which expired in 1894.

The lottery conducted by the Adams Brothers in London is mentioned in section 16, note 5. The prizes were not money, but houses, with their furniture and pictures. The sale of the tickets brought the sum of over two hundred and twenty–five thousand pounds.

TRAFFIC IN ALLEGED ANTIQUES

FRAUDS PERPETRATED BY UNSCRUPULOUS DEALERS—IMPOSITION UPON COLLECTORS

Consul Maxwell Blake, in writing from Dunfermline of the frauds which are still perpetrated on the inexperienced collector of old silver, china and period furniture by dealers throughout the United Kingdom and continental Europe says:

The United States is reputed by the well-informed to harbor more "artistic atrocities" that were purchased as genuine than any other country in the world, and we may see even a greater flux of pseudo works of art in American stores unless these frauds are detected by government experts or rejected by the public taste. The purpose of this article is to state facts, not opinions, and it is not addressed to the experienced collector. A real service, however, may possibly be conferred by warning the inexperienced—those who perhaps go abroad for the first time and find the curiosity shops places of interest, and many of whom doubtless can little afford to be so heavily penalized for their credulity by antique dealers.

MINIATURES AND SNUFF BOXES THE PRESENT VOGUE

Just now miniatures and decorated snuff and patchboxes are being most extensively collected by Americans. These and other such small "articles of vertu" are manufactured by dextrous copyists and are readily procurable by the gross. No one not possessing knowledge of the subject, great experience, and discrimination should ever allow himself to be tempted to purchase miniatures unless he is content to possess a cabinet of forgeries. The vast quantities of bijouterie, Dresden, and Battersea enamel ware that is just now flooding the market is made on the Continent, principally for the American trade. Apart from the painting on these, which is poor in quality and generally a crude copy of some original example, if one will observe closely it will be revealed that the rim to which the top is hinged is artificially colored and that the evidence of fresh glue extending from underneath is a further betrayal of its modern and hazy origin.

Color prints are almost as difficult to indulge as miniatures and snuff boxes since in the past they have been very legitimately and some times very beautifully copied. But many of these fine reproductions which originally were only intended as such, have been converted into "antiques" to be sold to the inexperienced at much enhanced prices. It may safely be accepted, on the authority of those who know, that genuine old prints and engravings are never to be found on the bargain counter by the amateur collector.

"OLD MARKS" ON CHINA MEANINGLESS

The collection of china, likewise, must inevitably lead the novice to an even more hopeless plight. Genuine examples of Dresden, Chelsea, Worcester, or Bow are worth more than their weight in gold; yet what one may fondly imagine to be a convincing piece, with its refined decoration and simple gilding, bearing the golden anchor, is not a bit of old Chelsea, but a "fake" made by well-known firms on the Continent. Only the uninitiated now put any reliance in "Old marks". They are meaningless, and are freely applied to modern copies with open and notorious forgery. There are occasionally some rare pieces of china and pottery yet to be procured, as well as genuine examples of the more recent periods of some of the notable factories (usually early Nineteenth Century), such as Derby, Worcester, Spode, Coalport, and Rockingham China, and Wedgwood, Spode, Mason and other Staffordshire potteries. These may possess some slight sentimental and antique value, and are well worth buying for practical use, but in themselves they cannot be called fine and are otherwise unworthy of collection. But even then such pieces should be purchased only under expert advice and with a written guaranty of genuineness.

Written Guaranty Upheld by Courts

With reference to the effectiveness of the written guaranty, the English courts have recently sustained the contention that if a false description of an antique is given in the invoice, the purchaser is entitled to full recovery. The written guaranty is therefore far from being valueless and should always be insisted on as a protection. Furthermore, any evasion or hesitation on the part of the dealer to give one should be accepted as a token of his dishonesty. (See also pages 1061 and 1063.)

Before leaving the subject of china it might be stated that Cromwellian coins of small denomination, wholly worthless to the numismatic collector, bring from 10 to 15 times their face value among purveyors of "fake" antiques, since they can be inbedded in a tray or the bottom of a punch or toddy ladle to convince the gullible of the genuineness of his purchase.

The forger of old English silver has been somewhat restrained by fear of the law, which makes the sophistication of hall–marks in Great Britain a very hazardous occupation. Likewise, the almost prohibitive prices for which early English silver is offered confine its collection, generally speaking, to connoisseurs. The ingenuity of the faker, however, is none the less occasionally exercised to insert into some late piece of modern copy old marks taken from an article of little value. Beyond the actual intrinsic value of the metal, specimens of the late Georgian period are worthless, yet they are now being extensively collected by many dealers throughout Great Britain for sale to American customers, who willingly pay from ten to twenty times their trade value.

Much Faked Sheffield Plate Offered

It is a difficult undertaking to dispel the threefold illusion that old Sheffield plate is to be found almost anywhere in the United Kingdom; that is as valuable as silver of the same period, and the genuine can easily be detected from the spurious by the fact that it has a discernible sub–surface of copper. Now the truth of the latter is that much modern electroplate is done on a copper body, as was the case with the old. The precise difference, however, between the old and new is that, with respect to the former, the silver was first fused and beaten on to a copper block, the whole slug afterwards being worked into shape by hand; whereas, after the discovery of the process of electroplating in 1840 or thereabouts, the article to be silvered was mechanically evolved and the silver instantaneously applied by means of the electro process. The results of these two methods are vastly dissimilar, for instead of the play and accident of light on the beaten and uneven surface, which imparts one of the chief charms to the hand–wrought process, there is, when the silver has been mechanically applied, only an assertiveness and garish regularity of surface. Genuine old Sheffield plate in its original and unrenovated condition is worth about 80 per cent as much as modern silver, and about 25 per cent of silver of a contemporary period. It is, however, worth five or six times the commercial value of "faked" Sheffield plate, with which in no other way can a comparison be made. Literally tons of faked Sheffield plate are now being manufactured, most of which, sooner or later, finds its way to America and the colonies.

With respect to pewter, the love for which did not assert itself until long after most of it had disappeared in the melting pot, it might safely be said that 95 per cent of all one could find through England and Scotland has been made within the last ten years. Likewise, practically all the "Old Dutch" brass articles, such as alms dishes, plaques, candlesticks, and jardiniers are of modern make, although they may reach the dealer via Holland. The production of "old masters" and ancestors continues a lucrative industry in Great Britain, it being a matter for serious regret that the talent, and sometimes even genius, suggested by these fraudulent works of art should be abased to such mean ends.

Clever Ruse of Antique Furniture Dealer

Difficulties thicken as the subject of old English furniture is approached. Large stakes are here frequently played for and the cunning of the dealer amounts to sheer genius. Illustrative of this, an instance of recent occurrence may be cited. What purported to be some exceptionally rare Chippendale chairs were sold by a well-known dealer to a certain nobleman, Lord X, who unhesitatingly accepted the dealer's word that they were genuine. Some time after this, however, the services of an expert were employed to further examine them, when it was revealed that a swindle had been perpetrated, the chairs being nothing more than fine modern copies. The customer informed the dealer of this discovery, demanding, on penalty of exposure, that the full purchase price be immediately refunded. Much to the purchaser's surprise the dealer refused to make restitution under circumstances which he alleged involved both his reputation and his honor. But to put it differently, if the customer would simply state his dissatisfaction with his purchase, then he, (the dealer) knowing the chairs to be genuine, would thank him for the privilege of being allowed to recover them, but it must be distinctly understood, only upon the terms and conditions of an ordinary sale. The dealer thereupon offered about $1,000 over and above the sum for which the chairs had previously been purchased. To this, of course, the nobleman demurred, protesting that he desired no profit from an unfortunate venture, but in the end, in order to secure the recovery of his money, he was prevailed upon to acquiesce in this extraordinary proposal.

The chairs having been duly returned, no great time elapsed before another customer took their purchase under consideration. The sale had now, however, become much simplified, for not only could the source of purchase be pointed to with pride, but actually the check was exhibited, showing beyond all doubt that the chairs had been purchased from Lord X, the well-known collector, at a price indicative of their apparent worth. Thus the dealer, shadowing his own dishonesty by this clever ruse, contrived to snatch even a further profit out of this second and more unscrupulous transaction.

It is no exaggeration to say that such episodes are a daily occurrence in the antique trade, except that, generally speaking, the ignorant purchaser seldom gets in exchange for his investment even so much as a good modern copy. Many so-called antique shops actually carry on business, without having one genuine piece of antique furniture in their establishment.

Other Pitfalls for the Inexperienced Collectors

In Holland old chests, cabinets, desks and chairs of little value are collected and, after being veneered with cheaply made marquetry, are sent to Great Britain. Old oak beams from demolished churches or granaries are likewise in constant demand for conversion into Jacobean refectory tables and Queen Anne furniture. Mid-Victorian pedestal sideboards are amputated to specimens of Robert Adam, and conventional inlay suitable for Sheraton furniture is cut out by machinery and supplied in any quantity to those who have skill and inclination to fabricate antiques. Grandfather clocks are frequently made up of such incongruities as a modern dial with a forged maker's name and date, an old case patched up and set off by modern inlay, and perhaps works of about fifty years ago. Grandfather chairs are also, almost without exception, modern, or old frames debauched by new cabriole or claw-and-ball legs. Violins signed Stradivarius or Jacobus Stainer, surreptitiously hidden in rubbish heaps, are replaced by others as soon as sold. "Old" armour, medals and medallions, all of modern origin, abound in rich profusion. "Antique" Spanish, Portuguese, and English paste jewelry everywhere intrudes itself. A flood of cheap and inartistic Japanese ware is also pouring out over the country; prints, gold lacquer, cloisonne enamel, ivory, and bronze contributing a full share in the swelling volume of alloys and commercial antiques.

To successfully collect nowadays requires expert knowledge and technical training. Those, therefore, who wish to secure genuine antiques would be better to make up their minds that it will be more satisfactory, and cheaper in the end, to purchase only on expert advice or of dealers willing to give a written stipulation that all articles sold are guaranteed to be approximately of the period represented; and with respect to English furniture, that no carving, inlay, or repairs not frankly admitted have been added; purchase money to be refunded should any of these statements prove on examination to be untrue. Furthermore, the services of this office are at the disposal of any person wishing more specific and detailed advice. (See also pages 1059 and 1063.)

The statements of the Consul are in harmony with the remark of Mr. Herbert Cescinsky on page 1 of his book entitled "The Gentle Art of Faking Furniture", where it is said that "one does not require an expert to tell the collector of English furniture that in one year more is shipped to America than could have been made in the whole of the eighteenth century." And on a preliminary page it is said that "The Buyer needs a thousand eyes; the Seller but one." An interesting story of an Italian dealer is in the note.[1]

Section 212. Advice to amateur collectors.—In almost all books on antique furniture the writers have thought it necessary, or at least proper, to give to the reader a chapter of well–meaning advice on how not to make mistakes in the purchase of articles said to be antique[1] and how to take care[2] of them if they are purchased. It is hoped that in the purchase of articles offered for sale as genuine antiques the readers of this book may be assisted by the advice in this section. The advice is plainly expressed and for convenience of reference the paragraphs are

---

1. In Mr. Nobili's "The gentle art of faking", pages 172–175, is a story of an Italian dealer and his skill in evading the Italian law which forbids the exportation of works of art from Italy without permission of the authorities and the payment of a tax. The dealer entered the Export Office with several antique bas–reliefs of a noted artist and handed his documents to the inspector, who examined the bas–reliefs and stated that being antiques they could not be exported. The dealer then scraped a piece of plaster from the apparently antique back of one of the pieces and showed that the plaster was new and was stamped with the name of a prominent Italian factory. The dealer said that the pieces were to go to America and that the smart Americans were fooled in believing they were getting antiques. The inspector then approved the shipment and did not discover that all the other bas–reliefs were genuine old antiques.

1. In the English books the subject of fakes and faking is plainly discussed and fakers are called fakers; in the American books, magazines and newspapers there seems to be some hesitation in calling a spade a spade. No American book has been published on "The Gentle Art of Faking Furniture", which is the title of a book by Mr. Cescinsky; nor has the book of Mr. Nobili, entitled "The Gentle Art of Faking" been widely circulated; nor has "An American Consul's Report", in section 211, been published or referred to as far as the writer has discovered, except a reference to it in Mr. Walter A. Dyer's book entitled "The Lure of the Antique", page 488. Reference may also be made to sections 7 and 8 in volume 1 of this book and "An American Consul's Report" in the section preceding this one.

    In the third volume of Mr. Wallace Nutting's "Furniture Treasury", the subject of "Pitfalls for the collector" occupies pages 262–272; and on pages 127–135 "The Art of Collecting" and "Method of Collecting" are considered.

2. As to the care of antique furniture, referring both to cabinet work and to the use of polishes or other preparations, the best printed advice is "Do not try to do the work yourself", unless you are experienced in such work; this refers to all kinds of decoration including gilding and painting; but if you prefer to try to repair or restore any of your antique furniture without trained help, consult the book referred to in section 10, note 1, entitled "Knowing, collecting and restoring early American furniture", by Mr. Henry Hammond Taylor, published in 1930 by J. B. Lippincott Company, Philadelphia. This book may assist you but will not make you a cabinet maker.

numbered. Section 209, entitled "Auction sales and prices", may be read to advantage in connection with this section.

The items of advice here presented to the amateur collector are meant as suggestions of some things to do and some things not to do in the fascinating pursuit of antique furniture. These items are all taken from serious books or magazine articles or from personal experiences of the writer and others.

1. Read all you can about the article in which you are specially interested at the time. No one can appreciate an article of antique furniture or realize what is fine and valuable and what is not, unless he knows something of the principal furniture periods and styles. Read this book, which is intended to give the information in a pleasing way; but if you do not find the subject interesting as here presented, get the smaller book entitled "Furniture of the Olden Time" by Miss Frances Clary Morse and read it.

2. Get fixed in your mind's eye, by examining the illustrations, the characteristic features of one or two articles, such as chairs or tables, during each of the furniture periods. When these features are once learned, you will never forget them and will be able to recognize them in other articles of the same periods.

3. Besides book learning, study real antiques in the homes of friends and acquaintances, and in museums and other collections. Almost every one who owns antiques, especially if they are family pieces, is glad to show them to others who are really interested.

4. Collect American furniture only, as advised in section 8 of this book. To put it the other way—do not collect foreign furniture; first, because we are Americans, and we naturally are more concerned in American things; second, because fine American furniture is as fine as European in many respects, although generally not so elaborate; third, because foreign furniture brought to America for sale here is often likely to be faked; fourth, because the value of American antique furniture will probably increase in value as the years pass by, whereas European furniture has a more settled standard of price and may not rise in value so readily. Alleged antique furniture has been imported in great quantities from England and is offered in many shops, but real and fine American antiques are not plentiful. See section 211.

5. Buy things in the rough rather than in a new condition. If repairs or restorations are necessary, have them made by your own cabinet maker, if he is experienced in working on antique furniture. If you buy things that have been skilfully restored and refinished for the purpose of sale, it is almost impossible for an amateur to know what parts of the article are original and what are new. This is especially true of gilded looking glasses. If you buy things in the rough you will have the satisfaction of seeing exactly what you pay for.

6. If you think of buying a piece of furniture which is not in the rough, always ask the owner, whether he is a dealer or not, what repairs and restorations have been made, and whether they were made by him or by some one else.

7. Examine in a bright light the inside and underside, as well as the outside, of anything you wish to buy. If the article is genuine, the owner will not object to the closest scrutiny. Moreover, it is well to carry with you a magnifying glass.

8. If you are a little doubtful about an article which is offered to you as a genuine antique, but you decide to buy it, you should require the seller to give you a written guarantee that it is genuine. The following form is legally binding when written on the bill and signed by the seller when the price is paid: "Received payment in full for the above article and for my guarantee, which I hereby give, that the said article is a genuine antique throughout, and if it is not, I will refund the purchase money on demand and return of the article." (See pages 1059 and 1061.)

9. Before buying an article about which you have serious doubt, have it examined for you by some one who is really an expert, preferably a cabinet maker or dealer of high standing and long experience with antique furniture. His fee may be trifling in comparison with the benefit to you.

10. If you have a number of articles of considerable value, whether acquired by inheritance or purchase, get an appraisement of them by two well informed persons, either dealers or appraisers. This is for fire insurance purposes and for possible use in the settlement of your estate. The appraisers' fees may be money well spent. Some of your things may have increased in value and others may have declined.

11. Do not buy a piece of antique furniture for yourself unless you have use for it in your home or elsewhere. Antique furniture should be bought for use or for its artistic interest, or both. Moreover, do not buy things which are too large for your rooms, for example, a bookcase which almost touches the ceiling. Also do not buy things which are not in themselves attractive. Mere age does not generally make articles of furniture attractive. Antique furniture which was crude and ugly when made is still crude and ugly now, and ought not to be in the home, although perhaps allowable in a museum in order to show changes of styles.

12. Do not buy any article of antique furniture unless its style is that of one of the recognized periods of American cabinet making. The history of furniture has been minutely studied and the styles are well known and are illustrated in many books. Articles in any of the antique styles, and made within the period, are valuable even though they are in a transition state; articles not made in one of such styles are not worth collecting. They may be desirable in a great museum, but not in your home. The amateur collector should confine himself to the established styles and periods; otherwise he will find himself possessed of a lot of junk.

13. Do not esteem "rarity" too highly. If the shape of a chair is unusual, the chair may be rare, but it does not follow that it is valuable. It may have been merely an experiment, an oddity; or it may have been made on the order of a customer who had a queer fancy. One may say "I never saw a chair like that in all my experience; it is a very rare piece." It may indeed be rare, but the reason for its rarity may be because few persons wanted chairs like that and there was little sale for them, and therefore only a few were made. Of course if Chippendale himself had made the chair it would be valuable, because anything that Chippendale made would now be valuable; but if not made by a well-known cabinet maker, the chair, in spite of its rarity, would be an almost worthless freak. It is well said that the rarity now desired is that of quality, not of kind. As to "quality" see section 214, L.

14. Do not buy an alleged article of antique furniture that is offered at a low price compared with the price elsewhere, unless you are very sure of what you will get. Dealers generally know what real antiques are worth and a very low price may be an indication that something is wrong.

15. Do not be influenced by lively bidding at an auction sale. The owner of the article may have his agent bidding against you, running it up. At some auction sales the articles are chiefly those of dealers or other owners who cannot get rid of them in their shops or homes. See section 209.

16. Unless there is a positive advertisement or statement by the auctioneer that an article is a genuine antique the purchaser has no redress if it should turn out to be a fake. The Latin legal phrase "Caveat emptor" controls, meaning "let the purchaser beware".

17. Do not pay as much for a veneered mahogany article as for a solid mahogany one. Veneer was and is made in thin strips which are sold by the yard. A veneered mahogany article may have a brilliant color, and show a fine grain, but its value never was, and is not now, equal to one made of the solid wood. You may know a veneered table by looking at the under side; if the wood and grain underneath is different from that on the surface, the surface is probably veneered. See section 32 as to veneer.

18. Do not make a new piece of furniture out of parts of one of a different kind nor change one piece into another. We sometimes find the heavy legs and other parts of a piano supporting a table; or a washstand converted into a telephone stand or a bedside table. A vase may no doubt be properly fitted with lighting appliances, or a necklace may be made into a bracelet; but we cannot make a decent new article of furniture out of an old one of a different kind. Any new article created in this manner is unworthy of a place in the home of a collector of fine antiques.

19. Do not paint an article of antique furniture if it was made without paint. The natural color of the wood may have been lost but an experienced cabinet maker will know what to do.

20. If you are fully satisfied with the antiquity of a certain article and it suits you exactly, buy it, as you may never find another. But if you are in doubt as to the desirability of the article, decide against it and you will not be obliged to explain to your visitors why you bought it. A dealer may buy such pieces without hesitation because he will probably have other customers who are not so well informed.

Quere. In many books and magazines the writers relate with glee their purchases from ignorant country people at a small fraction of the real values. If a collector is offered a chair for five dollars which he knows to be worth fifty, what is the honorable thing for him to do? Legally he need not pay the owner more than the owner asks, nor need he tell the owner that it is worth more—but how can any collector of antiques be proud of taking advantage of the ignorance of some poor old man or woman? One writer mentions that having discovered in a farm building the ball and claw feet of a chair protruding from the top of a wood pile, he almost lost his balance in his efforts to get it; and states that "with the duplicity learned in years of collecting" he concealed his emotions until the chair had been secured.

Section 213. Museums and Collections in New England open to the public.—Through the kindness of many persons interested we present a list of the museums and collections in New England which contain articles of American antique furniture. Although this list may not be complete, it includes as many of the principal places as the writer was able to find.

It is thought that this list will be of special value to the large number of visitors interested in antique furniture who have no means of knowing the locations of the treasure houses in New England.

A space is provided at the bottom of each page for the convenience of the reader in inserting other names.

CONNECTICUT

BRIDGEPORT
Bridgeport Scientific & Historical Society

CLINTON
Cow Hill Red School House
Stanton Memorial House

COLCHESTER
Nathaniel Foote House

DANBURY
Mary Wooster Chapter D. A. R.

EAST LYME
Thomas Lee House

FAIRFIELD
Fairfield Historical Society

FARMINGTON
Whitman Stanley House

GREENWICH
General Ebenezer Mead House
Holly House
Old Brice Mansion
Putnam Cottage
Thomas Lyon House

GROTON
Monument House

GUILFORD
Hyland House
Old Stone House

CONNECTICUT—Continued

HAMDEN
Jonathan Dickerman House

HARTFORD
Avery Memorial
Connecticut Historical Society
Wadsworth Athenaeum & Morgan Memorial

KILLINGWORTH
Old Ely House

LEBANON
Governor Jonathan Trumbull House
Lebanon War Office

LITCHFIELD
Judge Tapping Reeves House
Litchfield Historical Society
Quincy Memorial

MADISON
Bushnell Homestead
Madison Historical Society

MARLBOROUGH
Marlborough Tavern

MIDDLETOWN
Middlesex County Historical Society

MILFORD
Eells Stow House

CONNECTICUT—Continued

MORRIS
 James Morris House

MYSTIC
 Captain George Dennison House

NEW HAVEN
 New Haven Colony Historical Society
 Pardee Old Morris House
 Pierpont House
 Yale University
  Gallery of Fine Arts

NEW LONDON
 Nathan Hale School House
 Shaw Mansion

NEW MEDFORD
 New Medford Historical Society

NORWICH (CENTRAL)
 General Rockwell House

OLD LYME
 Wm. Noyes House

OLD SAYBROOK
 Acton Library Museum

PLAINVILLE
 John Cook Tavern

SIMSBURY
 Eno Memorial Hall

SOUTHINGTON
 Sylvia Bradley Memorial

STONINGTON
 Peleg Brown House or "Capt. Nat'
  Palmer House"

STRATFORD
 David Judson House

WALLINGFORD
 Old Royce House
 Wallingford Historical Society
 Washington Elm House

WATERBURY
 Mattatuck Historical Society

WESTBROOK
 David Bushnell House

CONNECTICUT—Continued

WESTBURY
 Bushnell House (Memorial Museum)

WETHERSFIELD
 Webb House
 Wethersfield Historical Society

WINDSOR
 Oliver Ellsworth House
 Walter Fyler Homestead

WINDSTEAD
 Solomon Rockwell House

WOODBURY
 Glebe House

MAINE

AUGUSTA
 Blaine Mansion

BERWICK
 Captain Jewett Mansion

BRUNSWICK
 Bowdoin College
  Museum of Fine Arts
 Pejepscot Historical Society

CASTINE
 Wilson Museum

COLUMBIA FALLS
 Ruggles House

DENNYSVILLE
 Lincoln Mansion

ELIOT
 William Fogg Library

ELLSWORTH
 Black Mansion

FORT KENT
 Fort Kent Historical Society

GORHAM
 Baxter House
 Longfellow Farm

MACHIAS
 Burham Tavern

NORTH BRIDGTON
 Bridgton Academy

MAINE—Continued

PEMAQUID BEACH
Fort William Henry

PORTLAND
Maine Historical Society
Sweat Memorial Art Museum
Tate House
Wadsworth–Longfellow House

SACO
York Institute

SOUTH BERWICK
Captain Jewett Mansion
General Goodwin House
Theodore Eastman Memorial

THOMASTON
Montpelier, Gen. Henry Knox Mansion

WATERVILLE
The Redington Museum

WINTHROP
Bishop Museum

YORK
Frost Garrison House
McIntyre Garrison House
York Museum

YORK VILLAGE
Old Gaol Museum

MASSACHUSETTS

ADAMS
Eleazer Brown Homestead

AMESBURY
Macy–Colby House
Whittier House

AMHERST
Historical Society Museum
Nehemiah Brown Strong House

ANDOVER
Andover Historical Society
Addison Gallery of American Art
Deacon Amos Blanchard House

ARLINGTON
Jason Russell House

MASSACHUSETTS—Continued

ATTLEBORO
Peck House

BARNSTABLE
Crocker House

BERNARDSTON
Ryther House

BEVERLY
Balch House
Cabot House

BILLERICA
Billerica Historical Society
Manning House

BOSTON
Boston Museum of Fine Arts
Fanueil Hall
Harrison Gray Otis House
King's Chapel
Massachusetts Historical Society
Museum of Fine Arts
Old South Meeting House
Old State House
Paul Revere House

BROOKLINE
Edward Devotion House

BURLINGTON
Francis Wyman House

CAMBRIDGE
Cambridge Historical Society
Cooper–Frost–Austin House
Craigie House (Longfellow House)
Fogg Museum

CHARLEMONT
Hall Tavern

CHATHAM
Atwood House

CHELMSFORD
Chelmsford Historical Society

CHELSEA
Cary House

COHASSET
Historical Society Museum

MASSACHUSETTS—Continued

CONCORD
  Antiquarian Society
  Art Centre
  Orchard House (Louisa Alcott House)
  The Wayside
DANVERS
  General Israel Putnam's Birthplace
  Page House
  Rebecca Nourse House
  Samuel Holton House
DANVERSPORT
  Samuel Fowler House
DEDHAM
  Dedham Historical Society
  Fairbanks House
DEERFIELD
  Pocumtuck Valley Memorial Asso.
DORCHESTER
  Blake House
  Dorchester Historical Society
DOVER
  Miller–Caryl House
DUXBURY
  John Alden House
EDGARTOWN
  Dukes County Historical Society
FAIRHAVEN
  Bennett House
FALMOUTH
  Falmouth Historical Society
FITCHBURG
  Fitchburg Art Centre
  Fitchburg Historical Society
FOXBORO
  Foxboro Historical Society
FRAMINGHAM
  Framingham Historical & Natural History Society
  Old Brown House
GREENFIELD
  Historical Society of Greenfield

MASSACHUSETTS—Continued

GROTON
  Groton Historical Society
GLOUCESTER
  Cape Ann Scientific & Historical Society
  Hammond Museum, Inc.
  Sargent–Murray–Gilman House
HADLEY
  Farm Museum
HANOVER CENTRE
  Hanover Historical Society
  Samuel Stetson House
HAVERHILL
  Buttonwoods
  Haverhill Historical Society
  John Ward House
  Whittier Birthplace
HARVARD
  Fruitlands
  Shaker House
HEATH
  Heath Historical Society
HINGHAM
  Hingham Historical Society
  Old Ordinary
  Old Ship Meeting House
HUDSON
  Hudson Public Library
IPSWICH
  Emerson–Howard House
  John Whipple House
KINGSTON
  Brewster House
  Major Bradford House
LEOMINSTER
  Leominster Historical Society
LEXINGTON
  Buckman Tavern
  Hancock–Clarke House
  Monroe Tavern
LOWELL
  Historical Society
  Whistler's Birthplace

MASSACHUSETTS—Continued

LYNN
Hyde–Mills House
Lynn Historical Society

MANSFIELD
Fisher–Richardson House

MARBLEHEAD
"King" Hooper Mansion
Lee Mansion

MARSHFIELD
Edward Winslow House

MEDFORD
Medford Historical Society
Peter Tufts House

MELROSE
Phineas Upham House

MENDON
Mendon Historical Society

MILTON
Milton Historical Society

NANTUCKET
Maria Mitchell Birthplace
Nantucket Historical Association Museum
Oldest House

NEW BEDFORD
Old Dartmouth Historical Society

NEWBURY
Coffin House
Jackson Willett House
Short House

NEWBURYPORT
Historical Society of Old Newbury
Pettengill–Fowler House

NORTH ADAMS
Fort Massachusetts Historical Society

NORTH ANDOVER
North Andover Historical Society

NORTHAMPTON
Northampton Historical Society
Wiggins Old Tavern

MASSACHUSETTS—Continued

NORTH WOBURN
Rumford House

NORWOOD
Historical Society

ORANGE
Historical Rooms

PEABODY
Foster House

PITTSFIELD
The Berkshire Museum

PLYMOUTH
Harbor House
John Howland House
Pilgrim House
Plymouth Antique Society
Richard Sparrow House
William Harlow House

PROVINCETOWN
Historical Society Museum

QUINCY
Adams Mansion
First Church, Unitarian
John Quincy Adams Birthplace
John Adams Birthplace
Quincy Homestead

READING
Parker Tavern

ROWLEY
Chaplin–Clarke–Williams House
Platt–Bradstreet House

ROXBURY
Dillaway House

RUTLAND
Rufus Putnam House

SALEM
Essex Institute
Gardner–Pingree House
John Ward House
Peirce Nichols House

MASSACHUSETTS—Continued

SALEM—Continued
  House of Seven Gables
    Hathaway House
      Retire Becket House
  Peabody Museum
  Richard Derby House
  Ropes Memorial
  Witch House

SANDWICH
  Sandwich Historical Society

SCITUATE
  Cudworth House

SHREWSBURY
  Artemus Ward House

SOUTHBRIDGE
  Wells Historical Museum

SOUTH HADLEY
  Skinner Museum

SOUTH LEE
  Old Tavern

SOUTH NATICK
  Natural History & Library Society

SOUTH SUDBURY
  Wayside Inn

SOUTH WEYMOUTH
  Fogg Library

SPRINGFIELD
  Pynchon Memorial Building
  Springfield Art Museum

STOCKBRIDGE
  Mission House

SWAMPSCOTT
  Humphrey House

TAUNTON
  Old Colony Historical Society

TEMPLETON
  Phelps House

TOPSFIELD
  Parson Capen House

MASSACHUSETTS—Continued

VINEYARD HAVEN
  Sea Coast Defense Chapter D. A. R. Rooms

WAKEFIELD
  Hartshorne House
  Wakefield Historical Society

WALTHAM
  Abraham Brown House
  Gore House

WATERTOWN
  Abraham Browne, Jr. House

WENHAM
  Claflin–Richards House

WEST BRIDGEWATER
  Old Bridgewater Historical Society

WESTBORO
  Historical Rooms

WESTFIELD
  Edwin Smith Historical Museum Westfield Athenaeum

WEST MEDWAY
  Medway Historical Society

WEST SPRINGFIELD
  Josiah Day House
  Storrowtown Houses

WEYMOUTH
  Weymouth Historical Society

WINTHROP
  Deane–Winthrop House

WOBURN
  Count Rumford Birthplace

WORCESTER
  American Antiquarian Society
  Art Museum
  Historical Society
  Stephen Salisbury House
  Timothy Paine House
  Worcester Historical Society

YARMOUTHPORT
  John Thatcher House
  Winslow–Crocker House

NEW HAMPSHIRE

CONCORD
New Hampshire Historical Society

DOVER
Woodman Institute

EXETER
Gilman Ladd House

FRANKLIN
Daniel Webster Birthplace

HOPKINTON
New Hampshire Antiquarian Society

MANCHESTER
Currier Gallery of Art
Manchester Historical Society

PETERBOROUGH
Peterborough Historical Society

PORTSMOUTH
John Paul Jones House
Moffatt–Ladd House
Portsmouth Athenaeum
Richard Jackson House
Tobias Lear House
Thomas Bailey Aldrich Memorial
Warner House

WENTWORTH
Gardner House

WOLFEBORO
Wolfeboro Historical Society House

RHODE ISLAND

ANTHONY
Gen. Nathaniel Greene Homestead

EAST GREENWICH
Daniel Howland House

MIDDLETOWN
Whitehall

NEWPORT
Old Colony House
Vernon House
Wanton–Lyman–Hazard House
Whitehall

NORTH KINGSTON
Gilbert Stuart Birthplace

RHODE ISLAND—Continued

PAWTUCKET
Daggett House
Pidge Tavern

PROVIDENCE
Ann Mary Brown Memorial
Betsy Williams Cottage
Brown University
John Carter Brown Library
John Hay Library
Esek Hopkins House
John Brown House
Rhode Island Historical Society
Museum
Rhode Island School of Design
Carrington House
Museum of Art
Pendleton House
Wickford

WAKEFIELD
Commodore Perry Museum

WARWICK
Nathaniel Greene Birthplace

WESTERLY
Dr. Babcock House
Library Building—Historical Society

VERMONT

BENNINGTON
Bennington Historical Museum

BROWNINGTON
Old Stone House

BURLINGTON
Robert Hull Fleming Museum

FERRISBURGH
Rokeby

MIDDLEBURG
Sheldon Museum

MONTPELIER
Vermont Historical Society

WINDSOR
Old Constitution House

Section 214. Other interesting items.—Many liberties have been taken with this book by remarks on subjects which are not relevant to "American Antique Furniture", but will probably be interesting to most of the readers. For example, the section entitled "English Hall Marks", which has no connection with antique furniture, is the subject of section 205, and section 206 on "The tradition of English bricks" and section 210 on "Lotteries" are, strictly speaking, out of place in this book. But these subjects are interesting and are briefly considered. In section 198, the first one in the Appendix, are somewhat similar remarks.

The present section, No. 214, is the last one in the Appendix. Its broad title, "Other interesting items", offers a final opportunity to refer to several subjects which the writer has noticed in the preparation of these two volumes.

A. The "William Camp label".—This label was loaned to the writer by Mrs. Miles White, Jr., who has contributed many fine illustrations to this book. The writer at once examined the old Baltimore City Directories and found that William Camp, the cabinet maker, was in business in Baltimore from about 1802 to 1822. Pursuing the investigation further, the writer next examined the Baltimore telephone directory in order to learn whether any descendants with the name of Camp could now be found, and thought himself fortunate in discovering the name of a Mr. "Camp, C." who is in the radio business, and also "Camp, Louise". Thinking that the Lady Louise would be interested in the family tree, the writer, by letter and telephone, endeavored to get in touch with her. Alas, he had a shock when he found that the "Louise Camp" was a summer resort for children and that "Louise" was merely the first part of the name of a benefactor.

In the third edition of Sheraton's "Drawing Book", published in 1802, several dated designs appear which were copied in this label. For example, the drawings of the two "Drawing Room" chairs on the right and left appear on plate 32 of Sheraton's book and are dated 1792. The "Side Board with Vase" is almost the same in design as the drawing by Sheraton on his plate No. 21, dated 1793. This label is referred to in section 54, note 2.

A similar label is shown in plate 432 in the book of Mr. W. M. Hornor, Jr., entitled "Philadelphia Furniture". In that label the engraved name of Joseph B. Barry of Philadelphia appears instead of William Camp.

It seems probable that fine and expensive engraved labels with a blank centre were prepared by engravers who for a small charge would print in the centre, as an advertisement, the name and address of any cabinet maker who desired to have his advertisement appear in a handsome label. The cost of the blank engraved labels and the printing would be much less than if an expensive engraving were made separately for each cabinet maker.

B. Pianos and Musical Glasses.—Photographs of several pianos and their forerunners, antique and semi–antique, were made for this book, but the writer found it difficult to present briefly a satisfactory display of the various articles, including spinets, virginals, dulcimers, clavichords and harpsichords. The Metropolitan Museum of Art, in New York, has a catalogue of the numerous musical instruments in its possession. An illustrated and interesting chapter on antique

2115. THE WILLIAM CAMP LABEL.

musical instruments is in "Furniture of the Olden Time", by Miss Frances Clary Morse, pages 280–314. The furniture styles of the cases of the American and English pianos may be ascertained approximately by the design of the legs and by the inlay, if any.

An illustrated article entitled "When is a Piano", by Edna Deu Pree Nelson, is in "Antiques", June, 1936, pages 245–249, in which it is well said that "to most people a small early piano is either a harpsichord or a spinet. . . All keyboard stringed instruments whose wires are vibrated by hammers qualify as pianos. Their size or shape has nothing to do with their naming. The significant and distinguishing characteristics of spinets and harpsichords is that their strings are vibrated not by hammers, but by little quill or leather plectra which, when operated by their respective keys, pluck the wires instead of striking them. This very simple point should be easy to remember."

Sets of "musical glasses" were popular about 1820–1840. These consisted of about twenty or more glasses, often in the shape of finger bowls, which were placed in a box on a pedestal and were tuned by pouring more or less water in them. The musical sounds were made by rubbing the tops of the glasses, each one giving out a different sound. This is well shown in Miss Morse's book, page 305. The cabinet work was in the Empire style.

C. Exclusively American Furniture.—Almost all important articles of American furniture originated in the furniture of England, but several of our articles are purely American. The most important of the latter are the butterfly tables, seen in section 156; the Philadelphia style highboys and lowboys seen in sections 87 and 92; and the block–front articles seen in sections 114–119. An illustrated article, by Mr. Edward Stratton Holloway, entitled "Furniture exclusively American" is in "Antiques", May, 1933, pages 182–183.

Certain other articles have seldom been made in our country although they had been in long and frequent use in England. These include wig–stands, such as No. 1677; tripod tables with fretwork around the top, as in No. 1343; spider–leg tables such as those shown in an illustrated article by Mr. Benjamin Ginsburg entitled "An American Spider–leg table" in "Antiques", December, 1934, pages 220–221; the very slender legs, or spider legs, seen on the nest of tables No. 1625 may also be considered.

Whether rocking chairs were invented in England or in our country has been a question of some uncertainty, as mentioned in section 63. Mantel clocks of the type shown as Nos. 1913–1915 were probably not made in our country.

D. Cleopatra's Barge.—This celebrated yacht, without the aid of the fair queen and not a product of Egyptian skill, was built at Salem, Massachusetts, in 1816, by a wealthy ship–owner, Captain George Crowninshield. The elegance and luxury of the furniture and other appointments of the boat attracted great attention. In the "Salem Gazette" of January 14, 1817, it was said that "you descend into a magnificent salon, finished with polished mahogany. . . The settees are of splendid workmanship; the backs are shaped like the ancient lyre and the seats are covered with crimson silk–velvet. . . Two splendid mirrors and a magnificent chandelier in the saloon give a richness of effect not easily surpassed." The settees were eleven feet long and there were five lyres in the back. The Sheraton style seems to have prevailed. Further details are in "The Furniture of Our Forefathers" by Miss Esther Singleton and in "Furniture of the Olden Time" by Miss Frances Clary Morse. An illustrated article on the subject by Mr. W. E. Keyes is in "Antiques", January, 1930, pages 29–33. It is said that the owner first chose the name "Car of Concordia", but later concluded that the name was not suitable for a sea–going ship.

E. Two Noted Houses. The Derby House.—Elias H. Derby was a wealthy citizen of Salem, Mass. His house, built about 1795–1799, and its furnishings, cost about $80,000. The house was designed by Samuel McIntire, who is more fully referred to on page 315. Soon after the house was completed Derby died, leaving a large estate. A number of the furnishings of the house, set forth in the court papers, are mentioned in "The Furniture of Our Forefathers", by Miss Esther Singleton. It is interesting to see that many of the chairs, settees and sofas were covered with horsehair cloth which was much used by Hepplewhite, as appears on pages 109 and 174. The house was torn down soon after the death of Derby, as none of the heirs desired to take such an expensive house. An article on the Derby furniture, by Mrs. Mabel M. Swan, is in "Antiques", November, 1931, page 280.

The Bingham House.—Another fine house with elegant furniture was that of William Bingham, a wealthy Philadelphian. An English visitor in 1794 had a letter of introduction to Bingham, and in his journal the visitor wrote: "I found a magnificent house and gardens in the best English style with elegant and even superb furniture. The chairs of the drawing room were four Seddon's (prominent cabinet–makers) in London, of the newest taste, the back in the form of a lyre." These and other interesting matters in this connection are mentioned in "The Homes of our Ancestors" by Halsey and Tower, pages 99 and 154, and in the book of Miss Esther Singleton, pages 562–564.

F. Noted Houses in Maryland and Virginia.—The Derby House of Salem and the Bingham House of Philadelphia were no doubt among the most elaborate and expensive houses of the times; but from an architectural point of view the palm must be given to several houses in Maryland and others in Virginia. Two illustrated books on the Colonial "Mansions" of Maryland are especially recommended to any one interested in the subject, namely "Colonial Mansions of Maryland and Delaware", by John Martin Hammond and "Tidewater Maryland, its History, its Tradition, its romantic Plantation Mansions", by Paul Wilstach.

Among the "mansions" in or near Annapolis, Maryland, are many elegant ones built by men of wealth and culture. One of these mansions is "Whitehall". On page 77 of Mr. Hammond's book it is said that "no considerations of economy of money or space hampered the building of Whitehall"; and Mr. R. T. H. Halsey has stated to the writer that the interior of Whitehall is superior to that of any other American mansion of the period.

G. Acanthus leaves.—These have probably been carved out of the solid wood more frequently than any other leaf design. From the time of Chippendale to that of Duncan Phyfe acanthus leaves were used on many articles of furniture, especially on chairs and tables. In addition to being a decorative feature the carved leaf may be useful as a means of covering an otherwise plain surface. Examples may be seen on the lyre–back chair of Duncan Phyfe, No. 326, and on his table No. 1530. In some cases the combination of acanthus leaves with other designs has not been pleasing, as in the table mentioned. On our furniture the leaves are more flat than those in the classical designs of the Greek and Roman architects who used the leaves as a basis of ornamental decoration in marble. The handsome plants are natives of the southern parts of Europe and in the neighborhood of the Mediterranean. It is said that an effort has been made to develop them in the "Field Museum of Natural History".

H. Exhibition of Fakes.—In the Bulletin of the Pennsylvania Museum for October, 1916, pages 56–57, is an interesting article entitled "The Collection of Fakes and Reproductions" from which the following is copied with the permission of the Museum.

"So much interest has been taken this summer in the display of fakes and reproductions at the Pennsylvania Museum, not only by collectors whom such an exhibit naturally most concerns, but also by the general public, that it has been deemed unwise to withdraw from view a feature the usefulness of which had been demonstrated by so marked a success. It will therefore be continued as a permanent exhibit."

"The commerce of spurious antiquities has reached such proportions that in every museum there should be a chance for the collector to test his judgment with regard to the real value of objects offered him. The expert antiquary in time acquires an instinctive 'feeling' about genuine objects which is sometimes bewildering to the untrained eye of the layman. But this cultivated instinct, which by the French is called 'flair', of late years has lost much of its value, owing to the class of men who have gone into the business of manufacturing spurious antiquities."

"The small collection of fakes displayed at the Pennsylvania Museum is intended as an educational feature of the institution. As it stands, it is but a beginning of what it is meant to be in time in all classes of ancient industrial or decorative art, and it contains as yet little more than ceramics. But in this class it is illuminating; and its development among all the lines taken up in the Museum is greatly to be desired."

I. A warning from England.—In section 211 is a paragraph in "An American Consul's Report", dated in 1909, in which the Consul referred to forgeries in English pottery. By a coincidence it happened that a few days after that paragraph was printed for this book a warning was sent by the president of the British Antique Dealers Association to Mr. Charles Messer Stow, of New York, Mr. William Germain Dooley, of Boston, and other American experts stating that old English pottery was being faked. The president wrote that "A number of clever forgeries of old English pottery are being passed off on unsuspecting collectors. The matter is the more serious in that high prices, amounting in some cases to hundreds of pounds, are being asked. The forgeries simulate pottery of the mid–eighteenth century, and . . have been identified as spurious. Collectors should exercise caution when offered such and similar types of highly priced pottery."

J.   In Mr. Cescinsky's book entitled "The Gentle Art of Faking Furniture", his gentle art of clever comment explains the details of many "detective methods" in questions as to whether certain articles are genuine antiques.[1] On pages 35–36 of that book a question was whether the article was the kind of thing which was made in the period in which such things were made, and Mr. Cescinsky writes in substance that "If a dealer possessed Queen Elizabeth's automobile, no one would believe it, even if it were smothered all over with Tudor roses. There are certain types of furniture which originated at certain definite periods, and are not found before. Thus the table on legs, as distinct from one of the trestle type, belongs to the late sixteenth century and after; . . the self–contained sideboard, with drawers and cellarettes, from 1780 onwards. Thus a Queen Anne sideboard, or even a Queen Anne dining–table, is just as unknown as a Tudor motor–car. Similarly, a fine bedstead without posts and a canopy was unheard of until the nineteenth century. Upholstery began, and very sparingly, in the reign of Charles I and did not become general until after 1680. Washstands (as distinct from the so–called wig–stands or powdering–stands shown in No. 1677) were as unknown in the eighteenth century as bathrooms. Baptism must have been the one bathing experience of our Georgian ancestors, if the testimony of their houses and furniture is to be believed."

K.   The beginning of our collecting.—Some of us attended the Centennial Exhibition held in Philadelphia in 1876 and are aware that the present interest in collecting American antiques began from that date. As expressed in the New York "Sun", by Mr. Charles Messer Stow, "At that display were exhibited specimens of American handicraft of the era before black walnut. Seeing them, many an observer was moved to remember that in the attic at home were similar pieces, discarded as old–fashioned when the fancy of the country turned to black walnut and poorer design. If they were worth showing in Philadelphia, there must be some merit in them, and a general rummaging took place at home later. Then their beauty did the rest and a generation of collectors came into being."

L.   The "quality" of an article of antique furniture.—This is occasionally referred to in connection with fine articles, such as the two "sample" chairs Nos. 116 and 117 on page 153. There are many meanings of the word "quality", as may

---

1.   The title of Mr. Cescinsky's book is partly drawn from the title of a book written by the celebrated English artist James A. McNeill Whistler, whose mother was one of the Baltimore family of Winans. In the eleventh edition of the Encyclopaedia Britannica, page 597, reference is made to the "controversial personality" of Whistler, and to his book entitled "The Gentle Art of Making Enemies", 1890. "The substance of this flippantly written and amusing outburst was an insistence on the liberty of the artist to do what was right in his artistic eyes, and the inability of the public or the critics to have any ideas about art worth considering at all." It is fortunate that a Whistler style of furniture did not become the fashion.

Mr. Cescinsky prepared the catalogue of the furniture of the late Viscount Leverhulme, a large collection which was brought to New York for sale at auction in 1926, and stated that "Everything that I considered a mistake has been removed" from the collection. In his "Gentle Art of Faking Furniture", published in 1931, it is said on page 127 that "The late Lord Leverhulme—who, considering the enormous amount of furniture which he bought (he had three or four great houses simply packed with pieces), seemed to have had a positive genius for buying fakes."

be seen in the pages of the Century Dictionary, in which one of the definitions is "a distinguished and characteristic excellence or superiority". Whether or not an article of furniture has a fine "quality" may depend upon the opinions of experts. It has been said that "the quality of an American Empire sofa is determined very largely by the skill with which its variously curving lines are harmonized in flow, the character of the wood used and the relative excellence of the carving". Another quotation is to the effect that "appreciation of quality may only very slowly be acquired by long–time observation and careful comparison. And even then, since it is usually influenced by personal preferences, it is seldom entirely trustworthy and may never conform to any absolute standard." From these quotations it is obvious that the word "quality" in connection with antique furniture is not a word to be lightly used, even though much good carving may have been applied as on the Philadelphia style highboys and lowboys shown in section 87 and 92. See the illustrated articles on the subject of "quality" in "Antiques", January, 1927, page 43, and November, 1932, page 190.

M.   The illustrations of the articles of furniture in this book have been reproduced through the courtesy of the following owners and others.

Abrams, Dr. Michael A.
Armstrong, Mrs. Alexander
Austen, Miss Lucille C.
Baily, Mrs. G. Frank
Baker, Mr. Henry Scott
Baldwin, Mrs. Rignal W.
Baltimore Museum of Art
Barroll, Mr. Morris K.
Bartlett, Miss Elisabeth H.
Benjamin Franklin Institute, Philadelphia
Berkley, Dr. Henry J.
Berry, Mr. & Mrs. J. Mauduit
Birckhead, Mr. & Mrs. Lennox
Bonsal, Miss Evelyn
Bonsal, Mr. Leigh
Bordley, Dr. James, Jr.
Bowie, Col. Washington, Jr.
Boyce, Mrs. F. G., Jr.
Brown, Mr. Alexander
Brown, Miss Mary Leigh
Brundige, Mrs. E. P.
Burns, Mr. F. Highlands
Buzby, Mrs. S. S.
Carey, Mrs. A. Morris
Carey, Mr. Charles H.
Carey, Miss Helen H.
Carey, Mr. & Mrs. James, Jr.
Carey, Mr. John E.
Carey, Miss Mary T.
Cary, Mr. & Mrs. Richard L.
Cescinsky, Mr. Herbert
Chase Home, Annapolis
Chew, Miss Harriett R.
Cohen, Miss Eleanor S.

Cohen, Estate of Miss B.
Cole, Mr. Arthur E.
Collinson, Dr. John
Colonial Dames, Maryland Society
Cottman, Mrs. L. W.
Cradock, Family of the late Thomas
Cradock, Miss Katherine
Davis, Miss Mary Dorsey
DeFord, Mrs. Wm.
Dixon, Mr. James
Dixon, Mr. & Mrs. Wm. A.
Drexel Institute, Philadelphia
Duer, Mr. & Mrs. A. Adgate
Duer, Mr. & Mrs. Henry Lay
Duncan, Mrs. John D. C.
Dunham, Mrs. Elizabeth N.
du Pont, Mr. Henry F.
Ellicott, Mr. Charles E.
Ellicott, Mr. & Mrs. Wm. M.
Eutaw Savings Bank
Evans, Mr. Geo. W., Jr.
Fenby, Dr. Edward
Fischer, Mrs. P. L. C.
Fitzhugh, Dr. Henry M.
Frost, Mrs. Wade Hampton
Fuchs, Mr. Fred.
Georgetown University
Gibbs, Mrs. John S., Jr.
Gibson, Mr. & Mrs. Edward Guest
Glenn, Mr. John, Jr.
Hale, Mrs. Arthur
Hammond–Harwood House, Annapolis
Hardy, Dr. George E.
Harris, Mr. & Mrs. J. Morrison

Harris, Mr. & Mrs. W. Hall
Hartshorne, Mrs. Murray Steuart
Helfenstein, Rt. Rev. & Mrs. Edward T.
Hinkley, Miss Mary K.
Howard, Mr. Benjamin Chew
Howard, Mr. Charles Morris
Howard Clock Co., The E.
Hubbard, Mr. Jos. K.
Hubbard, Mrs. Wilbur W.
Ingraham, Mr. Dudley S.
Ingraham Co., The E.
Johnson, Mr. C. W. L.
Kenmore Association, The
Kimmel, Miss Mary S.
Knight, Miss Ethel
Lanahan, Mr. William Wallace
Lindsay, Mrs. Thomas J.
Lockwood, Mr. Luke V.
Maginn, Mr. J. F. H.
Maryland Historical Society
Matthews, Mr. & Mrs. J. Marsh
McDaniel, Mr. John S.
McKeon, Mr. & Mrs. Edward H.
McLanahan, Mr. Austin
McLane, Mr. & Mrs. Charles E.
Metropolitan Museum of Art, New York
Miller, Mrs. Daniel
Miller, Miss Ethel M.
Miller, Mr. and Mrs. Henry C.
Miller, Mrs. Paul H.
Milligan, Mr. John J.
Morfit, Mr. & Mrs. Mason P.
Murdock, Miss Dora L.
Museum of Fine Arts, Boston
Myers, Miss Margaret L.
New Haven Clock Co.
Niver, Mrs. Edwin B.
Orphans Court of Baltimore City
Painter, Miss Margaret C.
Parke, Judge F. N.
Paul, Mr. J. Gilman D'Arcy
Pennington, Dr. Clapham
Petre, Mrs. Reginald W.
Pleasants, Dr. J. Hall
Pleasants, Mrs. J. P.
Poe, Mr. S. Johnson
Poultney, Mr. & Mrs. Wm. D.
Powell, Rev. & Mrs. A. C.
Powell, Mr. Paul R.
Randall, Mr. Blanchard
Randall, Mr. Daniel R.
Read, Mr. Benjamin H.
Redwood, Mrs. Francis T.
Reese, Mr. & Mrs. James P.

Roberts, Mrs. Wm. M.
Robinson, Mr. & Mrs. Ralph
Rodgers, Mrs. Maurice F.
Rogow, Mrs. Caroline Pennington
Ridgely, Mr. John of Hampton
Ridgely, Mr. John, Jr.
Rowland, Mrs. S. C.
Schwarz, Mr. John J.
Scott, Mrs. Townsend
Sheppard & Enoch Pratt Hospital
Shipley, Mr. & Mrs. George
Shoemaker, Mrs. Edward
Sill, Mrs. Howard
Simmons, Mr. Geo. Bradford
Smith, Mr. & Mrs Edmund L. R.
Smith, Mrs. Mabel Perry
Snyder, Mr. C. Edward
Speer, Mr. J. Ramsey
Steuart, Mrs. W. Donaldson
Steuart, Mr. James E.
Stokes, Mrs. John
Stokes, Mr. J. F.
Stein, Mr. C. F., Jr.
Taylor, Mrs. Robert, Jr.
Thomas, Mrs. Wm. H.
Thompson, Mr. H. Oliver
Tiffany, Mr. Herbert T.
Toland, Mr. John C.
Towers, Mr. Albert G.
Trimble, Mrs. Isaac Ridgeway
Turnbull, Mrs. A. Nisbet
Turnbull, Mr. & Mrs. Bayard
Tyson, Mr. A. Morris
Van Ness, Mr. & Mrs. Carroll
Wagner, Mrs. James V.
Walker, Mr. Edward A.
Wallace Collection, London
Walton, Miss Agnes M.
Ward, Mr. & Mrs. George
Wetherall, Mrs. Wm. G.
White, Mrs. Miles, Jr.
Whiteley, Est. of Mrs. J. H.
Whitely, Mr. James Gustavus
Whitridge, Mr. Morris
Williams, Mr. J. Ambler
Williams, Mrs. J. W.
Wilson, Mrs. James W.
Winslow, Dr. Randolph
Woollen, Mrs. Charles
Whyte, Mrs. Joseph
Wyatt, Mr. & Mrs. Charles H.
Wyse, Dr. Wm. P. E.
Yale University

INDEX

References are to pages unless otherwise specified

Volume I, pages 1–606; Volume II, pages 607–1106

References are to pages unless otherwise specified

Volume I, pages 1–606; Volume II, pages 607–1106

References are to pages unless otherwise specified

Volume I, pages 1–606; Volume II, pages 607–1106

References are to pages unless otherwise specified

Volume I, pages 1–606; Volume II, pages 607–1106

References are to pages unless otherwise specified
Volume I, pages 1–606; Volume II, pages 607–1106

References are to pages unless otherwise specified

Volume I, pages 1–606; Volume II, pages 607–1106

References are to pages unless otherwise specified

Volume I, pages 1–606; Volume II, pages 607–1106

References are to pages unless otherwise specified

Volume I, pages 1–606; Volume II, pages 607–1106

References are to pages unless otherwise specified

Volume I, pages 1–606; Volume II, pages 607–1106

References are to pages unless otherwise specified

Volume I, pages 1–606; Volume II, pages 607–1106

References are to pages unless otherwise specified

Volume I, pages 1–606; Volume II, pages 607–1106

References are to pages unless otherwise specified

Volume I, pages 1–606; Volume II, pages 607–1106

References are to pages unless otherwise specified

Volume I, pages 1–606; Volume II, pages 607–1106

References are to pages unless otherwise specified
Volume I, pages 1–606; Volume II, pages 607–1106

References are to pages unless otherwise specified

Volume I, pages 1–606; Volume II, pages 607–1106

References are to pages unless otherwise specified

Volume I, pages 1–606; Volume II, pages 607–1106

References are to pages unless otherwise specified

Volume I, pages 1–606; Volume II, pages 607–1106

References are to pages unless otherwise specified

Volume I, pages 1–606; Volume II, pages 607–1106

References are to pages unless otherwise specified

Volume I, pages 1–606; Volume II, pages 607–1106

References are to pages unless otherwise specified
Volume I, pages 1–606; Volume II, pages 607–1106

References are to pages unless otherwise specified

Volume I, pages 1–606; Volume II, pages 607–1106

References are to pages unless otherwise specified

Volume I, pages 1–606; Volume II, pages 607–1106

References are to pages unless otherwise specified

Volume I, pages 1–606; Volume II, pages 607–1106